DISCARD

DO NOT SPECIAL LOAN

*Projective Techniques*

*with Children*

# *Projective*

# *Techniques*

# *with Children*

*Edited by*

ALBERT I. RABIN

*and*

MARY R. HAWORTH

**GRUNE & STRATTON**

*A Subsidiary of Harcourt Brace Jovanovich, Publishers*

**New York   San Francisco   London**

GRUNE & STRATTON, INC.
111 Fifth Avenue, New York, New York 10003

Distributed in the United Kingdom by
Academic Press, Inc. (London) Ltd.
24/28 Oval Road, London NW1

*Library of Congress Catalog Card Number* 60-7253
*International Standard Book Number* 0-8089-0369-1

*Printed in the United States of America* (JU-B)

# Contents

PART I: INTRODUCTION

PART II: THE RORSCHACH METHOD

PART III: PICTURE TECHNIQUES

PART VI: THE USE OF PLAY MATERIALS

PART VII: FURTHER METHODS

PART VIII: PROJECTIVE PROCESSES IN THE CLINIC AND IN RESEARCH WITH CHILDREN

# Contributing Authors

**Crusa Adelman,† M.A.**
Research Fellow, Child Development Center, New York, N. Y.

**Charlotte H. Altman, Ph.D.**
Supervising Psychologist, Institute for Juvenile Research, Chicago, Ill.

**Leopold Bellak, M.D.**
Director of Psychiatry, City Hospital (at Elmhurst), New York, N. Y.; Adjunct Professor of Psychology, Graduate School, New York University.

**Gerald S. Blum, Ph.D.**
Professor of Psychology, University of Michigan, Ann Arbor, Mich.

**Paula Elkisch, Ph.D.**
Consultant and Psychotherapy Supervisor to the Division of Child Psychiatry, St. Luke's Hospital, New York, N. Y.

**Bertram R. Forer, Ph.D.**
Veterans Administration Mental Hygiene Clinic, Los Angeles, Calif.; Associate Clinical Professor, University of California at Los Angeles.

**Erika Fromm, Ph.D.**
Associate Professor, Department of Neurology and Psychiatry, Northwestern University Medical School, Chicago, Ill.

**Florence Halpern, Ph.D.**
Associate Professor, College of Medicine and Graduate School of Arts and Sciences, New York University, New York, N. Y.

**Emanuel F. Hammer, Ph.D.**
Head, Psychology Unit, Psychiatric Clinic, Court of Special Sessions, New York, N. Y.

**Mary R. Haworth, Ph.D.**
Assistant Professor of Psychology, Michigan State University, East Lansing, Mich.

**Marguerite R. Hertz, Ph.D.**
Clinical Professor of Psychology, Western Reserve University, and the Cleveland Psychiatric Institute and Hospitals, Cleveland, Ohio.

†Deceased

**Jerome Kagan, Ph.D.**

Chairman, Department of Psychology, Fels Research Institute, Yellow Springs, Ohio.

**Gerald F. King, Ph.D.**

Associate Professor of Psychology, Michigan State University, East Lansing, Mich.

**Vita Krall, Ph.D.**

Clinical Psychologist, Kansas Neurological Institute, Topeka, Kan.

**Karen Machover, M.A.**

Senior Psychologist, Kings County Hospital, Downstate Medical Center, Brooklyn, N. Y.

**Lois B. Murphy, Ph.D.**

Research Psychologist, The Menninger Foundation, Topeka, Kan.

**Albert I. Rabin, Ph.D.**

Professor of Psychology and Director of the Psychological Clinic Michigan State University, East Lansing, Mich.

**Saul Rosenzweig, Ph.D.**

Professor of Psychology, Washington University, St. Louis, Mo.

**Edwin S. Shneidman, Ph.D.**

Co-Principal Investigator, Central Research Unit, Veterans Administration Center, Los Angeles, Calif.; Research Associate, University of Southern California.

**Irving Sigel, Ph.D.**

Chairman of Research, The Merrill Palmer Institute, Detroit, Mich.

**Adolf G. Woltmann, M.S.**

Consulting Psychologist, New York, N. Y.

**Helmut Würsten, Ph.D.**

Chief Clinical Psychologist, Childrens Hospital Society of Los Angeles, Calif.; Clinical Associate, University of Southern California.

# Foreword

PROJECTIVE TESTS have been subjected to stormy gusts of criticism from the scientific community since Hermann Rorschach invented the first of them. Yet now, entering the fifth decade of their use in clinical psychology, they have not only weathered the storms but are staunchly flourishing, with their vigor and growth reflecting the valuable tools which they have proved themselves to be to the clinical psychologist. The clinical psychologist has remained aware, however, through these decades, of the soundness of some of the criticisms, and he has consistently bent his efforts toward strengthening the scientific validity of these instruments.

The volume which Rabin and Haworth have here organized, an exposition of projective tests as used with children, will fill a need which investigators have long been voicing. The present collection is a garden with plants of many species in this genus, projective techniques. They are in various stages of development: sturdy oaks, some with wide-reaching roots; others, frail shoots just sprouting blossoms. What is common to all is their reach for depth dynamics, a reflection of the ever-waxing influence of Freudian psychology.

The structure of this book as a whole demonstrates at the same time both important psychological concepts and the variety of the tests available. There is, on the one hand, discussion of the ego in children, their prepubertal development, psychopathology, the classical psychodynamics, and even a touch of philosophical origins; and, concerning method, the Rorschach, TAT, CAT, Blacky, films, stories, free art, free play, and puppetry are elucidated; and even that oldest, garden variety of psychological tests, the psychometric, is shown to have projective properties. Referring to the "oldest," one cannot but digress regarding the actually immemorial age of projective methods of communication in human annals. The Homeric poems, the Greek tragedies, the Hebraic religious literature, Renaissance painting, the music of Europe, what were they but projections of the artists and thinkers and nations that produced them? Modern psychology is only using its refined techniques, systematically, to penetrate and study formally what the sensitive and creative have long understood through that mysterious something which is genius.

The methods described in the present volume vary considerably in the degree to which they have been established as valid tests. This is necessarily to be expected in view of the comparative recency of some and the small number of psychologists as yet applying them. Another reason resides in the different and very difficult problems which they present, first in administration, then in subjecting the data to controlled and statistical ordering. The spirit of scholarship runs, however, as a salient characteristic throughout the chapters. Case presentations are cited in many. Some stand out by reason of their exposition of underlying concepts, and in doing so, they point up some theoretic problems that relate to all projective tests. Problems of further research are stated. Whatever the stages of scientific development of each, one cannot but admire the intellectual daring which they exemplify. We humans *will* pioneer into unknown lands. And what area has remained as unknown as the human mind?

A need for appraisal by their practitioners applies to the projective techniques as to other fields; recognition of this is an ingredient of the book in the final section, which centers about the idea of the "projective community." It is an interesting idea—new and even strange to the writer of this foreword —and yet arresting by reason of a self consciousness identifying the field. I can scent a hazard in such consciousness, that of cultism. The critical judgments with which this section is written, however, militate against these writers' straying into closed system devotions. The editors themselves comment on the essentially nascent, and therefore untested, state of some of the techniques. They reflect in this the wisdom of the seasoned exponent in this field. It is a recognition that no test can be better than the clinical psychologist making use of them. As an extension of this principle, we might add that projective tests will never be better than the general scientific state of psychology at the time.

Taken in overview, the book demonstrates the many avenues by which we can approach some understanding of the human personality. The neophyte in the field will find it opening many doors to this so-elusive subject. He will obtain leads as to the methodological pitfalls of which he must beware, the scientific cautions he must observe. And he will breathe excitement at the vistas in personality opening up to him, as well as glean provocative research ideas. Best of all, he will learn about those most fascinating denizens on the human scene—children.

*University of Chicago*
*Michael Reese Hospital*

SAMUEL J. BECK

# Preface

THIS BOOK has been designed to serve the needs of the clinical student, the practicing clinician and the research worker, insofar as their concern is with the use of projective techniques with children. Our assumption is that the reader is already familiar with some of the basic principles of projective theory and methodology. The focus, therefore, is upon clinical and research applications of some well known, and of other lesser known, projective methods with children.

The student will find a description of most tests, typical responses which they elicit from a variety of children and extensive references for further study. The clinician may draw upon the discussions of practical considerations in the selection, administration and interpretation of the entire range of projective techniques described in the volume. The researcher will probably be most interested in the relevant research findings, as well as the theoretical and methodological problems involved in the study of childhood personality and personality development by means of projective methods. The two final chapters of the book are particularly relevant in this connection.

All of the chapters are original contributions, especially written for this volume. Although the book was planned by the editors, needless to say the contributors are mainly responsible for making it a reality. We are deeply grateful for their painstaking efforts, patient cooperation and willingness to take time out of already crowded work schedules in order to make their contributions.

We are also grateful to those publishers who gave permission to quote or reproduce materials from previous publications. Specific acknowledgments appear in the individual chapters.

Finally, it is the hope of the editors that this volume will not only prove of practical value to the clinician and research worker, but that it will also serve to stimulate refinements and reformulations of existing methods, as well as to generate new and creative approaches to the study and assessment of personality in children.

ALBERT I. RABIN

MARY R. HAWORTH

# Part I: Introduction

# 1

## Projective Methods and Projection in Children

A. I. RABIN

NEARLY forty years after the publication of Rorschach's original mono-graph and more than twenty years since the appearance of Murray's *Explorations*, projective techniques continue to enjoy widespread application in research and in clinical practice. It was particularly during World War II that the rapidly developing profession of clinical psychology brought about a tremendous upsurge in the development and application of these techniques. It also stimulated a proliferation of new methods based on the projective hypothesis.

For a time the "projective movement" developed outside the confines of orthodox academic and traditional "scientific psychology." It received its impetus from the practice of allied professions, from psychoanalytic theory and other dynamic approaches to personality. Many techniques evolved from sheer empiricism and practical clinical observations rather than from complex and highly rigorous theoretical formulations. Whatever theory was involved, it was not that of the extant "general psychology," since the appliers of projective methods, especially the clinicians, were concerned with the uniqueness of personality.

From the very beginning of projective methodology, however, we have witnessed a developing and continuous process of interpenetration between academic psychology and the field of projective techniques. It has been, and is, a two-way process of mutual influence. On the one hand, workers with projective methods have become increasingly aware of, and concerned with, problems of validity, reliability and standardization of their methods. They have become more and more concerned with the scientific status of their methods and with the appropriate quantitative methodologies for their investigation. (The extensive literature in this area overwhelmingly attests to this trend.) Moreover, they have been laboring increasingly on the integration of the more empirical methods with existing personality theories. Outstanding examples of the latter trend in the case of the Rorschach are the contributions of Holt[10] and Schafer.[18] There are many others.

On the other hand, the aforementioned process of interpenetration extends in the other direction as well. Kutash[14] has described at some length "the impact of projective techniques on basic psychological science." Projective techniques and projective methodology are increasingly being used in the study and investigation of the more traditional psychological problems. For example, the work on motivation by McClelland and his associates[16]

2

and the research on perception by Witkin and his collaborators[19] are two outstanding instances of this direction. There are many other studies, too numerous to list, which have received their impetus from projective techniques and from the theoretical speculations which they have generated. Perhaps the "new look" in perception is in no small measure indebted to the conceptual climate due to projective methods. Moreover, contributions to the field of psychopathology, such as Beck's *Six Schizophrenias*,[3] open up new avenues to personality typology, normal and abnormal, employing projective methods as primary instruments.

It appears that this interpenetration of what originally tended to be disparate tendencies in psychology will develop into a fusion of a more unitary and consistent nature. The projective *antithesis* to the frequently sterile, mechanical, mechanistic and additive *thesis* in personality description and evaluation will contribute a new and more dynamic *synthesis*, consistent with the dialectic process apparent in many a historical movement.

## The Concept of Projection

Although it is not the purpose of this chapter, nor of this volume for that matter, to deal extensively with projective theory as such, some review of the projective hypothesis, especially in relation to children's behavior and experience, appears to be desirable. With regard to general projective theory, the discussions by Abt and Bellak[1] and some of the contributions to the volume edited by the Andersons[2] are still fundamental and pertinent at the present time.

The term projection is often considered a misnomer when applied to what has become known as projective techniques. Critics of the use of the term, however, seem to be attached to a rather circumscribed definition of projection. They consider it only in a pathogenic context, i.e., as a defense mechanism described by Freud and by psychoanalytic theory. Closer examination and more complete scrutiny of Freud's writings will reveal that he attributed a broader and more extended meaning to the term projection. Bellak treated this matter in some detail.[1]

In a paper dealing with the relationship between projective techniques and the theory of thinking, Rapaport[17] has also pointed out that a whole range of phenomena is reflected in the psychoanalytic use of the term projection. He states that ". . . phenomena subsumed under the psychoanalytic conception of projection . . . [are] paranoid projection, infantile projection, projection in transference phenomena . . . " He further elaborates by pointing out that these phenomena

". . . are rather a graduated continuum which becomes progressively more general extending from the externalization of a specific type of tension in paranoid projections to that of any kind of tension in infantile projection, to that of a whole system of attitudes and tensions in transference phenomena, to where it imperceptibly shades into the externalization in the form of a 'private world' defined by the organizing principles of one's personality" [reference 17, pages 270–271].

Thus, perhaps the broader term "externalization" is more appropriate in the case of projective techniques. It avoids the constricting misconception of projection as a mere defense mechanism pure and simple. It is in the sense of externalization that the originator of the term "projective methods"[6] employed the word "projection."

In this connection, we may note that others have also been concerned with a more precise designation of the processes involved in projective techniques. Bellak,[1] for instance, writes of "apperceptive distortions" and Cattell[2] of "dynaception" and "misperceptions." Perhaps the need for this modified terminology is obviated when we consider the process of externalization as a continuum and its involvement in the broad range of perceptual tasks, from the more strictly cognitive, with highly structured material, to the more apperceptive or misperceptive, with unstructured or less structured stimulus materials.

These issues will be touched upon to some degree in the next section, in which we will consider some of the processes involved in projective testing and in the projective test situation.

## The Projective Process

Before we consider specifically the issue of projection (as used in projective techniques) in children, it would be well to review this process in general and particularly as it takes place in adults. We shall not, at this juncture, consider a variety of other factors, such as the cooperativeness of the person in the testing situation, the effects of set, examiner-examinee interaction, etc. There is a voluminous literature in which these aspects are described and investigated with a good deal of sensitivity, insight and rigor.

The aim of projective testing in the clinic, with the exception of methods that are designed to shed light on specific variables, is to study and obtain an evaluation of the "total personality." In terms of modern dynamic psychology, we are concerned with an assessment of the ego, ego strength and defenses, assets and liabilities. Bolgar suggests" . . . that the proper field of investigation of projective psychology is character, its formation and its manifestations, and that the theoretical emphasis, insofar as it is psychoanalytic, should be the psychology of the ego and not the psychology of the id" (reference 11, page 656). There is no universal agreement with the latter part of the statement. Holt,[9] for instance, is concerned with the "gauging of primary processes" as well as the secondary processes of the ego. Perhaps it is a matter of emphasis, for it is difficult to evaluate the ego without reflecting certain implications with respect to the id.

Bolgar's emphasis, however, is consonant with modern theoretical developments in ego psychology and psychoanalysis. Hartmann[8] has particularly emphasized the role of the ego in psychoanalysis in recent years. The more complex and extended meaning of the ego encompasses relatively "autonomous" maturational (biological) processes, "secondary" autonomous functions, in addition to the learning that takes place vis-à-vis ego-id interaction. This theoretical elaboration is familiar to the reader acquainted with recent developments in theory.

Paradoxically, however, in order to penetrate the depths of character formation, of the ego and its defenses, in projective testing, an important prerequisite is the relaxation of some of the controls and the partial, voluntary surrender of the ego's secondary process. Here we have reference to Schafer's notion,[18] borrowed from Kris,[13] regarding "regression in the service of the ego."

In the projective test situation, as in states of artistic creativity, a person is expected to "make believe," to imagine, to tell what a stimulus "looks like" or to "tell a story," rather than to give a factual description of the picture or some other stimulus to which he is reacting. Of course, people vary to the extent that they are able to "regress" at the ego's behest in cooperation with the examiner's request. The degree of freedom with which this operation is undertaken, performed or accomplished and completed, is in itself an important index of the ego's freedom from threat, of the freedom of the individual to allow himself some "regression." Here, too, there is perhaps a continuum from which the degree of defensiveness may be inferred.

Defensiveness, however, is only one aspect of the total personality with which we are concerned. The modes of coping with reality, identification, interpersonal relations, methods of problem solving, "style," "the organizing principles of personality" and many other positive, nonpathologic or nonpathogenic aspects are to be included in the final personality evaluation based on intensive study by means of projective methods.

### Projection in Children

The projective or externalization process in childhood is somewhat less well understood. To begin with, we are not dealing with a relatively stable ego and character structure. The ego evolves rather gradually from an undifferentiated state to high levels of differentiation in the external and internal environments as a result of the constant interplay of learning and maturational processes. Development of the various ego functions is often saltatory. Moreover, there is often a lack of age-appropriateness in some functions as compared with others. Earlier levels of integration exist along with later ones. Such a fluid state in ego development dictates considerable caution in evaluation, diagnosis and prediction.

With children perhaps more than with adults, the nature of the requirements that each projective method imposes (differences in degree of structure, interaction with examiner, inquiry, etc.) upon the examinee is particularly crucial to the picture obtained. Also, the countertransference of the examiner-interpreter in specific testing situations may be crucial in the final evaluation. This point was well illustrated by Bolgar,[4] who advocates multiple testing with children for a complete and unbiased evaluation. She states:

The value of the multiple approach, however, derives not only from the increased opportunity for the child to display his problem-solving behavior and the successes and failures of his adaptive resources; perhaps the most important function of the multiple test approach lies in the control of the investigators' and clinicians' unconscious reactions to the child and his test behavior.

In a previous section we have discussed the occasional "regression in the service of the ego" in adult projective testing. With children who are just beginning to develop controls of the primary process and a rudimentary defensive structure against the unsanctioned id drives, this type of "regression" is not to be readily expected. If regressiveness occurs, it is not "in the service of the ego," but is probably due to the ego's immaturity and insufficiency. Hartmann addressed himself to this point by stating that in the relatively integrated adult ego regression may occasionally be so tolerated; however, "The child up to a certain age is not capable of using this mechanism, or feels threatened by its attempted use. I think this is probably one reason why the child fails vis-à-vis the demand of free association" (reference 8, page 26). But when an older child shows some of this "regressive," dreamlike content in his responses, along with many bits of evidence of realistic thinking and strong secondary process, our judgment with respect to his ego security may be strengthened.

Whereas the range of possible responses of adults on some of the more popular projective techniques and the resulting norms provide a frame of reference for making judgments of degree and level of ego integration, such information on children is not as readily available nor is it so easily applicable. The age norms for various test variables with children mask a good deal of the "unevenness" in the profiles of individual children on which they are based. A child's performance may spread over several age levels, reflecting the vicissitudes of his ego development, which is still in a state of flux. Except for the "private norms" of the clinician experienced with children, little information is available about the behavior of children in, and their responses to, a great many projective situations with different types of materials. In the last analysis, the individual clinician, or perhaps more than one, as Bolgar suggests above, needs to integrate the findings obtained, working consistently within some psychodynamic theoretical frame of reference.

As we have suggested above, a good deal of the material obtained, and the personality picture that results, depends on the task presented and the demands made, whether of child or adult. Some of these more specific issues in relation to particular methods are considered in some of the chapters that follow. Nevertheless, it may be of value to consider a classificatory framework for the vast array of projective methods—a task to be briefly undertaken in the subsequent sections.

### Proliferation of Methods

In an earlier section of the present chapter we have referred to a "proliferation" of projective methods. The trend of devising new methods, based on the projective hypothesis, has not yet run its course; more and more techniques, often devised for special purposes or for the assessment of some particular personality variable, find their way into the clinic, the research institution and the professional literature. Since, as Korner[12] pointed out, one of the major assumptions underlying projective techniques is " . . . that all behavior manifestations, including the most and least significant, are expressive of an individual's personality," then the possibilities of and potentialities for new methods are virtually unlimited. The same author further states with some degree of justification that " . . . we tend at times to lose ourselves in our pragmatic efforts, and to make only feeble or no attempst to relate our new discoveries to basic personality theory" (reference 12, page 619). Others[11] bemoan our tendency to create new "gadgets" without investigating sufficiently the ones which we already possess.

It is difficult not to be in sympathy with the concern of the authors referred to above. Yet we cannot but consider some legitimate, pragmatic though it may be, motivation for devising and experimenting with still newer techniques. Practicing clinicians, for example, may find that some of the existing methods are singularly unproductive with some patients or unsuitable for special groups of patients (the handicapped, for example); also, research workers may be concerned with the intensive investigation of some variable or group of variables (such as masculine versus feminine identification). The most cogent criticism is not the profusion of techniques per se but their tenuous relationship to systematic personality theory. Empiricism of this kind, however, is often justifiable historically, since practical instruments and devices have a way of stimulating theory and contributing to it; they often serve as building material for the theoretical edifice.

### Varieties of Projective Techniques

Since there is such a tremendous variety of projective techniques of different origins, utilizing different kinds of material, requiring different kinds of response and dictating various methods of interpretation, it has been tempting to put some order into this confusion of versatility. Frank[7] in his 1948 monograph augmented his earlier classification of projective methods and emerged with the following five categories: *constitutive, interpretative, cathartic, constructive* and *refractive*. These categories are based on the type of response that is elicited by the respective methods. However, considerable overlap between categories defining the variety of projective methods was inevitable. Other attempts at categorization using different frames of reference have recently been reviewed by Lindzey[15]. This author also makes a serious effort to analyze the several criteria which may serve as a basis for classification and then emerges with a newer and, probably, a more useful one. We shall follow Lindzey in the next few paragraphs and then examine the contents of the present volume in the light of this newer set of categories.

The six different approaches (or groups of criteria) which may be considered in the classification of projective techniques are as follows:

A. Classification based on *"attributes that inhere in the test material itself"*; i.e., degree of structure and sense modality involved.

B. The *"method by which the technique was devised"*; i.e., is it based on a theoretical rationale or mainly empirical?

C. *Method of interpretation* as a basis for classification; formal versus content analysis (or "sign" as opposed to holistic interpretation).

D. *"Purpose of test"*; general personality evaluation or the assessemnt of some specific personality variable.

E. *Mode of test administration*; group versus individual administration or self- versus examiner-administered.

F. *Type of response elicited*; e.g., association, completion, construction, etc.

If we were to consider a final classification of projective techniques combining all of the criteria and possible alternatives, we would come up with a very large number of multidimensional categories. The number would be so large as to be useless for all practical purposes (although it might be of value for large-scale research in the projective field).

We agree with Lindzey that, psychologically, the last criterion ("type of response") is the most meaningful and the most useful basis for the classification of the techniques involved. He suggests a categorization based on responses, which is somewhat parallel to the one proposed by Frank, and states that " . . . we find that the instruments brought into the same category have a general congruence and psychological consistency that makes it easily possible to conceive of similar underlying psychological processes" (reference 15, page 162). The types of response suggested as a basis for classification are: (1) association; (2) construction; (3) completion; (4) choice or ordering; and (5) expression.

## Classifying Projective Techniques with Children

We shall now attempt a brief description of the several categories listed above and then place some of the techniques described in the present volume in the appropriate classification. The schema, like many others, does not offer an opportunity for easy categorization of the entire array of projective methods now available, or even those included in the present volume. We have, consequently, not followed it in the arrangement of chapters in the book. The classification is primarily presented for heuristic purposes.

The *associative* techniques require that the examinee respond to stimuli presented with the "first word," image or idea, "as soon as possible." The most obvious technique that falls in this category is the word association test. The Rorschach also makes similar demands on the subject. Both techniques are discussed at length in the present volume.

*Construction* techniques make somewhat more complex demands upon the subject. He is expected to "make" or "make up" something, to "create." We have included a large sample of this type of method in our book. The Thematic Apperception Test (TAT), the Children's Apperception Test (CAT), the Blacky and the Make-A-Picture Story (MAPS) are examples.

The term *completion* techniques is readily self-explanatory. In these situations the examinee is presented with an incomplete product which he is expected to complete. This is, in many ways, a more structured type of method since certain requirements are imposed upon the subject (by the "unfinished" part—the stimulus). There is not as much freedom as in the case of the constructive situation. The children's form of the Picture-Frustration Study, the Story Completion method and the Sentence Completion test are some of the representatives of this category in our volume.

The *choice* or *ordering* techniques are in some ways closest to "psychometric" methods due to the considerable structure involved and because of the relatively limited and simple kind of response required. They probably allow the least amount of freedom and spontaneity on the part of the respondent. No separate chapters are devoted to individual techniques of this category, although the Szondi and the Kahn Symbol Arrangement Test are examples briefly considered in the "miscellaneous" chapter.

Finally, the *expressive* techniques, which are similar to those in Frank's "cathartic" category, offer the opportunity not only for projection (material for the examiner's interpretation of the personality) but for the subject's self-expression (catharsis!) as well. It is for this reason that Lindzey states that " . . . these methods represent a bridge between the diagnostic and therapeutic, for all of them play an active role in current therapeutic practice." He also adds that they differ from other methods by the emphasis "upon the style or manner in which the constructive process is carried out" (reference 15, page 164). Also, the emphasis here is much more on process than on product. Some of the chapters that reflect this category are the ones concerning free art expression, free play and the use of puppets.

Before closing this discussion, two comments are in order. In the first place, no classification is perfect, the present one included. The worker well acquainted with projective methods can easily point to some techniques which cut across more than one category. Some overlapping is inevitable. There is a degree of arbitrariness in any such classification. Some instruments, such as Rorschach, for example, though primarily *associative*, may involve some *construction* and even *expressive* processes as well. Also, some of the drawing techniques may be placed in the "construction" category; however, could they not, with some justification, be considered in the *expressive* rubric as well? Perhaps placement in a particular category would vary with the projective worker and with the relative emphasis on aspects of responses he places in his interpretation.

Secondly, considering this fivefold classification, we would have difficulty in placing some of the instruments, including "projective aspects of intelligence testing." Thus, the classification may be considered as suggestive, but hardly final or all-inclusive. Future efforts will perhaps be multidimensional and/or pattern-analytic approaches.

### The Categories and the Age Range

The very nature of the task with which a child is presented, and the response demands that are made upon him, are to no small degree dependent upon the age level and/or level of ego development in that child. We have quoted Hartmann earlier in connection with the young child's difficulty in regressing "in the service of the ego." *Associative* methods (including the Rorschach) are likely to be less revealing with the young preschool child than would other projective methods. The "magic wand" perseveration[10] of the young child on the Rorschach does not reveal much about his inner world. The older child, however, with a sturdier and less tenuous ego structure is more productive and self revealing. The same is true of the more *constructive* type of technique. This type of method requires a fairly persistent and continuous set as well as a good deal of cognitive activity. Most techniques in this category are most suitable for school-age children. Most of the *completion* techniques are suitable for older children. A notable exception may be the Story Completion Test when it is introduced as a game and when the child is considerably urged and prodded by the examiner.

In our judgment, the *expressive* methods are most rewarding when employed with very young children. These are least restrictive of the child and allow maximum freedom and spontaneity. They resemble most closely a natural play situation in our culture. Not only do they provide insight into the inner world of the child and his psychodynamics, but they give us important clues to the process of ego formation and consolidation. To quote Erikson, who paraphrased Freud—". . . we have called play the royal road to the understanding of the infantile ego's efforts at synthesis" (reference 5, page 182).

## Summary

In the preceding pages we have attempted an overview of the field of projective techniques with special emphasis on their application to children. We have attempted to describe briefly the developing relationship and interpenetration between projective methods and the field of psychology in general. The concept of "projection" as externalization was considered and its operation in projective techniques described. A psychologically meaningful schema of the categorization of projective techniques was also presented, discussed and scrutinized. These issues were considered especially in relation to children and to personality development from the viewpoint of ego psychology.

Throughout we are cognizant of the relationship between personality assessment and evaluation and personality theory. We also recognize the tentative nature and shortcomings of many techniques, as we do the relatively unintegrated, fractionated and incomplete status of personology and personality theory upon which they depend.

## References

1. Abt, L., & Bellak, L. (Eds.)  *Projective psychology.* New York: Alfred A. Knopf, 1950.
2. Anderson, H. H., & Anderson, G. L. (Eds.)  *An introduction to projective techniques.* New York: Prentice-Hall, 1951.
3. Beck, S. J.   The six schizophrenias. *Res. Monogr. Amer. Orthopsychiat. Ass.*, 1954, No. 6.

4. Bolgar, H.   Validity aspects of multiple projective techniques in child research. Paper read at the annual meetings of the Amer. Psychol. Ass., Chicago, 1956.

5. Erikson, E. H.   *Childhood and society.* New York: W. W. Norton, 1950.

6. Frank, L. K.   Projective methods for the study of personality. *J. Psychol.*, 1939, *8*, 389–413.

7. ———.   *Projective methods.* Springfield, Ill.: C. C Thomas, 1948.

8. Hartmann, H.   Mutual influences in the development of ego and id. *Psychoanal. Study Child*, 1952, *7*, 9–30.

9. Holt, R. R.   Gauging primary and secondary processes in Rorschach responses. *J. proj. Tech.*, 1956, *20*, 14–25.

10. Klopfer, B., Ainsworth, M. D., Klopfer, W. G., & Holt, R. R.   *Developments in the Rorschach technique.* Vol. I. *Technique and theory.* Yonkers-on-Hudson: World Book, 1954.

11. ———.   (Ed.)   *Developments in the Rorschach technique.* Vol. II. *Fields of application.* Yonkers-on-Hudson: World Book, 1956.

12. Korner, A. F.   Theoretical considerations concerning the scope and limitations of projective techniques. *J. abnorm. soc. Psychol.*, 1950, *45*, 619–627.

13. Kris, E.   *Psychoanalytic explorations in art.* New York: Int. Univer. Press, 1952.

14. Kutash, S. B.   The impact of projective techniques on basic psychological science. *J. proj. Tech.*, 1954, *18*, 453–469.

15. Lindzey, G.   On the classification of projective techniques. *Psychol. Bull.*, 1959, *56*, 158–168.

16. McClelland, D. C., Atkinson, J. W., Clark, R. A., & Lowell, E. L.   *The achievement motive.* New York: Appleton-Century-Crofts, 1953.

17. Rapaport, D.   Projective techniques and the theory of thinking. *J. proj. Tech.*, 1952, *16*, 269–275.

18. Schafer, R.   *Psychoanalytic interpretation in Rorschach testing.* New York: Grune & Stratton, 1954.

19. Witkin, H. A., Lewis, H. B., Hertzman, M., Machover, K., Meissner, P. B., & Wapner, S.   *Personality through perception.* New York: Harper, 1954.

Part II:  The Rorschach Method

**2**

## The Rorschach Test with Children

FLORENCE HALPERN

AS A METHOD for evaluating the personality of children the Rorschach serves at least two important functions. Not only does it provide a personality picture and a clinical diagnosis, as it does for adults, but it also sheds considerable light on the course of personality development. Children's Rorschach records afford very valuable evidence in support of many of our theories regarding personality growth. As such they are important to the student of child development, the psychologist concerned with personality in all its phases, and of course the clinical psychologist.

Actually the best way to understand children's Rorschachs is to deal with them in developmental terms. Has the child achieved the degree of control, the integrative and organizational ability, the emotional understanding of his peers? In contrast to what happens in primitive cultures, in our culture such an evaluation is not a simple matter. In relatively simple societies behavior patterns are rigidly defined, and the way the individual is expected to act at each age, what his childhood, adolescence and adulthood will be, how he will deal with his feelings, how he will relate to those about him, are all carefully prescribed. Departures from such blueprints are few, infrequent and relatively inconsequential.

In our culture, on the other hand, although there are certain commonly accepted realities and certain forms of behavior that are acceptable at various ages, the approved way of meeting life situations and filling the role that one chooses for oneself varies greatly. In fact, the big difference between our culture and the more primitive ones is that in ours the individual is encouraged to find and fulfill himself and, therefore, chooses his role up to a point, rather than having it defined for him; whereas in primitive society self awareness is not encouraged and the individual is taught to adapt himself totally to the prescribed mold. Certainly in our society there is no one absolute way of meeting life experiences, no one accepted mode of behavior for all children. Rather, many factors in the child's subculture, including his native endowment, socioeconomic level, religious background and rural or urban origin, will determine the standards and value systems that are taught to him and the modes of response that are expected of him.

The variations that can be anticipated in the character structure of children in this culture will of course become increasingly apparent as the child moves from a state of infantile dependence to one of greater self awareness and independence. It follows then that, while there will certainly be some individual differences even at very early ages (that is, at two and three), the general personality structure in the case of very young children will be far more homogeneous than it is by the time they reach the age of four or five.

For the student of child development and for the clinician, this homogeneity presents definite advantages along with some disadvantages. The advantages lie in the fact that if there are clearcut patterns of response typical for a given age level, deviations from this pattern in either a positive or a negative direction can easily be detected. The disadvantages of such homogeneity have to do with the fact that, at least at the very early ages, meaningful personality differences are not too clearly distinguishable.

In the following pages the course of personality development will be discussed and translated into Rorschach terms. Following this, some of the more typical deviations in development and their clinical significance will be presented. Of course, it should always be borne in mind that the Rorschach alone can certainly not give the full personality picture, just as no single test can. For this reason clinical evaluation must never be based solely on the Rorschach findings.

## Testing Procedure

In testing the preschool child, it is often well to modify some of the more usual procedures. For the youngest age group, that is the two and three year olds, it is often necessary to give the inquiry immediately after the response is given since such a young child rarely has the patience to go through the entire procedure a second time. Furthermore, even if his patience holds out, it is unlikely that his memory will. Rather than explain what he said before, he is far more likely to give an entirely new Rorschach.

The preschool child is often unable to point out with any clarity or definiteness the area of the blot that he used in giving a response. Here once again the examiner must be flexible because too much insistence will only disturb the child and prevent him from responding to subsequent blots. Far more important than the formal factors at this age are the associations that the child brings to his responses. It is therefore quite useful to use the responses almost as one might use a CAT picture. For instance, if the child interprets the card as "a bird," one might then say, "Tell me something about this bird." Since the stimulus in this case is even less well defined than in the usual pictures, the child obviously brings his own associations to the "bird." There is then much to be learned from these associations: whether it is seen as a bird flying away from a bigger bird that wants to devour it, or sitting in a tree waiting to be fed, etc.

Test behavior of the child during the Rorschach examination, even more so than in the case of the adult, is almost as important as his actual responses. The child is much less adept at hiding or disguising what he is experiencing, and so his total manner, his physical activity, his facial expression and his spontaneous comments acquire particular value. For example, after which

·blot does the child who has been apparently enjoying himself suddenly ask if his mother is still waiting for him, or if he may use the bathroom?

Because the Rorschach is in most instances a truly unfamiliar and anxiety-arousing experience for children, the child's response to the first card has very special significance. Very young children, in particular, frequently respond to the first blot with what might best be described as "initial" shock. This shock may manifest itself in a highly puzzled, anxious, frightened expression; in a drawing back from the examiner and from the blot; in a demand for the mother; in a refusal to go on; in semi-hysterical laughter employed by children in their attempts to deny anxiety, etc. The way the child exhibits his distress and the speed with which he overcomes this distress are of great significance in evaluating his ego strength and how he is likely to handle unexpected and disturbing situations. It is a particularly good criterion of the way the child will react when he first attends nursery school or kindergarten.

## Personality Development

In so far as the formal aspects of the test are concerned, the child's responses, beginning with two or two and one-half years of age and going on through childhood, should reflect his growing appreciation and acceptance of reality; his development of a concept of himself; his blossoming emotional life; and the particular mechanisms he develops for dealing with the problems he encounters. Acceleration or retardation in any of these areas can be easily detected when the child's reactions are compared with those of his peers.

### *Reality Awareness*

In the records of young children the lack of good reality testing is one of the most conspicuous features. His inability to go into a situation and analyze it and then reorganize it effectively manifests itself over and over in the large number of poor whole responses that this child offers, along with a high degree of perseveration. If the situation is unfamiliar and extremely puzzling to him, he is very likely to jump to some conclusion on the basis of some aspects of the situation that he has observed and recognized or thought he recognized, without testing this conclusion out against any firm, well established reality. Thus, although it is impossible to get this information from the child, it is very likely that many of his responses are of the *DW* order.

Poor reality testing is further aggravated by the fact that the child shows a strong tendency to perseverate. Perseveration stems in part from the fact that his first response, regardless of its nature, has been accepted and possibly even greeted with enthusiasm and so he feels he knows what is expected and thus gives the same answer over and over, hoping again to evoke from the environment the accepting attitude his initial answer produced. This is very like the behavior often encountered in young children. They do something that causes an adult to react in a pleased manner and the child then repeats his performance, often *ad nauseam*, regardless of its appropriateness, hoping in this way once again to stir up environmental enthusiasm. Still

another factor would seem to account for the child's emphasis on perseveration. As he sees it, all the Rorschach cards are the same size and have a
shiny white background. The fact that the shape of the superimposed blot
differs somewhat from card to card does not make too much impression
on the youngster for whom reality is still so unclear. In fact, it is very frequently only when the all-colored cards appear that some break in his
perseveration is likely to manifest itself.

Evidence for increasing appreciation of reality can be found in the gradual
disappearance of the perseverative tendency and a rise in good form responses. By the time the child is four and one-half or five years of age, he
should no longer perseverate, and his $F+$ percentage should have risen from
a low of 20 to 40 per cent to something approximating 50 or 60 per cent.

By six years of age, that is by the time the child is ready to enter the first
grade, he is well aware of the fact that there are realities which he must
respect, and he knows that he can no longer deal with his experiences exclusively or even primarily in terms of his own needs and in highly arbitrary
fashion. Thus, while the reactions of the six year old tend to be somewhat
concrete, at times even crude, and certainly lack the richness and subtlety
that older children and adults possess, there no longer is any appreciable
tendency to disregard or distort reality. In consequence his form level should
be quite good, form percentage relatively high, approximating about 80
per cent $F+$. From this time on any marked departures from reality can
only be considered as evidence of some disturbance. If such departures are
infrequent and not of a particularly gross or spectacular order, they may
simply reflect a momentary lack of judgment, a tendency to be overambi-
tious and daring, to overreach oneself; whereas comparatively frequent misperceptions or outright breaks with reality are evidence of more serious disturbance.

### Self Concept

The child's gradual development of a concept of himself as an independent
entity can also be traced through his reactions to the ink blots. In the very
young child the inability to go into a situation and analyze it adequately
reflects his inability to separate himself from his environment and recognize
himself as an object psychologically separate from that environment. Rather,
he can only conceive of himself as a biological entity, living from moment to
moment with little concept of past or future.

The child's lack of any sense of separateness is paralleled by his inability
to deal with the various aspects of his experiences in a way that reflects a
recognition of the presence of discrete units which may or may not be in
some way related to one another. In the Rorschach his limitations in this
respect can be seen in the overwhelming number of whole $(W)$ responses
that he offers.

The almost complete, or actually complete, absence of color responses
reinforces this picture of the child as still fused with the world about him.
If the self is the entire universe and the entire universe the self, there is no
need for an exchange of feelings, no need to attempt to bridge the emotional

gap that exists between one individual and another. Rather, the child can only assume that what he feels everyone feels, and what he wants everyone else wants. Along with this lack of any strong concept of self, there is also no human identification, and, correspondingly, on the test human interpretations are not likely to appear.

Somewhere between the age of four and five, depending upon many factors such as his mental endowment and the nature of his experiences with his environment, the child becomes increasingly aware of himself as a "self." In his test reactions evidence for this can be found in the appearance of some good large detail responses (D), pointing up his ability now to separate out aspects of his experiences rather than to deal with them in a vague, fused, indiscriminating fashion. Color responses are now also present, reflecting the child's need to relate to those about him. The fact that the way he relates is likely to be egocentric and demanding (that is, on $C$ and $CF$ basis) does not take away from the fact that he now recognizes some need to invest affect in others and share feelings with them rather than to assume that others feel exactly as he does at all times. Finally, as part of the growing awareness of self there may even be some attempts at internalizing feelings and impulses, some effort at dealing with them on symbolic and fantasy levels. It is possible that in at least some cases, a human movement response (M) will appear. Such a reaction definitely shows growing ego strength, since it gives evidence that the child now has a mechanism by means of which he can delay his responses and avoid direct acting-out as he did when he was younger. Such a reaction constitutes a big step forward on the road to maturity.

Again, by the time the child has reached school age, his concept of himself, while still somewhat crude, is relatively well developed. Certainly he knows that he is an individual in his own right, and he has a very definite picture of himself either as someone secure, loved, capable and comfortable or, in less fortunate cases, as someone only partially accepted, completely rejected, or inadequate in many respects, as the case may be.

The child's concept of himself, as in the instance of the adult, will find expression in a variety of ways. The kind of human responses that he gives will of course be important. However, since the child tends to identify strongly with animals and also with fairy and cartoon figures, the animals and mythologic folk that he interprets, the (H) answers that he gives will be most important in arriving at a concept of how he perceives and experiences himself. Actually it is the child's animal responses that are most likely to express his self concept, while his human responses are more likely to reveal his perception of those about him, expecially the adults in his immediate world. The wider the disparity between the child's picture of himself and the significant adults in his life, the more immature he probably is and the greater the difficulty he will probably have in his attempts at making identification. For example, the child who gives such interpretations as "crawling worms" or "rabbit" and whose only human response is that of a "giant" or "Frankenstein" is most probably the child who feels small and inadequate in the face of an overpowering, frightening adult world. He therefore has a long road to travel before he will feel strong enough to compete and identify with such overwhelming adults. In fact, without help it may well be that he will never achieve this. Not only does the type of animal the child interprets give indication of his self concept, the kind of activity in which that animal is engaged is also important. Certainly the child who identifies with the little bird that is waiting to be fed is quite different from the child that sees the bird as attacking another bird, fighting over a piece of food.

As the child moves along through the school years his concept of himself should become less and less primitive and more civilized and what we call "human." He should no longer see himself as little other than a big mouth waiting for oral supplies but as someone with strength and purpose, working with himself and with others in goal-directed fashion. Thus, while the six year old will give a high number of animal responses and some ($H$) responses, with relatively few real human interpretations, by the time the child is about 10 years old these more immature concepts should have been replaced by more adult ones.

### Emotionality

As has already been indicated, the child's emotional life begins to develop when the child recognizes that he is not omnipotent and that what he feels and wants is not necessarily what everyone else feels and wants. He then recognizes the need for sharing his feelings with others although, because of his immaturity and general lack of control, he can generally only do this in egocentric, impulsive fashion. Hence his first color responses are almost inevitably of the $C$ and $CF$ variety. As his appreciation of reality increases and his control grows, the $C$ responses should disappear and some $FC$ make their appearance. However, it is not until the age of 9 or 10 that the more controlled type of emotional response equals or outweighs the more impulsive reactions.

### Adjustment Mechanisms

The child's ways of dealing with his experiences and allaying the anxieties that are inevitable as he goes through the socializing process can also be discerned from his reactions to the Rorschach test. Denial and avoidance are prominent in the early years. Thus when the two or three year old is anxious because of the nature of the experience confronting him, he is very likely either to try to get away from the immediate situation or to do what he can to negate its anxiety-evoking properties. Some children will definitely make a statement to the effect that "It can't hurt you"; others get silly and ascribe to the objects they perceive positive qualities which are inappropriate.

By the time the child is four or five years of age, he attempts to exercise some control over anxiety-arousing impulses, but, as may be expected, his control is weak and intermittent. Thus, good form is likely to be punctuated by bad form and judgment swept away by a flood of impulse and feeling. Blocking and repression are also evident in the five and six year old. As has already been indicated, in at least some children the beginnings of attempts at internalization, at dealing with problems on symbolic levels, are evident in the appearance of $M$ responses.

In some children efforts at constriction and isolation become apparent at quite an early age. Once the child has learned to analyze his experiences and deal with certain limited aspects of them, he may exploit his ability in order to gain a sense of security. By confining himself to certain obvious concrete details of a situation he feels less threatened, better able to control himself and the circumstances in which he is placed. Thus, contrary to what is ordinarily seen in four and one-half to six year olds, there are some children who give a relatively high number of responses rather than the customary 15 or so, and the majority of these responses will be large details. Along with this recourse to constriction and this emphasis on the immediate and the practical, the form per cent is likely to be extremely high and possibly quite good. In these instances the beginnings of the obsessive-compulsive character structure can be clearly discerned.

## Deviations

While the personality structure in early childhood in most instances is not yet sufficiently well differentiated to permit the definition of clear character types, trends such as those described above in relation to the obsessive-compulsive character are certainly evident by the time the child is six or seven years of age. Thus, in contrast to the child who is already resorting to constriction and control, there is the child who dissociates himself from his unacceptable impulses, projects these onto the environment and then reacts in exaggeratedly phobic, hysterical fashion. There is the child who in the main shows little frustration tolerance and tends to act out as compared to the child who deals with his anxiety in self-punitive and self-destructive fashion: the behavior problem child in contrast to the bed-wetting, nail biting, stuttering child and the child with psychosomatic disorders.

In the main, children who do not suffer from a disorder of the central nervous system or who are not classified as schizophrenic but whose development has nevertheless not been of the expected healthy order are the children who have not learned how to make an effective adjustment between their own needs and the environmental demands. Such difficulties may be due to any number of causes: too much may be expected of them before they are able to meet such pressures; they may not be provided with enough emotional support; not enough positive response is offered to motivate them to make adequate adjustive efforts, etc. Inconsistency in the attitude of parents or parent surrogates is a very common cause of maladjustment. For example, the child is often expected to be good, compliant and conforming in certain situations, especially in the home and in the school, to show comparatively little initiative and self assertion but at the same time is required to be very independent and self sufficient in dealing with his peers.

The deviations that will result from failure to move along effectively in the developmental process will manifest themselves in many ways, depending upon the nature of the environment and the child's constitutional endowment, both of which certainly play an important part in shaping his "temperament." Lack of control with explosive emotional outbursts and low frustration tolerance may be the conspicuous features. In other cases, the emphasis may be on control and, because the child feels threatened, this control may be carried to exaggerated lengths and accompanied by much withdrawal and the turning back of all feeling on himself or complete repression of feeling and fantasy. While it is a gross oversimplification, children may be divided into two groups in terms of their reactions to emotional disturbance, namely, the acting out child who gives way to his impulses and the overcontrolled child whose behavior is characterized by exaggerated attempts to achieve, conform and comply.

If the behavior is almost completely of the acting out variety, there is unlikely to be any attempt at delay of feeling and impulse, little if any capacity for internalizing feelings, as well as little real feeling for others. In these cases emotional immaturity, egocentricity and instability will be of an exaggerated order. On the tests such weaknesses will show themselves either in explosive emotional outbursts (many $CF$'s and $C$'s) or in the absence of any affective investment in the environment and little awareness of, or response to, environmental pressure. Serious emotional impoverishment is therefore one of the most significant aspects of the Rorschach records of many acting out and delinquent children. Lacking a meaningful inner life and no pleasure in their contacts with the world about them, they give immediate expression to whatever impulse or feeling moves them. Their Rorschach protocols are therefore likely to consist largely of form responses and some animal movement responses $(FM)$, possibly interspersed by occasional $CF$'s and/or $C$'s.

It is important to distinguish between the impoverishment of the primitive acting out child and the barrenness that stems from the severe inhibition of affect, from the child's desperate attempt to control impulses and feelings in order that he may conform. In these latter cases depression as well as barrenness is evident. One distinguishing feature is of course the general behavior of the child as well as his performance on other tests and his life history. On the Rorschach itself the acting out child is very likely to be indifferent and arbitrary, producing vague, "cheap" whole responses and a number of poor form responses. The animals that he perceives are very likely to be "wild" ones, engaged in aggressive, destructive behavior. On the other hand, an exaggeratedly constricted, repressed and depressed child will approach the whole situation very slowly and carefully. His perceptions will be as good as his age and intellectual endowment permit, and the animals that he interprets will probably be more passive and timid, although angry, ferocious ones also occur, revealing the impulses he is striving so hard to repress.

In many cases the deviations that are encountered are less extreme than those cited above. Many children alternate between acting out and conforming. Thus there is likely to be evidence of strong efforts at control and conformity in their productions (high $F$ and $F+$, possibly some $FC$ and $M$) punctuated by sporadic emotional explosions when the stress that they are experiencing becomes too great to be contained. Such a picture is especially typical of children whose disturbances find indirect outlets in such channels as speech difficulties, tics and other neurotic manifestations.

One of the most common pictures encountered in clinics and private practise is that of the passive-aggressive child. This is the child who wants to conform, whose desperate need for environmental support and approval leads him to repress what he feels is undesirable and who tries at all times to do what he thinks is wanted. Yet he cannot exercise the control necessary for such behavior because of the resentment and hostility that he feels toward the environment. However, he rarely gives direct expression to this hostility, rarely strikes out verbally or physically against others. Instead, he finds many indirect ways of releasing his anger. These then are the bed wetters, the children of good intelligence who do not learn, and in some instances, the children with somatic complaints and the children who learn to control the environment through their weakness, their dependency and their passivity.

In the Rorschach records of these children there is likely to be a marked alternation between responses reflecting passive, dependent attitudes ("two animals clinging to the branches of a tree," "two animals holding onto a pole," "two birds in a nest with their mouths open waiting for the mother bird to bring them some worms," etc.) and responses revealing aggressive, destructive drives ("two animals stalking their prey," "two Mars men fighting over a rocket ship," "two boys sticking their tongues out at each other," etc.). The formal aspects of the test will reflect a shift from control of an exaggerated order to moments when control will be completely lost. Thus while emphasis is likely to be on form, sporadic $CF$'s, and $CF$'s accompanied by $M$, will probably occur.

In terms of the criteria of development described earlier in this chapter, namely the child's appreciation and acceptance of reality, his development of a concept of himself, the nature of his emotional life and the particular methods he has developed for dealing with the problems he encounters, the following would seem to be the case: The acting out, neurotic and so-called passive-aggressive children have great difficulty accepting the realities they are called on to face. In the acting out child there is likely to be a direct ignoring and defying of reality, a high-handed approach to experiences, whereas the neurotic child is likely to be overly aware of reality and the limits set by reality and fearful of any impulse toward pushing or rebelling against that reality. In consequence the poor form responses of the acting out child will be the result of carelessness, impulsiveness and indifference, whereas in the neurotic child the poor form interpretation will reflect his ineffectual effort at achieving some resolution between his own needs and the expectations of the environment. This is the child whose timidity and passivity in conjunction with his underlying anxiety-evoking hostility is likely to come up with such a response as "a little rabbit with horns on his head."

For the acting out child the concept of the self is likely to be of a very primitive order. For him the self is an object with many needs and wants which demand immediate satisfaction. On the whole he tends to experience himself as an isolated figure, giving and getting little if anything from the world about him. There is a kind of "lone wolf" quality to many of these children. In fact one of the responses sometimes given by these children is that of "a wolf with its head back howling at the moon."

The neurotic child, on the other hand, perceives himself as either small and helpless, or as a kind of "monster" who must conceal his "badness" and do what he can to compensate for it. The passive-aggressive child is likely to vacillate between experiencing himself as good, acceptable, passive and conforming, and contrariwise as bad, aggressive and defiant.

For all these children emotional development will inevitably be of a deviant order. Thus there is likely to be an almost complete absence of any emotional experience, either because all feeling experiences have been sharply repressed or because they have never been adequately developed. In other cases there is likely to be a flooding over of feeling which cannot be controlled. In some instances in which emphasis is on conformity, a kind of pseudo-precocity may manifest itself in the early appearance of *FC* responses, accompanied by a high *F* and *P* per cent and little else.

In so far as defensive operations are concerned, clearly defined defense systems are not usual in children. Rather, the child is likely to use a variety of defenses ranging from denial and projection in very young children to repression, blocking and sublimation in older children. When the child of six or more still relies heavily on denial and projection and lacks any capacity whatsoever for internalization and delay of impulse, he is certainly not developing in line with his peers and lacks the ego strength that most children his age can exercise. In Rorschach terms a child of six or seven who does not give a single *M* response and whose *F+* per cent is low is manifesting some disturbance in his development. When well developed and crystallized mechanisms, comparable to those found in adults, are seen in a child, one must assume that he has been under special stress, that his needs are of a desperate order and that he is really a very seriously disturbed individual.

### Schizophrenic Children

The schizophrenic child is the child with such severe defects in his ego structure that his functioning in all areas is crippled. In particular, perceptual disturbances, poor reality testing and weak integrative capacities make it practically impossible for this child to develop a stable, meaningful self concept and to achieve firm identification. Similarly, he cannot make order out of his experiences with the environment but instead perceives them in a distorted, confused and at times even bizarre fashion that bears little relation to commonly accepted reality. As part of his failure to find the "self," the schizophrenic child is unable to separate himself from the world about him, to experience himself as a discrete, independent unit with fixed limits. At best this "self" is a vague shadowy figure, always in danger of being swallowed up and lost in a vast, amorphous, boundless world. Consequently the child's confusion and anxiety are of extreme proportions. He lives a kind of nightmarish existence, always threatened by the possibility of complete annihilation.

The way the child copes with his disturbance depends upon a number of factors, including his age, the age at onset of illness, his intellectual endowment and his other resources, his past experiences and the support given him by his environment. Correspondingly, the behavior of these children differs. In some children withdrawal is the conspicuous feature, whereas in others there may be much acting out of a totally disorganized, unacceptable, even destructive order. The common factor in all these cases will be the disturbances noted above, namely the perceptual difficulties, the poor reality testing, the lack of an adequate, stable self concept and an inability to make meaningful identifications.

In his response to the Rorschach the schizophrenic child reveals not only his special difficulties but also his attempts at coping with them. The child who develops schizophrenia at two and one-half or three years, when he has not acquired the skills that would provide him with some ego strength, will even at a later age give test reactions that are meager and empty, in many ways like those of defectives. In fact, it is often difficult to distinguish such protocols from those of children with low IQ's. Sometimes the differential diagnosis can be made on the basis of the schizophrenic child's compulsive concern with numbers and/or his preoccupation with time and space, topics most unlikely to interest the defective child. Thus the schizophrenic child who is functioning at a low mental level may suddenly begin to count the wings on the butterfly at the top of Card VI or the feet on the caterpillar in the lower center area of Card X. Preoccupation with time and space may find expression in efforts at placing a figure "two feet up" or "a hundred years ago," responses which are in contrast to the generally flat, barren quality of most of the child's productions.

In some instances the child's failure to set limits and come to terms with reality leads to uncritical responses not based on any real perception of the stimulus. For example, there are schizophrenic children who give a response to Card I and then associate to that response rather than to the blot. If the first response is a bird, the following ones are likely to be "a black bird," "a blue bird," "a red bird," "a pigeon," "an eagle," "a duck," etc. Frequently the interpretations become less and less related to the stimulus. This kind of productivity is very likely to go on indefinitely and often has to be terminated by the examiner. Each blot may be handled in this way, showing an almost complete disregard of reality.

The child who shows the kind of pseudo-perseveration described above or who responds much in the manner of the defective child has few if any defenses against his illness and is more or less overwhelmed and disorganized by it. On the other hand, the child who has developed some strengths before he became ill will use the defenses employed by all children but will carry these efforts to extremes and apply his adjustive techniques in a nonconstructive fashion. In his recourse to denial he is likely to deny everything, and it is not unusual to get from the schizophrenic child a record in which each interpretation is negated almost before it is given. In particular, on inquiry such a child is likely to insist that he never made a given response or that he cannot find it now.

In his efforts to control his disturbing impulses and make order out of the confusion in which he is operating, the schizophrenic child of school age may use obsessive-compulsive defenses, selecting from his experiences certain aspects of them that correspond to his immediate needs and which he feels he can handle, while repressing many essential details of a situation. Such classically obsessive-compulsive pictures are not usual in children. Furthermore, in the schizophrenic child these efforts are very likely to be subject to sporadic and spectacular disruption when ego boundaries are lost and reality ignored. In these children the $D$ per cent and $F$ per cent will be high, but poor form will alternate with good form, and the poor form responses are likely to be of a particularly bizarre order.

Similarly, the child who seeks to allay his anxiety by projecting his unacceptable feelings and impulses onto others will carry these efforts to paranoid lengths. He is the child who in his Rorschach will see "devils," "monsters," "a man swallowing up the world," "God," "the sky falling down," etc. Such children often have grandiose ideas which find reflection not only in the content of the interpretations but in a high $W$ per cent, frequently in conjunction with a large number of $M$ responses. However, several of these $M$'s will probably be $M-$.

The schizophrenic child's inability to make a stable, satisfying identification is likely to manifest itself in any one of a number of ways. In some instances, particularly in the case of the child who has been ill since an early age and who is functioning intellectually, emotionally and socially at a very dull, inadequate level, there is likely to be a complete lack of any human interpretations. The child who is trying to control his feelings and impulses by isolating and repressing much that is threatening to him may also show no human responses or at best give just one. Occasionally, however, he may give a relatively large number of human detail answers, many of which are faces. Such responses not only reflect the child's emphasis on constriction but in their content reveal his feeling of being watched, criticized and possibly even punished and attacked.

In contrast to the schizophrenic child who gives few or no human interpretations, there is the child who is so obsessed with his need to find himself that he gives an overwhelming number of human and human movement responses. The seeming precocity of such interpretations is not supported by his other reactions since in many of these cases the numerous $M$ responses are not accompanied by an adequate number of $FM$'s. In fact, sometimes there are $M$'s but no $FM$'s at all. In other words, the child's efforts at identification have no sound underpinning. The fact that these many human and human movement responses are often found in conjunction with $CF$, $CF-$ and $C$ responses also attests to their deviant and nonconstructive nature. Very often the humans that these children perceive are of a most bizarre order, as when they give such responses as "a man with three heads and his tongue is reaching down to the ground, and someone shot him with a cannon ball and he has a big hole in his stomach."

An inability to cope adequately with his impulses often leads the schizophrenic child to offer direct sexual responses, something that is rare in a child's Rorschach. Likewise, the hostility that such a child experiences is very likely to find expression in a far more primitive, brutal fashion than is ordinarily encountered. Morbid preoccupations and concern with death is also characteristic of the Rorschach reactions of some schizophrenic children.

It is evident, then, that while the schizophrenic child's problems are in no way different from those of all children, he is not at all well equipped to meet these problems effectively. Consequently his conflicts are not resolved, and his anxiety is intense and continuous. In some instances he gives up the struggle altogether and makes no attempt to find himself and come to terms with reality, while in other instances his struggles produce much tension and highlight the deviant nature of his perceptions and reactions.

## Prepuberty

In concluding this discussion of children's Rorschachs it seems advisable to make brief mention of what happens to the prepuberty child and how his Rorschach record reflects the changes, physical and psychological, that he is experiencing. This seems especially important because the rather drastic alteration in the mode of response that characterizes the prepuberty child sometimes occurs as early as nine or 10 years of age.

Sometime around the age of 10 or 11 the child who has been finding satisfaction in the role that he is filling, who has been enjoying the companionship of his peers and the security that his environment has offered him, begins to question this role and to perceive himself and his relationships with others in less confident terms. The things he was sure about and comfortable with, his preference for the company of his own sex, his assurance about what it means to be a boy rather than a girl, his concept of his role, etc., no longer seem so definite and acceptable to him. Troubled by his shifting feelings and attitudes, he becomes uncertain and anxious. If he is not sure of himself, he is certainly not prepared to handle his relationships with others. When this state of affairs occurs, the child tends to react to it by withdrawing, stressing control and turning feeling back on himself. He becomes absorbed in himself and devotes much of his energy to refinding himself and redefining his role.

In some instances this need to refind the self leads the child to exercise much repression since he is anxious about everything he does and everything he is experiencing and feels safer when he deals with his experiences on purely formal intellectual levels. In such cases his Rorschach record will show a heavy emphasis on form and little else. Other children will turn their feelings back on themselves rather than invest affect in others. Their records will certainly show a drop in the number of color responses given, and evidence of an active emotional life will be found only in the presence of a number of human movement interpretations. These interpretations are very likely to be of a varying order, at times showing identification with vigorous active figures, at times with passive dependent ones, as the child tries on different roles in his attempts to refind himself. This kind of adjustive effort is likely to continue for a year or two, until the child is 12 or 13 and once more feels secure enough to move out actively and consistently in search of meaningful social and emotional relationships with others. It is during this period of emotional withdrawal and self involvement that for the first time the child's Experience Balance on the Rorschach will show emphasis on the movement side. Until this time, for most children the color answers definitely outweigh the human movement interpretations.

While all children seem to show this withdrawal and retreat into the self during prepuberty (girls more so than boys), there is a difference in the way the healthy child handles this troublesome period as compared with the way the maladjusted child reacts. The so-called "normal" child withdraws, but he is not so disturbed that he cannot accept reality. Consequently his good form percentage remains high. In disturbed but nonpsychotic children, the form percentage tends to drop, but the poor form responses are not grossly bizarre. In the schizophrenic child the poor form responses are likely to be numerous, or if the form remains relatively good the responses will never-theless be of a most atypical and unrealistic order. At this time, then, one of the chief criteria of strength is the ability to maintain contact with reality despite the pressures to which the child is being subjected as a result of physiologic and psychological changes.

It is at this time, during the prepuberty period, that the child becomes aware of the subtle nuances that play a part in many of his experiences and relationships. As part of this awareness he learns to make modifications in his responses and to alter his reactions in a way that will bring him the environmental acceptance that is so important to him. Thus, it is generally during this period, at about the age of 10 or 11, that shading responses are likely to appear. It is only rarely that they occur earlier except possibly in a vague, diffuse form, as in such responses as "clouds" or "sky." At this time, however, the relatively well adjusted child will see the bearskin rug on Cards IV or VI and indicate his awareness of the textured aspect of the blot. In the emotionally disturbed child such awareness is not likely to be present. If it is, it will not be accompanied by the control necessary to make such awareness a positive factor in the child's handling of his experiences. For the psychotic child such awareness is almost impossible.

### Final Comments

Throughout this discussion emphasis has been on developmental factors and the way in which these find expression in the child's test reactions. It is only from this vantage point, in terms of his level of development, in conjunction with his abilities and resources and his particular environment and the problems inherent in it, that the child's productions can be adequate-ly appreciated. With the child, therefore, even more than in the case of the adult, "blind" interpretations should not be undertaken. In addition to a knowledge of the child's age, sex and intellectual endowment, everything else that is known about him should be available to the tester. Such facts as his socioeconomic level, his religious and racial background, the number, age and sex of his siblings, whether or not he comes from an intact home, and the reasons why testing has been requested are all of vital importance in attempting to understand how the child perceives himself and his world and just what he is trying to do about his experiences and relationships. Only when the "realities" of the child's situation are known can his reactions to and handling of these realities be adequately evaluated, and the direction of his future growth charted.

## References

1. Ames, L. B., Learned, J., Métraux, R. W., & Walker, R. N. *Child Rorschach responses: developmental trends from two to ten years.* New York: Paul B. Hoeber, 1952.
2. Bender, L.   Childhood schizophrenia. *Amer. J. Orthopsychiat.*, 1947, *17*, 40–56.
3. Beck, S. J., Bender, L., Bettleheim, B., Szurek, S. A., Goldfarb, W., Braunstein, P., Lorge, I., Eisenberg, L., & Kanner, L.   Childhood schizophrenia. Symposium, 1955. *Amer. J. Orthopsychiat.*, 1956, *26*, 497–566.
4. Halpern, F.   *A clinical approach to children's Rorschachs.* New York: Grune & Stratton, 1953.
5. Marshall, J.   Children in the present world situation. *Amer. J. Orthopsychiat.*, 1953, *23*, 454–464.
6. Mead, M., & Wolfenstein, M.   *Childhood in contemporary cultures.* Chicago: Univer. Chicago Press, 1954.
7. Paulsen, A. A.   Personality development in the middle years of childhood: a ten-year longitudinal study of thirty public school children by means of Rorschach tests and social histories. *Amer. J. Orthopsychiat.*, 1954, *24*, 336–350.

# 3

## The Rorschach in Adolescence

### MARGUERITE R. HERTZ

IT MAY APPEAR highly artificial to demarcate one stage in the life of the child—adolescence—and treat in isolation the Rorschach studies which have been made on children in this period of their development. Adolescence is only a stage in the total life cycle of the developing child, one period in an ongoing process. Consideration of this stage without knowledge of prior stages which contribute to it may lead to superficial and even distorted generalizations.

While we keep in mind that the child is a growing organism and that there are no hard and fast lines between one stage of development and another, we also realize that there are periods in the life of the child when special conditions prevail and significant problems present themselves. These must be understood by the psychologist who has the responsibility of understanding and guiding his development.

Adolescence is one such stage of development in which many physiologic and psychological phenomena undergo both quantitative and qualitative changes. It appears legitimate, then, to concentrate on this relatively circumscribed period of development, to obtain descriptive and normative data, to determine common characteristics and differences between adolescents, to study growth trends and to analyze the various conditions which facilitate or retard their occurrence. Any clinical instrument which is of service in this task is valuable. The Rorschach is one tool which permits such study.

Unfortunately, there is no unanimity of opinion as to the age range or the conditions which distinguish adolescence from any other period of development. Some psychologists define it as the period between 11 and 16 years of age for girls and 12 and 17 years for boys. Others vary these ages by one to two years. On the other hand, adolescence is sometimes made coincident with the period after pubescence. Still other psychologists are content to speak of "the second decade of life."

Thus in Rorschach studies, as in other studies, age groups are somewhat arbitrarily selected in the teen years to represent adolescence, on the assumption that the characteristic behavior and the shifts noted take place during the years in which sexual maturity has been achieved or is about to be attained. It is assumed that the results obtained may be associated at least in part with developmental changes taking place during this period. Indeed, results are frequently interpreted in terms of pubertal status and changes. Only a few Rorschach studies [15, 24] have been made of children differentiated on the basis of physiologic development or stage of pubescence.

In the present chapter, studies of children in the second decade of life will be considered, with occasional references to children below 10 years of age and to adults. Discussion will be restricted to those studies in which the Rorschach method has been used (a) to describe the characteristics of the adolescent at various ages in terms of norms for the group and (b) to identify age and developmental changes taking place in the adolescent years.

### Need for Normative Data on the Adolescent Years

While some investigators apply normative data established on the basis of adult groups to adolescent Rorschach records (and to those of other ages), they should of course be appropriate to the age and developmental level. In adolescence, with the relatively sudden introduction of so many new factors in the developing personality which may precipitate developmental "crises" and produce stress and anxieties, it is especially important to have an appropriate frame of reference for evaluating an adolescent record and for determining whether or not Rorschach patterns fall within the normal range or whether they deviate radically. Unless appropriate Rorschach norms are utilized, Rorschach results cannot be characterized as typical or atypical of any one child or group of children. On the basis of adult norms, the adolescent may show many deviant patterns pointing to maladjustment, even pathology, which, when viewed in proper perspective, may not be deviant at all. Hence Rorschach norms for the adolescent age range are necessary.

Further, appropriate scoring criteria for the Rorschach factors which are relatively statistical in derivation, $D$, $F+$, $P$ and $O$, must likewise be established and utilized. Contrary to statements of Bohm[6] and Loosli-Usteri,[43] current research [1,22,30] shows many significant differences between the $D$ and the $Dr$ of children, adolescents and adults. This is similarly true of the $P$, [1,23] and it is obvious that it is true of the "original" score.

There are some investigators who contend that if the developmental aspects of the Rorschach data are to be studied, it is necessary to use the same scoring standards for these factors at every age level. Thus Bohm[6] in his criticism of the developmental studies of Ames et al.[1,2] finds it impossible to follow the changes of these test factors through the various ages of development. "Different scoring for children and adults would prohibit us from conducting investigations in psychological development as it is reflected in these factors" (reference 6, page 311).

It appears to us that the purpose for which we utilize normative data must be kept in mind. If we wish to compare the adolescent's performance with that of the adult, we utilize adult normative standards and adult norms. When we interpret our scores, however, we must keep in mind the procedure we have followed.

With the use of the Rorschach popular score, for example, it is one thing to indicate that there has been an increase in $P$ from childhood to late adolescence, the $P$ being developed on the basis of the performance of adult groups. It is another thing to say that there has been an increase in the ability of the individual to conform intellectually to the thinking of his group. If the adult populars are utilized, it would appear more accurate to indicate that there has been an increase in the ability of the child to conform intellectually to the thinking of the adult, perhaps in his ability to recognize adult social conventions. If, on the other hand, we want to judge the child's ability to adapt and to conform to the thinking of *his group as he matures*, it seems more appropriate to judge him in terms of his group with appropriate standards. Both procedures are valuable, but they must not be confused, as is done more often than not. Further, we see no incongruity in studying the development of the child in terms of populars (or normal details or originals) appropriately developed for the age group to which he belongs, despite the fact that some scoring criteria happen to be different for different ages. We study major aspects of the personality and functioning as the child grows, not scores per se.

### Normative and Developmental Studies

Rorschach[58] did not include norms for adolescents in his original monograph. He suggested, however, that different "Erlebnistypen" were characteristic of different age groups. He viewed the personality as relatively stable throughout the course of an individual's life. At stated intervals, however, one should anticipate profound shifts. Children in the early years were supposed to be ambiequal, with a balance between introversive and extratensive elements—a type of personality which reappeared at puberty.

Since Rorschach's early publication some workers have sought to establish normative data for various age groups. Others have preferred to work with an ideal concept of maturity and adjustment and have identified subjectively norms which purport to represent ideals for normality.[39,40]

The normative studies have, for the most part, used the cross sectional approach. A few longitudinal studies have likewise been reported. Most studies have presented norms in terms of means and/or medians. Some have included proportions of groups giving certain patterns. Also, since it is generally observed that boys and girls of similar age differ in physical, physiologic and psychological functioning in the second decade, many investigators report separate norms for the two sexes.

Finally, most of the Rorschach studies with adolescent subjects relate the characteristics observed and the changes noted in Rorschach patterns to psychological characteristics or processes derived from other sources.

Davidson and Klopfer[14] have summarized norms for children including those of the adolescent age range. These include the pioneer study by Behn-Eschenburg[5] and the studies by Loosli-Usteri[41,42] and Hertz.[21] This summary was followed by other studies published by Hertzman and Margulies,[35] Loosli-Usteri,[43] Cotte[8-10] and Mons.[47]

Normative data are likewise reported by Meili-Dworetzki,[45] Rabin and Beck,[54] Thetford, Molish and Beck[67] and Beck.[4] More recently, Steiner[15] has reported norms for 300 girls at three stages of development (prepubertal, pubertal and "adolescent"). In this study, however, the group Rorschach was used, and no statistical evidence for the results was included.

Norms for specific patterns are reported by Taulbee, Sisson and Gaston,[65] Bühler, LeFever, Kallstedt and Peak[7] and Kallstedt.[37] Hemmendinger's genetic study[19] of the structural aspects of perception may also be mentioned at this point.

The book *Adolescent Rorschach Responses*, by Ames, Métraux and Walker,[2] provides the most comprehensive Rorschach study of adolescents to date. Seven hundred records are analyzed and norms reported at each age level from 10 to 16 years. Unfortunately the records are mixed in the age groups, and some records represent the first Rorschach which the child has taken, while others are from the same child at more than one age. The study is a cross sectional one. Longitudinal data from the same children are not used in the analyses, except in a chapter devoted to individual cases. One of the first longitudinal studies was reported by Suares,[64] who retested children who had been tested earlier by Loosli-Usteri[41] and Shapiro.[62]

Early studies at the Brush Foundation based on 41 boys and 35 girls of high average intelligence and high socioeconomic status, tested at 12 and 15 years of age, include results for movement,[25] color patterns,[34] "Erlebnistypen,"[27,28] and "control" patterns.[33] Other normative data appear in mimeographed form.[29] Another study[24] is reported in summary form based on the records of 80 twelve year old and 100 fifteen year old girls identified on the basis of physical maturity as determined by the age at menarche. Twelve and 15 year old groups, prepubescent by and pubescent for 12, 18 and 24 months, are studied in terms of Rorschach color and movement patterns, "Erlebnistypen" and the stability-maturity index. These patterns are likewise studied in groups of girls of like pubescent status at 12 and 15 years with special comparison of the 15 year old "early" pubescents (pubescent for 36 to 60 months) and 15 year old "late" pubescents (pubescent for one to 24 months).

Paulsen[50] presents cross sectional norms for 30 school children as well as follow-up data 10.5 years later. Perhaps the most extensive longitudinal studies with adolescent groups have been made at the Institute of Child Welfare at the University of California and reported by McFate and Orr[44]. The report of Ranzoni, Grant and Ives[55] on "card pull" of the several age groups is invaluable in that it is the first systematic study of the potential of each card in terms of Rorschach factors. Data pertinent to adolescent development may also be found in Harrower's book, *Personality Change and Development as Measured by the Projective Techniques*.[18]

### Results of some Rorschach Studies of Children in the Second Decade

Obviously it is not possible to summarize all the studies made of children in the second decade of life. We shall instead refer to certain of these studies

which present normative data that permit us to make tentative generalizations as to the personality characteristics of children and the trends of development in this period of life. Reference must of course be made to the
original material for the means or medians discussed, for the statistics showing
significance between group means or medians, and for results reported in
which proportions of the groups are compared for the presence or absence
of specific scores. Table 1 summarizes the normative data amassed from
studies at the Brush Foundation which many investigators use for scoring
adolescent records.[29]

It cannot be overemphasized that norms must be considered only in
terms of the nature of the sample of the population on which they are based,
the method of administration and scoring, and in general in terms of the
many variations in procedure prevalent today[32]. While normative data can
be compared only in a rough manner, it is of interest to study the results
presented by various investigators and to note the developmental trends
which are suggested in these studies for the teen* years.

### Intellectual Organization and Functioning

Certain Rorschach patterns reveal the level and nature of intellectual
functioning and the degree to which ego control is attained. Hence the productivity, initial reaction time, the mental approach, form level, human
movement patterns, the popularity and originality of the responses and
various aspects of the content of the responses have been utilized in several
studies to evaluate intellectual organization and functioning.

#### Total R (Productivity)

In general, an increase is reported in the total number of responses as the
child progresses from year to year in the second decade. Thus an increase is
reported from 10 to 12 years,[50,54] from 10 to 16 years,[2] from 14 to 16 years
compared with 6 to 9 years[67] and from 11 to 18 years.[44] In the Hertz data,[29]
little difference is noted between the $R$ given by children at 12 and 15 years
of age, however, although girls at both ages tend to give more than boys.
For Ames et al.[2] also, girls give more $R$ at every age from 10 to 16 years,
with exception of 11 years. Again, the average $R$ for the girls of McFate and
Orr[44] was higher than that for boys at 11, 13, 15 and 18 years.

The 14 to 17 year group of Thetford et al.[67] shows a higher mean $R$ than
that of adults. Further, an increase in fluctuation of $R$ is reported in the
three groups studied with the greatest amount of fluctuation in the 14 to
17 year group.

It would appear, then, that as the child progresses in the teen years, he
becomes more productive, girls appearing to be more productive than boys.
At least in the age group 14 to 17 years, there seems to be considerable
unevenness of intellectual functioning.

#### Initial Reaction Times (Freedom of Approach, Facility in Reaction)

Children 14 to 17 years of age appear to be less variable in their initial
reactions to the blots when compared to younger groups, showing a lower

*The term "teen" is used broadly throughout this chapter to refer to the entire second
decade.

TABLE 1.—*Rorschach Norms* for 12 and 15 Year Old Adolescents

N = 96 (51 boys, 45 girls)

| | | 12 year | | | 15 year | | | | 12 year | | | 15 year | | |
|---|---|---|---|---|---|---|---|---|---|---|---|---|---|---|
| | | M | SD | Mdn | M | SD | Mdn | | M | SD | Mdn | M | SD | Mdn |
| R | b.† | 34.26 | 13.53 | | 38.87 | 13.66 | | RT(1)Sh | 16.17 | 9.09 | | 14.13 | 8.76 | |
| | g.† | 38.71 | 13.05 | | 41.38 | 17.34 | | | 13.78 | 6.34 | | 13.87 | 8.09 | |
| | tot.† | 36.43 | 13.48 | | 37.54 | 16.02 | | | 15.00 | 7.96 | | 14.00 | 8.44 | |
| RT(1)C | b. | 16.77 | 7.66 | | 16.94 | 9.59 | | RT(1) | 16.45 | 7.76 | | 15.51 | 8.41 | |
| | g. | 15.69 | 6.36 | | 13.40 | 9.02 | | | 14.80 | 5.51 | | 13.69 | 7.89 | |
| | tot. | 16.24 | 7.07 | | 15.20 | 9.48 | | | 15.64 | 6.81 | | 14.62 | 8.21 | |
| W | b. | 9.74 | 5.97 | | 7.72 | 4.62 | | %W | 32.06 | 20.00 | | 26.49 | 17.06 | |
| | g. | 8.96 | 5.39 | | 7.02 | 5.36 | | | 25.93 | 20.01 | | 21.73 | 19.49 | |
| | tot. | 9.36 | 5.71 | | 7.38 | 4.92 | | | 29.35 | 20.20 | | 24.75 | 19.10 | |
| D | b. | 17.62 | 8.90 | | 19.02 | 8.34 | | %D | 50.79 | 14.34 | | 56.04 | 11.58 | |
| | g. | 20.73 | 9.86 | | 23.07 | 10.83 | | | 51.73 | 15.44 | | 55.31 | 14.02 | |
| | tot. | 19.14 | 9.51 | | 21.00 | 9.85 | | | 51.25 | 14.90 | | 55.68 | 12.84 | |
| Ⓦ | b. | 4.38 | 3.54 | | 3.62 | 3.30 | | %Ⓦ | 14.23 | 11.76 | | 12.02 | 10.82 | |
| | g. | 4.00 | 3.01 | | 3.36 | 3.16 | | | 11.71 | 10.15 | | 10.27 | 11.69 | |
| | tot. | 4.20 | 3.30 | | 3.49 | 3.24 | | | 13.00 | 11.08 | | 11.16 | 8.43 | |
| Dr | b. | 4.77 | 5.58 | 3.38 | 4.89 | 5.52 | 3.36 | %Dr | 11.68 | 11.08 | 5.67 | 11.77 | 9.61 | 9.80 |
| | g. | 6.33 | 5.58 | 5.42 | 8.42 | 8.01 | 7.17 | | 15.64 | 12.00 | 11.50 | 16.82 | 12.61 | 16.60 |
| | tot. | 5.55 | 5.64 | 4.00 | 6.62 | 7.08 | 4.17 | | 13.33 | 11.66 | 8.50 | 14.24 | 11.22 | 11.43 |
| S(S) + s(s) | b. | | | 4.14 | | | 3.36 | %S(S) + s(s) | | | 11.40 | | | 9.80 |
| | g. | | | 4.21 | | | 3.50 | | | | 10.20 | | | 7.63 |
| | tot. | | | 4.20 | | | 3.40 | | | | 10.80 | | | 9.00 |

*Reference should be made to Hertz[26, 29-31] for a description of Rorschach scoring symbols and formulas. In addition Ⓦ reflects wholes which are not popular or vague and which do not involve minus forms. *Sh* is used for Shading in general.

† b. = boys; g = girls; tot. = total.

| | | | | | |
|---|---|---|---|---|---|
| g. | b. | 12.01 | 6.35 | 10.81 | 6.02 |
| | g. | 12.44 | 5.56 | 11.88 | 6.14 |
| | tot. | 12.22 | 5.98 | 11.33 | 6.11 |
| %F Prim | b. | 74.91 | 13.83 | 72.55 | 14.07 |
| | g. | 71.55 | 14.34 | 68.09 | 12.88 |
| | tot. | 73.27 | 14.19 | 70.37 | 13.68 |
| %F + Prim | b. | 82.59 | 11.60 | 87.30 | 8.73 |
| | g. | 83.78 | 9.64 | 87.27 | 7.90 |
| | tot. | 83.19 | 10.70 | 87.28 | 8.33 |
| %M | b. | 8.70 | 7.43 | 11.26 | 8.40 |
| | g. | 11.22 | 7.96 | 13.13 | 7.65 |
| | tot. | 9.93 | 7.80 | 12.17 | 8.10 |
| %FM | b. | 8.00 | 6.01 | 9.83 | 6.22 |
| | g. | 7.22 | 5.55 | 9.76 | 6.31 |
| | tot. | 7.62 | 5.80 | 9.79 | 6.26 |
| %C resp. | b. | 11.38 | 7.45 | 10.49 | 7.85 |
| | g. | 11.31 | 7.13 | 10.58 | 5.26 |
| | tot. | 11.35 | 7.30 | 10.53 | 6.71 |
| [FC − (C + CF)] wt. | b. | −1.20 | 2.16 | −0.14 | 2.25 |
| | g. | −1.80 | 2.95 | −0.59 | 2.14 |
| | tot. | −1.49 | 2.59 | −0.36 | 2.21 |
| FSh | b. | 6.23 | 4.32 | 7.55 | 4.91 |
| | g. | 6.33 | 3.10 | 10.16 | 6.23 |
| | tot. | 6.28 | 3.77 | 8.83 | 5.78 |

| | | | | | |
|---|---|---|---|---|---|
| %F crude | b. | 51.15 | 17.70 | 44.30 | 15.27 |
| | g. | 49.42 | 16.64 | 38.49 | 12.51 |
| | tot. | 50.30 | 17.21 | 41.46 | 14.29 |
| %F+ (Crude) | b. | 80.70 | 13.72 | 85.40 | 11.45 |
| | g. | 82.16 | 14.24 | 86.69 | 11.51 |
| | tot. | 81.41 | 14.00 | 86.03 | 11.50 |
| M | b. | 2.74 | 2.11 | 3.77 | 3.13 |
| | g. | 4.56 | 4.29 | 5.11 | 3.25 |
| | tot. | 3.63 | 3.48 | 4.42 | 3.26 |
| FM | b. | 2.70 | 1.87 | 3.26 | 2.50 |
| | g. | 2.64 | 2.08 | 3.78 | 2.32 |
| | tot. | 2.67 | 1.97 | 3.51 | 2.42 |
| C resp. | b. | 3.70 | 2.50 | 3.61 | 2.91 |
| | g. | 4.40 | 3.31 | 3.89 | 1.75 |
| | tot. | 4.04 | 2.95 | 3.75 | 2.42 |
| Sum C wt. | b. | 3.01 | 2.17 | 2.56 | 2.29 |
| | g. | 3.72 | 3.35 | 2.88 | 1.55 |
| | tot. | 3.36 | 2.83 | 2.72 | 1.97 |
| %VIII − X | b. | 33.49 | 7.29 | 33.57 | 7.47 |
| | g. | 34.69 | 7.01 | 34.26 | 7.26 |
| | tot. | 34.08 | 7.26 | 33.91 | 7.18 |
| %FSh | b. | 17.79 | 9.24 | 21.38 | 8.42 |
| | g. | 16.93 | 7.11 | 23.73 | 9.09 |
| | tot. | 17.37 | 8.28 | 22.53 | 8.83 |

TABLE 1.—*Continued*

| | 12 year | | | 15 year | | |
|---|---|---|---|---|---|---|
| | M | SD | Mdn | M | SD | Mdn |
| **F(C) + Fc** | | | | | | |
| b. | 5.19 | 3.93 | | 6.45 | 4.41 | |
| g. | 5.04 | 2.76 | | 8.73 | 5.42 | |
| tot. | 5.12 | 3.41 | | 7.56 | 5.06 | |
| **Sum Ch wt** | | | | | | |
| b. | | | .96 | | | 1.07 |
| g. | | | 1.25 | | | 1.60 |
| tot. | | | 1.04 | | | 1.25 |
| **M + Sum C wt.** | | | | | | |
| b. | 5.76 | 6.11 | | 6.12 | 4.39 | |
| g. | 8.26 | 7.98 | | 7.99 | 3.84 | |
| tot. | 6.98 | 7.03 | | 7.03 | 4.24 | |
| **Var** | | | | | | |
| b. | 9.93 | 3.14 | | 10.74 | 3.20 | |
| g. | 10.47 | 3.49 | | 10.60 | 3.41 | |
| tot. | 10.20 | 3.33 | | 10.67 | 3.31 | |
| **H** | | | | | | |
| b. | 3.04 | 2.15 | | 3.30 | 2.55 | |
| g. | 5.78 | 4.45 | | 5.42 | 4.10 | |
| tot. | 4.38 | 3.73 | | 4.34 | 3.56 | |
| **Hd** | | | | | | |
| b. | 2.85 | 3.28 | | 4.11 | 4.53 | |
| g. | 4.73 | 3.92 | | 7.11 | 7.00 | |
| tot. | 3.77 | 3.73 | | 5.58 | 6.06 | |
| **%H + Hd** | | | | | | |
| b. | 17.85 | 10.15 | | 21.06 | 9.69 | |
| g. | 26.11 | 10.91 | | 28.73 | 11.03 | |
| tot. | 21.89 | 11.31 | | 24.82 | 11.06 | |

| | 12 year | | | 15 year | | |
|---|---|---|---|---|---|---|
| | M | SD | Mdn | M | SD | Mdn |
| **%F(C) + Fc** | | | | | | |
| b. | 15.02 | 8.93 | | 18.17 | 7.47 | |
| g. | 13.08 | 5.89 | | 20.00 | 7.91 | |
| tot. | 14.08 | 7.66 | | 19.07 | 7.78 | |
| **M-Sum C wt.** | | | | | | |
| b. | - .26 | 2.59 | | + .82 | 3.06 | |
| g. | + .83 | 3.93 | | +2.21 | 3.33 | |
| tot. | + .28 | 3.36 | | +1.50 | 3.27 | |
| $\dfrac{\text{M} - \text{Sum C wt.}}{\text{M} + \text{Sum C wt.}}$ | | | | | | |
| b. | - .12 | .56 | | | | |
| g. | - .02 | .56 | | | | |
| tot. | - .07 | .56 | | | | |
| **%A + Ad** | | | | | | |
| b. | 47.30 | 12.38 | | 46.91 | 11.52 | |
| g. | 42.20 | 11.08 | | 43.40 | 12.73 | |
| tot. | 44.80 | 12.04 | | 45.20 | 12.25 | |
| **%H** | | | | | | |
| b. | 9.85 | 7.64 | | 10.64 | 7.78 | |
| g. | 14.64 | 8.31 | | 13.62 | 8.56 | |
| tot. | 12.20 | 8.33 | | 12.10 | 8.30 | |
| **%Hd** | | | | | | |
| b. | 7.47 | 8.43 | | 10.53 | 8.88 | |
| g. | 11.62 | 8.45 | | 14.98 | 11.24 | |
| tot. | 9.50 | 8.69 | | 12.71 | 10.35 | |
| **H - Hd** | | | | | | |
| b. | + .15 | 4.02 | | - .81 | 5.39 | |
| g. | +1.04 | 5.70 | | -1.69 | 7.45 | |
| tot. | + .58 | 4.93 | | -1.24 | 6.50 | |

| | | | | | |
|---|---|---|---|---|---|
| A + Ad/H + Hd | b. | 4.44 | 2.25 | | |
| | g. | 2.45 | 1.75 | | |
| | tot. | 3.25 | 1.96 | | |
| %Anat. | b. | 2.00 | 3.49 | 3.94 | 4.43 |
| | g. | 1.33 | 1.97 | 2.60 | 3.45 |
| | tot. | 1.67 | 2.87 | 3.28 | 4.04 |
| %obj. | b. | 13.02 | 7.93 | 10.15 | 6.90 |
| | g. | 9.98 | 7.22 | 9.76 | 7.40 |
| | tot. | 11.53 | 7.77 | 9.96 | 7.15 |
| O+ | b. | 3.04 | 2.71 | 2.77 | 3.63 |
| | g. | 3.40 | 2.99 | 3.62 | 3.07 |
| | tot. | 3.22 | 2.85 | 3.18 | 3.40 |
| Sum O | b. | 6.98 | 5.23 | 5.53 | 5.53 |
| | g. | 7.93 | 6.13 | 7.96 | 6.66 |
| | tot. | 7.45 | 5.71 | 6.71 | 6.23 |
| P | b. | 7.21 | 3.05 | 8.13 | 2.84 |
| | g. | 7.64 | 2.53 | 8.04 | 2.56 |
| | tot. | 7.42 | 2.82 | 8.09 | 2.70 |

| | | | | | |
|---|---|---|---|---|---|
| %Nat | b. | 16.74 | 12.13 | 11.60 | 7.68 |
| | g. | 16.16 | 12.37 | 11.96 | 9.97 |
| | tot. | 16.45 | 12.25 | 11.77 | 8.88 |
| %OBJ | b. | 32.00 | 15.68 | 28.47 | 11.09 |
| | g. | 29.67 | 13.48 | 25.24 | 12.51 |
| | tot. | 30.86 | 14.69 | 26.89 | 11.92 |
| %O+ | b. | 8.64 | 7.26 | 7.57 | 8.82 |
| | g. | 9.02 | 7.35 | 8.62 | 7.54 |
| | tot. | 8.83 | 7.31 | 8.09 | 8.24 |
| %Sum O | b. | 19.98 | 12.24 | 15.04 | 11.99 |
| | g. | 19.91 | 12.80 | 17.84 | 11.77 |
| | tot. | 19.95 | 12.32 | 16.41 | 11.96 |

mean fluctuation in initial reaction times.[67] They appear to have attained a greater measure of stability in their reactions to environmental stimuli.

While the Hertz data do not include a consideration of fluctuation, mean initial reaction times to the shading cards, color cards and to all cards combined for the 12 and 15 year groups show few reliable differences. A tendency is noted, however, for the boys as compared to the girls to show longer initial reaction times to the shading cards at 12 years of age, suggesting a greater amount of hesitation in responding to anxiety-laden stimuli. At 15 years, boys show, on the average, longer initial reaction times to the color cards, suggesting undue caution, blocking or disturbance because of the emotional implications of the cards.

### Mental Approach (Intellectual Procedure in Approaching the Situations)

Teen age children tend to give a lower per cent $W$,[7,37] as compared with adults. While the location categories show little mean change from 10 to 16 years of age for Thetford and his colleagues,[67] the 14 to 16 year group tend to emphasize $D$ at the expense of $W$ when compared with an adult group.

On the whole, the per cent $W$ tends to decrease in the teen years,[2,29] at least up to 16 years of age. Qualitative changes with age are also shown by Meili-Dworetzski,[45] who reports a decrease in $Wv$ ($W$'s based on the grey) from childhood to adulthood, with an increase in "superior globalizations" which result "from an articulated perceptual process." "Schematic superior $W$" based on the general outline used in a differentiated way and "impressionistic $W$," based on the chromatic or depth impression combined with form elements, appear from 13 years upward. Similarly, there is an increase in "combinatorial $W$'s," which result from complex differentiated perceptive processes which involve analysis, synthesis of the forms and logical integration of successive impressions into a well structured unit (reference 45, page 140).

Children in the teen years appear to show an increased attention to detail.[2,4,29,50]* Thus the per cent $D$ tends to increase for Ames et al.,[2] and children at 15 tend to give higher per cent $D$ than at 12 years in the Hertz data.[29] The mean per cent $Dd$ or the per cent $Dr$ does not appear to change.[2,29]

Marked sex differences are noted in the location categories. Boys tend to give more $W$ than girls in the age range 10 to 16,[2] and at 15 years as compared with 12 years of age.[29] Girls tend to give on an average more $D$ from 10 to 15 years,[2] and at 15 years.[29] Again, girls give more $Dr$ than boys on an average from 11 through 15 years,[2] 14 to 17 years[4] and at 15 years.[29]

The data of McFate and Orr[44] only partially bear out these results. While they find that $D$ significantly increases for girls 10 to 18 years of age, they also note that $W$ increases significantly with age for boys. They too report that $Dd$ is used increasingly at the later age levels, and that more

---

*The normal detail has the symbol $D$, the rare detail, $Dd$ or $Dr$. This latter generally includes Klopfer's small, usual and unusual details.[39] Unless otherwise noted, the normal space detail (symbol $S$ or $DS$) and the rare space detail (symbol $s$ or $Dds$) and the fragmentary details ($Do$ and $Dro$) are included in the $D$ or $Dr$, depending on their area.

girls than boys score on detail categories at almost all ages. They report a shift at the age of 13 for both sexes, $D$ and $Dr$ decreasing slightly while $W$ increases. Girls give a higher mean $W$ and $D$ than boys except for $W$ at 18 years.

It appears then that children in the second decade are still immature in their organizational ability and interest when compared with adults. They still do not show the mature ability to conceptualize and to abstract which is expected of adults. Indeed, there appears to be a decrease in this ability from 10 to 16 years of age. This may reflect an inability or an unwillingness to take an integrated view of their environment. Or it may point to a decrease in mental push and striving. Again, it may reflect an increase in attention to detail, so evident in this age range. Despite this immaturity which is still evident, qualitatively their mental procedure is of a higher level and more enriched than that of younger age groups. What evidence they show of organizational ability reflects an increase in complex differentiated perception of their world and in the ability to analyze their environment, to see the relationships between the various aspects of their experiences, and to achieve a more integrated view than children of younger ages. Boys appear to show more of the overall global approach to their environment than girls throughout the teen years.

In addition, there appears to be an increase in a matter-of-fact approach to the world with emphasis on the concrete and the practical. The mental procedure of children in this period is more differentiated, with more attention to minute detail. Their reaction to new situations is now expressed in a more flexible and differentiated manner. This is much more evident in girls than in boys.

*Space Details (Oppositional Trends Indicated in the Mental Approach)*

A progressive increase is reported for response to space when the primary space details and the additionals (or tendencies) are combined, groups 10 to 13 and 14 to 17 showing higher scores than the younger group.[67] Kallstedt's older girls, age 16 to 19 years, show more space responses than his younger girls, age 13 to 15.

Only a small proportion of the children of McFate and Orr use space. Those who do, however, show a significant decrease in the number of girls using space at 13 years, with a gradual increase after that age. In the Hertz data, little difference is noted in the median number of primary space and/or additional space responses used by children at 12 and 15 years of age $[S+s+(S+s)]$.*

It is suggested, then, that children 10 to 17 years, and especially after 13 years, increasingly show thinking of an oppositional nature which may manifest itself as self will or persistence, perhaps obstinacy or negativism. It may even show as doubt and indecision. Again, it may reflect a healthy tendency to want to see all aspects of a question, even the opposite side.

---

*Throughout the chapter I have attempted to retain the scoring symbols used by the investigators to whom reference is made. Where necessary, equivalent symbols are introduced.

*Form and Form Level (Impersonal Reactivity, Constriction, Ego Control, Reality Testing)*

When form is considered, it is especially necessary to keep in mind that different patterns are utilized by different investigators depending upon their system of scoring. Those who do not include animal movement or inanimate movement as separate scoring categories have different per cent $F$ and per cent $F+$ from those who use $FM$ and $m$ as separate scoring entities. Thus the per cent $F$ refined of Klopfer, the per cent $F$ crude of Hertz and the Lambda Index of Beck may be different although they all refer to the pure $F$, i.e., the $F$ where it appears without co-determinants regardless of form level. The per cent $F$ is based on the total $R$.

Again, today many clinicians utilize a more extensive per cent $F$ called $F$ Primary (Hertz), $F$ prevalent (Rapaport) or the extended $F$ (Schafer), all of which include the scoring categories involving $F$ whether it be the pure $F$ or $F$ as a co-determinant in scoring categories where $F$ is primary (i.e., $M$, $FM$, $Fm$, $FCh$, $FC$, $F(C)$, $Fc$, $FCh'$, $FCh''$, $FC$ or their corresponding symbols in other systems). The per cent $F+$ Primary (which consists of the proportion of $F+$ Primary to the total $F$ Primary) is really the best measure of fitness of form perception, reality testing and intellectual control.

Per cent $F$ crude corresponds to per cent $F$ refined of Klopfer and the Lambda Index of Beck. Most investigators find that children in the teen years show a higher per cent $F$ crude than adults. Within the teen years, children at the younger ages show a higher per cent $F$ crude. Thus children 10 to 13 years show the highest Lambda Index for Thetford et al., when compared with their younger and older groups. The 12 year old group of Hertz gives reliably higher per cent $F$ crude than the 15 year old group.

Contrary to these findings, McFate and Orr report a rise in mean $F$ from 11 to 18 years. The per cent $F$ crude remains relatively constant in the 10 to 16 year old groups of Ames et al., with a decrease at 16, although a tendency is noted for a higher median $F$ crude in girls 10 and 13 years and a lower median at the other ages.

When the per cent $F+$ is considered, there appears to be an increase from childhood to adolescence.[4,54,67] There is a decrease, however, in mean per cent $F+$ in the 14 to 17 year old group as compared with the 10 to 13 year old group.[67] Similarly, in the Hertz data, the 15 year old group gives a higher mean per cent $F+$ than the 12 year group. Ames et al.[2] find little variability in the mean per cent $F+$ from age to age, 10 to 16 years. They report that the norm for the groups approximates that of the adult.

Studies differ as to sex differences in the $F$ crude category. Thus, at both 12 and 15 years, boys show a higher per cent $F$ Primary than girls, and at 15 years they show a higher per cent $F$ crude in the Hertz data. Contrary to these findings, the McFate and Orr study shows the mean $F$ for girls to be higher than that for boys at ages 11, 13, 15 and 18 years.

For the per cent $F+$, the study by Ames et al. shows the mean per cent $F+$ for girls to be higher than that for boys at every age but 12. No sex differences are noted in the Hertz data for the 12 and 15 year groups.

Thus these studies point to the fact that children 10 to 13 years of age show considerably more constriction and rigidity of thought and more ego control than children somewhat older. They tend to repress spontaneity, using an impersonal matter-of-fact way of dealing with their environment. They appear to build ego defenses in the form of constriction of both impulse life and affective release. Paulsen thinks that this high degree of "conscious control" is a means of attaining stability and is an expression of ego strength.[50] Children 14, 15 and 16 years of age show a loosening up of these constrictive trends and a greater expansion of personality.

Again, some studies point to a greater increase in form accuracy, realistic thinking and intellectual control in children in the second decade as compared to younger children. The older children in this period, however, show less realistic thinking, less intellectual steadiness and more proneness to autistic thought than the younger children. This may reflect preoccupations with inner needs and conflicts which obscure or distort perception of reality, or disturbance in perception of reality because of the stresses and pressures of the outside world. It may even reflect a temporary shift in the level of functioning to a more primitive level in the form of "regression in the service of the ego."

*Human Movement (Imaginative Ability, Fantasy Life, Inner Control)*

As compared to adults, children in the second decade appear to give less $M$.[7,35,37]

Most investigators report mean $M$ increasing with age in the second decade. Thus McFate and Orr report mean $M$ significantly higher in the 18 year old group than in the younger age groups, 11, 13, and 15 years. Thetford and his colleagues find a continuous increase in the $M$ for the entire age range, the 14 to 17 year old group showing a higher mean and a larger proportion of older children giving $M-$ as compared with the other groups. The 15 year old group in the Hertz study gives higher mean $M$ and higher per cent $M$ than the 12 year old group. While the study of Ames et al. notes only a slight upward trend for mean $M$ from 10 to 16 years, they emphasize the fact that $M$ fluctuates from year to year, with the largest proportion of children giving $M$ at 14 and 16 years, mean $M$ dropping at 13 and 15 years.

Sex differences are likewise emphasized. Girls give more $M$ than boys at almost all the ages studied.[2,29,44] The study of girls of different pubescent status at 12 and 15 years of age suggests some interesting hypotheses. According to one study [24] more of the prepubescent 12 year old girls within 1 to 12 months of puberty (approaching puberty) tend to score higher in $M$ than girls who are more physically mature or less physically mature. The 15 year old pubescents who have been sexually mature for 37 months or more (early pubescents) score higher in $M$ than the 15 year old pubescent girls of lesser maturity (late pubescents). Again, the 15 year old girls pubescent for 1 to 24 months give significantly more $M$ than the 12 year old girls who have been pubescent for a similar period. More $M$ appears then (*a*) in the younger group approaching puberty when compared with girls less mature or more mature of the same age, (*b*) in the older girls who have been physically mature for a long time in comparison with girls of the same age who are less mature, and (c) in older girls rather than in the younger of like pubescent status.

Thus children in the second decade progressively utilize fantasy living and engage in intrapsychic activity, girls showing more of this inner living than boys. They are motivated more by stimuli from within, from drives, urges, ideas, fantasies, anxieties and powerful strivings which dominate their life at this time. They show greater capacity for creative mental activity which involves a high degree of mental effort and tension. This reflects the more mature intellectual functioning noted in other Rorschach patterns. This inner activity may take the form of constructive productivity or it may be a kind of creative activity which satisfies their need of the moment, as in daydreaming. It may even cause them to resort to autistic thinking on occasion. This increased emphasis on inner living may represent a kind of withdrawal from immediate involvement and emotional contacts which the adolescents do not understand or cannot handle.

Since it is hypothesized that human movement represents not only a more mature intellectual functioning and capacity to utilize imaginative resources but also an acceptance of one's inner urges and promptings, it may be said that adolescents of this age show a higher measure of inner control as they progress in the teen years. The greater tendency for girls to show more of this capacity than boys is in keeping with their more advanced physical development.

Finally, it is suggested by the Hertz data that this intensification of inner living depends both on chronologic age and pubescent status. In 12 year old girls, the year before the pubertal crisis is marked by this increase in inner living, which seems to be followed by a decrease with the onset of pubescence. At 15 years, girls who have been mature for a long time (early pubescents) show more intensified inner living than girls of lesser maturity (late pubescents). Again, the 15 year old girls show more intensive inner living than the 12 year old girls of like pubescent status.

### H and Hd: A and Ad

The proportion of human and animal forms reflects certain aspects of intellectual functioning, which will be considered under *Content*.

### W:M (External Striving and Achievement in Reference to Potential Capacity)

If the group means for $W$ and $M$ are used to compute the $W:M$ ratio, Hertz' 12 year old group as a whole shows a ratio of 2.6 as compared to the 1.6 for the 15 year old group. If the optimal relationship of 2:1 is taken, as Klopfer[39] suggests, the younger group shows an overweighting of $W$, and the older, overweighting of $M$. Boys show an even higher weighting of $W$ at 12 years, their ratio being 3.5 as compared with 2.05 at 15 years. Girls show 1.96 at 12 years, as against 1.37 at 15 years. On comparing the sexes, boys show a higher weighting of $W$ than girls at both 12 and 15 years.

It may be hypothesized that boys 12 years of age, when compared with 15 year old boys, tend to show more striving, possibly more competitive drive, which may be compensatory for real or imagined inadequacies.

Girls approximate the suggested norm, showing greater balance between their imaginative strivings and achievements. At 15 years of age, the group as a whole shows some imbalance, with greater emphasis on inner living and less on productive achievement. The 15 year old girls, especially, do not make use of their creative and productive abilities.

### Popular Response (Conformity with the Thinking of the Group)

Most studies indicate that older adolescents appear to give more $P$ than do younger ones[44,54,67]. In the Hertz data, little difference is noted between the 12 and the 15 year groups, however. Ames et al. also find that all but 10 per cent of their groups give four or more $P$, the middle 50 per cent of the group as a whole showing between 5 and 8 $P$.

Girls tend to give more $P$ than boys at 11, 13, 15 and especially at 18 years for McFate and Orr. In the Ames data, girls give higher median $P$ at 10 and 13, boys at 11 and 14; at other ages the sexes are about equal.

Thus, according to some studies, children in the teen years tend to show more and more intellectual conformity to the thinking of their group. They show progressive ability to participate in the common thinking of their group as they mature, becoming more socialized and more observant of the conventions of the group. Here we might see the normative influence of culture patterns. In our society, in large measure security comes with conformity. The adolescent, as he grows up, becomes more aware of and submits to those patterns of behavior and modes of thinking which are socially approved.

### Originality (O) (Deviate Thinking, Special Interests or Preoccupations and/ or Creativity)

Few studies include this pattern in their group data. In the Hertz data, children 12 years of age, especially the boys, give a higher median per cent $O$ than those 15 years of age. Since little difference is noted between the groups in per cent $O+$, the difference must be due to the minus form quality. While little difference is noted between the sexes at 12 years, there is a tendency for girls at 15 to give more $O$ than boys. We hypothesize that the 12 year old children, expecially the boys, tend to deviate more in their thinking than the older children. At 15 years, however, girls tend to show more deviate thinking than boys.

### Organizational Activity (Intellectual Ability, Intellectual Drive, Mental Effort)

Beck's organizational score, $Z$, which purports to measure mental effort or intellectual drive, shows a progressive increase in mean values with increase in age.[67] The differences between the means of the 14 to 17 year old group and the two younger groups are significantly reliable. The older teenagers then show more drive to organize percepts into meaningful and complex units, greater thinking power and intellectual effort.

The mean index of organization ability ($g$) utilized by Hertz,[31] which is weighted according to form level, complexity, vagueness, popularity and originality, shows little difference in the 12 and 15 year old groups. Each shows a range of scores which overlap. The organizational and integrative aspect of intellectual functioning represented by this organizational pattern does not seem to vary at these ages for the groups studied.

### Emotional Organization and Control

Several Rorschach patterns reflect the degree and kind of emotional balance which the individual displays, whether it be an intensification or constriction of inner living, or emotionally free responsiveness to outer stimuli, or restrained and muted responsiveness in the form of sensitivity, circumspection, passivity or anxiety. They reflect also the extent to which the individual achieves control of impulses and the emotions and in general the relative maturity and adaptability of the affective structure. These patterns include the $F$ crude and per cent $F+$, animal movement $(FM)$, movement in nature and artificial happenings $(m)$, the various color categories $(FC, CF$ and $C)$, and the "Erlebnistypen."

$F$ crude and per cent $F+$ have already been considered as indicators of control. They reflect the nature and degree of intellectual control and the extent to which children in the second decade are spontaneous or constricted in their emotional responsiveness. Similarly the human movement factor has been discussed as it reflects the extent to which the adolescent utilizes his imaginative resources, engages in fantasy living within realistic channels and achieves inner control.

### FM (Basic Primitive Impulses)

Little agreement is noted in the trends for $FM$ in the teen years as reported by different investigators. For some, $FM$ decreases with age,[44] for others $FM$ increases with age up to 12 years at least.[50] Ames et al. find little variation in the mean $FM$, although dips occur at 13, especially in girls and at 15, especially in boys. Boys give more $FM$ at 12, 13 and 14 years, girls more at 15 and 16 years. The Hertz data show the 15 year old group tending to give on an average a higher per cent $FM$ than the 12 year old group.

Most investigators agree that $FM$ is greater than $M$ in the early teen years.[2,37,50] By 12 years, there is a slight excess of $M$ over $FM$, and by 15 years $M$ is greater than $FM$.[2,29]

### m (Inner Tensions, Struggle Between Conflicting Impulses)

Some investigators report a larger proportion of $m$ in older adolescents than in younger.[7,37] Ames finds that the highest proportion of the groups gives $m$ at 12 years, the lowest at 15 years.

Thus, while the results are equivocal, children in the early teen years appear to show immaturity in that their basic impulses are not yet balanced by constructive fantasy living. It is suggested that older teen age children show a greater awareness of the promptings of the more basic drives, yet more control over them and more ability to sublimate and to structure impulses in a manner acceptable to themselves and to others. Hence, they display more maturity than younger teen age children. At the same time they show more tensions and conflicts than younger teen age children, no doubt due to struggles with impulses which are still unacceptable to them.

*Color (Emotional Responsiveness, Control and Maturity)*

For the total color score, i.e., Sum of Color responses and Sum Color weighted, higher Sum $C$ is reported in the 14 to 16 year old group as compared to younger groups.[67] On the other hand, the 15 year old group of Hertz tends to show less total color than the 12 year old group. While Ames et al. do not report marked age trends, less color seems to be used at 11, 13 and 15 years, and more at 16 years. For them, Sum $C$ tends to be higher in girls at every age (10 to 16 years) than in boys.

When the subcategories of color are considered, most investigators agree that children 14, 15 and perhaps 16 years of age show more $FC$ and $CF$ than the younger teen age children. The 14 to 16 year old groups of Thetford et al. show more $FC$ and $CF$ than do the younger groups. The proportion of the groups giving $FC$ increases from 10 to 16 years in the study of Ames et al. There is a decrease in the proportion giving $CF$ from 10 to 13 years, and then a gradual increase. In the Hertz data, more of the 15 year old group score lower in per cent $CF$ and in $C + CF$ and higher in $FC + F(C)$, and more of the older girls show $FC$ than the younger ones.

Most investigators find that $C$ crude diminishes with age.[2,29,44,45,67]

An increase in stability and maturity as evidenced by the color patterns is likewise reported. Paulsen[50] finds $FC$ greater than $CF$ from 10 years on; Hertz' 15 year old group shows a higher stability-maturity score $[FC - (CF + C)]$ wt. Rabin and Beck[54] also report an increase in their maturity ratio ($C + CF/FC$), the older groups showing a balance in favor of $FC$. Kallstedt's 16 to 19 year old groups[37] show favorable control of emotionality ($FC$ greater than $CF + C$), but a high $C + CF$ is still apparent in the group.

The per cent VIII-X pattern shows little variation at 12 and 15 years in the Hertz data. Thetford et al., however, report a higher affective ratio for the 14 to 16 year old group than for their youngest group.

Sex differences are reported for the color patterns. Girls tend to give more color than boys in the teen years.[2,29,44] Sum Color tends to be higher at every age from 10 to 16 years in girls, more girls giving $FC$ at almost every age.[2] While more boys give $CF$ at 12, more girls give $CF$ at every age 13 through 16 years.[2] In the Hertz data, more girls score higher in Sum $C$ and $FC + F(C)$. A tendency is reported for girls to give higher $C + CF$ than boys. McFate and Orr report approximately the same results.

In the study of girls grouped according to pubescent status,[24] it is of interest that at 12 years of age, more of the girls approaching pubescence show lower Sum $C$ than the more immature girls (prepubescent by 12 to 35 months) or the more mature girls (pubescent for 1 to 3 months). At 15 years the more mature girls consistently show higher Sum $C$ scores than groups of lesser maturity.

In the emotional stability-maturity pattern, the more immature 12 year old girls score less than groups nearer the pubertal crisis or than those already pubescent. At 15 years the more mature girls likewise exhibit higher stability scores than those of lesser maturity. On comparing the girls of like pubescent status at 12 and 15 years, little difference appears in the Sum

Color score. The 12 year old girls, however, consistently and reliably give higher stability-maturity scores than the 15 year old girls of like pubescent status.

Thus according to some results children in their early teen years show constriction of emotional responsiveness. When they are responsive, however, they are prone to be more excitable, egocentric and less controlled than older teen age children, although less so than younger children. Girls appear to be more emotionally responsive than boys at these ages.

Children 14 years of age and older show greater expansion and liberation of emotional energy, girls more so than boys. They show more labile and volatile affectivity. With this, however, they show greater emotional stability, adaptability and maturity than children in the younger teen years. They show greater capacity to identify emotionally with their fellows, girls more so than boys. They are more adequate to the demands of their environment and are more capable of channelizing their energies into forms of expression which are adaptive and socially acceptable.

We hypothesize that the emotional stability, adaptability and maturity noted depend on the pubescent status of the girls as well as age. Twelve year old girls approaching pubescence are more constrained and less emotionally responsive than girls who are more immature or who are already pubescent at this age. The more physically mature girls at 12 years are more stable emotionally than those of lesser maturity. Again, the more mature 15 year old girls are more emotionally responsive and more stable than those of lesser maturity. Twelve year old girls are more stable emotionally than 15 year old girls of like pubescent status.

*Shading (Sensitivity, Cautiousness, Contactual Effort, Passivity, Anxiety)*

With this category, it may seem difficult to evaluate findings since different symbols* are used to represent the same scoring criteria. Generally viewed, however, there is considerable agreement among investigators. Shading appears to increase conspicuously in the teen years.

Mean over-all shading responses (Hertz' *Sh*) are higher in the 15 than in the 12 year old group, with children at 15 giving more controlled shading (*FSh*) than those at 12 years.[29]

When the shading responses are broken into subcategories, for Ames et al. the $F(C)$ increases from 10 to 16 years of age. More children at 15 give $F(C) + Fc$ than at 12 years;[29] the 14 to 16 year old group shows higher Sum Vista than other groups studied, and the $FV$ shows a progressive increase at each age level.[67] Again, more boys use Vista in the later teen years than in the earlier, with more boys than girls giving these scores.[44]

Older teen age children likewise use more controlled texture responses. Texture responses lead in the 15 and 16 year old groups of Ames et al.;

*Beck employs $V$ for vista, $Y$ for greyness and diffusion and $T$ for texture. These correspond to Hertz' symbols $F(C)$, $Ch$ and $c$ respectively.[26, 31] Ames et al. differentiate between $F(C)$ for nondysphoric shading which seems to include vista and texture, and $Clob$, dysphoric shading.[1] McFate and Orr use Klopfer's scores of $FK$ for vista, $c$ for texture and $KF$ and $K$ for diffusion.[39] Hertz finds it convenient to have an over-all shading category $(Sh)$, which includes all types of shading.[31]

Kallsted's 16 to 19 year old group shows higher $Fc$ than the 13 to 15 year old group. For McFate and Orr the number of children scoring $cF$ decreases in their age range. The $cF$ responses seem to appear less frequently in the higher teen years.[37,44] Older teen age children show much less $c$ than the younger teen age children.[7,37]

Diffusion responses ($Ch$ or $Y$ or $K$) likewise appear to increase with age in the teen years. The 14 to 16 year old group shows more Sum $Y$ and more $FY$ than younger groups.[67] Girls tend to give more $YF$ in the 14 to 17 year old group, boys more $V$ in this age range.[4] More of the 15 year old group show higher Sum $Ch$ and higher $FCh$ than the 12 year old group.[29]

Summarizing, studies point to greater sensitivity to external stimuli on the part of children in the mid-teen and later teen years, manifested as cautiousness, circumspection, watchful adaptability, or inferiority consciousness and insecurity. There is greater effort to adjust to the environment. Children from about the middle teen years on are more self critical, more concerned with self and with moods and physical feelings. They are more aware of others around them and more concerned with their relationships with them. They show more inner disharmony and greater proneness to anxiety, which, however, tends to be under control.

### "Erlebnistypus" or Experience Balance (EB) (Introversive-Extratensive Orientation, Emotional Balance)

When the "Erlebnistypen" are differentiated in terms of type and degree of introversive-extratensive emphasis, or when they are described by numerical formulas, (e.g., $M$ − Sum $C$ wt, or $M$ − Sum $C$ wt / $M$ + sum $C$ wt), some studies emphasize a more constricted EB in the early teen years and for a few years before 10, some calling this period the "prepubescent years." [50,54,67] There is general agreement that there is an introversial swing in the mid-teen or later teen years, some investigators calling this period "adolescence."[2,27,28,50,67]

In the Hertz data[28] no one type EB appears characteristic of the group at 12 years of age, a very low proportion showing the constrictive type. In the 15 year old group, over half show the introversive EB. Change in EB from 12 to 15 years is noted in 68 per cent of the children, with more change taking place to the introversive emphasis than to any other. Over half of the group either remain introversive or change to the introversive pattern. Further contraction of one or both sides of the EB is in evidence in a large proportion of the children.

The introversial shift is noted by other investigators.[2,50] Ames et al. indicate, however, that the introversial swing is not a steady trend but appears around 13 years of age, with expansion and evidence of extraversion at 14, with introversion again at 15, and greater balance between introversive and extratensive trends at 16.

Results based on numerical scores point to little difference between the means for $M$ + Sum $C$ (index of constriction-dilation) in the 12 and 15 year old groups of Hertz[27] but with higher means for girls than boys at both ages. For McFate and Orr,[44] however, this index increases with age, expecially in girls at 18 years of age.

When the $M - \text{Sum } C$ pattern is computed, higher means are obtained at 15 than at 12 years, older children showing more introversiveness and more girls giving positive scores at both ages as compared to boys.[27]

In the study of girls of different pubescent status,[24] certain modifications of the above results are suggested. Girls within 24 months or less of pubescence are more introversive than girls who are more immature or more mature. Girls who have already attained puberty at 12 years of age are less introversive, or the introversive capacity has been restricted or repressed. The 15 year old late pubescents consistently score higher and are more introversive than the early pubescents. At 15 years of age there appears to be a definite intensification of introversiveness 1 to 18 months after the pubertal crisis. Again, 15 year old girls are more introversive than 12 year old girls of like pubescent status, when both have been pubescent 1 to 24 months.

When the dilation-constriction pattern is studied in the groups, the most immature 12 year old girls (prepubescent by 18 to 35 months) are more expansive and score higher than the more mature groups. Thus the more physically mature the girls are at 12, the more constricted the personality, with the exception of the group just prior to puberty which appears to expand in the introversive direction. The 15 year old early pubescents (pubescent for 35 to 48 months) score higher than those of lesser maturity. Thus the more mature 15 year old girls on the whole are more dilated than those of lesser maturity. Again, 15 year old girls are more expansive than 12 year old girls of like pubescent status.

Thus the constrictive pattern with some $M$ is more a prepubertal pattern in 12 year old girls just approaching puberty. Constriction appears to be more a pubertal pattern of chronologically early maturity. The introversial swing is not a pubertal pattern per se since it does not occur with puberty at 12 years of age but does appear with puberty at 15 years of age. It is a pattern more characteristic of late pubescence related to both age and pubescence. It is more an index of general maturity than of pubescence per se. It is related, no doubt, to factors in the social experience and in contact with the environment. It appears to be a forerunner of further expansion later in post-pubescence in older children. Dilation with its uninhibited inner living and freely expressed emotions appears to be a post-pubertal pattern in 15 year old girls at least.

### Content

In recent years, investigators have focused on content analysis, finding it fruitful for formulating hypotheses helpful in the interpretation of a response. They have studied the varieties of content as Rorschach originally suggested. In addition, some attempts have been made to emphasize other qualitative features, such as specific references, perseveration of specific themes, kinds of personal and self references, and personally saturated features of the responses, such as the feelings, emotions and attitudes expressed in conjunction with the figures and objects projected into the blots. Some have considered the stylistic features of the responses themselves—the kinds of perceptual and conceptual distortions, and style in mode of verbal communication.[51,52,61] Unfortunately these qualitative aspects of the responses have not been systematically attacked in research on adolescents. The book by Ames et al.[2] is perhaps the first attempt to make a rough quantitative analysis of specific content categories given in this age period with a consideration of additional qualitative features of the responses.

### Variety of Content Categories

Some investigators report on the number of different content categories (Variety, Hertz symbol $VAR$) used by adolescents. This depends, of course, on the number of content categories used in the scoring system. An increase in variety of content in the 10 to 16 year old range as compared to younger age groups is reported by Ames et al.[2] Girls appear to have a higher number of content categories from 12 to 16 years of age, the greatest variety showing at 14 and 16 years of age. In the Hertz data, little difference is noted between the mean $VAR$ in the 12 and 15 year old groups.

### H and Hd (Intellectual Ability, Interest in People and Human Problems)

Many studies report progressive increase in $H$ and $Hd$ or per cent $H + Hd$ in the teen years, with the $Hd$ greater than $H$.[29,44,54,67] Ames et al., however, find no consistent age trends in their 11 to 16 year old groups. For them, the per cent $H$ approaches the adult norm by 10 years of age. Girls show higher median per cent $H$ for every age 11 through 16. They observe many imaginary $H$ in their groups as a whole, girls tending to give more than boys. In this connection the hypothesis suggested by Phillips and Smith is of interest: "A group of mythology contents which includes 'dragon,' 'elves,' 'centaurs,' 'fairies' and the like are found in the records of female adolescents who are fearful of, and unable to face, the prospect of adult sexuality and who show rather childish attitudes, avoid peer contacts, daydream extensively . . . " (reference 51, page 148).

In the Hertz data, little difference appears between mean $H$ in 12 and 15 year old groups. The older group however shows higher mean $Hd$, per cent $H + Hd$ and scores lower in the $H - Hd$ formula. This is also seen in the Thetford data, in which more $Hd$ are given by children 10 to 16 years of age than by adults. At no time do children in these years show the expected adult ratio of $2 H : 1 Hd$ suggested by Klopfer et al.[39]

### Per cent A + Ad (Stereotypy of the Thought Processes, Constrictive Tendency)

Most studies observe little variation in the per cent $A + Ad$ in the teen years.[2,29,67] A tendency is noted for children 10 to 13 years of age to show a higher mean than groups younger or older.[2,67] McFate and Orr, however, report a tendency for the $A$ and $Ad$ to rise with age.

Boys tend to give higher per cent $A + Ad$ at 12 and 15 years of age.[29] According to Ames, too, this is true, boys showing higher scores at 12, 14, 15 and 16. Girls, however, score higher at the other ages.

*Other Content Categories*

Normative data for other content categories are sparse. For most investigators, most content categories cannot be subjected to statistical treatment because they occur with such infrequency in the adolescent records.

In the Hertz data[29] more 15 year old children give over one anatomy response than 12 year old children, with boys tending to give a higher percentage than girls at the 15 year old level. Beck[4] also finds that boys tend to give more anatomy than girls in his 14 to 17 year old group. Ames et al. observe this in boys at 11, 14 and 16 years of age.

In the Hertz data, the 12 year old group gives a higher mean per cent Nature and a higher per cent inanimate objects (symbol per cent $OBJ$) than the 15 year old groups. For artificial objects taken separately (symbol per cent $obj$), boys tend to give higher mean scores at 12 years of age than girls.

The content of the human and animal movement responses receives attention from some investigators. Piotrowski[52] hypothesizes a developmental change from a childhood assertive $M$ to the compliant $M$ of the adult, resulting from frustration and the need to adjust to powerful forces in the environment. Thetford[66] differentiates between extensor, flexor, static and ambivalent human movement in scoring 179 normal children and 50 schizophrenic children, separated into three groups, 6 to 9 years, 10 to 13 years and 14 years to 17 years 6 months. While the study is primarily a comparison of schizophrenic with normal children, he reports an increase in active $M$ in the adolescent group. On the basis of Zubin's seven step scale[70] which purports to measure the amount of energy involved in a response, he also finds that normal adolescents have the highest energy level, the 10 to 13 year old group the least, his youngest group scoring second. Stein[63] cannot substantiate Piotrowski's hypothesis in his study of 60 children, 20 tested at each of three levels (8, 12 and 16 years) selected to coincide with "latency," puberty and adolescence. He differentiates between extensor, flexor, static and ambivalent human and animal movement responses. Analysis is also made in terms of the purpose or meaning of the activity involved. There is no evidence for an increase in compliant $M$ or $FM$ responses within the age span tested. He notes, however, a significant rise in assertive $M$ responses of a hostile, aggressive nature with increased "sociable-cooperative" activities, and increased "static," "social-sexual" and "curiosity" responses at 16 years of age. He concludes that during puberty assertiveness has a hostile, aggressive quality, only partially compensated by cooperative attitudes. At 16 years of age, sexual interests appear. The "static" responses at this age may reflect the adolescent's way of handling inner conflicts at this stage of development.

Ames et al. also study the content of the $M$ and $FM$, differentiating them into static, extensor and flexor-passive groups. They find extensor movements predominant in the age range from 10 to 16 years for both $M$ and $FM$. Analyzing the content of the movement in nature category, $m$, they find tension content especially prominent in the 10 to 16 year old range.

*Symbolic Aspects of Content*

No investigations have been reported as yet on the symbolic significance of certain kinds of content projected by adolescents into the Rorschach blots. Interesting hypotheses have been suggested in the literature.[51,52,61] Piotrowski[52] reports an interesting hypothesis advanced by Rieti on the significance of size and type of animals produced by adolescents in relation to the nature and intensity of attitudes such as submission, aggression, rebelliousness, and critical and defiant attitudes toward parental discipline. Mention should be made of the Elizur method of assessment of anxiety and hostility content with adolescents suggested by Gorlow, Zimet and Fine,[17] which appears to be sufficiently valid in differentiating delinquent and non-delinquent adolescents. Ames et al.[2] discuss the sexual symbolism which might be implied in certain adolescent responses. They present a list of responses which may be considered as indications of interest in sex. These have not been subjected to systematic study, however. In this connection, most clinicians agree that few frank and uninhibited sex responses are given by children in the teen years. While this may reflect repression of sexual imagery, it would suggest to us a better degree of adjustment than when sex answers are given spontaneously.

*Other Qualitative Features of the Response*

Bühler and her colleagues[7] report that the content is more emotional for children in the teen years than for adults. Teen age children give more personal references, more symbolism and more references to injuries and gruesome scenes.

*Summary of Content*

In general, as teen age children grow older, their mental horizons broaden. They become more socialized as they advance in years, showing increasing interest in people and attempting to make more and more contact with people. They still show some anxiety in their relations with people, which tends to inhibit their full acceptance of adults (*Hd*).

In the early teen years, children are more constrained and show more stereotypy of the thought processes. Their interests tend to be more impersonal (*obj*), perhaps more intellectually evasive (*nature*). They gradually become more expansive, more flexible and less prone to stereotyped thinking, and attain a healthy degree of adaptability which compares favorably with that shown by adults (per cent *A* + *Ad*).

Children from 15 years on tend to show more body preoccupation and more anxiety concerning health and possibly sex than they did in the years before.

It may be hypothesized that at this time also, thought content shows more affective loading, more tension and more hostile assertion and aggression, although there is ample evidence of cooperative attitudes (content, *P*). It may reflect preoccupation with rebellious feelings, desire for power or status, resentment against authority. It may reflect dysphoric thinking, with emphasis on frightening, threatening and gruesome figures. Again, the content may reflect egocentric thoughts, with inability to consider people or situations apart from themselves and their own experience (*personal references*).

Unfortunately little has been done in this area of content analysis and affective symbolism. There is little doubt that a systematic analysis would reveal content reflective of keenly felt attitudes about self and environment, many self identifications and many important, pressing and perhaps disturbing conflicts.

### *"Neurotic" Indications*

Many studies emphasize considerable neurotic disturbance in the teen years. Children in the teen years appear to show many of the "neurotic signs" developed by Miale and Erickson[46] or few of the "adjustment signs" developed by Davidson.[13] Thus it is reported that high school boys show a greater number of neurotic signs than college men.[35] Groups of "normal" adolescents show a high incidence of neurotic signs in the report of Ives, Grant and Ranzoni.[36] Further, the adjustment signs of Davidson seem to vary in incidence in this study, with girls showing more adjustment.

Bühler et al.[7] report that the Basic Rorschach ($BR$) scores of "well adjusted adolescents" 13 to 15 years of age are similar to the scores of the adult neurotic. This is true to a lesser extent for the older adolescent (16 to 19 years). One pattern which appears consistently in the mean profiles which they developed involves more $FM$, $m$ and $c$ than the normal adult, pointing to "more unsatisfied instinctual needs, more tension and more insecurity" in the adolescents. They conclude that clinically the adolescent's Rorschach resembles that of an anxiety neurosis in adults. In the report of Kallstedt[37] the adolescent scores resemble those of the neurotic adult. Their $BR$ scores descrease with increase in age. Further their scores fall at the "level of conflict." Adolescents, as compared with adults, show greater lack of direction, stronger unsatisfied instinctual needs, more tensions, greater social and sexual insecurity and greater lack of inner organization. There are many individual differences among her adolescents and much more variety than in her normal adult Rorschachs. It may well be, many clinicians have pointed out, that the signs themselves are not valid for this age period, or that the "sign approach" distorts the data. It may be, of course, that there is much disturbance which is neurotic in nature in this age period.

### Summary of Normative and Developmental Studies

In general, studies of children in the second decade point to marked growth toward intellectual and emotional maturity with gradual expansion of personality, increase in ego strength and increased intellectual adaptability to the thinking of the group. Their functioning approaches that which is anticipated of the "normal" adult, although there is still evidence of instability, lack of inner organization and even some confusion.

In the early teen years, children are more productive than in the younger years and show considerable capacity for realistic and logical thinking. Compared to older teen age children, they tend to be impersonal and objective in approach to reality, often showing strong drive beyond their capacities, narrowed interests, emotional immaturity in fantasy structure and markedly rigid control of the thought processes.

From the middle teen years on, children become more intellectually and emotionally mature, on the whole. Thinking becomes more complex and differentiated; greater flexibility in reacting to the demands of the environment is noted; productivity and ability to organize and integrate experiences is increased; the approach to reality is less impersonal; the capacity for creative mental activity is considerable; and conformity and degree of socialization are increased.

The increased intrapsychic activity in the middle teens may result in constructive productivity and creative achievement. It may, however, take the form of fantasy living which satisfies only their personal needs, showing up as daydreaming and brooding, or as autistic-regressive lapses to a more infantile level.

In the middle to late teen years, children tend to be emotionally more responsive to their environment, approaching it with greater ease and flexibility. They appear to be less constricted, more labile, to have better emotional control and a capacity for channeling emotional energy into adaptive forms. They also show a greater awareness and understanding of their fellows than in the early teen years.

During the years of the second decade, marked shifts appear. Children in the early teens show a constricted personality structure. In the middle teen years the adjustment is in a basically introversive direction. An "introversial swing" appears to take place in personality structure, no doubt "in spurts and plateaus and even regressive movements," as Paulsen[50] suggested. In some adolescents, even in the middle teen years, there appears a marked contraction of the more spontaneous aspects of personality.

The results of the study on girls of different pubescent status cause us to think that the personality characteristics and shifts noted must be evaluated in terms of pubescent status as well as chronologic age. Constriction appears to be a prepubertal pattern of chronologically early maturity. The introversial swing appears to be indicative of late pubescence and may be an index of general maturity rather than a pubertal pattern per se. It appears to be a forerunner of further expansion later on in post-pubescence in older children. Dilation, with its uninhibited inner living and freely expressed emotions, appears to be a post-pubertal pattern, at least in older children.

There is clear evidence from a variety of Rorschach studies that there are marked sex differences in personality structure and functioning in the second decade. As expected, girls, because of their relatively more advanced physiologic development, show more progress toward emotional and intellectual maturity than boys of the same age. Girls are more productive and analytic, more realistic and logical than boys; they show a more differentiated and flexible approach to their environment, tend to be less stereotyped in thinking, show greater imaginative capacity and a higher degree of inner control. Girls are also more emotionally responsive, more introversive and show more anxiety than boys. A greater variety of interests, more interest in people and greater intellectual conformity are also more characteristic of girls.

In the middle teen years, boys are more hesitant, feel more inadequate and appear to be less productive than girls. They tend to be more global in their intellectual approach, are less accurate in their thinking, are more prone to be constrained and impersonal, show narrower interests and appear to show more anxiety concerning body, health and sex than girls.

Contrary to some of the popular conceptions, Rorschach studies indicate that for the most part adolescents, at least from the middle teen years on, have many adaptive strengths to cope with their new experiences. They show adequate inner and outer control, are able to direct their energies into effective and socially adequate channels and appear to achieve a more mature level of social identification.

There are of course many individual differences. And there are frequent deviations from the level of stability and maturity suggested by the group norms—excessive constriction, apprehensiveness, tensions, self consciousness, anxiety, autistic thinking, perhaps uncontrolled and inappropriate emotional reactions, confusion as to sex and social role, and the like. In a way, some adolescents may exhibit a picture akin to that of the neurotic which some workers emphasize.

These deviate patterns must of course be viewed in the light of what we know of this period of development and of the inner and outer pressures which impinge on the adolescent at this time. As already suggested, the imbalances may be the adolescent's attempt to attain balance and equilibrium. They may represent adjustive reactions, paradoxical as it may seem, whereby the adolescent attempts to reorient himself not only to the demands and pressures of his inner world and of his complicated environment, but also to wider horizons and newer experiences.

### Application of Normative and Developmental Rorschach Data

The studies which have been reviewed are not without their methodologic inadequacies. This is not the place, however, to evaluate them. We must be satisfied with a discussion of certain general problems which must be kept in mind when the norms are generalized to wider populations or applied to individual records.

The nature of the sample of children selected for study must, of course, be clearly understood, especially the "normality" of the children. As we have already pointed out, many studies with adolescent populations (as with other age groups) use "normal" subjects. Some investigators view the normal in a statistical sense. For others the term reflects the absence of pathologic traits or of behavior problem cases. Some include children distributed in respect to general intelligence. Others use groups of high intelligence. These factors must be considered when normative material is used.[16,32]

Again, many investigators restrict their studies of "adolescent" to normative data only. The distortion involved in restricting interpretation to scores and formulas has been emphasized again and again in the literature. There is ample evidence that it is most unrewarding to apply scores, signs, equations or formulas in mechanical fashion. To attain a valid interpretation of a record, we must take into account the configurational properties of the

Rorschach patterns and keep in mind at all times that different scores have different implications in different configurational contexts. The newer approach with the Rorschach in both research and clinical application is focused on the interpretation of scores, patterns, test behavior and content analysis, combined, integrated and studied simultaneously.

The shifts observed in Rorschach patterns must likewise be cautiously interpreted. Since it has been shown that many of the Rorschach categories depend upon the total number of responses in a record, the results reported in many studies may be biased by this dependence upon the $R$. Hence, when increase in certain patterns is noted, it may be due to nothing more than the increase in the total number of responses.

Again, changes noted from one age level to another frequently are interpreted as changes in physical maturity. Most of the studies are based on groups of different pubescent status, and while more of the younger teen age children may be prepubescent and more of the older teen age children pubescent, there obviously are mixtures of both at all ages. Of course, the investigator can select arbitrarily any age period, but he must interpret his results cautiously, keeping in mind the individual differences among children. Indeed, many phenomena observed at the various age levels may not be the result of physiologic changes but may be associated with puberty more by cultural circumstance and social environment.

Again we have ample research to show that there are many factors which condition and influence the Rorschach performance in a differential way. We know that the Rorschach is altered by different test attitudes and behavior on the part of the subject and examiner and that it is fundamentally influenced by different conditions which obtain in the immediate Rorschach situation.[32,59,61] This is true of adolescent records just as of other records. The adolescent's performance is an expression of his personality structure in conjunction with the immediate environment. This must be taken into consideration when Rorschach records are utilized for the purpose of amassing normative material and determining developmental changes. It must be kept in mind when normative data are applied in the interpretation of the individual record.

Finally, it must also be remembered that innumerable environmental and cultural factors influence the developing personality of the adolescent. Hence, the Rorschach performance must be interpreted in terms of these influences also. It has been emphasized that most studies on adolescents in this age period are from middle-class populations. It has been shown, for example, that the socioeconomic status of the adolescents influence their Rorschach scores. Auld[3] compared the results of Hertz[25] for upper middle-class 15 year old boys with those of Schachtel[60] for boys of similar mean age selected to represent a different social class. Results show different norms for several variables, especially $M$, $FM$, $FC$, $CF$ and $C$ responses. Of course, as Auld admits, other variables no doubt account for the differences obtained. There is, however, the possibility that social class may account in some measure for these differences.

On the other hand, Davidson's study[12] of boys and girls of high intelligence attending a New York City public school and a private school failed to show that income significantly influenced Rorschach patterns or degree of adjustment. Auld,[3] however, scrutinizing the data, points out differences. The children of higher income families show higher Sum $C$ scores, more of the unstable varieties of color and fewer popular responses than children of the lower income families.

Wertheimer[69] attacks this problem also. She asks: Is adolescent adjustment a function of sex, sociometric status and socioeconomic level? On the basis of a "new sociometric questionnaire" to determine degree of social acceptance and rejection, 200 high school students are differentiated. Group Rorschach records are analyzed for Davidson's signs of adjustment. No significant differences are found as a function of sex, sociometric status or socioeconomic level. Of course, the group Rorschach may obscure the more subtle nuances which appear in the individual Rorschach record.

Auld[3] and Sarason[59] have even made the additional point that the interpreter himself when he analyzes the Rorschach record may show a middle-class bias, and his interpretation may reflect his "middle-class centered values."

It has likewise been shown that other factors influence the development and adjustment of the child and hence his Rorschach performance. Thus, studies have been made on the effect of different varieties of maternal behavior[48] and the influence of parents when personalities show pathology to varying degrees.[49] Similar studies are in progress at the Fels Institute today.[56,57]

Cultural standards no doubt influence the Rorschach performance just as they affect the child who is giving the performance. The tremendous changes which have taken place in our social, economic, educational and even religious life in the past few decades certainly have had far-reaching impact on the social attitudes, values, standards and behavior of adolescents. The personalities they present reflect in large measure their cultural milieu. Cultural influences must be included in our analyses when we try to understand personality structure and dynamics on the basis of any test.

Thus, the defensive operations noted in Rorschach studies may be at least in part a development which has become a part of the personality structure of the adolescent, to prevent the emergence of the kind of emotional display which in his environment elicits social disapproval. The constriction so frequently observed may well reflect controls prevalent in, and approved by, middle-class groups. Similarly, repression of impulses, feelings and emotions, or the development of impersonal attitudes at certain ages, or the increased conformity in the teen years, may be characteristic of the personality structure and at the same time may be a response to the cultural *milieu*. Paradoxical as it may seem, these may be successful defensive operations for the adolescent at the time. In like measure, the greater flexibility and expansion of the later teen years may reflect not only basic personality change but American cultural attitudes toward these age groups.

Rabin's Rorschach study[53] of the personality maturity of Kibbutz (Israeli Collective Settlement) and non-Kibbutz children is pertinent to this discussion. On the basis of Rorschach results with children 9 to 11 years of age, obtained on the basis of appropriate normative material, he was able to evaluate the intellectual and emotional maturational processes. He could also show that the Kibbutz children, brought up with intermittent contacts with mother and family throughout childhood and adolescence, do not reflect the deleterious effects of early maternal deprivation which have been emphasized in studies in this country.

Research with other personality tests show the influence of cultural milieu, social class, economic status, child training, parental occupation, parental behavior, urban-rural residence and the like.[3] If similar influences have a differential effect on Rorschach scores—and we are sure that they do—norms which are applied in clinical procedure and in research must of course be appropriate to the group or the case and must be evaluated in terms of the cultural background and the personal and social values of the different subcultures of our society.

Finally, we would like to emphasize again the caution which must be exercised in the interpretation of patterns which deviate from the normative material available for children in the second decade. It is an elementary fact that norms are merely central tendencies of the group, and what is modal is not necessarily optimal, desirable or even healthy. We may and do find certain imbalances in the records of adolescents—tenuous ego controls, regressions to and resurgences of primitive thinking, immature affect, perhaps "unhealthy" defensive operations, and the like. We cannot and should not conclude at once that we have neurotic pictures or a more serious pathology. These deviations may represent temporary experimental and protective forms of adjustment and hence adaptive strengths, and while they must be identified and handled, pathology is not indicated without appropriate weighing of weaknesses and strengths, without consideration of the degree of resilience manifested in the record, and other relevant information. More often than not, deviations do not reflect serious or prolonged illness.

Vorhaus[68] has discussed some of these temporary disturbances in adolescents. In her article discussing the use of the Rorschach in preventive mental hygiene, she hypothesizes four different configurations of adolescent maladjustment and suggests ways of differentiating between temporary disturbances and more serious disorders.

There are, then, many factors which must be taken into consideration in applying Rorschach normative and developmental data. Fortunately, the responsible clinician is sensitive to them. Unfortunately, however, the research investigator does not always consider the general scope and limitations of normative material.

## Summary

The Rorschach studies in adolescence which are available are valuable in the sense that they furnish many fruitful hypotheses concerning the general personality dimensions of children in the second decade of life, the process of development, the normative changes which take place and the many individual patterns of development. Rorschach adolescent norms provide a frame of reference for the evaluation of the adjustment potentials of the individual child. They help in differentiating between temporary imbalances and the more pervasive mental disorders. When normative and developmental data are applied, however, the various factors which influence the Rorschach performance in a differential way must be taken into consideration.

Unfortunately, there has been no well designed programmatic approach to adolescence with the Rorschach method. As yet we have only miscellaneous and unrelated data for the most part, and a mass of isolated empirical studies, most of them score-centered. Few are longitudinal studies which, in our judgment, represent the only approach which will prove fruitful for the understanding of the growth processes. Few attack the developmental processes directly. Few start with testable hypotheses concerning personality development and work from them. Few are theoretically oriented. Many clinicians and research workers recognize these problems.[11,38,56,57,61]

There is need today to systematize our Rorschach data by structuring specific hypotheses within a theoretical framework so that we may interpret in a more meaningful fashion the valuable empirical data which have been accumulated over the course of the years. There is even greater need for well designed Rorschach research in which theoretically oriented hypotheses pertaining to the developmental processes taking place in the second decade (or at any other period) are formulated and subjected to study by systematically oriented and clinically trained research workers. In this way valuable data may be amassed on the phenomena and problems of adolescence. At the same time we may validate many aspects of the Rorschach which we find so helpful in the clinic and possibly add to its potentialities as an instrument of diagnosis and personality research.

## References

1. Ames, L. B., Learned, J., Métraux, R. W., & Walker, R. N. *Child Rorschach responses: developmental trends from two to ten years.* New York: Hoeber, 1952.
2. ——, Métraux, R. W., & Walker, R. N. *Adolescent Rorschach responses.* New York: Hoeber, 1959.
3. Auld, F. Influence of social class on personality test responses. *Psychol. Bull.,* 1952, *49,* 318–332.
4. Beck, S. J. The six schizophrenias. *Res. Monogr. Amer. Orthopsychiat. Ass.,* 1954, No. 6.
5. Behn-Eschenburg, H. *Psychische Schüleruntersuchungen mit dem Formdeutversuch.* Bern u. Leipzig: Ernst Bircher, 1921.
6. Bohm, E. *Rorschach test diagnosis* (Translated by Anne G. Beck & S. J. Beck). New York: Grune & Stratton, 1958.
7. Bühler, C., LeFever, D., Kallstedt, F. E., & Peak, H. M. Development of the basic Rorschach score. Supplementary monograph. Los Angeles, Calif.: Rorschach Standardization Studies, 1952, *iv* (Mimeo).
8. Cotte, S. Étude statistique sur les interprétations globales (G) dans le test psychologique de Rorschach. *G. Psichiat. Neuropatol.,* 1953, 3.
9. ——. Étude statistique sur les réponses zoomorphiques (A) dans le test de Rorschach des enfants impubères. *Bull. Group. Franç. Rorschach,* 1955, *7,* 5–8.
10. ——. Étude statistique sur les réponses anthropomorphiques (H) dans le test de Rorschach des enfants impubères de 7–11 ans. *Bull. Group. Franç. Rorschach,* 1956, *8,* 19–22.
11. Crandall, V. J. Observations on the use of projective techniques in child development research. *J. proj. Tech.,* 1956, *20,* 251–255.
12. Davidson, H. H. *Personality and economic background.* New York: King's Crown Press, 1943.
13. ——. A measure of adjustment obtained from the Rorschach protocol. *J. proj. Tech.,* 1950, *14,* 31–38.
14. ——, & Klopfer, B. Rorschach statistics, Part II: Normal children. *Rorschach Res. Exch.,* 1938, *3,* 37–43.
15. Frank, L. K., Harrison, R., Hellersberg, E., Machover, K. & Steiner, M. Personality development in adolescent girls. *Monogr. Soc. Res. Child Developm.,* 1951, *16,* No. 53.

16. Gallagher, J. J.  Normality and projective techniques. *J. abnorm. soc. Psychol.*, 1955, *50*, 250–264.
17. Gorlow, L., Zimet, C. N., & Fine, H. J.  The validity of anxiety and hostility Rorschach content scores among adolescents. *J. consult. Psychol.*, 1952, *16*, 73–75.
18. Harrower, M.  *Personality change and development as measured by the projective techniques.* New York: Grune & Stratton, 1958.
19. Hemmendinger, L.  Perceptual organization and development as reflected in the structure of Rorschach test responses. *J. proj. Tech.*, 1953, *17*, 162–170.
20. Hershenson, J. R.  Preference of adolescents for Rorschach figures. *Child Developm.*, 1949, *20*, 101–118.
21. Hertz, M. R.  Rorschach norms for an adolescent age group. *Child Developm.*, 1935, *6*, 69–76.
22. ———.  Scoring the Rorschach test with specific reference to the "normal detail" category. *Amer. J. Orthopsychiat.*, 1938, *8*, 100–121.
23. ———.  The "popular" response factor in the Rorschach scoring. *J. Psychol.*, 1938, *6*, 3–31.
24. ———.  Personality changes in 35 girls in various stages of pubescent development based on the Rorschach method. *Psychol. Bull.*, 1941, *38*, 705. (Abstract)
25. ———.  Personality patterns in adolescence as portrayed by the Rorschach ink-blot method: I. The movement factors. *J. gen. Psychol.*, 1942, *27*, 119–188.
26. ———.  The scoring of the Rorschach ink-blot method as developed by the Brush Foundation. *Rorschach Res. Exch.*, 1942, *6*, 16–27.
27. ———.  Personality patterns in adolescence as portrayed by the Rorschach ink-blot method: III. The "Erlebnistypus" (a normative study). *J. gen. Psychol.*, 1943, *28*, 225–276.
28. ———.  Personality patterns in adolescence as portrayed by the Rorschach method: IV. The "Erlebnistypus" (a typological study). *J. gen Psychol.*, 1943, *29*, 3–45.
29. ———.  Adolescent Rorschach norms. 1950 (Mimeo).
30. ———.  *Frequency tables for scoring responses to the Rorschach ink-blot test.* (3rd ed.) Cleveland, Ohio: Press of Western Reserve Univer., 1951.
31. ———.  Rorschach scoring symbols with definitions, scoring formulae and qualitative notations. 1953 (Mimeo).
32. ———.  The use and misuse of the Rorschach method. I. Variations in Rorschach procedure. *J. proj. Tech.*, 1959, *23*, 33–48.
33. ———, & Baker, E.  Personality changes in adolescence as revealed by the Rorschach method. "Control" patterns. *Psychol. Bull.*, 1941, *38*, 705. (Abstract)
34. ———, & ———.  Personality patterns in adolescence as portrayed by the Rorschach ink-blot method: II. The color factors. *J. gen. Psychol.*, 1943, *28*, 3–61.
35. Hertzman, M., & Margulies, H.  Developmental changes as reflected in Rorschach test responses. *J. genet. Psychol.*, 1943, *62*, 189–216.
36. Ives, V., Grant, M. Q., & Ranzoni, J. H.  The "neurotic" Rorschachs of normal adolescents. *J. genet. Psychol.*, 1953, *83*, 31–61.
37. Kallstedt, F. E.  A Rorschach study of sixty-six adolescents. *J. clin. Psychol.*, 1952, *8*, 129–132.
38. Kass, W.  Projective techniques as research tools in studies of normal personality development. *J. proj. Tech.*, 1956, *20*, 269–272.
39. Klopfer, B., Ainsworth, M. D., Klopfer, W. G., & Holt, R. R.  *Developments in the Rorschach technique. Vol. I. Technique and theory.* Yonkers-on-Hudson, N. Y.: World Book Co., 1954.
40. Klopfer, B. (Ed.)  *Developments in the Rorschach technique. Vol. II. Fields of application.* Yonkers-on-Hudson, N. Y.: World Book Co., 1956.
41. Loosli-Usteri, M.  Le test de Rorschach appliqués à différents groupes d'enfants de 10–13 ans. *Arch. Psychol., Genève*, 1929, *22*, 51–106.
42. ———.  *Le diagnostic individuel chez l'enfant au moyen du test de Rorschach.* Paris: Hermann, 1938.
43. ———.  Der Rorschach Test als Hilfsmittel des Kinder Psychologen. *Schweiz. Z. Psychol.*, 1942, *1*, 86–91.

44. McFate, M. Q., & Orr, F. G.   Through adolescence with the Rorschach. *Rorschach Res. Exch. & J. proj. Tech.*, 1949, *13*, 302–319.
45. Meili-Dworetzki, G.   The development of perception in the Rorschach. *In* B. Klopfer (Ed.), *Developments in the Rorschach technique.* Vol. II. Yonkers-on-Hudson, N. Y.: World Book Co., 1956. Pp. 104–176.
46. Miale, F. R., & Harrower-Erickson, M. R.   Personality structure in the psychoneuroses. *Rorschach Res. Exch.*, 1940, *4*, 71–74.
47. Mons, W. E. R.   Eine Normstudie des kindlichen Rorschach-Bildes. *Z. diagnost. Psychol.*, 1955, *3*, 177–180.
48. Montalto, F. D.   Maternal behavior and child personality: a Rorschach study. *J. proj. Tech.*, 1952, *16*, 151–178.
49. Morris, W. W., & Nicholas, A. L.   Intrafamilial personality configurations among children with primary behavior disorders and their parents: a Rorschach investigation. *J. clin. Psychol.*, 1950, *6*, 309–319.
50. Paulsen, A. A.   Personality development in the middle years of childhood: a ten-year longitudinal study of thirty public school children by means of Rorschach tests and social histories. *Amer. J. Orthopsychiat.*, 1954, *24*, 336–350.
51. Phillips, L., & Smith, J. G.   *Rorschach interpretation: advanced technique.* New York: Grune & Stratton, 1953.
52. Piotrowski, Z. A.   *Perceptanalysis.* New York: Macmillan, 1957.
53. Rabin, A. I.   Personality maturity of Kibbutz (Israeli Collective Settlement) and non-Kibbutz children as reflected in Rorschach findings. *J. proj. Tech.*, 1957, *21*, 148–153.
54. ——, & Beck, S. J.   Genetic aspects of some Rorschach factors. *Amer. J. Orthopsychiat.*, 1950, *20*, 595–599.
55. Ranzoni, J. H., Grant, M. Q., & Ives, V.   Rorschach "card-pull" in a normal adolescent population. *J. proj. Tech.*, 1950, *14*, 107–133.
56. Reichard, S.   Discussion: Projective techniques as research tools in studies of normal personality development. *J. proj. Tech.*, 1956, *20*, 265–268.
57. Ricciuti, H. N.   Use of the Rorschach test in longitudinal studies of personality development. *J. proj. Tech.*, 1956, *20*, 250–260.
58. Rorschach, H.   *Psychodiagnostics* (Translated by P. Lemkau & B. Kronenberg). Bern: Hans Huber, 1942.
59. Sarason, S. B.   *The clinical interaction: with special reference to the Rorschach.* New York: Harper, 1954.
60. Schachtel, F. G.   Notes on Rorschach tests of 500 juvenile delinquent adolescents. *J. proj. Tech.*, 1951, *15*, 144–172.
61. Shafer, R.   *Psychoanalytic interpretation in Rorschach testing: theory and application.* New York: Grune & Stratton, 1954.
62. Shapiro-Pollack, N.   *Contribution à l'étude psychologique de la puberté à l'aide du test de Rorschach.* Paris: Soc. Nouv. d'Imprimerie, 1935.
63. Stein, H.   Developmental changes in content of movement responses. *J. proj. Tech.*, 1956, *20*, 216–223.
64. Suares, N. D.   Personality development in adolescence. *Rorschach Res. Exch.*, 1938, *3*, 2–11.
65. Taulbee, E. S., Sisson, B. D., & Gaston, C. O.   Affective ratio and 8–9–10 per cent on the Rorschach test for normals and psychiatric groups. *J. consult. Psychol.*, 1956, *20*, 105–108.
66. Thetford, W. N.   Fantasy perception in the personality development of normal and deviant children. *Amer. J. Orthopsychiat.*, 1952, *22*, 542–550.
67. ——, Molish, H. B., & Beck, S. J.   Developmental aspects of personality structure in normal children. *J. proj. Tech.*, 1951, *15*, 58–78.
68. Vorhaus, P. G.   The use of the Rorschach in preventive mental hygiene. *J. proj. Tech.*, 1952, *16*, 179–192.
69. Wertheimer, R. R.   Relationships between specific Rorschach variables and sociometric data. *J. proj. Tech.*, 1957, *21*, 94–97.
70. Zubin, J., with Young, K. M.   *Manual of projective and cognate techniques.* Madison, Wis.: College Typing Co., 1948.

# Part III: Picture Techniques

# 4

## The Children's Apperception Test (CAT)

### LEOPOLD BELLAK AND CRUSA ADELMAN†

### Description of the CAT and Typical Responses to Pictures

THE CAT consists of 10 plates, accompanied by a manual (fig. 1). Below we present a description of each card and typically related themes:

*Picture 1: Chicks seated around a table on which is a large bowl of food. Off to one side is a large chicken, dimly outlined.*

Responses revolve around eating, being or not being sufficiently fed by either parent. Themes of sibling rivalry enter via themes of who gets more, who is well behaved or not, etc. Food may be seen as a reward or, inversely, the withholding of it may be seen as punishment; general problems of orality are dealt with; satisfaction or frustration, feeding problems per se.

*Picture 2: One bear pulling a rope on one side while another bear and a baby bear pull on the other side.*

It is interesting to observe whether the figure with whom the baby bear cooperates is identified (if at all) by the child as mother or father. The picture may be seen as a serious fight with accompanying fear of aggression; in other words, a projected fulfillment of the child's own aggressive or autonomous fantasies. More benignly, the card may be seen as describing a game (tug of war, for example). Sometimes the rope itself may be a source of concern, i.e., the "toy rope" might break, causing fear of subsequent punishment; or it may be seen as a symbol concerning masturbation, with the rope breaking representing castration fears.

*Picture 3: A lion with pipe and cane, sitting in a chair. In the lower right corner a little mouse appears in a hole.*

The lion is usually seen as a father figure equipped with such masculine symbols as pipe and cane; or, on the other hand, the cane may turn this paternal figure into an old, helpless creature, of whom one need not be afraid. This is usually a defense process against the child's acute awareness of father's strength. If the lion is viewed as a strong paternal figure, it will be important to note whether he is represented as benign or dangerous.

The mouse is often taken as the identification figure. In such a case—by tricks and circumstances—the mouse may be turned into the more powerful animal indeed. On the other hand, it may be totally at the lion's mercy. Some children identify with the lion, and there will be other subjects who will switch identification one or more times, suggesting conflicts between compliance and autonomy, etc.

†To our greatest regret, Miss Adelman died in the summer of 1959.

Fig. 1.—The CAT pictures.

*Picture 4: A kangaroo with a bonnet on her head, carrying a basket with a milk bottle; in her pouch is a baby kangaroo with a balloon; on a bicycle a larger kangaroo child.*

This usually elicits themes of sibling rivalry, and/or some concern with the origin of babies. In both cases, the child's relationship to the mother is an important feature. Sometimes an older sibling will identify with the pouch baby, thus indicating a wish to regress in order to be nearer the mother. On the other hand, a child who is in reality the younger may identify himself with the older one, thus signifying his wish for independence and mastery. The basket may give rise to themes of feeding. A theme of flight from danger may also occasionally be introduced. Our experience suggests, thus far, that this can be related to the child's unconscious fear of the primal scene—the pouch, basket, etc., suggesting pregnancy due to mother's sexual relationship to father.

*Picture 5: A darkened room with a large bed in the background; a crib in the foreground in which there are two baby bears.*

Productions concerning the primal scene in all variations are common here; the child is concerned with what goes on between the parents in bed. These stories reflect a good deal of conjecture, observation, confusion and emotional involvement on the child's part. The two baby bears in the crib lend themselves to themes of mutual manipulation and exploration between children.

*Picture 6: A darkened cave with two dimly outlined bear figures in the background; a baby bear lying in the foreground.*

This again is a picture eliciting stories concerning the primal scene. It is used in addition to picture 5 since experience has shown that picture 6 will add to what was held back in response to the previous picture. Jealousy in the triangle situation will at times be reflected. Problems of masturbation at bedtime may appear in response to either picture 5 or picture 6.

*Picture 7: A tiger with bared fangs and claws, leaping at a monkey which is also leaping through the air.*

Children's fears of aggression and their manner of dealing with these emotions are exposed here. The degree of anxiety associated with aggression often becomes apparent. It may be so great as to lead to rejection of the picture, or the defenses may be good enough (or unrealistic enough) to turn it into an innocuous story. The monkey may even outsmart the tiger. The animals' tails lend easily to the projection of fears or wishes concerning castration. Oral aggressive and incorporative themes predominate.

*Picture 8: Two adult monkeys sitting on a sofa drinking from tea cups. One adult monkey in the foreground is sitting on a hassock talking to a baby monkey.*

Here one often sees the role in which the child places himself, within the family constellation. It may also reflect the child's conception of adult social life. His interpretation of the dominant (foreground) monkey as either a father or mother figure becomes significant in relation to his perception of it as a benign or admonishing, inhibiting monkey. The tea cups will on occasion, give rise to oral themes again.

*Picture 9: A darkened room seen through an open door from a lighted room. In the darkened room there is a child's bed in which a rabbit sits up looking through the door.*

Common responses to this picture are: fear of darkness themes, of being left alone, desertion by parents, or significant curiosity as to what goes on in the next room.

*Picture 10: A baby dog lying across the knees of an adult dog; both figures with a minimum of expressive features. The figures are set in the foreground of a bathroom.*

This leads to stories of "crime and punishment," revealing something about the child's moral conceptions. There are frequent stories about toilet training as well as masturbation. Regressive trends will be more clearly revealed in this picture than in some others.

### Range of Application of the CAT

The CAT was designed with the idea in mind that its range of application extend from about *three years to 10 years of age*. A number of qualifying remarks need to be made with regard to this range.

By and large, few children below three will be sufficiently verbal to give adequate responses to the pictures. However, there are occasionally children of two and one-half whose verbal development is precocious enough to allow them to give excellent stories. As to the upper limits of the age range, the Symonds Picture-Story Test and/or the TAT can often take over advantageously. Children whose chronological age is 10 and whose mental age is considerably higher may not respond well to the CAT or at least not need it. Naturally, some children with an M.A. of 14 years may give excellent CAT stories, and some of lower C.A. or M.A. than 10 may have the particular kinds of defenses that force them to decline the CAT as too childish.

### Rationale for the CAT

There are three basic propositions involved in the rationale underlying the CAT.

The *first proposition* involves the basic projective hypothesis: When given a situation to handle, one with some degree of freedom, the person not only gives information which is meant to meet the requirements of the task, but in so doing, he also gives us information from which we can make inferences regarding his unique personality organization, including, of course, adaptive as well as defensive features. In essence, the first proposition can be stated as the belief that perception is a function of the total personality, and that a study of the individual differences of perceptual responses to stimuli will lead to an understanding of the subject's personality. Asking someone to respond freely (i.e., with a story) is likely to increase the individual differences, in contrast to asking for a precise description. A detailed statement of the subsidiary hypothesis and propositions involving the basic projective hypothesis (different types of projections—i.e., a reflection of the different kinds of personality constituents together with the different levels of consciousness and organization) is not included in the present limited discussion and can largely be found elsewhere.[1,11] The types of inferences are, in large measure, predicated upon the psychologist's theory of personality; for the present discussion, the psychoanalytic theory of personality is mainly used.

The *second proposition* involves the choice of particular scenes to be represented in the pictures. The selection of these is not independent of one's theoretical frame of reference.

The CAT pictures were designed the way they were because of preconceived ideas about problems, situations and roles that were especially relevant to children. It was assumed that, for example, an eating scene, a toilet scene, sleeping, etc., were stimuli that would elicit significant responses reflecting current and not so distant realities and fantasies. By using these situations it was hoped that one could come closer to learning something of the context of the child's preoccupations, troubles, wishful daydreams and of his body or self image, his identification "choices" (of both figures and activities), coping devices, and defensive and adaptive functioning. The usefulness of the CAT depends on the entire set with its chosen situations, special degree of ambiguity, appealing quality of the scenes and its "nontest" presentation to the child, that is, the fact that it is not a right-wrong school test.

The *third proposition* concerning the CAT relates to the choice of animal figures. This feature of the CAT is the third proposition because it is the relatively most subsidiary assumption. Nevertheless, the animal nature of the stimuli has caused considerable research.

On the basis of experience with children, it was expected that they would more readily relate to animals than to human figures. This assumption was predicated on the fact that the animals which children know are usually smaller than adult humans, or at any rate, are usually thought of as "underdogs" like children, and even below children, in our pecking order.

Animals play a prominent role in children's fantasies and phobias, and they become identification figures in children's dreams; on a conscious level, they figure importantly as children's friends, in stories and in reality. The primitivity of animal drives also increases their symbolic proximity for children. From the vantage point of a projective test, it was assumed that animals would offer some manifest disguise. Aggressive and other negative sentiments could more easily be ascribed to a lion than to a human father figure, and the child's own unacceptable wishes could be more easily projected onto the less transparent identification figure, in a picture stimulus, than onto a human child. Animals also lend themselves more easily to the age and sex ambiguity in the stimuli, which was desired.

The Rorschach records of young children show a high per cent of animal references and a relative absence of human figures. The use of animals as identification figures by some psychotics and in primitive cultures also tended to support the expectation of a high stimulus value.

A good deal of literature has been consistent with this idea. Goldfarb[48] expressed interest in the child's animal fantasy. He referred to the fact that

Freud found a close connection between the psychodynamics of the individual child and the kind of animal predominating in the child's fantasy. Bender and Rapoport,[19] on the basis of their clinical experience with normal and disturbed children, concluded that animal pictures were more productive. Olney and Cushing[72] found that the majority of children's picture books contained animal characters. Werner's discussions[94] of the mental organization of children, as well as quoted statements from source books on primitive man, also supported the proposition.

Some subsequent studies have been confirmatory. Spiegelman, Terwilliger and Fearing[85] reported that animals appeared in 50 per cent of all Sunday comic strips. Blum and Hunt[25] believed in the superiority of animal over human figures; the former more easily overcome the child's resistance, and thus projection of the child's feelings was facilitated. Bills[23] and Bills, Leiman and Thomas[24] in pioneer investigations compared TAT pictures with animal pictures, using children ranging from 5 to 10 years of age; they concluded that the animal picture was an easier situation for formulating projective stories.

On the other hand, some studies doubt the superiority of animal pictures over human pictures:

Biersdorf and Marcuse[22] used six pictures similar to the CAT (Cards 1, 2, 4, 5, 8 and 10) and had the same artist design corresponding human cards. The two sets were similar in other respects, although there were some shading and size differences. The human set was not nearly as ambiguous as the original CAT with respect to role and sex. On seven criteria of productivity no significant difference was found between the two sets of cards.

A second study was then done by Mainord and Marcuse[66] with the use of the same two sets of pictures but now administered to emotionally disturbed children. Four criteria, similar to the ones in the first study, failed to show significant differences, but judges' ratings of clinical usefulness showed that the human figures produced more clinical information. Of course, the human figures also used the total stimulus situation of the CAT but many details— such as the lack of ambiguity in the figure—raise doubts about the comparability of the results. These studies inadvertently underline the value of the animal pictures with regard to ambiguity in that the authors found it necessary to structure the human substitutes with more than their animal equivalents: in the equivalent to picture 1, the shadowy figure is clearly a woman; even worse, in the equivalent to picture 2 a woman and a little boy are matched against a man, pulling rope; in picture 10 a woman clearly has a little boy across her knee. By comparing stimuli structured in a way likely to produce stories (e.g., their picture of a woman with a little boy across her knee is very likely to produce stories of spanking as compared to the fact that the dog in the CAT card 10 is often seen as being brushed) to the more ambiguous stimuli of the CAT, the authors have produced an artifact that violates the basic principles of projective testing, and wrongly gives the impression that human figures are intrinsically superior to animal figures.

Furuya[42] used the Marcuse pictures with Japanese subjects. He too found that human figures produced better results, using criteria such as expression of feelings and expression of significant conflict. Aside from the doubts raised above, it must be mentioned that two of his three groups ranged well above 10 years in age—the upper limit for which the CAT claims some possible advantage to animal figures.

Light[63] tried to improve on the Marcuse and Biersdorf study by using more subjects and more qualitative criteria. He found better identification with human than animal figures. His subjects ranged from 9 years 8 months to 10 years 6 months, and he compared CAT cards with TAT cards, two reasons why his data are not particularly useful here.

Not a single one of the above studies used a child below 5 years 4 months, the bulk of the subject population being at least over eight and in the last two studies being close to and above 10 years of age.

The CAT was originally devised to meet the need of the young child. Although, as we have stated, it can be used for children from three to 10 years, the question of animal versus human pictures is relevant particularly for the lower half of this range. From a variety of clinical as well as empirical sources we know that animals are most often used as displacement figures by very young children. In addition, we have learned from the work of Piaget[74] that at about age seven, and perhaps earlier in our present-day culture, a new level of intelligence emerges, a transition from the sensori-motor to operational thinking. While we have no data regarding the animal-human controversy in connection with this emergent intelligence, one might speculate about its relationship to a readiness to become involved in animal pictures.

## Administration

In the administration of the CAT account must be taken of the general problems of child testing. Good rapport must be established with the child. This will, in general, be considerably more difficult with the younger children as well as with the more disturbed ones. Whenever possible, the CAT should be presented as a game, not a test. With children who are obviously aware that it is a test, whether from previous experience with such procedures or sophistication, it will be advisable to acknowledge this fact fully. However, it is important to explain carefully that this test, unlike those the child knows about from home or school, does not ask him to submit to approval, disapproval, competition or disciplinary action.

For the actual instruction, it may be best to tell the child that he is going to play a game in which he is to tell a story about pictures (thus suggesting even to the sophisticated child that this is no ordinary test), and that, accordingly, he should describe what is going on—what the animals are doing now. At suitable points, the child may be asked what happened in the story before and what will happen later.

It will probably be found that much encouragement and nonsuggestive prompting may be necessary as well as real-play interruptions. After all stories have been related, one may go over each of them asking for elaboration on specific points such as: why some animal or figure was given a certain name or age, names of places, or even about the outcome of a story. If a child's attention span does not permit this procedure, an attempt should be made at a time as soon after administration as possible.

All side remarks and activities should be noted as the story is told. A difficult situation to deal with may arise if the child wants the examiner to tell a story; this is primarily a request to be given something rather than to have to give, and is best dealt with in that light. While it may help to explain that we want to hear what the particular child can make of the picture, it may be necessary to promise to tell a story later (and to adhere to it); or to leave off testing until one can ingratiate oneself with the child—by giving in one way or another—and then to resume.

It is helpful to keep all the pictures out of sight except the one in use, since younger children may want to play with all the pictures at once or choose them at random for story telling. These pictures have been numbered and arranged in a particular sequence to maintain a uniform test situation.

If, however, a child is particularly restless and one has some indication as to what the current problems are, one may restrict the test to only those few cards which are likely to illuminate those specific areas. Thus, a child who apparently has sibling rivalry problems might be given cards 1 and 4.

## Interpretation of the CAT

The interpretation of the CAT can be approached from any number of avenues, theoretically and practically.[11] The approach discussed here is predicated upon clinical usefulness and mostly the concepts of psychoanalysis. As a frame of reference, a special Analysis Blank has been designed and will be used here for purposes of illustrating the interpretation of one entire protocol.

A short form of the original Bellak TAT and CAT Blank and Analysis Sheet has been published for the sake of economy and clinical convenience. It largely uses the same variables as the earlier blank, but consists only of a three-page form which folds into a single 11″ x 8½″ sheet, with all the summarized facts on the front (fig. 2).

When the Blank is completely unfolded, each of these variables can be recorded in appropriate boxes for all 10 stories and summarized consecutively, under the same headings, at the extreme right. The final report can be written with the summary sheet opened out in full view.

One of the main purposes of the Blank is to permit a safe transition from concrete primary data to summary of inference and final diagnosis, with a minimal danger of contamination by the interpreter's personality. The nature of the hypothetical inferences and the detailed process of the formation of the diagnosis are reported elsewhere.[11]

Each story should be scrutinized with the help of the 10 major categories listed in the blank, and the essential data recorded in the relevant box. The major categories and the details listed under them are used primarily as a frame of reference, a reminder to look for certain aspects. Naturally, not all aspects will be presented in every story, in which case, of course, the boxes are simply left empty. Also, occasionally, facets not mentioned in the Blank will occur and need recording.

### The Main Theme

We are interested in what a child makes of the pictures and *why* he gives this particular story. Rather than judge by one story, we will be on safer interpretive ground if we can find a common denominator or trend in a number of stories. That is, if the main hero of several stories is hungry, and resorts to stealing in order to satisfy himself, it is not unreasonable to conclude that this child is preoccupied with thoughts of not getting enough— food literally, or gratification generally—and in his fantasy wishes to take it away from others. We can speak of the theme of a story or of several stories, and the theme may be more or less complex. Also, a story may have more than one theme, all of which may be complexly interrelated. In children of three and four the theme is usually very simple.

### The Main Hero

A basic assumption in our reasoning thus far is that the story which our subject tells is, in essence, a reflection of himself. Since there can be a number of people in a story, it becomes necessary to state that we can speak of the hero as that figure with which our subject mainly identifies himself. We will have to specify some objective criteria for differentiating the hero from other figures. The hero is the figure about whom the story is primarily woven. He resembles the subject most in age and sex, and it is from his standpoint that the events are seen. While these statements hold true most of the time, they do not always. There may be more than one hero, and our subject may identify with both, or first with one and then with another. There may be a deviation in that a subject may identify with a hero of a different sex; it is important to note such identifications. Sometimes an identification figure secondary in importance may represent more deeply repressed unconscious attitudes of the subject. Probably the interests, wishes, deficiencies, gifts and abilities with which the hero is invested are those which the subject possesses, or wishes or fears that he might have. We will want to establish which of these is the most probable. It will be important to observe the adequacy of the hero—the ability to deal with circumstances in a way considered adequate by the society to which he belongs. The adequacy of the hero serves as the best single measure of ego strength, or, in many ways, of the subject's own adequacy. An exception is, of course, the case of the story which is a blatant compensatory wish fulfillment. Careful scrutiny will show the real inadequacy, in such cases.

### Self Image

By self image we mean the conception which the subject has of his body and of his entire self and social role. Schilder first described body image as the picture of one's own body in one's mind. The separation of the self from the outside world, and from the mother particularly, takes place slowly. Federn particularly contributed valuable ideas with his concept of ego boundaries and its defects in psychoses. The self image has found little systematic discussion so far, except for the concept of "role playing." Nevertheless it is most important, and may be revealed in the CAT, e.g., by the hero thinking of himself as dangerous, dirty, defective, etc.

### Main Needs of the Hero

*Behavioral Needs of the Hero (as in the Story)*

The story behavior of the hero may have one of a variety of relationships to the story-teller. The needs expressed may correspond directly to the needs of the child. These needs may be, at least in part, expressed behaviorally in real life, or they may be the direct opposite of real life expression and constitute the fantasy complement. In other words, very aggressive stories may be told sometimes by a very aggressive child, or by a rather meek, passive-aggressive one, who has fantasies of aggression. At least to a certain extent the needs of the hero may not reflect so much the needs of the story-teller as they do the drive quality which the child perceives in other people. He may be describing the aggression feared from various objects, or referring to idealized expectations, such as brilliance and fortitude, ascribed to significant figures in his life and only in part internalized in himself. In short, the behavioral needs of the hero expressed in the story have to be examined and understood in the light of all the varieties and vicissitudes of drive modification as subsumed under the broader concepts of projection or apperceptive distortion.[11]

It is the difficult task of the interpreter to determine to what extent the manifest needs of the hero correspond to various constituents of the story-teller's personality and what the relationship is to the narrator's manifest behavior. It is here that comparison with the actual clinical history is most useful and entirely appropriate under clinical circumstances (as distinct from a research setting). If a child is reported to be particularly shy, passive and withdrawn and the CAT stories overflow with aggression, the compensatory nature of the fantasy material is obvious. Of course, it must remain a goal of psychological science to develop further criteria which will make for increasingly valid predictions from the fantasy material to behavior. The study of ego functions is particularly useful in this respect. The relationship of drives expressed to their vicissitudes within the story may often serve as one clue; that is, if the sequence of the story shows an initial response with aggression which becomes entirely controlled by the end of the story, the chances are that this is a person who does not translate the fantasy or latent need into reality. There are other criteria helpful in attempting predictions about what one might call "acting out." The high degree of detail and realism in the description of needs may suggest the likelihood of the expression in reality. Vaguely structured needs of the hero are less likely to be related to reality.

*Figures, Objects or Circumstances Introduced*

A subject who introduces weapons of some sort or another in a number of stories (even without using them) or frequently refers to food (even without its being eaten) may be tentatively judged, on such evidence, as having a need for aggression or oral gratification, respectively. Similarly, the introduction of such figures as punisher, pursuer or benefactor, or such circumstances as injustice or deprivation may be similarly interpreted but with due regard to the rest of the record.

### Figures, Objects or Circumstances Omitted

If a subject omits references to objects, one may wish to infer a repressive operation. Of course, this level of inference can only be a tentative one until we have a large enough sample of norms, so that expectations regarding objects and themes introduced and/or omitted are possible.

## Conception of the Environment

This concept is, of course, a complex mixture of unconscious self perception and apperceptive distortion of stimuli by memory images of the past. The more consistent a picture of the environment appears in the CAT stories, the more reason we have to consider it an important constituent of our subject's personality and a useful clue to his reactions in everyday life. Usually, two or three descriptive terms will suffice, such as succorant, hostile, exploiting or exploitable, friendly, dangerous.

## Figures are seen as . . .

Here we are interested in the way the child sees the figures around him and how he reacts to them. We know something about the quality of object relationships—symbiotic, anaclitic, oral-dependent, ambivalent, etc., at different stages of development and in different personalities. However, in a broader scheme we may descriptively speak of supportive, competitive and other relationships.

## Significant Conflicts

We not only want to know the nature of the conflicts but also the defenses which the child uses against anxiety engendered by these conflicts. Here we have an excellent opportunity to study early character formation, and we may be able to derive ideas concerning prognosis.

There are those conflicts which all children experience as they grow from one phase into the next, each phase being characterized more or less by its concomitant conflict. For example, beginning at about age three, we ought not to be alarmed to find evidence of the oedipal struggle and defenses against the fantasied relationship. Also, we begin to see the seesaw of little-big, child-adult—the preparation for mastery and the frustrations because of lack of skill and mature intelligence.

## Nature of Anxieties

The importance of determining the main anxieties of a child hardly needs emphasizing. Anxieties related to physical harm, punishment and the fear of lacking or losing love (disapproval) and of being deserted (loneliness, lack of support) are probably the most important. The CAT may give us excellent clues regarding puzzling manifest behavior, resulting from unconscious wishes and defenses against them.

The nature of anxiety, as with all these variables, is to be viewed in terms of age-appropriateness. This frame of reference is particularly relevant to this factor or phase, since the kind of anxiety a child is beset with tells us about the level of psychosexual development, diagnosis and prognosis. If we see a young latency child whose CAT stories reflect anxiety about his body, his helplessness, or who is still concerned with the loss of the pre-oedipal love object and desertion, we would expect many other indices of pathology, and perhaps do a careful analysis of the formal features of the CAT as well as his intelligence test. Now, if another six or seven year old gave evidence of anxiety associated with superego authority and tried to work it out in a story which stressed rules and programs, we would certainly want to pursue this, but it would be at least the kind of anxiety many children of this age experience, as part of their development.

## Main Defenses

Stories should not be studied exclusively for drive content, but should, in addition, be examined for the defenses against anxieties and drives. Such a study of defenses may offer more information, in that the drives themselves may appear less clearly than the defenses against them. Also, the defensive structure may be more closely related to manifest behavior. By means of studying drives and defenses the CAT often permits an appraisal of the character structure of the subject.

Aside from a search for the main defense mechanisms, it is also valuable to study the molar aspects of the stories. For instance, some children choose obsessive defenses against a picture's disturbing content; they may produce four or five themes, each very short and descriptive, manifestly different but dynamically similar. Such a succession shows the attempt to deal with a disturbing conflict; successive stories may become more and more innocuous, showing an increase in defensive operation.

The concept of defense has to be understood in an increasingly broader sense, as has been discussed recently by Lois Murphy and her associates[71] in connection with coping (i.e., the person's general ability and mode of meeting external and internal stimuli). With the advance in ego psychology and a focus on problems of adaptation, a study of these broad defense functions is likely to play a dominant role in the exploration of projective methods. We not only want to know the nature of the defensive maneuvers but also the success with which they are employed and (or rather) the sacrifice such maneuvers demand from the functioning personality.

The concept of perceptual vigilance may be thought of in connection with projective methods. Various studies have suggested that not only the defensive projective function of the ego is increased in stress but also its cognitive acuity may be improved at the same time.

In the study of children's stories, it must be remembered that we view the nature of pathogenicity of defenses and other structural concepts in terms of age-appropriateness. What may be quite normal at one age may be pathologic at another age. In the absence of normative data some very rough, empirical guide lines must be considered.

## Severity of Superego

The relationship of the chosen punishment to the nature of the offense gives us an insight into the severity of the superego. A delinquent's hero who murders may receive no punishment other than a slight suggestion that he may have learned a lesson for later life, while a neurotic may have stories in which the hero is accidentally or intentionally killed or mangled or dies of illness following the slightest infraction or expression of aggression. On the other hand, a nonintegrated superego, sometimes too severe and sometimes too lenient, is also frequently met in neurotics. A formulation as to the circumstances under which a child's superego can be expected to be too severe, and under what other conditions it is likely to be too lenient is, of course, not only related to the difficult problem of "acting out" but, in general, a valuable piece of information.

## Integration of the Ego

This variable in its many aspects tells us about the general level of functioning; to what extent the child is able to compromise between drives and the demands of reality on the one hand and the commands of his superego on the other. The adequacy of the hero in dealing with the problems the story-teller confronted him with in the CAT is an important aspect of this variable.

We are interested also in how the stories are given and must remember that ego functioning must be considered in terms of the child's age. Is the subject able to tell age-appropriate stories, which constitute a certain amount of cognizance of the stimulus, or does he leave the stimulus completely and tell a story with no manifest relation to the picture because he is too preoccupied with his own problems? Does he find rescue and salvation from the anxiety pertaining to the test by giving very stereotyped responses, or is he psychologically healthy enough and intelligent enough to be creative and give more or less original stories? Having produced a plot, can he attain a solution of the conflict in the story which is adequate and realistic, or do his thought processes become unstructured or even bizarre under the impact of the problem? Does he have the ability to go from a past background of the story to a future resolution? How does the child meet the requirements of the task he is confronted with?

These observations, together with the content variables, permit an appraisal of the subject's ego strength, thus facilitating possible classification of the patient in one of the nosologic categories.

For practical purposes a separate consideration of a variety of ego functions such as drive control, frustration tolerance, anxiety tolerance, perceptual and motor adequacy and others[13] may be considered.

## The Summary and Final Report

After all the stories have been analyzed, the main data obtained from each should be noted down in the appropriate space on page 4 of the Blank. When the summary page is studied, a repetitive pattern in the subject's responses ordinarily becomes clear.

This final report can be written in full view of the summary page. It is suggested that the form of the final report follow the sequence of the 10 categories on the analysis sheet. The main themes, the second and third variables, permit a description of the *psychic structure and unconscious needs of the subject,* while the fourth and fifth variables show us his *conception of the world and significant figures* around him. Categories six, seven, eight, nine and ten may actually be used as headings for statements concerning the respective dimensions of personality.

The form of the final report will depend, of course, to a great extent on the person for whom it is intended. It is, however, strongly advised that empty phrases and erroneous inferences be avoided by the following procedure: The first half of the report may consist of general abstract statements; a second part of the report should then consist of specific documentation by excerpts from stories, from which the main abstract statements have been derived.

This arrangement is particularly useful in instances in which the psychologist reports as part of a team to psychiatrists and to social workers who may not have the time or the experience to read the stories themselves and for whom an abstracted statement will not be sufficiently meaningful.

If a diagnosis must be offered, we suggest that the following formulation be used: "The data represented in the CAT are *consistent with* the diagnosis of . . . . " This expresses our belief that the CAT is not primarily a diagnostic test and also, that preferably no diagnosis should ever be made on the basis of a single test or even any number of tests alone without integration with clinical data.

### Protocols and Clinical Data*

Below we will present all 10 stories of one child. The case presented does not necessarily represent ideal material for the CAT, nor is the interpretation meant to be exemplary in its exhaustiveness (fig. 2).

### James L.

#### Descriptive Data

Male, age 7 years 9 months, third grade, IQ 123, one sibling (brother, 10 years old). The first year teacher reported that James was overactive, had to be watched, and did not get along well with other children, since he fought a great deal. He told fantastic stories, e.g., brought in a toy and claimed his father had made it. The teacher later investigated this story and found it to be untrue. If someone said he had something, James boasted that he had two of the same thing. He constantly destroyed other children's creative play.

James' present teacher reports that his aggressive tendencies are not apparent now, but that the boy is not making use of his high IQ. He is retarded in all subjects. She has to prod him constantly to complete a job.

Not too much is known about the parents. His mother has a strong drive for social acceptance and always appears at school functions very beautifully dressed, though his family

*The senior author is indebted for these stories and the associated material to former students at the New School for Social Research, and at New York University. The cases were chosen, among other reasons, as ones not associated with the author, thus assuring anonymity. This need for anonymity prevents the acknowledgment of the specific students' contributions by name. Appreciation is nevertheless extended to these students, who often secured very fascinating case reports.

is not well off financially. It took all of two years to find out that the father was a chauffeur. Mother always side-stepped this question. The boy, too, must have been affected because his father often took on any occupation (in James' fantasy) that suited the moment; for example, if the children were playing with airplanes, his father was a pilot, etc. They lived in three very small rooms with not much space for the children to play in. His parents had very little home life together because of his father's irregular hours, and there were many arguments at home because the boys were noisy when father was sleeping, etc. Because of irregular hours, the father did not have time to spend with his two boys. Mother, however, spent a lot of time with them trying to "uplift" them. When called in to school because of her child's behavior, she refused to admit that there was any problem. She blamed it on the school in general and on the teacher in particular. She had been ill for some time, possibly with rheumatic fever and anemia. There had been some rivalry between the two boys. Mother described the brother as being "slower."

## CAT Stories

1. The rooster's gonna say, "Get some porridge from the big pot," and the chickens don't want to do it; so the chickens say to the rooster: "Go away on the fence and crow and we'll be eating our porridge." Then, the rooster comes back from crowing on the fence and the chickens didn't eat their porridge. So the rooster says: "Hurry up and eat your porridge. We're going to get some worms." And the chickies say again, "Go out on the fence and crow." [Inquiry: What will happen?] They're not gonna eat their porridge.

[Inquiry: What will happen to the chicks?] They're gonna get spanked.

2. These three bears went up on the mountain with a piece of rope and the father bear wanted to see if he was the strongest between the mother and the baby, and the mother and the baby was the strongest. And baby bear was helping his mama to pull rope but the baby bear could not pull it so hard as the mama bear and the baby bear nearly fell off the mountain. If mama bear hadn't been standing up straight father bear would have fallen off the mountain too. That's a tug of war.

[Inquiry: What will father do?] He fell down and banged his head on a rock.

3. One time there was the King Lion named King Richard—my brother's name is Richard. He thinks he was named after King Richard—and the little mouse's name was Peepsqueak. That's what they call Jimmy [a friend] and that's what I call a mouse. "Twas the night before Christmas when all through the house not a creature was stirring but only a mouse." And Peepsqueak was the little mouse who got on King Richard's nerves so he [King R.] called a doctor to get his nerve off. And then sitting on his throne, he laughed and said, "I think I'll smoke my pipe at last." And taking his cane and pushing his throne, he moved right near the mouse's home. Then he sat waiting for the doctor to come, but the funniest thing was the doctor didn't come at all. After the mouse came out of his house, he had a little hammer and he banged on King Richard's head and that's the end.

[Inquiry: What did the mouse do that got on King Richard's nerves?] He kept on banging him on the head. [Why didn't the doctor come?] He was afraid that the lion would eat him up if he didn't cure him. [What happens to the mouse?] The lion doesn't fool around with him any more. He's afraid of him.

4. One day Mother Kangaroo and Baby Kangaroo went for a picnic. Mother Kangaroo hopped. Baby Kangaroo went on his bicycle and the baby in mother's pouch had a balloon and Mother Kangaroo bursted the balloon and she (baby in pouch) made the milk bottle tip over and spill and Mother Kangaroo's sandwiches flew. One landed on a Christmas tree top and one landed in her face and the third one on her Sunday hat. Then, they went down the hill and got ready to leave but the little baby (in the pouch) tripped her feet and she fell down and threw the basket up and all the basket dumped over and spilled. Then, the little baby on the tricycle hit a rock and bumped his bill—I mean, nose. Then he got up and having nothing to eat, he stuck his nose in a beehive and smelled something good to eat. Just when he was reaching his little paw in, a bee came out and stinged him right on the

Fig. 2.—Analysis Blank for case of James L.

# SHORT FORM

## BELLAK T A T and C A T BLANK

### For Recording and Analyzing Thematic Apperception Test and Children's Apperception Test

Name___James L._____ Sex__M__ Age__7-9__ Date__May, 1959_____

Education___Third Grade_____ Occupation___Student_____ ; m. (s.) w. d.

Referred by_____Analysis by_____

After having obtained the stories analyze each story by using the variables on the left of Page 2. Not every story will furnish information regarding each variable: the variables are presented as a frame of reference to help avoid overlooking some dimension.

When all ten stories have been analyzed it is easy to check each variable from left to right for all ten stories and record an integrated summary on Page 4 under the appropriate headings. That way a final picture is obtained almost immediately.

Then, keeping Page 4 folded out, the Final Report: Diagnostic Impressions and Recommendations can be written on Page 1 by reference to Page 4. Page 5 gives available space for any other notations. The stories then can be stapled inside the blank against Page 5. For further instructions see Manual for TAT Interpretation, Psychological Corporation, by Leopold Bellak or Manual for the CAT, C.P.S. Company, or *The TAT and CAT in Clinical Use*, pp. 282, Grune and Stratton, 1954, N. Y. C. by Leopold Bellak;

### FINAL REPORT: Diagnostic Impressions and Recommendations

This boy shows a great deal of conflict with parental authority, particularly with mother. He feels coerced, aggressed-against and thus, feeling small, reacts with acting-out of aggression, denial of helplessness, and by making himself more important and stronger than reasonable, e.g., in story #1, 4, and 10.

There is some mild normal competitiveness with father in #2; in #7 it is accentuated with some question about the primal scene in which it may be the father indeed who comes to harm.

There is a suggestion of really felt and imagined superiority over the older brother, maybe over father, in story #3.

This boy is of superior intelligence which he uses both for self-inflation, by lying and showing off, but also constructively. His ego functioning is within neurotic limits; together with a rather unintegrated superego, his personality is consistent with a behavior disorder characterized by aggression and lying. His stories are usually well constructed, rather realistic, show good perceptual functioning and an absence of a thought disorder with an ability to be inventive and original.

| | Story No. 1 | Story No. 2 |
|---|---|---|
| 1. **Main Theme:** (diagnostic level: if descriptive and interpretative level are desired, use a scratch sheet or page 5) | Resists authority by (teasing) deception, expects punishment | Competitiveness with father, realizes own weakness, aggression against the father |
| 2. **Main hero:** age____ sex____ vocation____ abilities____ interests____ traits____ body image____ adequacy ($\sqrt{}$,$\sqrt{}\sqrt{}$,$\sqrt{}\sqrt{}\sqrt{}$) and/or self-image____ | deceptive, resistant | Adequate but small |
| 3. **Main needs of hero:**<br>a) behavioral needs of hero (as in story): ____ | to resist, to deceive | competitive, aggressive |
| b) figures, objects, or circumstances *introduced*: ____<br><br>implying need for or to: ____ | crowing, fence, showing off, suggesting need for exhibition | good perception |
| c) figures, objects or circumstances *omitted*: ____<br><br>implying need for or to: ____ | reference to other chickens is omitted in this story | |
| 4. **Conception of environment (world) as:** ____ | ? | |
| 5. a) Parental figures (m $\checkmark$___, f___) are seen as ____<br>and subject's reaction to a is ____<br>b) Contemp. figures (m___, f___) are seen as ____<br>and subject's reaction to b is ____<br>c) Junior figures (m___, f___) are seen as ____<br>and subject's reaction to c is ____ | Father (?) seen as directive, hero reacts with evasiveness, non-compliance, and is punished<br><br>Feels small | Father seen as competitor<br><br><br>wants to be big |
| 6. **Significant conflicts:** ____ | between need for resistance and compliance | wish to defeat father. Awareness of own smallness |
| 7. **Nature of anxieties:** ($\sqrt{}$)<br>of physical harm and/or punishment ____<br>of disapproval ____<br>of lack or loss of love ____of illness or injury ____<br>of being deserted ____of deprivation ____<br>of being overpowered and helpless ____<br>of being devoured ____other ____ | fear of punishment | Fear of physical harm |
| 8. **Main defenses against conflicts and fears:** ($\sqrt{}$)<br>repression____ reaction-formation____<br>regression____ denial____ introjection____<br>isolation____undoing____<br>rationalization ____other____ | lying, showing off | Rationalization: Father would have fallen too: not so strong |
| 9. **Severity of superego as manifested by:** ($\sqrt{}$)<br>punishment for "crime": ____<br>immediate____just____too severe____<br>delayed____unjust____too lenient____<br>delayed initial response or pauses,____stammer____ | slightly delayed, not severe superego | |
| 10. **Integration of the ego, manifesting itself in:** ($\sqrt{}$,$\sqrt{}\sqrt{}$,$\sqrt{}\sqrt{}\sqrt{}$)<br><br>Hero: adequate____inadequate____<br>outcome: happy____unhappy____<br>realistic____unrealistic____<br>drive control____<br>thought processes as revealed by plot being: ($\sqrt{}$,$\sqrt{}\sqrt{}$,$\sqrt{}\sqrt{}\sqrt{}$)<br>stereotyped____original____appropriate____<br>complete____incomplete____inappropriate____<br>($\sqrt{}$) syncretic____concrete____contaminated____<br>Intelligence____<br>Maturational level____ | fantasy adequate; outcome is realistic<br><br><br>appropriate<br><br><br>intelligence: above average | good ego<br><br><br>appropriate |

ear and all that time the little Kangaroo [on the tricycle] spent, his mother was back home getting on her new dress and then at the end, at night time, the little Kangaroo hopped to his feet and rides the tricycle home.

[Inquiry: How did the balloon break?] Mother stepped on it. [Is the little baby on the tricycle a he or a she?] He. [What happened when everything spilled?] Mother picked him up and went home but the baby on the bicycle got left there. [What happened when he got home?] Mother spanked him.

5. One time there was the house of the four little bears. Two baby bears slept in the cradle and two slept in the bed but when the baby bears were asleep the mother bear and the father bear woke up. They put on their clothes and went out to fish. They caught five fish and ate four, but while they were eating, there was a knock on the door and Father bear answered, but there was no one there. The knock kept coming and father bear got so angry that he fell down and sighed and when he was sighing sawdust came in his eyes. He went up on the rooftop and saw by his surprise Woody the woodpecker pecking very hard.

[Inquiry: Who was knocking?; first response] A little girl. [Then changed to] The woodpecker. [He put the card aside and said that was the end and so I didn't question further.]

6. This is some more bears, huh? Three bears were sleeping in a cave of their own, but when they were sleeping a dog came into their home. [Points to dark shadow on the right side of the card and says that is the dog.] The dog took all the bones the bears had taken from him. Then the dog dug a hole in the bear's home and buried them there so nobody would find them and when the bears go out for a walk in the woods, they leave baby bear sleeping so I can pounce on him. Then I can get my bones at last and bring them home and bury them in the grass. Then, my master will be pleased to see me and I'll drag home the bear [baby bear] by his tail. Then, the master will give me one more bone.

7. One day the lion was after the monk because the monk knew how to jump so the lion wanted to know how to jump so he wanted to get the monk to teach him how to jump and— three more, right? And the monk refused to teach the lion how to jump. Then the monkey got away and was ready to spring on a vine, but the lion came after him and missed him and fell on his nose. Then, he got angry and said to himself: "I'll get him on the other end and catch him with my mouth." He did that, but the idea didn't work, he got so angry that his throat began to hurt. Then he went home to his folks back home and said what happened so they all went out to the monk and then all the monks were up in the trees and when the lions came by, they took their sticks and banged the lions over the head. And then the monks said to the group, "There's not gonna be no more lions for us to fool with." Then all the monkeys went on the vine and waited till the natives came by. They took their clubs and walked right by with some of their stuff on their heads. Then the king lion came out and nearly got the monkey's tail but the monkey was fast and got away and the lion jumped right down into the middle of the natives and they said, "If you don't leave the monkey alone, we'll cut off your tail and use it for a sweeping brush." But the lion didn't agree and really went after the monkey, but before he got far, the natives cut off his tail and that was the end of the ferocious lion.

8. One day at a tea party, four monkeys sat—a grandfather with one child, with earrings on his ears like the natives. A mother monkey behind him drinking tea and the father monkey too, and they were having a chatter and laughing at the baby monkey because he looked so funny—then after a while you could see a round picture of grandma monkey with her night cap on and glasses, and she almost looked like the grandma at her house and the man monkey said to the chimp: "How old are you?," so the chimp said: "First let me count on my fingers, let me see now, 1, 2, 3, 4, 5, 6, 7, 8 years old." That's all. [James would not go on with this story.]

[Inquiry: Why did the baby monkey look funny?] Because he was laughing and he had his feet up.

9. One day the baby bunny saw a big creature coming in the door, but he didn't know what kind it was and he looked at the person and it looked like Santa Claus but it wasn't Santa Claus, it was only his mother dressed up like Santa Claus. Then, he (S. C.) said:

| Story No. 3 | Story No. 4 | Story No. 5 | Story No. 6 | Story No. 7 | Story No. 8 |
|---|---|---|---|---|---|
| Aggression against older brother | Aggression between mother and child; guilt, specifically Re: need for acquisition, mother seen as self-centered, interested in clothes | Curiosity; feels parents are eating at night. There are some noises when children are sleeping. Having to do when father being hungry, falling over. | Night time fears of being robbed and carried off | The little one is superior to the big one, the big one is angry. (Father, Brother) Big one loses, is castrated | The small one is Fanny and shows off, by being able to count. |
| Though small, powerful and aggressive; introduced as doctor, nerves and hammer | Aggressive, orally inquisitive | | Dog? Baby bear acquisitive, helpless | capable powerful | Hero is eight years old and can count |
| | aggressive | | dogs, bones, master | aggression, counteraction | |
| sees the bigger one as helpless and ill | orality, fear of aggression | eating, knocking, falling down, sawdust in eyes. Relates to fantasies about eating and noise and mishaps in relation to primary scene. | acquisition, aggression, approbation | pain in throat* peers | |
| implies need for self-aggrandizement | | | | is experienced with anger, need to be big, powerful | |
| | tooth for tooth | unknown things go on all the time | tooth for tooth | aggressive | |
| mother seen as helper —brother seen as helpless though bigger | mother is aggressive, punitive, self-centered | seen as secretive, sharing a meal | | inferior, demanding, aggression | chattering, interested in child |
| | | | | | ? |
| | aggression and guilt | | aggression and acquisition—fear of it | | |
| | | | desertion approbation helplessness— devoured? | fear of being hurt (castrated) | |
| denial projection Doctor is afraid | counter action; acting out, aggression | confabulation | counteraction | aggression, acting-out | performing: exhibits |
| too lenient, unrealistic outcome, original | has a quick interaction, some punishment. Superego not integrated. | | some primitivity: eye for eye non-integrated super-ego | little severity of super ego | |
| | good | good | | unrealistic outcome | |
| | | | | *The realistic detail suggests that he actually may at times experience pain in throat associated with anger. | |

| Story No. 9 | Story No. 10 | SUMMARY |
|---|---|---|
| Is there or is there not a Santa Claus. Wants tools of aggression | Aggressive, antagonistic to mother | **1-3. Unconscious structure and drives of subject (based on variable 1-3)** Is repeatedly concerned with conflict with authority—mother particularly—though also competitive and aggressive in relation to brother and father. He often feels small, aggressed against, and dominated. He meets these pressures with aggression, open antagonism/or teasing, showing off and self-inflation. |
| Tools, guns | Fearful, aggressive and compliant | |
| to get gifts tests reality | Black jack, pin | |
| Hammer, gun, Santa Claus, parents | fear of aggression Need for aggression | |
| need for reality testing, oral aggression | | |
| | | **4. Conception of world:** eye for eye, tooth for tooth |
| deceptive, giving | aggressive, hurting, feeling | **5. Relationship to others:** as described in 1-3 |
| | reactive aggression, compliance | |
| fantasy, reality | aggression, compliance | **6. Significant conflicts:** How to meet aggression: with counter aggression, guilt occasional compliance. Meets feeling of smallness and passivity and need for counter action by wishful thinking. |
| | fear of punishment, physical harm | **7. Nature of anxieties:** |
| denial | fantasy of power | **8. Main defenses used:** showing off, fantasy, (lying), denial, aggressive acting-out |
| ? | uneven, black jack is sorry; unintegrated—superego | **9. Superego structure:** unintegrated superego: in many ways too weak for appropriate control, and the again primitively retaliatory, probably more so than appropriate for his age. |
| ? | unrealistic powerful | **10. Integration and strength of ego:** good intelligence, inventive, perceptive and with a good structure of thought processes. Except where they are in the service of making himself bigger, then it leads to acting out and fancyful and wishful distortions. |

Where you find need for more extensive notations on any story (e.g. the main theme) please use this page for this purpose. (The pages on which the TAT stories were recorded may be enclosed or attached to this Blank)

### ADDITIONAL NOTES

1) If told to do something, resists by teasing, deceptive bargaining, (repeatedly) and expects punishment. Crowing on the fence: exhibitionism here; (is a liar). The need to show off is ascribed to mother but probably holds true for narrator: Displacement of projection from hero to secondary figure in a story usually involves particularly ego-alien unacceptable drives and is called object need (O.n.) by Henry Murray.

2) Sequence: how big is father
           I am small
           I could fall too (if in need of help!)

The test report itself should usually not be confounded by relating the test materials to the interview data. However, in an additional note, it is appropriate to point out that this boy's pathology results probably to a considerable extent from mother's pretentious need to "push" and insist on a higher socioeconomic status than the family has. She also probably encourages denial as a defense, and wishful thinking in the boy. Mother's self-centeredness and interest in being well dressed incidentally appears in the kangaroo story where she simply goes home and is concerned with dressing while the little kangaroo has its adventure with the bees, etc.

"Go to sleep or you won't get any presents." Then, after his mother dressed up like Santa Claus, she went out of the room and when he was asleep Santa Claus came in, but the baby was still awake and Santa Claus said, "Were you a good boy?" and the little bunny said: "Yes" and Santa Claus said, "What do you want?" and the bunny said: "I want a hammer and a pair of guns and a stuffed bunny just like me." So Santa Claus gave him all his presents and went into the other room with the presents. Then, at the last step, when at the head, he saw mother and daddy asleep at the head. Then, one reindeer clapped his feet and Santa Claus said "Whoa Rudolf! Rudolf! Rudolf! Stop, I'll be up there fast!"

10. One day the mother dog was washing her pup so always from now the pup didn't want to get washed. He didn't like to get washed because one day his mother scratched him like with a pen and he thought that every day mother would scratch him and he would get hurt. So every time his mother tried to wash him he ran away into the bathroom and taking the broom—the towel—he thought he could bang his mother over the head, but then he thought that wouldn't work so he took two socks and one shirt and said that the socks would be just the thing that would work. So he put one sock into the other and used it for a blackjack and hit his mother, but he didn't get away with it. He got washed that day and said: "Mother, I'm sorry I hit you and now I like to be washed every day."

## Martin O.

Below are a few stories by a boy five years and 11 months old who was referred to the school authority by two neighborhood mothers because he had been engaging their boys in sex play. They were particularly concerned because this child insisted on having objects, such as a toy car, placed into his rectum. Their speaking to the parents of the boy had been of no particular avail. This had happened in the spring, and in the fall still another parent reported that the boy asked her little girl to spank him on his "bare." He had used this word the previous spring in reference to his rectum with the boys. In kindergarten he had been observed by the teacher to be masturbating during the first part of the year; later on he came to attention only because of his immaturity in play and in learning. Otherwise, he behaved in a diligent and courteous way.

### Selected Stories

7. Oh, tigers and monkeys. The tigers were climbing from tree to tree. They climbed up the trees and the people didn't know what to do because they were in the trees and they couldn't get any apples. The bears said, "Let's go and eat the monkey up," but they couldn't because he was the grandest tiger in the world. Little Black Sambo said, "Here comes a tiger, what am I going to do? I think I'll give him my new shoes and he will be the grandest tiger in the world." Then another tiger came and he gave him his black coat and he was the grandest tiger in the world, and before he knew it along came some one else and he said, "Oh, oh, oh, I haven't anything else to give him," but it was a monkey instead of a tiger, so he said, "I'm going to get that monkey and put it on his ear." So he got the monkey and put it on his ear. "Give me that and I'll throw it on your face. Are there any other kinds of monkey? No, there isn't. This is the only sort of monkey in the whole wide world. Why? Just because I don't know. We'll see what you can do. I don't know what to do." Then the tiger started climbing on him and he climbed on the tiger. "Then, why don't you go crazy? You're the craziest tiger in the world." Why did they think that. The bear said, "I'm going to eat them up," and they ran from here to there and they didn't know what to do.

8. This looks like a big monkey. The monkey said, "Let's put the picture up and have some tea." "What about me?" said the little monkey. "You go out and play with your friends." The friends said, "I'm too busy," so he came back in and threw dishes and clothes and everything and broke them up in pieces and cleeses and he chopped down the monkey

again and he chopped his face and his face was bleeding, bleeding and the monkey said, "I'm going to chop you." "Oh, oh, you better not chop me." So the little monkey ran and ran and the little bear chased him. Then he said, "I'm going out and find some people to scratch." He scratched all the people and everybody. They went home and threw anyone out because they were so tired and they didn't know what to do. They were so so tired. "I'm going out and look for people to scratch," and he did. He wasn't satisfied so he didn't know what to do and he eated everybody up because he wanted to be the greatest tiger in the world. The only bear in the wide world because he just wasn't. The bear and the tiger and the monkey saw hunters who said to the other monkey, "What's the idea of chopping up all the mothers and fathers, grandmothers and grandfathers?" So they went out to smash people. "I'm going to smash that one," so they did. And when all the people saw that, they ran and ran. "Oh, dear, what am I going to do?" So he didn't know what to do. "Let's go to bed tonight and tomorrow night we'll go and see everybody because they won't know us." "No, they won't," said papa bear. "No, I'm afraid they won't." So they went to bed together. Then the grandfather clocks came. They were so silly. And they came with Christmas trees on top of them, doors on them, glasses on them, houses on them, dishes on them, mirrors on them, windows on them, shoes on them and everything. They decided to go to bed and they never got up again.

9. This is—Why do you write when I don't even say anything? "Let's go to bed." Baby bear said, "Leave my door open." "No, I'll shut that door," said Papa bear. "No, because you don't know what you're doing. See you tomorrow." "Why?" "I don't know. I guess I'm going to be silly tomorrow morning." He said, "I'm going to eat the people up. No, I'll eat Easter eggs and candy if I want to," so they did. "Now, well, I think I'll eat that bunny up. Why should I eat that nice bunny? I'll eat the candy instead." So he ate the bunny but the helpers ate the people up instead of the bunny. "Ho! Ho!" Then, he went home and told his mother, "This is awful crazy and I think I better go to bed. I'll get my flashlight and knock their heads off." Father said "Why do you act so silly?" "Because I just like to, because I like to." "I don't like the idea." "No, I know you don't." "Because you don't know what you're doing." "But why, why are you talking?" "I just don't know. I better go and see what I can do." "No, you won't," said the chick-chick. "If you do the chick-chick will come and chop you." "Oh no, I'll chop him instead of him chopping mine." "You be quiet." "No." "Why?" "I just don't want to. I just don't want to. I just don't want to." The quack-quack said "Why." "You are so silly." "Why did you say that I had to go to bed? I'll go see that you're never going. I'm going to count to 3 and if you don't count to 8 yourself, you'll be counting to 9." He shut his door and he went to sleep and didn't wake up for 5 weeks and he did wake up before he knew he did. So he didn't care, oh, no, no, no, no. Goodnight. "I'll see you in my dreams." "No you won't," said the bunny. "Why did you say I had to go to bed? I just don't want to." "Oh, dear, dear, why, why—I don't know. Goodnight, sight, might, kite, right, light. I'm going to find that bunny and go to bed with him."

10. Puppy dogs, cuppy dogs. Puppy dog said, "Let's go to bed, no I mean let's go out." "Not me." "Why?" said you. "I'm too lazy. Ha, ha." "Why?" "I just want to be. What did you say about being lazy?" "I said why don't you be lazy?" "I think I'll go to bed, I'll go find the bunnies." He found one bunny so he found all the others making the eggs and candy for Easter because he knew what he was doing. "What did you do again?" I said, "I think I'll go to bed. I think I'll go and wash my face." "No, you don't. Go to school." "All right."

He went to the little dog house. "This isn't dog school. I'll have to tell mother that this is not a dog school." "Why?" "I don't know." "Because you're silly." "I'll go and see what I'm going to do," so he did and he couldn't find anything to do and he went, he went, he went, he went, he went until he was so crazy he didn't know what to do. "Let's go out and have a game." They played a silly games, a silly game. Whoever stepped on the towel first won nothing, no, won the air. What a silly game. "You're crazy. You're going to crazy town." "I don't know where crazy town is. I don't know where Morris crazy town is." "You'll soon learn. But remember, be crazy or they won't want you. Why, why, why, why don't you brain your head out?" "No, no, no, n-o spells no. I think I'll go and see what they said to do." "Why?" "I don't know. I just don't want to." "Why? Why?" "Cuckoo, plucko.

I don't know because I just don't want to. Stop complaining. I'll leave you. Wait up bunny. I guess he's home. No, he isn't. He is gone West. I guess." "No, he isn't," said quack quack. "Why, why?" "I don't know." "I just don't want to," said puppy dog. "Let's go out and play today. Silly in the house and play with my cookies and towel, because I just WANT to."

## Brief Analysis

Stories 7, 8, 9 and 10 show the degree of underlying disturbance in this boy who constantly leaves the picture by the spontaneous introduction of extreme aggressiveness and destructiveness. Marked withdrawal and passivity is brought up in nearly all his stories by going to bed, usually with male figures.

Story 8: One might say that the main theme is as follows: "If one is rejected by family and friends, one becomes aggressively destructive, punishes father, sadistically hurts people, throws parents out and eats people up. People are afraid of one and one feels guilty and anxious because of one's aggressiveness and goes to bed with father." He seems to be saying that he is bothered at night by strange imagery and so withdraws (from reality) into bed; he wants never to relate again. Instead of feeling guilty, he says he feels dissatisfied and tired (tired is probably an equivalent to depressed).

Story 7: Climbing of one tiger on another is followed by ideas of going crazy. One might say that the theme suggests that one gives oneself up to an attacker (in a sexual way) and then goes crazy. In story 9, craziness, going to bed, extreme aggression, generally poor adaptiveness to the task and tremendous oral need for incorporation are again outstanding. The same may be said about story 10, with any number of references probably related to sexual play and certainly to passivity.

## TIMOTHY O.

Following are side by side the responses of a boy who at the time of first testing was 6 years 10 months, and at the time of the second testing 8 years 5 months. The boy was originally referred to the school psychologist because he was found extremely immature, showed off constantly, wanted to be different and to get attention, made silly noises, pushed other children and was found to be frequently inattentive. At the time of first testing his Stanford-Binet IQ was 124. He behaved in a very uneven fashion, shouted at the psychologist, wouldn't sit down, and engaged in some baby talk. The reason for his second test was that he was a classroom disturbance; he didn't conform, tripped and hit children and looked unhappy. He had few friends. His academic work was considered good, and the teacher thought he probably had an IQ of about 140.

### Stories

| *Age: 6 years 10 months* | *Age: 8 years 5 months* |
|---|---|
| 1. What are these, chickens? This chicken was eating badly and spilling and making work for the big chicken and the big chicken has to spank them and send them back to their grandfather. | 1. I wonder what it is. I know! The hen and the naughty little people, when the fox fell in the river! There were 3 and they were bad and they didn't want to help and they spilled crumbs. And one day the fox came and ate the mother hen |

*Age: 6 years 10 months (continued)*

*Age: 8 years 5 months (continued)*

up and then he fell asleep and they put rocks in him and he drowned. [Mother hen was out when they put rocks in?] Which would you rather have, 4 days of rain, fog or snow? [Which would you?] Snow, then we could have snowball fights. Which would you rather have, 3 days hot or 3 days of cold? [You?] Cold because I don't like short-sleeved shirts. [Want to look at the next one?] O.K.

3. You wouldn't be able to get near that would you? Would he eat a mouse? [Do you think so?] Yes, I think so but I don't know if the lion will find him or not. He's waiting for someone to come along that isn't looking what he's doing and he'll eat him.

3. [Timothy voluntarily picked up card 3, looked at it and said:] No, I don't want that, I feel like scaling it out of the window. A lion pooing on his chair. Somebody stole something of his and he was thinking what to do and there was a little mouse there and he bit his tail and the lion put dynamite in the hole and blew him up. Which would you rather have, calm or a hurricane? [Calm, and you?] I don't know, hurricane, maybe.

5. I guess it's the night time and someone must be away and it's just getting black and I don't know what this is, I'll call this smoke and there is a fire outside and when they come back they find their house is all burned down. That would make you cry, wouldn't it?

5. The mother bear and the daddy bear were out and 2 little bears came in and slept in this crib. And it was dark and after they slept they woke up and ran out the back door and when mother and father came home it was dark and they didn't know what was wrong and they never found 'em. Now, I have 32-38, here comes the kind of flag you have for 39-46. I like a fast wind that blows trees down, do you? [Not very much.] [Timothy picked up the next card.]

6. What is those, those swimming? Oh, a bear in his cave and the baby bear is with him. What eats bears, can you think of anything? [Can you?] No.

6. What's this! There's 3 bears and they have no house and they slept in a cave and one night someone put some mud over it and when they woke up they had to claw their way out. And the next night the same thing happened and the next night the little bear didn't go to sleep and he saw a man there. And the next day he told his mother and daddy and that night they ate the man up. 65, next is, no 55-65, no that isn't right. I'm the best in numbers in my class. [Timothy continued to write and say aloud, wind speeds to above 75.] Which would you rather have, above 75 with 10 below zero and cloudy or 8 to 12 with 70 and clear? [I'll take 10 below] Once it was zero and I ran all around, I am just about done, now I want to play a game with you.

## Brief Analysis

In both card 1 stories, the children eat badly, are naughty and antagonize the big chicken who punishes them and sends them away. In the second testing an aggressive animal is introduced, a fox, who eats up the mother and is, in turn, drowned for his misdeeds, whereupon the child reverted to an obsessive preoccupation with the weather which went all through the testing. In the story to picture 3, in the first session, he is anxiously concerned with the idea that one has to be careful or else one is devoured. In the second session, he wants to do away with the card altogether by scaling it out the window. There is much more evidence of violence and anal regression here with the lion "pooing" on his chair. The aggressive orality now relates specifically to the castrating notion of biting off the tail. There is also the suggestive evidence of explosive emotional tension in connection with the dynamite and the wish for a hurricane. In story 5, in the first testing, the reference to smoke and fire suggest a great deal of aggressive urethral sexual preoccupation, as does the reference to crying. This would be most suggestive of a history of enuresis (which we were unable to check on) but is certainly consistent with his aggressive behavior, including the aggressive need to show off. The second testing gives a much less clear-cut story except that the little bears run out when the parents come home and are never discovered. This is followed by some reference to figures and the discussion again of violent weather, in this case a fast wind.

Story 6, in the first session, introduces water, supporting the notion expressed in story 5, and again a preoccupation with oral incorporation. The second story 6 has to do with being walled up with mud and watchful night time observations. This is suggestive of insomnia perhaps associated with oral incorporation fantasies; and then again the preoccupation with numbers, windspeeds and the weather: his restlessness is also indicated by the reference to running.

An examination of the test material suggests not only the marked pathology consistent with the clinical report of aggression and showing off but also that the process is worsening. Judging by the leaving of the stimulus, the inappropriate material and very poor drive control, this boy is probably on the way towards a psychotic condition. Obsessive preoccupation and acting out have so far served as brakes on the ego disintegration. A school psychiatrist who saw the child suspected that he might be schizophrenic.

### HARRY S.

C.A. of 9 years 3 months, M.A. of 12 years 2 months and an IQ of 132. This boy has one older sister, a brother one year younger, a brother four years younger and a sister eight years younger. The boy was doing very poorly in school, and he needed remedial reading work. The mother considered him stupid. His responses to pictures 2 and 3 are particularly interesting.

## Stories

2. Well, the big bear called Toughie and the other two were called Weakie and Half. Strongie said, "I bet you couldn't win in a tug of war," and the other two said, "I'll bet we

could," and they brought the rope to a high cliff and they were gonna play a trick on him, but it wouldn't hurt him because they had a lot of mattresses and he went plump over the cliff and bounced back again but the next time he went down he grabbed a tree and threw it up and it pushed the other two down and he got even.

3. Well, I saw this on a cartoon. [Own story.] O.K. This old lion had one leg that wasn't too good and he had to use a cane and one day when he was walking along he met a strong lion and he made fun of him and threw rotten tomatoes at him and he got so mad he threw his cane at him and knocked him out. And when he woke up he said to him, "I hope that taught you not to pick on someone not as young and as strong as you."

### Brief Analysis

We are only interested in one particular feature, namely a markedly accentuated superego in response to a good deal of aggression. In story 2, though a trick is played on one of the participants, the story-teller makes sure that he wouldn't really get hurt because there are a lot of mattresses and in the other story, aggression against an older person, a lion, is very promptly punished and an explicit moral expressed. While there is no direct evidence, it is likely that his lack of achievement is related to his inhibition of aggression.

## ANTHONY B.

The next case involves a little boy who is characterized by his mother as being a very independent child, self sufficient, having a sweet and sunny disposition, playing well by himself and with other children. He showed excellent coordination, learned well and in every respect was found to be an undisturbed child by his parents, teachers and camp director. He had an IQ of 141, C.A. of 4 years 6 months and an M.A. of 6 years 4 months. The state of affairs is probably adequately reflected in his response to card 2.

### Story

2. Once upon a time three little bears had a fight with a rope, so two bears against one, is that fair? But the little one can't do it, can he? They tugged and tugged and see this one won because he was a good bear and these were bad. [Who is he?] He's a great papa.

### Analysis

He expresses his opinion that two against one isn't fair, showing a reasonable awareness of fair play. His reality testing is very good in that he says the little one can't do it and adds that the one winning was a good bear, and the two lost because they were bad. The good bear, he says is a great papa, suggesting a good relationship to father, an age-appropriate superego in a story which itself is without excessive aggression or punishment.

### Suggestions for Future Research

The following brief suggestions for future investigations with the CAT may be made: What is needed is a type of research that would make explicit what has been hitherto tacit and presumably implicit for clinicians who work with children. We have reference to a normative study, longitudinal and/or cross sectional, conceived within a theoretical framework, and designed to test hypotheses. Such a study should focus not only on statistical frequency of sameness, but should also consider and appreciate those differences and variabilities common to all normal children in all phases and areas of functioning. We would want to know about the formal changes in adaptive functioning;[74,94] the development of a cognitive style (Klein); the psychodynamic changes of drives; as well as the shifts from one organ mode to the next and the consequences involved.[39] We also would want to know about the building and preference of defenses, and about the latency period (extent of quiescence, time of onset and cessation, etc.). This is simply an enumeration of areas. However, data must be collected and handled so that established concepts can be checked and new formulations made possible.

The quest for such research is not new. Investigators have, in the past and are currently, engaged in such projects (Escalona, Macfarlane, Murphy, Witkin and others). We need more work of this kind. We need an exchange of findings and a greater familiarity with them. We also need to respond to a fascinating challenge—that of attempting to understand what the many threads are and how they play into those general and idiosyncratic qualities that come to endure throughout life.

## Foreign Versions of the CAT

The CAT is also published, together with respective manuals, in the following foreign languages: French, Italian, German and Spanish. There has also been an adaptation for India by Uma Chowdhury, with the assistance of B. S. Guha and L. Bellak. Figure 3 shows the Indian versions of Cards 1, 3, 4 and 9.

The Japanese modification, by Samiko Marui, is shown in figure 4.

## A Supplement to the Children's Apperception Test (the CAT-S)

The CAT Supplement (CAT-S) was designed by L. Bellak and Sonya S. Bellak to supply pictures which might illuminate situations not *necessarily pertaining to universal problems*, but which occur often enough to make it desirable to learn more about them as they exist in a good many children (fig. 5).

Ten pictures have been designed, any single one of which may be presented to children *in addition to* the regular CAT. For instance, CAT-S picture 5 may be given to children with a temporary or permanent physical disability or with a history of disability. It might permit one to learn about the psychological effects of this somatic problem upon the specific child. Or, children with any kind of psychosomatic disorder or hypochondriasis might project these onto the stimulus. Picture 10 may permit us to learn what fantasies a boy or girl may have about the mother's pregnancy. If, e.g., a child is brought to a clinic with a number of behavioral problems, and the history shows that the mother is currently pregnant or delivered relatively recently, then this picture may permit one to learn about the possible specific rela-

Fig. 3.—Indian adaptation of the CAT by Uma Chowdhury, Ph.D. (assisted by B. S. Guha, Ph.D., and L. Bellak, M.D.).

tions between the behavior problems and the fantasies concerning the family event. In short, the CAT Supplement may be used in specific situations for the purpose of eliciting specific themes, as indicated.

A further use of the CAT-S may lie in its usefulness as material for play techniques. Even though establishing proper rapport will obtain longer and better stories from children than the beginner is likely to think, there remain children severely enough disturbed to be unable to relate stories. For such subjects it may be expedient to make all the pictures of the CAT-S available at once, upon a table, (arranged from 1 to 10, in 3 rows, the last row having 4 pictures) and to let them see them, handle them, arrange and talk about them as they will. All of the child's remarks and behavior should be carefully recorded. Also, such use of the pictures may encourage story-telling in children less able to comply immediately with instructions. It should be cautioned, however, that this method would not be the most desirable procedure if the stories can be obtained in the regular manner.

Fig. 4.—Japanese adaptation of the CAT by Samiko Marui.

Fig. 5.—The CAT-S.

For the purpose of adapting it to this kind of play technique, the CAT-S has been constructed from washable material not too easily marred or destroyed.

The CAT-S is described in more detail in the *TAT and CAT in Clinical Use*.[11]

### References*

1. Abt, L., & Bellak, L. (Eds.)  *Projective psychology*. New York: Alfred Knopf, 1950.
2. Ainsworth, M. D., & Boston, M.  Psychodiagnostic assessments of a child after prolonged separation in early childhood. *Brit. J. med. Psychol.*, 1952, *25*, 169–201.
3. Ajuriaguerra, J. de, & Diatkive, et al.  *Le Psychiatrie de l'enfant.* Presse Universitaires, Vol. 1, Fasc. 1 and 2, 1958.
4. Amen, E. W.  Individual differences in apperceptive reaction: a study of the responses of pre-school children to pictures. *Genet. Psychol. Monogr.*, 1941, *23*, 319–385.
5. Armstrong, M. A. S.  Children's responses to animal and human figures in thematic pictures. *J. consult. Psychol.*, 1954, *18*, 67–70.

*The authors are indebted to A. C. Cain, who made available a bibliography of the CAT which he had compiled.

6. Balken, E. R., & Vander Veer, A. H. The clinical application of the TAT to neurotic children. *Amer. J. Orthopsychiat.*, 1944, *14*, 421–440.

7. Bell, J. E. Review of the CAT. *In* O. K. Buros (Ed.) *The fourth mental measurements yearbook.* Highland Park, N. J.: Gryphon Press, 1953. Pp. 103–104.

8. Bellak, L. The concept of projection: an experimental investigation and study of the concept. *Psychiatry,* 1944, *4*, 353–370.

9. ——. Projection and the Thematic Apperception Test. *In* Crafts, L. W., Schneirla, T. C., Robinson, E. E., & Gilbert, R. W. (Eds.) *Recent experiments in psychology.* (2nd ed.) New York: McGraw-Hill, 1950. Pp. 445–455.

10. ——. Thematic apperception: failures and the defenses. *Trans. New York Acad. Sci.,* 1950, *12*, 122–126.

11. ——. *The TAT and CAT in clinical use.* New York: Grune & Stratton, 1954.

12. ——. A study of limitations and "failures": toward an ego psychology of projective techniques. *J. proj. Tech.,* 1954, *18*, 279–292.

13. ——. The schizophrenic syndrome. *In* Bellak, L. (Ed.) *Schizophrenia: a review of the syndrome.* New York: Logos Press, 1959. Pp. 3–63.

14. ——, & Bellak, S. S. *Children's Apperception Test.* New York: C.P.S. Co., P.O. Box 42, Gracie Station, 1950.

15. ——, & ——. An introductory note on the Children's Apperception Test (CAT). *J. proj. Tech.,* 1950, *14*, 171–180.

16. ——, & ——. *CAT manual.* (2nd ed.) New York: C.P.S. Co., P.O. Box 42, Gracie Station, 1952.

17. ——, & ——. *Manual for the supplement to the CAT.* New York: C.P.S. Co., P.O. Box 42, Gracie Station, 1952.

18. ——, & Brower, D. Projective methods. *In* E. A. Spiegel (Ed.) *Progress in neurology and psychiatry.* Vol. 6. New York: Grune & Stratton, 1951. Pp. 465–477.

19. Bender, L. & Rapoport, J. Animal drawings of children. *Amer. J. Orthopsychiat.,* 1944, *14*, 521–527.

20. Bennett, E. M., & Johannsen, D. E. Psychodynamics of the diabetic child. *Psychol. Monogr.,* 1954, *68*, No. 11 (Whole No. 382).

21. Biber, B., Murphy, L. B., Woodcock, L. P., & Black, I. S. *Child life in school: a study of a seven-year-old group.* New York: Dutton, 1942.

22. Biersdorf, K. R., & Marcuse, F. L. Responses of children to human and to animal pictures. *J. proj. Tech.,* 1953, *17*, 455–459.

23. Bills, R. E. Animal pictures for obtaining children's projections. *J. clin. Psychol.,* 1950, *6*, 291–293.

24. ——, Leiman, C. J., & Thomas, R. W. A study of the validity of the TAT and a set of animal pictures. *J. clin. Psychol.,* 1950, *6*, 293–295.

25. Blum, G., & Hunt, H. F. The validity of the Blacky pictures. *Psychol. Bull.,* 1952, *49*, 238–250.

26. Booth, L. A normative comparison of the responses of Latin-American and Anglo-American children to the CAT. Unpublished doctoral dissertation, Texas Tech. Coll., Lubbock, Texas, 1953.

27. Boulanger-Balleyguier, G. Étude sur le CAT: influence du stimulus sur les récits d'enfants de 3 à 8 ans. *Rev. Psychol. Appliquée,* 1957, *7*, 1–28.

28. Braine, M. Piaget's formulation of the ontogenesis of certain logical operations tested by non-verbal methods. Unpublished doctoral dissertation, New York Univer.

29. Brody, S. *Patterns of mothering.* New York: Internat. Univer. Press, 1956.

30. Brower, J. F., & Bellak, L. Tabulating scheme for CAT-S. In Bellak, L. (Ed.) *The TAT and CAT in clinical use.* New York: Grune & Stratton, 1954. Pp. 255–268.

31. Buss, A. H., & Durkee, A. The association of animals with familial figures. *J. proj. Tech.,* 1957, *21*, 366–371.

32. Byrd, E., & Witherspoon, R. L. Responses of pre-school children to the Children's Apperception Test. *Child Develpm.,* 1954, *25*, 35–44.

33. Cain, A. C. The C.A.T. in childhood psychosis. (Unpublished). Univer. of Michigan.

34. ——. A supplementary 'dream' technique with the C.A.T. (Unpublished). Univer. of Michigan.

35. Caplan, G. *Emotional problems of early childhood*. New York: Basic Books, 1955.

36. Chowdhury, U. An Indian adaptation of the C.A.T. Delhi, India: Manasayan, 1960.

37. DeSousa, T. A comparison of responses of maladjusted and well-adjusted children on a Thematic Apperception Test. Unpublished master's dissertation, Loyola Univer., 1952.

38. Duhm, E. Erfahrungen mit dem CAT. *Diagnostica*, 1955, *1*, 14–15.

39. Erikson, E. H. *Childhood and society*. New York: Norton, 1951.

40. Fear, C. The CAT-S. Unpublished bachelor's dissertation, Vassar Coll., 1951.

41. Freud, A. *The ego and the mechanisms of defense*. London: Hogarth Press, 1937.

42. Furuya, K. Responses of school children to human and animal pictures. *J. proj. Tech.*, 1957, *21*, 248–252.

43. Genn, M. M. Review of the CAT. *Quart. J. child Behav.*, 1950, *2*, 469–470.

44. Gerard, M. Enuresis: a study in etiology. *In* Alexander, F. & French, T. (Eds.) *Studies in psychosomatic medicine*. New York: Ronald Press, 1948. Pp. 501–513.

45. Gesell, A., & Ilg, F. *The child from five to ten*. New York: Harper, 1946.

46. Gibson, R. M. An exploratory study of the effects of surgery and hospitalization in early infancy on personality development. Unpublished doctoral dissertation, Univer. of Michigan, 1958.

47. Ginsparg, H. T. A study of the CAT. *Dissertation Abstr.*, 1957, *17*, 3082–3083.

48. Goldfarb, W. The animal symbol in the Rorschach test and an animal association test. *Rorschach Res. Exch.*, 1945, *9*, 8–22.

49. Gurevitz, S., & Klapper, Z. S. Techniques for and evaluation of the responses of schizophrenic and cerebral palsied children to the Children's Apperception Test (CAT). *Quart. J. child Behav.*, 1951, *3*, 38–65.

50. Halpern, F. Projective tests in the personality investigation of children. *J. Pediatrics*, 1951, *38*, 770–775.

51. Harris, A. J., & Roswell, F. G. Clinical diagnosis of reading disability. *J. Psychol.*, 1953, *36*, 323–340.

52. Hartley, R. E., Frank, L. K., & Goldenson, R. M. *Understanding children's play*. New York: Columbia Univer. Press, 1952.

53. Hartmann, H. Comments on the psychoanalytic theory of the ego. *Psychoanal. Study Child*, 1950, *5*, 75–96.

54. Herman, H. Review of the CAT. *Amer. J. Psychiat.*, 1951, *108*, 317–318.

55. Holden, R. H. The CAT with cerebral palsied and normal children. *Child Develpm.*, 1956, *27*, 3–8.

56. Holt, R. R. Review: The CAT and manual. *J. proj. Tech.*, 1950, *14*, 200.

57. ——. TAT newsletter (special CAT issue). *J. proj. Tech.*, 1951, *15*, 537–544.

58. Isaacs, S. *Social development in young children*. London: Routledge & Kegan Paul, 1933.

59. Jersild, A. T., Markey, F. W., & Jersild, C. L. Children's fears, dreams, wishes, daydreams, likes, dislikes, pleasant and unpleasant memories. *Child Develpm. Monogr.*, No. 12. New York: Columbia Univer. Press, 1933.

60. Kaake, N. H. The relationship between intelligence level and responses to the CAT. Unpublished master's dissertation, Cornell Univer., 1951.

61. Katzenstein, B. Estudos individuais e orientarao psicopedagogica de Crianças acometidas de poliomidite. *Rev. Psicol. normal e patologica*, 1957, *3*, 77–85.

62. Koch, H. L. Social class differences in response to CAT. Unpublished research, Dept. of Child Psychol., Univer. of Chicago.

63. Light, B. H. Comparative study of a series of TAT and CAT cards. *J. clin. Psychol.*, 1954, *10*, 179–181.

64. Lumpkin, W. T. A sociometric and projective study of interpersonal relations among certain pupils at the Oglethorpe elementary school. Unpublished master's dissertation, Atlanta Univer., 1952.

65. Macfarlane, J. W., Allen, L., & Honzik, M. P.  *A developmental study of the behavior problems of normal children between twenty-one months and fourteen years.* Berkeley: Univer. California Press, 1954.

66. Mainord, F. R., & Marcuse, F. L.  Responses of disturbed children to human and animal pictures. *J. proj. Tech.*, 1954, *18*, 475–477.

67. Millar, M. A.  A study of common stories told by nursery school children on the CAT. Unpublished master's dissertation, Univer. of Alberta, 1952.

68. Moed, G.  *Special apperception pictures for disabled children.* Atlantic City: Seashore House, 1958.

69. Mueller, P.  *Le C.A.T.*, Bern: Hans Huber, 1958.

70. Murphy, L. B., & associates.  *Personality in young children.* New York: Basic Books, 1956. 2 vols.

71. ——, Heider, G., & Kass, W.  The Menninger Foundation 'coping project.' Papers read at A.P.A. meetings, September, 1956.

72. Olney, E. E., & Cushing, H. M.  A brief report of the responses of pre-school children to commercially available pictorial material. *Child Develpm.*, 1935, *6*, 52–55.

73. Peters, A., & Bellak, L.  Tabulation scheme for CAT. *In* Bellak, L. (Ed.)  *The TAT and CAT in clinical use.* New York: Grune & Stratton, 1954. Pp. 242–254.

74. Piaget, J.  *The language and thought of the child.* London: Routledge & Kegan Paul, 1932.

75. Raff, E.  Intrapsychic patterns of nursery-school children judged by their teachers to be best or worst adjusted in their group. Unpublished master's dissertation, Univer. of Chicago, 1951.

76. Rapaport, D., Gill, M., & Schafer, L.  *Diagnostic psychological testing.* Vol. II. Chicago: Year Book, 1946.

77. —— (Ed.)  *Organization and pathology of thought.* New York: Columbia Univer. Press, 1951.

78. ——.  Projective techniques and the theory of thinking. *J. proj. Tech.*, 1952, *16*, 269–275.

79. Shaffer, L. F.  Review of the CAT. *J. consult. Psychol.*, 1950, *14*, 161.

80. Shneidman, E. S.  TAT newsletter (CAT issue no. 2). *J. proj. Tech.*, 1953, *17*, 499–502.

81. ——.  Review: Bellak's *The TAT and CAT in clinical use. J. proj. Tech.*, 1955, *19*, 196–198.

82. Sidler, M.  Tierpantomimik durch Kinder. *Schweiz. Z. Psychol. Anwend.*, 1956, *15*, No. 3.

83. Simon, M. D.  Untersuchung an Kindern mit dem CAT von Bellak. Unpublished doctoral dissertation, Univer. of Vienna, 1952.

84. ——.  Der CAT bei gesunden und gestörten Kindern. *Z. Diagnost. Psychol.*, 1954, *11*, 195–219.

85. Spiegelman, M., Terwilliger, C., & Fearing, F.  The content of comic strips: a study of a mass communication. *J. soc. Psychol.*, 1952, *35*, 37–57.

86. Stern, W.  *Psychology of early childhood.* New York: Henry Holt, 1924.

87. Stokes, S. M.  An inquiry into the concept of identification. *J. genet. Psychol.*, 1950, *76*, 163–189.

88. Stone, L. J.  Review of the CAT. *In* Buros, O. K. (Ed.)  *The fourth mental measurements yearbook.* Highland Park, N. J.: Gryphon Press, 1953. Pp. 169–170.

89. ——, & Church, J.  *Childhood and adolescence.* New York: Random House, 1957.

90. Van Hove, W.  Praktijkervaringen met de CAT en met het CAT Supplement. *Tijdschr. Studie Beroepsoriënt*, 1957, *4*, 60–63.

91. Vuyk, R.  Projektionsphänomene bei Kindern. *Schweiz. Z. Psychol. Anwend.*, 1953, *12*, 124–134.

92. ——.  *Plaatjes als hulpmiddel bij het kinderpsychologisch onderzoek.* Leiden: H. E. Stenfert Kroese N.V., 1954.

93. Weisskopf-Joelson, E. A., & Lynn, D. B.  The effect of variations in ambiguity on projection in the CAT. *J. consult. Psychol.*, 1953, *17*, 67–70.

94. Werner, H.  *Comparative psychology of mental development.* New York: Follett, 1948.

95. ——, & Kaplan, E.   The acquisition of word meanings: a developmental study. *Mongr. Soc. Res. Child Develpm.*, 1952, *15*, No. 1 (Serial No. 51).

96. Witkin, H. A., Lewis, H. B., Hertzman, M., Machover, K., Meissner, P., & Wapner, S. *Personality through perception.* New York: Harper, 1954.

97. Wolff, W.   *The personality of the pre-school child.* New York: Grune & Stratton, 1946.

98. Woltmann, A. G.   Review of the CAT. *Amer. J. Orthopsychiat.*, 1950, *20*, 844–845.

# 5

# The Blacky Pictures with Children

GERALD S. BLUM

A DOG is traditionally man's best friend. "Man," of course, is used generically in this context to include men, women and children. Similarly Blacky, when first conceived in 1946, was destined to accompany little as well as big people along short-cut paths substituting for the tedious royal road to the unconscious.

Within the limits of this brief chapter, an attempt will be made to convey the flavor of responses to the pictures given by boys and girls at various age levels, to treat the issues of scoring and interpretation, reliability and validity, and finally to present a few illustrative research applications.

## Administration and Sample Responses

The Blacky Pictures Manual of Instructions[2] contains a section on "Adapting the Method for Use with Children." The following excerpt describes the necessary modifications in procedure for administering the test:

Directions to children must, of course, be altered to fit their understanding. Usually the set of using 'imagination' and 'telling stories' can be maintained even at the youngest levels. Cartoon preferences can also be carried out according to the adult directions. The major adaptation lies in the Inquiry, which generally cannot be given in multiple-choice form. Here the clinician must rely upon his own skill in phrasing items so as to obtain all the relevant data without confusing the child or "pushing" him excessively. A suggested revision of the Inquiry for children is given in Appendices B and C. Also, it is often advisable to omit the "discovering sex" introduction to Cartoon V since it may be disturbing.*

The types of stories told at ages 4 to 14 are reflected in the sample protocols given in figure 1.

## Scoring and Interpretation

The four sources of information on each test dimension are the spontaneous story, inquiry, cartoon preferences and related comments on other cartoons. The Manual offers some general guiding principles, equally applicable to children's protocols, for the integration of these sources:

Though these sources are intended to tap different levels of response within the patient, any interpretation on a given dimension must be able to encompass all four or else it is not correct. Since the separate sources are actually responses of the same individual, they can only be taken to reflect facets of a common core. Hence inferences from the four sources

*Reproduced with permission of the Psychological Corporation.

Fig. 1.—Sample protocols.

| | Age 4 (Male) (C) | Age 6 (Female) (N) | Age 9 (Female) (N) | Age 11 (Male) (N) | Age 14 (Male) (C) |
|---|---|---|---|---|---|
| **I Oral Eroticism** | B was coming this way [pointing toward M], tried to get him [pointing to T in background]. That's his bone [pointed to M's collar, then for a few seconds pointed to M's breasts], tried to get over on house so he can get in. | I see the M dog . . . spots on it . . . has a ribbon on it. B in picture . . . belt on neck . . . tail . . . legs. [E: What is B doing?] B got M down on back and he's just sitting there . . . trying to keep M down. That tail is simply awful! [E: anything else?] Dogs over here. B here (background) M here (also background). | B is getting some milk from his M. B is thinking that M doesn't like it. M is an awful lazy dog. She always sleeps all the time. All B does is eat and drink. | Well, M is laying down and she's sleeping and B is coming along and B is getting some milk from M and M doesn't know that B is getting milk from her and P is in the park getting some peanuts to bring home and . . . Is T the girl? [E: Whatever you think.] T doesn't like B very well and one time she almost got hit by a car and she almost broke her leg and she did break her leg and had to go to the hospital for three weeks but she still didn't like B. T has an expensive dog collar and can smell very well and M isn't all black. She has black and white spots and so does T and P and they don't have a very big yard to play in so they have to play in the streets. | That's a rather obvious picture . . . he seems to be nursing . . . [turns card over] . . . I don't do this too well . . . need a lot of action . . . [E encourages S]. She seems to be rather bored. [E: How does B feel?] Seems to be having a good time . . . what deductions can I draw from it? [E: anything you like.] He seems to be rather old for it. |
| **II Oral Sadism** | He's got your (Examiner's) belt. Mad at you (Examiner) because you took it from him and he had it first. [S then hit Blacky]. | He's chewing something . . . he has ears . . . has a hand . . . something here. [E: How does B feel?] He Doesn't like it. [E: Why?] Doesn't feel good to have to run away . . . will get a spanking . . . has his belt on. | M is very mad that B got her collar. M is trying so hard to get her collar back. But B can run faster than she can. B hides from M and digs a hole, puts the collar in, and fills it up again. But M is still trying to find her collar. | Uh . . . in this picture B has M's collar and he thinks it is a snake that was around M's neck and P is over here and he's laughing because he knows it is M's collar. M's master wants to get M a new collar and he unfastened the collar and it dropped to the ground like a snake. B is mad here because B kissed a girl dog and T was making fun of him. | [Looks away] All these related? He could be very put out with M . . . found her collar and chewed it to pieces . . . that seems to be about right. [E: Anything else?] From his attitude he doesn't like M very well . . . that's about all. |
| **III Anal Sadism** | B going to toilet. He was gonna pee-pee. That's his house [M's]. All his house. Gotta get that out [pointing to anus] so won't be bad. | She just tries to do this . . . whole bunch of houses . . . probably B is in one of them. [E: What is she doing?] Turning around and trying to play something . . . dishes . . . branches. | When B goes to the toilet he smells a dish of food. At first he runs to the food and then forgets all about having to go to the bathroom. P came out and ate his meal, and B and P got in a fight. Then M came out and broke up the fight, and that day, after lunch, they went on a picnic. | In this picture B had just gone down to the lake to get a drink of water and he fell in and P rescued him and the master had just put some milk in the bowls and P is getting some peanuts and T is off with a boy dog and B's girlfriend is over at the side but she doesn't even see her. P's doghouse is painted with green roof and red boards and M's is painted with a blue roof and pink and T's roof was red and painted black and B's roof has green again on it and painted blue. | Oh [laughs] I can't tell what the objects are in the picture. Are those his droppings? Looks like he's done it as far away from his own house as possible . . . natural instinct for dogs . . . bet some of my friends would like this picture. |

| | | | | | |
|---|---|---|---|---|---|
| **IV**<br>Oedipal Intensity | They trying to do a trick, shaking hands [hits card . . . (M and P)] . . . hit him (P) he's dead. | She probably wants to play with P. P is probably shaking hands with M. [E: How does B feel?] B is kind of crying or something. [E: Why?] Took the collar off M. | B is awful mad, because P and M are in love with each other. B says to himself, "Boy! I should get some of this smooching too." B goes and barks three times. "I want a kiss," B says and that day they went in the woods and lay down. They had supper there and then they went home, but first T had to go to the bathroom. | B is jealous because he wants more attention from P and M cause they're loving in this picture. Sometimes P gets jealous because he sees M with another dog and sometimes M gets jealous because she sees P giving B too much attention. Different season because the leaves are green and the sky cloudy. B is just extra mad there and he's mad at T too. B was careless this morning. He got in a fight with the neighbor's cat and got his nose scratched. The cat got mad because B was eating some of his food. P has real sharp claws and he used to chase cats too. | Well, from the picture it seems he's very jealous of them—either because he loves one parent or the other . . . becomes envious when that person gets more attention. |
| **V**<br>Masturbation Guilt | Licking himself, get clean, so he can go home . . . aren't mean now so can have some pudding . . . if he won't be mean give him some . . . he falls dead [S hits card]. | He's licking himself . . . probably washing himself. Paws up . . . front paw leaning over . . . tail's kind of crooked. [E: How does B feel?] He feels like he doesn't like himself. [E: Why?] Doing a bad trick . . . not supposed to do that. [E: What would happen?] If M there she would spank him. | B is feeling that her M is very proud of her washing herself. It's very hard for B to lick herself . . . she has to bend and bend her body. It's good exercise for her, though. P comes along and says, "It's time for dinner." B jumps right up because she likes dinner better than washing. | B got some fleas . . . his master hasn't put flea powder on for a long time and he's licking to get fleas off . . . B had just stepped on a stone and hurt himself. B just chased the neighbor's cat this morning again and the master spanked him . . . this was the third spanking this week . . . and T had run away and they couldn't find her. P and M and T all got new collars but B didn't. P has blue eyes and M has pink eyes and T has green eyes. | He's cleaning himself. [E: What else?] That's about all . . . or else he's chewing a flea. |
| **VI**<br>Castration Anxiety (M); Penis Envy (F) | Here comes a knife. He (B) can't stab him, [Takes hand and encircles knife] I locked it off. Knife will go back. Back already. B dead. T not dead, knife kills B. You (to E) stab him. | Now T has round thing on. Knife falling down. B sees it and doesn't know what to do. He's got a tail. B doesn't like way knife is falling on T. [E: Why?] Might hurt him . . . he's probably kind of crying. | B is saying, "I like to play with T, but that knife sure scares me. I'm going to go and see if T will play with me. He may come and eat lunch with me if M has it ready." Then B and T will go swimming. | B blindfolded T and told her to stand out there and B went into the house and bumped against the master and made her drop the knife out the window and it's coming down on her tail. B is smiling and T is scared and if M comes over she'll scold and tell him to go catch the knife real quick and if P comes over he'll be extra double mad and he'll say, "If you do that I'll just spank you and spank you and spank you until you are red." | Looks like T is having his tail docked . . . is that what's happening? Should be a hand connected to the knife. [E: Anything else?] T's nervous, you can tell from his expression . . . B looks curious. |

LEGEND: (C) = clinic patient; (N) = normal subject; P = Papa; M = Mama; B = Blacky; T = Tippy.

Fig. 1.—Continued

| | Age 4 (Male) (C) | Age 6 (Female) (N) | Age 9 (Female) (N) | Age 11 (Male) (N) | Age 14 (Male) (C) |
|---|---|---|---|---|---|
| **VII Identification Process** | Playing, "You go back to your room and go to sleep," B says. He knocks him down on the bed-floor. Superman flies in and saves toy and says, "You leave him alone." | He's pointing. Little dog has string. B's gonna pull it. It probably makes a noise. [E: How does B feel?] He feels nice because he has the toy. He has a nice tail. Got a curled up tail. | B is thinking that dog is real. So he tries biting it. Pretty soon the tail and all is all broken up. That was B's birthday present. M got it for him. | B is playing house with this other dog . . . he found this in the master's little girl's room and brought it outside and was pulling it along and playing house and he tripped and he lit on his face and the toy dog lit right on P's face . . . he was standing in front . . . and it made a purple spot right on P's face. This morning he gave B real hard spanking for biting T . . . This was the 6th one this week. | Looks like he's telling the toy dog where to get off . . . having trouble because toy won't listen to him. Looks like he's rather mad [Piles cards neatly]. |
| **VIII Sibling Rivalry** | B mean, M and P, T hungry too. Doesn't like (referring to B) . . . B cares. [S begins to hit picture]. | She (B) probably thinks it's nice. [E: Why?] Nice because P's playing with T. [E: How does B feel?] B feels nice about it. They both have a collar on. | B doesn't feel happy. T is getting all the loving and everything. B knows that M and P and T don't like him. So B ran away and he got so mad at himself he just wanted to throw stones and shoot himself. Next day he came home and only T was there. B asked T where P and M went and T said, "Down by the water . . . they have to clean themselves, cause they don't like to lick themselves." | B is sorta jealous and he doesn't like that with M and P around T like that. T scared B for chasing the cat and then B went in a corner and hid for a while and he had just come out. | They all seem to be petting T, who, by the way still has his tail or her tail . . . [E: How does B feel?] He's jealous . . . probably would be . . . probably think of some way of getting even with T. |
| **IX Guilt Feelings** | Crying, he wants some supper, he afraid dog will hit him. I'll hit him. [S hits picture]. | Ooh . . . what are these things? [Distracted by torn edge.] He doesn't like it . . . he's crying. Don't know who that is. B feels like he wants to bite that person. [E: Why?] This other person probably spanked him and said, "You be good." I think that's P. | B is dreaming that that is T up in the sky. But B doesn't feel good. He's all jiggly. His stomach aches and he didn't have a good meal and he sees that dog. He says to himself, "I want to be up in the sky too. But I have to do good deeds." | B is real scared cause this is his conscience cause he did something real terrible and got a spanking . . . his 27th . . . he'd bitten the neighbor's cat and the master was thinking more of sending him away. B is real scared cause his conscience is real mad and is telling him, "You'd better reform or you'll have to go away and not get good food." B says, "I'll do better. I'll do better and won't chase the neighbor's cat and I'll be better to M and P too." | Looks like his conscience is troubling him for some bad deed . . . that's about all. [Whistles] . . . seems to be rather worried. |

| | | | | |
|---|---|---|---|---|
| **X**<br>Ego<br>Ideal | Two B's . . . a big dog, he should hide (refers to dream figure). B to be dead, it's a man. [S begins hitting picture.] | She's dreaming about M and P. [E: What about them?] Spanking . . . time when they were spanking her and P said, "You be good." [E: How does B feel?] He feels like he wants to wake up. What are those little round things? [E: On the figure?] Ghost . . . a bad ghost . . . a P ghost I mean . . . big round circle around . . . big bubbles . . . He has a tail . . . ghost has a tail. | B wished he looked like that dog. He is thinking what that dog is going to do next, but then of course B is gonna do it. But that way B'll get into more and more troubles. B hears another dog barking. He wakes up and sees another real dog just like the dream. | B is in his dog house and dreaming of him being with his master's father and little girl out in the field and they were shooting ducks and he was the one who went and got the ducks. In this picture he's strong and can beat up all the other dogs and chase all the cats but on the other side of his mind he's still thinking of what his conscience said to him. | Looks like he's dreaming about himself . . . Are these abnormal answers . . . perverted or sadistic? . . . Can you tell? [E: How does B feel?] . . . Can't tell. |
| **XI**<br>Love<br>Object | Man-mamma and B. | He's probably dreaming with his paw under his head. He probably dreams about his collar coming off and how he took M's collar from her. Circle . . . bubbles . . . [E: who is the dream figure?] Probably M's ghost or something. [E: How does B feel?] He probably feels happy because he's dreaming about M's ghost instead of P's ghost. He has a tail you know . . . this one has a tail. | B is thinking some day he wished he could get a ribbon like that. But P comes along. "I'd better not wake B up, he's having a good dream." | Oh . . . he's dreaming of his mate come-to-be . . . what she'll look like and she'll look real strong like in the other dream and she'll be real pretty and she'll wear a ribbon around her neck. B had done better since this dream . . . he hasn't chased cats for two weeks and his M and his master like him better and she gives him better food now too. | Dreaming about a female dog . . . I don't see anything else . . . just a female dog . . . would like to go around with her . . . proper term for a female is "bitch." |

must be capable of complete integration. If a meaningful pattern does not emerge on a dimension, the sources must be examined until the inferences do fit together. Similarly, the dimensional interpretations must make sense when combined into the total personality configuration. Strict adherence to this congruent approach to the data reduces the possibility of interpretation error and makes attempted faking readily detectable. For clinical purposes, the data are thus most profitably handled in a qualitative fashion . . . . In this way, observations of the patient's behavior during the administration can also be taken into account.*

For research purposes, a standardized scoring system is obviously preferable. Such a system has always been available for the adult version of the test,[1,3] and accessibility to an electronic computer is now making possible a large-scale factor analysis of all responses to each cartoon. However, the more open-ended nature of the children's form makes quantification difficult. Typically, investigators have employed consensus of clinical judgments as to degree of disturbance along the various dimensions.

A first step toward objective scoring was undertaken by Winter,[13] who analyzed Blacky records of third and fourth grade boys and girls divided into two groups of 30 and 40 each. For criterion data she culled a number of measures routinely collected by the school, including intelligence and achievement tests, family and personal medical history, physical examinations and growth patterns, teacher ratings on behavior problems and social and educational development, journals of peer interaction and class behavior, and records of conferences with parents. From these sources criteria were selected to represent behavior relevant to the Blacky dimensions, and the criteria themselves were interrelated. For most of the cartoons it was possible to obtain a stable, positively interrelated cluster of measures. Next she analyzed the protocols of the first group of children for indicators of disturbance which predicted successfully to the criterion clusters, and finally cross validated those indicators on the second group. Detailed results are given in the reference cited above.

### Reliability

Granick and Scheflen[9] recently reported a series of investigations on the reliability of the Blacky Pictures with children ranging in age from 6 to 11 years. They performed three kinds of analyses: judgmental, temporal and split-half. In the first each of 10 judges sorted the stories of two cards into "strong" and "weak" categories of disturbance for 40 subjects. Their agreement is shown in table 1, reproduced from their article (reference 9, page 138).

Temporal reliability was assessed from retesting of 20 children at intervals varying from three to 12 months after the initial administration. Judges were asked to match test and retest on a gross basis, permitting utilization of language cues, story content and emotional patterns. All matchings but one were beyond chance expectation, though only three of seven were perfect. Another analysis pointed to significantly greater similarity of thematic productions between the two administrations than between single administra-

*Reproduced with permission of the Psychological Corporation.

TABLE 1.*—*Percentage Agreement of Judges in Rating Spontaneous Story*
*(Strong or Weak) of Each Card*
(N = 40)

| Card no. | % Agreement | p Value (binomial) |
|----------|-------------|---------------------|
| I | 75 | .01 |
| II | 58 | .34 |
| III | 90 | .001 |
| IV | 70 | .01 |
| V | 83 | .001 |
| VIA† | 83 | .001 |
| VIB | 80 | .001 |
| VII | 68 | .05 |
| VIII | 73 | .01 |
| IX | 60 | .21 |
| X | 95 | .001 |
| XI | 95 | .001 |

†Card VI was scored twice, A for "castration anxiety," B for "penis envy."

tions to different groups. Also, marked consistency over time was evidenced in the choice of cartoons "liked" and "disliked," with $p$ values of .001 in all 11 cases.

The split-half approach revealed a rank-order correlation of .92 between verbal fluency (measured by number of words in spontaneous stories) on odd- versus even-numbered cartoons. Finally, two judges scored each story of 40 records as to whether it was "structured" (utilized the central theme of the picture) or "unstructured" (failed to use the central theme). Agreement between judges was 100 per cent; and the phi coefficient between halves of the test was .67.

The authors conclude: "The results reported do not represent high level reliabilities, but since they are uniformly in the same direction they command some respect. Accordingly, the Blacky Pictures Test would seem to have a significant degree of reliability when used with a group of children" (reference 9, page 140).

## Validity

The topic of validity of the Blacky Pictures technique has been discussed earlier.[4] Essentially the argument was made for a type of approach which has since been elaborated and treated extensively by Cronbach and Meehl[7] under the rubric "construct validity." For example, the protocol of the nine year old girl presented in figure 1 indicates a very strong response to the first oral cartoon, and the spontaneous introduction of oral references on seven of the subsequent pictures. Clearly Margie qualifies for the psychoanalytic label "oral character": but how to validate such an inference?

In this instance the following pertinent data were immediately available, for she had been one of the subjects in a study of the concept of orality[5]:

*Table 1 reproduced, with permission of the publishers, from the *Journal of Consulting Psychology*, 1958, *22*, 137–141.

There were five general types of approach to the construct: ice cream consumption, teacher ratings, experimental situations, time-sampling, and sociometrics. In the first of these, the children were given a daily supply of one-ounce containers of vanilla ice cream and were allowed to eat as much as they liked. According to psychoanalytic theory, the oral character should rank high on this variable. Margie was 5th in a class of 26.

The second type of approach dealt with ratings made by teachers. The theory predicts that the oral character tends to give up easily in the face of frustration; Margie was ranked 7th by the teachers (in all of these ranks, 1 is the oral end of the continuum). Another prediction is poor leadership ability. Here she ranked 5th, again toward the oral end. On 'needs praise from others' she was 1st in the whole class; low self-reliance—5th; suggestibility—13th; difficulty in making choices—5th; hanging around teachers—5th; can't take disapproval—22nd; not being liked by other kids—5th. So out of 9 items rated by teachers, she ranked close to the oral extreme on 7.

A third approach consisted of a series of experimental situations. In a test of boredom, involving observations during a seemingless endless cross-out task, Margie ranked 9th out of 27—that is, in the oral direction of being easily bored or frustrated when no supplies are forthcoming. The theory also says that the oral character is continually in search of a magic helper. This was measured experimentally by having the children choose alternative endings to stories told in class. Here she again ranked 9th. In experimental tests of suggestibility (the oral character is presumed to be more suggestible), she was 3rd in taste suggestibility, 4th in auditory, and 7th in tactile suggestibility. Another experiment tested the prediction that oral characters can't say 'no' to requests from others. The situation was one in which the subject was asked to make some kind of picture out of a number of pieces of different shapes and colors. During this process the examiner interposed several suggestions with varying degrees of forcefulness and the subject's reactions were noted. Margie ranked 3rd in the class on this variable. The last experimental situation concerned the theoretical prediction that oral characters are preoccupied by gifts, and tend to be overly generous when there is hope of buying someone's affection. In a staged pencil drive, our heroine was 4th in the number of pencils she contributed.

The fourth general type of approach to the psychoanalytic concept of orality was through daily time-sampling in the classroom over a 3 week period. The dimensions observed were number of mouth movements, on which Margie was 24th; paying attention to observers, on which she ranked 1st; number of approaches to the teacher—13th; and approaches to other kids—6th.

The fifth procedure involved sociometrics. The theory leads to the prediction that oral characters, in view of their excessive demands for attention, will be rejected by their peers. Accordingly, a series of sociometric questions were administered to the group. Margie turned out to be the 2nd most rejected child in the class.

Summarizing these results, we see that of 20 variables she ranked in the most oral third of the group on 16. Furthermore, on 12 of the 20 she ranked in the top 5. It is also interesting to note that on two non-oral control variables—neatness and collecting tops in the ice cream situation—she was 23rd and 13th respectively.*

Greater opportunity for checking on the validity of any projective technique obviously exists in the clinical setting itself. Congruence of test findings with known case history material provides an important source of information. A published example of this method, written by Michal-Smith, Hammer and Spitz,[11] describes the case of a nine year old Negro boy with a history of stealing toys, spying on his mother and stepfather at night, masturbation and homosexual and heterosexual episodes. The Blacky protocol was filled with specific oedipal responses and perseverative references

*Based on a paper presented by G. S. Blum and D. R. Miller at the round table discussion on the Blacky Pictures held at the 1950 meetings of the American Psychological Association.

to Mama's collar. In their interpretation the authors stress the patient's strong ambivalence toward his mother, including retaliatory wishes accompanied by guilt, and his unconscious equating of toys, food and love, with an insatiable desire for all three. The article's summary states: "Our clinical experience indicates that the Blacky Pictures are very effective in stimulating projective productions in children" (reference 11, page 282).

## Illustrative Research Applications

Since the pictures are specifically designed to tap significant psychosexual dimensions, the technique lends itself to research problems involving psychoanalytic assumptions. The diversity of possible applications is illustrated in four studies which will be summarized briefly.

Hilgeman[10] investigated age and sex differences among 72 school pupils. Contrasting Blacky responses of equal numbers of 6 and 9 year old boys and girls, she discovered such differences as the following: more oral dependency in both sexes at the younger level; greater anal conflict in younger than older girls; 6 year old boys revealed more castration anxiety than did 9 year olds; and desire for identification with the father was stronger in younger than older girls.

Boyd[6] related personality factors to 23 matched pairs of good and poor readers in the fourth and fifth grades of elementary school. His results indicated that poor readers were not judged disturbed on a significantly larger number of Blacky dimensions. However, they did show evidence of greater conflict in the area of identification, that is, significantly more of the poor readers revealed confusion in sex role. Good readers, on the other hand, were more disturbed on the dimension of oral passivity.

In a very different setting, Rabin[12] compared responses of 27 Israeli Kibbutz-reared boys in the fourth grade to a control group of 27 fourth graders from non-Kibbutz villages in which the family structure was traditionally patriarchal. Consistent with his theoretical predictions, the former gave evidence of lesser oedipal involvement, more diffuse identification and less intense sibling rivalry.

Gibson[8] used the Blacky Pictures along with other projective techniques in a battery designed to explore the effects of surgery and hospitalization in early infancy on personality development. Three groups of children who had congenital anomalies in the alimentary tract were studied (all patients were between the ages of 5 and 8 at time of testing): 9 with divided esophagus, 15 with reduced pyloric opening and 5 with imperforate anus. A control group of 29 children was matched for sex, age and intelligence. The results indicated more emotional disturbance in the pyloric stenosis and imperforate anus groups when compared to their controls, but not in the atresia of the esophagus group.

## Summary

This chapter is written as a supplement to the Blacky Pictures Manual of Instructions,[2] extending the section on the technique's use with children.

Included are sample responses at various age levels, comments on scoring and interpretation, evidence bearing on reliability and validity, and illustrative research applications.

## References

1. Blum, G. S.   A study of the psychoanalytic theory of psychosexual development. *Genet. Psychol. Monogr.*, 1949, *39*, 3–99.
2. ——.   *The Blacky Pictures: a technique for the exploration of personality dynamics.* New York: The Psychological Corporation, 1950.
3. ——.   Revised scoring system for research use of the Blacky Pictures, 1951 (Mimeo).
4. ——, & Hunt, H. F.   The validity of the Blacky Pictures. *Psychol. Bull.*, 1952, *49*, 238–250.
5. ——, & Miller, D. R.   Exploring the psychoanalytic theory of the oral character. *J. Pers.*, 1952, *20*, 287–304.
6. Boyd, R. D.   Reading retardation as related to personality factors of children and their parents. Unpublished doctoral dissertation, Univer. of Michigan, 1953.
7. Cronbach, L. J., & Meehl, P. E.   Construct validity in psychological tests. *Psychol. Bull.*, 1955, *52*, 281–302.
8. Gibson, R. M.   An exploration of the effects of surgery and hospitalization in early infancy on personality development. Unpublished doctoral dissertation, Univer. of Michigan, 1958.
9. Granick, S., & Sheflen, N. A.   Approaches to reliability of projective tests with special reference to the Blacky Pictures test. *J. consult. Psychol.*, 1958, *22*, 137–141.
10. Hilgeman, L. M.   Developmental and sex variations in the Blacky test. Unpublished doctoral dissertation, Ohio State Univer., 1951.
11. Michal-Smith, H., Hammer, E., & Spitz, H.   Use of the Blacky Pictures with a child whose oedipal desires are close to consciousness. *J. clin. Psychol.*, 1951, *7*, 280–282.
12. Rabin, A. I.   Some psychosexual differences between Kibbutz and non-Kibbutz Israeli boys. *J. proj. Tech.*, 1958, *22*, 328–332.
13. Winter, L. M.   Development of a scoring system for the children's form of the Blacky Pictures. Unpublished doctoral dissertation, Univer. of Michigan, 1954.

**6**

## Thematic Apperceptive Techniques with Children

JEROME KAGAN

### Theoretical Considerations

APPERCEPTION is defined generally as the integration of a percept with the individual's past experience and current psychological state. However, the term "thematic apperceptive technique" has become synonymous with any task which requires story interpretations of pictures or simple scenes. The purposes of this chapter are to discuss the assumptions underlying the interpretation of apperceptive fantasy, to describe some of the tests used with children and to summarize research on the reliability and validity of fantasy derived variables.

### General Influences on Fantasy Production

Although we are primarily concerned with the factors influencing the production of apperceptive fantasy, it is commonly acknowledged that certain processes are common to all fantasy behavior. The individual's perception of the situation and his verbal ability are two such factors and both are of crucial importance when one is dealing with children.[64,66,137] The child is often more suspicious than the adult in a test situation, and the child's attitude toward the examiner, his hypothesis as to the purpose of the test and the physical surroundings can influence the length, content and language style of the fantasy response. Second, the child's fantasy interpretation is usually given orally, and his ability to express his thoughts can influence the length and content of his response. In research, it is common practice for the psychologist to devise molecular scoring schemes for a variety of content categories, and the probability of occurrence of specific categories may vary with the length of the story. Story length increases with age, and girls usually tell longer stories than boys from age six through early adolescence.

### Uniqueness of Apperceptive Fantasy

#### Nature of the Stimulus

Story interpretations of pictures differ from other categories of fantasy or projective behavior (Rorschach, draw-a-person, word association, spontaneous art) with respect to the nature of the eliciting stimulus and the type of response required of the subject. The importance of these two factors has been neglected by psychologists who use projective techniques. The motivational and symbolic content of the fantasy response has become the focus of interest, and this interest has been accompanied by a decreased concern both with the nature of the stimulus input and the cognitive process associated with the verbalized fantasy response. Thus the content, "These are two people fighting," to either a TAT or Rorschach card has been interpreted, at times, as similar in meaning despite the fact that the two stimuli differ on many dimensions. The fact that empirical research has failed to demonstrate any consistent correlations between similar contents on the Rorschach and TAT is not surprising when one considers the major differences in the stimulus impact on the child. The nature of the external stimulus plays a crucial role in response production, and research indicates that *the psychological significance of a fantasy response must be evaluated in terms of the stimulus impact and with knowledge of the normative reactions to the stimulus for different age and sex groupings.*[6,7,42,76,79,80,118,140]

### The Response Process

The type of response and cognitive activity demanded of the subject differs widely for various projective techniques. When the child is given a Rorschach card, for example, his task is to scan the stimulus for clues related to "real" objects. Baughman[14] has suggested that the form or outline of the stimulus is a crucial factor in this process. However, the cognitive process elicited by the TAT stimuli and instructions differs from the one associated with the Rorschach. On the TAT, the child's task is not to find a realistic shape, but to interpret relationships between people—to put order into human interaction. In the Rorschach the child tends to focus on the physical dimensions of the stimulus, i.e., color, shading and form outline. On the TAT he is instructed to focus on a dimension which is considerably less stimulus bound, i.e., the actions and motives of people and types of interpersonal relationships. These differences militate against the naive assumption that a given content area has the same psychological meaning regardless of the projective stimulus used to elicit the response.

## Use and Scoring of Apperceptive Fantasy

Because psychology lacks a well validated and generally accepted set of apperceptive variables, investigators have coded different aspects of the fantasy depending on their specific hypotheses and interests. The Murray[119] set of *need* and *press* variables has been used most frequently,[21,35,43,79,135] but there are many studies in which cognitive-expressive dimensions have been the focus of quantification.[5,7,12,60,90] In general, the major variables derived from apperceptive data include the following:

### The Assessment of Motive Strength

Psychologists have been most concerned with the fantasy motives of aggression, succorance, nurturance, achievement, passivity, affiliation, recognition, power, and autonomy.[79,81,123–125,135] These motives are either derived from or identical with Murray's need categories, and the reader is referred to Murray[119] and Sanford et al.[135] for definitions of these variables. A recent volume[9] contains detailed manuals for the scoring of *need* achievement, affiliation and power. In most scoring schemes all instances of a need category are summed across all stories, and repetitions of the same need or occurrence of different needs can be scored in one theme. Some investigators assign different weights to the intensity of various need-related activities, and in some schemes each theme is scored for a central need, in addition to the scoring of subsidiary ones. In the clinic, the explicit assumption has been that the more intense the fantasy expression of a motive and the more frequent its occurrence, the stronger the inferred motivation in this area. The validity of this assumption and of the above coding schemes will be discussed in a later section.

## The Child's Perception of the World

A second class of apperceptive variables concerns the child's perception of the environment and his expectancies with respect to the behavior of others. This fantasy dimension resembles Murray's *press* category, and the most popular press variables in research have dealt with aggression, rejection, dominance, nurturance, acceptance and punishment directed at the hero by different figures in the social environment.[31,60,78,79,86,123,124,126,135] In order to score these variables the hero or central figure must be predesignated, and action directed at the hero, in contrast to similar action by the hero, is assumed to reflect the child's perception of his environment.

## Assessment of Defensive Tendencies and Indices of Conflict

In recent years, psychologists have devised fantasy measures of defensive processes and areas of conflict. This trend parallels the theoretical shift from concern with unconscious motives to the role of the ego defenses in modifying their behavioral expression.[15] Some of the major variables studied include guilt over aggression and violation of prohibitions,[77,93,116,127,129,130] projection of aggression or blame,[36,70] and denial and repression of sources of anxiety.[49,56,60] The fantasy behaviors employed to assess these defensive processes include (a) themes of punishment for prohibited activity, (b) ratio of occurrence of punishment themes to occurrence of prohibited activity, (c) guilt attributed to fantasy figures, (d) absence of a conflictful theme to stimuli which suggest the conflict, (e) omission or distortion of figures or objects which are associated with conflict behaviors, and (f) failure to report a conflictful behavior following the verbal recognition of some instigation to the act.

## Cognitive-Expressive Styles

The term cognitive-expressive style refers to the child's preferred approach to the organization of the picture stimulus and the formal aspects of the language he used in his stories. The major dimensions for which individual differences have been established include (a) the degree to which the child describes concrete, physical aspects of the stimulus[5,13,60,63]; (b) degree of elaboration of the activity, thoughts and motives of the characters[5,7,34,60,61,63,64]; (c) the tendency to use specific classes of words, e.g., adjectives describing feeling or affect states, action words, nouns, specific verb tense forms[7,56,60,61,63]; (d) originality of plot and language[56,60,64]; (e) degree of distortion of the stimulus[5,13,34,56,60,76,90]; (f) length of story[54,60,61]; (g) degree to which story is based on the salient figures and objects illustrated[5,54,61,64]; (h) degree to which nonillustrated figures are introduced into the theme[56]; (i) tendency to give proper names to thematic figures or openly identify with one of the fantasy figures[104]; (j) degree of cooperation-resistance in the test situation.[60]

Although stylistic variables can be reliably coded, there is a serious lack of information pertaining to the construct and predictive validity of these dimensions. Some tentative hypotheses are that (a) story length reflects verbal fluency, (b) predominant use of a certain tense measures the child's time orientation to his environment, (c) a descriptive approach to the stimulus reflects an inability to understand the motives of others and/or personality constriction, (d) absence of language implying feeling or affect is an index of isolation and repression of affect, and (e) story incoherence and distortions of the stimuli are indices of pathologic thought processes.

Although the above hypotheses are still speculative, age differences in cognitive-expressive dimensions repeatedly have been reported. Children under nine to 10 years of age are likely to adopt a concrete, descriptive approach to stimuli while older ones tell more elaborate stories involving motives and feelings.[5,13,56] The fantasy of younger children is also likely to include more distortions and omissions than the fantasy of preadolescent children. The following set of three stories from one "normal" boy at ages 8 years 9 months, 9 years 10 months and 17 years 6 months to TAT card 3 BM illustrates some typical stylistic changes.

Protocol 1: Age 8 years 9 months: Well the boy—is that a boy? I'll have it be a boy and he's got his head laying on a step and he had black hair. And he's—the boy is crying because he's at home by himself and his mother and dad have went away and he came home from school and there wasn't anybody home. And that looks like a sword laying beside him and the house is white and his shoes are all colors and his belt is the same color as his shoes.

Protocol 2: Age 9 years 10 months: What's that right here? Looks like a gun. Well this little boy here, his mother and dad, well, they went away and he's here all by himself and they told him to lock the door and he didn't. He thought he'd be O.K. Somebody came along and they had been mean to this little boy. They went in the house and this little boy was all frightened and scared. They had a gun and he didn't know it. These men were robbers. And they had seen his mother and father come out of the house and leave him there. And so these men—this boy was frightened—these men shot the little boy and he was laying up against the bench when his mother and father come home.

Protocol 3: Age 17 years 6 months: This young man has just tried to commit suicide. He shot himself and he isn't dead. And they find him later on and they save his life. And they turn him against trying it again. He turns out to be a great success. He suicided because he and his parents didn't get along and he had no place to go.

In all three stories the hero is unhappy, and his parents are presented in a negative light. However, the concrete description of the boy's appearance on the first protocol was absent on the succeeding protocols; the ambiguous object which was seen initially as a sword was perceived more realistically at a later age; and affective states and motives were more elaborated on the last two protocols than on the initial one.

## The Rationale of Fantasy Interpretation

Despite more than twenty years of research with apperceptive stimuli, psychologists do not have an explicit set of rules on which to base their interpretations of fantasy. Lindzey[98] and Henry[64] have attempted to state the assumptions usually implicit in fantasy interpretations, and the following condensed statement is based, to some degree, on their more elaborate discussion.

### Assumption 1: Congruence between Fantasy Production and Personality

The most basic assumption is that the needs, presses, sources of anxiety, defenses, attitudes and behaviors attributed to the different characters in the stories bear a lawful relation to corresponding and analogous dimensions within the story-teller and in his view of the environment. It is acknowledged that displacement and condensation, i.e., symbolism, occur in the fantasy, and that this symbolism must be decoded in order to understand this correspondence. The type of language used in the fantasy also is assumed to be representative of the subject's language in other situations.

### Assumption 2: The Hero Assumption

For each stimulus, the subject perceives different degrees of similarity between himself and the various thematic figures. The figure with whom he perceives maximal similarity is regarded as the hero or central figure. Two important theorems or deductions follow from these first two assumptions. The first is that the attitudes, motives and actions of the hero have a closer relation to the child's own behavioral strivings than the attributes of other thematic figures. The second theorem states that if the subject perceives minimal similarity to all thematic figures, then the attributes assigned to the figures may be a poor index of the child's motive and action tendencies. *Thus, all stories are not equally revealing of the child's personality.*

The relevance of the hero assumption for the interpretation of fantasy cannot be overestimated. Assuming the validity of the hero assumption, one would not pool all the aggressive responses in a TAT protocol but would differentiate aggressive acts by the hero from aggressive acts directed at the hero. The evidence tends to favor the validity of the hero assumption[76,81,103]. Under test conditions in which the sex of the central figure was varied, both preschool and adolescent subjects produced the most elaborate and personally revealing material when the sex of the central figure corresponded to that of the story-teller.[5,40,149] Although the hero assumption involves a perception of similarity between the story-teller and fantasy figure, one must ask which dimensions of similarity are most relevant. It is suggested that similarities in sex, age, role and potential behavioral repertoire are most likely to facilitate identification of the child with a central figure.

Tests have been constructed for special populations, e.g., Negroes and crippled children, based on the assumption that the greater the degree of physical similarity between hero and story-teller, the more revealing the fantasy.[11,33,72,152,156] Excessive similarity in physical appearance between subject and hero may remove the "fantasy" element from the task and lead to suppression of anxiety-arousing material. Several studies suggest that productivity is not influenced by the use of fantasy figures which physically resemble the story teller.[133,156,158]

Bellak, in constructing the Children's Apperception Test, assumed that similarity between child and fantasy figure might interfere with the production of conflict-related themes, and he devised scenes illustrating animals rather than human figures.[16] Bellak argued that illustrations of children in conflictful activity might elicit sufficient anxiety to result in inhibition of revealing content, and that conflictful material would more likely be expressed when animals, rather than children, were the agents of action. Initial attempts at comparison of the child's fantasy to human and animal stimuli suggests that for story length and occurrence of selected content categories, pictures with animals are not superior to scenes with human figures.[8,18,22,50,96,107]

*Assumption 3: The Role of the External Stimulus*

*Evaluation of every fantasy response must take into account the nature of the stimulus, for every stimulus has a prepotent tendency to elicit specific content, mood and language categories regardless of its degree of ambiguity.*[44,84,163] A major theorem of this assumption is that similar contents may have different meaning depending on the type of stimulus to which they were reported. This assumption has been subjected to empirical validation and seems to be a sound, workable hypothesis. Incidence of aggressive themes to pictures which were ambiguous for aggression did not differentiate young boys (ages 6 to 10) who were rated high from those rated low on aggressive behavior. However, pictures which suggested aggressive action effectively differentiated these two groups, with the aggressive boys reporting more aggressive themes than the nonaggressive boys.[76] Related research with both children and adults[6,7,42,44,118,121,140] has yielded similar results and indicates that *a content area reported to a stimulus which is ambiguous for that content may have different psychological significance from the same theme told to a stimulus which is suggestive of that content.* This statement is supported by the theory relating the probability of occurrence of a conflictful response with the degree to which the external stimulus is goal related, i.e., its incentive value.[39] Thus, if a child is conflicted over a certain content, e.g., aggression, the probability of occurrence of the conflict theme decreases as the external stimulus becomes more suggestive of the conflict area. Of course, there is an optimal degree of stimulus ambiguity, and completely nonambiguous illustrations of a conflict area demand realistic and accurate interpretations. However, one implication of these statements is that the psychologist should adopt a critical attitude toward the earlier conception that only ambiguous stimuli can elicit significant aspects of personality functioning.

*Assumption 4: The Subject's Set and the Situation*

This assumption simply states that temporary sets and/or the nature of the testing situation can influence the content and style of the stories. Thus, type of instructions, administration, sex, age and role of the examiner, experimental interference, and temporary emotional states all may influence aspects of the thematic material. The work of McClelland, Atkinson and their colleagues[9,111,154] on the experimental production of achievement fantasy is ample evidence of the validity of this assumption.

*Assumption 5: Fantasy as the Product of Motive and Defense*

The final assumption concerns the theoretical position of a fantasy response. It states that *fantasy is an index of neither motive strength nor defensive tendencies but reflects the result of the interaction of these two processes.* Since Murray's initial schema, there has been a strong tendency to view fantasy contents as measures of motive strength, and the use of the label "need achievement" by McClelland and his colleagues is a demonstration of this conceptual preference. It is generally acknowledged that overt behavior is rarely an uncontaminated measure of motive but rather the result of the interaction of both motive and defensive processes. However, there has been a reluctance to view fantasy behavior in a similar fashion. Some psychologists have implicitly assumed that since the fantasy stimulus was ambiguous the effect of defensive processes on manifest fantasy content was minimal. This position is not defensible in the light of recent research.[34,42,60,76,80,94,118,127,129,140] Fantasy expression of a motive which is associated with a source of anxiety is subject to the same defensive modifications as any other overt response. Thus, absence of achievement fantasy does not necessarily indicate low achievement motivation but might, in some instances, indicate high anxiety associated with the acquisition of achievement goals. Four stories from another male subject in the Fels sample to Card 1 of the TAT (boy with violin) illustrate this point. Independent data from several sources revealed that this subject, as a boy, had strong needs to accomplish something important and as an adult was involved in many achievement-related activities. However, interview data indicated strong fear of failure and considerable doubt as to his ability to obtain the achievement goals he desired.

Protocol 1: Age 10 years 11 months: This guy is studying his violin and he's getting tired of it and he doesn't like it any too well. He's disgusted—he can't do his violin very well.

Protocol 2: Age 12 years 10 months: Well, looks like a boy that doesn't especially want to play the violin and he's supposed to. He's sorta sad, thinking about playing the violin. He'd rather be outside playing.

Protocol 3: Age 13 years 11 months: Well, this kid has been playing the violin—he doesn't like it very much and he's going to run away cause he doesn't like the violin.

Protocol 4: Age 28 years: He is supposed to be practicing but he wants to be outside playing ball and so after going after it diligently for a while he just took a little rest—daydreaming. . . . I could tell you another story about it. That's the first one that came to my mind because—he wishes he could play it but he can't—for some reason he can't—some physical reason—he enjoys music very much but—for some reason he's unable to play.

On the first protocol the hero was studying the violin but stopped because he felt he was not competent. On the following two protocols there was no mention of achievement motivation or behavior. On the final protocol, at age 28, the subject verbalized the conflict between desire for mastery and anxiety over failure and feelings of incompetence.

It is suggested that when a motive is believed to be associated with a source of anxiety, occurrence or nonoccurrence of the motive in fantasy may not be a sensitive index of motive strength. Perhaps if we place fantasy in the same conceptual scheme that we apply to all behavior we will be in a better position to understand the relationships between fantasy and other dimensions of personality functioning.

## The Tests

The present discussion of apperceptive instruments used with children will be limited to the (a) Thematic Apperception Test (TAT), (b) Michigan Picture Test (MPT), (c) Picture-Story Test (PST) and (d) special sets of pictures devised for specific research goals.

### Thematic Apperception Test (TAT)

The first set of TAT pictures was published in 1935, but the most widely used set of stimuli was published by Murray[120] in 1943 and consists of 30 pictures plus a blank card. The pictures were selected so that there was one set of 20 cards for the following four groups: boys under 14, girls under 14, males over 14 and females over 14. The primary basis for inclusion in a specific set appears to be based on the age and sex of the central figure. The manual by Murray[120] presents a description of each stimulus; it is assumed that the reader is familiar with the nature of the pictures. Most of the pictures are best suited for subjects who are at least 11 or 12 years of age. However, some of the stimuli are fairly productive with children between 7 and 11 years of age; these include Cards 1, 3 BM, 7 GF, 8 BM, 12 M, 13 B, 14 and 17 BM. The content categories usually told by young children to these stimuli include concern with achievement and status goals (1, 8 BM, 14, 17 BM), aggression to or from the hero (3 BM, 8 BM, 12 M, 14, 17 BM), concern with parental nurturance and rejection (3 BM, 7 GF, 13 B, 14), and parental punishment and attitudes toward parents (1, 3 BM, 7 GF, 14).

### The Picture-Story Test (PST)

In 1940 Symonds initiated a study of the fantasy of a small group of adolescents of high school age. A series of 42 drawings illustrating scenes with adolescent "heroes" were administered to 20 boys and 20 girls; Symonds' volume *Adolescent fantasy*[149] summarizes the results of the research. On the basis of these results the 20 best pictures were selected for general distribution.[148] The 20 pictures include sets A and B, with the B set judged to be diagnostically superior. Although the stimuli illustrate both adolescent girls and boys as central figures, Symonds suggested that all the stimuli be used for both male and female subjects. A brief description of each of the pictures follows. The writer has taken the liberty of suggesting the emotional expressions of the figures in those cases in which it seemed relatively unambiguous.

A 1. An adolescent boy holding a valise stands on an empty street.
A 2. An adolescent boy knocks on a door.
A 3. In the foreground an adolescent girl sits with a book in her lap; in the background a young couple are walking.
A 4. An older man with a somewhat angry expression and money in his hands stares at an adolescent boy who has one hand out toward the man.

A 5. An adolescent girl with books beside her sits on the ground.

A 6. An adolescent boy walking in a house at night with a shadowy figure in the background.

A 7. An older woman talks with an adolescent boy.

A 8. In the foreground an adolescent girl stares forward while in the back of her is a heavily made-up young woman.

A 9. A young woman in a domestic uniform holds a broom.

A10. A young couple stare into a crystal ball with a fortune teller beside them.

B 1. An adolescent boy with his fists clenched and the suggestion of an angry expression walks out of a door.

B 2. An adolescent girl looks into a mirror and an older woman stands beside her.

B 3. In the foreground an adolescent boy stares forward and in back of him is an older boy with a cigarette in his mouth and the suggestion of a sneer on his face.

B 4. An adolescent girl is holding a flower with an older woman and a younger girl beside her.

B 5. In the foreground stands a woman with the back of her head to the subject; in the background a young woman talks to the first woman.

B 6. An adolescent boy with the suggestion of an angry expression is slumped in a chair.

B 7. An adolescent girl is climbing the stairs at night and a shadow of a figure is at the top of the stairs.

B 8. An adolescent girl talks to an older man.

B 9. An adolescent boy is in a prison cell.

B10. An adolescent girl holding a book is walking on a street with the outline of a man in the background.

The reader will note that at least one-half of the stimuli would be expected to elicit themes of sadness, aggression or tragedy, especially pictures A 1, 4, 6, 8, and B 1, 3, 6, 7, 9, 10. The data reported by Symonds support this expectation.

## The Michigan Picture Test (MPT)

In 1948 the Michigan Department of Mental Health initiated a project whose major goal was the selection of a set of fantasy pictures to be used for the evaluation of degree of emotional adjustment in school children 8 to 14 years of age. This project was one of the most systematic attempts at standardization of a projective test, and a summary of the results can be found in a manual by Andrew, Hartwell, Hutt and Walton[7] and in shorter reports.[6,56,61,155] Over 1400 children were tested during the course of the research, and normative data for the major variables were based on samples of approximately 100 children. After preliminary testing with a large set of stimuli, 15 pictures plus a blank card were selected for commercial distribution. Four of the stimuli are used specifically with girls and four with boys, and each child is usually given 12 cards. There are four "core" stimuli on which most of the validation data are based, and these four pictures are recommended for brief screening tests. Discussion of the validity of the variables derived from the fantasy will be reserved for a later section. The original stimuli were photographs rather than drawings and are much more realistic than the pictures used in the TAT or PST. A brief description of each of the pictures follows:

1. (Core card) A family of four at a table. The man is reading the paper, a woman feeds a boy and an older girl looks on.

2. A boy and girl standing together. The boy holds a straw hat and the girl looks away from the boy.

3. A schoolroom scene with a teacher, pupils, and one boy standing.

4B. (For boys) A man and boy, with man seated and boy standing beside man with head bowed.

4G. (For girls—Card 7 GF of the TAT) A woman and a girl with a doll are seated on a couch.

5. A man and two naked boys in a bathroom.

6. (Core card) A mixed group of six children playing checkers.

7. A group of four boys walking up a road in the country.

8B. (For boys) A boy's head with chin resting in his hand and face staring upwards.

8G. (For girls) A girl at school desk with head in hands and the suggestion of a sad expression.

9. (Core card) A large streak of lightning on a black background.

10B. (For boys) A man standing behind a desk and a boy standing in front.

10G. (For girls) A man and young girl are seated with the girl reading.

11B. (For boys) A woman, boy and man are standing in a doorway with the man and boy seen from the back. The man's cap suggests that of a policeman.

11G. (For girls) A girl with pencil on her lips sitting at a school desk surrounded by a room of empty desks.

12. (Core card) Blank card.

These stimuli are not as suggestive of aggression, rejection or sadness as Symonds' pictures, and there are more stimuli which suggest achievement (Cards 3, 6, 8G, 10G, 11G) and concern with peer group affiliation (Cards 2, 3, 6, 7). If one selected specific pictures from the TAT, MPT and PST, one could sample a wider variety of clinically relevant need, press and conflict situations than is possible by using the pictures in any one of these tests

### Special Apperceptive Stimuli for Children

Many psychologists have devised special sets of pictures related to their research interests. These pictures have usually illustrated scenes designed to tap the child's perception of his parents and the family milieu [4,5,36,46,63,70,78,116] and the child's attitudes toward his teachers.[17,108] Other sets of stimuli have been constructed to assess (a) conflict over sexuality,[109] (b) attitudes toward alien racial groups,[72] (c) validity of psychoanalytic hypotheses about oedipal anxiety,[49] and (d) the tendency to express aggression to peers.[76,93] Pictures have also been devised for the testing of special diagnostic groups such as the physically handicapped.[11,33] The validity of these instruments will be discussed in a later section.

### Administration

The administration of apperceptive stimuli to children follows closely the procedure used with adults. For children over seven or eight years of age the instructions used by Andrew et al.[7] are appropriate:

I am going to show you some interesting pictures. I'd like you to make up a story about each picture. Any kind of a story will be all right. Just tell me what has happened in the picture and how it is going to turn out; just as if you were making up a whole story. You can tell me how the people in the story feel and what they are doing (reference 7, page 61).*

*Quoted with permission of the publishers, Science Research Associates.

Bellak[16] and Kagan[76] suggested that the child be told that this is a game in which he has to guess what's happening in the picture. For children under eight, emphasis on the gamelike quality of the task facilitates ego involvement and decreases the threatening nature of the task. Symonds[149] and Bellak[16] suggested that an inquiry be conducted after the child has told his themes. In the inquiry the examiner obtains the child's association to the story and a statement about the source of the story in order to better evaluate the significance of the theme. Several investigators[5,36,40,116,141,151] did not request a story at all but asked the child a series of structured questions about the pictures. It is often difficult to obtain a complete story with children four to six years of age, and the procedure of asking the child structured questions about single figures or simple scenes appears to be a promising method. Rejections are not uncommon in children under 10 years of age, and it is best not to press the child but to return to the rejected card after the other stimuli have been administered.

## Reliability

### Reliability of Content Categories

The question of the reliability of apperceptive fantasy only has meaning with respect to specific variables coded from specific stimuli. Some psychologists have concluded that apperceptive fantasy is unreliable because all the variables which were scored from a protocol did not show significant degrees of intraprotocol consistency or test-retest reliability. This conclusion is too severe since a specific set of pictures should not be expected to be a sensitive index of all possible themes. We do not expect a specific blood test to be a reliable index of all the compounds that are known to appear in the blood and accept the fact that only one factor can be reliably assessed by any one technique. Unfortunately there has been very little research on the reliability of children's fantasy, and reference will be made to research on both children and college students.

In one study with children[79] the long-term intraindividual stability of eight *need* and *press* variables was assessed for three TAT administrations (ages 8 years 9 months, 11 years 6 months, 14 years 6 months). Only achievement themes and acts of physical aggression by the hero showed a statistically significant degree of stability (phi coefficients in the .30's, $p < .01$), and these two thematic categories occurred primarily to TAT pictures which suggested these contents. The remaining six variables showed no definite tendency to be associated with any one TAT picture. It was concluded that the long-term stability of a fantasy content was dependent, in part, on the presence of a stimulus which suggested the theme in question.

In two separate studies,[87,115] pictures designed to elicit achievement themes were administered to college students and adolescent boys using test-retest intervals of 12 and 5 weeks, respectively. The test-retest reliability coefficients for occurrence of achievement themes were .26 and .50 ($p < .01$), with the higher coefficient associated with the shorter test-retest interval. Similarly, sets of stimuli structured to elicit fantasy hostility toward authority[73] and themes of achievement, security and hostility[68,74] showed reliability coefficients ranging from .42 to .73. Thus, when the stimuli were relatively nonambiguous for a specific content, reliability estimates were low but statistically significant. Two studies with college students[101,102] also point to a positive relationship between the reliability of a content on the TAT and the presence of stimuli which have a prepotent tendency to elicit that content. One implication of these data is that content categories reported to stimuli ambiguous for that content are not apt to be stable over time.

### Reliability of Cognitive-Expressive Variables

There has been embarrassingly little research on the reliability of cognitive-expressive dimensions in thematic material. Granick and Scheflen,[54] using the Blacky Pictures, found that length of story and type of story organization showed a high degree of intratest consistency for children 6 to 11 years of age. The author has unpublished data on older boys (ages 8 to 15) which indicate that the tendency to attribute affect and feeling states to TAT figures was moderately reliable ($r = .44$, $p < .05$) when the two protocols were separated by approximately two years.

## Validity

### Validity of Content Categories

As with the question of reliability, the validity of apperceptive fantasy can only be assessed with respect to specific variables derived from specific stimuli. Most of the research on children has centered on the fantasy variables of aggression, aggression anxiety, achievement, perception of the accepting or rejecting nature of the social environment and fantasy indices of maladjustment and pathology.

### Aggressive Fantasy and its Relation to Overt Aggressive Behavior

It is generally acknowledged that the relationship between aggressive fantasy and overt aggressive behavior is complex, and prediction and explanation of this relationship require either control or assessment of other variables. Two highly relevant variables are the ambiguity of the fantasy stimulus and the degree of anxiety associated with aggressive thoughts and behavior.

As noted earlier, Kagan[76] found that occurrence of aggressive themes to pictures which were ambiguous for aggression did not differentiate extremely aggressive from extremely nonaggressive boys. However, the former group reported significantly more aggressive themes than the latter to stimuli which suggested peer aggression. It was assumed that the aggressive boys were less anxious over reporting aggressive themes to the nonambiguous stimuli and, therefore, *intensity of aggression anxiety rather than strength of aggressive motivation was the major explanatory concept used in understanding these results.*

In a study with similar theoretical implications, Lesser[91,92] assessed the degree to which mothers encouraged or discouraged aggressive behavior in their prepubertal sons and had the boys tell stories to pictures illustrating boys in aggressive and nonaggressive situations. The measure of overt aggression in the boys was based on a sociometric technique. For the entire sample of 44 boys there was no relationship between overt and fantasy aggression. However, for the boys whose mothers encouraged aggression, the correlation between overt and fantasy aggression was $+.43$, $(p < .05)$, while for the boys whose mothers discouraged aggression the correlation was $-.41$ $(p < .10)$. If it is assumed that maternal discouragement of aggression produced aggression anxiety in the child, these results also indicate that degree of aggression anxiety is a highly relevant variable in the relationship between aggressive fantasy and behavior.

Other studies[70,78,94,127,129,130] reveal that when the psychologist evaluates fantasy measures of aggression anxiety (guilt, punishment for aggression, receptivity to socialization of aggression, inhibition of aggressive themes to pictures suggesting this content), he usually finds a significant inverse relation with overt aggressive behavior. Often a combined measure of aggression anxiety together with aggressive preoccupation, e.g., ratio of punishment themes to number of fantasy aggressive acts, shows an even better inverse relationship with overt aggression. However, the sum of all fantasy aggressive themes alone is generally not highly predictive of occurrence of overt aggression. These findings suggest that when apperceptive fantasy is used to assess conflict in a motive area, prediction of presence or absence of the corresponding behavior is better than when the fantasy is used to measure "motive strength." Clinicians faced with the problem of predicting overt aggression in children should attend closely to fantasy content which suggests anxiety over aggression and to distortions and abrupt changes in fantasy performance to stimuli which suggest aggressive behavior. It is also reasonable to assume that these conclusions about aggression are applicable to other conflict areas.

*Achievement Fantasy and Behavior*

Research on the relationship between achievement themes and aspects of achievement behavior in children tentatively suggests a positive relation between these two variables when the conditions are such as to arouse achievement motivation in relation to some task.[80,82,88,113,154] For example, achievement fantasy on the TAT was positively correlated with increases in IQ score during the years six through 10; this result suggests that achievement strivings can facilitate intelligence test performance.[80,82]

Milstein and Witt[113] found that lower-class adolescent boys with high "fear of failure" tended to be low in achievement fantasy whereas middle-class adolescent boys with high "fear of failure" were likely to report achievement themes. This research suggests not only that social class may be related to achievement imagery but also that occurrence of achievement fantasy may be inhibited by anxiety associated with failure.

Kagan and Moss[80] have looked into the historical determinants of achievement fantasy. They found that girls whose mothers showed concern with the child's mental and motor development for the first three years of life were more likely to tell TAT achievement themes at ages 9, 11 and 14 than girls whose mothers showed minimal concern with their child's early development. Winterbottom[162] used verbal stems rather than pictures as fantasy stimuli and found that eight year old boys who were high in achievement fantasy had mothers who placed more demands on the child prior to age eight than did the mothers of boys low in fantasy achievement. In summary, achievement fantasy shows both moderate reliability and a positive relationship with achievement strivings on intellectual tasks. For the clinician faced with the problem of evaluating readiness and motivation for school work, assessment of achievement fantasy may be a useful supplement to scores on standard intelligence and school achievement tests.

*Fantasy Indices of the Perception of the Social Environment*

There are some empirical data to support the assumption that the child's perceptions of different figures in his environment may be reflected in his description of thematic figures.

Both Cummings[36] and Jackson[70] have reported that neurotic children (ages 5 to 12) were more likely than "normals" to describe parent figures as rejecting and punishing. Similarly, Kagan[78] found that extremely aggressive boys (ages 6 to 10) described parent figures as more aggressive and less nurturant to children than a group of nonaggressive boys. In this latter study, nurturant behavior from all thematic figures did not differentiate the aggressive from the nonaggressive boys but occurrence of *parental* nurturance was significantly less frequent for the aggressive children. Thus, the psychologist should differentiate the actions of figures with respect to their social roles, since this procedure provides a more sensitive index of the child's view of the environment than a pooling of actions or presses without regard to the sex, age or role of the story figures.

Other research[141,167] indicates that asking the young child specific questions about thematic figures, e.g., "Why is the child crying?," "What is the mother doing to the child?," "Who is stronger, the daddy or the boy?," etc. can provide sensitive information as to the degree to which power and attitudes of rejection or acceptance are attributed to significant figures in the child's environment.

The child's perception of the peer milieu also may be reflected in fantasy. Themes of aggression and rejection directed at the hero by peer figures are higher for minority group children than for controls.[72,124] Furthermore, children who might be assumed to view the world as dangerous or rejecting, e.g., handicapped or physically immature children, report more fantasy themes indicating need for social acceptance[26] and rejection by others[125] than controls. However, the specific content which reflects the child's perception of a hostile world will vary with the specific pictures administered and the sex, age and class background of the subject. Thus, a perception of the environment as rejecting might be manifested in terms of physical or verbal aggression directed at the central figure depending on the structure of the stimuli administered.

*Other Personality Dimensions*

Several investigators have related fantasy variables to behavioral dimensions more global and clinically relevant than aggressive or achievement behavior. Temple and Amen[151] asked children (aged 3 to 10) to place either a "sad" or "happy" face on a hero figure and found that a clinical group with early traumatic experiences was more likely to view the child-hero as sad than were normal controls. The staff of the Michigan Picture Test project used adjustment-maladjustment as a behavioral criterion and related teacher ratings of adjustment in boys and girls 8 to 14 years of age to both content and cognitive-expressive scores.[7] The behaviors used in the teacher ratings of adjustment included social maturity, emotional security and a stable emotional mood. The two fantasy variables which discriminated the children in the upper third of the adjustment distribution from those in the lower third were (a) a "tension index" and (b) predominant use of the past tense, with high scores on these measures indicating maladjustment. A child's "tension index" was computed by summing all references (for the four core stimuli) to the need areas of affection, extrapunitive aggression, submission and personal adequacy. Although the total number of references to these four needs is the recommended index, extrapunitive aggression was disproportionately higher than affection themes for the poorly adjusted group. Andrew et al.[7] offered the interpretation that use of the past tense indicates a regressive tendency and avoidance of current conflicts whereas high tension indices reflect psychic tensions.* These interpretations require additional verification, for Hartman[60] has reported that adolescent boys with high "past tense" scores were rated as well adjusted and emotionally stable.

The failure of specific *need* or *press* variables to differentiate well adjusted from poorly adjusted children is in agreement with Symonds' data. Symonds[149] administered his special pictures to 40 adolescent boys and girls, used maladjustment as the major behavioral criterion and found that most content categories showed no relationship to ratings of maladjustment. As a matter of fact, contrary to expectation, the adjusted adolescents told more themes containing anxious elements than the maladjusted ones; this finding is in agreement with the research of Cox and Sargent.[34] Cox and Sargent[34] as well as Andrew et al.[7] warn that the clinician can make very poor predictions about a child's adjustment by using content measures of anxiety or conflict as indices of maladjustment, especially when normative data for the stimuli are not available.

---

*Andrew et al.[7] found that ratings of intensity of a need, in addition to discrete scoring of occurrence-nonoccurrence, did not improve the predictive power of the fantasy. Other research tentatively suggests that when one is working with discrete data, like thematic categories, scales measuring the intensity of a need or press do not always improve the power of prediction. The author has unpublished data on Rorschach content categories suggesting that scores based on an intensity scale were poorer predictors of a dependent variable than a simple summing of the frequency of occurrence of the content category.

## Validity of Cognitive-Expressive Categories

Cognitive-expressive variables have shown some promise of predictive power with respect to maladjustment and psychopathology. Cox and Sargent[34] reported that the stories of unstable boys contained less need-related content and less story elaboration than the themes of stable boys. This result seems inconsistent with the finding of Andrew et al.[7] that frequency of fantasy *need* references correlated with maladjustment. However, these differences might well be attributed to the differences in stimuli and definition of the criterion. Cox and Sargent[34] used TAT stimuli which contained scenes that are more difficult for children to interpret than those in the MPT. In addition, most of the boys in the Cox and Sargent unstable group had received psychiatric attention. Since aggressive behavior is the predominant cause of psychiatric referral, it is likely that their unstable sample contained more overtly aggressive boys than did the maladjusted school population in the Michigan Picture Test research. The lesson to be learned is that unless the stimuli and criterion groups are very similar, it is a bit dangerous to extrapolate any one result to populations and test conditions which differ markedly from those on which the data were originally based.

One common behavior which seems to correlate with maladjustment or pathology is a distortion or nonrealistic interpretation of the picture stimulus. Symonds' stimuli strongly suggested anxiety and aggression, and his poorly adjusted adolescents reported less anxious and aggressive content than did the adjusted ones. The Michigan "core" pictures did not strongly suggest aggression, and the maladjusted children in this sample were more likely to report this content than the adjusted subjects. Leitch and Schafer[90] reported that gross distortions of the stimulus were characteristic of the protocols of psychotic children, and Gurin[56] found that maladjusted children reported father-son conflict to pictures not suggesting this conflict but omitted this content to stimuli illustrating this type of scene. The most conclusive support for this hypothesis comes from a study[60] in which the TAT stories of delinquent boys were scored for both content and cognitive-expressive dimensions and these dimensions correlated with independent personality information. The best indicators of "emotional instability" were perceptual distortion of the TAT stimuli and attention to light or dark shading on the picture. Content categories for aggression, conflict and anxiety did not relate to ratings of maladjustment. However, the reporting of conflict themes to stimuli which suggested a conflict area, i.e., nondistortion of the scene, was positively related to ratings of adjustment and "ego strength." Oddly enough, the best fantasy correlate of an independent rating of "personal maturity" was not a content score, but vocabulary level ($r = .62$).

It appears that cognitive-expressive variables are predictive of aspects of psychopathology, and future research may indicate other behavioral correlates of these fantasy categories.*

---

*The author has unpublished data on adult and adolescent subjects which indicate that the use of adjectives describing affect and feeling states in TAT stories is positively correlated with interview ratings of introspectiveness and the production of Rorschach movement responses.

## Sex and Age Differences in Fantasy

The reported sex differences in apperceptive fantasy pertain to content and indicate that themes of *need* affiliation, *need* succorance and *press* nurturance are more frequent for girls than for boys at all ages.[75,135,161] There is some disagreement as to sex differences in aggressive content: Whitehouse[161] reported more aggressive themes for boys, whereas Kagan[79] and Sanford et al.[135] found no significant sex difference. Doll play data on preschool children consistently reveals more aggressive fantasy for young boys, and it is possible that the nature of the apperceptive stimuli used by Kagan and Sanford et al. (Murray TAT cards which did not show females in potentially aggressive situations) may account for these results. Prepubertal girls tell much longer stories than boys; this may be a function of the superior verbal facility usually ascribed to young girls. Both Cummings[36] and Friedman[49] found, for children 5 to 16, that girls viewed fantasy mother figures as less nurturant and more punishing than the boys; while boys viewed fantasy fathers more negatively than the girls. These data agree with interview data on children[75] and would be predicted from psychoanalytic hypotheses concerning identification and oedipal conflict.

Research on age differences in fantasy is somewhat spotty and usually restricted to cognitive variables. Preschool children (ages 2 to 5) show a general increase with age in the following variables: (a) description of the thoughts and activities of the thematic figures as opposed to a static description of the illustrated objects, (b) an interpretation of the entire scene as opposed to focusing on one detail of the picture and (c) identification with same sex thematic figures.[5] The data from the Michigan Picture Test project[7] on children 8 to 14 years of age produced similar conclusions. There was an increase, with age, in level of interpretation and number of fantasy needs. Thus, lack of cognitive elaboration of the motives and actions of thematic figures may be used as an index of immature psychological functioning.

## Conclusions

### Implications for Research

At present the methods of fantasy analysis differ somewhat, depending on whether the goal is to verify a research hypothesis or to make a clinical prediction. However, certain tentative guides seem relevant for both the laboratory and the clinic.

The hero assumption appears to be a sound, workable hypothesis, and new sets of stimuli should maximize similarity between story-teller and hero with respect to sex, age, role and behavioral repertoire. In addition, analysis of thematic actions should differentiate behaviors on the part of the hero from those directed at the hero.

Second, predictions from specific fantasy motives or defenses to a corresponding overt behavior have fared better than predictions from content categories to gross variables like "adjustment." Let us call this phenomenon "fantasy-behavior congruence." If one accepts the hero assumption and the notion of fantasy-behavior congruence, then an important methodologic task for psychology is the construction of sets of stimuli which vary with respect to both ambiguity and hero-nonhero figures for a variety of motivational areas.* The assessment of aggressive tendencies and conflict would then be based on a large sample of relevant stimuli, rather than on one or two pictures involving one type of aggression and one type of interpersonal relationship. We recognize that aggression can vary with respect to mode of expression and interpersonal situation, and fantasy stimuli should begin to sample some of these relevant dimensions.

### The Clinical Use of Fantasy

It was suggested earlier that apperceptive fantasy is a better index of conflict and preferred mode of defense than it is of motive strength. The clinician may obtain clues related to conflict and defense variables if he evaluates thematic content in relation to the relative ambiguity of the fantasy stimulus. The following paradigm, based on research,[39,140] is offered as a tentative guide to the interpretation of responses elicited by stimuli which are both ambiguous and nonambiguous for specific conflict areas, i.e., motives which are associated with anxiety.

|  |  | Stimuli nonambiguous for the motive | |
|---|---|---|---|
|  |  | Absence of motive in fantasy | Presence of motive in fantasy |
| Stimuli ambiguous for the motive | Presence of motive in fantasy | Conflict—moderate denial | Conflict—counterphobic defense |
|  | Absence of motive in fantasy | Conflict—strong denial | Low conflict—"realistic" |

The paradigm assumes that failure to report a motive to a stimulus which suggests it (nonambiguous stimulus) reflects not only conflict but the tendency to deny and/or inhibit expression of the motive. The denial response is strongest when the child avoids reference to the motive with both ambiguous and nonambiguous stimuli. The strength of the denial response is assumed to be somewhat weaker if the child does not report the motive to the unambiguous scenes but does to the ambiguous pictures. Occurrence of goal-related themes to ambiguous stimuli reflects preoccupation with the goal and potential conflict. However, occurrence or nonoccurrence of the motive in themes reported to nonambiguous stimuli provides additional information regarding the degree of conflict and preferred defense (phobic versus counterphobic) associated with the motive area.

It is urged that psychologists attend more carefully to the external stimulus in evaluating fantasy material and systematically vary "ambiguity" in testing procedures.

### Summary

This chapter has discussed the theoretical bases involved in the interpretation of thematic apperceptive fantasy, described some major in-

---

*Lesser[93] has shown that pictures suggesting aggression between boys can be effectively scaled for degree of ambiguity using Guttman's scaling procedures.

struments and reviewed research bearing on the reliability and validity of fantasy variables. It was stressed that the impact of the stimulus materials has been neglected in the interpretation of projective data and that similar contents told to different types of stimuli may have different meanings and involve different processes. The problem of picture "pull" seems crucial, for specific fantasy needs have different predictive validity depending on the ambiguity of the eliciting stimulus.

The question of reliability and validity of fantasy can only be applied to specific variables coded from specific stimuli and not to the "technique" as a whole. Under these conditions, certain need, press and cognitive-expressive variables show evidence of stability, predictive accuracy and construct validity. Although specific content categories are not predictive of maladjustment or pathology, cognitive measures like "distortion of the stimulus" do show consistent correlations with this behavioral criterion.

It was urged that the psychologist view the fantasy response as a result of interaction of both motive and defense processes and adopt a critical attitude toward the early projective hypothesis that fantasy was measuring "pure" motive strength independent of the subject's defenses and the nature of the stimulus materials. This earlier notion has held up progress in this area to a degree heretofore unsuspected.

## References

1. Albert, R. S.   The role of mass media and the effect of aggressive film content upon children's aggressive responses and identification choices. *Genet. Psychol. Monogr.*, 1957, *55*, 221–285.

2. Alexander, T.   The prediction of teacher-pupil interaction with a projective test. *J. clin. Psychol.*, 1950, *6*, 273–276.

3. ——.   Certain characteristics of the self as related to affection. *Child Develpm.*, 1951, *22*, 285–290.

4. ——.   The adult-child interaction test. *Monogr. Soc. Res. Child Develpm.*, 1952, *17*, No. 2 (Serial No. 55).

5. Amen, E. W.   Individual difference in apperceptive reaction: a study of the response of preschool children to pictures. *Genet. Psychol. Monogr.*, 1941, *23*, 319–385.

6. Andrew, G., Walton, R. E., Hartwell, S. W., & Hutt, M. L.   The Michigan Picture Test: the stimulus values of the cards. *J. consult. Psychol.*, 1951, *15*, 51–54.

7. ——, Hartwell, S. W., Hutt, M. L., & Walton, R. E.   *The Michigan Picture Test.* Chicago: Science Research Associates, 1953.

8. Armstrong, M. A. S.   Children's responses to animal and human figures in thematic pictures. *J. consult. Psychol.*, 1954, *18*, 67–70.

9. Atkinson, J. W. (Ed.).   *Motives in fantasy, action and society.* Princeton, N. J.: D. Van Nostrand, 1958.

10. Ausubel, D. P., Balthazor, E. E., Rosenthal, I., Blackman, L. S., Schpoont, S. H., & Welkowitz, J.   Perceived parent attitudes as determinants of children's ego structure. *Child Develpm.*, 1954, *25*, 173–183.

11. Bachrach, A. J. with the collaboration of Thompson, C. E.   *Experimental set, Thematic Apperception Test, modification for the handicapped, Series A: Child.* 16 cards and manual (6 pp. mimeo). The authors, 1949.

12. Balken, E. R., & Vander Veer, A. H.   The clinical application of a test of imagination to neurotic children. *Amer. J. Orthopsychiat.*, 1942, *12*, 68–80.

13. ——, & ——.   Clinical application of the Thematic Apperception Test to neurotic children. *Amer. J. Orthopsychiat.*, 1944, *14*, 421–440.

14. Baughman, E. E.   The role of the stimulus in Rorschach responses. *Psychol. Bull.*, 1958, *55*, 121–147.

15. Bellak, L.   Thematic apperception: failures and the defenses. *Trans. New York Acad. Sci.*, 1950, *12*, 122–126.

16. ——.   *The Thematic Apperception Test and the Children's Apperception Test in clinical use.* New York: Grune & Stratton, 1954.

17. Biber, B., & Lewis, C.   An experimental study of what young children expect from their teachers. *Genet. Psychol. Monogr.*, 1949, *40*, 3–97.

18. Biersdorf, K. R., & Marcuse, F. L.   Responses of children to human and to animal pictures. *J. proj. Tech.*, 1953, *17*, 455–459.

19. Bijou, S. W., & Kenny, D. T.   The ambiguity values of TAT cards. *J. consult. Psychol.*, 1951, *15*, 203–209.

20. Bills, R. E.   Animal pictures for obtaining children's projections. *J. clin. Psychol.*, 1950, *6*, 291–293.

21. ——, Leiman, C. J., & Thomas, R. W.   A study of the validity of the TAT and a set of animal pictures. *J. clin. Psychol.*, 1950, *6*, 293–295.

22. Boyd, N. A., & Mandler, G.   Children's responses to human and animal stories and pictures. *J. consult. Psychol.*, 1955, *19*, 367–371.

23. Brian, K.   Reactions of delinquent and other groups to experimentally induced frustration. *Brit. J. Delinqu.*, 1954, *4*, 245–264.

24. Brittain, H. L.   A study in imagination. *Pedag. Semin.*, 1907, *14*, 137–207.

25. Brackbill, G. A.   Some effects of color in thematic fantasy. *J. consult. Psychol.*, 1951, *15*, 412–418.

26. Broida, D. C., Izard, C. E., & Cruickshank, W. M.   Thematic apperception reactions of crippled children. *J. clin. Psychol.*, 1950, *6*, 243–248.

27. Buchanan, M. P.   A picture-interpretation personality test. *Brit. J. educ. Psychol.*, 1945, *15*, 151–152.

28. Byrd, E., & Witherspoon, R. L.   Responses of preschool children to Children's Apperception Test. *Child Develpm.*, 1954, *25*, 35–44.

29. Carlile, J. S. H.   The TAT applied to neurotic normal adolescent girls. *Brit. J. med. Psychol.*, 1925, *25*, 244–248.

30. Cava, E. L., & Raush, H. L.   Identification and the adolescent boy's perception of his father. *J. abnorm. soc. Psychol.*, 1952, *47*, 855–856.

31. Child, I. L., Frank, K. F., & Storm, T.   Self ratings and TAT: their relation to each other and to childhood background. *J. Pers.*, 1956, *25*, 96–114.

32. Coleman, W.   The Thematic Apperception Test: I. Effect of recent experience. II. Some quantitative observations. *J. clin. Psychol.*, 1947, *3*, 257–264.

33. Colli, A.   A group of plates to supplement TAT for crippled children. *Arch. Psicol. Neurol. Psichiat. Psicoter.*, 1951, *12*, 463–464.

34. Cox, B., & Sargent, H.   TAT responses of emotionally disturbed and emotionally stable children: clinical judgment versus normative data. *J. proj. Tech.*, 1950, *14*, 61–74.

35. Crandall, V. J.   Induced frustration and punishment reward expectancy in thematic apperception stories. *J. consult. Psychol.*, 1951, *15*, 400–404.

36. Cummings, J. D.   Family pictures: a projection test for children. *Brit. J. Psychol.*, 1952, *43*, 53–60.

37. Davidson, M. A., McInnes, R. G., & Parnell, R. W.   The distribution of personality traits in seven-year-old children: a combined psychological, psychiatric and somatotype study. *Brit. J. educ. Psychol.*, 1957, *27*, 48–61.

38. Despert, J. L., & Potter, H. W.   Technical approaches used in the study and treatment of emotional problems in children. Part I: The story, a form of directed phantasy. *Psychiat. Quart.*, 1936, *10*, 619–638.

39. Dollard, J., & Miller, N. E.   *Personality and psychotherapy.* New York: McGraw-Hill, 1950.

40. Dorkey, M., & Amen, E. W.   A continuation study of anxiety reactions in young children by means of a projective technique. *Genet. Psychol. Monogr.*, 1947, *35*, 139–186.

41. Eiserer, P. E.   The relative effectiveness of motion and still pictures as stimuli for eliciting fantasy stories about adolescent-parent relationships. *Genet. Psychol. Monogr.*, 1949, *39*, 205–278.

42. Epstein, S., & Smith, R.   Thematic apperception as a measure of the hunger drive. *J. proj. Tech.*, 1956, *20*, 372–384.

43. Eron, L. D.   A normative study of the Thematic Apperception Test. *Psychol. Monogr.*, 1950, *64*, No. 9 (Whole No. 315).

44. ——, Terry, D., & Callahan, R.   The use of rating scales for emotional tone of TAT stories. *J. consult. Psychol.*, 1950, *14*, 473–478.

45. Feshbach, S.   The drive reducing function of fantasy behavior. *J. abnorm. soc. Psychol.*, 1955, *50*, 3–11.

46. Finch, H. M.   Young children's concepts of parent roles. *J. Home Econ.*, 1955, *47*, 99–103.

47. Fitzgerald, P. C.   Success-failure and TAT reaction of orthopedically handicapped and physically normal adolescents. *Personality*, 1951, *1*, 67–83.

48. Frenkel-Brunswick, E.   Patterns of social and cognitive outlook in children and parents. *Amer. J. Orthopsychiat.*, 1951, *3*, 543–558.

49. Friedman, S. M.   An empirical study of the castration and oedipus complexes. *Genet. Psychol. Monogr.*, 1952, *46*, 61–130.

50. Furuya, K.   Responses of school children to human and animal pictures. *J. proj. Tech.*, 1957, *21*, 248–252.

51. Getzels, J. W., & Walsh, J. J.   The method of paired direct and projective questionnaires in the study of attitude structure and socialization. *Psychol. Monogr.*, 1958, *72*, No. 1 (Whole No. 454).

52. Gorlow, L., Zimet, C. N., & Fine, H. J.   The validity of anxiety and hostility Rorschach content scores among adolescents. *J. consult. Psychol.*, 1952, *16*, 73–75.

53. Gothberg, L. C.   A comparison of the personality of runaway girls with a control group as expressed in the themas of Murray's Thematic Apperception Test. *Amer. J. ment. Def.*, 1947, *51*, 627–631.

54. Granick, S., & Scheflen, N. A.   Approaches to reliability of projective tests with special reference to the Blacky Pictures Test. *J. consult. Psychol.*, 1958, *22*, 137–141.

55. Greenbaum, M., Qualtere, T., Carruth, B., & Cruickshank, W.   Evaluation of a modification of Thematic Apperception Test for use with physically handicapped children. *J. clin. Psychol.*, 1953, *9*, 40–44.

56. Gurin, M. G.   Differences in the psychological characteristics of latency and adolescence. Unpublished doctor's dissertation. Univer. of Michigan, 1953.

57. Haggard, E. A.   A projective technique using comic strip characters. *Charact. & Pers.*, 1942, *10*, 289–295.

58. Harrison, R., & Rotter, J. B.   A note on the reliability of the Thematic Apperception Test. *J. abnorm. soc. Psychol.*, 1945, *40*, 97–99.

59. Hartley, E. L., & Schwartz, S.   A pictorial-doll play approach for the study of children's intergroup attitudes. *Int. J. Opin. Attitude Res.*, 1951, *6*, 261–270.

60. Hartman, A. A.   An experimental examination of the thematic apperception technique in clinical diagnosis. *Psychol. Monogr.*, 1949, *63*, No. 8 (Whole No. 303).

61. Hartwell, S. W., Hutt, M. L., Andrew, G. & Walton, R. E.   The Michigan Picture Test: diagnostic and therapeutic possibilities of a new projective test in child guidance. *Amer. J. Orthopsychiat.*, 1951, *21*, 124–137.

62. Haworth, M. R.   The use of a filmed puppet show as a group projective technique for children. *Genet. Psychol. Monogr.*, 1957, *56*, 257–296.

63. Henry, W. E.   The Thematic Apperception Technique in the study of culture-personality relations. *Genet. Psychol. Monogr.*, 1947, *35*, 3–135.

64. ——. *The analysis of fantasy*. New York: Wiley, 1956.

65. Heppell, H. K., & Raimy, V. C.   Projective pictures as interview devices. *J. consult. Psychol.*, 1951, *15*, 405–411.

66. Holt, R. R.   The Thematic Apperception Test. *In* Anderson, H. H., & Anderson, G. L. (Eds.)   *An introduction to projective techniques.* New York: Prentice-Hall, 1951. Pp. 181–229.

67. Horowitz, R. E.   A pictorial method for study of self identification in pre-school children. *J. genet. Psychol.*, 1943, *62*, 135–149.

68. Hurley, J. R.   The Iowa Picture Interpretation Test: a multiple choice variation of the TAT. *J. consult. Psychol.*, 1955, *5*, 372–376.

69. Jackson, L.   A study of sado-masochistic attitudes in a group of delinquent girls by means of a specially designed projective test. *Brit. J. med. Psychol.*, 1949, *22*, 53–65.

70. ———.   Emotional attitudes towards the family of normal, neurotic and delinquent children. Part I. *Brit. J. Psychol.*, 1950, *41*, 35–51.

71. ———.   Emotional attitudes towards the family of normal, neurotic and delinquent children. Part II. *Brit. J. Psychol.*, 1950, *41*, 173–185.

72. Johnson, G. B.   An experimental projective technique for the analysis of racial attitudes. *J. educ. Psychol.*, 1950, *4*, 257–278.

73. Johnson, O. G., & Stanley, J. C.   Attitudes toward authority of delinquent and non-delinquent boys. *J. abnorm. soc. Psychol.*, 1955, *51*, 712–716.

74. Johnston, R. A.   A methodological analysis of several revised forms of the Iowa Picture Interpretation Test. *J. Pers.*, 1957, *25*, 283–293.

75. Kagan, J.   The child's perception of the parent. *J. abnorm. soc. Psychol.*, 1956, *53*, 257–258.

76. ———.   The measurement of overt aggression from fantasy. *J. abnorm. soc. Psychol.*, 1956, *52*, 390–393.

77. ———.   Psychological study of a school phobia in one of a pair of identical twins. *J. proj. Tech.*, 1956, *20*, 78–87.

78. ———.   Socialization of aggression and the perception of parents in fantasy. *Child Develpm.*, 1958, *29*, 311–320.

79. ———.   The stability of TAT fantasy and stimulus ambiguity. *J. consult. Psychol.* 1959, *23*, 266–271.

80. ———, & Moss, H. A.   The stability and validity of achievement fantasy. *J. abnorm. soc. Psychol.* 1959, *58*, 357–364.

81. ———, & Mussen, P. H.   Dependency themes on the TAT and group conformity. *J. consult. Psychol.*, 1956, *32*, 20–29.

82. ———, Sontag, L. W., Baker, C. T., & Nelson, V. L.   Personality and IQ change. *J. abnorm. soc. Psychol.*, 1958, *56*, 261–266.

83. Kates, S. L.   Suggestibility, submission to parents and peers, and extrapunitiveness, intropunitiveness and impunitiveness in children. *J. Psychol.*, 1951, *31*, 233–241.

84. Kenny, D. T., & Bijou, S. W.   Ambiguity of pictures and extent of personality factors in fantasy responses. *J. consult. Psychol.*, 1953, *17*, 283–288.

85. Kluckhohn, C., & Rosenzweig, J. C.   Two Navaho children over a five year period. *Amer. J. Orthopsychiat.*, 1949, *19*, 266–278.

86. Koppitz, E. M.   Relationships between some background factors and children's interpersonal attitudes. *J. genet. Psychol.*, 1957, *91*, 119–129.

87. Krumholtz, J. D., & Farquhar, W. W.   Reliability and validity on the n-Achievement test. *J. consult. Psychol.*, 1957, *21*, 226–229.

88. Lazarus, R. S., Baker, R. W., Broverman, D. M., & Mayer, J.   Personality and psychological stress. *J. Pers.*, 1957, *25*, 559–577.

89. Lebo, D., & Harrigan, M.   Visual and verbal presentation of TAT stimuli. *J. consult. Psychol.*, 1957, *21*, 339–342.

90. Leitch, M., & Schafer, S.   A study of the Thematic Apperception Tests of psychotic children. *Amer. J. Orthopsychiat.*, 1947, *17*, 337–342.

91. Lesser, G. S.   Maternal attitudes and practices and the aggressive behavior of children. Unpublished doctor's dissertation, Yale Univer., 1952.

92. ———.   The relationship between overt and fantasy aggression as a function of maternal response to aggression. *J. abnorm. soc. Psychol.*, 1957, *55*, 218–221.

93. ——. Application of Guttman's scaling method to aggressive fantasy in children. *Educ. psychol. Measmt.*, 1958, *18*, 543–552.

94. ——. Conflict analysis of fantasy aggression. *J. Pers.*, 1958, *26*, 29–41.

95. Liccione, J. V.   The changing family relationships of adolescent girls. *J. abnorm. soc. Psychol.*, 1955, *51*, 421–426.

96. Light, B. H.   Comparative study of a series of TAT and CAT cards. *J. clin. Psychol.*, 1954, *10*, 179–181.

97. Lindzey, G.   An experimental examination of the scapegoat theory of prejudice. *J. abnorm. soc. Psychol.*, 1950, *45*, 296–304.

98. ——. Thematic Apperception Test: interpretive assumptions and related empirical evidence. *Psychol. Bull.*, 1952, *49*, 1–25.

99. ——. Thematic Apperception Test: the strategy of research. *J. proj. Tech.*, 1958, *22*, 173–180.

100. ——, & Goldberg, M.   Motivational differences between male and female as measured by the Thematic Apperception Test. *J. Pers.*, 1953, *22*, 101–117.

101. ——, & Heinemann, S. H.   Thematic Apperception Test: individual and group administration. *J. Pers.*, 1955, *24*, 34–55.

102. ——, & Herman, P. S.   Thematic Apperception Test: a note on reliability and situational validity. *J. proj. Tech.*, 1955, *18*, 36–42.

103. ——, & Kalnins, D.   Thematic Apperception Test: some evidence bearing on the "hero assumption." *J. abnorm. soc. Psychol.*, 1958, *57*, 76–83.

104. ——, & Newburg, A. S.   Thematic Apperception Test: a tentative appraisal of some signs of anxiety. *J. consult. Psychol.*, 1954, *19*, 389–395.

105. ——, Tejessy, C., & Zamansky, H. S.   Thematic Apperception Test: an empirical examination of some indices of homosexuality. *J. abnorm. soc. Psychol.*, 1958, *57*, 67–75.

106. Lubins, N. M.   The effect of color in the TAT on productions of mentally retarded subjects. *Amer. J. ment. Def.*, 1955, *60*, 366–370.

107. Mainord, F. R., & Marcuse, F. L.   Responses of disturbed children to human and to animal pictures. *J. proj. Tech.*, 1954, *18*, 475–477.

108. Malpass, L. F.   Some relationships between students' perceptions of school and their achievement. *J. educ. Psychol.*, 1953, *44*, 475–482.

109. Mamiya, T.   Problem of the critical period of psychosexual development. *Jap. J. educ. Psychol.*, 1956, *4*, 21–27.

110. Mayman, M., & Kutner, B.   Reliability in analyzing Thematic Apperception Test stories. *J. abnorm. soc. Psychol.*, 1947, *42*, 365–368.

111. McClelland, D. C., Clark, R. A., Roby, T. B., & Atkinson, J. W.   The effect of the need for achievement on thematic apperception. *J. exp. Psychol.*, 1949, *37*, 242–255.

112. Meltzoff, J.   The effect of mental set and item structure upon response to a projective test. *J. abnorm. soc. Psychol.*, 1951, *46*, 177–189.

113. Milstein, A. F., & Witt, G.   Ambition and fear of failure. (Unpublished Manuscript).

114. Morgan, C. D., & Murray, H. A.   A method of investigating fantasies: the Thematic Apperception Test. *Arch. Neurol. & Psychiat.*, 1935, *34*, 289–306.

115. Morgan, H. H.   Measuring achievement motivation with picture interpretations. *J. consult Psychol.*, 1953, *17*, 289–292.

116. Morgan, P. K., & Gaier, E. L.   The direction of aggression in the mother-child punishment situation. *Child Develpm.*, 1956, *27*, 447–457.

117. ——, & Gaier, E. L.   Types of reactions in punishment situations in the mother-child relationship. *Child Develpm.*, 1957, *28*, 161–166.

118. Murray, E. J.   Thematic apperception during sleep deprivation. Paper read at meeting of Eastern Psychol. Ass., Philadelphia, 1958.

119. Murray, H. A.   *Explorations in personality.* New York: Oxford Univer. Press, 1938.

120. ——. *Thematic Apperception Test.* Cambridge: Harvard Univer. Press, 1943.

121. Murstein, B. I.   Non-projective determinants of perception on the TAT. *J. consult. Psychol.*, 1958, *22*, 195–198.

122. ——. The relationship of stimulus ambiguity on the TAT to productivity of themes. *J. consult. Psychol.*, 1958, *22*, 348.

123. Mussen, P. H. Some personality and social factors related to changes in children's attitudes toward Negroes. *J. abnorm. soc. Psychol.*, 1950, *45*, 423–441.

124. ——. Differences between the TAT responses of Negro and white boys. *J. consult. Psychol.*, 1953, *17*, 373–376.

125. ——, & Jones, M. C. Self-conceptions, motivations and interpersonal attitudes of late- and early-maturing boys. *Child Develpm.*, 1957, *28*, 243–256.

126. ——, & Kagan, J. Group conformity and perceptions of parents. *Child Develpm.*, 1958, *29*, 57–60.

127. ——, & Naylor, H. K. The relationship between overt and fantasy aggression. *J. abnorm. soc. Psychol.*, 1954, *49*, 235–240.

128. Palmer, J. O. A note on the intercard reliability of the TAT. *J. consult. Psychol.*, 1952, *16*, 473–474.

129. Pittluck, P. The relation between aggressive fantasy and overt behavior. Unpublished doctor's dissertation. Yale Univer., 1950.

130. Purcell, K. The TAT and antisocial behavior. *J. consult. Psychol.*, 1956, *20*, 449–456.

131. Rautman, A. L., & Brower, E. War themes in children's stories. *J. Psychol.*, 1945, *19*, 191–202.

132. ——, & ——. War themes in children's stories. II. Six years later. *J. Psychol.*, 1951, *31*, 263–270.

133. Riess, B. F., Schwartz, E. K., & Cottingham, A. An experimental critique of assumptions underlying the Negro version of the TAT. *J. abnorm. soc. Psychol.*, 1950, *45*, 700–709.

134. Sanford, F. H. Speech and personality: a comparative case study. *Charact. & Pers.*, 1942, *10*, 169–198.

135. Sanford, R. N., Adkins, M. M., Miller, R. B., & Cobb, E. A., et al. Physique, personality and scholarship: a cooperative study of school children. *Monogr. Soc. Res. Child Develpm.*, 1943, *8*, No. 1 (Serial No. 34).

136. Sarason, S. B. The use of the Thematic Apperception Test with mentally deficient children: a study of high grade girls. *Amer. J. ment. Def.*, 1943, *47*, 414–421.

137. ——. *The clinical interaction.* New York: Harper, 1954.

138. Schafer, S., & Leitch, M. An exploratory study of the usefulness of a battery of psychological tests with nursery school children. *Amer. J. Psychiat.*, 1948, *104*, 647–652.

139. Schoeppe, A., Haggard, E. A., & Havighurst, R. J. Some factors affecting sixteen-year-olds' success in five developmental tasks. *J. abnorm. soc. Psychol.*, 1953, *48*, 42–52.

140. Scott, W. A. The avoidance of threatening material in imaginative behavior. *J. abnorm. soc. Psychol.*, 1956, *52*, 338–346.

141. Shapiro, D. S. Perceptions of significant family and environmental relationships in aggressive and withdrawn children. *J. consult. Psychol.*, 1957, *21*, 381–385.

142. Siegel, A. E. The influence of violence in the mass media upon children's role expectations. *Child Develpm.*, 1958, *29*, 35–56.

143. Sigel, I. E., & Hoffman, M. L. The predictive potential of projective tests for non-clinical populations. *J. proj. Tech.*, 1956, *20*, 261–264.

144. Sontag, L. W., Crandall, V., & Lacey, J. I. Dynamics of personality: resolution of infantile dependent need. *Amer. J. Orthopsychiat.*, 1952, *22*, 534–541.

145. Symonds, P. M. Criteria for the selection of pictures for the investigation of adolescent phantasies. *J. abnorm. soc. Psychol.*, 1939, *34*, 271–274.

146. ——. Adolescent phantasy. *Psychol. Bull.*, 1941, *38*, 590–597.

147. ——. Inventory of themes in adolescent fantasy. *Amer. J. Orthopsychiat.*, 1945, *15*, 318–328.

148. ——. *Picture-Story Test:* Manual and set of 20 pictures. New York: Bureau of Publications, Columbia Univer. Press, 1948.

149. ——. *Adolescent fantasy.* New York: Columbia Univer. Press, 1949.

150. Symonds, R. F., Hughes, A. A., & Raabe, V. L. Measurable changes in empathy with age. *J. consult. Psychol.*, 1952, *16*, 202–206.

151. Temple, R., & Amen, E. W.   A study of anxiety reactions in young children by means of a projective technique. *Genet. Psychol. Monogr.*, 1944, *30*, 60–113.

152. Thompson, C. E.   The Thompson modification of the Thematic Apperception Test. *Rorschach Res. Exch.*, 1949, *13*, 469–478.

153. Tomkins, S. S.   The present status of the Thematic Apperception Test. *Amer. J. Orthopsychiat.*, 1949, *19*, 358–362.

154. Veroff, J., Wilcox, S., & Atkinson, J. W.   The achievement motive in high school and college age women. *J. abnorm. soc. Psychol.*, 1953, *48*, 108–119.

155. Walton, R. E., Andrew, G., Hartwell, S. W., & Hutt, M. L.   A tension index of adjustment based on picture stories elicited by the Michigan Picture Test. *J. abnorm. soc. Psychol.*, 1951, *46*, 438–441.

156. Weisskopf, E. A., & Dunlevy, G. P.   Bodily similarity between subject and central figure in the TAT as an influence on projection. *J. abnorm. soc. Psychol.*, 1952, *47*, 441–445.

157. Weisskopf-Joelson, E. A., & Lynn, D. B.   The effect of variations in ambiguity on projection in the Children's Apperception Test. *J. consult. Psychol.*, 1953, *17*, 67–70.

158. ——, & Morey, L.   Facial similarity between subject and central figure in the TAT as an influence on projection. *J. abnorm. soc. Psychol.*, 1953, *48*, 341–344.

159. Wells, H.   Differences between delinquent and nondelinquent boys as indicated by the Thematic Apperception Test. *Psychol. Bull.*, 1945, *42*, 534 (Abstract).

160. Wenar, C.   The effects of a motor handicap on personality: III. The effects on certain fantasies and adjustive techniques. *Child Develpm.*, 1956, *27*, 9–15.

161. Whitehouse, E.   Norms for certain aspects of the Thematic Apperception Test on a group of nine- and ten-year-old children. *Personality*, 1949, *1*, 12–15.

162. Winterbottom, M. B.   The relation of need for achievement to learning experiences in independence and mastery. Unpublished doctor's dissertation. Univer. of Michigan, 1953.

163. Wittenborn, J. R., & Eron, L. D.   An application of drive theory to TAT responses. *J. consult. Psychol.*, 1951, *15*, 45–50.

164. Wyatt, F.   The interpretation of the Thematic Apperception Test. *Rorschach Res. Exch.*, 1947, *11*, 21–25.

165. ——.   The scoring and analysis of the Thematic Apperception Test. *J. Psychol.*, 1947, *24*, 319–330.

166. Zucker, H. J.   Affectional identification and delinquency. *Arch. Psychol.*, 1943, *40*, No. 5 (Serial No. 286).

167. Zuckerman, M.   The effect of threat on perceptual affect in a group. *J. abnorm. soc. Psychol.*, 1951, *46*, 529–533.

# 7

## The MAPS Test with Children

EDWIN S. SHNEIDMAN

IT WOULD BE a happy circumstance if one could claim that any psychological diagnostic device (or any psychodiagnostician) were omnipotent, but unfortunately one has to content oneself with somewhat fallible techniques (and clinicians) of less than perfect validity. Thus the purposes of this chapter are simply (a) to present the reader with a description of the Make-A-Picture Story (MAPS) test materials and modes of administration, and (b) to relay our fairly firm impression (based on our experience, articles in the technical literature and informal communications from others) that this instrument seems to have special usefulness with children—eliciting what seem to be, in some cases, good rapport and very interesting (and seemingly rich) protocols.

The MAPS Test is essentially a variation of the TAT principle in which the backgrounds and the figures are separated, so that the subject is faced with the task of selecting one or more cut-out human-like figures from among many such figures, populating a background picture, and then (as he would in the TAT) telling his story. In a sense, therefore, the subject must respond to a stimulus situation which he has in part himself created, using a *dramatis personae* of his own choosing. The possibilities for vicarious psychodrama, in addition to the usual diagnostic uses of picture thematic materials, immediately present themselves to mind.[4,19]

### Materials

The complete MAPS method materials may be divided into two parts: the primary materials (the figures and the backgrounds) and the supplementary materials (the Figure Location Sheet, the Figure Identification Card, and the Theater Carrying Case). The materials may be described as follows:

#### Backgrounds

There are 22 background pictures, 8½ by 11 inches, printed achromatically on thin cardboard. With two exceptions, there are no figures in any of the pictures. (There is an ambiguous human head in the bottom left corner of the *Dream* background and a human-like lump in the bed of the *Bedroom* background.) The set includes unstructured or ambiguous backgrounds such as the *Blank* card, the abstract *Doorway* and the *Dream* background; semi-structured backgrounds such as the *Stage*, the *Forest*, the *Cave* and the

*Landscape;* and definitely structured backgrounds such as the *Living room, Street, Medical, Bathroom, Bridge, Bedroom, Closet, Schoolroom, Shanty, Camp, Raft, Cemetery, Attic,* etc. An attempt was made on an a priori basis to include background pictures which would allow for the possibility of eliciting information on most of the important specific problem areas and specific problem dynamics encountered in clinical practice. Some empirical data on the "card pull" of the various MAPS test background pictures are presented elsewhere.[17]

### Figures

A distinguishing feature of the MAPS method is that it offers the subject the opportunity to *select* the figures, as well as verbally to enliven and interpret them. There are 67 figures. A six foot human figure is 5½ inches tall, and all others are scaled proportionately. With few exceptions, the figures are shown as standing. Any figure can be placed on any background without violating realistic proportions. The figures are depicted with various facial expressions, and in various poses; some are partially clothed or nude. The type of figures, their identification letters, and the number of figures within each type are as follows: children (C), 12; male adult (M), 19; female adult (F), 11; minority group figures such as Negroes, Jews, Orientals (N), 10; animal figures (A), 2; figures of indeterminate sex (I), 2; legendary and fictitious characters (L), 6; and silhouettes and figures with blank faces (S), 5.

### Figure Location Sheet

This is a form on which there are lightly printed, reduced reproductions of all the background pictures. This form enables the examiner to record the subject's *choice* and *placement* of the test figures for later recapitulation of the subject's performance. The manner of recording is described in the section on administration, below. Reproduction of part of the *Figure Location Sheet* is presented in figure 1.

### Figure Identification Card

This card serves to group the figures and to identify each one by a code symbol so that the examiner may label them properly on the *Figure Location Sheet* as they are used by the subject. The figures are numbered consecutively within each letter category: thus "F-4" is the fourth female figure, "A-2" the second animal figure, and so on. No identifying marks appear on the figures themselves, as it is felt that such marks might have varying meanings to different subjects and thus be undesirable. In addition, marks on the figures are unnecessary if the suggestions indicated in the section on administering the test are followed. The *Figure Identification Card* has a verbal description of each test figure on one side and a miniature picture of each figure on the other side.

### Theater Carrying Case

This part of the materials ordinarily is used when the MAPS method is employed as part of a psychodramatic or psychotherapeutic procedure. It consists of a miniature wooden theater, which also can serve as a carrying

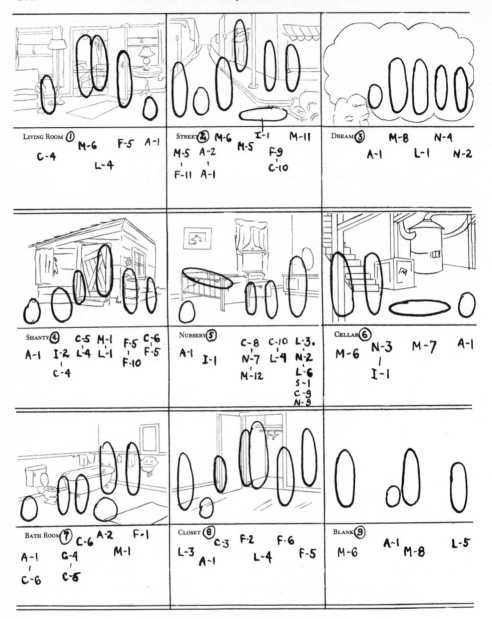

Fig. 1.—MAPS *Figure Location Sheet.*

case for the test materials. Its use makes it possible for the test figures to be placed erect on the "stage" on little bases at varying distances in front of the vertical background picture. The theater is not ordinarily employed in the psychodiagnostic use of the test materials.

## Administration

The following directions for administering the MAPS method refer specifically to the *diagnostic* use of the materials and do not relate to therapeutic or other uses of the materials. The test has been found applicable to subjects as young as three and one-half years of age,[20] although six years of age is the general baseline.

## MAPS Test—Directions for Administering

A. The S is seated in front of the desk. The E is seated to his side. At the beginning of the test administration, the test materials are on another chair near the E.

B. The E places the *Living room* background picture directly in front of the S (so that the bottom of the picture is along the edge of the table) and says: WHAT I AM GOING TO DO IS SHOW YOU PICTURES LIKE THIS, ONE AT A TIME.

C. The E pours or gently tosses all the figures on top of the background picture and says: YOU WILL HAVE FIGURES LIKE THIS AND YOUR JOB IS SIMPLY TO TAKE ONE OR MORE OF ANY OF THESE FIGURES AND PUT THEM ON THE BACKGROUND PICTURE AS THEY MIGHT BE IN REAL LIFE. YOU MIGHT START BY PUTTING THE FIGURES OUT ON THE TABLE SO THAT YOU SEE EACH ONE.

D. The E takes two or three figures and lays them on the table top so that the feet of the figures are toward the S. He then encourages the S to arrange the remainder of the figures: YOU PUT THE REST OUT. The E notes any peculiarities or evidences for "systems" in the S's arrangement of the figures on the table top.

E. After the S has put all the figures on the table top the E says: NOW I WOULD LIKE TO GO OVER THE INSTRUCTIONS IN A LITTLE MORE DETAIL. AS I SAID BEFORE, ALL YOU HAVE TO DO IS TAKE ONE OR MORE OF ANY OF THESE FIGURES, PUT THEM ON THE BACKGROUND AS THEY MIGHT BE IN REAL LIFE, AND TELL A STORY ABOUT THE SITUATION YOU HAVE MADE. IN TELLING YOUR STORY, TELL ME WHO THE CHARACTERS ARE, WHAT THEY ARE DOING AND THINKING AND FEELING, AND HOW THE WHOLE THING TURNS OUT. ALL RIGHT. GO AHEAD.

F. The E records the S's story verbatim. After the S has finished his story, the E records the S's choice and placement of test figures onto the *Figure Location Sheet*. The E then says: THAT WAS GOOD. YOU TOOK ONE OR MORE OF THE FIGURES AND PUT THEM ON THE BACKGROUND AND TOLD A STORY. IN YOUR OTHER STORIES WITH OTHER BACKGROUNDS YOU MAY USE EITHER THE SAME OR DIFFERENT FIGURES. ALL RIGHT. PUT THE FIGURES BACK—ANYWHERE ON THE TABLE. The E then takes the *Living room* picture from the table top and puts it with the other test materials.

G. The E selects the second background picture (usually the *Street*) and puts it in front of the S and says: TRY THIS ONE. The E records the S's stories, and, after each story for each new background is completed, the E records the *Figure Location Sheet* for that background. The E introduces each new background picture with the phrase: TRY THIS ONE.

H. For the *Blank* background (usually given after several other backgrounds have been given) the E says: THIS ONE IS A LITTLE DIFFERENT FROM THE OTHERS. IN ADDITION TO SELECTING THE FIGURES AND TELLING THE STORY, IN THIS CASE YOU ALSO MAKE UP WHAT THE BACKGROUND MIGHT BE. IT CAN BE ANYTHING. TELL ME, SOMETIME DURING YOUR STORY, WHAT BACKGROUND YOU HAVE IMAGINED. ALL RIGHT, GO AHEAD.

## Role of the MAPS in a Test Battery

The MAPS method will usually be administered as part of a group of psychological tests. It may be given as the only picture-thematic test in the battery, or, better, combined with other tests of similar type. Murray[16] has stated, "I am prompted to suggest that if the testing period must be limited . . ., a compound TAT-MAPS test might be most efficient." When the administration of the MAPS test is combined with the Thematic Apperception Test, the recommended procedure is to give a halfdozen or so TAT pictures first and then introduce the first (*Living room*) MAPS background as part of the same test, simply by saying to the subject: "Now in this next one, the figures are separate. Your task is simply to take one or more of any of these figures . . ." and so on. The advantages of using picture-thematic tests of different degrees of "structure"[12] and which demand different types of responses (prior to the telling of the story) should be obvious. Oftentimes, the differences in the quality of one subject's responses to the TAT and MAPS are extremely revealing.

When the MAPS method is administered as the sole picture-thematic test, 10 background pictures are ordinarily recommended. A suggested battery for adolescent subjects, normal or abnormal, is made up of the following cards in this order: *Living room, Street, Medical, Bathroom, Dream, Bridge, Bedroom, Blank,* and the ninth and tenth background pictures chosen by the subject himself from among the remaining pictures. ("Why don't you look through these pictures and select the one or two that you would like to do?") Regardless of the number of pictures used by the examiner, it appears to be a good procedure to use a few of the unstructured pictures such as the *Dream* or *Blank.* Where the TAT and MAPS test are combined, either TAT Card no. 16 or the MAPS Test *Blank* should be given in each record. It seems best not to introduce the unstructured backgrounds too early in the record nor to place them too close to one another. An abbreviated battery might consist of the *Living room, Street, Dream, Bathroom,* and one or two others. The examiner should feel free to make his own selections of background pictures in light of his own expectations regarding the significance of each picture, in light of problems which have prompted the testing session, and in light of the aspects of the subject which are revealed as the testing session progresses.

The stories tend to run between three and five minutes for each background picture. If they run over 10 minutes, the examiner may indicate to the subject that the stories can be shortened. The time for administration should not ordinarily be allowed to run much over one hour.

### The Inquiry

Inquiry on the MAPS stories may be done by the examiner in whatever fashion he does inquiry for TAT stories. It has been the author's practice, however, not to do an inquiry on the MAPS test stories. The rationale for this is simply that one is interested in the *subject's* responses and that questions asked by the examiner tend to introduce the examiner's personality and to influence, in unknown ways, the subject's subsequent performance. (The situation is dissimilar from that which occurs in the Rorschach test, in which information adequate for scoring location, determinant and content is obtained after the entire performance proper.) There are, however, two questions which might well be asked by the MAPS test examiner. The *first* is a general, nondirectional prompting question simply for more production, such as "Can you tell me more?," although one should recognize that paucity of production *is* an interpretable aspect of the subject's performance. The *second* question—one which is asked after each story—is for the title of the story. This question may be phrased as "What might you call this story?" or "If you were to give it a title, what would it be?" The titles given by the subject often give the clinician clues to the dynamic interpretation of the stories.

## Recording

The examiner's recording tasks are twofold: (a) to obtain an account of the story and other verbal interchange, and (b) to complete the *Figure Location Sheet*.

The account of the story should be verbatim and should include all verbal material, such as comments, mutterings, asides, questions, etc. Subjects who speak too rapidly for the examiner's writing speed should simply be asked to slow down or to stop for a moment.

The purpose of the *Figure Location Sheet* is to enable the examiner to record the subject's choice and placement of test figures on each background so that the subject's performance may be recapitulated at any time. This recording is done by drawing an ellipse to represent each test figure in the *corresponding* place on the reproduction of the background picture and by labeling it with the correct code symbol for the figure. Effort should be made to indicate both the exact placement of the figure and its exact proportions within the background. One good way to do this is to note especially the position of the top of the head and of the bottom of the feet of a figure on the test background and to reproduce these accurately on the *Figure Location Sheet*. Figure 1 illustrates the manner in which the *Figure Location Sheet* is completed by the examiner.

Two specific recommendations for procedure may be made which will greatly expedite the entire administration of the MAPS test. First, the *Figure Location Sheet* should be completed by the examiner for each test background *after* the subject has completed his story for that background. That is, the examiner should not worry about recording the rejections of figures, movements of figures, substitutions of figures, etc., which occur during the telling of a story. While the subject is telling the story he should attend solely to the recording of the story. After the story is finished, he should then take the *Figure Location Sheet* and draw the ellipses for choice and placement of figures and identify the figures. (If the subject starts to take the figures off the background picture and put them back on the table-top before the examiner has filled in the *Figure Location Sheet* for that background, the examiner can simply ask him to hold off for a moment.) This means, in effect, that the examiner takes a "snapshot" of the "tableau" of test figures for each test background as they were at the end of the subject's story. The second suggestion is that the examiner not be concerned with ascribing the *Figure Identification Card* code for each figure (such as F-6, C-3, L-4) during the administration of the test. During the test itself, the examiner should not look at the *Figure Identification Card*, simply because this slows up the test administration. The suggested technique is for the examiner to be sufficiently acquainted with the test figures so that he can, at the moment he draws the ellipse for a figure on the *Figure Location Sheet*, write down a word or two which will enable him to identify the figure from the Identification Card after the test is over (and the subject has gone). For example, for Figure F-6, he might write "female, apron"; for C-3, "girl, ribbon"; for L-4, "ghost" —or any other words which will allow him later to identify the figure and enter the code identification of the figures on the *Figure Location Sheet*.

## Review of the Literature

The review of the literature will be divided among three types of references: the basic manuals or tests for the MAPS Test in general; the references which have to do specifically with children (including adolescents); and other relevant references to the use of the MAPS Test.

There are three basic references to the MAPS Test. They are: (a) The monograph entitled *The Manual for the MAPS Method*[17] which presents the procedures for administering and recording (summarized in this chapter), some assumptions and suggestive procedures in the use of the MAPS Test, a detailed sample interpretation, and some clues in relation to the diagnosis of 12 different kinds of subjects (including normal males, paranoid schizophrenics, obsessive neurotics, etc.). (b) The second basic reference to the test is the text *Thematic Test Analysis.*[16] This text presents MAPS Test (and TAT) protocols for one 25 year old male subject and different "blind" detailed interpretations and analyses by 16 different thematic test experts. This reference is especially recommended for those who wish to see the breadth and scope of possible thematic interpretations and who wish, as it were, to "look over the shoulder" of the expert as he goes through his various cerebrations in arriving at his interpretations. (c) The third reference is the monograph entitled *Schizophrenia and the MAPS Test,*[14] which not only presents some MAPS Test differences between schizophrenic and normal adults but primarily demonstrates the procedure of deriving objective signs (almost entirely from the *Figure Location Sheet*) by which research and study with the MAPS Test can be done.

Specifically in relation to children, there are six studies with the MAPS Test which are available. Arranged chronologically, by age of the subjects, these studies are: (a) Spiegelman's study[20] with 64 outpatient clinic children ranging in age from three and one-half to 16, with a mean chronological age of 10; (b) Fine's study[7] of 30 asthmatic and nonasthmatic children ranging in age from 6 to 14, with a mean age of 10; (c) Hess' dissertation[10] on 48 adjusted, 48 maladjusted and 28 deaf children, 8 through 10 years of age, using a nonverbal administration of the test; (d) Fraimow's research[8] with 24 mentally retarded children and children of normal intelligence ranging in age from 9 to 22 years with a mean age of around 15; (e) Joel's study[11] of 50 emotionally disturbed children ranging in age from 11 to 18, with a mean age of 15 (of the total, 34 of the children were inpatients in a children's unit of a State Mental Hospital and 16 were in the outpatient clinic of the same hospital); (f) Bindon's paper[1] reporting her study of 36 children deaf after rubella, 15 children deaf from other causes and 30 children of normal hearing, all 15 years of age.

Other relevant literature, having to do with the use of the MAPS Test with adults,[2,3,5,6,9,13,21] is listed in the bibliography.

## Methods of Interpretation

As to interpretation of the MAPS Test, some general notions may be stated. It is believed that degree of competency in the interpretation of any projective technique depends on the interpreter's skills, understanding and experience in the following three areas: (a) his understanding of a comprehensive theory of personality to the extent that he understands the implications of the theory and can extrapolate from all kinds of language and logic and fantasy to their theoretical implications; (b) experience with normality and with a variety of psychopathologic types including various kinds of psychoses, character disorders, neurotics and individuals of various age and intelligence levels; (c) knowledge of the details of the test stimulus—the usual expectations as to what is elicited from various types of subjects by various aspects of test stimuli.

In general, one interprets a MAPS test protocol in the same ways as he would interpret a TAT protocol. There are, as is well known, over 30-odd different published ways of interpreting the TAT. Seventeen of these ways are presented systematically (built around the interpretation of a single case) in *Thematic Test Analysis*.[16] Although it is not the intention of this chapter to recapitulate these various methods in detail, it can be indicated that all these different methods can be subsumed under the following five general headings or approaches.

## General Approaches

### Normative Approach

The normative techniques are those which aim at quantifying thematic test interpretation. They are typically tabular and statistical in nature. The basic operation is that of comparing the tabulations derived from the test stories of the subject under study with the normative data for similar (or different) groups of subjects. The general purpose of such techniques is more often personality research than psychodiagnostic service. (Psychologists identified with this approach are Eron, Hartman, Klebanoff, et al.)

### Hero-Oriented Approach

Historically, this is the most important method, one which concentrates on the chief protagonists in the stories. It is a hero-oriented, need-press, or story-character analysis method. This type of approach emphasizes the story hero—his needs and pressures upon him, his defenses, his feelings, his interactions, his characteristics, his affects, his ego activities and his relations to other story characters. (Individuals identified with this approach are Murray, N. Sanford, Aron, Fine, Korchin, Sargent et al.)

### Intuitive Approach

The intuitive approach, based on psychoanalytic theory, is the most unstructured of the approaches. It uses the insightful empathy of the interpreter; it is often a kind of free association of the clinician's unconscious against the backdrop of the test protocol. It is the approach used most often in the clinical setting. (Clinicians identified with this approach are Bellak, Holt, Lasaga, Rotter, Symonds, et al.)

### Interpersonal Approach

In this approach, the interpersonal situations of the characters or the interpersonal feelings (such as hostility or warmth), or the subject's "social perception" of his story characters are analyzed. The interpersonal approach is a kind of psychodramatic variation, in which the interactions of the characters of the thematic drama hold the center of the stage, so to speak, for the clinician. (Individuals identified with this approach are Arnold, Joel, Ralph K. White et al.)

*Formal Approach*

This approach has to do with the formal aspects of the subject's production, such as perceptual distortions of the visual stimulus of the test materials, his idiosyncratic use of language, his peculiarities of thought or logic, or his loose or queer twists within the story. (Psychologists identified with this approach are Rapaport, Schafer, Holt, F. Sanford, et al.)

In brief, the present author believes that the best "method" is a *combination* of all these approaches.

## Report Areas

In addition to the types of approaches, one may focus on the psychological "areas" within each story, giving a different slant and a different organization of the same raw data. Nineteen report areas evolved from another study with the TAT and the MAPS Test and are reported in some detail elsewhere.[16] Practically all the statements that might be made in a psychological test report from the test protocol (eliminating the subject's behavior and manner during the testing session) can be thought of in terms of one of these 19 areas. These areas are not intended to represent areas of personality functioning nor are they subtopics in an integrated theory of personality; they are simply areas under which test report items can be classified.

Following is a list of the 19 report areas for psychological picture-thematic test analysis: (1) pressures; forces; press; (2) motivations; goals; drives; (3) outlooks; attitudes; beliefs; (4) frustrations; conflicts; fears; (5) affects; feelings; emotions— (a) general, other than hostile, and (b) hostile feelings; (6) sexual thought and behavior; (7) psychosexual level and development; (8) superego; values; ego ideal; (9) self control; ego strength; ego capacity; (10) self concept; insight into self; (11) personality defenses and personality mechanisms; (12) reality contact; orientation; (13) interpersonal relations and object relations; (14) quality of perception, fantasy, language, style and thought; (15) intellect; abilities; intellectual attainments; information; (16) symptoms; diagnoses; (17) etiology; (18) prognoses; predictions; treatment; (19) postdictions—(a) factual biographical data, and (b) psychological biographical data.

### The Figure Location Sheet

We have indicated that, by and large, one would interpret a MAPS test protocol in essentially the same way in which he would approach a TAT protocol—however that would be. A unique feature of the MAPS test, however, lies in the fact that the subject selects and places his own figures; this special characteristic is reflected in the *Figure Location Sheet*. The *FLS* (on which are printed miniature reproductions of the background pictures and on which the examiner draws in ellipses reproducing the placement of the test figures chosen by the subject) is essentially similar to a kind of photograph of the tableau of characters created by the subject (fig. 1). The interpreter's looking at a completed *FLS* is in some ways similar to the professional critic's looking at "still pictures" of the casts of characters of several plays by the same author (and attempting to "divine" the *playwright's* personality from his productions). It is assumed, as Thomas Carlyle said: "In every man's writings the character of the writer must lie recorded." The *FLS* gives the *dramatis personae* of the psychosocial aspects of the fantasy life of the subject.

In light of these feelings about the special role of the *FLS* in the total interpretation of the subject's MAPS test production, the following suggestions are made for clinical interpretation:

a. That the clinician inspect and interpret the *FLS before* he begins to interpret the protocol, so that the unique contribution of the *FLS* can be exploited.

b. That the clinician take the stimulus situation presented to him by the subject (as indicated on the *FLS*) and that he (the clinician) tell a story to this situation and then interpret his own story which he had been "forced to tell" by the tableau of characters chosen and placed by the subject.

c. That the clinician attend to the "formal" aspects of the completed *FLS*. These aspects would include such items as the following: the number of figures (paucity of figures, overinclusion); the placement of figures (upside down, off the background, at sharp angles, etc.); the inappropriateness of figures (e.g., a nude figure on the *Street*); the general "tenor" of the figures (hostile, sexual, frightened, etc.); conspicuous absence in choice of figures; relationships among figures (which kinds of figures are generally coupled with which other figures); any differences in the "figure handling" of the relatively unstructured backgrounds (such as the *Dream* and the *Blank*), as opposed to the ways in which the subject populates the specifically structured backgrounds. A *résumé* of these formal signs (especially as they apply to schizophrenic subjects) is given in a separate monograph.[14]

## Illustrative Case

In the sample case selected for presentation in this chapter, some of the special attributes of the *FLS* are illustrated. The case is that of a 13 year old girl who did not speak during the entire examination but was known to talk to her mother when in the confines of her own home. The psychological examiner reported that "There was no word at all ever uttered to me in the day and one-half that I saw her." Ordinarily this would present a formidable problem for psychological testing, especially if projective materials were desired. In this case, by virtue of the examiner's having established excellent rapport with the subject, an abundantly rich MAPS test *FLS* was obtained.

The following remarks were made "blind" in a training session at a children's hospital. These remarks were recorded, and the statements printed below represent a slightly edited and somewhat abridged version of the original extemporaneous comments. But first a brief description of our subject should be given.

## Background Information

The subject, a 13 year old Mexican-American girl, the youngest of four children, was referred to the psychiatric clinic of a children's hospital with the chief complaints of refusing to eat, refusing to talk, and not performing toilet functions while in school or anywhere away from home since about the age of 5 years. Since the age of 8 years she had been considered mentally retarded. She does respond to verbal directions. The mother claims that she speaks at home but in a somewhat immature manner. The patient has always been extremely shy, withdrawn and has preferred social isolation; she has never been a management problem. The physical examination revealed her to be well developed, well nourished, and well coordinated, an individual who gave the impression of mental retardation and complete withdrawal. At the time of the examination, the father, who is employed as a pipe finisher and has held the same job for 30 years, was 56, the mother 42, the brother 16, and two sisters 15 and 14. They all lived in a five room house which they owned. The brother and sisters occupied separate bedrooms, and the patient has slept in a small bed in the parents' room for the past four years because it was reported that she played roughly and was a source of antagonism to her older sisters. The mother reported that the patient ate and spoke at home except when company came over, and that she also spoke at the homes of friends when the family was invited as a group. She has never spoken at school, but she seemed happy and was cooperative there. The parents spoke both Spanish and English and seemed rather concerned with the patient's welfare. The patient was referred to the psychological service for testing, with special questions relating to the possibility of mental retardation. She did not utter a single word during all the testing, and her principal mode of communication was through smiling and nodding her head either affirmatively or negatively. On nonverbal tests of the Wechsler Intelligence Scale for Children (WISC), she performed at a low normal level with a rather wide scatter ranging from low normal to high average. The psychologist at the hospital felt that mental retardation in the sense of feeble-mindedness could be ruled out, that intellectual limitations were not the primary cause of her unwillingness to speak. It was at this point that the MAPS Test was administered to her, resulting in the performance indicated on the *Figure Location Sheet* (fig. 1). She made no verbalizations.

## Test Interpretation

The blind analysis of this subject's *Figure Location Sheet* was as follows.

1. *Living room.* Figures chosen: M-6 (Gangster, man with gun in hand); L-4 (Ghost); F-5 (Woman with both hands to mouth); C-4 (Girl, rear view, running); A-1 (Cocker Spaniel pup).

Before we begin our interpretation of the *Living room,* let us remind ourselves of the tactic of interpretation in which the interpreter tells a story around the stimulus situation presented to him by the subject. This procedure is based on the assumption that the interpreter's unconscious will somehow pick up some faint vibrations from the important psychodynamics expressed by the patient. Let us then go ahead and tell a story to the situation that our subject has created here. We would follow this procedure even if she had given a full verbal protocol. The point is that her stimulus material (on the *FLS*) makes us think of what it makes us think of, and the fact is that in as much as we are the interpreter, it is important to see what it is that she leads us to do with the materials she has selected. To begin with, an examination of the *Living room* tableau does not look like a normal, happily settled American home. The dominant figure is perhaps the man with the gun. We will say that he has come into the house and we can see that the woman of the house is terrified and suppressing a scream. The girl of the house is running, perhaps running from him. The only emotion that we can easily attribute to the girl is one of terror or fear. Worse than this, there is a supernatural feeling to the whole picture introduced by the ghost. One can only have compassion for an individual who would have to live in this kind of psychic environment. One sees that this is not a barren kind of imagination, but rather that this reflects a very active kind of fantasy life. Our subject is a girl living in a house of horror. It is like the kind of fun house one sees in an amusement zone, in which fun is used in this special chilling way, and whatever her story might have been, we can guess that it would pretty much have to follow along the lines that we have indicated. And we may also make the further assumption that our subject looked carefully over all 67 figures. In fact, we have an indication that she had previously sorted them, so that she had handled and seen each one, and so hers was a careful, almost "unconsciously advertent" selection of these figures. In terms of identification, we assume that there is global or diffuse (rather than focal) identification, and although our first choice would be to say that she identifies with the little girl in the picture, it may be that in part she also identifies with the ghost in the picture, so that she is able in some silent, almost magical way, to be a nonparticipant observer of the hostilities and the other interactions which occur in the home. This ghost may not only be a frightening figure for her but may also be the role which she plays. At any rate, one gets the feeling here of a kind of magical process, almost a primary process thinking on her part.

These remarks are, at this point, most tentative in nature. We shall want to see how in subsequent backgrounds some of these trends we think we have seen are either corroborated or denied. As yet we have no strong belief in what we said. We have only begun. Now we must continue and modify our first formulations in light of what we see in the subsequent figure-background situations.

2. *Street*. First set of figures chosen: M-5 (Policeman); M-6 (Gangster; man with gun in hand); I-1 (Supine figure in slacks or pants, left hand on belt); A-2 (Snake). Second set of figures chosen: M-5 (Policeman); M-11 (Man with right fist raised); F-9 (Woman, right hand to ear); F-11 (Young woman in defensive position, left elbow in air); C-10 (Boy, hands on chest, looking up); A-1 (Cocker Spaniel pup).

There seem to be two separate productions here. In the first one, someone has apparently been hit by the automobile, although this is not too clear because this person might also have been shot by the gangster. The policeman is standing in the scene. It so happens that the policeman is faced away from this action and there is also the inappropriate and/or magical figure of the snake. The placement of the snake can be appropriate in the *Forest*, and in one or two other places, but certainly not in the middle of this hostile *Street* situation. It is interesting to see what she changes this into, and if we can speculate that she withdraws in actual behavior from this kind of violence and hostility, then what we find is that these two situations for the *Street* scene are simply variations on the same theme. The second variation of the scene looks like a family fight. Father is shaking his fist, mother is standing there in a way that we are not quite sure of, either listening or also shaking her fist, the girl is apparently traumatized by this and seems to be the target of the abuse. She has her arm up to ward off either physical or verbal assault. The little boy also seems hurt by this. The policeman looks on, seemingly almost in a nonparticipant, spectator way. The dog, of course, can do nothing. And there is the highly symbolic snake in the corner of the picture. So that it almost seems as though these two are indeed variations on the same basic theme. To be explicit, the basic theme is rampant hostility. We notice in the second variation that the automobile plays very little role—in fact it is covered by the little boy and the snake. People—not things—kill or hurt one. Now we can entertain a rather unusual hypothesis, and that is that there might have been an early seduction of this child, when she was 4 or 5. We can rule out the brother since he is only three years older. This points to the father, or grandfather, or to the uncles, cousins or nephews who were in the house. It would not transcend imagination that this kind of episode might have occurred which shocked her into silence. At any rate, it would be worth investigating by asking the mother or other sources of information. It is interesting to note that in practically every one of these situations, a girl's best friend is her dog. The little puppy appears in all of the 10 productions. From this we could expect our subject to communicate with her doll, with her animals and with safe objects of that nature. One guess would be that, if therapy were done with this subject, play therapy would certainly be one of the modalities indicated. It would be indicated for other reasons also, but it would certainly be indicated for this reason.

3. *Dream.* Figures chosen: M-8 (Priestlike male in long robe); L-1 (King, sixteenth century costume); N-2 (Mammy-type Negress); N-4 (Negress in business suit); A-1 (Cocker Spaniel pup).

The figures chosen for the *Dream* are of interest. We will assume that she sees the head of someone imagining or fantasying or dreaming. In addition to the omnipresent canine, she selected a priest. We wonder whether this person plays the role of forgiving her or condemning her. In addition, there is a king, certainly a person of strength and one from whom she could expect sanctuary and protection. And then there are two female figures. These are clearly Negro figures, a young Negress and a mammy type. One wonders here what minority group people think. We refer not to her Mexican minority status, but rather to her schizophrenia minority status. All this has to do with being different, being Negro, being lowly, being unworthy, being in a really second-class position. Somehow it seems that in her own household she is the Negress of the house. We can go on and say that in this way she seems closer to her mother, but apparently this is not enough protection for her. Perhaps an additional comment about the priest in the dream ought to be made, and that is, whether this is a kind of superego figure or whether it betokens the excessive religious preoccupation of the schizophrenic; it is hard to say. We can assume that this Mexican girl has had a Catholic upbringing, and for her the priest may simply play a benign role.

4. *Shanty.* First set of figures chosen: M-1 (Nude male, rear view); F-5 (Both hands to mouth); C-5 (Nude girl); C-6 (Nude boy); I-2 (Rear view of seated figure, head resting on left arm); and A-1 (Cocker Spaniel pup). Second set of figures chosen: F-5 (Both hands to mouth); F-10 (Old lady with shawl); L-1 (King, 16th century costume); L-4 (Ghost); C-4 (Girl; rear view, running); A-1 (Cocker Spaniel pup).

Again there are two situations produced by the subject. The first is a very interesting one, of a nude male who seems to be presenting himself sexually to a nude female child, almost as though the male adult, if one looks at the situation, were exhibiting himself or masturbating himself, or behaving in a way that might be a prelude to sexual relations. There is also a kind of duplication of this with the nude male adult, right behind the nude male boy. These two figures in many ways duplicate the position and thus perhaps the activity of each other. Further, there is the figure who is grieving—at least he had his head in his arms. We might call this the Mexican counterpart of the Greek chorus, becoming the situation which is presented in the scene. It is almost as though the squalor and the degradation of the physical environment gives a kind of psychological permissiveness to this disturbing kind of almost incestuous sexuality. The second variation, as though the first were too disturbing for her, is rather different. The protecting King is there, the haunting ghost, the running child, the old lady, the frightened young woman and the ubiquitous dog. Here it almost seems as though the frightening thing, the only frightening aspect of the picture, would seem to be the ghost. He is perhaps the ghost of incest past. It is of interest to note that the figure directly substituted for the nude girl, who may indeed be the one assaulted, is the ghost, so that our formula might almost read that when she is a human female she is assaulted, and her protection is to become almost a magical or ethereal or unreal, a ghostlike person, that is to pretend that the whole thing did not really happen. This procedure may permit her not only to frighten others, but also to have a fantasy companion, the good old King, whoever he is, by her side. The tragedy is that her protector is only a fantasy figure, so unreal and so unattainable, and cannot help her in real life situations, whereas the real males in her life are seen as potential instruments of assault and hurt. She is without real friend or ally.

5. *Nursery.* First set of figures chosen: I-1 (Supine figure in slacks or pants, left hand on belt); L-3 (Santa Claus); C-8 (Boy with left fist raised); C-10 (Boy, both arms outstretched, bandage on left leg); A-1 (Cocker Spaniel pup). Second set of figures chosen: M-12 (Man with both hands to left cheek); N-2 (Mammy-type Negress); N-7 (Pious figure with beard and skull-cap); N-9 (Latin-American female, bracelets on left arm); L-4 (Ghost); L-6 (Witch, ugly old woman); S-1 (Solid black male silhouette); I-1 (Supine figure in slacks or pants, left hand on belt); C-9 (Boy with left hand to eye); C-11 (Boy; hands on chest, looking up).

Here in the nursery scene we can again attempt to use the method of difference and capitalize on the comparisons which occur between the figures which are moved or substituted for, and the figures for which there is a sequence of substitution. The one figure that has not been moved is the figure in the bed. All the others are substituted for, even the dog. At the beginning we see a scene in the nursery in which there is a benign Santa Claus, a couple of boys who are either somewhat frightened or somewhat agitated or fighting with each other. This becomes changed to some rather sad or sober-sided figures, a male adult, a mammy female, and then this becomes changed to a ghost—the ghost that is either frightening or observing—and the sad male (M-7) is changed into a sadder male (M-12), the mammy becomes the witch (L-6) and she in turn becomes the all-black silhouette (S-1) who changes into the seductive female (N-9). Crying children (C-9 and C-11) enter the scene. All this wonderful, mysterious sequence of individuals seems to be in response to this one person in the crib. It's also of interest to note who is in the crib. The person in the crib is large for the crib; whether the person is male or female may be difficult to tell because it is an indeterminate figure. It is most assuredly not a baby, almost an adult, and these events, these ghosts, these witches, these silhouettes, the joy of Santa Claus, turn into a kind of sadness, so that one gets some feeling here of her being responded to, not with the happiness she would want, but with a kind of bizarre, sad feeling. It is difficult to say exactly what this story communicates, except that it has a kind of pervasive, unsettling quality about it. This is not a joyful reaction to the person in the crib, nor could the person in the crib, if she or he were to witness what is happening in the nursery, take any joy or any comfort from the figures which troop though it.

6. *Cellar*. Figures chosen: M-6 (Gangster, man with gun in hand); M-7 (Supine figure with blood spots); N-3 (Negro man reading paper); A-1 (Cocker Spaniel pup). N-3 becomes I-1 (Indeterminate figure).

Here in the cellar, this dark and mysterious dungeon for tabooed feelings, we see mainly aspects of naked hostility. The man with the gun and his victim, the supine figure covered with blood spots. We see here two other figures who play something of a similar role—the role of incongruity. That is, the dog really doesn't know what is going on, and thus can be happy in the midst of sadness and can feel fairly comfortable in the midst of rampant hostility. One sees something of this same incongruity in the figure of the Negro male (N-3) who is reading something. It would be of great interest to know whether he is reading something to the person who has been shot down or whether he is aside from the scene. At any rate, when the subject changes the picture, she removes the Figure N-3 and substitutes the other supine figure. Let us recall that this was the figure she placed in the crib. And so, the murderer, whoever *he* is, not only has one victim, but two. In a sense he also killed the baby of the nursery scene. We can infer here the tremendous amount of fear she must have. It can also be inferred that in addition to being a frightened person, she is also an angry person. She is, *in fantasy*, a murderously hostile person. The possibility might be that in reality she would not hurt a fly. Thus, we can guess that she is frightened by her own fantasies of hostility. Indeed, part of her magical thinking might be that if she talked, she would appear so vile and so angry that she would destroy others, who might in turn, sensing this potential destruction from her, completely destroy her. One gets the feeling that she not only is frightened by others in her environment, but that she has very angry fantasies which occupy her a great deal and that she is frightened by her own fantasies.

7. *Bathroom.* First set of figures chosen: M-1 (Nude male, rear view); F-1 (Nude female); A-1 (Cocker Spaniel pup); A-2 (Snake); C-4 (Girl, rear view, running); C-6 (Nude boy). Second set of figures: A-1 becomes C-6. C-4 becomes C-5.

As it is often supposed to happen in the *Bathroom* scene of the MAPS test, the attitude just below the surface concerning sexuality comes out on this scene. What is of some interest is that no one seems to be using the bathroom facility. This is rather almost a tableau, using the feeling of the bathroom, rather than the specific details of the bathroom. There is a nude male adult, a nude female adult, a nude male child, and the female child who is running and who has been frightened, and who was substituted for this figure, the nude female child. So we have the four nudes, the ever-present dog, and, very interestingly, the snake who is put on top of the nude male adult figure. This last bit of open symbolism from a psychologically naive and completely unsophisticated subject becomes something which we can take as having welled directly out of her unconscious, and in general betokens a type of control which is consistent with a picture of childhood schizophrenia. Now it was in this particular scene that an item of actual behavior took place, which should be noted: The examiner asked her, pointing to Figure M-1, if this was daddy, and the subject responded by shaking her head in the affirmative. The examiner then asked her if she liked snakes, and the subject responded by smiling spontaneously and shaking her head in the negative. The examiner then posed a third question, if she *liked* daddy, and the subject's response to this was a frozen expression, almost like a masked face. Now at this point, we don't have so much a feeling of a story, as we have a feeling of a tableau. That is, it is almost as though the subject is no longer thinking in terms of situations—in this case the situation is one of a lot of sexuality. All this might be a normal, happy, sophisticated, modern, contemporary family situation, in which nudity is no issue, except for the presence of the snake and except for what we know she has done with these figures in the preceding background.

8. *Closet.* Figures chosen: F-2 (Female undressing); F-6 (Female, bending over, arms up, apron); L-3 (Santa Claus); L-4 (Ghost); C-3 (Girl with ribbon in hair); A-1 (Cocker Spaniel pup); L-3 becomes F-5 (Female, both hands to mouth).

In this situation, unlike the previous one, one again gets the feeling that there is a narrative here. This heightens our feeling that the *Bathroom* and its attendant sexuality is especially traumatic for her. The *Closet* background can be described as fairly neat, although conspicuously barren. There is no furniture and there are no clothes hanging in the closet. Our subject gives us a situation of a young woman in brassiere and panties and a benign male figure, Santa Claus, who is perhaps giving her things. It may be then that our subject is most centrally identified with the young woman, who needs pretty clothes and things like this. But this fantasy does not continue, the frightened female with her hands to her mouth is substituted for Santa Claus and there is another woman (F-6), both of them looking toward the duo of female figures, F-2 and the little girl with the ribbon in her hair (C-3). It is of special interest that Figure F-2 is not substituted for by the ghost, but rather that the ghost is superimposed on Figure F-2, as though F-2 were literally covered by the ghost or becomes the ghost. This is what happens when people disapprove of one. She becomes ethereal in the sense that she transmits into ectoplasm, and thus escapes in this way. This would be our story to this particular background. Again we see the continued use of this mechanism of magical process, betokening not a reaction to mental retardation, but rather a kind of set of elaborate defenses and coping mechanisms to a serious kind of psychic disorder.

9. *Blank.* Figures chosen: M-6 (Gangster, man with gun in hand); M-8 (Priestlike male in long robe); L-5 (Futureman, with cape and tights); A-1 (Cocker Spaniel pup).

This is the blank card. It is of direct relevance to note that the subject was told by the examiner that this was the last card she would be given. I say this to indicate that this tells the subject that if she is going to do anything in this test situation, this is her last chance to do it, so that it gives some slightly special meaning to this card, in addition to the special meaning that the unstructured blank card gives. There are four figures selected for this background: the gunman, the priest, superman and the dog. Here is her continuous preoccupation with violence and hostility. On one side, the man with the gun, the man who looks aggressive and who can kill, and on the other side, there is the priest and her friend, the dog, hovering close to the priest. We can legitimately make something of the special relationships here; it is no accident that the dog is almost in the robes of the priest, rather than near the gunman or the other figure. The other figure, of course, is a person that most people, even devout Catholics, might agree was even more powerful than the priest, namely, superman, so that what is happening here is that naked violence, in the form of the gunman, is pitted against the forces of almost omnipotent, magical good.

### Over-all Impression

Our over-all impression from this "figure reading" of this subject's MAPS Test *Figure Location Sheet* is that she is a frightened, lonely, isolated person; a girl whose fantasies are peopled with hostile and sexually assaultive figures; an individual who is frightened also of her own hostile impulses and feelings— and of the retaliation that she fantasies that open expression of these feelings would bring; and a person whose "adjustment" mechanisms include such maladaptive techniques as magical and dereistic thinking, fantasies of transparency and emptiness, dichotomization of other people into good or evil, etc. The possibility of actual early sexual trauma (probably seduction by the father or uncle) was mentioned. The level and "richness" of the fantasy production did not seem consistent with amentia. An over-all quality of psychic functioning consistent with a schizophrenic disorder was suggested.

All these are my free-floating "thoughts" about this subject. What I would write in a *report* might, of course, be quite different, modified to take into account my own sense of confidence in these various notions, to whom the report was going, in what setting the report was being made, and other general dictates of the professional situation.

It is only necessary to add that in the ordinary case of MAPS testing, one could now turn to the *piéce de résistance*, the verbatim account of the stories that the subject had dictated to the fascinating figure-background situations which she had created.

### A Final Note

Granted that the above remarks in the sample case contain some rather far-reaching speculations, it is important to indicate that the purpose in presenting this example of a "blind" interpretation was not to demonstrate the "validity" (however defined) of these comments; rather the purpose was simply to illustrate a process or *modus operandi* by which one test interpreter could permit himself to make some off-the-cuff psychodynamic comments based solely on the subject's choice and placement of the figures as recapitulated on the MAPS Test *Figure Location Sheet*.

### Summary

This chapter is intended to present an overview of the Make-A-Picture-Story (MAPS) Test, particularly in relation to the use of the test materials for younger subjects. In this chapter, the materials of the test were described, the usual method for the psychodiagnostic use of the test was delineated, and a sample interpretation focusing on the attributes of the *Figure Location Sheet* was presented. In summary, it is proposed that the MAPS Test can serve two useful functions in the armamentarium of the clinician who works with children: as a psychodiagnostic tool, with its special characteristics bordering on play techniques and vicarious psychodrama which tend to enhance test interest and rapport; and as a set of materials which can be employed in psychotherapy, especially to overcome resistances and to clarify specific areas of the subject's psychodynamics.

### References

1. Bindon, D. M.   Make-A-Picture-Story (MAPS) test findings for rubella deaf children. *J. abnorm. soc. Psychol.*, 1957, *55*, 38–42.
2. Conant, J. C.   A comparison of thematic fantasy among normals, neurotics and schizophrenics. Unpublished doctoral dissertation, Univer. of Southern California, 1950.
3. Edgar, C. L., & Shneidman, E. S.   Some relationships among thematic projective tests of various degrees of structuredness and behavior in a group situation. *J. proj. Tech.*, 1958, *22*, 3–12.
4. Fantel, E., & Shneidman, E. S.   Psychodrama and the MAPS Test. *Rorschach Res. Exch. & J. proj. Tech.*, 1947, *11*, 42–67.
5. Farberow, N. L.   Personality patterns of suicidal mental hospital patients. *Genet. Psychol. Monogr.*, 1950, *42*, 3–79.
6. Fine, R.   Interpretation of Jay's Make-A-Picture-Story method. *In* Shneidman, E. S., et al. The case of Jay: Interpretation and discussion. *J. proj. Tech.*, 1952, *16*, 444–475.

7. ——. A scoring scheme for the TAT and other verbal projective techniques. *J. proj. Tech.*, 1955, *19*, 306–309.

8. Fraimow, I. S. The use of the MAPS Test with mentally retarded children and children of normal intellectual development. Unpublished master's thesis, Pennsylvania State College, 1950.

9. Goldenberg, H. C. A resume of some MAPS test results. *J. proj. Tech.*, 1951, *15*, 79–87.

10. Hess, D. W. Personality development and adjustment in a group of young deaf children as reflected by a non-verbal modification of Shneidman's Make-A-Picture-Story (MAPS) Test. Dissertation in process, Univer. of Rochester, 1959.

11. Joel, W. The use of the MAPS Test with disturbed adolescents. *Rorschach Res. Exch. & J. proj. Tech.*, 1948, *12*, 155–164.

12. Proud, A. P. Response to picture thematic material as a function of stimulus structure. Unpublished doctoral dissertation, Univer. of California at Los Angeles, 1955.

13. Roth, A. Erfahrungen mit dem Make A Picture Story von Edwin S. Shneidman. *Diagnostica*, 1956, *2*, 21–30.

14. Shneidman, E. S. Schizophrenia and the MAPS Test. *Genet. Psychol. Monogr.*, 1948, *38*, 145–223.

15. ——. *The Make A Picture Story Test.* New York: Psychological Corp., 1949.

16. —— (Ed.) *Thematic test analysis.* New York: Grune & Stratton, 1951.

17. ——. Manual for the MAPS Method. *Proj. Tech. Monogr.*, 1952, *1*, No. 2.

18. ——. Some relationships between the Rorschach technique and other psychodiagnostic tests. *In* Klopfer, B. (Ed.) *Developments in the Rorschach technique*, vol. 2. Yonkers-on-Hudson: World Book Co., 1956. Pp. 595–642.

19. Spiegelman, J. M. Jungian theory and the analysis of thematic tests. *J. proj. Tech.*, 1955, *19*, 253–263.

20. ——. A note on the use of Fine's scoring system with the MAPS tests of children. *J. proj. Tech.*, 1956, *20*, 442–444.

21. Walker, R. G. A comparison of clinical manifestations of hostility with Rorschach and MAPS test performances. *J. proj. Tech.*, 1951, *15*, 444–460.

8

# The Rosenzweig Picture-Frustration Study, Children's Form

SAUL ROSENZWEIG

## Historical Background

THE Rosenzweig Picture-Frustration Study, Children's Form, is a direct outgrowth of theoretically oriented, experimental research, a glance at which will serve as an introduction to this account of the technique.

Beginning in 1928, the author became interested in the psychology of philosophers (Schopenhauer, Nietzsche, Bergson) as focused on the interrelationships of personal frustrations, needs and creative productions. This interest led naturally to a concern with psychoanalytic theory, first in its application to the philosophies under scrutiny but soon afterwards in an attempt experimentally to validate the clinically derived concepts of Freud (experimental psychoanalysis). Laboratory investigations of repression, displacement and projection[35,36] threw into relief the phenomena of *frustration* as best epitomizing the psychodynamic approach in its experimental implications. A heuristic classification of types of reaction to frustration[47] was followed by the development of a behavioral test for tapping these patterns.[34,46] At about this time was also performed an experiment on repression with special reference to the hypothetical distinction between ego-defense and need-persistence,[37] a distinction that later provided two of the chief categories employed in scoring the Picture-Frustration Study. In a subsequent A.P.A. symposium on frustration which, along with the author, included Roger Barker, Quin Curtis, G. M. Haslerud and O. H. Mowrer, clarification of this concept was achieved from the standpoint of several investigative approaches, and it was there that the construct of frustration tolerance was introduced.[48] In brief, then, a psychoanalytic psychology of philosophic formulations via the biography and life experience of the formulators instigated an experimental attack on the concepts of psychoanalysis itself and, finally, produced a tentative formulation of frustration theory as an experimentally oriented psychodynamic schema.

But while this development with reference to the content of psychodynamics was transpiring, the formal side of the original problem was being expressed in studies of the techniques later dubbed "projective." Exploration of word association (as in the above-mentioned investigations of projection), the Rorschach Method and the just emerging Thematic Apperception Test

It is gratifying to acknowledge the invaluable assistance of Louise Rosenzweig in the preparation of this chapter. Three of the projects in the section on Validity, here described in print for the first time, were partially supported by generous grants from the Children's Research Foundation of St. Louis.

paved the way for the assessment of types of reaction to frustration and of frustration tolerance by a projective device—the present Picture-Frustration Study. In its earliest form this technique was part of a battery known as the F-Test consisting of four parts. The first was a version of the previously cited behavioral test (Part B). Then came two questionnaires or "optionaries" (listing for each item several options of typical response together with a free space), devoted to the subject's conception of (a) what he thought he was likely to say in frustrating situations (Part R—for Real) and (b) what he would like to think of himself as saying in such situations (Part I—for Ideal). This distinction between R and I had previously been delineated by the author as a suggestion for raising the validity of questionnaires.[45] The fourth part of the battery (Part P—for Projective) was the immediate forerunner of the present Picture-Frustration (P-F) Study. Cartoon-like drawings were employed as unstructured pictorial stimuli to elicit the subject's first associations when given the set: What would these anonymous characters say in the pictured (frustrating) situations? Part P of the F-Test was first systematically employed in an investigation of the triadic hypothesis in 1941—a hypothesis relating susceptibility to hypnosis, as a personality trait, to preferred mechanisms of ego defense, on the one hand, and to modes of immediate reactions to frustration, on the other.[36,54] It will be noted that this F-Test, as part of which the P-F first originated, posited as its organizing basis four coexistent levels of response—levels that reappeared in subsequent P-F research. But during the early 1940's the results of Part P appeared so fruitful and became so absorbing in themselves that the other three parts of the original battery were for the time being abandoned. The P-F Study was thus singled out for further development.

In 1944 an outline of frustration theory as it had by now crystallized was published.[41] In the same year appeared the first edition of the Picture-Frustration Study, Adult Form; a brief description of the technique (the first),[47a] and, immediately thereafter, the basic article describing the picture-association method with special reference to the assessment of reactions to frustration.[42] In 1947–48 the revised (and present) Adult Form of the P-F was published.[49] At this time the Form for Children, which had been devised and constructed during the four preceding years, was introduced.[50]

### Rationale

On the basis of the foregoing background it will be evident that the Children's Form of the Picture-Frustration Study was not in the first instance designed as a clinical tool but as a method for (a) exploring concepts of frustration theory and (b) examining some dimensions of projective methodology. Such conceptual validity as the instrument possesses derives from this provenance. As a projective technique the P-F lies midway between the Word Association Test—historically the first of the projective methods— and the Thematic Apperception Test; it resembles the former in the association set induced by the instructions and the latter by virtue of the pictorial nature of the stimuli. But in comparison with the TAT, which has the advantages of being both more global and more probing, it has the merit of lending itself more readily to quantitative research. The stimuli employed and the responses elicited are circumscribed in comparison with the TAT or the Rorschach. For these reasons the P-F has been extensively used in investigations of psychodynamics and of projective methodology. At the same time the clinical applications of the instrument soon became apparent and actually ran far ahead of original expectations in this regard.

Since research has frequently invoked the Adult Form of the P-F in addition to or instead of the Children's Form, it should be noted that the present account, for obvious reasons of space limitation as well as of relevance in the context, will refer but little to the Adult Form. It should not, however, be overlooked that the work done on and with this latter form bears directly upon the reliability, validity and general significance of the Children's Form. It follows that fully adequate use of the Children's Form presupposes some acquaintance with the Adult Form, and this recommendation is particularly apposite when research objectives are in question.

The basic assumption of the P-F Study, which it shares in some measure with the other projective techniques, is that the subject will "project" himself into the stimulus situation and possibly "identify" with the central figure of it, i.e., the frustrated character in each of the test items. In giving his first response—the one that first enters his mind as most likely to be made by the frustrated persons pictured—the subject will, it is assumed, respond in some sense more or less unconsciously for himself. His several responses to the P-F items may then be taken as a sample of his repertoire of reaction patterns in situations of frustration. But it still remains an open question in what sense the subject in any projective method "projects"— to what extent and in what way he reads himself into the stimulus situation. The point is a vital one as regards the interpretation of results, though it has received much less systematic attention than it deserves. In the research with the P-F this problem of *levels of behavior* has been made conceptually explicit[39] and has been submitted to some experimental investigation. The topic will of necessity be considered again in connection with P-F interpretation.

### Description of P-F Study

This technique is, in the Children's Form, intended for the age range 4 through 13. (Beginning with age 14 the Adult Form is employed and is therefore inclusive of the adolescent period which will accordingly not be covered in the present account.) The Study consists of 24 cartoon-like pictures, each of which represents an everyday frustrating situation involving two persons (fig. 1). It was anticipated that, particularly with children, this format would have a definite face appeal. One of the pictured individuals, on the left of the item, is shown saying something which either frustrates or helps to describe the frustration of the other character; and this other individual is drawn with a blank balloon or caption box above his head which the subject is instructed to fill. He is to do so by writing the very first words that it occurs to him the character might say in that situation. Facial features, etc., are purposely left vague in the drawings to facilitate projective structuring by the subject.

Fig. 1. Two items from the Rosenzweig Picture-Frustration Study, Children's Form (Copyright, 1948, by Saul Rosenzweig).

In selecting the items a large number were first devised and tried experimentally; then extensive investigation was made with a 32 item form that was finally reduced to the present 24 item Study. Care was taken to include a sampling of the range of needs frustrated more or less often in the life of the average child, e.g., the needs for approval, freedom, nurture, etc., as well as the various formal types of frustration, i.e., privation, deprivation and conflict. While in every instance it was a child who was represented as frustrated, in approximately half the items the individual inflicting the frustration or otherwise associated with it was likewise a child while in the other half he was an adult. The sex of both frustrated and frustrating characters was deliberately varied to show boy or girl, father or mother figures. Moreover, the situations were constructed to maintain a distinction between *ego-blocking* and *superego-blocking*. Ego-blocking is involved in 14 items in which some personal or impersonal obstacle directly frustrates the identification figure; superego-blocking enters into 8 of the remaining 10 items, in which some accusation or incrimination is represented. (Two items are ambiguous in this regard.) But the distinction is not absolute and is always subject to the interpretation implicitly given by the examinee. To facilitate comparison with the Adult Form for clinical or research purposes, it was further attempted to make a majority of the items of the Children's Form parallel to those of the Adult Form. This parallelism is specified in the Manual.[50]

## Administration

The P-F Study is printed in an eight page leaflet (the Examination Blank) of which the first page is devoted to Instructions; each of the next six shows four of the above-described items. In the standard procedure the examiner hands the subject an Examination Blank, has him read over the Instructions or, if the child is too young to read himself, reads them to him. The Instructions call the P-F a "game" to be played: the leaflet is described as containing pictures of people doing and saying different things. In each picture one person is always shown talking. The game is to write in the empty space the first thing you think of that the other person would answer. The leaflet is then opened, the first item is read aloud, and the subject asked, as a demonstration, what answer first comes to his mind. He is then told to write that answer in the blank caption box. Then he is instructed to proceed with the rest of the items silently by himself. The demonstration is important in order to reinforce the Instructions, particularly with regard to giving the very first response that comes to mind.

This procedure presents no difficulty with the vast majority of children eight years old or over. With younger subjects who cannot read or write well enough to carry out the task alone, it is permissible for the examiner to read the Instructions and the items aloud for the subject and to write at dictation the responses given. But even in these circumstances it is advisable for the answers to be written directly in the Examination Blank so that the simulated "game," intended to encourage projection, is not spoiled. Whenever possible, however, the subject should read and write for himself, since experimentation with matched groups has shown that oral administration is apt to increase censorship in the direction of polite or "acceptable" answers. This possible effect of the oral administration is perhaps less pronounced at ages 4 to 7, and, in any event, the norms at these earlier ages were of necessity established by such administration.

The examiner records the total time spent by the subject in completing the leaflet. He then conducts an Inquiry. The child is asked to read aloud, one at a time, the responses he has written and the examiner interjects nonleading questions that will help in scoring ambiguous or very brief answers. He also notes tonal inflections that indicate sarcasm, petulance, humility, etc., for use in the later scoring. This Inquiry often crucially affects the scoring and is strongly recommended, particularly if research is in question.

Beginning with age 9 it is possible to administer the P-F Study to groups when individual administration would be impractical. However, even then subjects should be allowed to work at their individual speed and to turn in completed blanks as soon as finished; subjects are asked to raise their hands as a signal for the examiner to pick up the leaflets. Total time can then be recorded as in individual administration. Again, if it can be arranged, inquiry should be conducted with the subjects as soon as convenient after the group session and before scoring is attempted.

## Scoring: Definition of Categories, Factors and Patterns

No attempt will here be made to duplicate the detailed scoring instructions given in the Manual. A general discussion of the rubrics and aims of the scoring must suffice.

The responses given by the subject are scored along two main dimensions: *Direction of Aggression* and *Type of Aggression*. Direction of Aggression is divisible into extrapunitive or E (when the subject turns aggression outward), intropunitive or I (when aggression is turned inward) and impunitive or M (where all expression of aggression is avoided or evaded). Blaming some person or circumstance for the frustration is, for example, extrapunitive; blaming oneself is intropunitive, while glossing over blame ("It couldn't be helped") is impunitive. Type of Aggression is divisible into obstacle-dominance or O-D (when the response indicates only a perseveration at or insistence upon the presence of the obstacle), ego-defense or E-D (when the response refers to the blameworthiness or inviolacy of the ego), and need-persistence or N-P (when the response involves in some fashion the satisfaction of the frustrated need). From the combination of the three *categories* in each of the two chief dimensions, nine scoring *factors* result, each of which represents a combination of Type and Direction of Aggression.

It should be observed that the term "type of aggression" here employed supersedes "type of reaction" previously used in writings concerned with the P-F Study. The new terminology implies that obstacle-dominance, ego-defense and need-persistence are all to be regarded as forms of aggression. This clarification implies a prior one according to which *aggression* must be clearly distinguished from *hostility* as only one mode of aggression. Generically aggression is closer to *enterprise* or *assertion* than to hostility though dynamically oriented psychologists, in particular, have often concentrated their attention upon the negative species of the genus. In the present context a distinction is definitely intended between *constructive* or positive and *destructive* or negative aggression, the former being conceptualized as need-persistence and the latter as ego-defense. Obstacle-dominance would then represent a type of aggression in which the response is curtailed or inhibited before either of the other two modes can be actuated, possibly because of a conflict between them. In the combination of the three types of aggression with the three directions, it now becomes possible to provide a consistent terminology as follows: *extrapunitive, intropunitive* and *impunitive* would refer only to the three directions of ego-defensiveness, while for the three directions of obstacle-dominance the terms *extrapeditive, intropeditive* and *impeditive* would be employed, and for the three directions of need-persistence the terms *extrapersistive, intropersistive* and *impersistive* would serve.

The verbal responses as given in the blank caption boxes are, with the aid of the Inquiry, scored for the nine possible factors. (At this point in the treatment of the data, deep interpretation is avoided—the verbal response is scored at its face value. Cues as to underlying psychodynamics are, of course, noted for use in the final qualitative interpretation of the protocol.) Usually one or two of the scoring factors completely suffice to characterize a given response. To facilitate the use of the system and to insure consistency among examiners, extensive scoring samples for each item have been provided in the Manual. The reliability of the scoring system is indicated by the finding that when the records of the first 300 subjects, of the approximately 500 employed for the work of standardization, were independently scored by two individuals, over 80 per cent of the assigned scores were in agreement; the remainder were agreed upon in conference between the scorers. (A published study on the reliability of the scoring of the Adult Form[5] found initial agreement of approximately 85 per cent.)

After the individual items have been scored, the Record Blank—a summary of the results—is completed by the examiner. (Full directions are given in the Manual.) The inventory of item scores is used for the calculation of percentage scores under the main scoring dimensions as well as to derive certain composite scores or patterns. Both the percentage scores for categories and factors and the composite scores are interpreted according to the norms made available by the standardization. One of the composite scores is the Group Conformity Rating (GCR) derived by comparing each of the subject's item scores with the modal responses yielded by the norm population. A rough measure of the examinee's social adjustment is thus obtained—an index of his tendency to apperceive and respond to frustrating situations as the majority do. Another composite type of score is obtained by comparing the so-called superego responses; the patterns here derived tend to highlight the subject's sense of responsibility by comparing the frequency of responses in which he assumes blame, absolves himself from blame or attributes it to others. Finally may be mentioned the Trends, which take account of any tendency to shift from one prevalent mode of reaction in the first half of the record to another prevalent mode in the second half. The hypothesis involved is that not only should responses be considered discreetly, item by item, but cumulatively, i.e., the subject's later responses may well represent a reaction to his earlier ones as, for example, when an individual who has been blaming others rather consistently grows aware, more or less consciously, of this tendency and begins altering his responses in the direction of intropunitiveness or impunitiveness. Five such types of Trend are provided for on the Record Blank.

## Available Norms

The original standardization group included 256 children ranging in age from 4 through 13 years and yielded norms for the several scoring categories, factors and patterns in two-year intervals.[50] All the subjects were attending school in grades ranging from nursery classes through eighth grade. Of these, 131 were males and 125 females. Since sex differences when analyzed proved to be insignificant, the sexes were not distinguished in the compiled norms. It is not, however, to be concluded that sex differences do not exist in this area; research on an adolescent population has revealed such differences, and these conceivably reflect the well-known comparative difference in maturation rate of girls and boys. It is possible that an investigation with larger samples at the various age intervals would show significant differences during childhood also. But one investigator[61] who undertook to examine the problem of P-F sex differences in elementary school pupils, comparing 50 boys with 50 girls, confirmed the earlier negative result. However, he did obtain some interesting sex differences when child-vesus-child items and adult-versus-child items were scored separately (see below, pages 171–172).

A second set of norms has been made available for 162 child guidance patients, 103 males and 59 females.[53] (The difference in sex frequency, males preponderating, reflects the similar frequency difference in child guidance referrals for the two sexes and came into play in this investigation because the design of it called for a consecutive series of cases during a given time interval.) These data, compiled in two-year intervals like those for the original standardization group, showed significant differences from the normal that are helpful for the interpretation of similar cases. Also available are norms for 102 mentally retarded children[3] who were compared with the P-F normal standardization group.

In addition to these American norms, there are available norms based on large groups of French,[32] Italian,[9] German,[7] Japanese[11] and Indian[31] children. These data have been compiled in the authorized adaptations and standardizations of the Picture-Frustration Study in the respective countries. Other national or cultural normative studies have been published as follows: on 245 African Congo children,[16] a Finnish group,[63] 161 Sicilian[55] and 150 Dutch children.[10] The majority of the latter investigations include comparisons with the American norms.

Of interest from all the normative studies are the consistently found developmental changes in the expression of aggression as to both type and direction. The norms compiled by age level all show a steady decrease in extrapunitiveness and corresponding increases in intropunitiveness and impunitiveness. In like fashion the Composite Group Conformity Rating tends to increase with age in the 4 to 9 year range. In some measure these developmental results reflect favorably on the validity of the instrument since they show that in the course of growth, children tend, as commonly supposed, to inhibit hostile reactions to frustration and to acquire patterns of social conformity and personal responsibility.

## Interpretation

The general concepts employed in the interpretation of results obtained from the P-F Study were introduced in several of the previously cited papers.[34,36,37,41,42] Further criteria have been described in the Manual. The available norms by age level for the scoring categories, factors and patterns obviously provide the most direct interpretive guides. The Group Conformity Rating, as already mentioned, is regarded as an *approximate* index of social adjustment.

But the most problematic aspect of interpretation concerns the behavioral level represented by the responses of the subject. As indicated above, this problem has been recognized from the outset, and on more than one occasion research has been devoted to it. Some of this work will be described in a succeeding section. Three possible levels of response must be considered in the evaluation of any protocol.[39] There is, first, the *opinion* level, on which the subject gives self-critically censored answers such as he might make in the usual self-report questionnaire. A second and more naive level of response is the *overt*, which corresponds to what the person would actually say in a real life situation. (For general purposes, where contravening information does not exist, it is this overt level that may be assumed to be represented in performance on the Children's Form of the P-F Study.) Finally, the subject's answers may reflect the *implicit*, covert or fantasy level of the personality. It is seldom possible in any projective method to differentiate these levels of response with certainty; the P-F Study shares this common fate. But the Inquiry which is to be conducted at the end of the administration may often be usefully extended to shed light in the given case on this vexing question. After the Inquiry for scoring purposes, as above described, has been concluded, it is possible to ask casually and without leading implications what the subject was thinking as he gave his answers; further, was he thinking of what he himself might say in the situations? or, again, whether he thinks that the answers he gave are those he would actually give in real life. This sort of interrogation is, of course, by no means a direct approach to the goal in view—the replies must themselves be clinically interpreted since rationalizations are quite as possible here as in the item responses themselves, perhaps more so. Nevertheless, the replies are on occasion enlightening, as, for example, when the subject expresses naive surprise as he says that, of course, he was thinking of himself in the picture situations or, when, with equally disarming frankness, he allows that he was simply playing the game of saying what the pictured characters might say. When, however, no other clues as to level are in hand, it is advisable to assume, as above mentioned, that the second or overt level has been tapped.

Skill in clinical interpretation is acquired through clinical experience. The foregoing general remarks will hence be amplified by reviewing several actual P-F protocols as seen in the light of the presenting picture of the subject's personality. A normal, a prepsychotic and a neurotic child are included in this illustrative sample.

## Illustrative Protocols

### Normal Case

Reference may first be made to the sample case employed in the Manual (reference 50, page 178 f.) as a basis for explaining the compilation of the Record Blank. Some interpretive discussion not there included will be given here.

The case was that of an 11 year old boy, son of a physician, of superior intelligence, successful in his school work but having some minor problems of family and social adjustment. He was somewhat withdrawn and ill at ease in social situations, though said not to be seriously disturbed. The father referred the boy privately to obtain informal counseling for his own guidance in dealing with his son.

Inspection of the Profile in table 1 reveals several deviations, mostly within normal limits, that confirm the father's concern. The total extrapunitive score was close to the mean, as was the intropunitive score, but the impunitive bordered on significant deviation in the elevated direction. The figures for type of aggression were more significantly out of line. While obstacle-dominance was normal, the ego-defense figure was clearly depressed (46 per cent as compared to the norm of 57 per cent) and the need-persistence score was notably high (42 per cent as compared to the norm of 27 per cent). On the whole, the results up to this point reflected some tendency to gloss over frustration with evasiveness, to decompensate, as it were, and to escape into fantasy. (This last interpretation is based largely on the elevated need-persistence score which research has indicated often to have not a constructive but a somewhat regressive significance when found during the adolescent period.) The interpretation is corroborated by the other results. There was a significant fifth Trend in the direction of increased obstacle-dominance (he became more blocked as frustration continued), and the Group Conformity Rating was depressed to a significant degree (54 per cent as compared to the norm of 65 per cent for his age). That the boy needed psychological help at this critical prepubertal period of his development, so that he might enter adolescence more realistically and more courageously, was indicated even from the P-F results alone though this was not, of course, the only diagnostic device employed in advising the father.

TABLE 1.—*P-F Profile of an Eleven Year Old Boy with Minor Adjustment Problems*

| Profile and deviation pattern | | | | | S–E patterns | Trends |
|---|---|---|---|---|---|---|
| | O–D | E–D | N–P | Total | % | $\underline{E} = 2 = 8\%$ | 1. none |
| E | 0 | 5 | 4 | 9 | 38 | $\underline{I} = 0 = 0\%$ | 2. none |
| I | 1 | 1 | 4 | 6 | 25 | $\underline{E} + \underline{I} = 2 = 8\%$ | 3. none |
| M | 2 | 5 | 2 | 9 | 38 | $E - \underline{E} = 3 = 12\%$ | 4. none |
| Total | 3 | 11 | 10 | 24 | 101 | $I - \underline{I} = 1 = 4\%$ | 5. $\xrightarrow{-.67}$ O–D |
| % | 12 | 46 | 42 | 100 | | $M + \underline{I} = 9 = 38\%$ | *Total pattern* |
| GCR = 13 = 54%. | | | | | | | (E = M) > (e = i) |

## Prepsychotic Case

The second case is that of a 9 year old boy who was referred for psychodiagnostic re-evaluation after two years of therapy at a child guidance clinic.

When first seen he was severely disturbed. His behavior was impulsive and erratic. When he started school at about age six, he had to be removed after about two months, since his nervous, excitable and uncontrollable outbursts could not be tolerated in that situation. He ran about the classroom screaming and striking other children. His speech was disturbed by stuttering and word repetitions of a perseverative kind. The diagnostic study brought up the possibility of organic brain damage—he had once been diagnosed as suffering from chorea —but his schizophrenic-like symptoms seemed to take precedence over this possibility. On either basis he was regarded as close to psychosis.

His trouble seemed to have started with the birth of a sister when he was three and one-half years old. He openly resented and protested her presence. At his own birth, as the first child of a late marriage, he had a mother of 32 and a remarried father of 45. The father appeared to be a somewhat schizoid person who for a long time failed to admit the problem of his son and who, in fact, tended to encourage it in various ways. He read long fairy tales to the boy at inopportune times and gave him books that intensified an already excessive fantasy life, e.g., *The Pied Piper of Hamelin*. The mother was a dependent and somewhat hostile person who found herself at a total loss in dealing with her son's bizarre behavior.

The therapy began with a gross "acting out" in the playroom of the patient's much disorganized fantasy in which hostility toward both his parents could be readily discerned. Envy of the father's close relationship to the mother appeared to instigate this hostility toward them both. Gradually it became possible to achieve some limitation of the boy's fantasies by the use of drawing, play technique with dolls, etc. He then revealed and partially worked through the "tricks" (his term) which he habitually used in coping with his environment. Slowly but surely the patient formed a strong relationship to his therapist. After about a year of treatment he was able to return to school and, though still clearly disturbed, to control his more bizarre and impulsive behavior in that situation. He became progressively more controlled during the next year of therapy, at the end of which time he was referred for the re-evaluation here in question.

In table 2 will be found the Profile of the patient's scores on the P-F Study. The findings revealed that he was still markedly hostile (extrapunitive score of 67 per cent, in comparison with a norm of 48 per cent); intropunitiveness was normal but impunitiveness was depressed (12.5 per cent as against the norm of 30 per cent). There was some elevation of obstacle-dominance. The Group Conformity Rating was significantly low (46 per cent as compared to the norm of 64 per cent) and reflected his obviously poor social adjustment. The Superego Patterns were notable for their marked deviation on nearly every count: The third pattern was depressed (8 per cent as compared to 18 per cent), the fourth elevated (33 per cent as compared to 17 per cent), and the sixth greatly depressed (17 per cent as compared to a norm of 35 per cent). It was concluded that the patient was still far from having

TABLE 2.—*P-F Profile of a Nine Year Old Prepsychotic Boy*

| Profile and deviation pattern | | | | | | S–E patterns | Trends |
|---|---|---|---|---|---|---|---|
| | O–D | E–D | N–P | Total | % | $\underline{E} = 1 = 4\%$ | 1. none |
| E | 2 | 10 | 4 | 16 | 67 | $\underline{I} = 1 = 4\%$ | 2. none |
| I | 1 | 3 | 1 | 5 | 21 | $\underline{E} + \underline{I} = 2 = 8\%$ | 3. $e\overset{+1.00}{\leftarrow}$ |
| M | 2 | 0 | 1 | 3 | 12 | $\underline{E} - \underline{E} = 8 = 33\%$ | 4. none |
| Total | 5 | 13 | 6 | 24 | 100 | $\underline{I} - \underline{I} = 1 = 4\%$ | 5. $\begin{array}{l} O\text{–}D \overset{+ .60}{\leftarrow} \\ N\text{–}P \overset{+ .67}{\leftarrow} \end{array}$ |
| % | 21 | 54 | 25 | 100 | | $M + \underline{I} = 4 = 17\%$ | *Total pattern* |
| GCR = 11 = 46%. | | | | | | | E > e > I |

acquired adequate aggressive control, his typical patterns of response reflecting excessive hostility and generally low frustration tolerance. In the same vein the further results showed three Trends: One of these was away from need-persistence while a corresponding one was toward obstacle-dominance; and both could be more closely interpreted in terms of the third Trend, which moved away from extrapunitive need-persistence (e). In plainer words, as the patient in the course of progressive frustration attempted to abandon an initial adjustment of dependent aggressiveness—an attempt that may have been reflecting the effects of his therapy—he became increasingly blocked and, at a loss for any response at all, he soon resorted (as evident in the Item Scores not here reproduced) to a consistently hostile or extrapunitive mode of response.

### Neurotic Case

The third case, affording opportunity for more subtle analytic interpretation, will be discussed in some detail. It is that of a child guidance patient whose problem was twice diagnosed, once before and again after therapy.

The patient was a 7 year old girl who was neurotically obsessed with the fear that she might harm someone and that she had "bad thoughts about people." A hand-washing ritual had been part of her behavior for about two years. Still, she was at the top of her second-grade school class, in which she took her lessons with the utmost seriousness. A perfectionist in everything she did, she feared all possible mistakes and took any general criticism as aimed at her individually. Religion was an important part of her defensive system for combating her fears, but while she prayed to God, she also "hated Him for letting her have such bad thoughts." Intolerant of any imperfection, she hated her father because he wore glasses. Her hand washing started after seeing a health film; in the dynamic background were recent experiences of sex play with an older girl and with a male cousin a year or more previously. The father was himself a highly perfectionistic person whose view was that the patient must learn to live with her perfectionism as he had learned to live with his. The mother, a somewhat immature individual who giggled readily, seemed much less involved in the patient's problem than the father. The relationship between the parents was reportedly excellent. There was one sibling, a boy of 16, from a previous marriage of the father.

The test battery administered at the first evaluation included the Wechsler Intelligence Scale for Children (which yielded a full-scale IQ of 131), the Rorschach, the TAT and the P-F Study. The Profile of her P-F scores is shown in table 3, part I. As will be observed, the patient had a very slightly elevated total extrapunitive score and a correspondingly depressed intropunitive one. More notable was the high ego-defense score (68 per cent as compared to the norm of 60 per cent for her age) and the low need-persistence score (15 per cent as compared to the norm of 23 per cent); but even these results were not significantly deviant

TABLE 3.—*P-F Profiles of a Seven Year Old Girl with Obsessive-Compulsive Symptoms, Before and After Treatment*

### Part I.   (*Before Treatment*)

| Profile and deviation pattern | | | | | S–E patterns | Trends |
|---|---|---|---|---|---|---|
| | O–D | E–D | N–P | Total  % | E = 0 = 0% | 1. none |
| E | 2.5 | 8.5 | 2.5 | 13.5    56 | I = 3 = 13% | 2. $\xrightarrow{-.50}$ I;M $\xleftarrow{+.75}$ |
| I | 0 | 4 | .5 | 4.5    19 | E + I = 3 = 13% | 3. $\xrightarrow{-.50}$ e |
| M | 1 | 4 | 1 | 6    25 | E − E = 9.5 = 39% | 4. M $\xleftarrow{+.50}$ |
| Total | 4 | 16.5 | 3.5 | 24    100 | I − I = −2 = −8% | 5. none |
| % | 17 | 68 | 15 | 100 | M + I = 8.5 = 35% | *Total pattern* E > (I = M) |
| GCR = 15.5 = 64%. | | | | | | |

### Part II.   (*After Treatment*)

| Profile and deviation pattern | | | | | S–E patterns | Trends |
|---|---|---|---|---|---|---|
| | O–D | E–D | N–P | Total  % | E = 0 = 0% | 1. none |
| E | 0 | 1 | 6 | 7    29 | I = 1 = 4% | 2. I $\xleftarrow{+.33}$ |
| I | 0 | 7 | 1 | 8    33 | E + I = 1 = 4% | 3. none |
| M | 2 | 5 | 2 | 9    37 | E − E = 1 = 4% | 4. none |
| Total | 2 | 13 | 9 | 24    99 | I − I = 5 = 21% | 5. none |
| % | 8 | 54 | 37 | 99 | M + I = 8 = 33% | *Total pattern* I > e > M |
| GCR = 13 = 54%. | | | | | | |

on a statistical basis. When, however, the more indirect measures were examined, the child's idiosyncrasies emerged clearly: under Trends, four that were significant appeared—a Trend away from impunitiveness and a corresponding one toward intropunitiveness, and another toward dependent extrapunitiveness (e). As the examination proceeded, she had apparently become less capable of glossing over frustration and assumed blame herself or shifted responsibility onto others for solving her problems. A further peculiarity of the record consisted in three instances in which she obsessively responded by giving two alternative answers (e.g., in picture 9, in which a boy says he has won the game and claims the spoils, the response was, "O.K. or I won it"; and in picture 11, in which the father figure admonishes the child to stop beating his drum—mother wants to sleep, the response was, "I don't care or I will stop it"). Particularly when taken in the light of the total test battery, it became evident that the patient was in conflict regarding the expression of aggression, was struggling to control her hostility and resorted finally to hostile dependence as one way out. But the Group Conformity Rating was 64 per cent, i.e., no more deviant than the category scores above cited. It was evident that with her superior intelligence the child could in social situations, e.g., the schoolroom, mask her inner conflicts and perform acceptably.

The patient was approved for treatment at the clinic. Therapy lasted for three months, when it was discontinued because of her excellent progress. She had profited from the sessions by ventilating her aggressive conflicts and gaining considerable mastery over them. Symptoms had markedly decreased. She showed little scrupulosity and fewer guilt feelings. Her compulsiveness, though still present, was not emotionally crippling. She was now almost too compliant, but there were signs of maturation toward a balanced (though obsessive) type of "normal" personality. In discontinuing her treatment it was recommended that a diagnostic re-evaluation be made in about six months to determine how stable the gains had been.

The same battery of tests was administered at this second evaluation, which occurred eight months after therapy (15 months after the initial testing). The P-F Study yielded markedly different results, as shown in table 3, part II. The total extrapunitive score of 29 per cent was now about half the previous one and significantly below the norm for her present age (48 per cent); intropunitiveness was correspondingly high (33 per cent as compared to a norm of 23 per cent), and impunitiveness was barely within normal limits. Egodefensiveness was reduced, need-persistence increased, and obstacle-dominance at 8 per cent was clearly decreased (significantly below the norm of 17 per cent). The findings warranted the interpretation that she had mastered her hostile aggressiveness almost too well. But again, in terms of the more indirect indicators, it was apparent that this mastery was not accompanied by energy-depleting conflict. As compared to the previous record, in which there had been several qualified responses necessitating composite scoring (6 instances) and three responses with alternatives given for the same item, there were now no such alternatives and not even one composite response. (The profiles reflect this difference in the round numbers of part II as compared to the decimals of part I.) Again, while the earlier record included four Trends, the present profile showed only one (away from intropunitiveness, at the level of borderline significance). The Group Conformity Rating was still normal. The total record reflected a personality that was overcompliant but was not characterized by the previously pathognomonic emotional conflicts. The other projective techniques corroborated the P-F results, and all together demonstrated that the therapy gains had thus far been lasting. Perhaps, as the father had earlier maintained, the girl was learning to live with her obsessional personality structure even if a radical cure had not been effected.*

## Reliability

The reliability of the Children's Form of the Picture-Frustration Study has been investigated by both the split-half and retest methods. As is apparent

*There is here observable a striking paradox that highlights the psychodynamic import of projective techniques. Before therapy the patient had a more "normal" P-F score profile (by group norms) than she had after brief treatment! (She had now learned to relax her defenses and to tolerate their outward appearance.) It is surmised that had therapy been continued to a more complete outcome her profile might have reverted again toward *normality*, now in the more intrinsic or idiodynamic sense of that concept.

from the most superficial consideration of the structure of the projective method in comparison with the psychometric test—a point fully discussed elsewhere[38,43]—the approach by split-half correlation violates the deliberately nonlinear plan of a technique like the P-F in which the items, though they do aim to elicit certain general functions or traits, are also intentionally *diverse* so as to sample various aspects of experience. Moreover, as already mentioned in the discussion of Trends, in the projective method the configuration of the entire succession of item responses is vital—a fact that contradicts an approach to reliability based on the correlation of first and second halves of the test and, to a lesser extent, of odd-even item correlation. For that matter, even the approach by retest is open to question since many of the personality functions tapped by a projective technique are admittedly subject to change from one occasion to the next. It is thus inevitable that reliability figures for these techniques when obtained by the conventional statistical approaches must have a far more limited meaning than in the pure psychometric test and will assuredly be quantitatively smaller.

In one project two groups of elementary public school children were investigated. In one group there were 88 subjects, ranging in age from 10 to 13 years, who were given a second P-F three months after an initial administration; another group of 45, 9 to 13 years of age, had their second P-F 10 months after the first. Data from the former group were analyzed for two year age levels both by odd-even item and by retest correlation. Product-moment correlations, corrected for attenuation, on the percentage scores of the six scoring categories and GCR for the 10-11 year group (n = 44) were as follows: E = .82; I = .57; M = .62. (All these figures were significant at the .01 level.) O-D = − .04; E-D = .28; N-P = .46. (The results for O-D and E-D were not statistically significant, but that for N-P was significant at the .01 level.) GCR = .35 (significant at the .05 level). For the 12 to 13 year group (n = 45), the correlations were as follows: E = .68; I = .32; M = .60; O-D = .36; E-D = .23; N-P = .13; GCR = .16. (The first and third figures were significant at the .01 level, the second and fourth at the .05 level, while the last three failed to reach either level.) It will be observed that the results for direction of aggression tended to be more reliable than those for type of aggression. In the light of the preceding general comment, these findings on odd-even reliability are as significant as could have been anticipated. On the same basis it would be expected that the retest method should yield better results, and the correlations bear out this expectation: For the 10 to 11 year group E = .69; I = .65; M = .57; O-D = .32; E-D = .56; N-P = .51; GCR = .53. For the 12 to 13 year group E = .64; I = .46; M = .59; O-D = .33; E-D = .40; N-P = .50; GCR = .26. (Of these 14 figures, only three failed to reach significance at the .01 level: .32 and .26 being insignificant and .33 being significant at the .05 level.) These quite significant figures are approximated by the correlations for retest scores in the second group of subjects, ages 9 through 13, above mentioned when treated as a whole: E = .44; I = .25; M = .50; O-D = .18; E-D = .55; N-P = .49; GCR = .22. (The results for E, M, E-D and N-P were significant at the .01 level, the others being insignificant.) It may be concluded that even by these only partially applicable methods of assay, the P-F is as reliable as could well be expected; the unreliability remainder could be readily rationalized as representing features of the projective method that do not come under the psychometric aegis.

## Validity of the P-F Study

If reliability as a psychometric concept is problematic when applied to projective techniques, validity is even more so—and more importantly. Questions have repeatedly been raised as to the relevance of the traditional psychometric concept.[38,43] It has, for instance, been asked: How valid is the validity criterion itself? Or, again, in what sense is the indicated criterion relevant to the intent of the projective technique? Uncritical applications of validity criteria which are themselves in need of validation or that are actually beside the point to which the projective method directs itself contribute nothing but confusion. But, on the other hand, projective methodologists have themselves often been guilty of practices that reflect a different prejudice but an equal nebulosity of approach. Thus one finds numerous examples of the attempt to validate one projective method in terms of another—the blind leading the halt and arriving hopefully at the same undefined destination. One does detect even here the essential axiom of idiodynamics that personality is at its deeper levels self consistent, but the trait or function in respect to which the consistency consists has not been determined.

One important distinction bearing on validity that has seldom been made explicit highlights the dual function of the projective method as *test* in the psychometric sense or as *tool* in the broader clinical one. As test the technique will be judged by the usual psychometric criteria (group norms, etc.). In so far, however, as it is also a tool in the clinical sense, its validity will depend largely upon the skill of the clinician; it may have more validity with one clinician than with another. Again, it may as a tool elicit different aspects of personality, and with different degrees of effectiveness, from different subjects so that a univocal validity is automatically ruled out. In these latter respects *individual norms* largely supersede group norms in defining the validity of the technique. Investigations of the validity of projective methods are thus confronted with a far more complex problem than the corresponding one in the purely psychometric area.

With this background it will be readily understood that the validity of the Picture-Frustration Study has of necessity followed both conventional and unconventional routes. The conventional methods have involved the correlation of personality judgments or ratings with scores on the P-F; but even here the question insistently arose as to the meaning of the criterion judgments and ratings—their relevance and their own validity. The unconventional methods of validation depended largely on the invention of new approaches, e.g., that of successive clinical predictions. Throughout it was necessary to keep in mind the bearing of *levels of behavior* on the significance of the separate and the composite scores to be validated.

Finally, it remains to be recognized that the validity of a projective technique like the P-F Study is to a certain extent not statable in terms other than the success that it enjoys clinically—an implicit expression of the degree to which it permits clinicians to use it for these various individualized ends. It is likewise important to note that the validity of the P-F increases—its potentialities are maximized—when employed in a battery of tests on the same subject, since by this circumstance the population of events from which the individual interpretive norms must be deduced is increased.

Emphasis will be placed in this section on several investigations of P-F validity performed by the author or under his supervision. Though none of these studies has as yet been fully published, only brief reports can here be given. Related investigations of others will be mentioned incidentally.

### Elementary School Project

In a private school several classes consisting of 60 pupils who ranged in age from 4 through 7 years and were attending nursery through second grade were investigated. The Children's Form of the P-F Study was administered orally and the results related to the teachers' independently written semester reports on the behavior of each child. These reports were analyzed with primary reference to the social habits and adjustment of the children, this emphasis being selected because observations along this line were noted fairly consistently and were considered to be as free from teacher bias as anything that might be reported. On this basis the subjects were classified into five social adjustment groups: I. (n = 18) *Socially adequate* (*unaggressive*), including those pupils who were, in general, characterized by good social relations, acceptance by their peers, but without special qualities of aggressive leadership or dominance. II. (n = 9) *Socially adequate* (*aggressive*), including those who were likewise accepted by their peers but assumed a role of dominant leadership. III. (n = 13) *Shy, timid* and *insecure*, including those who, while desiring acceptance from the group, had a variable relationship to others based on lack of assurance. IV. (n = 6) *Destructively aggressive*, including those characterized by poor social adjustment with hostility toward others expressed in teasing and sometimes by physical force. V. (n = 7) *Asocial or withdrawn*, including those with little interest in social contacts and with preference for playing alone, silent reading, etc. (Seven cases resisted classification by the available information.)

When the scores of the P-F Study were related to these five classifications by group the following general results were obtained: Group I (socially adequate—unaggressive) had relatively low extrapunitive scores, high intropunitive and low impunitive ones. The extrapunitiveness tended to be of the obstacle-dominant type when it did appear. On the other hand, the intropunitiveness tended to be of the ego-defensive type and the impunitiveness of the need-persistive or conforming type. Group II (socially adequate—aggressive), on the other hand, revealed elevated extrapunitive scores with low intropunitive and impunitive ones. The extrapunitiveness tended to be of the ego-defensive type and the impunitiveness of the need-persistive or conforming type. Group III (shy, timid, insecure) had relatively high intro-punitive and impunitive scores with low extrapunitive ones. Such extra-punitiveness as did appear was of the obstacle-dominant variety while the intropunitiveness was ego-defensive. Impunitiveness was of the need-persistive or conforming type. Group IV (destructively aggressive) was characterized by high extrapunitive, low intropunitive and relatively high impunitive scores. The extrapunitiveness in this group, while chiefly of the ego-defensive type, was also commonly need-persistive. Group V (asocial, withdrawn) was comparatively low in extrapunitiveness, high in intro-punitiveness and impunitiveness as well as in need-persistence. The Group Conformity Ratings of the first three groups were higher than those of the other two, the most marked difference appearing between Groups III and V. A separate analysis[52] revealed that Trends were most frequent in Groups III and IV—classified together in the published report as "socially in-adequate"—while the other three groups had about the same number of Trends. In the cases of both the shy and insecure and the destructively aggressive groups, the presence of Trends was thus taken to indicate in-stability and poor adjustment.

While none of these findings excluded one group from the others, the general results could be reconciled with the classification based on the teachers' reports. But it is not to be denied that the slight comparative differences, while readily rationalized, were far from conclusive in their bearing on P-F validity. Here as elsewhere, however, one could, of course, question the objectivity of the teachers' reports as well as the relevance of these judgments to the variable level of the P-F tapped in the individual cases.

### Validation of P-F Trend Scores

The published report on Trends just mentioned[52] dealt only incidentally with the Trend scores in the Elementary School Project. It was based mainly on the records of 272 children, ranging in age from 4 through 13 years, and yielded the following results: The mean number of Trends was found to be slightly over 2 per subject, with a range from 0 to 7. After age five a signifi-cant rise in the number of cases with Trends appeared and was interpreted as reflecting the process of socialization with an attendant suppression of infantile aggressiveness and arousal of conflict in reacting to frustration. The predominant type of Trend at every age was that toward obstacle dominance. Trends toward extrapunitiveness were found only in the youngest children while those away from extrapunitiveness and those toward intro-punitiveness occurred in the older subjects. The effects of increased socializa-tion seemed here again to be appearing. There were also some interesting relationships between other P-F scores and the presence or absence of Trends. Records showing no Trends were comparatively lower in extrapuni-tive and higher in intropunitive and obstacle-dominance scores—a finding interpreted as indicating that the presence of Trends is commonly associated with the inhibition of hostility and increase of guilt feelings.

## Child Guidance Patients Compared with Normals

In the previously mentioned investigation of problem children as compared with normals,[53] 162 children seen at a child guidance clinic, at which they had been administered the P-F Study routinely, were compared in respect to P-F scores with the normal standardization group. Consistent differences between these problem children and the normals were found, the patients showing somewhat higher extrapunitive scores than the normals at every age level and correspondingly lower intropunitive scores. Similarly, the Group Conformity Ratings were lower for patients than for normals. The categories for type of aggression revealed less consistent differences. Trends, on the other hand, proved to be significantly less frequent in the problem children than in normal ones (means of 1.77 and 2.07, respectively, with a difference significant at the .05 level). This finding was interpreted as indicating the relative immaturity of the problem children, since it had previously been determined that the frequency of subjects with Trends at ages 4 to 5 was significantly less than at later age levels. Moreover, this specific interpretation was in line with the general conclusion that, as indicated by their relatively higher extrapunitive and lower intropunitive scores and their lower Group Conformity Ratings, the patients appeared belated in learning to react to frustrating situations. But the qualification was noted that the problem, as compared with the normal, children showed as a group far greater variability—a result that underlines the possibility of sometimes encountering individual child guidance patients who are over-conforming and excessively self-controlling.

In a related investigation Ferguson[8] studied 32 children with serious behavior problems and compared their P-F scores with the anamneses in their bearing on home and parental stability. He singled out the superego patterns of the P-F and showed that the half of the subjects with the lowest superego scores had the highest frequency of home and parental instability. The P-F was thus presumably able to differentiate the two groups of children with poorer or better home backgrounds. It should be added that the total group of 32 were not, to judge from the incomplete data presented in the report, clearly different from the normal standardization group.

## Validity of the P-F Study with Special Reference to Levels of Behavior

A dissertation project by Wechsberg[67] investigated (a) the level or levels evoked by the P-F Study in two different populations of 7 to 12 year old children—a group of 22 normal children living in welfare homes and another with an equal number of maladjusted children who had been referred for diagnosis or treatment to a psychiatric clinic; and (b) the relationship of the opinion level and the implicit level in the personality structure of the normal as compared to that of the maladjusted child. The procedure was threefold: (a) The P-F Study was first administered individually. (b) Between three to eight weeks later each subject was observed in a series of playlets intended to elicit fantasy reactions (implicit level). These playlets were dramatized adaptations of the first 12 items of the P-F Study and were administered in a fashion designed to promote unconscious identification with the frustrated doll-figure. The frustrating scene of each situation was dramatized by the experimenter and completed by the subject. It thus became possible to score the playlets in P-F terms. (c) One to three weeks after (b), opinion behavior was explored by employing two questionnaires paralleling the 24 P-F items. The first questionnaire was designed with instructions to reveal the child's *self-concept* (corresponding to Part R of the above-mentioned F-Test) while the second questionnaire was oriented to elicit *ego-ideal* responses to the same items (compare Part I of the F-Test). The scoring system of the P-F Study was thus again applicable to these questionnaires. The data were treated by comparing intra-individually the scores of each subject at the two aspects (self-concept and ego-ideal) of the opinion level, the implicit level of the playlets and the undetermined level of the P-F Study itself; and, further, by comparing the results of the normal group with those of the patient group.

In brief, it was found that the results obtained from the two populations were quite different. In the normal group the self-concept and the ego-ideal opinion sublevels were significantly disparate, the former being characterized by high extrapunitive and low intropunitive and impunitive scores while the latter yielded low extrapunitive and high intropunitive and impunitive ones. The implicit level of the playlets was distinguished by exaggerated extrapunitiveness and showed few intropunitive or impunitive reactions. This implicit level was clearly differentiated from the opinion level. When the undefined P-F was compared with these levels, close agreement between the P-F and the self-concept scores appeared.

In the patient group consistently different scores for the several levels did not, however, appear. There was, for one thing, much closer agreement between the self-concept and the ego-ideal in this group than in the normal group, and, for another, the scores at the implicit level of the playlets were not clearly differentiated from the opinion level. The P-F scores as such showed no consistent similarity to the self-concept or ego-ideal opinion sublevels; they more closely resembled the implicit or fantasy level of the playlets. But despite these differences between the normal and the patient groups treated by intra-individual analysis, there were no stable differences obtained in any scoring category when *general* results on the undefined P-F, the opinion level questionnaires or the implicit level playlets were compared. It was only through an intra-individual analysis of relationships among the various levels that the normal subjects were differentiated from the maladjusted ones.

It was concluded that the Picture-Frustration Study elicited different levels of behavior in normals as compared to patients, the self-concept opinion level being more frequently tapped in the former group; and that this difference was in turn referable to differences of personality integration in the two groups. The patient group was regarded as having less well differentiated personalities, less frustration tolerance and less capacity for conceptual or abstract thinking than the normals. Given such differences in personality structure, the P-F Study was seen to be utilized differently in the performance of these two groups when that performance was scrutinized by intra-individual analysis.

Another investigation with a bearing on level was performed quite early with the experimental 32 item version mentioned in an earlier section. The aim of the project was to compare the P-F Study in its ordinary pictorial form with a matched open-ended questionnaire (similar to Part R of the F-Test but not in optionary form) as to their relative efficacy in predicting a subject's everyday behavior. The subjects were 40 children, aged 9 through 13, who were attending the fourth and fifth grades of a public school and who were all well known for at least a year to each of three teachers. The children were first administered the P-F Study. Approximately four months later the questionnaire was given. Both instruments were group administered. For each item the pairs of responses with the names of the subjects were compiled, questionnaire and P-F responses being recorded randomly in the two possible orders. The three teachers were then individually asked to go through the sheets and indicate by a check mark which of the two responses for a given child seemed to be more characteristic of his everyday behavior as *overtly* observed. The judgments of the three teachers were combined and analyzed by the chi-square technique. It was assumed that if there were no real difference between the P-F and the questionnaire, the judgments would distribute themselves equally. The analysis showed, however, that in 14 of the 32 items the P-F was clearly favored over the questionnaire (differences significant at the .01 or .05 levels). On only one item was the questionnaire significantly favored. When the judgments for the 32 items as a whole were similarly treated, there resulted a predominance in favor of the P-F which was highly significant (.01 level). It was concluded from this blind test that the overt behavior of these children, as known to the three teachers, was demonstrably closer to the pictorial P-F than to the questionnaire responses, and that the P-F was superior to the matched questionnaire in tapping the overt level of behavior.

### Validation of the P-F Study by the Method of Successive Clinical Predictions

The purpose of this dissertation research by Mirmow[23] was to examine the Method of Successive Clincial Predictions[40] by applying it to the investigation of the validity of the Children's Form of the P-F Study. The method was introduced as a possible means of reducing some of the obstacles hitherto standing in the way of the systematic determination of validity in the projective instruments, and of permitting their validation in a configurational-theoretical framework consistent with the principles underlying their construction and use.

Briefly, "the method of successive clinical predictions" may be described as follows: (a) A number of investigators, in conference, attempt to predict, on the basis of case history and other test data, the responses of a given subject to the projective instrument which is to be validated. (The foundation for this prediction is derived from previously formulated hypotheses concerning the significance of the instrument and its relation to the other data under consideration.) (b) The degree of attained success or failure in prediction is determined from inspection of the actual responses of the subject to the instrument under investigation. (This new information then becomes the basis for explicit or implicit revision of previous hypotheses concerning the meaning of the instrument.) (c) These revised hypotheses are tested in a second prediction of the results of another subject, and this process is then repeated with a succession of subjects. It is assumed that, as the experiment progresses, the new device, if valid at all, will gradually "define its own validity," and that the predictions of the judges will therefore become increasingly accurate. The validity of the instrument—or, rather, of the hypotheses concerning the dynamic significance of the instrument—is thus measurable not only in terms of the over-all success with which the judges are able to predict, but also on the basis of the extent to which improvement may be demonstrated to have occurred during the course of the investigation.

In the present experiment a group of three psychologists who were familiar with psychodiagnosis in general and with the P-F Study in particular attempted, on the basis of anamnestic and psychological test data with which they were provided, to predict the P-F scores of a series of 24 children (7 to 14 years of age) referred to a child guidance clinic. In addition, these numerical predictions of the various P-F scores were supplemented for the last 19 cases by an attempt to identify the complete P-F protocol of each child within a group of five unidentified Record Blanks. The predictions of the judges once made, the actual P-F of the subject in question was scored and the results compared with the predictions. Discrepancies were noted and discussed. On this foundation the hypotheses previously employed in making the P-F predictions were re-evaluated. A new predictive attempt was then made with another case, and so on throughout the series.

The results were as follows: The blind identification of the total P-F blank was found to be significantly more successful for the last 9 than for the first 10 subjects on whom this task was performed. There was thus demonstrated a clear gain in ability to recognize the total P-F. As regards the validity of the P-F, apart from the increased accuracy of the judges in the experimental series, the findings showed that in 10 of 19 cases the composite judgment correctly identified the P-F of the subject (a result which, by chi-square test, was significant at the .01 level).

Correlations of composite predictions and actual scores revealed significant correspondence for the P-F categories under Direction of Aggression (E, I and M) and for GCR, but the coefficients for the categories under Type of Aggression were not significant. It was also found that the judges showed consistently different ability, as well as improvement, in the course of the experiment. (Only the composite judgments have been considered in this brief report.)

By and large, the results of this investigation throw a favorable light on the gross validity of the P-F Study. Even when allowance is made for differences in the ability of the several judges, the findings proved that total P-F protocols as well as certain specific P-F scores could be meaningfully predicted well beyond chance expectation. Furthermore, it was indicated that the categories under Direction of Aggression and the Group Conformity Rating had superior validity to the categories under Type of Aggression—within the limits of this investigation. This research also demonstrated the feasibility of employing a global approach to the validation of projective methods, including the P-F Study, which can at the same time be treated quantitatively.

## Research Applications

The Children's Form of the Picture-Frustration Study has been found useful in a variety of clinical and nonclinical research applications. A brief summary of representative investigations will be offered.

In several laboratories, particularly in connection with child guidance, there has been experimentation in the conjoint use of the Children's and the Adult Forms to shed light on parent-child relationships. A variation involves the administration of the Children's Form to the parent, usually the mother, with instruction to respond as the child might do. By comparing responses and scores of a parent and child it is hoped to discover similarities or differences with dynamic implications. A related departure is found in an unpublished study of Siegel[56] who investigated the interchangeability of the Children's and Adult Forms at three levels of development. It is conceivable that older subjects can meaningfully project regressively on the Children's Form and, conversely, that the child is capable of a corresponding progressive projection.

In a research on enuresis in boys, Lord[20] found mean differences in ego-defensive extrapunitiveness for persistent wetters (42 per cent), for recurrent wetters (54 per cent) and for nonwetters (65 per cent). This result is interesting in relation to his major finding that enuretic subjects demonstrated, by other measures, a more frequent feminine identification and more fear of women than nonwetters; the depressed extrapunitive score of the wetters might in this context have been reflecting their nonaggressive femininity.

In a study of 102 mentally retarded children, aged 6 through 13, Angelino and Shedd[3] obtained some significant differences from the normal that point in the same direction as the above findings on problem children when compared to normals. They concluded that their retarded subjects were delayed in socialization, as reflected in P-F scores, about one age group (two years) behind the norms. Another investigation devoted to the mentally retarded was reported by Portnoy and Stacy[33] on a group of Negro as compared to one of white subnormals. Their analysis of P-F Trends revealed that both groups tended away from extrapunitiveness and moved toward impunitiveness and obstacle-dominance.

Spache[57,59,60] has made extensive use of the P-F in work with retarded readers in which he reports the findings to be extremely helpful in diagnostic and remedial efforts. In one investigation he found a highly significant difference in total extrapunitiveness: nonreaders had a mean score of 55 per cent as compared to a normal mean of 46 per cent (difference significant at the .001 level). His interpretation was that, as shown by the P-F and by other findings, retarded readers are apt to be more negativistic toward authority figures and, in general, more aggressive and defensive than normal readers.

Children with handicaps have been studied by Van Roy[65] with the aid of the P-F Study, and Krall[14] has employed it in an investigation of accident-proneness. Johannsen and Bennett[12] applied the P-F in research on diabetic children with the finding that they had lower GCR scores and higher obstacle-dominant ones than the controls.

Delinquency has been one of the areas in which the P-F Study has had extensive application, presumably on the hypothesis, correct or incorrect, that such social deviants err in being generally negativistic or nonconforming to cultural standards. Typically this work has been done with adolescent groups for which the Adult Form of the P-F has been employed. But an interesting investigation reported by Lindzey and Goldwyn[19] compared 40 delinquent boys, 12 to 13 years of age, with 50 nondelinquents. They found that, contrary to expectation, the delinquents had elevated intropunitive and impunitive scores, depressed extrapunitive ones and comparatively high Group Conformity Ratings. Since these results accord rather well with those in other work using the Adult Form, the consistency of the findings merits comment. For one thing, it is fairly obvious that delinquent subjects in detention might well be motivated to put a good face on their P-F responses and would accordingly produce the type of record that these investigators had not anticipated. That the P-F is not immune to such distortion has already been implied in the several references to the various possible levels of response given above. Vane,[64] in an investigation of 95 delinquent girls who were compared with 50 nondelinquents, made just such an interpretation. But it is also necessary to bear in mind that social deviation in children and adolescents may in many instances proceed as much from docility as from hostility—in which case even undistorted P-F scores at the overt level might not be different from those found by these investigators. Moreover, there is the further possibility, stemming from psychoanalytic theory, that criminal acts may be inspired by an unconscious sense of guilt; the P-F, if reflecting the implicit level, might then yield elevated intropunitive scores. Delinquency is thus an area of research that well exemplifies the importance of considering the potential multiplicity of dynamics for any manifest behavior with which P-F scores are to be related. Until one has determined the dynamics of the behavior in question as related to the several possible levels of performance on the P-F, one cannot advance any tenable hypothesis as to expected P-F scores.

In addition to the foregoing research applications of a primarily clinical relevance, there have been a number of studies in which the P-F has been used with normal children for one or another theoretical purpose. One such investigation was that of Spache,[61] who explored sex differences by administering the P-F to 50 boys and 50 girls with a mean age of 9 years. Analysis of the results confirmed the findings reported in the Manual:

consistent sex differences did not appear. However, when the investigator treated separately the child-versus-child and the adult-versus-child P-F items by a differential method of scoring which he devised,[58] he obtained some positive results. Girls were found to show significantly more outward aggressiveness toward other children than toward adults; both sexes were more ready to acknowledge or accept blame when in conflict with adults than with children. Boys tended to project hostility upon the environment when in conflict with adults but toward the other individual when the frustrater was a child. Spache concluded that the sex differences he found through his differential scoring method bore out the common experience that boys get involved in more frequent conflict among themselves than do girls; and that children of both sexes show more deferent behavior to adults than to other children, with boys behaving thus more characteristically. The differential scoring recommended by Spache is similar to that described by Cox,[6] who distinguished home and peer regions on the P-F for separate scoring. The suggestion for such separate scoring has useful clinical implications; in keeping with the design of the technique, the sex of the frustrating figure may, in individual cases, reveal a particular complex of the subject, and even isolated items may by virtue of content be productive of significant clinical leads.

In a project involving 157 fifth grade pupils Levitt and Lyle[18] established relationships between a Problems Situations Test (PST) of their own devising and P-F scores. The PST required the subject to check multiple-choice responses to a series of hypothetical situations covering typical misbehavior of children. The responses were designed to be scored as punitive or nonpunitive. From the results of this scale two extreme subgroups were selected—24 with the highest and 28 with the lowest scores (high or low punitiveness). The P-F was administered to these 52 subjects about a year afterwards. Comparison revealed that the high and the low groups on the PST differed significantly in their P-F scores for extrapunitiveness, intropunitiveness and impunitiveness, the former group having distinctly higher E, lower I and lower M scores. Type of Aggression also distinguished the two groups: the high PST scorers had significantly higher ego-defense scores and lower need-persistence scores, but the two groups were found not to differ in obstacle-dominance or GCR. The conclusion was reached that the findings reflected favorably on the validity of the P-F but one can, of course, still question the unknown validity of the PST with which the correlations were established.

Lesser[17] studied population differences in construct validity, employing the P-F as one of his instruments. His subjects were 44 boys, with ages from 10 to 13, along with their mothers. He first distinguished two populations—one with Low Anxiety and one with High Anxiety as defined by maternal attitudes and practices that *encourage* or *discourage* aggression in the child, respectively. More validity was then demonstrated for the P-F in the former than in the latter group. In the Low Anxiety group, E correlated with I $-.74$, while in the High Anxiety group a lower correlation of $-.59$ was obtained; similarly, there was a correlation of $-.89$ of E with M for the Low Anxiety and of $-.68$ for the High Anxiety group. He concluded that it is inaccurate to describe personality assessment techniques as valid or not in an over-all sense, since any given type of measure may have different degrees of validity for different populations. The conditions of his experiment also suggest another interpretation: the children of mothers who encouraged aggression learned to use extrapunitiveness more consistently than did the children of mothers who discouraged or were ambivalent about aggressive behavior.

An investigation that has a bearing on the previously mentioned *triadic hypothesis* was carried out by Kates[13] on 31 elementary school subjects ranging in age from 8 to 12 years. The children were administered the P-F Study and also a test of suggestibility devised by the investigator. He found that the subjects with the higher suggestibility scores had lower extrapunitive and higher impunitive scores than the low suggestibility group (E of 49.8 per cent versus 57.6 per cent and M of 50.6 per cent versus 43.9 per cent, both differences being significant at the .05 level). These results lend some support to the triadic hypothesis and indirectly to the validity of the P-F.

A study by Mensh and Mason[22] of the relation of school atmosphere to reactions in frustrating situations brought incidental validation of the P-F Group Conformity Rating. Working with two groups of children, one consisting of 110 pupils attending a *traditional* school and another of 75 in a *progressive* school, these investigators found a statistically significant difference between them (at the .01 level) in mean GCR. While both groups were within the normal range, the mean for the traditional school children was 15.24, while that for the progressive school group was 13.81 (scored by number of item agreements rather than by percentage of total). Other P-F scores did not significantly differ for the two groups. It was concluded that the GCR score differences were a reflection of the difference in the traditional school atmosphere as compared with the progressive one, the former producing more social conformity than the latter. A modicum of validation for the GCR may be derived from this research.

A final area in which the P-F Study has had and can have further research applications is that of cross-cultural comparisons. In view of the several foreign standardized adaptations mentioned above, such comparative application of the P-F to the explication of cultural patterns becomes readily possible. Several studies of this type have been cited above (page 156). Pareek[28,29] has made an interesting comparison of children in American, Japanese and Indian cultures. Using the American standardization and the Japanese norms compiled by Hayashi and Sumida,[11] this investigator found that Indian children are, in approximate terms, more extrapunitive and less intropunitive than American ones, while, as compared to these latter, the Japanese are even more intropunitive and less extrapunitive. These results were interpreted in terms of general cultural differences. A comparison of children in Hawaii with those on the American mainland made by Lyon and Vinacke[21] by means of the P-F also brought out significant differences. In particular, they found that Hawaiian boys were less intropunitive and ego-defensive and more extrapunitive than their American peers. In consequence of these findings they recommended the establishment of local norms for Hawaii—a step that has, of course, been taken in the foreign adaptations previously cited. The availability of comparable versions of the P-F Study for several nationalities and languages should prove useful to cultural anthropology and related endeavors.

In addition to the representative work cited in the foregoing survey, there are numerous other investigations in progress employing the P-F Study as a primary or ancillary technique. The instrument appears to have found a place both for clinical and research purposes in clinics and hospitals, schools and remedial institutions, and in various other settings in which the personality of the child in his reactions to frustration is in focus.

# References

1. Angelino, H. R.   The validity of the Rosenzweig Picture-Frustration Study (Children's Form). Unpublished doctoral dissertation, Univer. of Nebraska, 1951.
2. ——, & Shedd, C. L.   Reactions to frustration among normal and superior children. *J. int. Counc. except. Child.*, 1955, *21*, 215–218, 229–230.
3. ——, & ——.   A study of the reactions to "frustration" of a group of mentally retarded children as measured by the Rosenzweig Picture-Frustration Study. *Psychol. Newsltr.*, 1956, *8*, 49–54.
4. Clarke, H. J.   The Rosenzweig Picture-Frustration Study. *In* Anderson, H. H., & Anderson, G. L. (Eds.)   *An introduction to projective techniques.* New York: Prentice-Hall, 1951. Pp. 312–323.
5. ——, Rosenzweig, S., & Fleming, E. E.   The reliability of the scoring of the Rosenzweig Picture-Frustration Study. *J. clin. Psychol.*, 1947, *3*, 364–370.
6. Cox, F. N.   The Rosenzweig Picture-Frustration Study (Child Form). *Austrl. J. Psychol.*, 1957, *9*, 141–148.
7. Duhm, E., & Hansen, J.   *Der Rosenzweig P-F Test. Form für Kinder.* Göttingen: Verlag für Psychologie, 1957. (German translation of the Manual for the Children's Form of the P-F Study.)
8. Ferguson, R. G.   Some developmental factors in childhood aggression. *J. educ. Res.*, 1954, *48*, 15–27.
9. Ferracuti, F.   *Del Test P-F Study (Picture Frustration) di Rosenzweig.* (Il tipo per fanciulli) Manuale. Firenze: Organizzazioni Speciali, 1955. (Italian translation of the Manual for the Children's Form of the P-F Study.)
9a. Foster, A. L.   The relationship between EEG abnormality, some psychological factors and delinquent behavior. *J. proj. Tech.*, 1958, *22*, 276–280.
10. Habets, J. J. G. M.   Enige bevindingen over de Rosenzweig "Picture-Frustration Study" voor Kinderen. (Some experiences with the Rosenzweig Picture-Frustration Study for children.) *Ned Tijdschr. Psychol.*, 1958, *13*, 205–228.
11. Hayashi, K., & Sumida, K.   *The Rosenzweig P-F Study, Children's Form.* Kyoto City, Japan: Sankyobo, 1956. (Japanese translation of the Manual, with a Preface by S. Rosenzweig.)
12. Johannsen, D. E., & Bennett, E. M.   The personality of diabetic children. *J. genet. Psychol.*, 1955, *87*, 175–185.
13. Kates, S. L.   Suggestibility, submission to parents and peers, and extrapunitiveness, intropunitiveness, and impunitiveness in children. *J. Psychol.*, 1951, *31*, 233–241.
14. Krall, V.   Personality factors in accident prone and accident free children. Unpublished doctoral dissertation, Univer. of Rochester, 1951.
15. Lebbolo, F.   Contributo allo studio del "P.F. Study—Children form" di Saul Rosenzweig. *Publicazioni dell' Universita Cattolicà del S. Cuore.* (Milan, Italy) 1955, *49* (Nuova Serie), 300–402.
16. Leblanc, M.   Adaptation africaine et comparison interculturelle d'une èpreuve projective: Test de Rosenzweig. *Rev. Psychol. appl.*, 1956, *6*, 91–109.
17. Lesser, G.   Population differences in construct validity. *J. consult. Psychol.*, 1959, *23*, 60–65.

18. Levitt, E. E., & Lyle, W. H., Jr.   Evidence for the validity of the Children's Form of the Picture-Frustration Study. *J. consult. Psychol.*, 1955, *19*, 381–386.

19. Lindzey, G., & Goldwyn, R. M.   Validity of the Rosenzweig Picture-Frustration Study. *J. Pers.*, 1954, *22*, 519–547.

20. Lord, J. P.   Psychological correlates of nocturnal enuresis in male children. Unpublished doctoral dissertation, Harvard Univer., 1952.

21. Lyon, W., & Vinacke, W. E.   Picture-Frustration Study responses of institutionalized and non-institutionalized boys in Hawaii. *J. soc. Psychol.*, 1955, *41*, 71–83.

22. Mensh, I. N., & Mason, E. P.   Relationships of school atmosphere to reactions in frustrating situations. *J. educ. Res.*, 1951, *45*, 275–286.

23. Mirmow, E. L.   The method of successive clinical predictions in the validation of projective techniques with special reference to the Rosenzweig Picture-Frustration Study. Unpublished doctoral dissertation, Washington Univer., 1952.

24. ——.   The Rosenzweig Picture-Frustration Study. *In* Brower, D., and Abt, L. E. (Eds.)   *Progress in clinical psychology.* Vol. I, New York: Grune & Stratton, 1952. Ch. 13.

24a. Němec, J.   Contributions to the study of the motivational background of hyperkinetic dysphonia in childhood. *Logos* (Bull. Nat'l. Hosp. Speech Disorders), 1960, *3* (in press).

25. Pareek, U.   Reliability of the Indian adaptation of the Rosenzweig P-F Study (Children's Form). *J. psychol. Res.* (Madras, India), 1958, *2*, 18–23.

26. ——.   Scoring samples of Indian children on Rosenzweig P-F Study: *Naya Shikshak,* (Bikaner, India), April, 1959.

27. ——.   Some preliminary data about the Indian adaptation of the Rosenzweig P-F Study (Children's Form). *Educ. & Psychol.* (Delhi, India), 1958, *5*, 105–113.

28. ——.   A study of children's reactions to frustration with the help of Rosenzweig Picture-Frustration Study technique. Unpublished doctoral dissertation, Delhi Univer., India, 1958.

29. ——.   Studying cultural differences in personality development with the help of the Rosenzweig P-F Study. *Pratibha* (Bangalore, India), 1958, *2*, 115–123.

30. ——.   Validity of the Indian adaptation of the Rosenzweig P-F Study (Children's Form). *Psychol. Newsltr.*, 1958, *10*, 28–40.

31. ——, & Rosenzweig, S.   *Manual of the Indian adaptation of the Rosenzweig P-F Study (Children's Form).* Delhi, India: Manasayan, 1959.

32. Pichot, P., Freson, V., & Danjon, S.   *Le test de frustration de Rosenzweig (Forme pour enfants).* Paris, France: Centre de Psychologie Appliquée, 1956. (French translation of the Manual for the Children's Form of the P-F Study; appeared originally in *Rev. Psychol. appl.*, 1956, *6*, 111–138.)

33. Portnoy, B., & Stacey, C. L.   A comparative study of Negro and white subnormals on the children's form of the Rosenzweig P-F test. *Amer. J. ment. Defic.*, 1954, *59*, 272–278.

34. Rosenzweig, S.   The experimental measurement of types of reaction to frustration. *In* Murray, H. A. (Ed.)   *Explorations in personality.* New York: Oxford Univer. Press, 1938. Pp. 585–599.

35. ——.   The experimental study of psychoanalytic concepts. *Charact. & Pers.*, 1937, *6*, 61–71.

36. ——.   The experimental study of repression. *In* Murray, H. A. (Ed.)   *Explorations in personality.* New York: Oxford Univer. Press, 1938. Pp. 472–490.

37. ——.   An experimental study of 'repression' with special reference to need-persistive and ego-defensive reactions to frustration. *J. exp. Psychol.*, 1943, *32*, 64–74.

38. ——.   Idiodynamics in personality theory with special reference to projective methods. *Psychol. Rev.*, 1951, *58*, 213–223.

39. ——.   Levels of behavior in psychodiagnosis with special reference to the Picture-Frustration Study. *Amer. J. Orthopsychiat.*, 1950, *20*, 63–72.

40. ——.   A method of validation by successive clinical predictions. *J. abnorm. soc. Psychol.*, 1950, *45*, 507–509.

41. ——.   An outline of frustration theory. *In* Hunt, J. McV. (Ed.)   *Personality and the behavior disorders.* Vol. I. New York: Ronald Press, 1944. Pp. 379–388.

42. Rosenzweig, S.  The picture-association method and its application in a study of reactions to frustration. *J. Pers.*, 1945, *14*, 3–23.

43. ——.  Projective methods and psychometric criteria: a note of reply to J. P. Sutcliffe. *Austrl. J. Psychol.*, 1956, *8*, 152–155.

44. ——.  Rosenzweig Picture-Frustration Study. *In* Weider, A. (Ed.) *Contributions toward medical psychology*. Vol. II. New York: Ronald Press, 1953. Pp. 650–659.

45. ——.  A suggestion for making verbal personality tests more valid. *Psychol. Rev.*, 1934, *41*, 400–401.

46. ——.  A test for types of reaction to frustration. *Amer. J. Orthopsychiat.*, 1935, *5*, 395–403.

47. ——.  Types of reaction to frustration: an heuristic classification. *J. abnorm. soc. Psychol.*, 1934, *29*, 298–300.

47a. ——, Bundas, L. E., Lumry, K., & Davidson, H. W.  An elementary syllabus of psychological tests. *J. Psychol.*, 1944, *18*, 9–40 (see pp. 28–29).

48. ——, Mowrer, O. H., Haslerud, G. M., Curtis, Q. F., & Barker, R. G.  Frustration as an experimental problem. *Charact. & Pers.*, 1938, *7*, 126–160.

49. ——, Fleming, E. E., & Clarke, H. J.  *Revised scoring manual for the Rosenzweig Picture-Frustration Study*. St. Louis, Mo.: Published by Saul Rosenzweig, 1947. (Manual for the Adult Form. Appeared originally in *J. Psychol.*, 1947, *24*, 165–208.)

50. ——, ——, & Rosenzweig, L.  *The Children's Form of the Rosenzweig Picture-Frustration Study*. St. Louis, Mo.: Published by Saul Rosenzweig, 1948. (Manual for the Children's Form. Appeared originally in *J. Psychol.*, 1948, *26*, 141–191.)

51. ——, with Kogan, K.  *Psychodiagnosis*. New York: Grune & Stratton, 1949. Pp. 167–182.

52. ——, & Mirmow, E. L.  The validation of trends in the Children's Form of the Rosenzweig Picture-Frustration Study. *J. Pers.*, 1950, *18*, 306–314.

53. ——, & Rosenzweig, L.  Aggression in problem children and normals as evaluated by the Rosenzweig P-F Study. *J. abnorm. soc. Psychol.*, 1952, *47*, 683–687.

54. ——, & Sarason, S.  An experimental study of the triadic hypothesis: reaction to frustration, ego-defense, and hypnotizability. I. Correlational approach. II. Thematic apperception approach. *Charact. & Pers.*, 1942, *11*, 1–19; 150–165.

55. Sacco, F.  Studio della frustrazione col P-F test di Rosenzweig nei siciliani in età evolutiva. (Study of frustration by means of the Rosenzweig P-F Study, form for children, in Sicilian children.) *Infanz. anorm.*, 1955, *11*, 146–166.

56. Siegel, N. F.  An investigation of the interchangeable use of the Adult Form and the Children's Form of the Rosenzweig P-F Study on three levels of development. Unpublished master's thesis, The Pennsylvania State College, 1951.

57. Spache, G. D.  Appraising the personality of remedial pupils. In *Education in a free world*. Washington, D. C.: American Council on Education, 1955. Pp. 122–131.

58. ——.  Differential scoring of the Rosenzweig Picture-Frustration Study. *J. clin. Psychol.*, 1950, *6*, 406–408.

59. ——.  Personality characteristics of retarded readers as measured by the Picture-Frustration Study. *Educ. psychol. Measmt.*, 1954, *14*, 186–192.

60. ——.  Personality patterns of retarded readers. *J. educ. Res.*, 1957, *50*, 461–469.

61. ——.  Sex differences in the Rosenzweig P-F Study, Children's Form. *J. clin. Psychol.*, 1951, *7*, 235–238.

62. Stern, E.  Le test de Rosenzweig en neuro-psychiatrie infantile. *Psyché* (Paris), 1954, *87*, 35–46.

62a. Stoltz, R. E., & Smith, M. D.  Some effects of socioeconomic, age and sex factors on children's responses to the Rosenzweig Picture-Frustration Study. *J. clin. Psychol.*, 1959, *15*, 200–203.

63. Takala, A., & Takala, M.  Finnish children's reactions to frustration in the Rosenzweig test: an ethnic and cultural comparison. *Acta psychol.*, 1957, *13*, 43–50.

64. Vane, J. R.  Implications of the performance of delinquent girls on the Rosenzweig Picture-Frustration Study. *J. consult. Psychol.*, 1954, *18*, 414.

65. Van Roy, F.  *L'Enfant Infirme, son Handicap, son Drame, sa Guérison*. Paris: Delachaux & Niestlé S. A., 1954 (Especially Part Two, Chapters III and IV).

66. Watson, R. I.  *The clinical method in psychology*. New York: Harper, 1951, Ch. 15.

67. Wechsberg, F. O.  An experimental investigation of levels of behavior with special reference to the Rosenzweig Picture-Frustration Study. Unpublished doctoral dissertation, Washington Univer., 1951.

9

# Films as a Group Technique

MARY R. HAWORTH

THE EFFECTIVENESS of drama in revealing hidden feelings and conflicts was recognized by the world's greatest playwrights long before
the term "projection" was coined and applied to clinical phenomena.
Shakespeare stated the projective concept in the well known lines:

> The play's the thing
> Wherein I'll catch the conscience of the king.

Goethe, in the Prelude to *Faust*, suggests the selective participation of
the audience:

> Each tender soul, with sentimental power,
> Sucks melancholy food from your creation;
> And now in this, now that, the leaven works,
> For each beholds what in his bosom lurks.
> They still are moved at once to weeping or to laughter.

Even more than adults, children seem to identify closely with characters
in a drama and continue to impersonate them in subsequent free play and
games. Movement and action appeal to children; they "live" a play with
real intensity.

## Film Dynamics

The use of a filmed play as a projective technique seems to offer real
promise in work with children. The appeal of drama and animation is combined with a standard stimulus that can be "produced" with the flick of a
switch. The child-subject need not create a whole story but is stimulated to
respond to the characters and activities portrayed on the screen. Studies
of the film-viewing process indicate that this method may be an aid in reaching unconscious levels of personality. Similarities to the hypnotic state have
been pointed out.[11,28] The dark room, the focusing on a bright light and the
reduction of extraneous distractions all combine to weaken defenses.

### Children's Reactions to Films

Various methods have been employed to assess children's reactions to
films, both in this country and abroad. Early studies, in the 1930's, focussed
on physiologic concomitants.[8,22] French investigators[13,14,20] have been
concerned with age differences in overt manifestations, i.e., laughing, clap-

ping, restlessness, talking to neighbors, verbal comments and ease of distraction. Infrared photography has been used in the United States, England, France, Germany and Denmark[7,10,15] to take continuous pictures of child-audiences while watching films.

It has been found that both adults[5] and children[9,36] give more dynamic verbal responses to films than to still pictures. The progression from simple description to a more interpretive approach occurs at a much earlier age with films than with still pictures.

When scenes in a film touched problem areas actually experienced by a clinic group, Heuyer et al.[21] found the children would object to these scenes or omit them in retelling the story of the film, although other details were accurately recalled.

## Identification with Film Characters

The extent of identification has been a major subject of interest. Studies with adult psychiatric patients[29,34] indicate strong emotional identifications with the central film character. In an experimental approach, McIntyre[26] found that increasing the similarity of film protagonist to viewer did not increase projection. Stein[33] found that the sex of the film character was no barrier to identification.

Studies of children's film identifications by Albert[1] and Maccoby and Wilson[27] concur in finding strongest identifications with like-sexed protagonists. Actions and words of the "identificand" were recalled the most frequently.[27]

With but one exception,[5] all of the filmed projective tests to be discussed have avoided the use of human actors. Instead, animated cartoons,[12] silhouettes,[9] canaries[11] and puppets[18,23] have been used. Fulchignoni[11] feels quite strongly that if any film character should remind the subject of someone close to him in real life, this would interfere with the identification process.

## Use of Films in Therapy

Films have been successfully used in therapy with adults as a means of "loosening up" and so facilitating access to repressed material. Prados[28] sees this as a way of enabling the patient to become aware of his own emotions without fear or guilt, since the group situation gives a feeling of safety and reassurance. Rome[3] and Schwartz[32] showed combat scenes to subjects with war neurosis and found that the original fear and panic reactions could be safely relived and then worked through in follow-up group sessions. Rubin and Katz[31] developed "auroratone" films (abstract color patterns combined with music) to create moods which aided rapport and stimulated the subjects' participation in subsequent individual or group therapy.

### Filmed Projective Techniques

The earliest attempt at using a film as a projective technique was briefly reported in 1941 by Lerner and Murphy.[23] As part of a comprehensive personality study of preschool children, they presented a marionette film, noting children's reactions during the showing and their subsequent play with similar real puppets. Since 1949, six films have been specifically designed as projective techniques, three for use with adults and three with children.

## Adult Tests

Lundin[24,25] has produced a film test, somewhat analogous to the Rorschach, in which patterned movements are produced by placing iron filings over magnets. He found the test responses discriminated between normal and clinical adult groups. Gemelli,[12] in Italy, filmed TAT situations using animated cartoons. In 1955, Cohen-Séat and Rébeillard[5] published their Test Filmique Thématique in France. This consists of a series of short, filmed sequences without sound in which human actors are used. The subject is asked to describe each scene and complete its story. Formal aspects of the stories are noted, as well as the identification figures, emotions and attitudes of the characters and the types of endings.

## Children's Tests

Eiserer[9] designed a projective device employing silhouettes to determine the relative merits of filmed or still pictures. He prepared two parallel series of adolescent-parent situations which he presented to 50 adolescent boys. He concluded that the filmed sequences elicited more psychologically meaningful material than did the still pictures.

Fulchignoni,[11] in Italy, developed a film depicting the activities of a family of canaries. After the showing, the child subjects are asked a standard set of questions designed to reveal attitudes toward parents and siblings, dependency needs, anxieties, fears of abandonment and self punitiveness.

Haworth[17,18] has worked with the filmed puppet play *Rock-A-Bye, Baby*, produced by Haworth and Woltmann.[19] The play was originally one of a series of live puppet shows written and given by Woltmann[2,35] in the Children's Observation Ward of the Psychiatric Division of Bellevue Hospital. The filmed version can be used as a group screening device for school children and will be discussed in more detail in later sections of this chapter.

## Inquiry Methods in Film Presentations

Four general methods have been used for securing responses in film studies:

a. The film is stopped at a critical point, and the audience is asked to suggest endings to the story.[4,18] This is usually referred to as the "half-show" technique.

b. The subject supplies endings to each of a series of short sequences.[5,9,12]

c. A standard set of questions is asked after the complete film showing.[11,13,18]

d. The subject is asked to retell the story immediately afterwards[14,20,21,36] or at a later date.[6,16,27,29]

## Rock-A-Bye, Baby

As previously stated, live puppet plays have been used as a group technique for diagnosis and therapy[2,3,35] and seemed a logical choice for conversion into film. *Rock-A-Bye, Baby,* originally written by Woltmann[35] for use at Bellevue, was made into a 35 minute, 16 mm. sound film.[19]* Scenes from the film are shown in figure 1.

Fig. 1.—Scenes from *Rock-A-Bye, Baby:* (A) Casper with his mother and father; (B) Mother leaves the baby with Casper.

## Synopsis of the Film†

Casper is the main figure in a story based on sibling rivalry. In the early scenes he is shown arriving home from school, kissing his mother and eager to play with her. She resists his rough play and finally tells him that he will soon have a baby brother or sister and must now take more responsibility for himself, such as going to the toilet and washing his own hands before dinner.

*Adolf G. Woltmann played the parts of Casper, the father and the witch, while Adaline Harriman played the mother.

†The complete film script is given in Woltmann[35] and was used in the film with the permission of the publisher, Prentice-Hall, Inc.

Fig. 1 (*continued*)—(*C*) Witch puts a spell on the milk; (*D*) Casper gives the milk to the baby; (*E*) Casper forces the witch to remove the spell; (*F*) Casper resolves to take care of the baby.

The next scene opens with mother holding the baby and asking the child-audience to help her put the baby to sleep by singing "Rock-a-Bye, Baby." Casper rushes in, yelling and shouting, and is told to be quiet and take a nap beside the baby. He repeatedly gets up and makes noises while his mother's back is turned. After mother exits he scolds the baby and finally hits her in a wave of jealousy.

Mother comes in and comforts the baby, then leaves Casper in charge while she goes to the store. He calls the witch and asks her to take the baby. She refuses to do this but does cast a spell on the baby's milk and then disappears. The baby cries as Casper gives her the bottle; mother returns and rushes the baby to the hospital. Overcome with remorse, Casper asks the audience what he should do. (At this point the film is stopped for the half-show discussion and then resumed.)

Casper calls back the witch, tells her he made a terrible mistake and begs her to remove the spell. He beats her with a huge stick until she says the magic words, then completes her demise. Mother returns with the healthy baby, and father joins in the happy homecoming while Casper is given some of his favorite ice cream.

In the final scene Casper, holding the baby, tells the audience how glad he is that the baby is well; how sorry he feels for what he has done; and that he will never think of harming her again. As a final gesture, he asks the children to help him sing the baby to sleep with "Rock-a-Bye, Baby."

### Significance of the Characters

In a sense the puppet characters in the film are analogous to the ambiguous representations of persons in the still-picture tests; both can be viewed as prototypes of persons in general, in situations in which realistic characters might be too threatening. Bender and Woltmann[2,3,35] emphasize that each of the puppet figures represents a single attitude, emotion or aspect of personality. The symbolic, fantasy nature of puppets is seen as an aid in identification. In addition, various emotional situations which would be difficult to portray verbally can be easily communicated to children through actions and gestures.

Casper could be *any* boy between the ages of five and 12, with features more caricatured than real and with clothes that do not tie him to any period of fashion. He can defend himself against dangers and always finds solutions to his problems. His stick, bequeathed to him by previous generations of Kasperlen, Guignols and Harlequins, is a phallic symbol of vitality and power.

On the assumption that children see their parents as having a combination of both good and bad qualities, the witch personifies the bad part of the mother. On her, the child can project all that is harsh, demanding, refusing and unloving in his own mother. It is safe and acceptable to destroy this symbolic figure. Woltmann[35] points out that it is only the truly fantasy characters (witch, crocodile, giant) that are killed in the puppet plays. These killing sequences employ the use of countless repetitions which seem to have a cathartic effect that would be missed if the death was sudden and complete.

Casper's parents represent his superego. The detective father symbolizes authority in the home and the sanctions of society. These "good" parents are loving, protecting, and the givers of food.

### Technique of Administering the Film

Detailed suggestions for presenting the film and scoring the protocols are given in the manual.[19] The film seems most suitable for children from five to 10 years of age. Groups should be kept fairly small (usually from 9 to 16 children), depending on the number of adults available for the follow-up inquiry. Each adult can interview three or four children. A complete testing session usually takes an hour.

Responses are secured at two points: (a) during the "half-show" when the film is stopped and the children are given the opportunity, as a group, to suggest endings for the story; (b) after the showing is completed when each child is asked, individually, the following questions*:

No.  1 (Like): What did you like best about the show?
No.  2 (Not like): What did you not like about the show?
No.  3 (Identif): Which one of the people in the show would you most like to be? Why?
No.  4 (Mother): What did Casper think of his mother?

*Each question is preceded by the abbreviation to be used in subsequent discussions of individual protocols.

No.  5 (Father): What did Casper think of his father?

No.  6 (Have Ba): What did Casper think when his mother told him he was going to have a baby sister?

No.  7 (Witch): How did you like the witch? Why?

No.  8 (Ba sick): How did Casper feel when the baby got sick?

No.  9 (Punish): Should Casper be punished for what he did? Why? How should he be punished?

No. 10 (What say): What should Casper say if his mother asks him about the baby's sickness?

No. 11 (Get rid): Why did Casper try to get rid of his baby sister?

No. 12 (Ba well): How did Casper feel when the baby got well?

No. 13 (What next): What will happen next if the show goes on?

An Analysis Sheet (fig. 2) is used as an aid in evaluating the child's responses. Each index has been developed on the basis of patterns of deviate responses secured in the testing of 500 children. The purpose of these indices is not to arrive at a numerical score but rather to highlight areas in which the child's answers stand out as being atypical for his age or sex group. After an initial screening by means of the film, it is suggested that those children who show high "scores" in two or more areas should then be given a more complete diagnostic evaluation with an individual projective battery.

## Illustrative Protocols*

Examples will be given of protocols which would be scored high on the various indices and of portions of others which are qualitatively significant in view of known facts about the child's real-life situation. All are taken from a sample of "normal" school children.

### Jealousy

*Jerry*, aged six, was a serious, quiet and very sensitive little boy, the oldest of three children. He had been quite upset, at the age of four, when the last baby was born. During the show he became excited and involved with the action, talked a great deal to the puppets, and showed strong guilt feelings by scolding Casper and telling on him in response to the puppet-mother's questioning. In the subsequent inquiry, he revealed an almost pathetic desire to be the baby again (no. 3, no. 11). In the half-show, the initial guilt and need for punishment is followed by an expression of aggression against the baby. Note also the constant concern with the witch as the agent for eliminating the baby; feelings of rejection by the mother (no. 4); and the glaringly obvious slip of the tongue on no. 9.

Half-show: Casper and the witch would die, I think the baby would too.

No.  1 (Like): When the witch got hit with the log.

No.  2 (Not like): When witch made baby sick.

No.  3 (Identif): Baby, I'd like to be holded.

No.  4 (Mother): That she wouldn't talk to him and he didn't like it.

No.  5 (Father): He would put him in jail.

No.  6 (Have Ba): Don't know. (Q) Funny. (Q) Didn't like.

No.  7 (Witch): I hated her. (Q) Ugly and had white eyes.

No.  8 (Ba sick): He felt bad.

No.  9 (Punish): No, because he killed the baby—not the baby but the witch.

No. 10 (What say): The witch made her sick.

No. 11 (Get rid): He didn't like her, he wanted to be a little baby.

No. 12 (Ba well): Fine.

No. 13 (What next): Don't know. (Q) You'd see the witch. (Q) That's all.

*Several of the protocols have appeared previously in *Genetic Psychology Monographs* (1957, *56*, 257–296) and are reproduced here with the permission of the publishers.

Fig. 2.—Analysis Sheet for *Rock-A-Bye, Baby.*

Name:       Birthdate:       Age:       Sex:

Date of test:       School:       Grade:       Sib. R:

## TEST BEHAVIOR

During film showing:

..........1) Talks to puppets

..........2) Suggests aggression to baby

..........3) Scolds or tells on Casper

..........4) Confuses witch with parents

..........5) Autoerotic activity (masturbate, wet)

..........6) Unusually excited, tense, upset

During inquiry:

..........7) Autoerotic activity

       (Masturbate, wet, thumb suck)

## SELF CONCEPT

A. *Identification,* #3

1) Usual:

..........a) Casper

..........b) Same-sex parent

2) Deviant for sex and age:

..........a) Baby (Boys from 5 years)

       (Girls from 8 years)

..........b) Witch (Boys from 8 years)

       (Girls from 6 years)

..........c) Casper to aggress vs. witch

       (Boys from 8 years)

       (Girls at all ages)

3) Always deviant:

..........a) Opposite-sex parent

..........b) Punitive parent

..........c) Intropunitive

..........d) Aggressive

..........e) Refusal

B. *Attitudes to Casper*

..........1) Bodily injury to Casper

..........2) Catastrophes to Casper

..........3) Punished or not loved by parents

..........4) Superior to Casper (# or during show)

..........5) Casper loved and accepted

## JEALOUSY INDEX

(High score = 3 or more)

..........1) Jealousy (one check)

..........2) Identif. with baby, #3 (boys only)

..........3) Two defensive signs, HS, #6, 8–13

       (one check)

  (a)..........Slips

  (b)..........Evasions

  (c)..........Ambivalences

  (d)..........Personal references

Aggression against baby:

..........4) During show    ..........8) #7 Witch/

..........5) Half-show    ..........9) #8 Ba sick/

..........6) #1 Like/    ..........10) #12 Ba well/

..........7) #3 Identif/    ..........11) #13 What

                next/

## AGGRESSION TO PARENTS

..........1) At half-show or #13

..........2) Dislike parents, #2

..........3) Hostility or aggression in inquiry

## GUILT INDEX

(High score = 2 or more)

..........1) Mother didn't know, #9

..........2) Bed or sleep

..........3) Father rejects Casper

..........4) Guilt and/or restitution

..........5) Baby stinks

..........6) Casper or baby in water

..........7) Kissing

## ANXIETY INDEX

(High score = 2 or more)

.......... 1) Identif. with witch, #3

.......... 2) Identif. with Casper to hit witch, #3

.......... 3) Witch aggress vs. Casper

.......... 4) Casper punished for killing witch

.......... 5) Casper punished with stick

.......... 6) Witch should be punished

.......... 7) Witch symbolism

.......... 8) Spy on witch

.......... 9) Confuse witch with parent (# or during

       show)

..........10) Bodily injury to Casper

## INDEX OF OBSESSIVE TRENDS

(High score = 7 or more)

Must have five checks:

..........1) Usual identif. for age and sex, #3

..........2) Casper should be punished, #9

..........3) Ambivalent to parent

..........4) Ambivalent to baby

..........5) One other ambivalent or balanced

       response

At least two checks:

..........6) Blocks or evades

..........7) Details, quotes, or additions

..........8) Superior to Casper (# or during show)

..........9) No method of punishment or two, #9

## Children from Broken Homes

*Billy* and *Johnny* (each aged six) lived with their mothers, and each reacted with strong feelings of guilt and rejection with respect to the father figure. *Billy* gave a deviant, punitive reason for wishing to be the father: "So I can lick the boy," and said Casper should be punished (no. 9) by having "his *dad* lick him and put him to bed."

Excerpts from *Johnny's* protocol reveal feelings of rejection by both his mother and father, jealousy of his own younger sister and the need for self punishment (half-show):

Half-show: Casper will get put in jail, the baby will live.
No. 4 (Mother): She only wanted the baby.
No. 5 (Father): He didn't want Casper (twisted neck of sweater).
No. 11 (Get rid): She was getting too much attention (twisted neck of sweater).

Five year old *Judy* lived with her working mother and seldom saw her father. Any mention of the kissing scenes has proved to be a very rare response and seems to signify the arousal of strong affect (see no. 5). *Judy* (an "only" child) has emphasized the mother's role in the hospital sequence as a means of expressing her own anxiety when mother leaves for work and her relief when mother returns.

No. 5 (Father): Casper liked him. (Q) Because he was kissing him.
No. 11 (Get rid): He didn't like her, because she was always crying. (Q) Mother took the baby to the hospital and he didn't want his mother to go.
No. 12 (Ba well): He felt better, happy for the mother to get back and because the baby felt better.

## Guilt

Certain patterns of responses were given significantly more often by the small proportion of children who engaged in autoerotic practices during the film showing or the inquiry period. The film scene which elicits many of the "guilty" responses is the one in which Casper keeps getting up from his bed at naptime to play or make noises behind his mother's back. The appearance of a cluster of such responses in a protocol would seem to indicate the presence of strong guilt feelings probably, but not necessarily, related to masturbatory and other autoerotic activities.

*Nancy* (aged six) was the only child, of 500 who have been tested, who requested to go to the bathroom before answering the questions. In view of her subsequent masturbation during the inquiry (see no. 5), she would appear to be easily aroused in the genital area.

Half-show: Mother will *wake up* the boy, Father will come and *get* the little boy.
No. 1 (Like): Where the baby was crying.
No. 2 (Not like): Boy and the witch. (Q) The boy made the witch die.
No. 3 (Identif): *The Daddy*, because he took the little boy to wash his hands.
No. 4 (Mother): The boy made a noise, the mother came and said "What's that noise?" He thinks *his mother would lick him.*
No. 5 (Father): (Child tugged on belt and elastic of underpants with skirt up.) Father came and *kissed the baby and picked the baby up* (masturbated).
No. 6 (Have Ba): (Refused to answer.)
No. 7 (Witch): Didn't like it. (Q) He's funny. (Q) He had a *long nose.*
No. 8 (Ba sick): He felt bad.
No. 9 (Punish): Yes, because he made the baby cry. (How punish?) Get a licking.
No. 10 (What say): Don't know.
No. 11 (Get rid): Didn't like it. (Q) It didn't have no hair.
No. 12 (Ba well): Pretty good.
No. 13 (What next): Father and mother. (Q) Baby too. (Q) Casper will get another bottle and give it to the baby.

Qualitative aspects of *Nancy's* protocol lend credibility to the hypothesis of masturbatory guilt. The half-show response brings both parents into a bedroom scene, while the answer to no. 4 shows preoccupation with the napping sequence and the expectation of a "licking" for whatever is going on there. It is quite unusual for a girl to identify with the father on no. 3 and also to give punitive reasons for such an identification. The deviant kissing response (no. 5), which in this case also implies less attention being shown to Casper by the father, was the point at which masturbation was obvious. Her agitation or self absorption was sufficient to cause blocking and refusal on the following question and to produce the symbolic masturbatory-phallic response of the witch's "long nose" on no. 7.

During a follow-up study a year later, the teacher reported that the family had moved but that in *Nancy's* last few months at school she had become extremely sensitive and withdrawn, crying if "anyone even looked at her."

## Anxiety

The witch, in fairy tales and dreams, is generally regarded as a symbol of the bad or castrating mother. Certain children showed unusual preoccupation with this character in the film story, and their responses reflect identification with the witch, the desire to express aggression against her, the expectation of punishment in kind (via the stick) and fears of personal attack or bodily injury. These responses were most often given by boys from broken homes, "only" children, children rated by their teachers as "most aggressive," and those with a record of previous or current bed wetting.

*Tommy* (aged six) was rated by his teacher as being very aggressive. His complete protocol mentioned four spankings for Casper and two "boppings" for the witch.

No. 3 (Identif): The witch, I'd like to *see* how those witches act. I'd like to go *into their house* and *steal* some of their *magic*.

No. 4 (Mother): Don't really know. (Q) He thought his *mother* would give him a *spanking*.

No. 12 (Ba well): The *witch needed a good bopping* to take care of the witch.

No. 13 (What next): (Long pause) Casper would get a *spanking*.

The reasons given for his identification—wanting to see, to enter the witches' house and to steal from women—suggest fear of the mother as castrator. Immediately following this response he suggests the mother will spank. Finally, on no. 12, he can express hostility toward this witch-mother, for which due punishment is again received on no. 13.

*Malcolm*, in a different showing, gave a response similar to *Tommy's* no. 3, which strongly suggests voyeurism and castration fears: "I'd like to *see* the witch *stand on her head* and make some *things disappear*."

## Obsessive Indications

A few children gave protocols containing numerous obsessive features: meticulous attention to details, direct quotations, lengthy and highly elabororated responses, expressions of doubt and indecision, critical comments, doing and undoing, and moralizations.

*Charles* was a fifth grade boy. Note the unusually detailed answer to no. 1, the blocking on no. 10, and the weighing and balancing of phrases throughout.

Half-show: While the witch got away, Casper tells his mother, his mother tells his father. The father goes out and finds the witch. He's a detective and doesn't make any noise. He finds a book and can find a spell to take the spell away and make the baby well.

No. 1 (Like): First, when the witch changed the baby to make it sick. Later, when mother was trying to get Casper to go to sleep and he'd keep getting up, and when the detective came home and said, "Where is everyone?" and Casper lied. Also it would be better if he'd tell the truth, he'd get along better. I also liked when the witch came in and the second time when Casper was pounding her.

No. 2 (Not like): I liked all of it.

No. 3 (Identif): Casper, he seems funny, enjoyable.

No. 4 (Mother): He thought she didn't like him very well, just didn't care for him as much.

No. 5 (Father): Just about the same. I think he thought his father was a little nicer but thought his mother didn't care for him as much.

No. 6 (Have Ba): He thought that he didn't want her. I think that's right. He'd like to have a baby sister. But in the second part he didn't like her and wanted to kill her.

No. 7 (Witch): I liked the parts when she was funny, laughing. I didn't like it when she changed the baby to be sick and blue in the head.

No. 8 (Ba sick): Sorry that he made witch do that and wished he hadn't done it.

No. 9 (Punish): Well, yes and no. One way, yes, because he should think of sister better. No, because the second time he was sorry.

No. 10 (What say): He lied to his father. What did you say? (Q was repeated.) She'd want to find out what happened? (Q—would Casper tell her?) I don't think so because he didn't like her then.

No. 11 (Get rid): He didn't like her, he didn't want one.

No. 12 (Ba well): Pretty good, pretty nice.

No. 13 (What next): Let's see, maybe the witch had a sister and found Casper killed her sister. She's a bad witch and will get her powers and try to get Casper. (Q—will she?) No, I don't think so.

## Research with Rock-A-Bye, Baby

*Rock-A-Bye, Baby* was originally shown to approximately 250 children attending nursery school, first, third and fifth grades.[18] Age and sex norms were determined, and deviant responses (those given by less than 10 per cent of cases) were incorporated into various indices for scoring purposes. Subsequently the film has been shown to a new sample of 250 kindergarteners, first and second graders.

### Comparison of Samples

The proportion of children scoring high on each index was determined for each grade level of each sample. (Results for the nursery school group were not included, as many of the four year olds did not respond adequately). Except for one aspect of identification, no significant differences in percentages of high scores were found between the two first grade samples.

The incidence of obsessive indicators, jealousy and deviant identifications showed no differences throughout the total age range. A significant drop in amount of aggression expressed toward the parents occurred between kindergarten and first grade and was maintained through the fifth grade, thus pointing to the strengthening of controls and defenses during the socialization process. The proportions of children receiving high scores on the anxiety and guilt indices showed significant decreases between the second and third grade. In terms of the film responses, it would seem that high scores on these two indices in the early latency period are reflecting specific aspects of anxiety (i.e., castration) and guilt (i.e., masturbation) in those children who may be experiencing more than the usual difficulties in the resolution of the Oedipal situation. The markedly few high scores (around 2 per cent) beyond the second grade become especially significant, since general conditions of stability and conformity seem to be established for most children by the ages of 8 or 10.

## Effect of the Group

The extent to which a child might be influenced by responses of the other children was studied in a first grade sample of 112 children.[18] While 28 per cent of half-show responses were repetitions of responses previously given, only an infinitesimal proportion of the final inquiry statements were borrowed from either "own" or "other's" previous comments at the half-show. There was also some evidence that shy children feel supported and encouraged to respond as a result of the group situation.

## Evidences of Projection

Study was made of any differences that might exist between those children who had experienced a situation similar to Casper's (i.e., the arrival of a younger sibling in the family) and youngest or "only" children. Significant differences with respect to the baby and to the parents were found, as well as sex differences within and between sibling groupings.[18]

## Superego Development

A pilot study[18] suggests that the particular problem story presented in this film may lend itself to a meaningful differentiation in terms of levels of superego attainment. A Superego Scale was developed whereby protocols could be scored for the proportions of responses indicating immature, severe or adequate stages of development. (Most protocols contained varying numbers of responses that could be scored for each stage.) For normal children, age progressions were apparent in the direction of less "immature" and more "adequate" responses, with the "severe" level remaining fairly low. In contrast, at all age levels, the obsessive children had an outstandingly high proportion of "severe" indicators. The anxiety and guilt groupings showed equal proportions of "immature" and "severe" responses which were also greater than the "adequate" ones. It may well be that the presence of a large proportion of severe level responses may be an indication of emotional disturbance. "Normal" children, at least in response to this test, did not give indications of experiencing a phase of development in which the superego level was predominantly severe.

## Validation Procedures

The validity of personality assessment based on the film responses has been studied by various means: teacher rankings, anecdotes and problems mentioned in school records, followup observations, comparisons with clinic cases, differential responses of various sibling groupings, and the responses of children displaying autoerotic habits.

A more carefully controlled project is currently under way. Experimental groups consisting of children scoring high on the Obsessive Index and those scoring high on both Anxiety and Guilt are being compared with controls (matched for age and sex) who did not score high on any index. A battery

of projective tests—Rorschach, CAT, Despert Fables and Draw-a-Person—
is being administered individually to each child.

*Reliability*

Inter-scorer reliability for three judges scoring the Jealousy, Guilt,
Anxiety and Obsessive Indices yielded average reliability coefficients of
.94, .83, .92 and .91, respectively. (The markedly lower coefficient on the
Guilt Index could be consistently traced to oversight of a very objectively
defined criterion for one of the items. Increased "vigilance" with respect to
the presence of this response would result in almost equivalent reliability
measures for all four indices.)

## Summary

The use of film as a projective medium is still in its infancy but already
has demonstrated merit in that meaningful material can be elicited from
young children, and large numbers of children can be assessed in a short
period of time. As an initial screening device, it should serve a useful purpose
in school settings.

Many promising possibilities for future research can be envisaged: studying
the relative effectiveness of animal, puppet or Disney-like characters;
exploring the projective possibilities of a series of short action sequences;
further study of the identification process; and consideration of the dynamic
aspects of group participation in the film-viewing situation.

## References

1. Albert, R. S.  The role of mass media and the effect of aggressive film content upon
   children's aggressive responses and identification choices. *Genet. Psychol. Monogr.*,
   1957, *55*, 221–285.
2. Bender, L., & Woltmann, A. G.  The use of puppet shows as a psychotherapeutic
   method for behavior problems in children. *Amer. J. Orthopsychiat.*, 1936, *6*, 341–354.
3. ——, & ——.  Play and psychotherapy. *Nerv. Child*, 1941, *1*, 17–42.
4. Bouman, J. C., Heuyer, G., & Lebovici, S.  Une expérience d'étude de groupes. Le
   process de l'identification et l'importance de la suggestibilité dans la situation cinéma-
   tographique. *Rev. int. Filmol.*, 1953, *4*, 111–141.
5. Cohen-Séat, G., & Rébeillard, M.  Test Filmique Thématique. *Rev. int. Filmol.*, 1955,
   *6*, 111–118.
6. Conrad, H. S., & Jones, H. E.  Psychological studies of motion pictures: III. Fidelity
   of report as a measure of adult intelligence. *Univer. California Publ. Psychol.*, 1929,
   *3*, No. 7.
7. Dawson, Margaret G.  *The children's film library and special children's programs.*
   (4th ed.) New York: National Children's Film Library, 1949.
8. Dysinger, W. S., & Ruckmick, C. A.  *The emotional responses of children to the motion
   picture situation.* New York: Macmillan, 1933.
9. Eiserer, P. E.  The relative effectiveness of motion and still pictures as stimuli for
   eliciting fantasy stories about adolescent-parent relationships. *Genet. Psychol. Monogr.*,
   1949, *39*, 205–278.
10. Field, M.  *Children and films.* Dunfermline, Fife, Scotland: Carnegie United Kingdom
    Trust, 1954.
11. Fulchignoni, E.  Examen d'un test filmique. *Rev. int. Filmol.*, 1951, *2*, 173–183.
12. Gemelli, A.  Le film, procédé d'analyse projective. *Rev. int. Filmol.*, 1951, *2*, 135–138.

13. Gratiot-Alphandéry, H.   L'enfant et le film. *Rev. int. Filmol.*, 1951, *2*, 171–172.
14. ——.   Jeunes spectateurs. *Rev. int. Filmol.*, 1951, *2*, 257–263.
15. Greenhill, L. P.   The recording of audience reactions by infra-red photography. Technical Report—SPECDEVCEN 269-7-56. Instructional Film Research Program, The Pennsylvania State University, 1955.
16. Haladay, P. W., & Stoddard, G. D.   *Getting ideas from the movies.* New York: Macmillan, 1933.
17. Haworth, M. R.   Les recherches filmologiques et les situations de test projectif appliquées aux enfants. *Rev. int. Filmol.*, 1956, *7*, 177–192.
18. ——.   The use of a filmed puppet show as a group projective technique for children. *Genet. Psychol. Monogr.*, 1957, *56*, 257–296.
19. ——, & Woltmann, A. G.   *Rock-A-Bye, Baby: A group projective test for children.* Manual and film (16 mm, 35 min., black and white, sound). University Park, Pa.: Psychological Cinema Register, 1959.
20. Herbinière-Lebert, S.   Pourquoi et comment nous avons fait *Maine Blanchez.* Premières expériences avec un film éducatif réalise spécialement pour les moins de sept ans. *Rev. int. Filmol.*, 1951, *2*, 247–255.
21. Heuyer, G., Lebovici, S., & Bertagna, L.   Sur quelques réactions d'enfants inadaptés. *Rev. int. Filmol.*, 1952, *3*, 71–79.
22. Kleitman, N.   The effect of motion pictures on body temperature. *Science*, 1945, *101*, 507–508.
23. Lerner, E., & Murphy, L. B.   Methods for the study of personality in young children. *Monogr. Soc. Res. Child Developm.*, 1941, *6*, No. 4 (Serial No. 30).
24. Lundin, W. H.   Projective movement sequences: motion pictures as a projective technique. *J. consult. Psychol.*, 1949, *13*, 407–411.
25. ——.   Projective movement sequences in the study of personality. *J. proj. Tech.*, 1954, *18*, 208–220.
26. McIntyre, C. J.   Sex, age and iconicity as factors in projective film tests. *J. consult. Psychol.*, 1954, *18*, 337–343.
27. Maccoby, E. E., & Wilson, W. C.   Identification and observational learning from films. *J. abnorm. soc. Psychol.*, 1957, *55*, 76–87.
28. Prados, M.   The use of films in psychotherapy. *Amer. J. Orthopsychiat.*, 1951, *21*, 36–46.
29. ——.   The use of pictorial images in group therapy. *Amer. J. Psychother.*, 1951, *5*, 196–214.
30. Rome, H. P.   Therapeutic films and group psychotherapy. *Sociometry*, 1945, *8*, 485–492.
31. Rubin, R. E., & Katz, E.   Auroratone films for the treatment of psychotic depressions in an Army General Hospital. *J. clin. Psychol.*, 1946, *2*, 333–340.
32. Schwartz, L. A.   Group psychotherapy in the war neuroses. *Amer. J. Psychiatry*, 1945, *101*, 498–500.
33. Stein, E. M.   The influence of the sex variable in the perception of two mental health motion pictures. Unpublished master's thesis, The Pennsylvania State College, 1952.
34. ——.   An exploratory investigation of the use of motion pictures in the treatment of hospitalized psychiatric patients. Unpublished doctoral dissertation, The Pennsylvania State University, 1954.
35. Woltmann, A. G.   The use of puppetry as a projective method in therapy. *In* Anderson, H. H., & Anderson, G. L. (Eds.) *An introduction to projective techniques.* New York: Prentice-Hall, 1951. Pp. 606–638.
36. Zazzo, B., & Zazzo, R.   Une expérience sur la compréhension du film. *Rev. int. Filmol.*, 1951, *2*, 159–170.

# Part IV: Verbal Methods

**10**

## Story Completions: Madeleine Thomas Stories and Similar Methods

HELMUT WÜRSTEN

WHAT METHODS are available to explore the inner world of the child? How can we evaluate the type and extent of emotional conflicts that are interfering with the healthy functioning and adjustment of the child? Madeleine Thomas, a clinical psychologist and psychoanalyst in Switzerland, asked herself these questions. In one of her papers,[24] published in 1937, she briefly points out the limitations of the direct interview, and the very helpful but extremely time-consuming aspects of the psychoanalytic methods as used by Anna Freud and Melanie Klein. Madeleine Thomas noticed the need for a useful, subtle method of investigation which could be applied effectively in a busy child guidance clinic. Dr. André Rey of the University of Geneva suggested that a series of incomplete short stories be constructed which would depict various aspects of the child's everyday life. The subject would be invited to complete the stories and thus have ample opportunity to use his fantasy and imagination.

A method was devised which would permit exploration of the child's inner world and of his possible areas of conflict and yet not involve the examiner in this process too much and not intensify the patient's defenses excessively. By orienting the stories towards some possible or probable conflict area in a subtle way, it might be possible to discover some of the child's emotional difficulties, problems and conflicts which the patient might ordinarily be very reluctant to reveal or to admit in a direct conversation, and which might take a long time to elicit through psychoanalytic play methods.

Fifteen stories or items were selected by Madeleine Thomas. They represent samples of everyday activities and problems encountered at home and school, as well as samples of the fantasy life and dream world experienced by a fictitious child of the same sex and similar age as the patient. The stories were translated by the present author in 1947 and have been used extensively with both European and American children. Mills [9-12] and others have used the stories in the United States.

### The Stories

1. A boy (or girl) goes to school. During recess he does not play with the other children, he stays by himself in a corner. Why?
2. A boy fights with his brother. Mother comes. What is going to happen?
3. A boy is at the table with his parents. Father suddenly gets angry. Why?

4. One day, Mother and Father are a bit angry with each other. They have been arguing. Why?

5. Sometimes he likes to tell funny stories (a) to his friends (b) to his parents. What kind?

6. A boy has gotten bad grades in school. He returns home. To whom is he going to show his report card? Who is going to scold him most?

7. It is Sunday. This boy has been taken for a ride with Mother and Father. Upon their return home, Mother is sad. Why?

8. This boy has a friend whom he likes very much. One day his friend tells him: (a) "Come with me, I am going to show you something, but it is a secret. Don't tell anybody." What is he going to show him? (b) "Listen, I am going to tell you something, but it is a secret, don't tell anybody." What is he going to tell him?

9. It is evening. The boy is in bed, the day is ended, the light turned off. (a) What does he do before going to sleep? (b) What is he thinking about? (c) One evening he cries, he is sad. What about?

10. Then he goes to sleep. What does he dream about?

11. He wakes up in the middle of the night. He is very much afraid. What of?

12. He goes back to sleep, and this time has a very nice dream. A good fairy comes to him and says, "I can do anything for you! Tell me what you want, I am going to touch you with my magic rod, and all you may wish for is going to come true!" What does he ask for?

13. The boy is growing up. Is he anxious to be a big boy soon, or would he rather remain a little boy for awhile? Why? What is he going to be when he grows up?

14. Among all the fairy tales that have been told to him, which one does he like the best of all?*

15. Do you remember when you were a little boy? Which is the first thing that you can remember now?

Madeleine Thomas specifies in her paper[24] that she did not design a test, but that her stories represent a clinical method of investigation. We hope the reader and clinician will use these stories with that intention in mind.

### Administration of the Madeleine Thomas Stories (M.T.S.)

In administering the M.T.S. the examiner suggests to the child that they make up some stories together. We have used the following approach quite successfully: "You and I are going to make up some stories, all kinds of stories. I am going to start the story, and you will help me finish it. It's fun— you will see. It is about a little boy [a little girl]. Here is the first one—."

We may add reassuring statements indicating that it is not hard to make up stories, that there are no right or wrong answers because we are just making it up. Ordinarily reference to the specific age of the child should not be made, as such a reference might only result in an intensification of the already alerted defense system and make it more difficult for the patient to identify himself with the fictitious child. Nevertheless, in certain circumstances, when the patient does not seem to know anything about "that little boy," it may be necessary to be more specific; we have stated, for instance, that "this little boy is about eight years old [or whatever the patient's age is]. . . I bet you know a lot about boys that age," or occasionally we have gone a little further and said, "This little boy is about eight years old, just the same age as you are. I bet you know a lot about what he thinks and wants to do."

This is a clinical method, not a "test," and therefore the approach should

*Often fairy tales are not familiar to American children nowadays. We then substitute "stories" or "TV programs."

be flexible, be adapted to the particular individual child, and even be modified in the process of the clinical exploration. We have found it helpful to
start with some of the first items, but not necessarily in the listed sequence,
nor is it always indicated or advisable to use all the items.

Thomas[24] points out that it is not sufficient simply to administer the
stories and thus attempt or expect to automatically "collect deep-seated
conflicts." The method is infinitely more subtle, is intended to gently lead
the child to express some aspects of his emotional life, some preoccupations
and conflicts in the form of fantasies and stories. The clinician has to be
continuously aware of various leads offered by the child and be prepared to
follow some of these clues. At other times, he must avoid all further questioning in order not to block the flow from unconscious areas of the psyche. The
attitude of the examiner throughout the interview should be one of calm
reassurance and warm interest. It is essential not to pressure the child. On
the other hand, some children, after long pauses and obvious difficulties in
dealing with a specific story, may need some further help from the examiner,
perhaps some encouragement. It may even become necessary for the inter-
viewer to abandon that particular story and go on to another one. Decisions
of this sort are of course done at the discretion of the interviewing clinician,
depending upon his intuition and grasp of the psychological process operating
at that time in the child. We are reluctant to put in writing too many specific
recommendations regarding administration of this method; it might be
applied too rigidly and become a "test," instead of a clinical method. There
are times when a story can be expanded with great advantage, when specific
leads offered by the child are worthwhile following. This can be easily done
by applying the same principles of indirect approach, avoiding confronting
the child too directly with what we suspect of possibly being his own conflicts,
and very definitely not attempting to interpret the content of stories offered
by him.

As with other methods of personality study, there are times when a
patient's M.T.S. record is unusually barren, and only a limited incomplete
diagnostic impression can be formed. In such instances we have simply used
whatever other methods or tests seemed indicated in order to complete our
evaluation. We have at times added some stories of our own in order to
explore some specific aspects of our patient's life, or we have combined it
occasionally with our own selection of pictorial thematic material. The
M.T.S. method can be varied in a great many ways and adapted to many
different circumstances, since it lends itself to unlimited combinations. It
can prove extremely helpful and fruitful if used skillfully by an experienced
clinician. A word of caution is indicated, however. This flexible technique
may be rather confusing and perhaps even disastrous in the hands of a
beginner. It may lead to much fumbling or excessive, untimely exploration
that may upset the patient. A child can be encouraged to reveal more than
he is actually prepared to cope with. The examiner should be continually
aware of these risks.

The clinician should be closely aware of the many psychological factors
constantly interacting during the interview (including those relating to his

own personality), and be able to adopt a flexible attitude, to adjust to what the child may be trying to tell him through the stories and the difficulties and resistances he encounters. The stories are recorded verbatim, unless a patient objects very strongly. Usually it is quite easy to explain why we write the stories down, "because they are so interesting, . . . you have so much imagination, I couldn't possibly remember all the things you tell me . . . ," etc.

Usually the M.T.S. require less than 30 minutes, unless a child is unusually productive.

## The Rationale

Thomas[24] states that all products of our fantasy life obey a certain determinism. By means of inductive thinking, one can determine the cause from which the fantasies originated. Thomas' basic rationale is both genetic and psychoanalytic in the Freudian sense. Thomas is well aware that each child is likely to look at the stories in his own subjective way, with all the accompanying individual distortions brought about by his own conflicts. At the same time, Thomas' concepts of child development (from a psychological viewpoint) have been strongly influenced by the teachings of Claparède, and particularly by Piaget and Rey. Madeleine Thomas is less concerned about proving any particular theory than she is in finding a way to lead children to express some of their difficulties, especially unconscious conflicts, in an indirect and symbolic way with a minimum of discomfort.

We can examine her rationale from several viewpoints: intellectual aspects, emotional aspects, the defense system, and symbolism.

### Intellectual Aspects

In order to participate meaningfully, the child must be able to comprehend what is expected of him in these stories, be able to adapt to the request and to identify with the individuals or situations described in these stories. Thomas found that children below four and one-half years of age tend to react to "making up stories" in two ways; passive (listening to the story and echoing), or active (telling his own story but in an erratic manner with much confabulation).

Between 4 and 6 years, children comprehend the request but still seem to have some difficulty adapting to it. Thomas attributes this essentially to the child's egocentric way of thinking, as described by Piaget.[17,18] Identification with others through stories remains difficult for children until this egocentricity has been conquered or outgrown. Identification with some of the stories is possible at that age, but mostly when the incident or situation described in the story is directly related to a personal experience of the subject.

### Emotional Aspects

The process of identification necessitates a certain minimum of intelligence. In the case of these stories, a mental age of about 5 years seems necessary to assure meaningful results. It also requires ability to adapt to the request. Identification may take various forms, and unfortunately not always the hoped for objectivation of the child's own conflict. Those forms could be described as follows:

1. Child expresses some of his own preoccupations directly, but without involving himself (called "direct reaction" by Thomas).

Examples: *Serge*, 6½ years: no. 2—"My brother did the same thing!" No. 4—"At home, my Daddy kicked my Mommie too" (reference 24, page 217).

2. Direct objectivation or projection of one's own conflicts, with involvement of the subject.

Example: *Crista*, 8 years: no. 6—"To Mommie and Daddy." (To whom first?) "To both." (Who will scold the most?) "Daddy will. My Daddy scolds the most. My Daddy slaps me with his belt. My, does it hurt!"*

3. Partial objectivation of subject's conflicts, still involving himself (described by Thomas as an intermediary stage, not yet complete objectivation or projection found later on).

Example: *Daisy*, 5½ years: no. 9—"She sings or sleeps. She thinks about her Mommie, that Mommie will come; then she goes to sleep all by herself when she thinks that Mommie is coming, and one evening I called her real loud, but she did not come" (reference 24, page 217).

4. Objectivation of one's problems without involving oneself directly.

Examples: *Jack*, 11 years: no. 4—"Argues about—come over here! I am going to give you a spanking! (Arguing about giving the boy a spanking?) Yes, the apartment thing—the boy runs up there, and gets a toy-thing, and takes a rock and rolls it down. Rolls it down on father, and father gets hurt and the hospital comes to get him. The police get the little boy." No. 13—"Be big like me. He wants to be a little boy, tell Mommie and Daddy . . . he wants . . . ." Patient becomes very vague, stares into space. (When grown up?) "He'll be a killer monster like Frankenstein. Kill his Mommie and Daddy if they are in their room asleep. Daddy might get under the covers to hide his head."†

Sometimes this objectivation and projection takes essentially symbolic form, as in dreams.

Example: *Fanny*, 6 years: Tells a dream about a house: "Everybody has gone, only my maid stayed. There was a nice lady in the house, she did this (Fanny puts her finger close to her face indicating by gesture, "no-no!"). (What did the lady mean?) That means that she does not allow us to go into the house" (reference 24, page 243).

In this particular case, Thomas interpreted the dream as a symbolic expression of sexual fantasies, forbidden desire to masturbate (which had been a reality problem for Fanny).

5. Negative identification (defense reaction). The child refuses to express any conflicts verbally. We find this manifested in a direct and also in an indirect manner.

Examples: Direct manner—*Roberta*, 11 years: No. 3—"That never happens!" No. 4—"My parents never get mad at each other!" Indirect manner—expressed in statements like, "It is too hard!" "I can't find the ending. I can start the story, but I can't finish it" (reference 24, page 243).

*For a fuller discussion of this case, see pages 205–206.

†For a fuller discussion of this case, see pages 207–208.

The process of identification presents many intricate and complex aspects. Complete identification with a conflict situation and projection of one's own personal feelings is often hindered by a system of resistance and defense that operates in various ways. Identification also is partly age determined, as we shall describe below (see *Age Considerations*).

### Defense System

Thomas[24] states that if a child of normal intelligence has "nothing to say" in response to the stories, it is usually not because of lack of ideas or absence of imagination, but because the child cannot or will not face certain inner conflicts. She noticed that some of her subjects became much more productive during a second interview. They declared that at first they just did not know what to say. Their statement, "I don't know," was essentially a form of resistance.

Madeleine Thomas did not focus exclusively on ways to elicit "conflicts," but was fully aware of the presence and importance of the mechanisms of resistance and defense and the need to observe their manifestation in the course of the story interview. The mechanism of defense can take many forms, varying from the most obvious (definite refusal) to a somewhat more hidden type (passive resistance: "I don't know," or distractibility and playfulness), to signs of obvious uneasiness in the patient's thinking in specific stories, to clever intellectualization and avoidance of all emotional participation, to great verbal productivity of totally irrelevant type, completely disconnected from the initial story or situation. Continuous awareness by the examiner of these processes is essential if a good understanding of the child's psychological functioning in a broad sense is to be obtained.

### Symbolism

Some of the stories have been constructed in such a way as to give the patient opportunity to use his fantasy life extensively, and thus perhaps reveal some of his inner preoccupations indirectly in symbolic form. The interpretation of such symbolism presents many problems. For instance, in regard to *dream interpretation*, Thomas states[24] that dreams are indeed anchored in the past, as Freud postulated, but also turned towards the future simultaneously (Jung), and one's thinking, when it returns to the unconscious, assumes a more primitive and more symbolic form (Piaget[16]).

In our experience, we found that children speak quite willingly of their dreams, provided good rapport has been established between patient and examiner. How one interprets these dreams will depend of course to a large extent on one's background, orientation, training and insight, and on the child's age and history. Thomas[24] lists certain types of dreams which are often given by children as part of the M.T.S., and which the clinician might expect to encounter.

### Nightmares

These seem to be mostly about animals and occur between the ages of five and one-half to eight and one-half years. Before 5 years of age, it is generally difficult to obtain real dreams. The child usually cannot remember them well and fills in details by means of confabulation. (Of course, such a product can be of considerable clinical value also, just like the dream itself.) Often there is little disguise, and direct wish fulfillment is expressed. The older the child, the greater the need for association in order to understand the meaning of a particular dream.

### Dreams of Self Punishment

These appear often at 6 years, and the climax is reached by 10 years, though still found in adolescence. Why do such dreams appear at 6 years in particular? Thomas feels that at that age the child becomes socialized, which involves giving up self centeredness and pleasures of various types. Society forbids free satisfaction of sex libido and of death wishes. These dreams are partly the result of guilt felt from forbidden wishes of this type.

### Dreams of Naive Realization

Such dreams are most often found between 8 and 10 years. They are nondisguised realization of a desire.

### Symbolic Dreams

We find them mostly after 6 years of age. They are increasingly more detailed, refined, subtle and disguised as the child gets older. They are difficult to interpret. Thomas warns that one should not expect to find any one to one relationship between a specific symbol and a specific meaning.

In evaluating children psychologically, it is often necessary to explore some of the hostility that may have accumulated over a period of time. Hostility can be expressed in many ways in the M.T.S., from very direct, overt, obvious statements to extremely disguised forms. Hostility is at times expressed in the form of death wishes. Though no question is asked in the stories about death, children nevertheless quite often express fantasies about death, at times actual death wishes. Thomas lists the following examples of death wishes:

1. Death wishes against somebody who is in the way, or more specifically aimed at one or both parents or parental figures. Sometimes these are expressed directly, without apparent guilt, but often feelings of guilt appear in later stories.

Examples: *Serge,* 6½ years: Described by Thomas as very pleasant and gentle during examination, was also known to be a big tease and quite shrewd when not supervised by adults. His mother suffers from a serious cardiac condition, might die if someone were to upset her emotionally. Serge knows this. On no. 4, he says, "My Daddy kicked my Mommie too!" In no. 5 (jokes), he mentions that the father was mean to the mother, they argued and fought a lot. The little boy took a sword and killed the father. Further questioning revealed that the little boy had wanted to kill his father for a long, long time, even when he was a baby, "because he spanked me." The examiner then added a story of her own, mentioned that "one day the little boy overhears a conversation that is not meant for his ears. What was it all about?" Serge answered, "His parents are arguing about him, they are going to put him in jail, they are going to leave him there till he is all dead!" The feeling of guilt, not evident at all at first, actually is brought out. Further questioning reveals Serge's wishful thinking that the little boy later on will love his father. He adds questioningly, "Did the fairy make him a nice boy? He'll love his Daddy" (reference 24, page 254).

2. Death wishes at times may be much more disguised and distorted.

Example: *Don*, 6½ years: On no. 10 he related the following dream: "About witches, taking him out of bed and knocking him out of the house. (?) He wakes up, goes outside to find the witch and kill her. He takes Mommie's broomstick and flies after her. She has a broomstick too. He finally killed the witch. There was a lot of witches. He couldn't kill all. They chased him, he died, there were so many of them. (?) He got hit by one of the broomsticks."

3. Death wishes may be indirectly suspected in the child who cannot say enough nice and wonderful things about a certain sibling.

4. Death wishes have been found to be the basis of exaggerated fears of accidents in children. Sometimes such a wish, when about to be expressed, is quickly transferred to some other object, sometimes an animal instead of the human being it was originally aimed at.

5. Deeply buried death wishes may at times appear in burial fantasies. They usually represent strongly repressed sadistic fantasies. Of course, the child's concept of death differs considerably from that of adults. Death, to him, does not necessarily imply an irreversible condition, but often only a temporary absence.

## Age Considerations

The M.T.S. involves identification with an imagined situation, a story, and not with a direct action or attitude. This type of identification is usually too complex for the average four year old child. It also requires a certain ability to channel one's thinking within a given framework. At 4 years, the child is more likely to get one concept and to build upon it a confabulation, forgetting the examiner's requests during that time. His thinking is egocentric, and not particularly theme-oriented in a manner that can be successfully tapped by the M.T.S.

At 5 years, according to Thomas,[24] there is a first attempt at adaptation to the examiner's instructions. It is still difficult for children of that age to objectify their feelings. We found this to be true of American children too.

In the age groups of 7 to 10 years, objectivation and identification has become much easier. Sometimes this projection leads to subjective identification. In listening carefully to the child's verbalization, we often found a switch from subjective identification to less personal, more disguised identification, a switch back and forth from one to the other. This often presents valuable leads.

Thomas obtained the best results with her methods with children between the ages of 8 and 10 years. We have found them most useful between the ages of 6 and 11 years.

The 11 to 13 year age group is usually a less productive age, with less originality, many more statements like, "I don't know," "maybe," and general evasiveness being common. Patients often realize at that age that we want to get them to talk, and they tend to barricade themselves, often very effectively. There are several reasons for the lessening of productivity.

Increased resistance and introspection contribute to a large extent. Probably the stories are also too simple, too naive or otherwise inadequate for that particular age group. We hope that further attempts will be made to explore the possibilities of using this method with older groups, especially adolescents. It has been used successfully with college students by Mills.[12]

## Interpretation

To our knowledge there is no well established specific method for analysis and interpretation of the M.T.S. However, there are several approaches that can be successfully used, even simultaneously, in studying a M.T.S. record. What Shneidman,[23] Klopfer,[7] Schafer,[21] Forer,[6] Wyatt,[27] Rapaport[19] and many others have said about methods of interpretation of thematic tests applies here also. We have found it useful to survey both the total record and to study individual responses as well. We proceed with the analysis while administering and recording the stories, during the interview itself. This type of progressive analysis permits one to form working hypotheses fairly early. It alerts the clinician to some of the child's processes and areas of particular sensitivity. We search for the major psychodynamic themes and look for repetition of these themes. We explore what the child may have revealed in regard to relationships with others (family members, people at school) and also watch for the things our patient definitely avoided mentioning. We search for possible traumatic experiences and attitudes related to his own personal experiences. We study various aspects of the psychological processes that have been exposed by him in the stories (reasoning, level of verbalization, reality contact, process of identification), and all along we look for possible unusual or bizarre concepts. We keep in mind some of the child's known background (the biographic material) and compare it with his fantasy life as expressed in the M.T.S.

Mills[11] has explored the frequency with which certain themes occur and has listed them as follows: Manners and moral conduct, fantasy life, parent-child tensions, parental discipline, anxiety, social adjustment (good and bad), likes, parental conflict, sibling rivalry, aggression, home stability and instability, sex awareness, parent-child understanding, escape, fears, school conduct, teacher-child relationships, deep loss.

We found it helpful to keep in mind these various themes. We do not feel, however, that this particular order of frequency carries any specific diagnostic implication. We also found that the theme which occurs the most often in a given child's record is not necessarily the one that holds the major key to the child's problems, or will necessarily be of the most pertinent diagnostic importance. Sometimes the psychological process exposed in only one story or even a single response proves to be the most revealing. The child's behavior in itself is usually very significant and should be observed carefully.

In formulating our impressions, we keep in mind that we are dealing with a child, an organism in the process of development and therefore subject to many changes and influences. What we obtain through the M.T.S. are only samples of his fantasy life. We make inferences from them about our patient's personality, such as its organization and disorganization of thought, affect and probable interpersonal relationships. In formulating an interpretation, a vast process of screening is involved: the M.T.S. themselves are selected, the child chooses from his great wealth of fantasy only a certain number and type. We collect them under specific conditions and interpret them according to what we have been taught. In addition, there is undoubtedly another distorting factor present; namely, the "personal equation," that is, our own viewpoint influenced by our personality and our various needs. This has been remarkably well described by Schafer.[21] We cannot avoid all these errors. Perhaps all that can be done to reduce some of the distorting subjective elements at present is to understand better in which direction we, as clinicians, tend to err and then make the necessary allowance for it.

Interpretation of the M.T.S. should be done in the light of a total psychological test battery and biographical data. Even then the personality picture will remain incomplete. It seems, for example, very doubtful that we can describe, from these stories, what a certain child's overt behavior is like or predict what it will be in the future under specific conditions.

The clinician, in using and interpreting the M.T.S. (or other projective methods) is often torn between dual roles; as a clinician he desires to understand his patient and to give as clear a personality description as possible, with appropriate recommendations; as a scientist, he continuously questions (or should question and verify) the basic assumptions of the theories he depends on. This dilemma need not force us to abandon all efforts at interpreting or drawing temporary conclusions from the clinical material available. It simply calls for careful scrutinizing of all existing case material and for awareness of both the advantages and limitations of present-day psychodiagnostic methods.

## Raven's Controlled Projection for Children

Raven,[20] in England, has presented a slightly different version of the Thomas Story Completions and has modified the presentation by asking the child to draw while responding to the stories. Raven calls this method "Controlled Projection."

The verbal responses to the standard set of questions have been tabulated for 50 school children (25 boys, 25 girls) at each of these age levels: six and one-half, nine and one-half, and twelve and one-half. Raven feels that after the normal or characteristic responses to each question have been determined, the unique or atypical answers can then be designated. It is possible to derive a "coefficient of conformity" for each child which reflects the degree to which his stories resemble those given by other children of his age and sex.

The responses of the school children were used as norms for comparison with four special groups of 20 boys each: clinic groups of "nervous" and "inhibited" subjects, and institutionalized groups of orphans and mentally defective delinquents. The similarities and differences between normal and special groups are presented both in tabular form and as composite, descriptive narratives or "digests."

The drawings seemed to add little to the understanding of the stories and often were unrelated to the story content. The method of drawing analysis reported by Raven[20] did discriminate between the clinical groups in terms of the drawings per se.

## Düss (Despert) Fables

The Düss Fables were developed by Louisa Düss,[3] of Geneva, Switzerland, and published in 1940. Later they were translated into English. Louise Despert has used them and discussed them repeatedly in psychoanalytic literature. Since then they have become better known as the "Despert Fables."[2,5] Düss designed them to elicit specific emotional conflicts in children of various ages. We include our own translation of the Fables from the original French text.

1. The Bird (to investigate the child's attachment to one of the parents, or his independence). A daddy and mommy bird and their little baby bird are sleeping in a nest on a branch of a tree. All of a sudden a big wind comes along and shakes the tree, and the nest falls to the ground. The three birds wake up brusquely. The daddy flies to a pine tree, the mother to another pine tree—what is the little bird going to do? He already knows how to fly a little bit.

2. Wedding Anniversary (to verify whether or not the subject has experienced an emotional shock in the parents' room; jealousy of the parents' union). It is the daddy's and mommy's wedding anniversary. They love each other very much and are having a beautiful party. During the party the child gets up and all alone goes to the very end of the back-yard. Why?

3. The Lamb (to explore the weaning complex and the brother and sister complex). There is a mother sheep and her baby lamb in the meadow. All day long the little lamb plays next to the mother. Every evening the mother gives him good warm milk, which he likes very much. But he also eats grass. One day, someone brings to the mother sheep a very tiny lamb who is hungry and needs to be fed some milk. But the mother sheep does not have enough milk for both of the lambs, and she says to her big lamb, "I don't have enough milk for both of you, so you go and eat the fresh grass." What does this lamb do? (To judge only the weaning complex: Leave out the arrival of the little lamb and say that the mother sheep no longer has any milk and that the lamb must now start to eat grass.)

4. The Funeral (to investigate aggressiveness, death wish, feelings of guilt, self punishment). A funeral procession is passing by in the village street and people are asking, "Who has died?" Someone answers, "It is someone in the family who lives over there in that house." Who is it? (One can mention the members of the family.)

5. Fear (to explore anxiety and self punishment). Here is a child who says very softly, "Oh, but I am afraid!" What is he/she afraid of?

6. The Elephant (to study castration fears). A child has a little elephant, which he loves very much. The elephant is very pretty with its long trunk. One day when he returns from a walk, the child comes into his room and finds that his elephant has changed. In what way has the elephant changed? And why is he changed?

7. The Handmade Object (to explore possessiveness and stubbornness; anal complex). A child has succeeded in making something out of clay (a tower) which he finds very, very pretty. What does he do with it? His mother asks him to give it to her. He is free to decide —will he give it to his mother?

8. A Walk with Mother or Father (to disclose the Oedipus complex). A boy (or a girl) took a very nice walk in the woods alone with his mother (or her father, for the girl). They had lots of fun together. When he returned home the boy found that his father did not look as he usually did. Why? (Similarly, upon returning the girl finds that the mother doesn't look the same as usual.)

9. News (to discover some of the desires and fears of the child). A child comes home from

school (or from a walk). Mother says to him (her), "Don't start your homework right away —I have something to tell you!" What is the mother going to say to the child?

10. Bad Dreams (control for preceding fables). A child wakes up in the morning all tired and says, "Oh, what a bad dream I've had!" What did he dream about?

Düss administered the stories to 43 children varying in ages from 3 to 15, and to 22 adults from 17 to 50 years of age. The Fables were found to be very helpful with preschool children, but by no means limited to that age group. The basic rationale is essentially Freudian. Düss used the following six criteria as indicators of some specific emotional conflict in the child: (1) immediate and unexpected response; (2) perseveration of the complex in other fables; (3) whispered response, given rapidly; (4) refusal to answer to one of the fables; (5) silence and resistance; and (6) the subject wishes to start the examination all over.

Düss was impressed by the self assurance with which neurotic subjects expressed their conflicts unconsciously. They seemed to be persuaded that their answers were correct, the only logical ones, and that everybody else answered as they did. She also felt that the answers she obtained by means of her Fables represented essentially individual responses determined by specific complexes.

A very recent communication from Louisa Düss informed us that her Fables are being used extensively in most European countries and also in South America.

Mosse[13] discusses each of the Düss fables at length, giving sample responses and numerous diagnostic interpretations. She also suggests letting a young child draw or paint while he talks or giving him appropriate dolls and toy animals with which to dramatize the stories.

Fine[5] presents both Rorschach and Fables responses for three different children to show how material from each technique supplements the other. Schwartz[22] uses a similar approach, presenting Rorschach, Despert Fables, H-T-P, and Stanford-Binet protocols for one 10 year old boy. He demonstrates that while the Rorschach and H-T-P give a general personality picture, the Fables present more concretely the direction of aggressive drives and the interrelationships within the family. One's confidence in projective findings is confirmed when indicators and themes occur on several tests.

## Research Data

Research and statistical data are rather scarce. Thomas[24] established her method with a group of 30 subjects, then tested it thoroughly with a group of 31 children who were boarders in a children's home. Her diagnostic impressions were carefully checked against reports and descriptions of the children as given by the director and staff of that particular home. Conferences were held on each child. Thomas claims that in 90 per cent of the cases there was general agreement between examiner and staff. In 3.6 per cent the diagnostic impression obtained with the M.T.S. did not seem to agree with the staff's impression and with what was known about the child's difficulties. In 6.4 per cent of the cases, no specific or clear picture of the child's personality or his difficulties could be obtained from the M.T.S.

Mills[9] studied 50 American elementary school children, 25 boys and 25 girls, from kindergarten to the sixth grade inclusive. He found that the stories elicited highly instructive material about the emotional life of the child. His conclusions were very similar to those of Thomas and our own. The method was found to be quite applicable to American children. Mills[10,11] analyzed very carefully what the various items explored (type of problem or conflict) and what kind of psychological processes were involved.

Vivian Williams[26] also studied a number of children in the Claremont Schools, and made a most thorough item analysis of the M.T.S.

A modification of the Thomas method was tried with college students by Mills.[12] It was administered to 312 history and psychology students in three liberal arts colleges, and a theme analysis was made of the responses. He reported that these stories often provided helpful clues. They also were found to be quite unthreatening and therefore particularly useful in preparing the student for a series of tests such as the Rorschach and the TAT, which seem to be far more threatening than these stories.

Several research studies with the Düss Fables have been published. In 1943 Düss used her Fables for an experimental study on problems of resistance in the psychoanalysis of children. This paper was published in book form, together with the Fables.[4] Düss found that her method enabled one to discover manifestations of resistance and to obtain excellent insight into the subject's mechanisms of defense. She strongly advised against using the Fables during psychoanalytic treatment, as they seem to provoke an intensification of resistance and make it difficult for subconscious and unconscious material to emerge in symbolic form. In general she found the Fables most useful with children between the ages of 3 and 7, but actually usable with individuals of any age, provided they are administered skillfully.

Despert[2] used the Fables as part of a study of 50 stuttering children in 1946. Reuben Fine[5] revised the Fables, expanding them to 20 in all, and administered them to 100 children between the ages of 4 and 14.

Peixotto,[14] using the Fine revision, studied the test-retest reliability of the eight psychodynamic variables described by Fine. She concluded that 14 of the 20 Fables gave reliable results and that certain Fables are reliable at some ages and not at others. She also presented normative data[15] based on the responses of 442 children (aged 6 to 14). Responses occurring with a frequency of 25 per cent or more for any sex or age grouping were considered to be typical or "popular." Each fable is discussed in terms of its usefulness in eliciting dynamic and atypical responses, its appropriateness for various age levels, and its reliability as determined in her previous study.[14] She concluded that the test, as it stands, seems most suitable for children under eight years of age and suggested that the Fables be revised by dropping some and adding other more suitable ones.

## Conclusions

We have found the Madeleine Thomas Stories very useful as a clinical method for studying children between the ages of 6 and 11 years. These stories seem to be relatively unthreatening and permit us to explore many aspects of the child's fantasy life. We consider this particular method most effective when used in conjunction with a test battery and detailed biographic data. The Madeleine Thomas Stories are not intended as a quick diagnostic test for nosologic classification.

The rationale and system of interpretation are similar to those used with other projective methods. Like other techniques, the story completion method has shortcomings. The rationale and methods of interpretation need continuous improvement and verification. These reservations, however, should not discourage clinicians from using story completions extensively.

## Illustrative Case Material

### Crista (8½ years)

Caucasian adopted girl. Referred because of restlessness, hyperactivity, purposeless and destructive movements, rebellious, nonconforming behavior, aggressive and sadistic behavior towards other children, tendencies to larceny, daily temper tantrums, lack of genuine warmth in relation to others, but insatiable need for affection. History of poor response to anticonvulsants and tranquilizers. Physically very attractive. Intelligence testing: Wide scatter; superior in verbal abilities; difficulties in some tests involving spatial organization; at times rather confused, with difficulty in channeling her mental processes. Full psychological test battery, medical and psychiatric examinations led to psychiatric diagnosis of "chronic brain syndrome, of unknown etiology, with behavioral reaction; emotional problems superimposed on an organically disturbed personality."

### Samples of the M.T.S.

No. 2—"The mother will spank her! Or the mother could tell her not to do that anymore. That's all. (Do you know of such situations?) Oh yes, because when I am naughty to my sister, my mother spanks me. (Does sister get pretty naughty sometimes?) No, she does not. She is real cute, she is real nice. Her name is Marcia Sue, she is 4 years old."

No. 3—"She did something wrong at the table. She said, 'I don't like this food!' (What happens?) Daddy tells her to leave the table. (How does she feel about it?) She is real sad. (Mad, too?) No, just sad. She goes to her room and cries on her pillow."

No. 4—"They are mad at each other. About . . . well, because their little girl is so naughty. (?) She is bad at the table and stuff. (How about school?) She is not at school. They don't want her at school. (?) Because she is so bad."

No. 6—"To Mamma and Daddy. (First?) To both. (Who scolds?) Daddy will. My Daddy slaps me with his belt. My does it hurt! He would do it! I never had bad things on my report card yet."

No. 9c—"That she was so naughty. She wants to be good."

No. 10—"If only she could be good, everybody would like her more. (?) What happens is the Angel tells her to be good."

No. 13—"A big girl. (?) She wants to be nice, a big girl like her friends. She wants to be like her friends, she wants them to like her."

No. 14—"About a girl, when she was naughty and she turned out to be good."

### Psychological Material

Responses to the Rorschach, TAT, CAT, Pigem and drawings point to an immature, poorly integrated total personality, impulse-ridden, preoccupied with very hostile (even sadistic) fantasies, showing infantile needs for oral gratification, attention and affection, probably afraid of her own hostile impulses and having many morbid preoccupations. There is little object relationship evident, though superficially she relates quite well. The M.T.S. confirms much of the general impression, and in addition, reveals preoccupations about being "bad." (She also expressed such concern directly during the interviews, stating that she thought there must be something wrong with her head, that it made her do things she did not really want to do, but that she just could not help it.) Parental figures are seen as very punishing, especially father. It is difficult for her to accept and face her own hostility directed towards parents and sister. There is much concern about not being accepted by others and wanting to be liked. In direct interview, she denies lacking friends: "I have lots and lots of friends!" According to parents and teachers, this is not true, in fact she is definitely rejected by peers. We can therefore assume that the wishful thinking expressed by the little girl in various stories reflects her own, that she has many needs that are difficult for her to admit openly.

### Ben (7½ years)

Referred because of precocious sexual development at 5 years (adult secondary sex characteristics). Shy, sensitive, lonely boy. Problem of school placement—can he be enrolled in regular class, what effect will it have on other children? How to help him with his own adjustment? Only child of Mexican parents. No behavior problem. Parents greatly concerned about his future, especially about his being socially accepted. Complete medical-psychological-psychiatric study revealed a boy with superior intelligence, precocious physical development that was confusing to him. He seemed to be struggling at different age levels within himself, has had little opportunity to actually be a little boy and a child his own age.

### Selections from the M.T.S.

No. 1—"Well, I think this one goes along with me, when I started school! When you go to school for the first day, it's kind of scary. You don't know anybody at school—it's kind of scary—you hold back making friends, that's how I was. It took me about two years to get acquainted with the whole school. In fact, I know the whole school now. I am in the fourth grade. The first day you are sort of jumbled up inside. Things go on quite well at home, but it shakes you up the first day. I didn't know what to expect."

No. 2—"Hmm—ooh! (patient laughed). I may be put up on this one, a little—maybe I'll tell you later. (What do you think the mother might do?) As usual, a little bit of spanking, on both of them! They get a good bawling out after that. I know a kid—Gerald. He has a little brother, he fights with him all the time. He does not let the little brother take the spanking, he takes it himself. (Whose fault is it?) Gerald's brother's fault. (How do you feel yourself about a boy who takes all the blame and punishment like that?)—I don't know, it's silly to do that."

No. 6a—"Kind of way out of my line, almost! (?) I don't want to sound like bragging, but the last three years, I did not have one bad thing on my report card! (How about this boy?) It's like this, he'll show it to his mother, that's what I do, then when the mother sees my report card, then my daddy sees it." (b) "Oho! Well—I guess the second one that gets home—father. (?) Father always likes his children to get good grades. (?) It's true at my home too."

No. 7—"Oho! Well—this would come under my field! I am usually the one who is sad, when we come back from a trip. I hate to leave grandmother—she is in bad health now, almost 80—no, 77 last year. (And why is mother sad in the story?) Well, she likes to—she never knew how it would feel without her own mother, kind of hard to leave when you have been some place and enjoyed it, so much. I try to keep a straight face when leaving, but sometimes I can't. Sometimes I feel a little sad. Sometimes I break down and I cry!"

No. 8a—"Well, like you know when you have a secret, you don't want to show it to anybody or give it away, like a gold mine. It would be an old house he found or a gun relic, or something—that means old, real old. A guy who worked at my father's place found a flintlock gun in the desert. The year inscribed on it was 1787."

No. 9a—"Well—kind of common occasion with me! (Patient laughed.) He washes his face, brushes his teeth, says his prayers and goes to sleep."

No. 11—"Well—this is one of my own problems, another boy's problems, I mean. His parents had put him to bed, left for a movie show, a drive-in. When they came back, the boy was crying. On top of his bed, there was a rattlesnake, just coiling up when they drove up. They had heard something when they got up to the screen door. It sounded like some rattling noise. They saw the boy in the bedroom, they found the snake, a rattlesnake.

Father got the gun and shot it. The boy had had a dream, woke up crying. He didn't know a rattlesnake was there. (And the dream?) I don't know what it was about. (Can you imagine what it might have been about?) Well, it was like those pictures, "The Night the World Exploded."

No. 13b—"My question. My alley. (?) Every boy's ambition is to be as good as Mickey Mantle. (?) The famous baseball player. He can hit both ways. That's my ambition too." (Patient talks at some length about some of his baseball exploits, and how he was the best, how he also can beat his father.)

## Contribution from the M.T.S.

Other findings are confirmed (MAPS, CAT, Rorschach, TAT). In addition, the M.T.S. reveal marked anxiety about his physical condition, his aggressive impulses which are not acceptable to him and have to be controlled at all times. (Parents expect him to be very good.) Very ambitious, perhaps more so than he really would care to be. He seems to be under pressure to please others and to achieve a great deal, and we suspect excessive demands and expectations on part of the parents. He has adolescent drives and preoccupations, also the needs of a much younger child that probably have not been fully satisfied. There is much more curiosity and concern about his sexual development than the parents are willing or able to admit.

## Jack (11 years)

Referred because of poor learning ability in school; restlessness, short attention span; withdrawal when in a large group; a preference to play with much younger children. He vomits when excited. School psychologist reported that psychological tests indicated mental retardation, possibly autistic behavior. He has been very difficult to handle at home. Medical, psychological and psychiatric examinations concluded: "Chronic brain syndrome of unknown etiology, with psychotic reaction." Psychometric data: IQ 68 on Stanford-Binet in 1955. In 1958, verbal IQ 47 on WISC, performance IQ 57, range of scaled scores from 0 to 4 mostly, with exception of Maze Test (8 points). These findings were considered only indicators of his intellectual functioning level rather than representing his true potential, in view of his severely disorganized erratic behavior and bizarreness of thinking. His difficulties in tests requiring perceptual organization and spatial organization were of the kind often found in children with certain types of brain pathology.

## Samples of the M.T.S.

No. 4—"He argues about—come over here! I am going to give you a spanking! (Giving the boy a spanking?) Yes, the apartment thing—the boy runs up there and gets on a toy thing and takes a rock and rolls it down. He rolls it down on father, and father gets hurt and the hospital comes to get him. The police will get the little boy."

No. 6—"To Daddy and Mommy . . . they will say, 'What a bad report card! I'll give you a spanking.' (What does the boy do?) He cries and he gets locked upstairs in his room. He does something . . ." (Patient vaguely trails off.)

No. 7—"They didn't take the boy."

No. 8a—"He showed him—let's go get your Mom and Daddy, and my Mommy and Daddy and sock your Daddy and lock the doors so they can't get out." (b) "Let's go over to your house and climb in the attic window where Daddy and Mommy are asleep. If Daddy gets up, take one of the bricks and throw it at his head. Shut the window of the attic and lock it, so he can't get in. Cut a hole and climb out and get on top of the roof and on top of the roof . . . if Daddy gets out there . . . What if the boy friend throws one of those things and pushes his fingers off and he'll get hurt. He'll die, I guess. (?) The boy will."

No. 9a—"He gets scared. (?) Some spooky by the window, he might be screaming. Father and mother are out in the living room and listen to the noise of his screams. Father says, 'Well, little boy, what happened?' and he says, 'There is a monster by the window and it terrifies me.' The father says, 'Well, son, if you don't scream, there are no monsters around these courts.'"

No. 12—"He wishes for a motor boat (do with it?). Going to a lake on it. (?) He is going to play there." (Unusually appropriate response.)

No. 13b—"Be big like me. He wants to be a little boy, tell my Mommy and Daddy . . . he wants . . . (Patient trails off, stares vaguely into space.) (When he grows up?) He'll be a killer monster, like Frankenstein. He'll kill his Mommy and Daddy, if they are in their room asleep. Daddy might get under the covers to hid his head."

## Contribution of the M.T.S.

Jack's ability to verbalize and his insight into various situations are much more mature than one could expect from a truly feeble-minded child of 11 years. On the other hand, the difficulties in reasoning, the arbitrary logic and difficulty in channeling his mental processes noticed in intelligence tests can be observed here also. Jack's anxiety overwhelms him, he reaches a point of panic. We suspect that this is due partly to the intensity of his aggressive-hostile feelings and his inability to cope with such feelings. He seems to feel the lack of parental support and control, and it has made him insecure. Human and superhuman forces are aligned against him and will punish him, not only for what he did, but also for what he is and what he thinks. Though psychological tests and the M.T.S. alone would not permit a clear-cut differential diagnosis between predominantly an organic pathologic disturbance and essentially severe emotional maladjustment, we can definitely state here that Jack presents a picture of a very serious disturbance affecting his total personality organization. We also can state that his severe learning difficulties are not explainable on the basis of intellectual deficiency alone.

## References

1. Despert, J. L.   Dreams in children of preschool age. *Psychoanal. Study Child.*, 1949, *3/4*, 141–180.
2. ——.   Psychosomatic study of fifty stuttering children. *Amer. J. Orthopsychiat.*, 1946, *16*, 100–113.
3. Düss, L.   La méthode des fables en psychanalyse. *Arch. Psychol., Genève*, 1940, *28*, 1–51.
4. ——.   *La méthode des fables en psychanalyse infantile.* Paris: Editions de l'Arche, 1950.
5. Fine, R.   Use of the Despert Fables (Revised Form) in diagnostic work with children. *Rorschach Res. Exch. & J. proj. Tech.*, 1948, *12*, 106–118.
6. Forer, B. M.   Research with projective techniques, some trends. *J. proj. Tech.*, 1957, *21*, 358–361.
7. Klopfer, B., et al.   *Developments in the Rorschach technique.* Yonkers-on-Hudson, N. Y.: World Book Co., 1954–1956. 2 vols.
8. Lippman, H. S.   The use of dreams in psychiatric work with children. *Psychoanal. Study Child.*, 1945, *1*, 233–245.
9. Mills, E. S.   A study of the Madeleine Thomas Completion Stories Test with fifty elementary school children. Unpublished master's thesis, Claremont College, Claremont, Calif., 1949.
10. ——.   The Madeleine Thomas Test as an aid in reading children. *Fourteenth Yearb.*, Claremont College Reading Conf., Claremont, Calif., 1949.
11. ——.   The Madeleine Thomas Completion Stories Test. *J. consult. Psychol.*, 1953, *17*, 139–141.
12. ——.   A story completion test for college students. *J. clin. Psychol.*, 1954, *10*, 18–22.
13. Mosse, H. L.   The Duess Test. *Amer. J. Psychother.*, 1954, *8*, 251–264.
14. Peixotto, H. E.   Reliability of the Despert Fables, a story completion projective test for children. *J. clin. Psychol.*, 1956, *12*, 75–78.
15. ——.   Popular responses for the Despert Fables. *J. clin. Psychol.*, 1957, *13*, 73–79.
16. Piaget, J.   La pensée symbolique et la pensée de l'enfant. *Arch. Psychol., Genève*, 1923, *18*, 273–304.
17. ——.   Ch. 6. Principal factors determining intellectual evolution from childhood to adult life. Ch. 7. The biological problem of intelligence. *In* Rapaport, D. (Ed.)   *Or-*

*ganization and pathology of thought.* New York: Columbia Univer. Press, 1951. Pp. 154–192.

18. ——, & Inhelder, B.   *The growth of logical thinking from childhood to adolescence.* New York: Basic Books, 1958.

19. Rapaport, D.   Projective techniques and the theory of thinking. *In* Knight, R. P., & Friedman, C. R. (Eds.)   *Psychoanalytic psychiatry and psychology.* Vol. 1. New York: Int. Univer. Press, 1954. Pp. 196–203.

20. Raven, J. C.   *Controlled projection for children.* (2nd ed.) London: H. K. Lewis, 1951.

21. Schafer, R.   Psychological tests in clinical research. *In* Knight, R. P., & Friedman, C. R. (Eds.)   *Psychoanalytic psychiatry and psychology.* Vol. 1. New York: Int. Univer. Press, 1954. Pp. 204–212.

22. Schwartz, A. A.   Some interrelationships among four tests comprising a test battery: a comparative study. *J. proj. Tech.*, 1950, *14*, 153–172.

23. Shneidman, E. S.   *Thematic test analysis.* New York: Grune & Stratton, 1951.

24. Thomas, M.   Méthode des histoires à compléter pour le dépistage des complexes et des conflits affectifs enfantins. *Arch. Psychol., Genève*, 1937, *26*, 209–284.

25. Wickes, F. G.   *The inner world of childhood.* New York: D. Appleton-Century, 1927.

26. Williams, V. C.   A study of the inter-relationships between the mental, emotional and social characteristics of thirty problem children, as revealed by sociometry and the modified Madeleine Thomas Completion Stories methods. Unpublished master's thesis. Claremont College, Claremont, Calif., 1958.

27. Wyatt, F.   A principle for the interpretation of fantasy. *J. proj. Tech.*, 1958, *22*, 229–245.

11

# Word Association and Sentence Completion Methods

BERTRAM R. FORER

## Word Association Methods

THE USE of verbal associations to stimulus words as a psychological measure antedated its use as a projective instrument. Since Galton[5] through Wundt[29] and Cattell and Bryant,[2] data on response frequency and reaction time to stimulus words have been collected. The focus of these and many related studies was the experimental investigation of general psychological characteristics of previously acquired associations. A few pre-psychoanalytic clinicians—for example, Sommer[27] and Kraepelin[9]—experimented with word associations for individual diagnostic purposes, observing the influence on associations of special psychological and physiologic conditions.

It was Jung[7] who formulated the word association method as a standardized diagnostic instrument having some properties of a projective method. The stimuli consisted of 100 words which were presented orally. Reaction times and responses were recorded. Subsequently subjects were requested to recall their original responses to stimulus words. Interpretation was based upon an analysis of (a) variations in reaction time to the various stimulus words, (b) nonverbal manifestations of affect or discomfort, and (c) content, classified on the basis of logical categories. Idiosyncratic and slow responses were taken as cues to the existence of unconscious complexes.

A somewhat different, quasi-clinical approach was developed by Kent and Rosanoff.[8] Rather than relying upon reaction time and response classifications, they employed a normative approach with frequency tables of responses to their own list of words. Their measure of commonness of responses to a given word proved to be of discriminative value in the comparison of groups but of minimal utility in individual diagnosis. Schafer[24-26] and Rapaport, Gill and Schafer[19] brought the word association method far from its experimental, psychometric and crude clinical origins into the framework of modern ego psychology and particularly Rapaport's formulation of the thought processes. They jettisoned the earlier concern for historically acquired associative residues and complexes (which had been seen as interferences with association) for interest in the ways by which affective, motivational and particularly ego processes organize, select and distort stimulus information and shape the process of fulfilling the assigned task. Although their word list contains many highly charged sexual and emotional words, they discovered early in their investigations that diagnostic

210

information gleaned from content was more sparse than had been anticipated. Schafer[24] and later Rapaport, Gill and Schafer[19] described in detail the clinical implications of formal characteristics which conceptualize the psychological process intervening between stimulus and response under the set to associate. Their analysis of the forms of associative disturbance provides a psychological rationale for the use of word associations which may promote a resurrection of the technique which has been largely superseded by others. Fairly detailed summaries of the methodology and ramifications of word association methods appear in Bell,[1] Rotter[22] and Schafer.[26]

## Word Association Methods with Children

One finds little in the literature to suggest the systematic clinical use of word associations with children. One can guess that Schafer[25] and others include it in their test batteries with adolescents. Its primary use seems to have been as a research tool for the investigation of age, sex, intellectual and diagnostic determinants of associations as measured by reaction time, logical classification of responses and commonness of response.

The Rosanoffs[20] and Otis[17] were able to demonstrate a developmental sequence in the nature of associations which attained an adult pattern by age 11. Characteristic of children's responses are: multiword responses,[17, 20] individualized responses,[20] slower reaction times,[12,13] failures to respond[17, 21] and perseverations and neologisms.[17] While Kent and Rosanoff[8] found perseveration and neologisms most common among neurotics and psychotics, Otis[17] found them so common among children as to require caution in taking them as indicators of pathology. For normal children the ontogenetic changes in word association are in the direction of closer adherence to the task and increased conformity of the associations to norms which appear to be part of normal social identification. Mitchell and Rosanoff[16] found the associations of Negro children to be more individual in content and to contain fewer failures to respond.

Woodrow and Lowell[28] with a modified Kent-Rosanoff list studied the associations of 1000 children from ages 9 through 12 and the preferred responses for each word at each age. They described developmental fluctuations in the use of 22 response categories, fluctuations which we would regard now as more or less descriptive of stages of socialization or ego development. A sophisticated recent study by Dörken[3] employed a conformity index for nine age groups from 10 to 79. With 10 stimulus words, common associations increased in frequency with age, with a subsequent decrement in conformity in the 40 to 50 age group. A provocative comparison with earlier studies employing the same words revealed a progressive rise in common associations since 1910, which the author attributes to the conformity engendered by mass communication.

A fairly widespread use of word association testing with children has been in the study of intellectual deficit. Woodrow and Lowell[28] found that retarded children's associations resemble those of younger normal children with slower reaction, perseveration, multiword responses and infrequent rhyming.

Others[4,6,11,16,17] corroborated the findings. McHale[14] found defective children to be less influenced in their associations by the insertion of "slanted" words into the series.

McDowell[10] found no significant differences between the associations of stuttering and nonstuttering children. McGee's study[12] of age and sex differences showed boys to be quicker in response at all ages. In another study[13] he found the classic logical and grammatical categories to be non-discriminating between the sexes. Girls did, however, manifest fewer individual responses and an earlier approximation to adult norms—not surprising in view of the earlier social maturation of girls. Meltzer[15] used word associations to investigate children's attitudes toward their parents. More elaborately, Powell[18] set up groups of stimulus words to investigate differential developmental rates of boys and girls in seven adjustment areas. Using reaction time differences between neutral and critical word groups for each individual, he was able to plot curves from ages 10 to 30 in each critical area for each sex. The methodology here resembles that of lie detection and research in cognitive dynamics, burgeoning offshoots whose discussion is not relevant to this chapter.

We are forced to conclude at this time that the word association method with children has had its historic importance but has not proved clinically profitable. It has, perhaps, served its purpose by preparing a research background for the later emergence of projective methods. It was congenial to the psychometric and experimental psychology of the times and it now finds a rationale for study of the individual. Perhaps within the framework of projective theory and newer dynamic psychologies it will be found of some use with children. More likely it will continue to be a useful experimental technique whose derivative in the form of sentence completions will attain its original clinical objective.

## Sentence Completion Methods

Word association methods have not fulfilled early hopes for their diagnostic value, particularly with children. The fact that individual responses to a given stimulus word converge early in life to a narrow range of popular words and that the use of a single word stimulus restricts the scope of appropriate responses precludes the emergence of subtle individuality.[35] Content interpretation is rarely possible,[52,57] particularly if the ego is strong. The diagnostic possibilities of a projective method are limited by the inter-individual variability in response to the stimulus. The more popular the responses to test stimuli, the rarer will be the qualitative deviations which reveal individuality, even though a massing of popular responses in a protocol will be of diagnostic import.

Payne[52] and Tendler[59] were among the first to desert the simplicity of single word stimuli for more complex phrases whose completion in the form of a sentence comprised the subject's response. In the sentence-completing task the projective method began to take form. Sentence stems permit a wider variety of appropriate responses than do single words, and the relationship between stimulus and response is less predetermined by cultural stereotypes and logical structure. While the same kinds of impediments to, and distortions of, thought processes can be discovered in sentence completions as in word associations, the sentence completion method has the added virtue of supplying content which contains rich diagnostic information.

Related to this advantage is the fact that the sentence stems provide varied sets[53] and direct associations roughly along lines which can be predetermined by the investigator, even though permitting considerable latitude of response. Although custom-building of incomplete sentences for specific research or diagnostic purposes may interfere somewhat with validity studies, many authors have relied upon content validity. In a sense, nonstandardized sentence completion methods function as exploratory open-ended attitude questionnaires.

## Review of Research

Sanford and his coworkers[57] employed 30 sentences as part of a battery in the study of personality and scholarship among children in grades three through eight. Correlation tables reveal relationships among family press syndromes, needs and performance. Wilson[60] found suggestive content differences in sentence completions between well adjusted and maladjusted adolescents in their attitudes toward study, success and status. Costin and Eiserer[34] investigated attitudes toward teachers, identifications and school among boys and girls in the eleventh grade. They converted content into a rating scheme of positive, negative and neutral following Rotter's procedure.[56] Another study, by Harris and Tseng,[46] used this scoring method with sentences designed to investigate age and sex differences in attitudes toward peers and parents. Cobb[32] used incomplete wish sentences to study age and sex differences in children from four to twelve. Adolescent underachievers and controls differed significantly in Kimball's study.[47] Her sentences were structured around attitudes toward parents, determinants of aggression and guilt, and forms of aggression. Malpass' study[50] of school attitudes among eighth graders revealed a positive relationship between perception of the school situation and academic success. An investigation carried out by Bene[30] explored differences in school attitudes as a function of age.

A somewhat different use of incomplete sentences was devised by Copple,[33] who converted sentence completions into a measure of "effective intelligence." Scoring reliabilities were above .90, and correlation of scores with the Stanford Achievement Test was .53. Another more clearly specialized approach was Cruickshank's[36-38] use of incomplete sentences to study fear and guilt reactions among children suffering from various disabilities and the effects of such disabilities on personal aspirations. Similarly, Freed and Cruickshank[42] found differences in attitudes toward parents of cardiac patients and normal children. Cass[31] found relationships between maternal attitudes and conflicts of adolescent girls to be manifested in sentence completions.

In an attempt to test hypotheses about the nature of aggression, Graham and colleagues[44] used sentences structured in varying degrees of press aggression and types of instigators to aggression. Getzels[43] and later Hanfmann and Getzels[45] provided thoughtful discussions of the sentence completion method, which they employed in a series of experiments with white and Negro high school girls in a study first of prejudice and later of the meaning of sentence completion responses. They found that much of the content was referred to the self. A series of inquiries into the meaning of the responses indicated that ego-alien material which was revealed in the test tended to be attributed to others.

The studies summarized thus far exemplify the varied uses of sentence completions as research tools. They assume implicitly or explicitly that the content of projective technique responses is to some extent determined by the test stimuli and that a single "standardized" projective technique has serious limitations in the study of psychological specificities. A similar view is gaining currency that the Rorschach can not be expected to provide evidence regarding every psychological function.

There are, however, a few sentence completion forms for adults and for children whose function is somewhat broader and more specifically clinical and diagnostic than the forms that have been constructed for examining specific attitudes or dynamics.

### Clinical Application of Sentence Completion Tests

Rohde[54,55] has been working for some time with a 65 item sentence completion form for adults and adolescents as a general utility projective technique. She attempted the large job of standardization on 690 ninth grade students. Her scoring system, based on Murray's system,[51] as was Sanford's,[57] consists of need variables rated in three degrees of intensity, inner states and traits, need integrates and environmental forces. A check list is provided for notation and totalling of ratings on the variables. Interscorer reliability of two raters of 36 protocols yielded 95 per cent agreement. A retest reliability study of a small sample after an eight month interval yielded mean correlation coefficients of .80 for girls and .76 for boys on the many variables. Criteria for validation were teacher ratings on a sample of 100. Mean validity coefficients were .78 for girls and .82 for boys with ranges among the variables from .30 to .96. Rohde also found significant differences between Los Angeles and New York samples. Rohde devotes half of her book[55] to a discussion, with clinical examples, of the diagnostic use of her sentence completion method and scoring system with a variety of clinical entities and including a few adolescents. Normative data on all of her variables, but independent of the specific test items, are presented as a frame of reference for clinical interpretation.

The Machovers[48,49] described their own form for diagnostic work with children.

Rotter[56] developed an adolescent form of 40 items, based on his earlier adult form, for the specified purpose of screening maladjusted students. Scoring of each item was accomplished by means of a seven point scale of degree of conflict. Scoring samples were developed. Odd-even reliabilities of the scale on 50 boys and 50 girls in his entire high school sample were .74

for boys and .86 for girls. Inter-scorer reliabilities were .96 and .97, respectively. Total test scores were validated (a) on ratings of adjustment from interviews (Boys: $r = .20$; Girls: $r = .37$); (b) against sociometric scores (Boys: $r = .20$; Girls: $r = .32$); and (c) in terms of the test's ability to differentiate between the norm sample and a class of maladjusted students.

The sentence completion forms offered by this writer are adaptations of his adult forms instigated by the need for a general clinical instrument for older children and adolescents. Three related considerations were kept in mind in formulation of the adult, the children's and the vocational forms.

First, the kind of scoring which Rotter uses provides a single scale designed for screening rather than clinical description, and hence this method was rejected. Rohde's method consists of classifying responses into needs with total scores for each need. While such neatness facilitates validation, the evidence in the research literature is that the sheer occurrence of magnitudes of drives or traits has little predictive utility. Particularly does this appear to be the case because such labeling or quantification of needs provides no evidence of the likelihood or conditions or forms of expression of these needs.[41] Rather, a growing focus in description of the personality deals with the enduring, organizing aspects, often conceptualized as the ego or the self.

The second consideration is that evaluation of a person's test response, whether it be used to describe inner processes or to make predictions about behavior, is bound inevitably to the stimulus which elicits the response. The response "... hit him with a brick," will be interpreted differently when given to the following sentence stems: (a) "When they looked at me, I ... ," (b) "When others made fun of him, he ... ," (c) "After they knocked him down, he ...." The response is overtly aggressive and destructive, but it is more appropriate to stem (c) than stem (a). Interpretively, it might be said that the stimulus quality of item (a) has lower properties for instigating aggression than (b) or (c) and that a violent response to (a) implies a low threshold for aggression. In each case Rohde's method would score *need aggression*. If the same response had been given to the first item on the blank (see below), "When he was completely on his own, he ... hit him with a brick," we should entertain the hypothesis of excessive readiness to admit to aggressive fantasy and question the appropriateness of the aggressive feelings. We should wonder about impulse control and speculate about deficiencies in reality testing. If such responses were massed and appeared to disregard the set suggested by the stimuli, we should think of the responses as so "distant"[53] as to suggest overt psychosis. That is, the client would be expressing endogenous processes with virtually no regard for differences in stimuli; the threshold for fantasy aggression would approach zero.

An unpublished and incomplete study of the dynamics of stimulus-response relationships in sentence completions revealed no significant differences among schizophrenic, obsessive-compulsive and anxious adults in the number of aggression responses. There was, however, a significant difference between schizophrenics and the other two groups in "causes of aggression," the schizophrenics more often expressing aggression to trivial instigators. Other similar evidence corroborates the thesis that the relationship between stimulus and response is more diagnostic than the response alone.

The third consideration is the degree of structuredness of the sentence stems. An implication of Rapaport's findings[53] regarding word associations is that when a stimulus is unstructured, the clinician can not easily determine at which phase of the attention, perceiving, selecting, organizing, thinking, communicating process the disturbance lies. When stimulus material is moderately structured, the specific ways in which the ego works with it can be more clearly delineated.

### Children's Form of Forer's Structured Sentence Completion Test

It was with such considerations in mind that the children's form[40] was set up. The organization of items described below is clearly shown in the check sheet (fig. 1), which locates particular sentence stems under their appropriate content areas.

Fig. 1.—Check Sheet for the Forer Structured Sentence Completion Test.

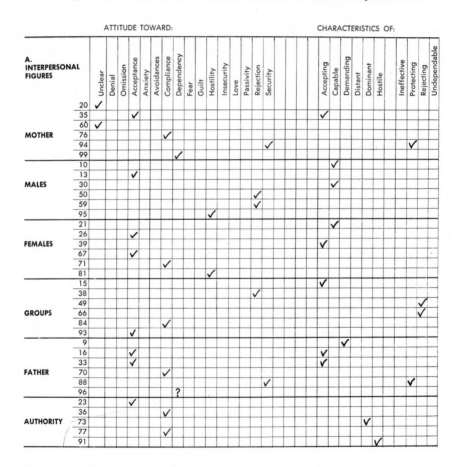

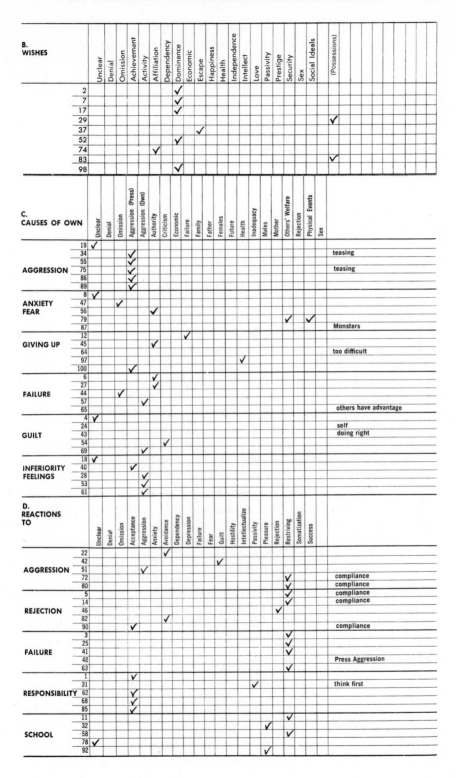

### B. WISHES

| | Unclear | Denial | Omission | Achievement | Activity | Affiliation | Dependency | Dominance | Economic | Escape | Happiness | Health | Independence | Intellect | Love | Passivity | Prestige | Security | Sex | Social Ideals | (Possessions) |
|---|---|---|---|---|---|---|---|---|---|---|---|---|---|---|---|---|---|---|---|---|---|
| 2 | | | | | | | | ✓ | | | | | | | | | | | | | |
| 7 | | | | | | | ✓ | | | | | | | | | | | | | | |
| 17 | | | | | | | ✓ | | | | | | | | | | | | | | |
| 29 | | | | | | | | | | | | | | | | | | ✓ | | | |
| 37 | | | | | | | | | | ✓ | | | | | | | | | | | |
| 52 | | | | | | | | ✓ | | | | | | | | | | | | | |
| 74 | | | | | ✓ | | | | | | | | | | | | | | | | |
| 83 | | | | | | | | | | | | | | | | | | ✓ | | | |
| 98 | | | | | | | | ✓ | | | | | | | | | | | | | |

### C. CAUSES OF OWN

| | Unclear | Denial | Omission | Aggression (Press) | Aggression (Own) | Authority | Criticism | Economic | Failure | Family | Father | Females | Future | Health | Inadequacy | Males | Mother | Others' Welfare | Rejection | Physical Events | Sex | |
|---|---|---|---|---|---|---|---|---|---|---|---|---|---|---|---|---|---|---|---|---|---|---|
| **AGGRESSION** 19 | ✓ | | | | | | | | | | | | | | | | | | | | | |
| 34 | | | | ✓ | | | | | | | | | | | | | | | | | | teasing |
| 55 | | | | ✓ | | | | | | | | | | | | | | | | | | |
| 75 | | | | ✓ | | | | | | | | | | | | | | | | | | teasing |
| 86 | | | | ✓ | | | | | | | | | | | | | | | | | | |
| 89 | | | | ✓ | | | | | | | | | | | | | | | | | | |
| **ANXIETY FEAR** 8 | ✓ | | | | | | | | | | | | | | | | | | | | | |
| 47 | | | ✓ | | | | | | | | | | | | | | | | | | | |
| 56 | | | | | | ✓ | | | | | | | | | | | | | | | | |
| 79 | | | | | | | | | | | | | | | | | | ✓ | | ✓ | | |
| 87 | | | | | | | | | | | | | | | | | | | | | | Monsters |
| **GIVING UP** 12 | | | | | | | | ✓ | | | | | | | | | | | | | | |
| 45 | | | | | | ✓ | | | | | | | | | | | | | | | | |
| 64 | | | | | | | | | | | | | | | | | | | | | | too difficult |
| 97 | | | | | | | | | | | | | | ✓ | | | | | | | | |
| 100 | | | ✓ | | | | | | | | | | | | | | | | | | | |
| **FAILURE** 6 | | | | | ✓ | | | | | | | | | | | | | | | | | |
| 27 | | | | | ✓ | | | | | | | | | | | | | | | | | |
| 44 | | | ✓ | | | | | | | | | | | | | | | | | | | |
| 57 | | | | ✓ | | | | | | | | | | | | | | | | | | |
| 65 | | | | | | | | | | | | | | | | | | | | | | others have advantage |
| **GUILT** 4 | ✓ | | | | | | | | | | | | | | | | | | | | | |
| 24 | | | | | | | | | | | | | | | | | | | | | | self |
| 43 | | | | | | | | | | | | | | | | | | | | | | doing right |
| 54 | | | | | | ✓ | | | | | | | | | | | | | | | | |
| 69 | | | | ✓ | | | | | | | | | | | | | | | | | | |
| **INFERIORITY FEELINGS** 18 | ✓ | | | | | | | | | | | | | | | | | | | | | |
| 40 | | | | ✓ | | | | | | | | | | | | | | | | | | |
| 28 | | | | | ✓ | | | | | | | | | | | | | | | | | |
| 53 | | | | | ✓ | | | | | | | | | | | | | | | | | |
| 61 | | | | | ✓ | | | | | | | | | | | | | | | | | |

### D. REACTIONS TO

| | Unclear | Denial | Omission | Acceptance | Aggression | Anxiety | Avoidance | Dependency | Depression | Failure | Fear | Guilt | Hostility | Intellectualize | Passivity | Pleasure | Rejection | Restriving | Somatization | Success | |
|---|---|---|---|---|---|---|---|---|---|---|---|---|---|---|---|---|---|---|---|---|---|
| **AGGRESSION** 22 | | | | | | | ✓ | | | | | | | | | | | | | | |
| 42 | | | | | | | | | | | | ✓ | | | | | | | | | |
| 51 | | | | ✓ | | | | | | | | | | | | | | | | | |
| 72 | | | | | | | | | | | | | | | | | | ✓ | | | compliance |
| 80 | | | | | | | | | | | | | | | | | | ✓ | | | compliance |
| **REJECTION** 5 | | | | | | | | | | | | | | | | | | ✓ | | | compliance |
| 14 | | | | | | | | | | | | | | | | | | ✓ | | | compliance |
| 46 | | | | | | | | | | | | | | | | | ✓ | | | | |
| 82 | | | | | | | ✓ | | | | | | | | | | | | | | |
| 90 | | | | ✓ | | | | | | | | | | | | | | | | | compliance |
| **FAILURE** 3 | | | | | | | | | | | | | | | | | | ✓ | | | |
| 25 | | | | | | | | | | | | | | | | | | ✓ | | | |
| 41 | | | | | | | | | | | | | | | | | | ✓ | | | |
| 48 | | | | | | | | | | | | | | | | | | | | | Press Aggression |
| 63 | | | | | | | | | | | | | | | | | | ✓ | | | |
| **RESPONSIBILITY** 1 | | | | ✓ | | | | | | | | | | | | | | | | | |
| 31 | | | | | | | | | | | | | | | ✓ | | | | | | think first |
| 62 | | | | ✓ | | | | | | | | | | | | | | | | | |
| 68 | | | | ✓ | | | | | | | | | | | | | | | | | |
| 85 | | | | ✓ | | | | | | | | | | | | | | | | | |
| **SCHOOL** 11 | | | | | | | | | | | | | | | | | | ✓ | | | |
| 32 | | | | | | | | | | | | | | | | | ✓ | ✓ | | | |
| 58 | | | | | | | | | | | | | | | | | | ✓ | | | |
| 78 | ✓ | | | | | | | | | | | | | | | | | | | | |
| 92 | | | | | | | | | | | | | | | | | ✓ | | | | |

*A. Attitudes Toward and Characteristics of Interpersonal Figures (35 Items)*

Blocks of items are allocated to father, mother, males, females, groups and authorities. Examination of these items as subgroups enables the exploration of various facets of object relationships, transference attitudes, displacements and the like.

*B. Wishes (9 Items)*

These items provide an opportunity for the client to express wishes to less structured stimuli than in the rest of the blank.

*C. Causes of One's Own Feeling or Action (31 Items)*

The client is assigned a response or feeling and is asked to specify the instigating circumstances. That is, he describes the conditions under which he is likely to express aggression, guilt, anxiety or fear, giving up, failure and inferiority feelings. Such an ego assignment is often a fruitful source of information about ego-defensive operations.

*D. Reactions to External States (25 Items)*

The child is asked to react to press aggression, rejection, failure, responsibility and school conditions. These items define important typical situations with which the child can be expected to have to contend. While the sentence completions can not be expected to be directly representative of his overt reaction in reality situations, they provide clues to the nature of his characteristic coping techniques and his conflicts.

The check list indicates the numbers of the sentences and the areas in which they fall. A list of common dimensions for classification is supplied so that each item and each group of items can be compared. In addition, the categories of *unclear, denial* and *omission* are printed onto the form because these, too, are diagnostically important, particularly with reference to their differential occurrence among the content areas. The response classifications ought not to be taken too seriously. Their function is partly convenience, partly a means of focusing clinical attention on variations among responses to the group of items. It is often useful to write the responses onto the check sheet, particularly when they are uncommon in content or form, along with interpretations or clinical hypotheses.

We have not the space to discuss in detail the many techniques and theoretical considerations that go into interpretation of a protocol. Some ideas are presented in the writer's adult test manual,[39,40] and others will be exemplified below in the case illustration. Many of the cogent ideas in Rapaport, Gill and Schafer[53] and Schafer[58] are applicable.

### Case Illustration

The following protocol was obtained from a nine year old boy whose mother took him to a university psychological clinic for assistance. In this case the test was administered orally. The check list (fig. 1) has been filled out for demonstration purposes, but many of the examiner's classifications of responses can legitimately be disputed. In addition to the check list the writer compares and summarizes the responses within each group of items and between groups of related items, sometimes writing hypotheses and dynamics on a separate sheet of paper for later synthesis.

FORER STRUCTURED SENTENCE COMPLETION TEST        Form B

Age __9__ Sex __M__ Grade_____ _____

INSTRUCTIONS: Finish the following sentences as fast as you can. Write down the first thing you think of. Please finish all 100 sentences.

1. *When he was completely on his own, he* . . . brought his own things
2. *He often wished he could* . . . be a man
3. *It looked impossible, so he* . . . went to see
4. *He felt to blame when* . . . saw it
5. *When she refused him, he* . . . did it
6. *I used to feel I was being held back by* . . . school teacher
7. *He felt proud that he* . . . was a man
8. *As a child my greatest fear was* . . . never here
9. *My father always* . . . say to me that you must be a man
10. *The ideal man* . . . knows things
11. *Whenever I have to study, I* . . . do it
12. *He felt like quitting when* . . . he didn't finish
13. *My first reaction to him was* . . . hello
14. *When she turned me down, I* . . . did it
15. *His new classmates were* . . . friendly
16. *Most fathers* . . . are good
17. *Sometimes he wished he* . . . was a policeman
18. *He felt pretty useless when* . . . he saw this
19. *I was most annoyed when* . . . I heard that
20. *His earliest memory of his mother was* . . . yes, yes, mother
21. *The ideal girl* . . . is smart
22. *When others made fun of him, he* . . . ignored them
23. *When he met his principal, he* . . . said hello
24. *When I think back, I am ashamed that* . . . to tell
25. *If I think the class is too hard for me, I* . . . still do it
26. *When she invited me, I* . . . came
27. *His poor grades were due to* . . . principal
28. *He felt inferior whenever* . . . he was bad
29. *His greatest wish was* . . . a dog
30. *Most men* . . . are smart
31. *When I have to make a decision, I* . . . think before I say it
32. *School is* . . . fun
33. *My earliest memory of my father* . . . was a good man to you
34. *I could hate a person who* . . . makes faces at you
35. *Most mothers* . . . are good. Like any of the mothers, my mother is good
36. *Taking orders* . . . is the right thing to do
37. *If I had my way, I would* . . . not do it
38. *When they looked at me, I* . . . ignored them
39. *Most girls* . . . are friendly
40. *He felt unpopular because* . . . she was mad
41. *If I can't get what I want, I* . . . save my money and buy it
42. *When I am criticized, I* . . . am sorry
43. *He felt he had done wrong when he* . . . did right
44. *He knew he couldn't succeed unless* . . . (Omitted by client)

45. *He wanted to get away when* . . . someone caught him
46. *When they didn't invite me, I* . . . didn't invite them
47. *He felt very tense when* . . . (Omitted by client)
48. *When he found he had failed the test, he* . . . got scolded
49. *People seem to think I* . . . silly
50. *When he asked me along, I* . . . didn't answer
51. *After they knocked him down, he* . . . knocked them down
52. *I'd like most to be* . . . a policeman
53. *My worst failing is* . . . that I'd done something wrong
54. *His conscience bothered him most when* . . . his friends talk to him
55. *He felt he could murder a man who* . . . tried to take him
56. *At times he worried about* . . . telling a policeman
57. *He did a poor job because* . . . wouldn't listen
58. *I wish that school* . . . was out
59. *While he was speaking to me I* . . . ignored him
60. *My mother always* . . . tells me when they come over here, you don't always have to go over there
61. *They didn't like him because* . . . he was bad
62. *When they asked my opinion, I* . . . told them
63. *Whenever he did poorly, he* . . . did it over again
64. *He didn't study because* . . . too hard
65. *I lost out because* . . . he had a head start
66. *In a group of people, I generally feel* . . . ignored
67. *My first reaction to her was* . . . yes
68. *When they put me in charge, I* . . . did it
69. *I feel guilty about* . . . doing wrong
70. *When my father came home, I* . . . told him what I did; had to tell
71. *As she spoke to him, he* . . . answered. Sometimes she send him to the corner and make him put knees on popcorn
72. *When he was punished by his mother, he* . . . went to place where mother told him
73. *People in authority are* . . . policemen
74. *I used to daydream about* . . . my best friend
75. *He boiled up when* . . . his friends made faces
76. *When my mother came home, I* . . . asked her could I go to my friend's home
77. *When they told him what to do, he* . . . did it
78. *The trouble with school is* . . . it's old
79. *His greatest worry was* . . . fire. Many people get killed in a fire
80. *When he was punished by his father, he* . . . went to do it, whatever father told him to do
81. *Most girls act as though* . . . they're smart. Some of them don't even know 2 and 2
82. *When I feel that others don't like me, I* . . . don't pay any attention to them
83. *More than anything else, he needed* . . . something like a toy on being punished
84. *When he was with the group, he* . . . did what the group did—whatever assigned to do
85. *When his turn came to speak, he* . . . did it, so the kids could hear him, and the teacher
86. *I could lose my temper if* . . . my friends were mean to me
87. *I am afraid of* . . . monsters
88. *Whenever he was with his father, he felt* . . . that nothing would harm him
89. *A fellow has a right to hit a girl who* . . . hits him. But boys don't fight girls. If they fight me, I'll take a rope, tie them up, lead them like a horse to the principal, put on my gun and go bang-bang.
90. *When they told him to get out, he* . . . got out
91. *Sometimes I feel that my teacher* . . . is mean to me
92. *When I joined the new class, I* . . . am proud
93. *Whenever he is introduced to people, he* . . . introduces himself
94. *When he was with his mother, he felt* . . . nothing would touch him
95. *Most fellows act as though* . . . they're great, but they aren't
96. *I wish that my father* . . . was a policeman

97. *He wanted to give up when* . . . he was tired
98. *If I were king, I would* . . . tell them what to do
99. *I wish that my mother* . . . was a nurse.
100. *I feel like running away when* . . . my mother is rude to me

## Interpretation

Instead of a complete test evaluation, which would be a dubious practice without data from other tests as well, or a thorough sequential analysis of the items, a sample of interpretive statements may better exemplify the procedure.

On the first half of the test the boy is rather accepting of parents and peers. Later, as defenses are penetrated by the succession of items, he gives indications of deeper feelings of hostility, distrust, transference expectations of rejection and excessive demands from others. Emphasis on parental power and protection (plus the need for parental approval) along with signs of increasing negative feelings toward peers suggests repression of these feelings toward the parents (who recently informed him that he is adopted) and their displacement to more distant objects. The father is seen clearly as the source of a demanding ego ideal of masculine strength and achievement which is less ego syntonic than it appears at first. Evidence is abundant that the boy is attempting to comply with others' wishes as he perceives them rather than expressing his own wishes. Items such as 36 and 37 suggest an underlying rebellion. Many responses, including 28, 43, 53, 54, 61 and 79, suggest a pervasive feeling of guilt which is augmented by the hostility counteracted by his compliance. In addition he employs denial and some projection as a defense against admitting his failure to attain the expected standards. (His parents have intellectual ambitions which his low average IQ cannot substantiate. And they are intolerant of normal childish wishes.)

Identification with the aggressor looms as an important defense. The wish for dominance has the component of fulfilling parental, i.e., ego ideal, expectations and of stemming the aggressive feelings which threaten him. (Play therapy revealed considerable anxiety, expressed in stuttering and body tension, fluctuating compliance and covert behavioral aggression in the handling of toys, and destructive fantasies with alternating identification with the "bad guys" and the "cops").

While there are two omitted items and several unclear responses, all responses seem fairly relevant to the stimuli. The threshold for aggression is somewhat low and is linked to transference feelings of press rejection and criticism. "Causes of anxiety and fear" elicit one omission and one unclear response, ambivalent concern about others' welfare and fear of monsters. These items together suggest considerable anxiety and relate it to aggressive feelings.

There is much more information in the protocol, and many additional clinical inferences and behavioral predictions could be drawn. The aim of this chapter, however, has been simply to describe the historical development of the techniques described and to demonstrate some of the diagnostic properties that they possess.

# References

## *Word Association Tests*

1. Bell, J.  *Projective methods.* New York: Longmans, Green, 1948.
2. Cattell, J. M., & Bryant, S.  Mental association investigated by experiment. *Mind,* 1889, *14,* 203–250.
3. Dörken, H., Jr.  Frequency of common associations. *Psychol. Rep.,* 1956, *2,* 407–408.
4. Eastman, F. C., & Rosanoff, A. J.  Association in feebleminded and delinquent children. *Amer. J. Insan.,* 1912, *69,* 125–141.
5. Galton, F.  Psychometric experiments. *Brain,* 1879, *2,* 149–162.
6. Horan, E. M.  Word association frequency tables of mentally retarded children. *J. consult. Psychol.,* 1956, *20,* 22.
7. Jung, C. G.  *Studies in word association.* (Engl. transl.) London: Heinemann, 1918.
8. Kent, G. H., & Rosanoff, A. J.  A study of association in insanity. *Amer. J. Insan.,* 1910, *67,* 37–96, 317–390.
9. Kraepelin, E.  *Ueber die Beimflussung einfacher psychischer Vorgange durch einige Arzneimittel; experimentelle Untersuchungen.* Jena: Fischer, 1892.
10. McDowell, E. D.  *Educational and emotional adjustments of stuttering children.* New York: Columbia Univer. Press, 1928.
11. McElvee, E. W.  Association in normal and subnormal adolescents. *Amer. J. Psychiat.,* 1941, *11,* 318–331.
12. McGehee, W. M.  The free word association of elementary school children: 1. Reaction times. *J. genet. Psychol.,* 1937, *50,* 441–455.
13. ———.  The free word association of elementary school children: 2. Verbal responses. *J. genet. Psychol.,* 1938, *52,* 361–374.
14. McHale, J. L.  Set as a determinant in the associations of normal and retarded children. *Dissert. Abstr.,* 1956, *16,* 1941–1942.
15. Meltzer, H.  Children's attitudes to parents. *Amer. J. Orthopsychiat.,* 1935, *5,* 244–265.
16. Mitchell, I., Rosanoff, I., & Rosanoff, A. J.  A study of association in negro children. *Psychol. Rev.,* 1919, *26,* 354–359.
17. Otis, M.  A study of associations in defectives. *J. educ. Psychol.,* 1915, *6,* 271–288.
18. Powell, M.  Age and sex differences in degree of conflict within certain areas of psychological adjustment. *Psychol. Monogr.,* 1955, *69,* No. 2 (Whole No. 387).
19. Rapaport, D., Gill, M., & Schafer, R.  *Diagnostic psychological testing.* Vol. 2. Chicago: Year Book, 1946.
20. Rosanoff, I., & Rosanoff, A. J.  A study of associations in children. *Psychol. Rev.,* 1913, *20,* 43–80.
21. Rosanoff, A. J.  *Manual of psychiatry.* (Rev. ed.) New York: Wiley, 1938.
22. Rotter, J. B.  Word association and sentence completion methods. *In* Anderson, H. H., & Anderson, G. L. (Eds.)  *An introduction to projective techniques.* New York: Prentice-Hall, 1951. Pp. 279–311.
23. Rusk, R. R.  Experiments on mental associations in children. *Brit. J. Psychol.,* 1909, *3,* 349–385.
24. Schafer, R.  Clinical evaluation of a word association test. *Bull. Menninger Clin.,* 1945, *9,* 84–88.
25. ———.  *The clinical application of psychological tests.* New York: Int. Univer. Press, 1948.
26. ———.  Tests of personality: word association test. *In* Weider, A. (Ed.)  *Contributions toward medical psychology.* Vol. 1. New York: Ronald, 1953. Pp. 577–589.
27. Sommer, K. R.  *Lehrbuch der psychopatischen Untersuchungensmethoden.* Berlin: Urban-Schwartzenberg, 1899.
28. Woodrow, H., & Lowell, F.  Children's association frequency tables. *Psychol. Monogr.,* 1916, *22,* No. 5 (Whole No. 97).
29. Wundt, W.  *Grundzuge der physiologischen Psychologie.* Vol. 3. Leipzig: Engelmann, 1911. Pp. 436–456, 519–543.

## Sentence Completion Methods

30. Bene, E.  The objective use of a projective technique, illustrated by a study of the difference in attitudes between pupils of grammar school and of secondary modern schools. *Brit. J. educ. Psychol.*, 1957, *27*, 89–100.

31. Cass, L. K.  An investigation of parent-child relationships in terms of awareness, identification, projection and control. *Amer. J. Orthopsychiat.*, 1952, *22*, 305–313.

32. Cobb, H. V.  Role wishes and general wishes of children and adolescents. *Child Develpm.*, 1954, *25*, 161–172.

33. Copple, G. E.  Effective intelligence as measured by an unstructured sentence completion technique. *J. consult. Psychol.*, 1956, *20*, 357–360.

34. Costin, F., & Eiserer, P. E.  Students' attitudes toward school life as revealed by a sentence completion test. *Amer. Psychol.*, 1949, *4*, 289 (Abstract).

35. Cromwell, R. L., & Lundy, R. M.  Productivity of clinical hypotheses on a sentence completion test. *J. clin. Psychol.*, 1954, *18*, 421–424.

36. Cruickshank, W. M.  The effect of physical disability on personal aspiration. *Quart. J. Child Behav.*, 1951, *3*, 323–333.

37. ———.  The relation of physical disability to fear and guilt feelings. *Child Develpm.*, 1951, *22*, 291–298.

38. ———.  The relationship of physical disability to fear and guilt feelings. *Cerebr. Palsy Rev.*, 1952, *13*, 9–13.

39. Forer, B. R.  A structured sentence completion test. *J. proj. Tech.*, 1950, *14*, 15–30.

40. ———.  *The Forer Structured Sentence Completion Tests.* Santa Monica, Calif.: Western Psychological Services, 1957. (Adult male, adult female, boys', girls' forms, and male and female Vocational surveys.)

41. ———.  Research with projective techniques: some trends. *J. proj. Tech.*, 1957, *21*, 358–361.

42. Freed, E. X., & Cruickshank, W. M.  The relation of cardiac disease to feelings of fear. *J. Pediatr.*, 1953, *43*, 483–488.

43. Getzels, J. W.  The assessment of personality and prejudice by the method of paired direct and projective questions. Unpublished doctoral dissertation, Harvard Univer., 1951.

44. Graham, F. K., Charwat, W. A., Honig, A. S., & Weltz, P. A.  Aggression as a function of the attack and the attacker. *J. abnorm. soc. Psychol.*, 1951, *46*, 512–520.

45. Hanfmann, E., & Getzels, J. W.  Studies of the sentence completion test. *J. proj. Tech.*, 1953, *17*, 280–294.

46. Harris, D. B., & Tseng, S. C.  Children's attitudes toward peers and parents as revealed by sentence completions. *Child Develpm.*, 1957, *28*, 401–411.

47. Kimball, B.  The sentence-completion technique in a study of scholastic underachievement. *J. consult. Psychol.*, 1952, *16*, 353–358.

48. Machover, K.  *The C Z I Sentence Completion Test.* New York: Kings County Hospital, 1949.

49. Machover, S. (Ed.)  Case reports in clinical psychology. *Case Rep. clin. Psychol.*, 1949, *1*, No. 1.

50. Malpass, L. F.  Some relationships between students' perception of school and their achievement. *J. educ. Psychol.*, 1953, *44*, 475–482.

51. Murray, H. A.  *Explorations in personality.* New York: Oxford, 1938.

52. Payne, A. F.  *Sentence completions.* New York: N. Y. Guidance Clinic, 1928.

53. Rapaport, D., Gill, M., & Schafer, R.  *Diagnostic psychological testing.* Vol. 2. Chicago: Year Book, 1946.

54. Rohde, A. R.  Explorations in personality by the sentence completion method. *J. appl. Psychol.*, 1946, *30*, 169–181.

55. ———.  *The sentence completion method.* New York: Ronald, 1957.

56. Rotter, J. B., Rafferty, J. E., & Lotsof, A. B.  The validity of the Rotter Incomplete Sentences Blank  High School Form. *J. consult. Psychol.*, 1954, *18*, 105–111.

57. Sanford, R. N., Adkins, M. M., Miller, R. B., & Cobb, E. A.   Physique, personality and scholarship. *Monogr. Soc. Res. Child Develpm.*, 1943, *8*, No. 1 (Serial No. 34).

58. Schafer, R.   *The clinical application of psychological tests.* New York: Int. Univer. Press, 1948.

59. Tendler, A. D.   A preliminary report on a test for emotional insight. *J. appl. Psychol.*, 1930, *14*, 123–136.

60. Wilson, I.   The use of a sentence completion test in differentiating between well-adjusted and maladjusted secondary school pupils. *J. consult. Psychol.*, 1949, *13*, 400–402.

## 12

## Projective Aspects of Intelligence Testing

INTELLIGENCE for many years was considered to be an inborn faculty of the human being, separate from his personality and its dynamics. Consequently, a cleavage has existed in psychology between the fields of intelligence testing and projective techniques. Intelligence tests were assumed to measure intellectual ability only, and were used statically for this purpose; while projective techniques were employed dynamically as a means of gaining insight into a patient's personality, the nature of his drives, his ego organization, his areas of conflict and his defenses.

However, intelligence does not exist as a separate entity in splendid isolation from personality. And the assumption of the constancy of the IQ, so long a prime credo of intelligence testing, is a fallacious one.* IQ's do change, and intellect can be measured as little in isolation from personality as the function of seeing can be studied on an eye that has been removed out of the living human being and ceased to be a part of it. Intelligence is a *function* of the total personality, mutually interdependent with education, life experiences, emotions, conscious and unconscious wishes and yearnings, attitudes and conflicts.

Since the middle forties dynamically oriented clinical psychologists have again challenged the concept that intelligence tests measure intelligence only. In the United States Rapaport and his co-workers,[16,19-21] Lois Murphy,[17] Gladys Anderson,[1] Breiger[4] and the author of this chapter and her collaborators[10-12] extended the projective principle to intelligence testing. Simultaneously, and apparently independently, a similar trend was set into motion in Holland by Chorus[6] and in South Africa by Lejeune.[14]

The "projective hypothesis"[7] states that any reaction of an individual potentially reflects basic aspects of his unique personality organization. It is the principle underlying projective techniques. But it is not only applicable to the manner in which a person structures unstructured material such as the Rorschach cards. It applies to *all* reactions or responses a person gives, be the stimulus a projective test, a real life situation or a question on an

---

*The first attack on the idea of the constancy of the IQ did not come from Wellman in 1940,[23] as we erroneously stated in an earlier publication (reference 11, page 4), but in 1911, from the originator of intelligence testing himself, Alfred Binet.[3] Binet was also the first to devise projective techniques. In an elaborate study of personality differences and the functioning of intelligence,[2] he experimented with the interpretation of ink blots, with sentence completion and word association tests and with a TAT-like method of letting his teen age daughters tell stories about pictures. But somehow these projective aspects of his work on intelligence quickly sank into oblivion.

intelligence test. True, the stimuli on projective tests are less structured than standard intelligence test questions and therefore lend themselves more easily to projection. However, the dynamically oriented clinical psychologist who stops to look at more than just the "pass" or "fail" aspects of answers given to subtest questions on intelligence tests must soon realize that the variety of responses he receives from different children to the same intelligence test questions, and the qualitative aspects of the responses, cannot be a function of intelligence alone. To the great majority of intelligence test questions there is not just one possible correct answer and one wrong one. Though the constructors of these tests have striven to pose their test questions so that there should be little or no ambiguity, qualitatively widely differing responses are given to nearly every subtest in the "pass" as well as the "fail" category. It must therefore be possible to interpret intelligence tests in a projective manner.

Let us give an example of projective aspects of intelligence tests from the vocabulary of the Stanford-Binet.[22] When asked "What is an orange?" a 12 year old boy produced the following dissertation:

An orange is a round citrus fruit weighing approximately four ounces. It is orange in color. It was unknown to the Western World until the 13th Century, when Marco Polo discovered it on his travel to China and brought it back with him to Europe. From there, several centuries later, it was brought to the United States and it has now become a most important product of the orchard industries in the states of California, Florida, and Texas. Philologically speaking, its origin still is commemorated in the root of the Dutch word for orange, which is sinaasappel and which is a mutilation of the Dutch words for 'Chinese apple.'

In the quantitative test analysis this youngster's answer is given the same plus score as the more common response, "an orange is a fruit," or "an orange is to eat." But on hearing this answer, the psychologist should start to think about more than a "pass" or a "fail." He should ask himself, what are the personality dynamics of this boy? Is he a compulsive individual, a perfectionist or an exhibitionist who wants to show off all he knows? Is he an anxious and insecure person who has the need to impress the examiner because he lacks self esteem and is craving for approval? These are possibilities; they become working hypotheses to be tested by carefully watching and weighing all the verbatim answers the child gives to other questions on the same test, and on other tests. Such evaluation can and should be done not only with the "unusual" responses but with the ordinary ones as well.

On the Stanford-Binet, year VII, the Comprehension question "What would you do if another boy (girl) hit you without meaning to do it?" frequently elicits one of the following responses:

1. "Tell them I know they didn't mean to hurt me." (Good reality awareness and judgment, mature ego.)

2. "Say: never mind; it didn't hurt me." (Considerateness; denial of pain.)

3. "I wouldn't hit back." (Defense against own aggressive impulses which may be easily aroused.)

4. "Hit him back." (Aggressive.)

5. "Tell my Mama." (Infantile and dependent.)

The first three answers are all correct and scored plus, the last two are minus. As denoted in the parentheses, each of the five is the expression of a somewhat different personality. As far as strength of aggressive drives is concerned, the child who gives the failing response "Hit him back" is closely related to the one who says "I wouldn't hit back." But the latter has a stronger ego and with it has built up a defense system which enables him to control his easily aroused aggressive impulses, while the former has not. By thus qualitatively analyzing the specific, individual responses a child gives to subtest questions, we make projective use of intelligence tests and cull out of them personality factors. The clinical psychologist should always assess the total integrated personality and not artificially separated parts of it such as intelligence per se. He can make this assessment not only by means of any projective test such as the Rorschach or the TAT, but also by using intelligence tests. The so-called intelligence tests elicit personality data as well, *if* one is able and willing to listen with a clinical ear to qualitative nuances.

In a less dynamic, more typologic sense, Porteus[18] has applied this thesis to his Maze Test since 1942; and Solomon Machover[15] stated it in 1943 with particular emphasis on cultural and racial variables.

In order to interpret intelligence tests projectively, one must discard the shackles of the old attitude of looking only for the *single* factor with which each subtest question supposedly is loaded. Instead, in our own research[10,12] we have asked: What are *all* the variables, intellectual as well as emotional, that could possibly be involved in a child's passing or failing each subtest item of a given intelligence test and *the way in which* he fails or succeeds on them?

Through posing the question in this unorthodox way, we tried to open the door wider to systematic thinking about personality variables which enter into the giving of a response on intelligence tests. We systematically thought about each subtest question and the great variety of answers we had been given to each of them by the hundreds of children we have tested in our years of clinical work with normal, emotionally disturbed and brain-injured children. We tried to analyze the underlying meaning of these answers. Through this means of theoretical analysis, and through interrater agreement of from two to four experienced psychologists (some of the tests were analyzed by two raters independently, some by four), we arrived at 43 personality variables playing a role on intelligence tests. Some stem from the id, the majority of them represent functions of the developing ego, some are superego variables, and some variables are culturally or sociologically determined.

Table 1 gives the list of these 43 personality variables and the categories under which they can be grouped.

Table 2 shows the role the variables play on the three month level of the Cattell Infant Intelligence Scale[5] and the nine year level of the Stanford-Binet, Form L.

Table 1.—*List of Categories and Variables*

| | |
|---|---|
| A. Id-Ego Variables | B. Ego Development—*(Continued)* |
|   1. Primary motivation (1) |       b) reality-centered concept formation (21) |
|   2. Gratification of impulse (2) |       c) categorical thinking (22) |
|   3. Primary anxiety (3) |     (2) abstraction (23) |
| B. Ego Development |     (3) judgment (24) |
|   1. Sensory perception |     (4) flexibility (25) |
|     *a.* visual perception (4) |     (5) learning (26) |
|     *b.* auditory perception (5) |     (6) insight (either planned solution or "aha!" experience ) (27) |
|     *c.* kinesthetic, touch, taste, smell perception (6) |     (7) fantasy (28) |
|   2. Adaptation to reality and integrative behavior |   3. Ego ideal (29) |
|     *a.* reality awareness (7) |   4. Anxiety, either as an affect or as an ego defense (30) |
|     *b.* reality testing (8) |   5. Ego defenses |
|     *c.* reality mastery (9) |     *a.* blocking (31) |
|     *d.* goal-directed motivation (10) |     *b.* repetition compulsion (32) |
|     *e.* motor mastery of own body (11) |     *c.* perseveration (33) |
|     *f.* body image (12) |     *d.* meticulosity (34) |
|     *g.* memory |     *e.* stimulus boundness (35) |
|       (1) rote memory (13) |     *f.* denial (36) |
|       (2) memory for meaningful objects and materials (14) |     *g.* self criticism (37) |
|     *h.* attention span (15) | C. Superego Variables |
|     *i.* identification (16) |   1. Superego motivation (38) |
|     *j.* interpersonal relations (rapport) (17) |   2. Social habits (39) |
|     *k.* language development |   3. Following commands (40) |
|       (1) language understanding (18) |   4. Delay of impulsive action (41) |
|       (2) language mastery (19) |   5. Judgment, moral values (42) |
|     *l.* thinking | D. Cultural Influences (43) |
|       (1) concept formation | |
|         a) need-centered concept formation (20) | |

## Personality Variables

Let us now discuss in what way these personality variables can play a role in a child's passing or failing subtest items and how they can be used for the projective interpretation of intelligence tests.

### Id-Ego Variables

*Primary motivation* is the drive to achieve homeostasis within the organism by discharging tension without delay. In pure culture it is a characteristic of the very earliest stages of development. It is not directed towards a *specific* object (e.g., the child takes *any* test toy into his mouth), and it may not require an outside object for gratification at all (as in defecation or autistic rocking). If the three month old infant has severe gas pain, he is much more likely to cry, fret or try to expel what bothers him than to have the serenity and the interest in the outside world which would enable him to follow the Ring in Circular Motion with his eyes, to Regard a Cube or Spoon, to Inspect His Fingers or to Hold His Head Steady. Thus, if *primary motivation* is present, it is potentially involved in failure on the Cattell subtests 1, 3, 4, 5 and 6 at the three month level, and therefore these tests are marked (x) in the category for *primary motivation* in table 2. However, on subtest 2, hunger is a necessary condition for successfully passing the test; the satiated infant will show no excitement when he sees the breast or the bottle. Therefore a check mark is placed in this box under subtest 2. As hunger is not the only possible primary motivation, and all others we could think of might interfere with success on this subtest, an (x) beside the check mark indicates that one primary motivation, satiation of hunger, necessarily is involved in success on subtest 2 while other primary motivations may lead to failure.

On the six subtests of the 9 year level of the Stanford-Binet any type of *primary motivation may* become a deterrent and lead to failure. If a child masturbates while he is asked to repeat digits reversed, he is likely to forget or mix up the numbers due to the interference of his instinctual needs; but not necessarily so. His masturbating indicates that he is driven by primary motivation or by the desire to gratify an impulse immediately. But it is possible that, while masturbating, he may still listen to the numbers and repeat them in reversed order. Similarly, on subtest 2 the nine year old may have an aggressive impulse to tear up the test material rather than to reproduce the designs.

*Gratification of instinct* is closely related to *primary motivation*.

*Primary Anxiety* is a state of being flooded with such overwhelming excitement that the organism can do nothing but passively endure it. If present, *primary anxiety* will always interfere with the solution of a test task, except that it possibly may make the infant turn to the breast or bottle for solace.

In accordance with the new psychoanalytic concepts of Anna Freud,[8] Hartmann[13] and others, these three variables were classified as id-ego rather than as pure id variables. The id must always go through some ego channels in order to manifest itself.

### Ego Functions

In the whole inventory of intelligence tests there is hardly a subtest which does not involve *sensory perception* of one form or another. A child must hear the instructions and/or see the test material to which he is supposed to react. One of the few exceptions is the last test on the three month level of the Cattell: even a blind and deaf infant can hold its head steady as soon as his neuromuscular development has progressed to a certain point.

By far the most important variable the subtests 1 to 4 measure on the three month level of the Cattell is *reality awareness*. Without it, the infant cannot possibly pass them. Reality, the outside world, must exist for him at least as consisting of objects worthwhile to regard. We have reason to assume also that just in order to differentiate the "I" and the "not-I" at this age he Inspects his Fingers and Hands moving about. Therefore *reality awareness* and *reality testing* are also checked under subtest 5. Any subtest in which actual test material is presented to the subject requires,

## PERSONALITY DEVELOPMENT

### EGO DEVELOPMENT

### ADAPTATION TO REALITY AND INTE-

**LANGUAGE DEVELOPMENT**
- 18. Language understanding
- 19. Language mastery

**THINKING**
- 20. Need-centered concept formation
- 21. Reality-centered concept formation
- 22. Categorical thinking
- 23. Abstraction
- 24. Judgment
- 25. Flexibility
- 26. Learning
- 27. Insight
- 28. Fantasy

**EGO-IDEAL**
- 29. Ego-ideal

**ANXIETY**
- 30. Anxiety

**EGO DEFENSES**
- 31. Blocking
- 32. Repetition compulsion
- 33. Perseveration
- 34. Meticulosity
- 35. Stimulus-boundness
- 36. Denial
- 37. Self criticism

**SUPEREGO VARIABLES**
- 38. Superego motivation
- 39. Habits, social
- 40. Following commands
- 41. Delay of action
- 42. Judgment, moral values

**CULTURAL VARIABLES**
- 43. Cultural influences

## TABLE 2.— SAMPLE ITEM ANALYSES.

**LEGEND**

✓ enters necessarily in success
(✓) potentially involved in success
Blank: involved neither in success nor failure
✗ if present, definitely involved in failure
(✗) if present, potentially involved in failure

**PERSONALITY DEVELOPMENT**

- EGO DEVELOPMENT
- [INTE]GRATIVE BEHAVIOR
- MEMORY
- PERCEPTION*
- ID-EGO VARIABLES

| PERSONALITY VARIABLES | Primary motivation (1) | Gratification of impulse (2) | Primary anxiety (3) | Visual perception (4) | Auditory perception (5) | Kinesthetic, touch, taste, smell perception (6) | Reality awareness (7) | Reality testing (8) | Reality mastery (9) | Goal-directed motivation (10) | Motor mastery of own body (11) | Body image (12) | Rote memory (13) | Memory for meaningful objects & materials (14) | Attention span (15) | Identification (16) | Interpersonal relations (17) |
|---|---|---|---|---|---|---|---|---|---|---|---|---|---|---|---|---|---|
| **CATTELL INFANT INTELLIGENCE SCALE 3 MONTH LEVEL** | | | | | | | | | | | | | | | | | |
| 1. FOLLOWS RING IN CIRCULAR MOTION | (✗) | (✗) | ✗ | ✓ | | | ✓ | ✓ | | | ✓ | | | (✓) | ✓ | | (✗) |
| 2. ANTICIPATES FEEDING | (✗) | ✓ | (✓) | ✓ | | | ✓ | (✓) | | | (✓) | | ✓ | ✓ | | | (✗) |
| 3. REGARDS CUBE | ✗ | ✗ | ✗ | ✓ | | | ✓ | (✓) | (✓) | | ✓ | | | (✓) | ✓ | | (✗) |
| 4. REGARDS SPOON | ✗ | ✗ | ✗ | ✓ | | | ✓ | (✓) | (✓) | | ✓ | | | (✓) | ✓ | | (✗) |
| 5. INSPECTS FINGERS | ✗ | ✗ | ✗ | ✓ | | | ✓ | | | | (✓) | (✓) | | (✓) | ✓ | | |
| 6. HOLDS HEAD STEADY | (✗) | (✗) | ✗ | | | | | | | | ✓ | | | | | | (✗) |
| **1937 STANFORD-BINET FORM L 9 YEAR LEVEL** | | | | | | | | | | | | | | | | | |
| 1. PAPER CUTTING | (✗) | (✗) | ✗ | ✓ | | ✓ | (✓) | ✓ | | ✓ | ✓ | | ✓ | (✓) | ✓ | | (✓) |
| 2. VERBAL ABSURDITIES II | (✗) | (✗) | ✗ | | ✓ | | (✓) | ✓ | | (✓) | | | ✓ | (✓) | ✓ | | (✓) |
| 3. MEMORY FOR DESIGN | (✗) | (✗) | ✗ | ✓ | ✓ | ✓ | (✓) | ✓ | ✓ | ✓ | ✓ | | ✓ | (✓) | ✓ | | (✓) |
| 4. RHYMES | (✗) | (✗) | ✗ | | ✓ | ✓ | | (✓) | | ✓ | | | ✓ | (✓) | ✓ | | (✓) |
| 5. MAKING CHANGE | (✗) | (✗) | ✗ | ✓ | ✓ | ✓ | ✓ | (✓) | | ✓ | | | ✓ | (✓) | ✓ | | (✓) |
| 6. REPEATING DIGITS REVERSED | (✗) | (✗) | ✗ | | ✓ | | (✓) | | (✓) | ✓ | | | ✓ | (✓) | ✓ | | (✓) |

of course, that the subject is aware of the material—that is, of a piece of reality. While such tests (e.g., Stanford-Binet IX, subtests 1 and 3) involve *reality awareness* in the sense of actual perception of an object, a somewhat different form of *reality awareness*, knowledge of reality, is a *sine qua non* in order to pass Verbal Absurdities and Rhymes. A child may be blind, but he must realize that there are animals roaming this world called bear, hare and mare, and a color named red—or he cannot successfully pass this test on Rhymes. And only when and because he is aware of reality as it really is can he recognize Absurdities.

*Reality awareness* can never be a hindrance to the intellectual solution of a test question. However, it may not enter into a solution at all. Digits can be repeated successfully, forwards or backwards, as if they were non-sense syllables.

On all subtests on which a child succeeds after one or two faulty attempts, *reality testing* and *learning* play a role in the solution before mastery. The child who passes a subtest on the first trial as well as on all succeeding ones shows that he does not need to test reality, he fully masters this reality task.

When a child succeeds on any one of the subtests on the nine year level of the Stanford-Binet, some form of ego motivation is likely to be at least a part-incentive. The child may be motivated by the interest the intellectual task itself arouses in him (*goal-directed motivation*); by his *interpersonal relationship* to the examiner; or by his *ego ideal* ("I'd lose respect for myself if I could not do this"). All these motivations imply that the reality principle in the child has won out over the pleasure principle. Only the child who has learned to delay immediate gratification of impulse (such as, e.g., the wish to go out and play) for the sake of ultimate greater satisfaction (e.g., the wish to solve a knotty problem, the wish to have a pleasant relationship with the examiner, pride in his own achievement) can stick to any of these tasks. In the infant, *goal-directed motivation* and *interpersonal relations* may play a role too. The infant will only gaze at the cube if he is interested in finding out about it; and only a friendly examiner to whose warmth the infant reacts with a feeling of comfort and well being will get scorable responses from the infants he tests. However, in the infant the pleasure principle still prevails. He can succeed on test tasks only if they do not interfere with his instinctual needs. *Ego ideal* and *superego variables* play no role in an infant's passing or failing a test, as these personality facets are not yet developed at this age. No infant says to himself: "I ought to be able to follow the ring in circular motion with my eyes," or "I want to be a big boy and be able to regard the cube."

*Motor mastery of own body* always has to be thought of in relation to the child's chronologic age level. (The same applies to most other ego and all superego functions.) It would be absurd to diagnose a three month old infant as lacking in motor mastery of his own body because he cannot draw with a pencil. But a 9 year old with cerebral palsy who cannot do this may fail the Paper Cutting test and Memory for Design because he does not have the smooth motor coordination commensurate with his age. He may also have too much of a perceptual disturbance. A certain type of motor mastery, namely that over vocal cords, is involved in success on all items requiring speech. In table 2, on the first five subtests of the three month level, the check in the column for *motor mastery* refers only to coordinated eye movements and the ability to focus.

*Body image*, that is, the mental picture or representation the child has of his own body, begins to develop at about three months, in a testing-out way, when the infant inspects has hands in motion. *Body image* may also be involved in the successful solution of the question about Bill Jones' feet and his trousers on the Stanford-Binet. Sometimes one sees a youngster going through certain motions with hands, head and trunk, as if, in imagery, with his own body, he were trying out how Bill Jones can put on his trousers over his head.

*Memory for meaningful*, i.e. for cathected, *material* as well as *rote memory* are ego functions. What role memory plays on intelligence tests in general is too well known to all psychologists to merit discussion here. This applies also to *attention span*, another ego function.

Space does not allow us to discuss the rest of the personality variables systematically one by one. Instead, we shall in the following select a few of the *tests* from table 2 and show how some of the remaining personality variables play a role in them, (i.e., take some columns from table 2 vertically rather than continue horizontally).

On the Paper Cutting test an eight year old struggled for a while with the solution. She drew one cut incorrectly, looked at it critically and said, "No, I don't think I have it right." She erased it. She thus showed that, among other variables, she employed *judgment* and *self criticism* in striving for the correct solution. Had she stopped after the first trial with the remarks "Oh, well, I never can do things right," her self criticism would have been an unhealthy one and would have been involved in her failing the item. Instead, she asked the examiner: "Do you know how to do it?" The examiner said she did. The little girl replied in an eager voice, "If you can do it, I want to be able to learn to do it by myself too." Thus she also used the mechanism of *identification* in spurring herself on towards success. She sat there thinking for a few more moments, and suddenly, with a flash of *insight* (variable 27), exclaimed, "Oh, I know how it goes!" Then she drew the correct pattern. In addition to the variables already discussed, others were involved in her success: *language understanding*—she understood the instructions; *reality-centered concept formation*—she asked herself what is the thing, what does the paper look like when it is opened; and *flexibility of thinking*, which is necessary in order to proceed from the actual stimulus, the folded paper, to the imagined visualization of the opened paper.

Failure on any test can be due to the *absence* of one or more of the variables marked with a check as well as to the *presence* of any variable marked with a cross, or a cross in parentheses. Thus, a child who uses the ego defenses of *repetition compulsion, perseveration* or *stimulus boundness* will not pass Paper Cutting. He may *block* completely on it (variable 31) and thus fail; or he may *block* only temporarily, then rally the integrative forces of his ego and still succeed. A bit of *anxiety* (variable 30) may motivate him to do his utter best; but too much *anxiety*, or certain types of anxiety, e.g., castration fear, may paralyze him so that he cannot think productively and draw a "cut." *Fantasy* may help him in visualizing the opened paper; but irrealistic wild flights of *fantasy* may make him distort the cut or the creases he is supposed to draw. Similarly, a certain amount of *meticulosity* helps. However, compulsive *meticulosity* may incur failure.

On the Verbal Absurdities Test qualitative analysis of the responses and the way in which they are given often easily reveal personality dynamics. A 10 year old impulse-ridden boy whose ego was lacking in constructive defense mechanisms gleefully replied to the story about the fireman, "Boy-oh-boy, he'll start a second fire with his cigar! And pretty soon the houses next door will burn down, and then the whole city will burn up like Chicago did when Mrs. O'Leary's cow kicked over the kerosene lamp." In answer to the question about the melting icebergs he stated: "They couldn't have told you that, because when the icebergs melted the water rushed all over the boat and everybody drowned." Hostile-aggressive impulses which were uncontrolled and close to the surface are clearly evident in this answer, as well as wild, destructive fantasy; the test question makes no mention of a boat or of drowning people. In a somewhat similar sounding but dynamically quite different response, an adolescent girl revealed her instinctual anxiety (dread of the strength of her own sexual feelings) and her religious defense against them by saying: "God would not allow icebergs to melt when I am so near that I could see them, because God does not want me to get drowned."

Responses such as these simply beg to be interpreted in the same manner as TAT responses, and they reveal the child's personality dynamics as clearly as those given on projective tests. As on projective tests, one single answer can provide only a clue, a working hypothesis, and not a conclusive picture of a child's personality make-up. In order to arrive at this we must compare the answer that gave us the clue with other responses, weigh them against each other and check and recheck rigorously for internal consistency with every bit of material the child produces. We must either verify or discard the hypothesis, just as we do in projective techniques.[9] Beginners in the use of projective techniques, or in the projective uses of intelligence tests often have difficulty in abandoning a first intuitive hypothesis.

### Superego Variables

*Superego* components are evident in responses to the fireman story such as: "He ought to put out the fire as soon as he got there—even if he'd rather smoke a cigar" (a pass); or, to the story about Bill Jones' feet: "You should never put on your trousers over your head; it isn't nice" (a fail). The comprehension question on the seven year level of the Stanford-Binet, "What is the thing for you to do when you have broken something that belongs to someone else?" also frequently and particularly clearly brings out superego facets in passing responses such as: "Give him something that belongs to you in exchange, so you don't need to feel guilty any longer," or in failing ones such as "Feel bad." Lack of superego development, or superego lacunae, are shown by answers like "Tell him it was broken already" or "Hide it quietly and run away."

As potentially involved in success, superego variables may be found on any subtest in the sense that the child feels he ought to do whatever the adult desires him to do, or he ought to *submit to commands*, or he must conform and *delay*, till after the test, any action he would wish to undertake now. Less frequently, perhaps, they may play a role in preventing a child from arriving at correct answers, e.g., in cases of children who unconsciously feel they ought not to use their full intellectual powers so as not to compete with a parent (reference 11, pp. 18–21, 28–29). This occurs in many children whose neurotic symptom is a learning inhibition.

Two of the hypotheses in our earlier investigations were that intelligence tests—if they really test personality facets and not only intellectual ability—should reveal a higher differentiation of the ego on the middle and later childhood levels than on infancy levels; and that they should show the presence of superego components only on the levels beyond early childhood. A mere glance at table 2 shows that the analyses bore out these hypotheses.

## Summary

1. The dynamic approach to intelligence testing bridges the gap that has heretofore existed between intelligence testing and projective techniques.

2. The clinical psychologist who employs intelligence tests solely to ascertain the numerical IQ of a child and pays no attention to the dynamic personality data he can derive from its projective aspects wastes a great potential source of information. Intelligence and developmental tests actually tap much wider dimensions of the total personality than intelligence alone. Each subtest item of the standardized intelligence tests can reveal id, superego and a great variety of ego dimensions.

3. In our studies we carefully analyzed many subtest items of infants' and children's intelligence tests. Rather than asking: What single factor is this item loaded with? we asked: What besides intellectual ability are *all the possible* variables that may play a role in a child's passing or failing this subtest? We arrived at 43 variables. Three of them are expressions of the id-ego; 33 tap the perceptual, reality-adaptive, integrative and defensive functions of the ego; one is related to the ego ideal; five represent superego functions; and one cultural influences.

The list is by no means a closed one. More personality variables are probably involved in intelligence tests, particularly more ego variables. The field is a rich one for more extended research. Controlled studies with different nosologic groups of neurotic, psychotic and brain-injured children should lead to the establishing of diagnostic syndromes for children; and longitudinal studies could contribute to our so far rather scant knowledge of the normal stages of ego development at progressive age levels.

# References

1. Anderson, G. L.   Qualitative aspects of the Stanford-Binet. *In* Anderson, H. H., & Anderson, G. L. (Eds.)   *An introduction to projective techniques.* New York: Prentice-Hall, 1951. Pp. 581–603.
2. Binet, A.   *L'étude experimentale de l'intelligence.* Paris: Alfred Costes, 1902.
3. ——.   *Les idées modernes sur les enfants.* Paris: Ernest Flammarion, 1911.
4. Breiger, B.   The use of the W-B picture arrangement subtest as a projective technique. *J. consult. Psychol.*, 1956, *20*, 132.
5. Cattell, P.   *The measurement of intelligence of infants and young children.* New York: Psychological Corp., 1940.
6. Chorus, A.   *Intelligentie onderzoek en zijn kwalitatieve verdieping.* (Intelligence testing and its qualitative enrichment.) Utrecht: Het Spectrum, 1948.
7. Frank, L. K.   Projective methods for the study of personality. *Trans. N. Y. Acad. Sci.*, 1939, *1*, 129–132.
8. Freud, A.   The mutual influences in the development of ego and id: Introduction to the discussion. *Psychoanal. Study Child*, 1952, *7*, 42–50.
9. Fromm, E.   The psychoanalytic interpretation of dreams and projective techniques. *Amer. J. Orthopsychiat.*, 1958, *28*, 67–72.
10. ——, Hartman, L. D., & Marschak, M.   A contribution to a dynamic theory of intelligence testing. *J. Clin. & Exp. Psychopath.*, 1954, *15*, 73–95.
11. ——, & ——.   *Intelligence—a dynamic approach.* New York: Random House, 1955.
12. ——, ——, & Marschak, M.   Children's intelligence tests as a measure of dynamic personality functioning. *Amer. J. Orthopsychiat.*, 1957, *27*, 134–144.
13. Hartmann, H.   The mutual influences in the development of ego and id. *Psychoanal. Study Child*, 1952, *7*, 9–30.
14. Lejeune, Y. A.   Projective interpretation of intelligence tests. *J. S. Afric. Logopedic Soc.*, 1955, *3*, 9–12.
15. Machover, S.   Cultural and racial variations in patterns of intellect. *Teach. Coll. Contr. Educ.*, 1943, No. 875.
16. Mayman, M., Schafer, R., & Rapaport, D.   Interpretation of the Wechsler-Bellevue Intelligence Scale in personality appraisal. *In* Anderson, H. H., & Anderson, G. L. (Eds.)   *An introduction to projective techniques.* New York: Prentice-Hall, 1951, Pp. 541–580.
17. Murphy, L. B.   The appraisal of child personality. *J. consult. Psychol.*, 1948, *12*, 16–19.
18. Porteus, S. D.   *Qualitative performance in the Maze Test.* Vineland, N. J.: Smith Printing House, 1942.
19. Rapaport, D.   Principles underlying non-projective tests of personality. *Ann. N. Y. Acad. Sci.*, 1946, *46*, 643–652.
20. ——, Gill, M., & Schafer, R.   *Diagnostic psychological testing.* Vol. 1. Chicago: Year Book Publishers, 1945.
21. Schafer, R.   The expression of personality and maladjustment in intelligence test results. *Ann. N. Y. Acad. Sci.*, 1946, *46*, 609–623.
22. Terman, L. M., & Merrill, M. A.   *Measuring intelligence.* Boston: Houghton Mifflin, 1937.
23. Wellman, B.   Iowa studies on the effects of schooling. *39th Yearb. Nat. Soc. Stud. Educ.*, 1940. *39*. Part 2.

# Part V: Graphic and Artistic Procedures

## 13

## Sex Differences in the Developmental Pattern of Children as seen in Human Figure Drawings

KAREN MACHOVER

THIS CHAPTER will be devoted to a major area of consideration (i.e. sex differences) that has emerged from a comprehensive normative study.* Human figure drawings were obtained from middle class, white, urban children of ages 5 through 12, who were of at least average intelligence. Comparative studies of different cultural and racial groups are in progress. It was anticipated that the drawings not only would provide concrete normative guides but, considering the intimacy of body image projection, might well shed light upon known theories and behavioral facts of child development while, in addition, perhaps raising new questions.

One hundred sets (male and female) of drawings (50 boys and 50 girls) obtained in group classroom situations from children at each age level were classified with regard to 45 major graphic variables covering structural and content aspects of the figures drawn. These were organized into personality syndromes sufficiently comprehensive to offer a fairly solid picture of prevailing age trends. Principles of interpretation followed those developed by the author. It is assumed that the reader has sufficient orientation in the special language of body image and body function terms, indigenous to the method of human figure drawing interpretation, to follow references to specific drawing features made in the course of discussion.

In processing the drawings, it was discovered that differences between the sexes at each age were not only as important as age level differences, but often were more striking and dramatic. It is not my intention to persuade the reader that there are sex differences and that they are here to stay, but rather to point out that, despite the persistent encounter of these differences in daily clinical practice, they have, heretofore, not been taken into serious account in the development and application of such dynamic instruments as projective techniques. Statements of biologic differences are mostly buried in actuarial statistics, and sex differences, when noted, are dismissed with "boys will be boys" (when the boy is aggressive) or "that's a woman for

*The author is indebted to Helen Anderson, assisted by Alvin Wolf, whose ingenuity and persistent efforts have made available the mass of data upon which the study is based. She also extends her gratitude to the New York City Board of Education for their generous cooperation.

you" (when a woman changes her mind, which was never really hers, since it was always made up for her).

## General Developmental Patterns in Boys and Girls

The group trends that will be discussed briefly for each age group will, to be sure, not account for the individual child. As usual, it has been difficult to select a single drawing that would, in detail, portray composite group trends. A brief overview of the findings place the prepubertal girl in a highly privileged and triumphant position with regard to her less fortunate brother of similar age, intelligence and background. Her advantages in maturity, efficiency and prestige are most prominent at the peak of "latency" of the boy, at ages 7 and 8, and they register least at periods of high physiological loading and urgency, such as at Oedipal periods of 4 and 5 and pubertal thresholds of 11 and 12. In general, it may be said that when the environment is most regulated, persistent and demanding, the growing girl prospers with this structure, while the boy squirms with restless incoordination or else "plays possum," offering a deflated, ineffectual and harmless version of himself. The data suggest that the boy, although often reacting with disorganization and even panic to the pressure of his impulses, derives greatest ego strength at the "energetic" periods when he keeps active contact with his impulses, such as at 5, 11, 12 and 13.

From the earliest years, with accelerated differential, the drawings of girls are more mature in body concept, are more realistic and detailed, and express greater fluency, more flexibility and composure than do those of boys. Orderliness, tidiness, emphasis of facial features, cosmetics and clothing display mark the well groomed girl child in both drawing projection and in behavior. With such competent use of surface defenses, the girl can afford to draw sexual characteristics and show male-female differentiation more actively and at an earlier age than do the boys. A mood of apologetic compromise is often communicated in the relatively deflated and frequently crude and diffuse productions offered by the boys in early school years. Their self drawings shrink drastically in size, are hidden at the bottom and often left (timid or self-conscious) side of the page and are singularly lacking in vigor of limbs, posture or extension. Limbs are short, often weak, cut off and poorly integrated with the trunk. Substituting for the vitality of hair growth there is most often a silly or oversized hat in a feeble attempt to offer social stature. The female is most often given hair, more clothing detail and is made larger and more forceful. Since it is clearly a female government at home and at school, the girl displays her supremacy by drawing her self figure with greater detail and skill, while not neglecting the male of the pair in these respects. Although she may draw him smaller, less mature in appearance and perhaps give him a "beanie" rather than a prestige hat, she seems, after a spurt of rivalry at 5, to show increasing interest in cultivating him as a sex object. She gives him wide shoulders, crotch formation, strong limbs, appropriate coiffure, clothing, ties, belts and buckles, earlier and more frequently than the boy gives it to his own sex.

The boy, after his bold and often reckless self assertion at 4 and 5, seems to settle down to a career of female domination with varying degrees of resentment and various methods of coping with the constant threat. There is throughout, even in the early school years when he offers the most deflated drawings, some subtle or meek warning that the fires are only banked. They are not out. In dealing with the evidence offered by body projection, it is difficult to see latency as anything but a description of comparative shifting of balance of forces between the inner pressures and the environmental demands, for which the boys offer the major battlefield. The struggle is paced unevenly through the school years. There is constant graphic evidence of either biding time or gathering courage for the "putsch" against the domination of the female. While the girl is free to cultivate the male figure as a potential love object, the boy, in his constant struggle to liberate himself from libidinal dependency upon his mother, is most likely to build up exaggerated hatred toward the female. His campaign has two aspects. One is to project upon, to punish and to denounce the female, and the other is to accumulate (and test out) his powerful masculinity, which, by sheer force, will overcome female authority. The drawings suggest that, despite the tumult that is associated with pubertal development, the biologic and cultural advantages, for the first time in the growing boy's career, are basically his. The increase of physical magnitude and power, though frightening, seems more positive and growth-inspiring for the boy. The girl, however, approaching the exciting, yet frightening responsibility of sex and reproduction, retreats from "the curse." She has lost her emotionally subsidized childhood, in which she reigned supreme. She perhaps clings to the "princess" enchantment in her daydreams.

## Psychodynamic and Cultural Considerations

Before proceeding with a more detailed age level discussion of boy-girl differences seen in the drawings, it may be useful to inquire about the "why" and the "wherefore." Ego goals of the male in our culture revolve mostly about opportunities to use his potentials (intellectual, physical, sexual) in competitive masculinity. He constantly doubts his capacities "to measure up." In terms of space dynamics, it may be seen, in line with masculine play and interest patterns, as vertical ego striving. The girl, on the other hand, is generally more horizontal and involving-of-others in her play, interests and ego extensions. She is more concerned about her competitive power, not to achieve, create or fulfill potentials, but rather to seduce and command possessions, love, prestige and power. Rather than herself making any effort for attainment and distinction, she will insist that her man work for it. In her marriage vows, the female is instructed to love, honor and obey (as she did her mother); but whom? Not herself! Her self respect is measured only by what she can get. Goals for the female are essentially geared to building up a source of supply that is plentiful and secure, and to developing a sort of king-father figure, who will select her as a mate and thus offer a perfect Oedipal solution. It is in such rich and unrealistic fantasy soil that seeds of fears, depression, sexual frigidity, anxieties, postpartum reactions and suicides breed into the grave emotional disorders that beset the adult female. The male who "cannot make it" is more likely to veer off into ego-alienating symptoms, into addictions and/or antisocial behavior. In dealing with his ambition, the male may reap the somatic consequences of heart disease and in coping with his angry dependencies he may pay with ulcers.

So much for the differences in adult patterns. In childhood, the benefits of cultivated dependency are many for the girl and dangerous for the development of the boy. In many cases, the hazards of "receiving" interfere with the process of learning. The boy shows more difficulties in modification and control while the girl develops more indirect and subtle expression of countering or passively resisting authority. She will "throw up," refuse food or "faint" when overcome with an impulse. The boy, on the other hand, is more likely to submit or to rebel more openly, thus placing himself more frequently in the path of apprehension and punishment. Techniques of self expression must, for the boy, usually develop independently and sub-terraneously, since they are bound to be met with sharp disapproval. In drawings, as well as in behavior, the boy lunges into self assertions and fearful retreats more bluntly and ineffectively than does the girl. She traverses a well practiced middle ground, with her eye constantly fixed on authority (mother or teacher). The boy gives more trouble to the community in every area. In his body symptomatology the boy expresses primarily the consequences of restraint of aggression. Thus enuresis, nailbiting, stammers and tics are more common in boys, as are the physical acting out and learning difficulties that constitute our "problem" children. Even the allergic symptoms (such as asthma) for which boys are frequently referred are most often mixed with behavior disorders. It seems that the boys never fully lose contact with their raw impulses and the mandates of their growing bodies. Although this creates troublesome problems of control and discipline in childhood, it may constitute a source of ego power and creativity that is culturally appropriate for the adult male and not for the female.

For the girl, child or adult, aggressive and sexual drives are never appropriate as areas of enjoyment or self expression, while orderliness, control, display and surface talents are cultivated as her major social currency. She is thus more naturally coordinated with the passive values of *childhood*, while the male is more coordinated with the culturally more aggressive values of *adulthood*. The girl glides through childhood smoothly with approval and rewards, while the boy stumbles through, always the victim of conflicting standards. Expected to achieve the divergent goals of independence and power on the one hand, and full submission and organization on the other, it is no surprise that the boy, in his drawing and in his behavior, achieves neither. He is thus more awkward, slower to learn, more of a social problem and less mature in development of sexual interests. Considering the sources and background, opportunities for role identification are, unlike those for the girl, sporadic and confusing for the boy. His childhood government is all female. What is a man? What is his task, and how does he learn to perform it? In our urban, middle class culture, the father is often a weak, shadowy figure who may, on occasion, behave like a competitive big brother or as the executioner of a sentence substantially imposed by the mother. He is often a mechanical source of provisions and is accorded only token respect and prestige. Unlike the girl, the boy does not have a concrete model of manhood and thus, most often resorts to stereotyped figures such as policemen, cowboys, soldiers or spacemen (each with individual dynamic significance). The persistence of unrealistic fantasy models of a masculine ego woven in childhood, usually rigid and exaggerated, may produce lasting neurosis in adulthood.

In contrast to the boy, sex-role identifications for the girl are, in most middle class families, concrete, direct and rewarding. The girl most often assumes the position of first lieutenant to "the boss," and is encouraged to follow an established and consistent set of standards modeled continuously, and in detail, by her mother or her teacher, with the ever implicit promise that some day she will be given the reins. Actually, she is a perpetual "mother's helper" and is never trained for independent decisions or authority. The girl participates in accepting (with conflict) this role of safe security. She rehearses with house and doll play, and details are always subject to correction. She learns too well the lesson of gaining love and recognition by doing what mother and teacher ask of her. Her own sensations and feelings are unimportant and unladylike, and her personal decisions are usually regarded as inadequate. For childhood, this silent agreement seems satisfactory. Having the gratifications of love and effective sublimation in learning experiences, the girl does not seem to be under as great inner pressure as does the boy. The girl can secure love and possession equivalents by just being decorative, quiet and useful. It is in marriage, when she is told to make independent decisions and to accept such "sinful" impulses as sex, that panic and anxiety may ensue. On the one hand, she demands to be given the authority she had accorded her mother, and on the other, she looks to her husband to reward her as her mother did, thus she is feeding marital disharmony with her inconsistent demands to be both mother and child.

Since weakness is a quality that is rewarded, the girl has learned to make a positive virtue of it by cosmetization and display. In her drawings, she will, for example, often shape a dependent, concave mouth into a cupid bow. Instead of the dark, irascible line the boy draws to separate the sexual area of the body from the chest, the girl more often will deftly convert her restraint into a fashionable and seductive tight waistline. Dependency upon the mother, symbolically expressed in a navel button, is wrought into a socialized buckle which the girl offers at an early age. Disarray of the hair suggestive of sexual excitation, may be offered by the young girl with a crown, a bow, a fancy hat or a feather to top off the display. Similarly, sexual preoccupation conveyed in shading of the skirt, will most often appear as decoratively designed shading with flowers and plant themes on the skirt, perhaps, to suggest active pregnancy fantasies. The boy does not have the girl's subtlety or talent for socialization. He chafes with his weakness and dependencies and hides his struggles or inadequacies in profile evasion earlier and more often than does the girl. There is a more persistent rumble of his body impulses, and the boy cannot use the niceties of clothing or detail as a source of pleasure or defense.

At this point, it may be well to outline briefly the sexual differences as they are reflected in the developmental picture at successive age levels. Since, as has already been noted, it is the boy who is constantly gaining the attention of authorities (usually negative) and who reflects a more stormy pattern of development in his drawing projections, it will be he that gets more attention in this study than the girl. The girl continues to gain steadily in goals and methods that are established quite early in development. Minor retreats and adjustments, as well as differences in the pace of improvement, punctuate the growth record. It is only at 12 when the girl, under the threatening impact of puberty, finds her defenses strained and her resources not too adaptable that the boy-girl pattern shifts against her favor. At this age, the boy is seen looking to his own strength as a means of transcending female authority.

### Four and Five Year Olds

Children of 4 and 5, who are not as yet members of the outside or school community, exhibit less differences between the sexes than at any other age. The familial Oedipal drama, exaggerated by the imminence of school placement and loosening of family ties, is reflected in a rather "excited" body-image projection for both the boy and girl. For the *girl*, the projections are, in accordance with her more passive disposition, less bold, less assertive, less disorganized and more self conscious and insecure. Although both sexes draw fairly large figures, shade them with pressureful anxiety and guilt and are concerned with body extensions, the *girl* will draw more small figures, with lighter lines, place them more to the left of the page, introduce multiple figures for support and place them in toppling stance. In terms of control, she will attempt some clothing, accessories, give more double dimension arms, legs and fingers and more frequently draw hands with which to grip things. Arms of her figures extend from a more controlling area of the trunk and are less mechanical in extension than are those drawn by the boys. The *boy*, on the other hand, having more interest in his body stimulations and less of an eye for integration with the environment than does the girl, projects his figures in larger size, heavier line, in middle or right, acting out placement and with more aggressive and disorganized shading. Arms are flung out in single dimension, mechanically, often from the lower (impulse) level of the trunk, ending in heavy and long, spanning, stick-fingers. There is poor modification and control. Rarely is there a neck with which to integrate the raucous body needs with the controlling head, nor are there hands to direct the manipulating fingers. The boy does not avail himself of clothing with which to cover his needs but rather, in stark display of his anxious dependency, he often draws large shaded buttons down the middle of the trunk,

Fig. 1.—Male and female figure drawings produced by boys and girls 4 to 12 years of age: (a) Four year olds; (b) Five year olds; (c) Six year olds; (d) Seven year olds.

Male I                  Female II    Female I                 Male II

a          Four year old boy              Four year old girl

Male I                  Female II    Female I                 Male II

b          Five year old boy              Five year old girl

Male I                  Female II    Female I                 Male II

c          Six year old boy              Six year old girl

Male I                  Female II    Female I                 Male II

d          Seven year old boy              Seven year old girl

Fig. 1. (continued)—Male and female figure drawings produced by boys and girls 4 to 12 years of age: (e) Eight year olds; (f) Nine year olds*; (g) Ten year olds; (h) Eleven year olds.

*See figure 2 for responses given by this same nine year old boy to the inquiry about his male and female figures.

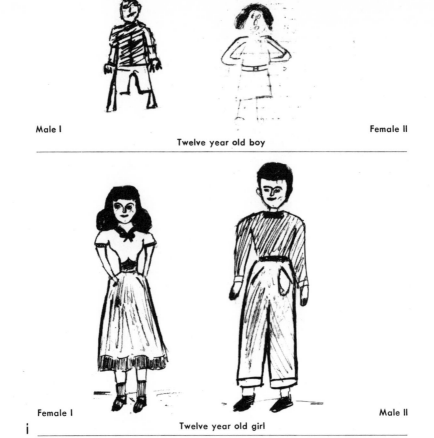

Male I

Female II

**Twelve year old boy**

Female I

Male II

**Twelve year old girl**

Fig. 1. (*continued*)—Male and female figure drawings produced by boys and girls 4 to 12 years of age: (*i*) Twelve year olds.

balanced by a hat for stature. Sexual stimulation is conveyed through voyeurism (transparent or shaded skirt, popeyes) or passive sensual enmeshment in disordered hair. Oversized noses, exactly "counted out" five fingers, and large extensions constitute restitutive repair. The head, as a self signature, is large and misshapen with bulging fantasies and with tortured attempts to resolve the unrealistic aspirations for masculinity characteristic of the Oedipal storm. The female of the set will often be drawn with a larger and oververticalized head, adding a note of menace.

The *girl* also draws large heads for control, but they are more round, more even in contour and enhanced with decorative or cosmetic touches. She, too, makes the female more important. Although the girl does not deface or mutilate her male figure, she may express her contempt by making him much smaller, more childish, putting a dunce cap on him, or depicting him as a clown. Envy of the boy is reflected in the fact that the five year old girl draws the opposite sex first more often than at any of the school ages until the age of 12. Also she assigns an older age to the male figure of the set more frequently than in succeeding years. Even at this rivalrous age, her figures are better integrated and controlled than are those of the boy. Like the boys, she may display oral aggression by drawing teeth, but while the boy scatters his teeth in a large, overactive and loosely drawn mouth, suggesting primitive eating habits and profanity, the five year old girl, drawing teeth, stacks them neatly in a reserved mouth as if to create a deliberate barrier against "intake" (of food?).

## Six Year Olds

After five, when the acuteness of the Oedipal excitement has subsided in varying degrees with the boy and more promptly for the girl, whose reaction was milder initially, the conspicuous difference in self concept and style of expression between the boy and the girl enters a decisive phase which is best described as a capitulation to female supremacy. This supremacy continues throughout the early and middle school ages with mild rebuffs imposed by the boy's sporadic, restless breaking of his restraints and by feeble efforts to declare himself as a male. At six and seven, as if in resolution to settle down to learning and regulation and to make room for 40 or more children in their class, boys and girls draw smaller, more controlled tidy figures in more reserved or withdrawn placement. Action potentials are all minimized. The *girl*, with her gratifications from control and from modelling after the teacher as she does after the mother, learns readily with pleasure and reward. The *boy*, on the other hand, having retreated or been thrown back from his bold self projection, views learning from the sulky dissatisfaction of defeat. The figures, though meek, are quiet and composed, raising the possibility of secondary gains being derived from the position of protected retreat. Judging from subsequent trends, the small figure in a quiet corner, with a small dot eye, may be studying the field and assessing the tolerance of the school environment as compared with his home. Emphasis upon limbs and bold or acting out placement diminish sharply, while the female of the set is drawn larger, more mature and given the wider, more assertive stance. Venturing so little, there is little expression of conflict. A feeble attempt is made to hold the line by attributing either the same or even older ages to the smaller and weaker self sex figures. An increase in phallically extended hair coiffure on the female figure suggests consolidation of sex and aggression which, at five, was expressed more bluntly. The six year old boy seems pleasantly disposed toward the more powerful female figure, while giving anger, fear and worry to his deflated self figure. Active, oversensitized ears appear less frequently as does the deep, wide arc mouth of contrived placation. Even the distorted head shapes (and fantasies) of the five year phase have faded out.

The six year old *girl* accepts the surrender, thus creating a wide gap in confidence of self projection between the two sexes—a gap which continues to widen for several years. Her drawings, particularly of her own sex, are now larger, more skilled, placed more boldly on the page, heavier in line and wider and firmer in stance. Although the girl has less to tidy up from the five year phase, she too is more controlled. Not only does she give the male a hat as she did at five, but she now adds a hat and a pocketbook to her self figure as if ready to go out and command the world. She is now a full-fledged member of the female club. In her self-confident stride, the six year old girl sharpens her passive techniques of seductive display while adding action features, such as strong limbs, active postures and outward (toward action) foot direction. Sensuality is underplayed. She either over-tightens her hair in corkscrew style or gives outline indication of curly hair, avoiding the substance. She draws more mature and intense eyes and accents them with the social commentary of brows more often. Mouths are less frequently concave and are set in a moderate arc line, suggesting the determined congeniality of contained pleasure of the triumphant. She is more attentive to the clothing, hair and sexual characteristics of her male figure, while often drawing him smaller, younger, with a "droopy" crotch or dunce cap. She is clearly in conflict.

### Seven Year Olds

Although all seven year olds, at the peak of learning and "receiving," offer small and passive drawings, boy-girl differences continue. The *boys* draw one-third opposite sex first, and play down such assets as body vigor, aggression and boldness even more than they did at six. Their figures are unlively images, more shrunken in size and hug the bottom of the page. They are lacking in sensuousness. Arms are weak, tentatively attached to more controlling areas of the trunk, and sockets are closed off. Feet point in all directions as if the figure is without a rudder. Facial features are brief and noncommittal, suggesting defensive social exchange. The seven year old boy watches himself and the female from a distance. An increase in short and mildly designed skirts betrays a simmering sex interest, while an increase in "father-replacement" heads and a tendency toward geometric object and clothing-equivalents of phallus-like forms give suggestion of restless stirring. His interest in external symbols suggests a greater readiness for learning.

The *girl* of seven advances further in her displayful, detailed and ordered self presentation. She seems content with her age and shows less interest in parent ages or "parent-replacement" heads than does the boy. She gives her male figure more sexual characteristics, more ties, hats and more masculine clothing. The masculine strength features she borrowed at six are now returned to him. Less of a rival, he is being cultivated for a role suitable to the pregnancy fantasies and princess daydreams which she rehearses in her doll play at this age. The seven year old girl manages rather well the integration of her childhood competency with stimulated fantasies of being grown up. She puts crowns and bows on her hair often, as if to signal her success. One cannot, however, help but see in her drawings such evidences of strain as increase in brittleness of control, more frequent defensive arm position, more inquiring head tilting, more sober eyebrow emphasis and more expressions of worry and sadness. It may be said that at seven the girls seem to control too much, and the boys to repress too much.

## Eight Year Olds

Although at eight the *boy* continues to draw passive and weak body forms, he gives fewer unrelieved apologetic figures than he did at seven. He draws fewer round, passive heads on the self sex and revives the more active and distorted head (full of ideas) seen at five. The body parts are still weak. The eight year old boy draws more circular body forms, more buttons, more small and round feet, more small noses, small and concave mouths and empty eyes, but he is beginning to pack a gun "in case." In contrast to the apparent submission at seven, the boy of eight is beginning to serve notice that he is dissatisfied with the balance of power and intends to do something about it. There is much labeling, balloon talking and strident humor with which he announces verbally his declaration of rights. There is still reliance upon outer symbols of stature and activity such as hats, heels and holding of sticks as at seven, but more active postures and shoulders for strength and responsibility do appear on the self sex, bringing in their train more conflict and anxiety. Thus we find the eight year old boy reviving background, multiple figures, holding things and active erasures in his drawings. His female figure, still drawn larger, is given the more assertive stance, is indicated as the older of the set more often and is drawn first more than at any other age (40 per cent). She is revived, though not as vividly as at five, as an object of threat and stimulation and is handled with greater sex detail, aggression, anxious and guilty shading and restless erasures. More control features such as neck, hand (to grip with) and waistline and hemline demarcations enter to cope with the added stimulations. Despite the greater disarray and diffusion on the female figure, the drawings offered by the eight year old boy are more mature and skilled. He has literally gotten off the ground, exchanging his "sunken" bottom placement for a more cautious but active left placement on the page. He is now less amiable toward the female and more frequently gives her angry expressions to replace the contrived pleasantness given her at six and seven.

The eight year old *girl* consolidates her gains. She takes hold of her superior position, adding sturdiness and physical activity at the same time that she cultivates further the more feminine assets such as clothing, jewelry, hair coiffuring, shaded lips, horizontal and intense eyes and emphatic brows. She takes herself quite seriously, and rather than being disorganized by a growth spurt, as the boys are, she increases her controls and her efficiency, leaving the boys behind more than ever. This age probably is seen as the height of differential between the adjustment of the boy and the girl in school and at home. The girl seems less preoccupied with themes of marriage and babies than she was at seven and, on the whole, shows greater realism. Her interest in the male as a potential sex object is increased. There is least evidence of rivalry. On her self figure, she draws fewer fanciful costumes, less dress and skirt designs and shows less hemline emphasis. She is well sublimated. In general, the eight year old girl shows less body arousal than is evident in the boy. She seems more highly satisfied with herself, more firmly controlled and is deriving more gratification from her positive achievements.

This burden of adequacy does, however, produce an increase in expressions of worry and fear on the self sex.

## Nine Year Olds

Following the verbal notice and restless sniping at the dominant female at eight, the *boy* of nine presses further into the struggle. Although the female is still strong and there is an increase in aggressive and sexual interest in her, the boy introduces himself more vigorously as a worthy contestant. While at eight the primary emphasis centered around protest and anger against the female, and the drawings tended to get "noisy" and disorganized, the nine year old boy balances his attack upon the female with more active explorations of his own body strengths. With this positive approach, the drawings become more varied and less shallow than in previous ages, and improve in skill. More open sockets, more flexibly extended arms (integrated at the shoulder level) and more hair shading add to the flavor of self expressiveness. More active themes underscore the impression of a heated campaign. There is, as at eight, still much labeling and "talking." Graphic features of dependency offer contradiction to manifestations of manliness. Thus, along with "father replacement" heads, parent ages, heavier lines, more dignified hats and brief cases, heels, cigarettes and phallic objects, we see much emphasis on food, sucking and talking. Mouths, in fact, become larger and more uncontrolled, teeth reappear, and more midlines and buttons enter as evidence of increase in body sensitivity. The female continues to be presented as sexually exciting with wide stance, diffusely shaded and erased hair and skirt, phallically extended hair, and a cigarette, stick or broom frequently stuck in her hand. Whereas, at seven and eight he draws a meek phallic object symbol with his self sex figure, at nine the boy seems more actively fighting the female for his phallus. Judging from the graphic evidence of noisy, orally aggressive, attention seeking and disorganized behavior, nine is a troublesome disciplinary age. While toying with father roles, he offers, rather gratuitously, the theme of a tree, solid in trunk, whose branches are bare and sharply truncated, with a self sex figure beside it, holding a hatchet as if he has just chopped down the mother tree. (It was not Washington's birthday.) The balance of power is being challenged energetically, although the move is essentially a "bootstrap operation" with the feet of the figure going in all directions. Figure 2 presents inquiry responses of a nine year old boy.

The nine year old *girl* is not unaffected by the mounting disparagement and active challenge of the boy. She, too, is becoming more interested in body functions and is no longer content with just reading and spelling better than the boy. The nine year old girl is less smug and composed under the impact of the boy's assertiveness and increasing awareness of her own developing body. She draws smaller figures than at eight and now gives the male figure more active recognition for the special qualities of physical sturdiness, some of which she would previously appropriate for the self figure. The male figure is, at nine, more often given the wider stance, more bold placement, heavier line, is made larger and indicated as the older of

Fig. 2. (*a*)—Inquiry responses given by a nine year old boy to the female figure.

1. *What is she doing?*    standing
2. *How old is she?*    22 year old
3. *Is she married?*    No
4. *Does she have children?*    No
5. *How many girls?*    0
6. *How many boys?*    0
7. *What kind of work does she do?*    college work
8. *What class is she in?*    11B
9. *What does she want to be when she grows up?*    Nerce.
10. *How smart is she?*    very smart
11. *How healthy is she?*    regular
12. *How goodlooking is she?*    very pretty
13. *What is the best part of her body?*    Her face
14. *What is the worst part of her body?*    Hair
15. *How happy is she?*    very happy
16. *What does she worry about?*    nothing
17. *What makes her mad?*    nothing
18. *What are the three worst things she ever did?*    nothing
19. *What are the nicest things about her?*    Her legs face build up
20. *How many girl friends does she have?*    60
21. *How old are they?*    20 and 21
22. *What do people say about her?*  nice things
23. *How much fun does she have with her family?*    she doesn't have a family
24. *How much does she like school?*    very much
25. *How many boy friends does she have?*    75 to a 100
26. *What does she call a good time?*    reading
27. *Will she get married?*    Yes
28. *How old will she be when she gets married?*    23
29. *What kind of a boy will she marry?*    a nice boy
30. *What are her three best wishes?*
      1. nothing        2. nothing        3. nothing
31. *Is she like somebody you know?*    no
32. *Who is she like?*    No Body
33. *Would you like to be like her?*    no    *Why?*    she is a girl I am a boy

Fig. 2. (*b*)—Inquiry responses given by a nine year old boy to the male figure.

1. *What is he doing?*  He is standing.
2. *How old is he?*  He is 37 years old
3. *Is he married?*  No, He isn't.
4. *Does he have children?*    no
5. *How many boys?*    0
6. *How many girls?*    0
7. *What kind of work does he do?*    He makes blouses.
8. *What class is he in?*    He is not in eny class.
9. *What does he want to be when he grows up?*    He is grown up already
10. *How smart is he?*    very smart
11. *How healthy is he?*    very healthy
12. *How goodlooking is he?*    very goodlooking.
13. *What is the best part of his body?*    His whole body is good

14. *What is the worst part of his body?*      He has know worst part
15. *How happy is he?*      very happy.
16. *What does he worry about?*      a private house.
17. *What makes him mad?*      fight's make him very mad
18. *What are the three worst things he ever did?*      yelled fought got C in homework
19. *What are the nicest things about him?*      He's very good.
20. *How many boy friends does he have?*      50
21. *How old are they?*      20, 21, 22 and ma more
22. *What do people say about him?*      very nice things.
23. *How much fun does he have with his family?*      He doesn't have a family
24. *How much does he like school?*      He's out of scool already
25. *How many girl friends does he have?*      55 girl friends
26. *What does he call a good time?*      playing baseball.
27. *Will he get married?*      yes
28. *How old will he be when he gets married?*      38
29. *What kind of a girl will he marry?*      tall, dark and pretty
30. *What are his three best wishes?*
    1. sucses      2. Happunes.      3. and children
31. *Is he like somebody you know?*      No, He isn't.
32. *Who is he like?*      No Body
33. *Would you like to be like him?*      No *Why?*      He is to nicelooking.

the set. At eight, the girl was secure in her superiority. At nine, with an increase in respect for the male figure, she mingles envy with anger. Thus, while giving him a crotch more frequently, she will either draw it low, scooped out or make it like a skirt. She may give him a "beanie" for a hat. Her greater insecurity is reflected in an increase in use of background as well as the defensive, overcontrolled self sex figure that she offers, with arms frequently at side or glued to body walls. Eyes are more often small and intense, while the mouth, contrary to the mouth of the boy, is most often small, cosmetized and faintly placating. In this sober mood, she places more figures toward the "magical" upper part of the page, and dresses her figures more primly. On occasion, she will engage in a "princess" daydream lingering from or returning to the seven year phase. This fails, however, to relieve the tension. There is evidence of brooding body concern. Eyes look to the side for approval, and overemphasized ears on the male testify to her sensitivity concerning his opinion of her. The male is a more serious contender. To handle her increased tension, the girl resorts to more overcompulsive detail, while sharpening her techniques of passive seduction.

## 10 Year Olds

While the eight year old boy served warning, and the nine year old boy combined high rebellion against female supremacy with a search for his masculinity, the 10 year old shows a definite advance in the direction of concentration on self assets. When the focus is largely upon outside points of reference, the *boy* presents a rather tame and constricted image. When it is upon his own feelings, graphic expressions of conflict become more numerous. Judging from the large increase in restless erasures, impatient reinforcements and islands of heavy shading on the figures, both sexes seem to be carrying a heavy load of body growth and sex sensitivities. There is, too, massing evidence of masturbatory tension. Increase in sexual arousal is seen in the greater number of diffusely shaded or near transparent skirts, emphasized waistlines and disordered hair on the female figures drawn by the boy. Occupied with the problem of building up his own stature, the boy appears to be less threatened by the sexually provocative female than he was in weaker states. He ventures more. He is free to indicate more sex characteristics on both figures and draws his self sex figure with greater maturity, skill and detail than he did at nine. Though he displays a substantial interest in body development and does not look to a large head or a tight bottleneck for control as he did in earlier years, the 10 year old boy, still lacking in body confidence, experiments with outer credentials of manhood, such as uniforms, insignia, elaborated belts and buckles, impressive hats. He draws his figures at an active postural slant as if they are in a hurry to get there. His figures are larger, placed more boldly toward the middle and are more detailed. Moreover, the self sex is given larger feet, wider stance, shoulders and more open sockets, and is cast in an active theme. He is beyond the gingerly testing of ground seen at nine, and "talking" protests of the eight year boy. He is now involved in actively mapping out his manhood. The boy seems to be catching up with the girl in many respects, and draws fewer of the opposite sex first.

Although the 10 year old boy thrives on this display of self assertion, and the girl takes appropriate notice of his challenge and makes room for him, the enterprise increases conflict and fear. The limbs may be stronger, but they are smudged with erasures or heavy shading. With the more frequent indication of crotch formation comes disturbance in that area. In his energetic attempts at masculinity, the boy needs to draw a line under the figure more frequently to sustain him. He no longer involves clouds, rain, cut-off trees, people or objects for support as the nine year old did. His fight is beginning to be more consciously with himself than with his environment. The burden shows in the increase in negative expressions, worry lines and turning aside to evasive profile more often. The developmental sequence may be described as follows: The seven year old boy draws quiet phallic object replacement of his emasculation. The eight year old boy is planning an offensive, mostly with "Am I going to tell her off!" fantasies. The nine year old is talking tough and becomes offensive to the female while beginning to inquire about his masculine strength, and the 10 year old seems to be actively trying out roles for manhood and is less oriented toward sheer rebellion.

The 10 year old *girl* views her growing body with more threat than promise. She vies less for stature, physical power or prestige and seems to cling more to her practical feminine virtues. She focuses increasingly on grown-up and seductive clothing, jewelry, special coiffure styles, bangs, cosmetized mouths and lashes. More hips are drawn, hemline problems (growth implicating) increase, and the breast area receives more attention, albeit in still indirect forms such as pockets, reinforced chest walls, and such bilateral symbols as bows or Peter-Pan collars. Under the stress of heightened body sensitivities, the girl tightens her controls and increases detail. She tightens and elaborates her waistline and designs her skirt more actively, rationalizing her anxiety about sex. She reserves for herself more of the small, weak and demure body features, except for still giving the girl wider shoulders (responsibility?). Some strong legs enter to suggest a prepubertal athletic thrust. She clothes her male more and shows more interest in sex characteristics and differences, but continues to express rivalry along with her respect by wrapping the boy up in a tight collar, giving him a weak tie, mostly immature crotch formation and frequently has his trousers too short for his legs. She imposes upon him the midline body sensitivity and button indications of dependency as if in sullen scapegoating. At 10, the boy is more challenging and the girl less amiable.

## 11 Year Olds

The strained, heroic and often poorly organized attempts at manliness projected by the 10 year old *boy* continue at 11 with more realism than the stereotype models with uniform offer. This sobering up brings into its wake a more manifest conflict between growth strivings and powerful dependencies which inevitably stir up the ever-present problems around the infantile patterns of sex and aggression. Body tensions press the environment into the background, except for increasing anger at the female whom he holds responsible for his growth difficulties. Both sexes strongly identify with their own, resisting the influence of the other. Sex differences between the male and female figures are more actively indicated. Stronger body parts and more fluency in self assertion are apparent, but there are false starts, and many of the figures withdraw toward left, self-conscious placement, must use a line for ground support and are heavily erased. More frequent midlines attest to increased sensitivity to body processes. More hair and fewer hats appear. An increase in clothing, collar and neckline demarcations add control features. Sex characteristics are more frequently indicated. The crotch formations are, however, essentially immature or disturbed. The mood has, for the 11 year old boy, quieted down. Overlarge heads, bottlenecks, arms up and at side and more rationalization of shading mark the greater control and reserve. It seems that throughout this process of emancipation seen in the later school years, the rhythm of self assertion wavers in its forcefulness. Disorganized advance may be followed by a reflective pause. Thoughts point to growth ahead. The 11 year old boy assigns older ages to his self figure. Although the figures look more active, the feet positions are static and the figure is most often described as doing nothing, standing or just looking.

The *girl* of 11 is also extremely aware of her growing body and communicates increased disturbance by her many erasures, areas of tightly controlled shading, disturbed lines and strong masturbatory tension, as revealed by mutilated fingers and repetitive clothing designs. If the girl has reached puberty, her disturbance is generally more severe. Legs may be pressed tightly and defensively together and hands are often hidden behind the back. In a hurry to grow up, the girl intensifies seductive features while fearfully looking to see the effect. She fights dependency and fears sensual involvement, drawing more empty hair (while the boy gives hair more substance than previously). She gives most items pertaining to physical vigor to the male of her set, more often casting him in athletic roles, giving him suits and manly ties. In other respects, she will express her rivalry by giving the male of the set the immature eyes and weak crotch formation, imposing upon him the midline and buttons, and presenting him as childish and carefree. It is as if she were taking advantage of the slightly less aggressive posture of the 11 year boy as compared with that of the 10 year old.

### 12 Year Olds

The 12 year old *boy* continues to battle with the twofold task: (a) he must free himself from female domination and its libidinal complications, and (b) he must examine, assess and construct a self image adequate to the task of manhood—a task that is confused and inflated in its standards. These central themes are presented in various balances and interplay from the age of 9. As the crisis ripens, patterns of the balance of forces and the methods of coping become numerous and variegated. Conflict continues to rise in intensity, and repressions, useful in former years, are less effective. There is, however, underlying the struggle a positive growth striving. After a brief pause at 11 for self accounting, the 12 year old gives more large drawings and places them more boldly in the center of the page, as if ready to do battle with the enemy. The line is active and disturbed. Extension is of primary concern and much conflict is expressed in what type of arms to make and where to place them. Often they are thrust out rigidly in phallic extension. With the rapid pace of physiologic changes pressing upon his awareness, the 12 year old boy presents particularly disturbed and disorganized projections. Line is shredded with lack of clear boundaries of head and trunk, shading is diffuse, joining and integration are careless, and the drawings are smudged with critical erasures and anxious, often diffuse, shading. Facial features are frequently uncomposed and overactive, and the face bears many marks and scars as if in the thick of an uncompromising battle. The "elements" are menacing with clouds and rain, and there is active background for thematic emphasis. Badges, merit ribbons, athletic letters and verbal balloon threats add to the heat and noise of the struggle. The picture bears a similarity to the surge at 10, but is more intense. It is as if it were a combination of all the efforts at self assertion made in previous years. Large, active mouths reappear, as well as a groundline for support, and figures are often holding "something." This dependency and need for support always enter in the height of battle and may be viewed as a mobilization of deeper and more primitive sources of strength for the critical task of ego survival.

The female of the set is also jolted out of the relative reserve with which the 11 year old boy drew her. She now is presented as a worthy contender to justify the display of injury shown on his self figure. She is often angry, the skirt area is actively erased, diffusely shaded, or almost transparent, and hair is drawn roughly and disordered, conveying acute sexual excitement. To return to the boy's self presentation, we find the male in two major stages of the battle. He is either castrated with broken limbs, disturbed crotch, perhaps small in size, or else he is a compensated figure of large size, often in the battle array of a two-gun cowboy, a marine with a sharp bayonet, a prizefighter or a muscle artist. The self figure is now drawn larger more often and is given the wider stance of the set. Despite improved male-female differentiation, the boy tends to masculinize his female and the girl feminizes her male, perhaps as a reflection of their acutely egocentric self reference at this age. The boy's drawings, though more disorganized, do advance in maturity and in strength of body features. Fewer weak noses, weak legs, small feet and more shoulders and crotch formations are drawn on the self sex. Necks with which to control appear more frequently. There is also control by evasive hiding of the commotion, as reflected in an increase of profiles.

The 12 year old *girl* struggles primarily with her own growing body sensations. Her drawings differ, depending upon her pubertal status. The girl, unlike the boy, does not project her "storm" upon background "elements." Nor can she use the reassurance of the environment in which, as a child, she was dominant. A decrease in object interest parallels her increased concern about body processes. Fewer hands with which to grasp are drawn. The 12 year old girl falters markedly in her poise and is worried about her future. In her drawing of 36 per cent opposite-sex first, in contrast to the usual 5 per cent, she expresses protest against her role. Her mood is essentially sober. She draws relatively large figures, suggesting active self esteem elements, but they are placed on the left of the page. Her growth task, unlike that of the boy, is not to overthrow female domination and to build masculine strengths. She must preserve the mother as a model while attempting to differentiate herself from her as an individual. Her effective childhood adjustment gave her contrary training. The drawings reflect uncertainty, depressive brooding and some withdrawal. Under stress, she increases her controls and most often reacts intrapunitively, while the boy disorganizes and often acts out upon others. The girl continues to persist in her interest in maturity. She displays determination, intense viewing, feet forward and outward, although her controls are under strain. The neck is often tense and erased and fingers compressed. Her clothing is, however, more mature, she depicts hips and breasts, and will assign teen ages to her figures.

Compulsive detail, binding, legs tightly pressed together, combine with the unstable line and nostril emphasis to suggest temper outbursts. No longer does she unload her dependency upon the male figure, but rather accepts upon her own figure the burden of her weakness. Mouths become more immature, with a small line-arc suggesting truce. She now seems to have less confidence in the seductive detail. She draws shorter, narrower skirts, prim, Peter-Pan collars and sleeves, as if suddenly ashamed of her body. She gives herself fewer curls, bangs, lashes, cosmetic lips, fancy dresses, jewelry or seductive poses. Sensuality, as reflected in hair substance, cannot be evaded or denied by suggestive outlines as it was by the 11 year old girl. As with the boy, hair is now heavily shaded. There is much fussing with hair at this age.

Sexually she is, as in earlier years, more interested in her peers than are the boys who rather fear girls since their fantasies and arousals are more linked with revived Oedipal problems. The 12 year old girl accords to the male less grudgingly the advantages of strength, self assertion and freedom from load. She reinforces his figure, dresses him more with suits and ties, assigns an older age to him, shows more sexual interest in him and emphasizes his ears. She is much concerned about his opinion of her and seeks out approval from her father at this age.

## References

1. Frank, L. K., Harrison, R., Hellersberg, E., Machover, K., & Steiner, M.    Personality development in adolescent girls. *Monogr. Soc. Res. Child Develpm.*, 1951, *16*, Serial No. 53.
2. Machover, K.    *Personality projection in the drawing of the human figure.* Springfield, Ill.: Charles C Thomas, 1949.
3. ——.    Drawing of the human figure: A method of personality investigation. *In* Anderson, H. H., & Anderson, G. L. (Eds.)    *An introduction to projective techniques.* New York: Prentice-Hall, 1951, Pp. 341–369.
4. ——.    Human figure drawings of children. *J. proj. Tech.*, 1953, *17*, 85–92.
5. ——.    The body image in art communication. *J. proj. Tech.*, 1956, *19*, 453–460.
6. ——.    A destructive juvenile delinquent. *In* Burton, A., & Harris, R. E. (Eds.)    *Clinical studies of personality.* New York: Harper, 1955.
7. Witkin, H. A., Lewis, H. B., Hertzman, M., Machover, K., Meissner, P. B., & Wapner, S. (Eds.)    *Personality through perception.* New York: Harper, 1954.
8. Wolff, W.    *Personality of the preschool child.* New York: Grune & Stratton, 1946.

**14**

## The House-Tree-Person (H-T-P) Drawings as a
## Projective Technique with Children*

EMANUEL F. HAMMER

CHILDREN like to draw! When projective drawings are included in the battery, they take quite readily to this task, since drawing is a favorite play activity. For the child, the request to draw is very likely to reduce tension in the psychological examination. He responds to it with pleasure and enthusiasm as well as with feelings of security, for it is an activity in which he feels at home.

### Function of Drawings

Within the projective battery, drawings thus serve a special function by providing a minimally threatening yet maximally absorbing introduction to the testing procedure. If employed as the first projective technique in the battery, drawings serve as an easy bridge to the clinical examination; the drawing task allows uncomfortable subjects to exclude the examiner, in a relative sense, during the initial phase of getting used to the new surroundings and to the stranger on the other side of the desk. To borrow from the observations of a nonprofessional psychologist, one may note that Winston Churchill (reference 23, page 32) speaks of drawings as "complete as a distraction." He continues, "I know of nothing which . . . more entirely absorbs the mind. . . . All one's mental light such as it is, becomes concentrated on the task."

The writer has found that children with emotional difficulties can be led more easily from drawing to verbal expression. Drawings also serve as a means of more easily establishing rapport and are a good "ice breaker" with the shy or negative child.

The drawing page serves as a canvas upon which the subject may project a glimpse of his inner world, his traits and attitudes, his behavioral characteristics, his personality strengths and weaknesses. Children find it easier to communicate through drawings than through the verbal projective techniques much that is important to them and much that troubles them.

Both children and primitive people consistently draw elements which they consider essential and drop out others which do not concern them. They then include aspects which are known to be there but are not visible.

*Appreciation is extended to Charles C Thomas, publisher, for permission to use material from the author's book.[15]

The goal, thus, of both child and primitive is not "objective realism" but what Luquet calls "mental realism."[22]

Projective drawings, basically a nonverbal technique, have the obvious advantages of greater relative applicability not only to young children but to the more poorly educated child, the mentally defective child, the non-English-speaking child, the mute, the painfully shy or withdrawn child, the child with a predominantly concrete orientation and the child from a relatively barren and underprivileged sociocultural background who frequently is wracked by feelings of inadequacy concerning his capacity for verbal expression. In addition, we may add to this list the case of the child referred for a psychological evaluation because of remedial reading problems. Bender[2] points out that children with reading difficulties often show compensatory adeptness in artistic ability to make articulate their emotional and social problems and needs.

### Projective Aspects of Drawings

At first, drawings were employed by clinicians as a form of intelligence scale based mainly on the number of details put into the drawings. Soon, however, it became apparent that the drawings were tapping personality factors in addition to intellectual capabilities. In fact, emotional factors even more than intellectual ones were constantly pressing into view. In crediting a drawing for the inclusion of a hand, the same quantitative score was given for a balled-up, clenched fist, or a delicate and open hand in a feminine gesture patting the cheek, and so important qualitative clues to the functioning of the total personality were being ignored. The subject was granted identical quantitative credit whether he drew his Person with the arms crossed defiantly over the chest, hanging flexibly at the sides or placed timidly behind the back, but the fact that these several arm positions had vastly different affective implications was not taken into account, and much valuable diagnostic material was overlooked. Similarly, the large range of facial expressions, size, placement on the page, etc., seemed to offer more information about nonintellectual components than about intellectual capabilities.

The writer recalls a child who had to walk with the aid of crutches. When asked to draw a Person, although he did not draw someone leaning upon crutches, he did draw an extra line suggesting a long spike extending from the heel of the shoe into the ground, as if through this device to gain greater stability of posture than the subject himself experienced. While the subject was not consciously drawing himself, he nevertheless projected his inner feeling that one cannot stand without the help of something additional upon which to lean. His need for physical bolstering pressed forward onto the drawing page.

Another subject, who was born missing his left arm, though he did not draw a one-armed Person, did give a distinct treatment to the left arm of the drawn Person which rendered it withered, foreshortened, crippled and conspicuously less effective than the right arm. When asked to draw a tree, he drew one in which a truncated limb protruded from the trunk of the tree. And if additional support for the projective thesis be needed, the amputated limb of the tree appeared on the same side as both the missing limb of our subject and the crippled arm of the Person he drew.

We have observed that obese children tend either to draw obese-looking Persons or else to fly to the other extreme—representation of an extremely lithe, slim and/or athletic looking Person. The depiction of an ego-ideal represents a more positive prognostic indication. Such children, it has been found, still actively entertain ideas of conquering their weight problem and have not yet given in to a self concept involving sluggishness, passivity and overweight.

In terms of expressive aspects, children's movements have diagnostic potential whether they are gross (as in the play therapy room) or confined (as on the drawing page). A child may withdraw into a corner of the room or sit on the edge of the chair, as though he were ready to run away; if he is given a big sheet of paper, he may follow suit by drawing cautiously in one corner of the page only. At the other extreme, a child may sit at a table as though he wished to occupy the whole space, showing no consideration for the other children there. No paper is big enough for him either, and his drawings expand beyond the drawing sheet. Projective drawings thus "capture" and record expressive movements on paper.

The size of drawings is a particularly important variable with children. Those children who draw small, or even tiny, objects and Persons tend to suffer from intensified awareness of the fact that they have been born pigmies in a world of giants. Their Persons are drawn as weak and insignificant and are protected or reinforced by guns, canes, etc. Feelings of inferiority and insignificance have been more deeply ingrained, via interpersonal experiences, in such children than in those who draw with adequate size. Whereas the aggressive child draws big, dangerous arms with long fingers, the inadequate or withdrawn child forgets to draw hands at all—as though the subject had not experienced helping hands when he needed them, or as if hands were guilty things which may be used to do something which is labeled as taboo in our culture.

As a reflection of their virility strivings, delinquent children frequently draw soldiers or cowboys as symbols of status attained through the use of force and aggression. One child who was referred to the writer because of excessive truancy, the flaunting of rules in school and generally rebellious behavior reflected his characteristic role in life in his drawing of a Person. As a reflection of the subject's need for greater status, prestige and recognition than he felt he possessed, the drawn male was dressed in a soldier's outfit with his back turned on the world. A regulation (see the "No Spitting" sign, figure 1) was introduced so that the drawn person might disobey it. This clearly paralleled the subject's manner of seeking out rules and regulations merely to break them, proving to himself and others that he was bigger and better than the rules and the people who made them.

Fig. 1.—Person, by adolescent boy.

With many children, drawings assume the character of an overemphasized, exaggerated portrait of strength or importance. Within the normal range, children and adolescents tend to draw themselves as more forceful, more glamorous, bigger, or older than they actually are—a depiction indicative of their own wishes about themselves. They put into the picture a promise of that reality which they desire.

Before leaving the topic of size, figure 2 may serve as an example of a drawing reflecting acute feelings of psychological tininess. The figure is so small that the reader may have trouble locating it; it will be found at the very bottom, center, of the drawing page.

Whereas some children portray small figures as a graphic reflector of feelings of inadequacy, figure 2 reflects feelings of total insignificance. Not only by the miniscule size, but also by the light line pressure which causes the drawn Person to all but fade from view, our subject conveys to us his feelings of being wholly without worth, status or recognition as a person. He feels painfully constricted and in danger of being totally overlooked by others.

This drawing was made by a 12 year old boy with an IQ of 150. His father held a Ph.D. in one of the social sciences, and his mother a master's degree in an allied area. They so pushed the child to attainments above even his clearly superior capabilities that he soon crystalized the self concept of

Fig. 2.—Person, by 12 year old boy.

someone who was, by comparison with these high standards, clearly inadequate. Obvious preference was shown to the subject's younger sibling, which served to reinforce the subject's feelings of insignificance as a person. Also, his parents held to the philosophy that watching TV, reading comic books or drinking a soda would spoil the child. Here, too, their behavior led him to believe that his needs were to be forever overlooked, just as the drawn Person he rendered is so easily overlooked. Close inspection of the drawing reveals inadequate, puny arms that cannot accomplish anything for himself, a head that is bowed in dejection and a sad facial expression.

## Administration of H-T-P

A No. 2 pencil and a sheet of paper are handed the subject. His drawing of a House is requested, with the longer axis of the sheet placed horizontally before the subject. His drawings of a Tree and Person, in turn, are then obtained on separate sheets of paper with the longer axis placed vertically. The subject is asked to draw as well as he can, but he is not told what kind of House, Tree and Person to draw.

If the subject protests that he is not an artist, he is assured that the H-T-P is not a test of artistic ability at all but that we are interested, rather, in how he does things. Any questions he asks are reflected back to him in such a way as to indicate that there is no right or wrong method of proceeding but that he may do the drawing in any manner he wishes.

After he draws the Person, the subject is then handed another sheet of paper and this time told to draw a Person of the sex opposite to that of the first Person drawn. With children, we may occasionally also ask for a drawing of an animal.[15]

## House

The House, as a dwelling place, has been found to arouse within the subject associations concerning home life and intrafamilial relationships. In children, it has been found to tap their attitudes concerning the home situation and their relationships to parents and siblings. One child drew a House with profuse and very heavily shaded smoke pouring forth from the chimney as a reflection of the hot and turbulent emotional atmosphere he experienced in the home situation.

## Tree

The drawing of the Tree appears to reflect the subject's relatively deeper and more unconscious feelings about himself, whereas the drawn Person becomes the vehicle for conveying the subject's closer-to-conscious view of himself and his relationship to his environment. In this manner, the elicited conflicts and defenses may be assigned to levels in the hierarcy of the subject's personality structure.

The view that the Tree taps more basic and long-standing feelings is supported by the fact that the Tree is less susceptible to change on retesting.[4,11] Whereas psychotherapy of a nonintensive kind will frequently bring improvement as indicated by the decrease of pathologic signs in the drawn Person, only deep and extensive psychoanalytic collaboration (or highly significant alterations in a life situation) will produce any but minor changes in the Tree.

Clinical experience also suggests that it is easier for a subject to attribute more conflicting or emotionally disturbing negative traits and attitudes to the drawn Tree than to the drawn Person because the former is less "close to home" as a self portrait. The deeper or more forbidden feelings can more readily be projected onto the Tree than onto the Person, with less fear of revealing oneself and less need for ego-defensive maneuvering.

A subject may, for instance, more readily and unwittingly portray his feeling of emotional trauma by scarring the drawn Tree's trunk and truncating its branches, than by a parallel mutilation of the drawn Person's face and body and similar distortion of the drawn Person's arms.

The clinical finding that forbidden feelings can be projected more readily onto the Tree than onto the Person is similar to the rationale behind Blum's Blacky Picture Test, Bellak's Children's Apperception Test and the Despert Fables. The animal figures in these thematic techniques seem to lend themselves to the projection of deeper and more negative feelings (with less threat to the subject) than do the human figures of the TAT.

Thus, a comparison of the subject's responses to the animal as opposed to the human TAT-type stimuli and a comparison of the subject's drawn Tree with his drawn Person provide data which enable the clinician to appraise the relative levels from which the subject's different projected feelings come.

Figure 3 illustrates the projection of negative feelings onto the Tree drawing; this picture was offered by an 11 year old boy who had been referred because he had been observed picking up baby pigs with the prongs of a pitchfork, throwing down baby chicks and crushing them under the heel of his shoe and at one time setting fire to a bale of hay underneath a cow. In addition, he had recently released a tractor to roll down a hill onto some children. (Fortunately, the children dodged the vehicle in time.)

His drawn Tree speaks as eloquently as does his behavior. His drawing is a graphic communication saying in distinct and unequivocal language: "Keep away from me!" Spearlike branches with thornlike "leaves" decorate a sharply pointed Tree trunk. The branches reach out aggressively in a promise of inflicting acute harm to all those who come within reach. The drawing is steeped in sadism, aggression and angry resentment, and could well have been used as an emblem of Hitler's Storm Troopers.

In contrast to aggressive Tree drawings, children sometimes depict beaten-up, mutilated, damaged or scarred entities.

The most extreme instance of scarring that the writer has encountered was offered by a 12 year old boy. He placed a ravaging wound approximately half-way up the height of the Tree trunk. Subsequent psychotherapeutic collaboration with the youngster revealed that his mother's death, occurring when he was five years of age, was unconsciously felt as an abandonment and left him with a deep hurt. This feeling of an aching wound was etched into the self portrait which his drawn Tree represented.

If the projective examination occurs some weeks after the initial phase of psychotherapy has begun, it is frequently found that the Tree trunk itself is truncated and that tiny branches grow from the stump. This type of Tree drawing reflects stunted emotional growth, but with beginning—although tentative and rather feeble—efforts at regrowth, stimulated by the initial phase of the therapeutic relationship. Some of these children, at the completion of therapy, render Tree drawings whose full bloom expresses their regained feelings of capability, fulfillment and optimism regarding future growth.

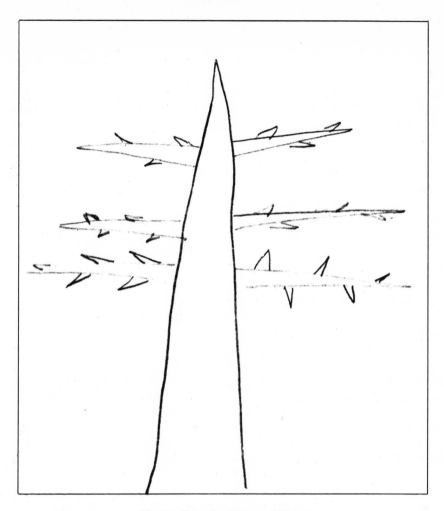

Fig. 3.—Tree, by 11 year old boy.

In children's drawings particularly, branches are sometimes drawn as if reaching appealingly to the sun. This has occurred with those youngsters who have shown other evidence of marked and frustrated needs for affection. The Tree stretches out its arms hungrily for warmth from some significant authority figure.

Occasionally a child will draw a Tree as bending away from a large and low-placed sun, which seems to be bearing down upon the Tree. This depiction is offered by subjects who shy away from domination by a parental or other authority figure who makes the subject feel painfully controlled, subjugated and inadequate.

### Person

In regard to theme, the drawing of a Person tends to elicit principally three types: a self portrait, an ideal self, and a depiction of one's perception of significant others (parents, siblings, etc.).

### Self Portrait

The subject draws what he feels himself to be. Body contours, whether obese or thin, areas of sensitivity such as a hooked nose, a cauliflower ear, a pockmarked skin, or a club foot are often reproduced faithfully and exactly in the drawn Person. Subjects of average or below average intelligence will usually reproduce these features upon their drawn Persons in mirror image, i.e., if the subject has a withered right hand, he will reproduce this condition on the drawn Person's left hand. Abstract ability allows the nonmirror image depiction, i.e., the subject's right side to be portrayed by the drawn Person's right side, and is seldom found in subjects of less than high average intelligence.

It has been noticed, however, that physical flaws or disabilities are reproduced in the drawing of the person *only* if they have impinged upon the subject's self concept and have created an area of psychological sensitivity.

Along with his projection of feelings of physical defects, the subject *also projects his assets*: broad shoulders, muscular development, attractive physiognomy. This is done to the point at which an amazing likeness frequently results, even in artistically incapable individuals.

In addition to the physical self, the subject projects a picture of the psychological self into his drawing of the Person. Subjects of adequate or superior height may draw a tiny figure, with arms dangling rather helplessly away from the sides and a beseeching facial expression. Here the subject is projecting his psychological view of himself as tiny, insignificant, helpless, dependent and in need of support, his physical self notwithstanding.

Other examples are: the toppling Person, losing equilibrium, offered by a preschizophrenic child; the manikin-like clothes dummy suggesting feelings of depersonalization; the adolescent's drawn Person carrying a baseball bat in one hand, a tennis racket in the other and wearing a mustache on his lip, revealing by his yearning for so many badges of virility his underlying feelings of inadequacy in this area; the drawing of a clown as a fusion of the child's attempts to depict the harmlessness of his instinctual impulses and the secondary use of this concept as an attention-getting maneuver; the reduced energy and drive suggested by the drawn Person slumped into a chair or sitting on the curb of the street—all these themes support the thesis that the drawn Person may represent a psychological self portrait.

### Ego Ideal

Rather than a picture of what the subject presently feels himself to be, he may draw his ego ideal.

A slender, rather frail, intensely paranoid male drew a boxer whose shoulders, before he was through, extended to the dimensions of a Hercules.

An unmarried, pregnant, 15 year old girl, suffering feelings of terrible shame in regard to the stomach contour which was so revealing of her condition, drew a lithe, graceful, slender dancer twirling unencumbered by any burden.

Adolescent boys frequently draw muscular athletes attired in bathing suits, and adolescent girls draw female movie stars wearing evening gowns—the ideal states longed for by adolescents. Healthy children tend to draw Persons two or three years older than their own ages as an index of their striving for forward growth.

### Significant Others

The subject depicts a significant person in his contemporary or past environment, usually because of that person's strong positive or negative valence for the subject. This pressing forward into the drawing page of the subject's perception of significant figures in the environment, in contrast to the perception of one's self, occurs more often in the drawings of children than of adolescents or adults. (At times the same drawing may yield a fused image of self and others.) The "other" Person children represent in their drawing is almost invariably a parental figure and probably represents the great importance of the parent in the child's life and the need for a model to identify with and to incorporate into his self concept. The kind of mother or father figure the child reveals in his drawing is often a prophesying element and predicts the traits which retest drawings, years later, frequently indicate the child incorporates.

One 8 year old boy, referred because of excessive bullying of his classmates, drew a man who was menacing in every aspect: bared teeth sharpened to a point, a club in one hand, the other hand coming to an end not in conventional fingers but in a clear depiction of what looked like the ends of scissors—a weapon which might shear off and do damage to vital parts of the subject. The social worker's investigation of the father revealed that he was a despot in every way, cruel, punitive and domineering. The bullying attitudes the subject had picked up suggested that he had already begun to defend himself against the threat of the destruction-invested father through the universal mechanism of incorporation. In an understandable self-protective maneuver, he donned his enemy's cloak so that he could put himself out of harm's way. He became the bully, rather than the bullied. The process of incorporation became the bridge across which the subject sought to travel to comparative safety.

In this manner, projective drawings tend to reveal the felt self, the ideal self and—one is tempted to say—the future self (barring the intervention of psychotherapy or significant changes in the environmental situation).

### Use of Crayons

The chromatic phase of the H-T-P involves a new set of drawings, in that the clinician collects the drawings previously made with pencil and now presents new sheets of paper and crayons. Some children approach the crayons with the hesitant anxiety characteristic of their customary everyday patterns of behavior. Their crayon lines are faint and uncertain with the color choices restricted to the safer black, brown or blue. They reveal their personality constriction and interpersonal uncertainties by not daring to open up with the bolder reds, oranges and yellows. Such color usage places these subjects at the end of the personality continuum at which over-cautiousness in exchanging pleasure or pain with others prevails.

Psychologically healthier subjects, by contrast, plunge more deeply into the chromatic task, confidently employ the warmer colors, utilize a firm, sure pressure on the crayon and thus reflect their greater self assurance in the emotional areas that colors represent.

On the other side of this healthier middle range in the continuum are those subjects who employ an almost savage pressure (frequently bearing down so heavily that they snap the crayons) and a clash of inharmonious, hot colors. Excessive lability, turbulent emotions and jarring inner needs in a tension-laden setting characterize the psychological state of the subjects in this group.

From a normative standpoint, the use of from three to five colors for the House represents the average range, as does two to three for the Tree, and three to five for the Person.

An inhibited use of color, below this average range, is exhibited by subjects unable to make warm, sharing personal relationships freely. The most "emotion-shy" subjects tend to use crayon as if it were a pencil, employing no coloring-in whatsoever.

A more expansive use of color than the normative middle range, particularly if combined with an unconventional employment of the colors, occurs most frequently in those manifesting an inability to exercise adequate control over their emotional impulses. One psychotic subject indicated his inadequate control, as well as his break with conventional reality, by drawing each of the eight windows in his House a different color.

## A Case Study

Although some clinicians interpret each drawing of a Person as a projection of the body image or self concept, the writer's experience has been that not all such drawings involve self portraiture. A figure drawing may at times, particularly with children, be a reflection of perceptions of significant people in one's environment, as indicated above.

The case of Leonard, a 12 year old who stayed away from school because he felt the teachers were picking on him, may serve as illustration (fig. 4). The tensions within the boy were reflected behaviorally in his doubting eyes, taut face, unceasing and jerky chatter and complete self centeredness. Knowing no other way to establish himself, he tried to do it by bravado, belligerence and a refusal to abide by the rules. It was for this latter reason that he was referred to the writer. Lenny soon earned from his peers the nickname of "Rocky." Behind Rocky's tendency to misinterpret the actions of people in authority was a series of childhood traumatizing experiences with a cold, harsh and often brutal set of parents; his mother was bitingly sarcastic and his father physically abusive.

This perception of his parental figures is expressed in the subject's two figure drawings. The mother is clearly presented as orally aggressive and capable of inflicting severe damage with her mouth. The hands are absent, reflecting Rocky's perception of his mother as not reaching out to him—ungiving and rejecting. She is perceived in unappealing and frightening tones. Rocky's father figure, on the other hand, while not orally aggressive, is apperceived as capable of inflicting severe physical damage to one's vital parts. The scissor-like fingers seem capable of cutting off anything that protrudes from Rocky's body. The implications

Fig. 4.—Drawings by a 12 year old boy: (*a*) Female; (*b*) Male; (*c*) House.

of castration anxiety are supported by the drawing of a House in which Rocky projects onto the chimney his feelings that any protrusion from his own body is likewise flimsily attached and vulnerable to separation from the body. The chimney hangs onto the body of the House by a mere thread; it is as unattached as one can draw a chimney and still keep it part of the House. Rocky's feelings of vulnerability are also expressed in the House drawing by its quality of thinness, lack of substance and lack of capacity to withstand the pressures and forces of the environment. On one side the House already buckles.

It should be noted that the subject dresses the male drawing in the authoritarian role (military uniform of the Russians) in which he apperceives his father to parade. He then adds the dictatorial aspects of his father image by labeling the drawn male "Stalin." From the facial expression of the male figure, it is apparent that Rocky, somewhere within himself, perceives the underlying passivity and ineffectuality of his father beneath his father's authoritarian cloak. Rocky appears to have some awareness, perhaps only unconsciously, of the compensatory nature of his father's aggressive role.

Apparently Rocky's experiences with his parents have torn a deep gash in his feelings of adequacy and have left him with no one to turn to for help in tending the aching wound. The drawings suggest the intensity of the dowry of antagonism with which Rocky had to start off in life. And once a boy has suffered rejection, he will find rejection even where it does not exist. The boy's fear of, and expectation of, mistreatment at the hands of authority figures rippled outward to include the teachers with whom he had so much trouble. So Rocky built a wall of isolation and toughness around himself, strong enough—he hoped—to defend himself against the world.

In response to the request to draw an animal, he began by drawing what he described as "a timid rabbit running away" on one side of the page; he then appeared displeased with the drawing, turned the page over and on the other side drew what he described as "a little wildcat." Here we see the two sides of the coin of Rocky's inner view of himself. His basic feeling of fearfulness and lack of adequacy ("a timid rabbit running away"), he attempts to hide behind the tough-guy facade of "a little wildcat."

One of the early dreams the patient reported after about six therapy sessions was a nightmare in which he tried to kill someone and then fell out of bed. He reported, "I'm always trying to kill someone in my dreams. I was beating up a guy in this dream. I had him on the floor and was kicking him, almost killing him." He then followed this with a degree of insight: "I was afraid of the guy, but I just hit him. When I hit him, I wasn't afraid any more." Thus, in his dreams, Rocky offers us support for the interpretive deductions made on the basis of his animal drawings, in which he attempts to hide his feelings of being the "timid rabbit" behind the cloak of "a little wildcat."

## Experimental Studies

Space limitations permit only the briefest passing mention of experimental studies in the area of projective drawings.

Central to the core thesis of drawings as a projective device are the studies by Lehner and Silver,[19] indicating that one's own age tends to be projected in drawings; by Hammer,[13] suggesting that one's felt or subjective psycho-maturational age tends to be projected; by Lehner and Gunderson,[18] finding that the height of the drawing is related to the degree of feelings of bodily adequacy; by Lyons,[20] showing a correlation between age at which psychic trauma was experienced and height up the Tree trunk where a scar is placed; by Kotkov and Goodman,[17] demonstrating more "obese" drawings by the more obese subjects; by Berman and Laffel,[3] who reported significant correlations between body type of the subject and figure drawn; by Hammer,[9] finding significantly more indices of castration anxiety in the drawings made by subjects after sterilization than before they knew of the impending operation; by Barker et al.,[1] who reported greater hostility toward women in drawings by homosexuals than in drawings by "normals"; by De Martino,[6] who found more feminine features in homosexuals' drawings of a male person; by Fisher and Fisher,[7] who uncovered a relationship between the femininity expressed in females' figure drawings and their psychosexual adjustment; by Hammer,[10] who showed the H-T-P to differentiate aggressive from control groups; by Tolor and Tolor,[24] who showed that popular and unpopular children projected associated traits into their drawings; by Cook,[5] who substantiated Machover's hypothesis that the drawing of the head area reflects the degree of social dominance of the subject; and by a number of investigators[6,12,16,21,25] who demonstrated that subjects, when asked to draw a person, drew a person of their own sex.

For a more complete presentation of research in the area of the H-T-P, and for a presentation of the H-T-P reorganized into a tool for research purposes, the reader is referred to *The H-T-P Clinical Research Manual*.[14]

## Summary

Armed with the knowledge that man's deeper needs color his creative efforts and show an affinity for speaking in pictorial images, the clinician and/or experimenter has at his disposal a rapidly and easily administered technique for eliciting submerged levels of feelings. Basically, the subject's relative emphasis of different elements within his drawings, in addition to his global drawing performance, tells us a good deal of what matters to him, what it does to him, and what he does about it.

By examining the creative art work of a number of individuals, we have observed that subjects tend to express in their projective drawings quite unwittingly (and at times, unwillingly) their view of themselves *as they are, as they fear they might become* or *as they would like to be*.

Drawings represent a form of symbolic speech which taps a relatively primitive layer within the subject. In the words of Tunnelle, "The artist does not see things as they are, but as he is." Hubbard, another artist, expressed it in much the same way: "When an artist paints a portrait, he paints two, himself and the sitter."

For advanced considerations of topics treated in this chapter, the interested reader is referred to *The Clinical Application of Projective Drawings*.[15] There the reader can also find a discussion of aspects which, because of space limitations, could not be included in this chapter, mainly developmental levels of children as these levels influence their projective drawings, the meaning of sub-items within the drawn House, Tree and Person, the individual symbolism of the different colors, the deeper personality level tapped by chromatic drawings and fuller treatment of experimental studies.

## References

1. Barker, A. J., Mathis, J. K., & Powers, C. A.  Drawings characteristic of male homosexuals. *J. clin. Psychol.*, 1953, *9*, 185–188.
2. Bender, L.  *Child psychiatric techniques*. Springfield, Ill.: Charles C Thomas, 1952.

3. Berman, S., & Laffel, J.  Body types and figure drawing. *J. clin. Psychol.*, 1953, *9*, 368–370.

4. Buck, J. N.  The H-T-P technique: A quantitative and qualitative scoring manual. *J. clin. Psychol. Monogr. Suppl.*, 1948, No. 5.

5. Cook, M.  A preliminary study of the relationship of differential treatment of male and female headsize in figure drawing to the degree of attribution of the social function of the female. *Psychol. Newsletter*, 1951, 34, 1–5.

6. DeMartino, M. F.  Human figure drawings by mentally retarded males. *J. clin. Psychol.*, 1954, *10*, 241–244.

7. Fisher, S., & Fisher, R. L.  Style of sexual adjustment in disturbed women and its expression in figure drawings. *J. Psychol.*, 1952, *34*, 169–179.

8. Fox, R.  Psychotherapeutics of alcoholism. *In* Bychowski, G., & Despert, J. L. (Eds.) *Specialized techniques in psychotherapy.* New York: Basic Books, 1952. Pp. 239–260.

9. Hammer, E. F.  An investigation of sexual symbolism—a study of H-T-P's of eugenically sterilized subjects. *J. proj. Tech.*, 1953, *17*, 401–413.

10. ——.  Frustration-aggression hypothesis extended to socio-racial areas: comparison of Negro and white children's H-T-P's. *Psychiat. Quart.*, 1953, *27*, 597–607.

11. ——.  The role of the H-T-P in the prognostic battery. *J. clin. Psychol.*, 1953, *9*, 371–374.

12. ——.  Guide for qualitative research with the H-T-P. *J. genet. Psychol.*, 1954, *51*, 41–60.

13. ——.  A comparison of the H-T-P's of rapists and pedophiles: III. The "dead" tree as an index of psychopathology. *J. clin. Psychol.*, 1955, *11*, 67–69.

14. ——.  *The H-T-P clinical research manual.* Beverly Hills, Calif.: Western Psychological Services, 1955.

15. ——.  *The clinical application of projective drawings.* Springfield, Ill.: Charles C Thomas, 1958.

16. Jolles, I.  A study of the validity of some hypotheses for the qualitative interpretation of the H-T-P for children of elementary school age. I. Sexual identification. *J. clin. Psychol.*, 1952, *8*, 113–118.

17. Kotkov, B., & Goodman, M.  Prediction of trait ranks from Draw-A-Person measurements of obese and nonobese women. *J. clin. Psychol.*, 1953, *9*, 365–367.

18. Lehner, G. F., & Gunderson, E. K.  Reliability of graphic indices in a projective test (DAP). *J. clin. Psychol.*, 1952, *8*, 125–128.

19. ——, & Silver, H.  Age relationships on the Draw-A-Person Test. *J. Pers.*, 1948, *17*, 199–209.

20. Lyons, J.  The scar on the H-T-P tree. *J. clin. Psychol.*, 1955, *11*, 267–270.

21. Mainord, F. B.  A note on the use of figure drawings in the diagnosis of sexual inversion. *J. clin. Psychol.*, 1953, *9*, 188–189.

22. Naumburg, M.  Art as symbolic speech. *J. Aesthetics and Art Criticism*, 1955, *13*, 435–450.

23. Ray, M. B.  You can be an amateur painter. *Coronet*, 1954, *35*(5), 82–104.

24. Tolor, A., & Tolor, B.  Judgment of children's popularity from human figure drawings. *J. proj. Tech.*, 1955, *19*, 170–176.

25. Weider, A., & Noller, P. A.  Objective studies of children's drawings of human figures. I. Sex awareness and socio-economic level. *J. clin. Psychol.*, 1950, *6*, 319–325.

# 15

## Free Art Expression

PAULA ELKISCH

A T THE OUTSET the title, "Free Art Expression," should be discussed. The designation "art" is here a rather ambiguous, if not an inappropriate, term for what it is supposed to convey; yet it is commonly used for certain means of expression of people being observed (tested or treated) in a clinical setting. "Free art" within that frame of reference should be understood in terms of *Ausdrucksbewegungen*, expressive movements* which are projected unwittingly by an individual through graphic media (pencil or paint) onto paper or canvas, or through some modelling activity. Since the term "Ausdrucksbewegungen" comprises any kind of motor behavior, including even movements which can hardly be circumscribed in words, it may also be applied to drawing or painting or modelling, similarly to the way it has been applied to handwriting.[16] If these activities are being considered under the aspect of Ausdrucksbewegungen, "expressive movements," they reveal an element which one may call unconscious, instinctual, primitive, archaic and which relates to a person's body feelings and body image,[17,23] an element which is void of any conscious deliberate intent, of any "tendency toward order."[14] Being thus excluded from a concept which would refer to "order," to deliberate intent, to "Gestaltung" (the latter qualities are inherent in genuine artistic production), "Ausdrucks-bewegungen" should be unequivocally differentiated from "art"; and drawing, painting or modelling in a clinical setting should be conceived of without any reference to "art." For the most comprehensive exploration of this subject see Kris;[17] Hartmann's discussion touches on these problems within the context of ego psychology.[14]

It is true, however, that the phrase *"free* art" modifies the concept of "art." And we may ask: What does the word "free" mean here? We may think of it in terms of "freedom from the regulation by the external world" (Hartmann, reference 14, page 78) as in play, as well as freedom from the regulation set by art. Both these freedoms make the application of the term "art" within a clinical setting more acceptable. In fact, the word "free" represents here a bridge which one may safely step on if one is to bow to the common linguistic usage of the concept "free art" employed for drawing, painting or modelling in a clinical setting, the concept which from now on I shall use myself after having discussed the semantic dilemma.

---

*The term "expressive movements," consisting of an adjective and a noun, is not precisely an equivalent for the German term *Ausdrucksbewegungen*, which is a composite noun.

Free art expression in a clinical setting suggests two possible approaches, one pertaining to psychodiagnosis, the other one to psychotherapy. Both of these approaches may be combined,[10,11] or they may be employed separately, i.e., independent of one another.[8,9] In the following the attempt will be made to give a description of the diagnostic method which is based on the author's own experience with children and the study of their free expressions in art.

### Diagnostic Criteria in Children's Free Art Work
### (With Special Reference to their Ego Functions)

For diagnostic use, free art expression as a projective instrument might be considered an approach complementary to the House-Tree-Person Test by Buck[6] and to Machover's Draw-A-Person.[19] In both of these tests, the manifest content of the subject's production is evident and may be evaluated as such. By contrast, in free art expression, the clinician is confronted with content whose evaluation is hardly possible. For he has to ask himself questions such as the following: Does the represented object perhaps stand for another object the patient did not want to or was unable to represent? And if so, what is the unrepresented object and what is its meaning? To cite an example: This author[7,8] was asked to give an account of the representation of the human figure in children's spontaneous art work. In response to this inquiry I searched the material which I had collected (about 2200 free drawings and paintings from 30 children, 22 boys and 8 girls). In the content analysis of these drawings and paintings it appeared that, if the drawing situation was determined by the child's spontaneous response, the representation of the human figure was very rare. It was outnumbered by far by the drawings of machines or of anything pertaining to a machine. In the attempt to evaluate this numerical predominance not only quantitatively but also as a qualitative factor, the relationship between the concept of the human figure and that of the machine proved to be significant.[12]

Since the contentual evaluation of the child's free art expression in general meets with unknown features as demonstrated by the example just given, it seems best to disregard content analysis and, instead, to give undivided attention to the form elements in the child's production. The fundamental importance of the recognition of form elements has been noted by Münz and Löwenfeld,[20] who state that the form experience which the blind achieve through the sense of touch pertains to a universal and primordial law of formal comprehension which applies equally for the blind and the seeing.

Now, what does a study of form elements imply? "A study of form would have to deal with the fundamentals of human expression as they may be inherent in expressive movements. A child who uses paper and pencil or paint freely without being directed will reveal himself through the style of his motion, i.e., through his expressive movements. . . . [These movements] have come to a standstill in his drawings and paintings [and can be interpreted]. The 'frozen' graphic elements offer the possibility of becoming 'dissolved' again, as it were, and of being treated as though they were fluid and in motion" (reference 8, page 2).

The method of form evaluation was employed by this author in a clinical study of 30 normal school children between 9 and 12 years of age.[7] In addition to the study of these children's immediate drawings and paintings produced during their individual sessions with the author, 2200 graphic art products made by the same children throughout their school life—some of them from 3 through 10 years of age—were analyzed with regard to their form quality. These form analyses, which were correlated with methods used by Olson and Hughes[21] and Bronfenbrenner[5] for judging these children's problem behavior, appeared to be significantly discriminative regarding their ability or disability for adjustment. They seemed to indicate the child's ego state and, if understood aright, might reveal fixations on earlier stages in psychosexual development. The recognition and evaluation of form expressions yielded the establishment of certain diagnostic criteria in the free drawings and paintings of children between the ages of three and twelve years. Of five pairs of criteria, four pertain strictly to form; the fifth one, although on the surface concerned with content, actually has many formal implications. Two sets of Criteria have been defined: Criteria A and Criteria B.

## Criteria A

### I. Rhythm versus Rule

1. *Rhythm* (fig. 1)* is expressed
   (a) explicitly through a flexible quality of the stroke (kinesthetically resulting from free relaxed movements);
   (b) implicitly through the pleasingly proportioned distribution of the represented object within the space at hand.

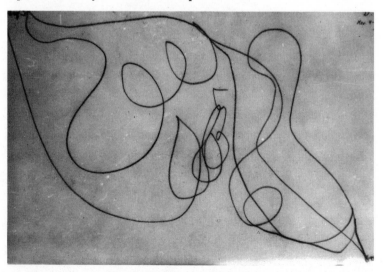

Fig. 1.—Rhythm. B. A. (age 7–8)

*The following plates originally appeared in *Psychological Monographs*, 1945, *58*, No. 1 (Whole No. 266) and are reproduced here with the permission of the publishers.

The graphic expression of Rhythm conveys a sensitivity to the functioning of time within space. Rhythm—Greek "rheo"—means "flowing"; flowing refers to the essence of time. The form expression of Rhythm elicits in the beholder the impression of *genetus non factus* (created, not made).

2. *Rule* is expressed in two ways, one opposing the other: Rigidity and Inertness.

 (a) Rule as Rigidity (fig. 2) is expressed through a rigid (torpid) quality of the stroke (kinesthetically affected by tight spasmodic movements which often become automatic, mechanical);

 (b) Rule as Inertness (fig. 3) is expressed through a smeary, sloppy quality of the stroke (kinesthetically affected by looseness). Inertness

Fig. 2.—Rule, (a) Rigidity. B. J. (age 7–3)

Fig. 3.—Rule, (b) Inertness. B. J. (age 5–1)

seems completely to be dropping out from the ruling control of
Rigidity.

In Rule there is no feeling for the dynamic functioning of the space, nor is
any connection with the time element suggested. Things have come to a
standstill.

*Suggested Symptomatology*

A child's ability to express himself rhythmically, as well as his spontaneous
response to Rhythm, suggests flexibility. One may expect an adaptive ego
which, although sensitive and in the moulding stage, is developing clear
boundaries, i.e., healthy ego defenses.

The two expressions of Rule—Rigidity and Inertness—are related to one
another in a compensatory way. Both are symptomatic of a weak ego.

Rigidity indicates that the defenses are too strong and too early established—repression is dominant; the superego harsh. Phobic features, elements
of an obsessive-compulsive neurosis, may be suspected here. However,
Rigidity, if combined with traits which are positive in nature, indicates that
the ego boundaries are intact, although rather inflexible.

Inertness indicates that the defenses are not strong enough, repression not
satisfactorily established. Since the ability to repress is an essential achievement during latency, Inertness during that time is a more serious symptom
than Rigidity, especially if there is no compensatory form expression in the
child. Without compensatory traits, Inertness, in latency, may indicate
regression, defective ego boundaries, possibly delinquent tendencies. In
terms of the psychosexual development, both Rigidity and Inertness pertain
to disturbances on the earliest developmental levels.

## II. Complexity versus Simplexity

1. *Complexity* (fig. 4) is expressed
   (a) through the tendency toward a rather complete, sometimes detailed,
       representation of the object, its individualization and differentiation;

Fig. 4.—Complexity. B. A. (age 5–9)

(*b*) structurally, through an imaginative feeling for form and Gestalt patterns.

2. *Simplexity* (fig. 5) is expressed by reducing the differentiated object, or structural form, to its simplest pattern, to its scheme. This expression conveys an impoverishment regarding form differentiation.

Fig. 5.—Simplexity. B. L. (age 6–7)

*Suggested Symptomatology*

While Complexity indicates potentially good object relations, Simplexity suggests fixation onto earlier stages of development, archaism, perhaps regression.

### III. Expansion versus Compression

1. *Expansion* is expressed in four ways:
   (*a*) through the widening (opening) of the space at the drawer's disposal, by presenting only a part of the object which has to be completed by imagination (fig. 6);
   (*b*) through the creation of a "spacious" background (fig. 7);
   (*c*) through the representation of an object that "bursts" (fig. 8);
   (*d*) through the representation of an object that seems to be coming from outside into "vision" (the space at disposal). This is a kind of "inverted expansion" (fig. 9).
2. *Compression* is based on a meticulous, fearful concept of space, expressed
   (*a*) in the spatial appearance of the object itself (fig. 10);
   (*b*) in its spatial relationship to other objects (fig. 11).

Compression conveys a feeling of discomfort, of being shut-in, of pressure and compulsion.

*Suggested Symptomatology*

Expansion indicates well established ego boundaries within which not only good object relations are likely to occur but also spontaneity, independence,

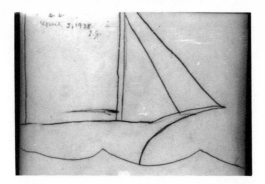

Fig. 6.—Expansion, (a). B. B. (age 7-3)

Fig. 8.—Expansion, (c). B. A. (age 5-9)

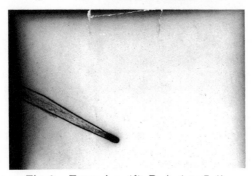

Fig. 9.—Expansion, (d). B. A. (age 7-1)

Fig. 10.—Compression, (a). B. J. (age 8-1)

Fig. 11.—Compression, (b). B. J. (age 10-7)

a striving toward making contact, forcefulness. It is noteworthy that the form expression (b) which is less spontaneous, less reaching out than is (a) may nevertheless be indicative of a good, though introverted, ego development; (c) and (d), which have an explosive quality, indicate vigor, healthy aggressiveness, dynamism, provided that these form expressions also convey a certain control and organization.

Compression betrays a harshly restricted ego given to phobic and/or obsessional compulsive disturbances, depression or schizoid withdrawal.

### IV. Integration versus Disintegration

    1. *Integration* is based on inner organization. It may appear in two ways:
       (a) as a merely synthetic or combinative function, designated as "Synthesis." The feeling for the "whole" is noticeable although the so-called artistic expression of such feeling may be poor (fig. 12);

Fig. 12.—Integration, (a) Synthesis. B. J. (age 8–5)

Fig. 13.—Integration, (b) Centricity. B. A. (age 9–2)

(b) Integration may be expressed on a level which is comparable to that of genuine art work. This expression is designated "Centricity" (fig. 13).

The beholder feels gratified that things (objects as well as their graphic equivalents) seem to be in the "right" place, in the right proportion and relationship to one another. Each of them is an indispensable part of the whole which dynamically and simultaneously is centered in both the represented object and the representing subject.

2. *Disintegration* is based on inner disorganization. It may appear in various forms of expression, all of which are lacking the synthetic function, and consequently "Centricity." Things (as well as their graphic equivalents) may be represented

Fig. 14.—Disintegration, (a) Piecemeal. B. 28. (age 6–4)

Fig. 15.—Disintegration, (b) Condensation. B. 28. (age 6–3)

(a) in a piecemeal way: things, apparently once connected, are disconnected; they fall asunder. Nothing is related to anything (fig. 14);

(b) in a contaminated way ("condensation"), i.e., two or more things are represented as one without, however, having become a oneness (fig. 15).

The product does not make any "sense," it conveys coldness, it alienates the beholder.

*Suggested Symptomatology*

The form expression of Integration would show the highest potentials for maturing, i.e., the capacity to relate and combine, to assimilate, unify, organize. Integration (especially Centricity) refers to complex and meaningful activities of mind and psyche, to the ability for sublimation. There might be a "promise" or a suggestion of originality, of a creative mind, of decisive power for self realization. Only a child with a healthily defended ego and considerable additional talents would express Centricity throughout latency. However, there may be a pitfall regarding the evaluation of this form expression. For the artistically talented child, judged merely by his art products, might give the impression of greater maturity (adjustability) than he exhibits in reality. Valuable as his talent may be for him on the emotional plane, diagnostically its validity has to be carefully scrutinized.

The symptomatology of Disintegration is obviously as serious as Integration (Centricity) seems promising. Disintegration signifies defective ego boundaries, distorted object relations, total absence of Gestaltung. For instance, in "condensation" the boundaries of one object are also the boundaries of another one, or of two or more objects. Such productions originate within primary process thinking, i.e., on an early level of development to which the subject of such products may have regressed.

### V. Realism versus Symbolism

1. *Realism* is shown when the representational element prevails over the structural one. An interest in the world of objects is dominant. There is a reality-related structural counterpart which is expressed in a kind of "mechanical" imaginative drawing. For example: boys tend to draw machines more often than human figures; girls make "pretty designs," "ornaments," "jewels."

2. *Symbolism* exists when the represented object obviously stands for something else, or when the structural element prevails throughout in a child's art work.

Criterion V essentially refers to content. However, as soon as an analysis of the content is attempted, *formal* aspects must be employed. They concern:

(a)  Choice of object(s)
   (1) animate versus inanimate objects
   (2) merely structural figures: squares, triangles, circles, etc. This form of expression is strikingly prevalent in the art work of schizophrenics[1,2] and borderline child patients.
   (3) "contamination" of objects (see Criterion IV, 2)
(b)  Interacting versus insulated objects
   Central figure (if any) in its relationship (if any) to the environment, i.e., to other figures and total space (see Criterion III)
(c)  Repetitiousness versus variety of themes
(d)  Size
   (1) the huge
   (2) the minute
   (For content analysis it may be considered that there is often a reversal of the two at work: reaction formation)
(e)  Perspective
   (1) Background (see Criterion III, 1, b)
   (2) Bird's eye view

(f)  Shading
    (1) particularly noticeable
    (2) totally absent
(g)  Color
    (The significance of color has not been dealt with in this study.)

The Diagnostic Criteria have been defined in terms of a positive and a negative aspect, respectively, with reference to human behavior and its relationship to the individual's survival. In employing the Criteria one should be conscious of their frame of reference. Moreover, one should be aware of the dynamic antinomy inseparably associated with the pairs of opposites, sometimes even within one of the pairs. There is an intrinsic tension within each pair. The relationship between one principle and its opposite becomes fully evident if one considers that a positive as well as a negative aspect may be ascribed to each of these concepts. There are elements which point to negative traits in each of the five criteria indicative of positive personality traits; and there are elements which point to positive traits in each of the five criteria indicative of negative personality traits. In order to employ such criteria legitimately one has to conceive their antinomic quality. Only against the background of the reversibility of their aspects may they function and be kept alive. In the following, the criteria will be considered under reversed aspects.

## Criteria B*

### I. Rhythm versus Rule

*1. Rhythm.* Krötzsch[18] and Prinzhorn[22] observed that occasionally the expression of rhythm appeared in cases of diminished consciousness, when the will was absent or feeble. In these cases rhythm is nothing but rhythmic motion; its essential characteristic is that there is no tendency toward any form. Krötzsch states: "Continuous rhythmic motion without attempting formation, or continuous sliding back into rhythmic motion is indicative of mental disturbance" (reference 18, page 17).

*2. Rule.* The statics inherent in the concept of rule is needed for any construction, for any steadiness. Furthermore, uniformity, as far as it is conformity, is desirable.

### II. Complexity versus Simplexity

*1. Complexity* might become too manifold, too diverse. It may express meticulousness or an undue emphasis on detail.

*2. Simplexity* being understood as *Simplicity* would have a most positive connotation. Simplicity strikes us, for instance, in the sketches of the great masters who with a simple line have brought to life a "complex" figure or landscape, etc. Such simplicity means the summation and unification of the

---

*Much of the material in Criteria B is taken from the author's original article in *Psychological Monographs*, 1945, *58*, No. 1 (Whole No. 266), Pp. 19–20, with permission of the publishers.

possible complex forms or patterns. Diversity has been overcome here in such a fashion that nothing seems lost; for the essence of the manifold is preserved and present. ("Simplexity"—Criteria A—suggests a quality which has never "overcome" the manifold items; which never has reached the level of differentiation).

### III. Expansion versus Compression

*1. Expansion* may appear as a flight of ideas, or as escaping one's self. If it is combined with dynamics which are not controlled, it may suggest states of elation, inflation, aggressiveness; in a milder and more passive form, too great a suggestibility.

*2. Compression.* There is a necessity for confinement, positively expressed in self discipline. This expression suggests good control over Id impulses.

### IV. Integration versus Disintegration

*1. Integration* is in danger of becoming stilted or stagnant.

*2. Disintegration* is necessary as a "reminder." It should be always close to integration as a possible danger; otherwise integration becomes sterile. In fact, integration and disintegration have to be intrinsically related to one another. (The disintegrated "art" of some of the modern expressionists may be considered a revolution against a stilted perfection.)

### V. Realism versus Symbolism

*1. Realism* may distract and divert the individual from his inner world.

*2. Symbolism* gives meaning to everything. "Alles Vergängliche ist nur ein Gleichnis" (Goethe). Realism is only meaningful if it is symbolic at the same time. Symbolic expression on this level speaks of artistic mastery, Gestaltung, guided intention. The primary process imagery has been integrated. Id impulses have been sublimated.

The antinomic conception of the criteria is related to Bleuler's[3,4] psychiatric concept of "ambitendency" to which he as well as Jung[15] refers in physiologic terms, saying that one should bear in mind that even the most primitive motor impulse is an antinomic (ambitendentious) one; as, for example, "in the act of extension, the flexor muscles also become innervated" (reference 15, page 167). This normal ambitendency never leads to an inhibition or prevention of the intended act; in fact "it is the indispensable preliminary requirement for its perfection and coordination" (reference 15, page 167). In regard to the form expressions it is equally true: the most undisturbed expression is an ambitendentious one. Rhythm, for example, cannot become "rhythmic motion" if the statics inherent in the concept of Rule (No. I, Criteria B) govern the rhythmic expression to a certain extent. Rule, on the other hand, will not appear as rigidity, or inertness, if the statics of the phenomenon of Rule tend to "move" or to "flow" as they do in Rhythm (No. I, Criteria A). It is the absence of ambitendency that indicates disturbance. When ambitendency is present, it results in a certain predominance of those characteristics which have been considered under the positive aspects in Criteria A. On account of this fact Criteria A are the guiding measures by which to judge.

In judging, however, there is a crucial consideration to be kept in mind. It concerns the judging of the combination of the characteristics which the examination of the drawings has yielded. That is to say, each characteristic feature has to be evaluated under the aspect of "What other traits or tendencies are combined with this feature?" To give an example: the explosive quality in No. III (c) and (d), Criteria A, has a positive value only if the drawing in which it occurs can be rated positively also on Rhythm and Integration (both Criteria A). Likewise, in other personality tests, such as the Rorschach, diagnostic evaluation does not simply take into account the specific scores per se but assesses them in the light of their interrelationship, judged quantitatively as well as qualitatively.

It appears that the consideration of "form" which is topical in the Diagnostic Criteria is being reiterated or "recurs" here on a different plane, in a global way, as it were. Namely, after each form criterion has been rated by the examiner, the sum total of the Criteria has to be responded to and evaluated once more under the aspect of "form." Judging the combination and interrelatedness of the various characteristics, traits or tendencies, the context in which they occur, and the uniqueness of the specific expressiveness in the child, means, in a comprehensive way, judging the form *niveau*.*

Since the discrimination value of the Diagnostic Criteria specifically refers to the child's ego functioning, it should be noted that the Criteria can be understood in terms of the "essential ego functions" listed by Anna Freud (reference 13, page 144) as: "testing of inner and outer reality; building up of memory; the synthesis function of the ego; and ego control of motility." Each of these designations of the ego functions can be matched with the concepts of the Diagnostic Criteria: *"Testing of inner and outer reality"* is referred to in Criterion A No. V, Realism versus Symbolism. The evaluation of the *"building up of memory"* function pertains to Criterion A No. II, Complexity versus Simplexity. The *"synthesis function of the ego"* is examined in Criterion A No. IV, Integration versus Disintegration. The term *"ego control of motility"* points perhaps in the most general, yet also most direct, way to the fact, or possibility, that one may read the child's ego state from his expressive movements. Anna Freud's statement (reference 13, page 144) that "a strict ego control of motility permanently deprives the instinctual forces in the id of their former free expression," falls completely in line with the concept "Rhythm versus Rule," Criterion No. I, its formulation and implications.

Not only in their specific formulations and meaning, but also in their deeper implications, the Diagnostic Criteria seem to bear out Anna Freud's concept of the ego functions. Her formulation of the conflict the child is exposed to by his new ego achievements which bring about an overwhelmingly great "amount of pain, discomfort and anxiety," as well as "instinct gratification . . . and some mastery of his environment" (reference 13,

---

*For further practical advice on how to use the Criteria, the reader is referred to the author's monograph.[8] There he will also find a scale for rating the adjustment and significance of children's drawings. Practical application of the Criteria has been explicitly demonstrated by the author.[10]

page 144) expresses on the part of the subject the antinomic quality objectively inherent in the Diagnostic Criteria. "Each of the new functions has its disagreeable consequences" (reference 13, page 144), as each one of the positive aspects in a pair of opposites of the Diagnostic Criteria is being counteracted by a negative aspect. The ability or inability to deal with the "disagreeable consequences" is a measure of ego strength or weakness, respectively. The conflict is not mastered by casting out what is disagreeable to the ego, but by being able to carry the negative with the positive, to unify, to assimilate both forces that oppose one another, into the ego. Therefore, ego strength may be measured by the ability to combine the opposites, to bear the conflict. For "the synthetic function of the ego . . . aims at unifying and centralizing all mental processes" (reference 13, page 144). This concept of the ego function equals Bleuler's and Jung's concept of ambitendency. It also refers to the solution of the antinomy, that is the dynamically carrying agent of the Diagnostic Criteria. For *an antinomy is the objective phenomenon of conflict subjectively experienced by the individual,* a conflict that may never be entirely resolved yet possibly be carried to an optimal solution.

At the end a word may be said concerning the frame of reference of the Diagnostic Criteria. The reader will have noticed that the concept of adjustability to which they refer connotes the concept of survival; this is a biologic concept. The implication then is that "adjustability" means here the individual's ability to adjust himself to *any* life situation. The "worth" of the given situation is not a topic of discussion here.

## References

1. Bender, L.   Art and therapy in the mental disturbances of children. *J. Nerv. ment. Dis.,* 1937, *86,* 249–263.
2. ——.   Childhood schizophrenia. *Amer. J. Orthopsychiat.,* 1947, *17,* 40–56.
3. Bleuler, E.   Zur Theorie des schizophrenen Negativismus. *Psychiatr.-Neurolog. Wochenschrift,* 1910, *12,* Nr. 18–21.
4. ——.   Über Ambivalenz (Autoreferat). *Psychiatr.-Neurolog. Wochenschrift,* 1910, *12,* Nr. 43.
5. Bronfenbrenner, U. A.   A constant frame of reference for sociometric research. *Sociometry,* 1943, *6,* 363–397.
6. Buck, J. N.   The H-T-P technique: a qualitative and quantitative scoring manual. *J. clin. Psychol., Monogr. Suppl.,* 1948, No. 5.
7. Elkisch, P.   Certain projective techniques as a means of investigating the psychodynamic status of children. Unpublished doctoral dissertation, Univer. of Michigan, 1943.
8. ——.   Children's drawings in a projective technique. *Psychol. Monogr.,* 1945, *58,* No. 1 (Whole No. 266).
9. ——.   The emotional significance of children's art work. *Childh. Educ.,* 1947, *23,* 236–241.
10. ——.   Diagnostic and therapeutic value of projective techniques. *Amer. J. Psychother., Monogr. Series,* 1948, No. 2.
11. ——.   The "Scribbling Game"—a projective method. *Nerv. Child,* 1948, *7,* 247–256.
12. ——.   Significant relationship between the human figure and the machine in the drawings of boys. *Amer. J. Orthopsychiat.,* 1952, *22,* 379–385.

13. Freud, A.   Indications for child analysis. *Psychoanal. Stud. Child*, 1945, *1*, 127–149.

14. Hartmann, H.   *Ego psychology and the problem of adaptation.* New York: Int. Univer. Press, 1958. (First published, 1939, in *Intern. Zeitschrift für Psychoanalyse.*)

15. Jung, C. G.   *Wandlungen und Symbole der Libido.* (3rd ed.) Leipzig & Wien: Franz Deuticke, 1938.

16. Klages, L.   *Handschrift und Charakter.* Leipzig: J. A. Barth, 1923.

17. Kris, E.   *Psychoanalytic explorations in art.* New York: Int. Univer. Press, 1952.

18. Krötzsch, W.   *Rhythmus und Form in der freien Kinderzeichnung.* Leipzig: A. Haase, 1917.

19. Machover, K.   *Personality projection in the drawing of the human figure.* Springfield, Ill.: C. C Thomas, 1949.

20. Münz, L., & Löwenfeld, V.   *Plastische Arbeiten Blinder.* Brünn: Rudolf M. Rohrer, 1934.

21. Olson, W. C., & Hughes, B. O.   Growth of the child as a whole. *In* Barker, R. G., Kounin, J. S., & Wright, H. F. (Eds.)   *Child behavior and development.* New York: McGraw-Hill, 1943.

22. Prinzhorn, H.   *Bildnerei der Geisteskranken.* (2nd ed.) Berlin: J. Springer, 1923.

23. Schilder, P.   *The image and appearance of the human body.* London: Kegan Paul, Trench & Trubner, 1935.

# Part VI:  The Use of Play Materials

**16**

## Free Play as a Projective Tool

LOIS B. MURPHY AND VITA KRALL

PLAY with miniature toys (suitable for constructing a "microcosmic" world) or large toys (suitable for interaction on a "macrocosmic" level) provides data on the child's relationships to and ways of dealing with things, and with persons; concepts about the world and human experiences; style of expressing himself—both bodily and verbally; methods of coping with conflicts and anxieties; creativity and capacity to restructure situations—as well as, by implication, his perceptions, preferences and needs. Thus play may well be considered the richest approach to diagnosis of the child's level of functioning. Cognitive, affective, motor aspects of response can be sorted out and judged at least roughly, or more precisely when individuals from a selected sample are being closely compared.

Since speech is not entirely necessary, and the concreteness of toys helps to avoid the ambiguities often involved in the interpretation of painting, play may be one of the methods of choice for the diagnostic study of deaf and other nonspeaking children, or any children whose problems of communication have precluded the use of intelligence tests, CAT and other approaches relying upon speech.

Sometimes autistic, schizophrenic and psychogenically retarded children can communicate much through play with toys and other objects, although many autistic children have achieved so little cathexis of objects in the external world that typical play procedures are not useful; special methods have to be devised for this group.

Since the child's use of play may express the most personal, idiosyncratic experience reflected in any medium, no standardized set of criteria, signs or scores can offer an adequate approach to the evaluation of play. Just as the analyst is constantly on the lookout for new experiences not previously discussed in the literature, the psychologist who evaluates the play of a child needs to be sensitive to the unforeseen events which may carry him closer to the experience of the child than scores on standard lists could do. Anyone undertaking to use play for general diagnostic purposes should be thoroughly familiar with the discussions by Erikson,[42,72,85,86] Peller,[57,58,103] Despert,[5,83,84] Murphy[19,91] and Loomis,[112] at a minimum; these deal with a range from normal to psychotic children and will help to prevent premature conclusions in the early stages of experience with play.

Play was recognized by Melanie Klein,[12-14] Anna Freud,[6] Erikson[85,86] and others as a major if not the major *therapeutic* medium for children before it was recognized as a major approach for evaluation and diagnosis. For this reason, most of the discussions of children's play available to clinical people are primarily concerned with the preoccupations, conflicts, disturbances and needs which are revealed through the themes of the child's play; here the child's verbalized fantasy is given the major consideration. Only a few writers (Erikson, [42,72,85,86] Murphy[19,91] and Meissner[101]) have paid attention to the larger picture of the way in which the individual child experiences and structures his world and functions within it, which is revealed in part through his play. We cannot give a detailed and comprehensive description of all the many facets of the child's behavior which we can see in play; we can simply indicate a variety of directions in which our attention may be turned with the hope of stimulating the reader to explore the available discussions of children's play, with the attached list of selected references serving as a guide.

## Factors Affecting Play

It is necessary to remember that what the child does in any play situation is influenced by the nature of the situation, the feeling tone and atmosphere of it, the materials available, the child's feeling as he enters the situation, his expectations and assumptions regarding what he is allowed to do or is free to do, and the interaction between him and the examiner, however covert or open this may be. A child will behave differently in a room full of many different kinds and levels of toys (which may be overstimulating) from the way he will behave with a more carefully selected range of toys which lend themselves to integration at only one or two levels. A child seldom plays as richly with miniature life toys when these are included in a very wide range of toys of different sizes suited to more realistic or macrocosmic or aggressive play as he does when he has an opportunity to play with miniature toys without the distractions of other things around. Similarly miniature life toys, precisely because they offer so little threat in terms of their size, may not stimulate certain kinds of aggressive behavior which large toys like Bobo, almost as big as or bigger than the child, will stimulate.

If there is no sensory material available, we are not likely to get as adequate a picture of the preferred sensory areas, the areas associated with pleasure and gratification as compared with those avoided or associated with pro-hibitions or disgust, as we can when a wide variety of sensory toy materials is made available, again without too much competition from other kinds of materials. We cannot get as clear an idea of the extent to which a child tends to impose arbitrary patterns on plastic unstructured material (such as cold cream or finger paints) as compared with a tendency to be relaxed and soothed by such media unless these materials are available. Miniature life toys, structured, realistic and evocative as they are, do not substitute for plastic or sensory materials; they provide an avenue to that portion of the real world cathected by the child and to the thoughts, feelings and fantasies he has about it and his ways of dealing with some of the problems with which it confronts him.

We cannot judge the child's preferred medium unless he is offered a wide range of media. The choice of medium in itself may be important in that a child's fear of plastic materials like finger paints, sand, water, paint, clay, plasticene, etc., may be related to other problems.

Similarly, a child's preference for a macrocosmic level of play which may be closer to reality or give room for more full-bodied acting out or interchange with the experimenter may lie behind his rejection of miniature toys where another child will prefer the latter because they are so easily mastered and lend themselves to innocuous ranges of fantasy precisely because they are too little to be dangerous and their very smallness creates a certain safe distance.

Different toys have different values, and a range of sizes, possibilities for activity, sensory qualities, and people surrogates is needed in order to tap all of the child's resources. One child will be most released by miniature toys that can easily be mastered, but such toys will seem unreal to other children who respond more to larger ones. Children who are too shy with strange adults to express their longing for affection may show it with cuddly animals or soft textures; and a capacity for healthy fantasy may be released by musical toys or those with interesting noise and sound possibilities. Children who do not cooperate well with intelligence test procedures may show certain cognitive abilities—such as an ability to organize, classify and see relationships, make an intelligible story-sequence, etc.—through their use of toys.

Some children will produce similar structures in any or all media—round or square or oblong, skewed or balanced—whether they play with blocks, fingerpaints, miniature life toys, or something else. In such instances the child may be creating a body image, for example, a curved spine or a pregnant mother (an enclosure with a baby thing inside), with every medium. Such persistence may bespeak a serious problem although we find this type of repetitiousness over short periods of time even with normal young children when under a strong impact from the environment, as when the mother is absorbed in her pregnancy or going off to the hospital to have a baby or when the child has had a severe illness.

Other children, more guided by the characteristics of the medium, perhaps even to the extent of being "stimulus bound," will produce a different structure in each medium. External data will help indicate importance of each one.

The old assumption that a child can use almost anything to express his fantasy—"he can make a doll out of a stick"—has some validity, but it is often carried much too far at the expense of giving the clinician an opportunity to make a genuinely thorough exploration of the diagnostically important structural aspects of the child's play as well as the communications which come through the themes of his dramatic acts. Only if there is a sufficiently wide range of materials and equipment available in a series of suitably planned experiences is it possible to elicit an adequate sample of the motor-energy-perceptual responses and cognitive integrations characteristic of the child's ego functioning, in addition to the content of needs, conflicts and anxiety.

The child's play will also be influenced not only by the materials and structure of the immediate situation in which he is playing, but also by the typical experiences in the community in which he lives. Children in a small town may use policemen much more rarely than children who have grown up in or near a large city. In the latter instance, in which almost every child uses policemen to represent limits, control of traffic or the authority who stands for order in life, this emphasis may not be nearly as significant for the individual problems of the child as would be true for a child living in a small town.

Similarly, rural children may play much more actively and intensely with wild animals than do city children; when a city child does play with great intensity with wild animals and in a way which is not typical for the children in his community, we have to consider more closely what this means to him. A distinction always should be made between the things that are more or less customary, habitual or everyday, for most of the children in a given area, as compared with the play actions which are unusual or individual and more likely to be important clues to special preoccupations of the particular child.

## Play Materials

In the playroom there are toys of many kinds: the "microcosmic" toys (to use Erikson's term for miniature toys which can be easily mastered and arranged to project a microcosm of the child's world or at least of the parts which have emotional salience at the moment) include miniature housekeeping and family toys, such as babies, mothers, fathers and child dolls of different sizes, furniture for every room, suitable beds and cribs, and all major items of bathroom and kitchen furniture. Town toys include cars, taxis, planes, locomotives, boats, etc. Soldiers, wild animals, or even tame animals, may be used to deal with aggressive impulses or fantasies, methods of control and ideas of punishment.

Among other kinds of play materials available, one will want to include the following general categories:

1. Materials which will permit regressive play in conjunction with miniature life toys, e.g., sand, water, clay.

2. Larger toys for more realistic play: (a) "construction transportation toys"—cars, trucks, wagons, blocks, people, etc.; (b) "doll equipment"—a mirror, blanket, nursing bottle, doll bed, people and other doll furniture.

3. Materials which will permit aggressive play—guns, rubber knives, punch bag, "Bobo the Clown."

4. "Junk toys" containing fragments such as pegs, light switches, string, tops, ball.

5. Materials which permit communication and expression—toy telephone, crayons, pencil and paper, chalk, paints, finger paints.

## The Play Session

### *Role of the Examiner*

Some of the children will be very inhibited and find it extremely difficult to play with anything at all. Sometimes they can do nothing unless the adult himself begins to play, then gradually the examiner's activity may either permit or invite the child to enter into some play activity of his own. The child's awareness of and responsiveness to the examiner will have much to do with this. The child is always very well aware of the fact that someone is with him, but sometimes he reacts to this by completely excluding the examiner as though he were trying to deny the latter's existence, while at other times he will be active in suggesting that the examiner join him in any sort of enterprise he may undertake. In contrast, some children will always attempt to include the examiner in their play. Active and passive roles of the examiner serve very different functions.

After the first introduction of the child to the toys, the role of the examiner should be quietly accepting, passive, meeting the child to the extent that the child asks for contact or for explanation, but otherwise allowing the child a free rein in order to have some picture of how he handles freedom. This permissiveness should be continued if feasible for several sessions; active participation of an adult in play alters the psychodynamics of the situation and consequently alters the play. It should be handled carefully when specific points are to be tested. If the adult takes a passive role, play is generally more spontaneous, original and representative of the child. Play is natural for the child and failure to play might be pathologic, especially in the earlier years.

### *Observing Play*

Some of the areas of the play which need to be observed have been delineated by Loomis, Hilgeman and Meyer[112]:

1. *What toys and what spaces* (in the room) are used and combined.

2. *What actions and interactions* (physical movements) occur. Child's functions in relation to objects played with or used (including skill).

3. *Affect:* emotional tone and involvement as shown in overt behavior and involvement with toy, examiner and task.

4. *Organization:* awareness of and use of the potentials and possibilities built into each toy; abilities in evaluating varieties of uses of toys and toy combinations; sensitivity to suggestive qualities of toys for socially meaningful construction and play utilization; judgment regarding reality nature of toys and toy situations, appropriateness in using them; grasp of purpose for which materials were intended; degree of inventiveness. (Probably a measure of reality testing and capacity to use association creatively and realistically.)

5. *Configurations and patterns:* spatial design and/or temporal sequence and their evident relevance to psychosexual zones and *modes* (Erikson).

6. *Content and theme:* dramatized or verbalized thematic content [reference 112, page 695].*

*Quoted, with permission of the publishers, from the *American Journal of Orthopsychiatry*.

## Evaluating a Child's Play

### *Developmental Level and Reality Situation*

The soundness of our inferences from a play session will be influenced not only by the breadth and depth of the concepts we bring to it, but also by the knowledge of normal children in the light of which we evaluate the behavior of the child we are studying. Normal children make airplanes crash, trains go off the track, doll people fight, and the like, but after the age of five or six all these activities are controlled within limits short of destructiveness. Ordinarily play sessions of normal children are free from disruptive explosions or extreme obsessive tendencies. The normal child is generally able to discharge his anger or to protect himself against his feared threat in such a way as to be free to go on to other activities or to complete a plan; it is important to watch the points at which strong feelings emerge which interfere with constructive activity of the child. To be angry, to be scared, to be jealous, are normal feelings; only if they paralyze the child, immobilize or disrupt him are they considered disturbing.

We have to be aware of the relation between the behavior of the individual child and that of other children of the same age level. Four year olds may destroy babies, mothers or female authorities, tear off tigers' tails or other appendages, or pull apart cribs; such behavior at the peak of emotional intensity in this developmental stage is not the cause for concern which it would be at the age of eight or nine. Play themes of this sort indicate the trouble spots; by themselves they do not give us a basis for evaluating the severity of the child's difficulty.

Just as it is important to watch the child's way of dealing with frustration—his ability to put up with it, cope with it, protest effectively against it or enlist adult support—so it is also important to watch the child's ability to use support and to respond to opportunities of gratification. With tense, anxious, constricted or disorganized children, it is particularly important to watch for evidences of increasing integration in response to the support and satisfactions of play sessions throughout the evaluation. A child may go through definite cycles, first able to discharge tension more freely and then quieting down toward the end of the evaluation. All such capacity for change is important in evaluating the child's ability to use help over a longer period of time.

Structural aspects of the child's play and fantasy—concern with *order* or tendency towards *disorganization*, spontaneous qualities of *clarity* as contrasted with tendencies toward *confusion*—are especially important as evidence of problems which interfere with the child's capacity for integration and smooth handling of his feelings. Here again we have to judge in terms of the degree of organization to be expected of a child of that age.

Fluidity or lack of organization may not indicate a problem in a child from subculture groups living in a fluid or disorganized way, or in a young child with short attention span and a primarily exploratory orientation toward new experience. Five people in one bed may be very unrealistic and individual for a middle or upper middle class child living in a community in which each individual has a bed of his own or at most two sleep together in one bed. In a poor family, living in a crowded area, four or five together in one bed may be an actual representation of conditions as the child knows them. Without some knowledge of the actual circumstances of the child's life, we cannot safely draw inferences regarding what is reality, what is wish, or even what is fear, unless the child is explicit in the affect which he is expressing along with the play.

Punishment experiences may be either more or less representative of actual experiences the child has lived through, they may represent fears or guilty feelings, or a need or desire for punishment as a help toward control. Evaluation of such meanings is likely to be most accurate when it is made not only in terms of the total behavior of the child in the play situation but also in relation to a comparison between the play and the actual experience of the child, when this can be ascertained.

## Ego Functioning

Although play records lack the easy scoring of tests, they often provide a wide spectrum of the range in the child's functioning. Perception, memory, communication, social interaction and reality testing, the extent of fine and gross motor control, and a variety of integrative and executive functions of the ego are seen through the range of activities appearing in a play session. Still more clearly than is possible in intelligence tests, we can watch the variations in ego functioning under the impact of frustration and disturbing emotional events or affective associations.

Intelligence tests typically give no opportunity for spontaneous constructions or creative activities. Only within narrow limits do they give an opportunity to observe deviations from realism which may be typical of the child. Play gives a wider opportunity for observing functions of reality perception, testing and manipulation, both in terms of control and of creative modification.

Thus we need to observe the child's *choice of media*, toys and other objects and their affective value to him; *forms* which he creates (abstract or concrete, realistic or unrealistic, etc.); degree of and qualities of *structure* (simplicity or complexity, fluidity or rigidity); degree of any kind of *organization;* motor, manipulative, verbal, facial *expressive patterns;* content and sequences of *fantasy* in relation to shifts in all of the above as well as shifts in the relation with the examiner, and the child's absorption in or detachment from the situation, and ways of protecting or defending himself. Strategies of keeping his distance or of eliciting support all need to be observed.

As part of clarifying the total picture of *ego functioning of the child* in play it is important to watch tempo, smoothness or jerkiness of energy discharge; rhythms and sequences of activity and passivity, and of control and impulsive action; the use and meaning to the child of different modalities of response (visual, auditory, tactual, kinesthetic, rhythmic); gratification, fear, suspicion, or conflict associated with different modalities; the areas of sharp as contrasted with confused perception and the emotional context and responses connected with each of these. Both positive and negative qualities may be used defensively; either a high degree of clarity or a casual, easy-going perceptual and response pattern may appear during the more relaxed moments with different children.

It is particularly important to watch variations in ego functioning of the child *in varying contexts of support from the examiner* as compared with times when the child is left to his own devices. Variations from the first session to the last as well as from the beginning of the hour to the end and in relation to different moods in the child's relationship with the examiner are all important.

At certain times during the play experiences there will be spontaneous frustrations—certain toys are broken, a block building will fall down, a fence will not fit together. These are good situations for watching *frustration tolerance* and the child's ability to cope with everyday disasters.

## Differential Diagnosis

Criteria for the differential diagnosis of disturbed children via their play have been discussed by Loomis, Hilgeman and Meyer[112] in the following terms:

Despite the lack of fully developed methods of objectifying them, numerous clinical impressions point to play impairment and distortion as almost universal concomitants of severe ego disorders in childhood. One confirmation of this impression is revealed in Shugart's anamneses of childhood play impairment in schizophrenic adolescents. These accounts disclose at least two major "play styles" among preschizophrenic children, which appear to be characteristic of this group and of schizophrenic children, but to be absent as dominant themes among nonpsychotic and nonretarded children.

The "autistic play style," or that seen in certain phases of early infantile autism, reveals both early impairment in the ability to play "playfully" and marked evidence of ignoring, destroying, or "perverting" toys. Typically the child was limited to repetitive and all-excluding use of moving parts or objects, concentrating on turning wheels and doorknobs, clicking switches, and/or collecting tiny fragments. Preoccupation with "small details" versus "wholes" in his life space, together with hoarding of his fractured treasures, was pronounced. Toy choice and use were perseverative in character. Inter-personal or social play other than response to skin or kinesthetic stimulation was virtually absent.

The "symbiotic play style" appeared at certain stages of the illness known as symbiotic psychosis. Characteristically the play of these children was limited almost exclusively to mimicry of parents' activities and duties, particularly the mother's. They became pathologically attached to vacuum cleaners, sewing machines and electric mixers, in contrast to generally accepted age-appropriate toys. They usually preferred to spin *large* rather than *small* wheels. They could be drawn into social play very briefly or only by the symbiotic partner.

Variations of the style did occur in the form of mixtures with each other and with age-conventional play styles. However, clear-cut patterns appeared consistently in the clinically most disturbed children [reference 112, page 691–692].*

The following groups of children have also been observed to play in characteristic fashion:

*Brain-damaged children* will often show evidences of perceptual distortion or deficiencies, motor instability, incoordination, etc. Difficulties in spatial

*Quoted, with permission of the publishers, from the *American Journal of Orthopsychiatry*.

relationships may be seen along with inability to construct things because of impaired coordination. Speech difficulties and sensory deficits appear in the play situation; the aphasic child may try to communicate by drawing, gesture and so forth.

*Retarded children* will show a lack of creativity in their play, evidence that limited fantasy life is available to them.

*Neurotic children* may be meticulous in the arrangement of toys, arrange them compulsively and anxiously, reveal areas of fears and phobias. Children who refuse to use human figures are apt to be very anxious and fearful of letting their instinctual drives find expression. The *area* covered by play is important; toys are generally spread widely by an expansive child; toys are handled in a constricted way by an inhibited child.

All these categories of illness may of course show features of the others; rarely does one see a clear-cut disease entity or one distinct style or pattern of play.

### Process of Play

The *process* characteristic of a given child's play can be meaningful and revealing. Molly comes to play because her teachers are worried about a tic; she has been blinking for a couple of months and her mother, too, is worried. The content of her play is focused on all the appendages—the cow's udders, other animals' tails. Finally she rips off the rubber tiger's tail and says, "I'm through," and leaves to blink no more. Just as important as the envy in her play is her way of handling it. Her play tackled the problem directly and developed a crescendo to the point of an aggressive climax and release without guilt.

This is quite different from the frequent sequence pattern of Robert, illustrated in the movie *This Is Robert*. With him, freedom to act out impulses also led to a crescendo; however, in his case it was often a crescendo without climax or release, but accompanied by acute anxiety and guilt so that intervention was necessary.

The process of play tells us what values play has for the child, or with what difficulties it may be necessary to help him. The process analysis tells us what the child is doing with his play—whether a discharge of aggression is followed by relaxation and constructive activity, by peace-making efforts and restoration, by fear of retaliation, by guilt, or just by more and more aggression. If the child's play gets him somewhere—so that he is freer, more constructive or happier afterward, we can infer the likelihood that he can handle and work through his own problems. If his play results in getting bogged down, repetitiously going through the same rituals again and again with no release, or if he scatters all over the place without being able to get his ideas into focus, we may conclude that he needs help. Play in therapy then may be the first medium of communication between the child and the therapist, but we would not expect play by itself to accomplish therapy in these cases.

Good Rorschach analysis includes an integration of process analysis (e.g., what is the carryover after threatening card IV; or after the initial defense or stimulus of the first card; or after the first color shock?) with the overall scoring of formal characteristics of the response and of content. This same overall integration, testing the implications found in one level of analysis against those from other levels, is also needed in the evaluation of play. In this way we can judge how a child is handling his wishes or anxieties and whether his defenses and coping techniques are functioning in a healthy way or in a way that will create more trouble for him; e.g., healthy regression is relaxing and releases energy for further growth; unhealthy regression stops growth.

The process analysis can also tell us other things about how the child copes with strong feelings. In one child's play emotionally toned themes alternate rhythmically with safe, neutral themes so that he never becomes emotionally flooded. He can shift gears emotionally, giving himself a rest from intensities until he is ready to come back and face them again. Other children have other designs for coping with intense emotion, easing in gradually, or going off on a siding, as it were, for a long period, later returning to the problem themes. Children who can do this, who can control their emotional preoccupations by shifting gears to neutral areas, resting, or taking time out to be silly, are apt to cope with their emotional problems more effectively than children who get caught in quicksand and cannot get out. When children do not spontaneously shift gears, it is possible to test the limits to see whether they are able to do so when stimulated by an adult.

# References

## General References on Play Techniques

1. Allen, F. H.  *Psychotherapy with children.* New York: Norton, 1942.
2. ——.  Some basic principles of psychotherapy with children. *Amer. J. Psychother.*, 1950, *4*, 325–334.
3. Axline, V. M.  *Play therapy.* Boston: Houghton Mifflin Co., 1947.
4. ——.  Play therapy experiences as described by child participants. *J. consult. Psychol.*, 1950, *14*, 53–63.
5. Despert, J. L.  Play therapy. *Nerv. Child*, 1948, *7*, 287–295.
6. Freud, A.  Introduction to the technique of child analysis. *Nerv. & ment. Dis. Monogr.*, 1928, No. 48.
7. ——, Hartmann, H., & Kris, E. (Eds.)  *The psychoanalytic study of the child.* Vol. 3/4. New York: Int. Univer. Press, 1949.
8. Hambridge, G., Jr.  Structured play therapy. *Amer. J. Orthopsychiat.*, 1955, *25*, 601–617.
9. Harms, E.  Play diagnosis: preliminary considerations for a sound approach. *Nerv. Child*, 1948, *7*, 233–246.
10. Hartley, R. E., Frank, L. K., & Goldenson, R. M.  *Understanding children's play.* New York: Columbia Univer. Press, 1952.
11. Jackson, L., & Todd, K. M.  *Child treatment and the therapy of play.* London: Methuen, 1946.
12. Klein, M.  *The psychoanalysis of children.* London: Hogarth Press, 1932.
13. ——.  *Contributions to psycho-analysis, 1921–1945.* London: Hogarth Press, 1948.
14. ——.  The psychoanalytic play technique. *Amer. J. Orthopsychiat.*, 1955, *25*, 223–237.

15. Lebo, D.   The development of play as a form of therapy: from Rousseau to Rogers. *Amer. J. Psychiat.*, 1955, *112*, 418–422.
16. Liss, E.   Play techniques in child analysis. *Amer. J. Orthopsychiat.*, 1936, *6*, 17–22.
17. Lowenfeld, M.   The theory and use of play in the psychotherapy of childhood. *J. ment. Sci.*, 1938, *84*, 1057–1058.
18. Moustakas, C. E.   *Children in play therapy.* New York: McGraw-Hill, 1953.
19. Murphy, L. B., & associates.   *Personality in young children.* New York: Basic Books, 1956. 2 vols.
20. Rogerson, C. H.   *Play therapy in childhood.* New York: Oxford Univer. Press, 1939.
21. Solomon, J. C.   Trends in orthopsychiatric therapy. IV. Play technique. *Amer. J. Orthopsychiat.*, 1948, *18*, 402–413.
22. ——.   Play technique as a differential therapeutic medium. *Nerv. Child.*, 1948, *7*, 296–300.
23. Taft, J.   *The dynamics of therapy in a controlled relationship.* New York: Macmillan, 1933.
24. Tallman, F. F., & Goldensohn, L. N.   Play techniques. *Amer. J. Orthopsychiat.*, 1941, *11*, 551–561.
25. Todd, K. M.   The therapy of play. *Ment. Health, Lond.*, 1944, *5*, 3–7.
26. Weiss-Frankl, A. B.   Play interviews with nursery school children. *Amer. J. Orthopsychiat.*, 1941, *11*, 33–40.
27. Woltmann, A. G.   Play and related techniques. *In* Brower, D., & Abt, L. E. (Eds.) *Progress in clinical psychology*, Vol. 2. New York: Grune & Stratton, 1956. Pp. 180–196.
28. Wright, D. G.   Dickie and his trains: an example of the therapeutic function of play. *Menninger Quart.*, 1955, *9* (2), 9–18.

## Factors Affecting Play

29. Ackerman, N. W.   Constructive and destructive tendencies in children. *Amer. J. Orthopsychiat.*, 1937, *7*, 301–319.
30. ——.   Constructive and destructive tendencies in children: an experimental study. *Amer. J. Orthopsychiat.*, 1938, *8*, 265–285.
31. Amen, E. W., & Renison, N.   A study of the relationship between play patterns and anxiety in young children. *Genet. Psychol. Monogr.*, 1954, *50*, 3–41.
32. Ammons, C. H., & Ammons, R. B.   Aggression in doll-play: interviews of two- to six-year-old white males. *J. genet. Psychol.*, 1953, *82*, 205–213.
33. Ammons, R. B., & Ammons, H. S.   Parent preferences in young children's doll-play interviews. *J. abnorm. soc. Psychol.*, 1949, *44*, 490–505.
34. Bach, G. R.   Father-fantasies and father-typing in father-separated children. *Child. Developm.*, 1946, *17*, 63–80.
35. ——, & Bremer, G.   Projective father fantasies of pre-adolescent, delinquent children. *J. Psychol.*, 1947, *24*, 3–17.
36. Barker, R., Dembo, T., & Lewin, K.   Frustration and regression: an experiment with young children. *Univer. Iowa Stud. Child Welf.*, 1941, *18*, (1).
37. Baruch, D. W.   Aggression during doll play in a preschool. *Amer. J. Orthopsychiat.*, 1941, *11*, 252–260.
38. Bender, L., & Schilder, P.   Form as a principle in the play of children. *J. genet. Psychol.*, 1936, *49*, 254–261.
39. Bonte, E. P., & Musgrove, M.   Influences of war as evidenced in children's play. *Child Developm.*, 1943, *14*, 179–200.
40. Bookbinder, K. F.   The relation of social status and punishment as observed in stories obtained with the Driscoll playkit. *Dissertation Abstr.*, 1955, *15*, 1252–1253.
41. Bender, L., Keiser, S., & Schilder, P.   Studies in aggressiveness. *Genet. Psychol. Monogr.*, 1936, *18*, 361–564.
42. Erikson, E. H.   Sex differences in the play configuration of preadolescents. *Amer. J. Orthopsychiat.*, 1951, *21*, 667–692.

43. Finch, H. M.   Young children's concepts of parent roles. *J. Home Econ.*, 1955, *47*, 99–103.

44. Gewirtz, J. L.   An investigation of aggressive behavior in the doll play of young Sac and Fox Indian children and a comparison to the aggression of midwestern white pre-school children. *Amer. Psychologist*, 1950, *5*, 294–295 (Abstract).

45. Graham, T. F.   Doll play phantasies of Negro and white primary school children. *J. clin. Psychol.*, 1955, *11*, 29–33.

46. ——.   Doll play phantasies of Negro and white primary school children. *Rev. Univer. Ottawa*, 1955, *23*, 229–242.

47. Hollenberg, E., & Sperry, M.   Some antecedents of aggression and effects of frustra-tion in doll play. *Personality*, 1951, *1*, 32–43.

48. Holway, A. R.   Early self-regulation of infants and later behavior in play interviews. *Amer. J. Orthopsychiat.*, 1949, *19*, 612–623.

49. Honzik, M. P.   Sex differences in the occurrence of materials in the play constructions of preadolescents. *Child Developm.*, 1951, *22*, 15–36.

50. Isch, M. J.   Fantasied mother-child interaction in doll play. *J. genet. Psychol.*, 1952, *81*, 233–258.

51. Korner, A. F.   *Some aspects of hostility in young children.* New York: Grune & Strat-ton, 1949.

52. Lebo, D.   The relationship of response categories in play therapy to chronological age. *J. child Psychiat.*, 1952, *2*, 330–336.

53. Levin, H., & Sears, R. R.   Identification as a determinant of doll play aggression. *Child Developm.*, 1956, *27*, 135–153.

54. ——, & Turgeon, V. F.   The influence of the mother's presence on children's doll play aggression. *J. abnorm. soc. Psychol.*, 1957, *55*, 304–308.

55. Merrill, B.   A measurement of mother-child interaction. *J. abnorm. soc. Psychol.*, 1946, *41*, 37–49.

56. Moustakas, C. E., & Schalock, H. D.   An analysis of therapist-child interaction in play therapy. *Child Developm.*, 1955, *2*, 143–157.

57. Peller, L. E.   Libidinal phases, ego development, and play. *Psychoanal. Study Child*, 1954, *9*, 178–198.

58. ——.   Libidinal development as reflected in play. *Psychoanalysis*, 1955, *3* (3), 3–12.

59. Phillips, R.   Doll play as a function of the realism of the materials and the length of the experimental session. *Child Developm.*, 1945, *16*, 123–143.

60. Pintler, M. H.   Doll play as a function of the experimenter-child interaction and the initial organization of materials. *Child Developm.*, 1945, *16*, 145–166.

61. ——, Phillips, R., & Sears, R. R.   Sex differences in the projective doll play of pre-school children. *J. Psychol.*, 1946, *21*, 73–80.

62. Robinson, E. F.   Doll play as a function of the doll family constellation. *Child De-velopm.*, 1946, *17*, 99–119.

63. Sears, P. S.   Doll play aggression in normal young children: influence of sex, age, sibling status, father's absence. *Psychol. Monogr.*, 1951, *65*, No. 6 (Whole No. 323).

64. Sears, R. R.   Symposium on genetic psychology. III. Effects of frustration and anxiety on fantasy aggression. *Amer. J. Orthopsychiat.*, 1951, *21*, 498–505.

65. ——.   Influence of methodological factors on doll play performance. *Child Developm.*, 1947, *18*, 190–197.

66. ——, Pintler, M. H., & Sears, P. S.   Effect of father separation on pre-school chil-dren's doll play aggression. *Child Developm.*, 1946, *17*, 219–243.

67. Siegel, A. E.   Aggressive behavior of young children in the absence of an adult. *Child Developm.*, 1957, *28*, 371–378.

68. Winstel, B.   The use of a controlled play situation in determining certain effects of maternal attitudes on children. *Child Developm.*, 1951, *22*, 299–311.

69. Wright, M. E.   Constructiveness of play as affected by group organization and frus-tration. *Charact. & Pers.*, 1942, *11*, 40–49.

70. Yarrow, L. J.   The effect of antecedent frustration on projective play. *Psychol. Monogr.*, 1948, *62*, No. 6 (Whole No. 293).

## Play Materials

71. Driscoll, G. P.　*The Driscoll play kit.* New York: Psychological Corp.
72. Erikson, E. H.　*Childhood and society.* New York: Norton, 1950. (Chapter VI, Toys and Reasons).
73. Lebo, D.　The expressive value of toys recommended for nondirective play therapy. *J. clin. Psychol.*, 1955, *11*, 144–148.

## Specialized Approaches to the Evaluation of Play

74. Ammons, C. H., & Ammons, R. B.　Research and clinical applications of the doll play interview. *J. Pers.*, 1952, *21*, 85–90.
75. Ammons, R. B.　Reactions in a projective doll play interview of white males two to six years of age to differences in skin color and facial features. *J. genet. Psychol.*, 1950, *76*, 323–341.
76. Axline, V. M.　Play therapy procedures and results. *Amer. J. Orthopsychiat.*, 1955, *25*, 618–626.
77. Bach, G. R.　Young children's play fantasies. *Psychol. Monogr.*, 1945, *59*, No. 2 (Whole No. 272).
78. Bühler, C.　National differences in "World Test" projection patterns. *J. proj. Tech.*, 1952, *16*, 42–55.
79. ——, & Kelley, G.　*The World Test. A measurement of emotional disturbance.* New York: Psychological Corp., 1941.
80. Conn, J. H.　The child reveals himself through play: the method of the play interview. *Ment. Hyg., N. Y.*, 1939, *23*, 49–69.
81. ——.　The play interview. A method of studying children's attitudes. *Amer. J. Dis. Child.*, 1939, *58*, 1199–1214.
82. ——.　The play interview as an investigative and therapeutic procedure. *Nerv. Child*, 1948, *7*, 257–286.
83. Despert, J. L.　Technical approaches used in the study and treatment of emotional problems in children. *Psychiat. Quart.*, 1937, *11*, 111–130; 267–294; 491–506; 677–693.
84. ——.　A method for the study of personality reactions in pre-school age children by means of analysis of their play. *J. Psychol.*, 1940, *9*, 17–29.
85. Erikson, E. H.　Configurations in play—clinical notes. *Psychoanal. Quart.*, 1937, *6*, 138–214.
86. ——.　Studies in the interpretation of play. I. Clinical observation of play disruption in young children. *Genet. Psychol. Monogr.*, 1940, *22*, 557–671.
87. Hartley, E. L., & Schwartz, S. A.　A pictorial-doll play approach for the study of children's intergroup attitudes. *Int. J. Opin. Attitude Res.*, 1951, *5*, 261–270.
88. Henry, J., & Henry, Z.　Doll play of Pilagá Indian children. *Res. Monogr. Amer. Orthopsychiat. Assoc.*, 1944, No. 4.
89. Lebo, D.　The present status of research on nondirective play therapy. *J. consult. Psychol.*, 1953, *17*, 177–183.
90. ——.　Quantification of the nondirective play therapy process. *J. genet. Psychol.*, 1955, *8*, 375–378.
91. Lerner, E., & Murphy, L. B. (Eds.)　Methods for the study of personality in young children. *Monogr. Soc. Res. Child Developm.*, 1941, *6*, No. 4 (Whole No. 30).
92. Levy, D. M.　Use of play technique as experimental procedure. *Amer. J. Orthopsychiat.*, 1933, *3*, 266–277.
93. ——.　Hostility patterns in sibling rivalry experiments. *Amer. J. Orthopsychiat.*, 1936, *6*, 183–257.
94. ——.　Studies in sibling rivalry. *Res. Monogr. Amer. Orthopsychiat. Assoc.*, 1937, No. 2.
95. ——.　"Release therapy" in young children. *Psychiatry*, 1938, *1*, 387–390.
96. ——.　Sibling rivalry studies in children of primitive groups. *Amer. J. Orthopsychiat.*, 1939, *9*, 205–214.

97. ——. Hostility patterns. *Amer. J. Orthopsychiat.*, 1943, *13*, 441–461.

98. ——. *Maternal overprotection*. New York: Columbia Univer. Press, 1943.

99. Lowenfeld, M. The World pictures of children: a method of recording and studying them. *Brit. J. med. Psychol.*, 1939, *18*, 65–101.

100. Lynn, D. B. Development and validation of a structured Doll Play Test for children. *The Quart. Bull., Indiana Univer. Med. Center*, Jan., 1955.

101. Meissner, P. B. The miniature-toy play situation. *In* Witkin, H. A., Lewis, H. B., Hertzman, M., Machover, K., Meissner, P. B., & Wapner, S. (Eds.) *Personality through perception*. New York: Harper, 1954. Pp. 376–425.

102. Munro, L. Steps in ego-integration observed in play-analysis. *Int. J. Psycho-Anal.*, 1954, *35*, 202–205.

103. Peller, L. E. Models of children's play. *Ment. Hyg., N.Y.*, 1952, *36*, 66–83.

104. Rosenzweig, S., & Shakow, D. Play technique in schizophrenia and other psychoses. I. Rationale. II. An experimental study of schizophrenic constructions with play materials. *Amer. J. Orthopsychiat.*, 1937, *7*, 32–47.

105. Solomon, J. C. Active play therapy. *Amer. J. Orthopsychiat.*, 1938, *8*, 479–498.

106. ——. Active play therapy. *Amer. J. Orthopsychiat.*, 1940, *10*, 763–782.

107. Taft, J. An experiment in a therapeutically limited relationship with a seven-year-old girl. *Psychoanal. Rev.*, 1932, *19*, 361–417.

108. Traill, P. M. An account of Lowenfeld technique in a child guidance clinic, with a survey of therapeutic play technique in G. B. & U. S. A. *J. ment. Sci.*, 1945, *91*, 43–78.

## *Differential Diagnosis*

109. Axline, V. M. Mental deficiency—symptom or disease? *J. consult. Psychol.*, 1949, *13*, 313–327.

110. Johnson, E. Z. The clinical use of Raven's Progressive Matrices to appraise potential for progress in play therapy: a study of institutionalized mentally and educationally retarded children. *Amer. J. Orthopsychiat.*, 1953, *23*, 391–405.

111. Kanner, L. Play investigations and play treatment of children's behavior disorders. *J. Pediat.*, 1940, *17*, 533–546.

112. Loomis, E. A., Hilgeman, L. M., & Meyer, L. R. Childhood psychosis. 2. Play patterns as nonverbal indices of ego functions: a preliminary report. *Amer. J. Orthopsychiat.*, 1957, *27*, 691–700.

113. Maisner, E. A. Contributions of play therapy techniques to total rehabilitative design in an institution for high-grade mentally deficient and borderline children. *Amer. J. ment. Def.*, 1950, *55*, 235–250.

114. Meister, D. Adjustment of children as reflected in play performance. *J. genet. Psychol.*, 1948, *73*, 141–155.

115. Miller, H. E. Play therapy for the institutional child. *Nerv. Child*, 1948, *7*, 311–317.

116. Miller, H., & Baruch, D. W. Psychosomatic studies of children with allergic manifestations. *Psychosom. Med.*, 1948, *10*, 275–278.

117. ——, & ——. A study of hostility in allergic children. *Amer. J. Orthopsychiat.*, 1950, *20*, 506–519.

118. ——, & ——. The emotional problems of childhood and their relation to asthma. *A.M.A.J. Dis Child.*, 1957, *93*, 242–245.

119. Moustakas, C. E. Situational play therapy with normal children. *J. consult. Psychol.*, 1951, *15*, 225–230.

120. ——. Emotional adjustment and the play therapy process. *J. genet. Psychol.*, 1955, *8*, 79–99.

121. ——. The frequency and intensity of negative attitudes expressed in play therapy: a comparison of well-adjusted and disturbed children. *J. genet. Psychol.*, 1955, *86*, 309–325.

122. Ricciuti, F. B. A study in differential diagnosis using a modified play technique. *Train. Sch. Bull.*, 1954, *51*, 135–145.

123. von Staabs, G.  *Der Scenotest.* (The Sceno-test.) Stuttgart: S. Hirzel, 1951.
124. ———.  Stotterheilung durch Wiederholung der einzelnen kindlichen Entwicklungs-
phasen im Erlebnis einer Scenotest-Spiel-therapie. (Treatment of stuttering by repetition of single child growth phases in experience with the Sceno-test play therapy.)
*Psyche*, 1952 (Feb.), 688–706.

# 17

# Spontaneous Puppetry by Children as a Projective Method

ADOLF G. WOLTMANN

PUPPETRY is as old as the folk song, the fairy tale and the folk dance. It has been known to and practiced by most cultures. Puppetry is composed of miniature reproductions and approximations of human beings, animals and imaginary creatures who appear to be lifelike through the movements and speech of the puppeteer or manipulator.

Puppets are often thought of as toys or play things for children. This is a misconception because, through the ages, puppets have been made and played by adults for various audiences which often included children. There have been, of course, exceptions in which children themselves found pleasure and satisfaction through giving puppet shows, as we know, for instance, from the written accounts of Goethe and George Sand. However, by and large, puppetry has been the domain of adults who determined what children would like. This line of thinking is not new.

Many theories about the nature of children's play, as the present author[8] has pointed out, have been expounded by grown-ups who approached this topic from the point of view of the adult philosopher and educator, forgetting that the growing child goes through cycles of maturation in which each new play activity is an enlightening upward thrust and a step closer to a fuller perception and mastery of the environment. Such speculations likewise do not consider the fact that the growing child not only grows physically, but also emotionally. A fuller understanding of children's play activities, which includes playing with puppets, must go hand in hand with a thorough knowledge of child development. It should take its clues from the child's activities and not be based on a preconceived idea as to what children should play.

The use of puppetry as a projective method in therapy has been described by Woltmann.[6] For the greater part he deals with puppet shows written and played by adults for children. The reactions of children quoted by him are the expressions of children to the adult puppet show. It is true that each show was modified and rewritten numerous times to suit the needs, desires and understanding of children, but the fact remains that the impetus to write these plays, to make the puppets and to construct the stage was the work of adults. Haworth[4] records the reactions of children to a filmed puppet show in her study, but here also the children express their emotional involvement to a puppet show produced by adults.

## Varieties of Puppets

Before going into a discussion of puppet plays by children, a few words about puppets themselves are necessary. Human-like figures or imaginary creatures, whether moved by sticks, strings or hands are called collectively "puppets." This is a generic term which leaves out important characteristics specific to each type of puppet. Puppets are divided into shadow puppets, rod puppets, marionettes and hand puppets. Shadow and rod puppets have not been too popular in this country and are therefore excluded from this discussion.

The marionette is a string puppet. It is the perfect puppet in the sense that it has a full body and is in full view of the audience. Its operation requires a very well developed coordination of both hands to make its motions appear to be lifelike. The marionette, like all puppets, being made of wood or *papier-mâché* and cloth, has no life of its own but, due to the fact that it hangs and is directed from above, does follow the laws of gravity. It is capable of pendular motions which can interfere with the action of the puppeteer. Lifelike action has to be projected onto the marionette from the outside by moving strings.

The hand puppet, in contrast to the marionette, consists of a head and a garment from which the arms and hands protrude. It is not a complete puppet like the marionette, and never in full view of the audience. However, whereas the string puppet has a pseudo-life projected onto it from outside, the hand puppet contains something inside of it which is organic and living: the hand of the puppeteer. It is this living hand which makes the puppet a part of the living person who operates it. It is this physical closeness to the puppeteer which enables the hand puppet to be simple, direct, obvious and forceful in its movements. What the hand puppet lacks in puppet-like completeness, it makes up for in its wider range of movement possibilities. Since there are no strings attached, the hand puppet can walk, amble, crawl, run, jump, lie down, wave its hands, fight, pick up and hold objects, shake hands, stroke the face of another puppet, kiss, dance, and perform many lifelike motions.

The simplicity of the hand puppet's anatomy is another reason why this type of puppet is ideally suited for spontaneous plays produced by children. Instead of spending weeks and even months in the careful construction of a marionette, it takes minutes to make a hand puppet. The *Puppet Theatre Handbook* by Marjorie Batchelder[1] and the New York City Board of Education Series on *Puppetry in the Curriculum*[2] offer many valuable suggestions about the construction of diverse types of puppets. Paper bags, vegetables, rubber balls and stockings form ready bases for puppet heads. A piece of cloth that covers the hand may suffice as a costume. Ordinary rag dolls can be altered so that a child can easily place his whole hand into the back and manipulate the (doll) puppet. This type of puppet cannot move its arms, but it certainly is capable of a lot of action. The same simplicity holds true for stagecraft. Anything that hides the puppeteer from sight, be it the back of a high chair or a blanket stretched between two door posts, will serve the purpose.

## Projective Aspects of Puppetry

Let us briefly remind ourselves that we are here concerned with puppet shows played by children. A great deal of the child's play is on a "make-believe" level in which fantasy and wishful thinking fill the gap left open by reality. The less structured the stimulus, the greater are the possibilities for projection. This basic tenet, which holds for all projective techniques certainly also applies to puppet shows, whether played for children, or produced by children themselves. Children who play cowboys and Indians, for instance, do not need horses, a stage coach and a landscape covered with sagebrush and cacti. They are merely acting out a human conflict between might and right, between skill and endurance, between aggression and defense. A piece of wood or an extended forefinger serves as a gun. Sounds imitate the whizzing by of bullets. Dramatic gestures accompany the act of being hit and falling to the ground. Similarly, in puppetry played by children, it is neither the artistically created puppet, nor the elaborate stage, nor the beautifully painted scenery that makes a puppet play a success. It is the dramatic portrayal of an idea that contains the core of a successful puppet show.

Yet, acting alone without sound is pantomime. Children are not quiet in their play activities and naturally are not silent when they let their puppet characters act out situations and episodes. We must remember that children are not born with a perfect knowledge of speech. It takes a number of years before the child acquires a somewhat adequate vocabulary and attains mastery of a meaningful, sustained and continuous level of verbal communication. It thus follows that a puppet show put on by a five year old child cannot exhibit the same smooth, modulated speech pattern that we may expect from a 10 year old child. On the contrary, the puppet show of a younger child usually contains more action and less talk than that of a youngster twice his age. If puppet shows by children are to be used as projective methods, then they certainly should be spontaneous and un-rehearsed. The child, who speaks for his puppet, uses his normal mode of verbal expression.

Several important elements, necessary for using puppet shows by children as a projective method, have been mentioned. It was demonstrated that the hand puppet is best suited for this kind of activity, because it is easily made and manipulated. It is guided by the hand of the puppeteer and therefore capable of direct, obvious, simple and forceful action. Taken into account also is the fact that the child goes through cycles of physical maturation which include the arms and the hands. Between the grasping reflex in infancy and learning to hold and to properly manipulate a spoon, between the combing of the hair and the tying of shoelaces lie periods of trial and error in which the hand must learn to move, reach, bend and twist. Before the child realizes that the hand is the social mediator between himself and the environment, he more often than not uses these "appendages" as a means of aggression and defense. Since his hand is the moving guide inside the puppet, he will use the puppet in accordance with his own level of maturation. This explains why children on the nursery school, or kindergarten, level often use puppets as an extended boxing glove and engage in endlessly repetitious hitting and beating of each other. In contrast, the moving of a string puppet requires thorough coordination of the movement of both hands, something which seldom is acquired before pre-adolescence.

Another important reason why hand puppet shows by children can be so readily used as a projective method lies in the fact that the simplicity of the puppet itself, the plain, makeshift stage, and the absence of scenery allow the "make-believe" element, so vital to the child's play, to appear.

The emphasis is on spontaneity. Correct, dramatic speech is not a prerequisite for puppet shows played by children. As a matter of fact, the puppet, the stage, the actions and the spoken word are only a means to an end. They are the media through which the child expresses and brings to a tangible level some of his ideas, concepts, modes of action, perceptions and levels of understanding, as well as his fears, his anxieties and his reaching out for love and acceptance. In drawing pictures the child achieves this through a combination of lines, forms and color. The handling of plastic material adds a three dimensional quality to his creation which gives it a more realistic effect. In playing with toys, whether doll house or so-called "world" or environmental toys (soldiers, airplanes, cars, animals, etc.), the child puts toys into relationships to each other and plays by projecting action into the play set up. In giving puppet shows the child actively enters into the play by using either all of himself or at least part of himself, his hand. The combination of his hand movements and his voice is then the carrier of an idea. It does not matter whether or not the child follows a carefully constructed dramatic build-up that leads to a climax. Important is the fact that the child feels free enough to let the puppets act for him what he thinks, how he would like to handle situations, or how he would meet and overcome obstacles.

Woltmann[7,8] states that children's play activities are a specific kind of language through which the child communicates his concepts and attitudes, and in which movement, acoustics, selection of play patterns, duration and intensity of the play, together with verbalizations, take the place of grammar, syntax and vocabulary of the spoken language. In order to use puppet plays given by children successfully as a projective method, the observer must first learn to understand this specific language of the child.

Suppose a nursery school child uses puppets like a boxing glove and engages in endless hitting. What inferences can the observer draw from this activity? In the first place, one would like to know whether this child is always aggressive, or whether it is the puppet that provokes this type of behavior. Secondly, is it just any puppet which brings forth this type of aggressive behavior, or is it a specific type such as a mother figure, or the witch, or perhaps a crocodile which is responsible for the aggression? Is the child a poor loser? Does he continue to fight in the face of obstacles? Are there some puppets of which he is afraid? With which puppet does he identify? Does the nursery child react, in his puppet handling (you could hardly call it a puppet play), to all of the children in his group? Is the nursery group—where the child is among his contemporaries—a safe place to express aggression, in contrast to the home, where such behavior might not be tolerated? If demonstrated to him, could the child stop his aggressive behavior and change to a more sociable, loving handling of the puppet? And last but not least, it must be remembered that at the nursery school level the child's motor apparatus has not yet developed sufficiently to allow for a smooth coordination of the hand, wrist and fingers. By the same token the child's verbalizations may not be too clear or logical in sequence and may contain many repetitions. The experienced child worker knows that repetition is a part of the child's learning process through which mastery is achieved. An evaluation of the child's handling of puppets should be guided by a statement of Hartley,[3] which says:

No behavior on the part of any child is truly random, and no fragment of behavior can be fully understood by itself. Nor is there a rigid set of rules for interpreting children's play, because for each child the materials he uses have unique values dependent on associations with his past and on his ability to project meaning and use symbols [reference 3, page iii].

Like other projective methods, puppet shows given by children can be used both diagnostically and therapeutically. Puppetry is primarily a group activity and should be used as such. There will be a few remarks later on in which the application of puppet handling and puppet shows in individual settings are discussed.

One would think that children, once they have witnessed a puppet show given by adult puppeteers, would repeat the themes in their own play activities with puppets. The experiences of the author do not bear this out. Regardless of how many puppet shows children have watched and reacted to, in their own handling of the puppets they invariably pick out those characters and scenes which made the greatest impressions on them. Many children were observed identifying with the crocodile, for instance, and using this puppet animal as an overgrown mouth that could bite and swallow. Others let their aggression out on the witch by killing her over and over again.

## Illustrative Protocols

### Children with Special Disabilities

A five year old boy, whose physical growth had been retarded, took great delight in playing the giant in endless repetitions. He liked this puppet because, through identification with and projecting onto himself the giant's physical prowess, he could, in his play, carry sacks of coal into houses like his father, and he also could beat up everybody.

A nine year old deaf girl, who had been rejected by her parents since early childhood, played out scenes in which the crocodile would attack and carry away in its mouth the mother who neglected her baby.

A 10 year old girl had been admitted to the Children's Observation Ward of Bellevue Hospital with a history of doubtful epileptic attacks. The child herself denied having suffered such attacks, and none were observed during several weeks in which the girl was a patient. One day this girl and a friend of hers decided to give a puppet show. She played the role of a puppet boy, while the other girl manipulated the (puppet) monkey. Both puppets wandered aimlessly around the puppet-stage, presumably playing hookey from school. They entered a make-believe fruit store with the intention of stealing some apples. Just then, the boy puppet called the monkey puppet for help, stating that he was not feeling well. Before the amazed author, this girl acted out, through her puppet, the sensations of an aura and an epileptic fit. The girl herself was physically well at this point and did not suffer a seizure.

What she played out on the puppet stage was clearly the projection of a past experience, of something that actually had happened to her, and which she could not have known either through having read about it or having observed in someone else.

## Group Activity

Many of the children who had been cared for at the Observation Ward were transferred to a newly opened Children's Division of a state hospital. For about one year the author worked part-time at this state hospital, having close contact with the very same children who knew him and who had seen his puppet shows at the Observation Ward in the city. When these children were encouraged to give their own puppet shows, they did not act out the same dramatic plots they previously had seen. Instead, the doctors, nurses, teachers, occasional visitors and the children themselves were portrayed through puppets. Adjustments to the state hospital routine, violations of hospital rules, attempted escapes, objections to medical and psychiatric treatment and aggressive conflicts with teachers, visitors and other children formed a never-ending source of material for their puppet shows.

Spontaneous puppet shows were supervised by the author in a New York City Junior High School for girls in the hope that these adolescents, most of whom had severe personality problems, would expose through their own puppet shows some of the roots of their maladjustments. The school was located in a slum area whose population was composed of a mixture of Jewish, Italian, Negro and Puerto Rican families. After being briefly instructed about the possibilities of hand puppet acting, these girls, ranging from 12 to 15 years of age, made up their own shows. Usually a few girls would gather around in a corner of the class room, hold a brief discussion and, without benefit of written notes, proceed to put on a show. Although the author had played a number of his own puppet shows for these girls, they did not respond to them. Instead, they acted out, through the puppets, their own most pressing problems.

The spontaneous puppet shows of Jewish and Negro girls were repetitions of scenes in which the parents felt that their daughters were treated unfairly at school, that their children were entitled to better report cards and that they should be promoted to the next higher grade. Invariably, on the puppet stage, the parents would come to school, argue with and then beat up the teacher and the principal.

Most of the Italian girls would portray an unfeeling, dictatorial father who would forbid his daughter to go out after dark. The crying girl would then be comforted by the mother, who would tell her child that she would leave the back door open so that the girl could sneak into the house without the father's knowledge.

The Puerto Rican girls displayed social contempt. In one of their shows the witch casts a spell on a Puerto Rican girl and on a girl from a very well-to-do neighborhood. The Puerto Rican girl goes to the "rich" house and is dined and wined. The financially rich and socially prominent girl goes to a Puerto Rican family where she too is invited for dinner. However, instead of soup, these girls serve her urine and tell her that the main dish consists of a special variety of Puerto Rican rice. Only the Puerto Rican girls know that the unsuspecting "rich" girl is eating their feces.

## Individual Use of Puppets

It was stated above that puppetry is a group activity and therefore most effective when the child puppeteer plays to an audience. Are spontaneous puppet plays effective in individual therapy in which only the child and the therapist are present? Yes, they are, provided the therapist first introduces the puppets to the child and demonstrates how the puppets move, act and use language. It is not important that a stage be used or that the child and the therapist handle the puppets as they would toys. Puppetry in such a setting is not entertainment but a medium through which the child can express some of his feelings. To say something is one thing, to combine the spoken word with action is another.

The author was painfully reminded of this many years ago when a 10 year old boy under his care, who acted out his relationship with his father through puppets, decided to reverse the situation. Previously, the therapist had to play the father, bawl out the boy and even spank him. As soon as this child took over the father puppet, he gave a vicious, vigorous beating to the boy puppet and to the puppeteer. It was not the puppet show per se, but the amount of aggression towards the father which provided the opening wedge into this boy's problems.

The mother of a nine year old girl wanted treatment for her child because, in her own words, "We don't get along with each other." The mother could not state specific situations, nor could she give reasons why she wanted Mary to be treated. Mary was found to be an intelligent, perceptive person with an excellent school record. Her drawings of persons were the stereotype "Betty Boop" type of female glorification, and her doll house play was unimaginative and unrevealing. One day she was shown the puppets. Immediately she selected a girl puppet, the witch and a boy puppet. From then on, for a period of several weeks, she played out, intensely, situations in which the girl (puppet) was sleeping. The witch would come and carry her away, presumably to eat her. In some of these plays the girl would try to talk the witch out of eating her, in other versions she would cry for help. The puppeteer-therapist, with the boy puppet on his hand, would then rush to the rescue, kill the witch and free the girl. The important part in this "Hansel and Gretel" reversal was the fact that the girl showed great fears about the witch. Little by little, she was able to talk about her relationship to her mother, which was based on a fear that the mother would either do away with Mary or ignore her. The mother's noncommittal attitude and Mary's inability to verbalize about this relationship now became clear. There was no love emanating from the mother to the child. Mary was aware of this lack of love but could not express it. She felt that she was responsible for being rejected by the mother. At the same time she retaliated with aggression towards the maternal neglect.

A five year old boy was brought into treatment because he showed signs of sibling rivalry towards his six month old baby sister. He picked out a boy puppet and a little baby doll which the author used in his *Rock-A-Bye, Baby* show. This boy took off the baby's clothes and placed her on a chair. Then, with the boy puppet on his right arm, he would stand in front of the chair, grimace, laugh out loud and talk unintelligibly to an imaginary audience. At first he refused to tell what was going on, but after several repetitions of such scenes he told the therapist that the baby girl was in a cage in the zoo. Since she wore no clothes, all the visitors could see her "pee-pee." Because the baby girl had no place to hide, the visitors would watch her urinate and defecate. It was through this spontaneous puppet acting that the whole problem of sibling rivalry could be discussed with Charles. First, the working through was continued with the puppets taking an active part. Charles was placed alternately in the place of the boy and of the girl. Slowly, therapy focused on Charles' home situation, on his own Oedipal development and his sexual curiosity.

Bill, a six year old boy from a broken family, played excessively with the puppet crocodile and the puppet cat. Both animals, in his play, were great friends. The crocodile would place the cat on its back and take it for rides around an imaginary lake. The cat, in return, would cook for the crocodile. Puppets representing people were hardly ever used. Now and then the crocodile would bite and chase them away. Bill lived with his mother and two older sisters. He visited with his father every other weekend. Outwardly he liked his parents, but his puppet plays and subsequent discussions disclosed that he disliked both parents for not being together and for not giving him a family as other children had.

Dick, an 11 year old boy, was referred for treatment because his mother found it difficult to manage him. Again, as in the case of Mary's mother, she could not voice specific complaints. It seemed that Dick's relationship towards his mother was one of continuous passive resistance. Outwardly obedient, Dick would dilly and dally and never finish what mother wanted him to do. He showed the same type of behavior in school. His teachers complained that this boy was daydreaming. By the time the class would finish an assignment, Dick would begin to get his paper and pencil ready for work. In the beginning of therapy, nothing startling happened. Dick's play activity would consist of burning paper in a cook pot. He watched the flames and smoke in fascination but would not reveal whom he was burning or what this type of play meant to him. When puppets were shown to him, he picked out the witch, the crocodile and a boy puppet for play. He always manipulated the crocodile, while the author moved the witch and the boy. In his repetitions the witch would always attack the boy and bawl him out for not doing his work properly. The boy would then feebly try to defend himself. This would enrage the witch to a point at which she would holler, scream and hit the boy. At this point the crocodile would come to the boy's rescue and drive away the witch. Since the witch would return, Dick would make believe that the crocodile had two tubes leading from his bowels to the mouth, filled with urine and feces. Whenever the witch would attack the puppet boy, the crocodile would shower her with excretions. Since this was not too effective because the witch would wash herself and change her clothing, Dick added a third tube, containing arsenic, to the crocodile's mouth. Only through the combination of excretions with poison could the witch be killed. After a while Dick would call the witch by a name which was identical with that of his last year's teacher. Attempts on the part of the therapist to gain a better understanding of Dick's relationship to this teacher were fruitless. Then, one day, Dick reverted back to his paper burning. As he watched a piece of paper go up in flames and smoke, he said to himself: "This takes care of the witch." When asked why the witch was now being burned, Dick answered that through burning, the witch really would be destroyed and could not return to do harm to—of all people—the therapist. The following discussion brought out that for Dick the puppet witch had been his own mother. He found her driving, forcing him to do his homework and household tasks and making him go to bed at a time which he considered to be too early. Dick felt that he had to protect the therapist from the witch because Dick really liked him. He did not want his mother to domineer the therapist in the way in which she had been wielding her power over her son. He found similarities between his mother and his last year's teacher. To him, both women had witchlike qualities against which one had to defend oneself. He had to defend the therapist, who had become his ally in the destruction of the witch and thereby had laid himself open to punishment.

## Summary

It was stated earlier in this chapter that puppetry is a means to an end, and not an end in itself. It is the means through which ideas, situations and problems can be expressed. One should not assume that every time a child plays with toys or gives a puppet show, he is wrestling with great problems. Play activities of children are their natural modes of expressions. Therapists, teachers and people working with children have learned that these activities, when used as projective methods or techniques, enable the child to tell us what he thinks and feels. How these expressions are used for understanding, clarification and therapy is a matter of training and skill. The emphasis is on the child. His language is action, and what he does with a wide variety of materials can communicate even more richly and directly to us what he might communicate through words.[5]

## References

1. Batchelder, M.   *The puppet theatre handbook.* New York: Harper, 1947.
2. Board of Education, City of New York. *Puppetry in the curriculum.* Curriculum Series, 1947–1948. No. 1.
3. Hartley, R.   *Growing through play.* New York: Columbia Univer. Press, 1952.
4. Haworth, M. R.   The use of a filmed puppet show as a group projective technique for children. *Genet. Psychol. Monogr.,* 1957, *56,* 257–296.
5. Murphy, L. B., & associates.   *Personality in young children.* Vol. 1. New York: Basic Books, 1956.
6. Woltmann, A. G.   The use of puppetry as a projective method in therapy. *In* Anderson, H. H., & Anderson, G. L. (Eds.)   *An introduction to projective techniques.* New York: Prentice-Hall, 1951, Pp. 606–638.
7. ——.   Concepts of play therapy techniques. *Amer. J. Orthopsychiat.,* 1955, *25,* 771–783.
8. ——.   Play therapy and related techniques. *In* Brower, D., & Abt, L. E. (Eds.)   *Progress in clinical psychology,* Vol. 3. New York: Grune & Stratton, 1958. Pp. 184–196.

Part VII:  Further Methods

# 18

## Miscellaneous Techniques

MARY R. HAWORTH AND ALBERT I. RABIN

EACH of the previous chapters in this volume deals with a projective method which is employed quite widely in clinical work and research with children. Some of these methods were especially devised for, and are applicable to, the study of children. This list does not exhaust, however, the whole gamut of methods and techniques requiring varying degrees of projection which have been proposed and investigated by a group of creative and ingenious workers during the past two decades. It is the purpose of the present chapter to present briefly a sizable selection of these new methods.

Some of the methods included have been primarily employed with adults but have engaged the interest of workers with children as well. Others have been productive of some interesting research and seem to show promise for special applications in the clinic. Still other methods are included simply because they represent some intriguing ideas and possibilities; they appear to be potentially useful in research and in clinical work with children.

Very few of these methods are "tests" in the strict sense of the word. Research and normative information are lacking to a large extent. Their rationale may be somewhat nebulous and incomplete. Yet, their empiricism and potential in eliciting meaningful clinical material and personality projection may be of interest and, perhaps, of value to the clinician and to the student of personality dynamics.

In keeping with the organizational treatment of the other chapters, these miscellaneous techniques have been grouped under similar headings, i.e., picture techniques, verbal methods, graphic and artistic procedures, and play materials. This latter heading has been expanded to include methods requiring the manipulation of objects. For ease in reference, the names of the methods are arranged alphabetically in the list of references, and the appropriate bibliographic entries are grouped accordingly.

### Picture Techniques

#### Test of Family Attitudes

Jackson,[64] in England, has devised a series of projective pictures to probe the child's emotional attitudes toward various family members. Eight pencil sketches present parent-child situations such as the parents conversing together while a child stands to one side; parents holding a small baby; a child sitting on a stool outside a closed door; a child reaching for an object and not seeing the father approaching from the rear. The pictures are suitable for children from 6 to 12 years of age.

Research[62,63,65] conducted with this instrument has compared the responses of 40 normal, 40 neurotic and 30 delinquent children. When types of responses were tabulated, no sex differences were found, but significant differences were noted between the nosologic groupings. The normal group gave the most positive picture of family life. The neurotic children saw the child figures as naughty and as being severely punished and/or rejected by the parents. Strong sibling rivalry, as well as anxiety, insecurity and fear of the parents, was shown by the neurotic group.

In contrast to the first two groups, the delinquents showed more detachment from the family situation. They saw the child as being bad and receiving more specific and severe punishments than did the neurotics. They gave more stories of the child being locked up or running away.

The normal group responded easily and gave stories that were generally reality oriented and ended happily. The neurotics lacked confidence and needed urging to produce. Their stories were often of the fairy tale type or tales of adventure. The delinquents seemed the most inhibited by the story-telling task.

### It Scale for Children (ITSC)

The It Scale for Children (ITSC) was designed by Brown[36] to "investigate and analyze the nature and extent of young children's preference for objects and activities characteristic of their own or the opposite sex. The concept, *sex-role preference*, may be operationally defined in terms of the preferential responses of children to sex-typed objects and activities" (reference 36, page 4). Sex-role *preference* is thus differentiated from sex-role *identification* which refers to the introjection of behavior appropriate to one of the sexes. Brown suggests that it may be possible for a person to identify with one sex, yet prefer the activities and objects generally associated with the opposite sex.

The test consists of 36 picture cards of various toys, articles, costumes and activities representing typical male or female roles. As these cards are presented, the subject makes choices in terms of the fantasied preferences of "It," an asexual stick-figure drawing of a child. The first selection consists of choosing from various sex-typed toys those "It" would like. Then follow eight pairs of pictures: Indians (male and female); clothes (male and female); sewing materials and airplane parts; cosmetic and shaving articles, etc. The final task requires the child to make a choice as to whom "It" would like to be: a boy, a girl, a boy dressed as a girl, or a girl dressed as a boy.

The scoring system provides a range from 0 (exclusively feminine) to 84 (exclusively masculine), with a score of 42 representing no strong preference in either direction. Data have been presented for a kindergarten group[36] of 78 boys and 68 girls, and another sample[37] of 613 children from kindergarten through fifth grade. The mean scores for boys in both studies and at all ages ranged from 66 to 76. The girls' mean scores, from kindergarten through fourth grade, ranged from 38 to 59, thus falling in the intermediate zone or moving toward the masculine pole. The fifth grade girls, on the other hand, had a mean score of 22, decidedly feminine. Differences between boys and girls were significant at each age level, and girls were more variable than boys in their sex-role preference.

The test assumes that children ascribe a sex role to "It" appropriate to their image of their own sex, yet when asked to name "It" (after the test was completed with the original kindergarten sample) 85 per cent of the boys gave a masculine name, while only 45 per cent of the girls gave a feminine name. Whether this can be interpreted as additional evidence of masculine preference on the part of girls, or as due to technical aspects of the drawing which may produce a bias toward its perception as masculine, remains for further research to determine. The difficulty may prove to be insurmountable as a function of a cultural response set toward assigning masculine gender to most neuter figures.

Nevertheless, the basic structure of the test is intriguing, it has interest value for children and, even in its present form, provides at least a rough measure of the consistency or confusion with which a child perceives sex roles. While a high masculine score received by a girl might not be diagnostically significant, certainly disturbance would be indicated if a boy perceived and assigned consistent feminine attributes to the present "It" figure.

### The Szondi Test

The publication of Deri's manual[54] of the Szondi Test in 1949, and the appearance of the English translation of Szondi's *Experimental Diagnostics* in 1952[51] have stimulated a flurry of activity, clinical work and research, with this technique. However, the interest in the Szondi method which surged up in the late forties and early fifties has been waning in recent years. Perhaps the fact that some of the questions that have been raised[56] concerning the Szondi remain unanswered, or were answered in a manner that casts considerable doubt as to its validity, is responsible for the reduced enthusiasm for the method.

Although the work of Szondi and Deri contained many scattered references to children and to the relative loading of the "factors" and "vectors" in their profiles, little systematic work exclusively and specifically with children has been reported. David's 1954 bibliography,[53] which contains over 300 titles, includes relatively few references to work with children. The same is true of the review of Borstelmann and Klopfer.[52]

The descriptive material presented by Spitz[60] and Schubert's comparison[57] of the choices of Szondi's pictures by American and Mid-Eastern children are interesting but shed little light on the usefulness of the test in psychodiagnosis. The same is true of the report by Simpson and Hill[59] on "The effects of verbal reward and punishment upon picture selection on the Szondi Test."

Some work with older children is also available. Deri[55] demonstrated the usefulness of the Szondi in the differential diagnosis of delinquents. However, Scott's study[58] of 1200 adolescent boys and girls failed to confirm Deri's prediction that their profiles would be characterized by $-E$, $-Hy$ and $-M$. Some confirmation that $+M$ is a "counterindication of delinquency" was obtained. A byproduct of the study was the clear indication of sex differences. However, Scott's conclusion is that many of the findings are inconsistent with Deri's theoretical formulations.

The status of the Szondi Test, in general, is rather precarious. Most of the well designed studies with adults failed to support the basic claims of the originator of the technique. Even more serious questions are raised about his genetic hypotheses regarding the effectiveness of the recessive genes. The few studies with children fail to give the method the strong support it would need to make it acceptable to the public of psychological practitioners. Here and there a few enthusiasts, who have developed an affinity for the test and a hitherto unverbalized and unreported "rule of the thumb," continue to employ the Szondi as part of their test battery. But it is fair to say that it is not part of the standard armamentarium of the clinical psychologist working with children. Moreover, there is little to support an expectation that the Szondi will become more acceptable in the future.

## Verbal Methods

### The Pigem Test*

D. Arn. van Krevelen[48] describes the use of a wishing test published in 1949 by José M. Pigem, a Barcelona psychiatrist, and gives his own practical experience and suggestions.

Pigem's basic assumption is that any person may be characterized by assigning to him the traits of some animal. Animals, on the other hand, are also considered to possess psychological traits. This is expressed frequently in everyday language, by adults and children.

The Pigem test consists of two questions: (1) wish expression and (2) wish symbol. Pigem presents it like this: "What would you like to be if you had to return to this world and you could not be a person? You may be whatever you like. Choose from everything that exists. What would you like to be?"

Van Krevelen[48] modifies the form of presentation when he uses it with children and introduces it in a casual way during the examination as part of the discussion. This is his version:

"Imagine that a magician—you know what that is? (If necessary, give an explanation)—comes to you and wants to turn you into something and you are allowed to say what you would like to be, what would you say? You could choose anything there is." If the child chooses a human being, Van Krevelen adds, "It is very nice that you made your choice, but now I see that I have forgotten something very important. The magician I told you of cannot make persons. That means you cannot choose a boy nor a man, a girl nor a woman." After the child is given the opportunity to make another choice, the examiner proceeds: "Now you must imagine that the magician cannot turn you into the thing you wanted to be. Then he says to you, 'I am sorry but that is not possible. I must turn you into something else, but I promise you that I am not going to turn you into something you do not like. So, tell me what would you never like to be.' "

In this manner one can obtain in a majority of cases two wishes, or even more, so to say—a positive wish and a negative one.

*This section was contributed by Helmut Würsten.

Needless to say, the form of the question must be adapted to the child's age, and to the situation and must be presented in such a way as to bring his inner desires to light. Since animals can represent different characteristics, another question is usually added: namely, the wish symbol. It can be stated as follows: "Now tell me, why would you like to be that? Why would it be so pleasant to be that particular animal (or thing)?"

Van Krevelen states that many objects, chosen by people as their wish, have conventional meanings (for instance, the bird represents independence, the fish symbolizes freedom, horses indicate domestic utility, etc.). In addition, the choice made by the *child* may be provoked by some specific aspect of the object which has a highly individual and personal meaning for *him*. What the symbol then really means has to be explored further and cannot be interpreted mechanically. This method can easily be used as part of a casual interview, or be incorporated very successfully into the Madeleine Thomas Stories (see chapter 10). In this respect it is another form of clinical interviewing and investigation rather than a specific test. For further discussion of this technique, especially as applied to adults, the reader is referred to David.[47]

## Graphic and Artistic Procedures

### Drawing Completions

Several tests have been designed in which straight lines, curves or dots are arranged in patterns or as separate stimuli for the subject to complete and make into a "picture." While none of these tests was developed specifically for use with children, data from young subjects have been reported.

The *Horn-Hellersberg Test* consists of 12 squares in which a series of disconnected lines have been reproduced from well known paintings. Hellersberg[35] feels the completion task gives insight into the individual's ability to adjust to the demands of reality.

Ames and Hellersberg[32] have given this test to 225 children from three to 11 years of age. They report age levels for 17 commonly occurring stages of development which range from random scribbling by the youngest children to unified scenes or designs at later levels.

The most commonly drawn items at each age level are listed. Trees, flowers and buildings are drawn at all ages, with persons, clouds, smoke and common everyday objects appearing at most ages. Items whose appearance decreases with age are domestic animals, snakes, doors and windows, numbers and letters. Items which show a definite increase around the tenth and eleventh years are water, buildings or hills, bridges and tunnels, roads and boats. These are generally viewed as being prepubertal symbols.

As a result of this normative study it was felt that the test was not suitable for use with children under five years of age. By the time a child is nine years old his productions approximate those of adults, and adequate diagnoses can be made.

Hellersberg[33] analyzed the drawing completions of 300 prepubertal, pubertal and adolescent girls who were given intensive personality evaluations in a study conducted by the Caroline Zachary Institute. Blind interpretations were made of the drawings and conclusions derived as to the inner tensions and anxieties of the subjects and their relative ability to handle reality situations during these crucial developmental periods. Certain symptoms of tension, self consciousness and control were noted: single figures and especially single heads, connecting all lines to form an enclosure, rigidity and compulsiveness of approach, abstractions or designs. The capacity for release and expressiveness was evidenced by pictures showing action, movement and interaction between people and/or animals. Emotionality was demonstrated by landscapes and flowers. Depicting violent action or nature elements, such as storms, lightning, waves and waterfalls, also demonstrates ability to release tension.

Certain symbolic expressions were studied statistically and revealed differences between the three groups of girls. For instance, drawings of a house seem to represent a projection of the girls' self images. The manner of drawing roads leading to the house underwent dramatic changes: at prepuberty a vertical approach was predominant (so that the house seemed to be elevated on stilts); the pubertal period showed a preponderance of zigzag roads or fences as obstacles to reaching the house; during the final adolescent period the roads were drawn running horizontally and leading to the vertical door (as an indication of female maturity and an acceptance of sex role).

Suns, especially over hills and valleys, were prominent at prepuberty; drawings of horizons showed a marked drop during puberty (being replaced by crowded, close-up landscapes); distant landscapes, rolling hills, and openness were characteristic features during adolescence.

The pubertal girls showed an immense amount of phallic symbolism, much use of shading, and fantasy representations of both male and female figures. On the other hand, the adolescents' social maturity was evidenced by more romanticism and idealism and by an increase in movement and interaction between characters.

The *Symbol Elaboration Test* (S.E.T.) reported by Krout[51] consists of 11 stimulus patterns, each designed to represent a "basic human experience." Each stimulus pattern is seen as symbolically representing a specific attitude or relationship, such as: femaleness, attitudes toward males, intimate heterosexual situations, self concept, general anxiety and aggression.

The original study reports data on 157 subjects from 6 to 69 years of age. Interpretations of the drawings were validated against material from case histories, other projective tests and therapy notes for the clinical cases included in the sample. Factors of sex, age, emotional stability, cultural background and sequence of presentation were also considered.

Wartegg's *Drawing-Completion Test* was administered by Kinget[20] to 383 adult subjects and 200 children between the ages of seven and 12. The stimulus designs are presented in eight white squares on a black background. Scoring blanks are provided in which numerous variables are organized under the general headings of emotion, imagination, intellect and activity. No data or norms are reported for the sample of children.

## The Bender Visual Motor Gestalt Test

The author of this test[6] did not originally intend it to be a method of personality assessment. Bender considered it a visual-motor performance test, which requires the response of the "integrated organism." There is no denying the relationship between what we term personality and the integrated organism. It is probably for this reason that Bell[7] included the Bender-Gestalt in his extensive survey of projective techniques.

Several attempts to establish an objective scoring method for this technique have been made. One of the more extensive studies, which included children, is that of Pascal and Suttell.[11] The standardization population on which the scoring system is based, however, does not include young children; a sizable group of adolescents, ages 15 to 19, is included. Some illustrative material of the performance of younger children and a comparison of their deviations with those of normal and psychotic adults is contained in one of the sections of this book.

More recently, Byrd[8] reported results of a comparison of 200 children recommended for psychotherapy with 200 who were judged to be "well adjusted." Using 15 factors selected from Hutt's list,[10] significant differences between the groups, at the several age levels (from 8 to 16), were obtained by means of the Chi-square method. The well adjusted children show " . . . more use of orderly sequence . . . less change in curvature, closure difficulty and rotation" than do the children in need of psychotherapy. However, the author concludes that "Investigation of specific psychodynamic interpretation of test factors remains to be done" (reference 8, page 135).

A partial attempt to fill the gap of psychodynamic interpretation of Bender-Gestalt productions of children was made by Clawson.[9] In comparing 80 children who were clients in a child guidance clinic with a like number of controls, this investigator was able to confirm several interpretive hypotheses. A relationship between "expansive organization" and "horizontal page" and acting out was obtained. Also found was a positive relationship between "compressed organization" and "decreased figure size" and the symptom complex of withdrawal. Some additional significant relationships between Bender-Gestalt factors and personality factors gleaned from the Rorschach were teased out from the data.

In summary it may be stated that many Bender-Gestalt scoring factors differentiate between clinical and nonclinical groups of children. However, the study of the possible relationship between the several factors and personality-psychodynamic variables is still at its inception. There is also a need for an adequate rationale that is to underlie such a linkage if in fact it is empirically found.

## Animal Drawings

Repeated references have been made throughout the previous chapters to the use of animal stimuli with children. The CAT and Blacky Test employ pictures of animals; Fulchignoni's projective film depicts a family of canaries; the Düss (Despert) Fables contain some animal situations; children's responses to the Pigem questions are often given in terms of the animal they would, or would not, like to be. Animal responses are prominent in the Rorschach records of children, while the $A\%$ normally decreases with age. Animal fantasies are a universal feature of myths, totems and fairy tales, not to mention dreams and, especially, nightmares of children.

The child will readily respond to the task of drawing an animal, and further insight can be gained by asking him to draw the animal he would most like to be and the animal he would least like to be.

Schwartz and Rosenberg[5] suggest a sequence of H-T-P-P-A, adding the opposite sex person to the H-T-P and then an animal. They feel that animal drawings reveal the subject's primary impulses and that insight into the specific symbolism can be derived from the structural features of the animals, their acknowledged disposition and temperament, their role function and ascribed status in legend and real life, and their customary habitat. For example, the tail usually has phallic significance, while the handling of head and rump may throw light on oral and anal problems. The treatment of skin, hair and fur finds parallels in Rorschach shading responses.

The symbolic significance of various species of animals and types (aggressive, nonaggressive, birds in flight, etc.) is discussed by Bender and Rapoport,[1,2] Hammer,[3] Levy and Levy,[4] and Schwartz and Rosenberg.[5] Levy and Levy[4] caution against too literal imputation of meanings to specific animals and emphasize the *"multidimensionality* of all symbols including animal symbols."

All users of this technique agree in feeling that animal drawings tend to circumvent the ego's defenses and to reveal deeper, and often more negative, aspects of personality. Because of the intrinsic appeal of this task, even very young children will readily cooperate.

### Family Drawings

Hulse[22,23] has secured interesting material by asking children to draw their families. Oedipal conflicts, as well as affective attitudes toward various family members, are often clearly revealed. The child's perception of his own role in the family and his concept of self are similarly reflected. Drawings secured in the initial stages of therapy, and again several months later, help to measure changes in the child's interpersonal relationships.

It is important to observe both the absolute and relative size of the figures, their placement on the page (i.e., whether facing each other, or turned away), and the distances between various figures. Exaggerations of persons or features, omissions of family members, erasures, shading, drawing persons as if seen from the rear, should all be noted. Behavior and verbalizations during and after the drawing are important.

Intimation of the child's concept of self can be gleaned from the size of the self figure and its placement. Sometimes the child does not put himself in the picture at all or complains about having difficulty in finding space to draw himself.

Hulse[22] reports that in cases in which parents are known to be seductive the children indicate their awareness of this relationship by the posture or facial expression of the drawn parent. Rejected children tend to draw parents as dominating the family group. Children raised by several relatives may include many persons unrelated to the immediate family. Severely distorted human figures are generally indicative of severe pathology.

A normative study[24] was conducted with 100 second-grade children of low and middle socioeconomic status, including both Negro and white subjects. Significant sex differences were revealed by the boys more often placing themselves in the center of the family group, and more often omitting the mother figure or drawing her without arms. No sex differences were found in measures of dependency (buttons, pockets), use of profile or amount of movement and activity portrayed. Negro children more frequently omitted fingers and excluded siblings. Socioeconomic differences were the most pronounced. The lower-class children more often drew the self figure as smallest, drew people as if floating in air, omitted the mother figure, made the oldest sibling the largest, and drew the father without arms.

Hammer[21] sees this technique as tapping, via drawings, social and interpersonal variables similar to those obtained verbally with the TAT. He presents a family drawing of a normal child for comparison with drawings produced by clinic cases.

### Cartoons

The use of cartoon drawings has been suggested in the literature as offering a situation with considerable appeal, especially to preadolescent boys who might be disdainful and hesitant about entering into other "test" situations. The use of cartoons as a stimulus was initiated by Haggard[12] as a verbal technique. The child was asked to tell a story involving his favorite comic strip character. Such stories were analyzed for variations or distortions from the activities usually associated with that particular character.

Solomon[14] and his co-workers[13] have adapted this procedure by asking the child to draw his own cartoon or "movie." Paper is ruled off into appropriate rows of squares. If the child is hesitant as to how to proceed, the examiner can make stick drawings of a man, woman and child, and suggest the child then make up his own story about them. While this approach has been used largely as part of the therapeutic process, it could also serve a useful purpose in diagnostic evaluations.

### Clay

Clay and plasticene are plastic, three-dimensional media which foster active, physical expression by virtue of both the malleability and resistance inherent in the material. Bender and Woltmann[16] suggest that plastic media allow direct expression of aggressive and destructive impulses and of rhythmic movements. They also point out that play with mud and clay provides satisfying avenues of expression for early repressed desires to play with bodily products; opportunities to experiment with curiosities, feelings and sensations associated with various body parts; experiences with problems of posture, motility and body image; and a means of dramatizing family and social interactions.

The ease with which a mass of clay responds to the child's manipulation facilitates projective expressions via this material. Figures can be quickly represented and as suddenly attacked or destroyed. Such procedures can be repeated endlessly. Verbalizations are not necessary, and less technical skill is required to produce a recognizable facsimile than is true for crayons or paints. Whole "scenes" are frequently made which incorporate many objects, rich symbolism and imaginative "playing-out" of a story or episode.

Hartley, Frank and Goldenson[17] devote a chapter to a discussion of clay, particularly as used by pre-school children. They emphasize the value of clay in serving as a channel for the expression of destructive impulses without associated guilt feelings and as a means of constructing something with satisfaction. These authors, as well as Bender and Woltmann,[16] stress the frequency with which disturbed children express preoccupation with toilet functions or interest in body parts when playing with clay. Happy, well adjusted children were frequently observed creating representations of foods, while troubled and troublesome children made such things as guns and crocodiles. For pre-school children, the manner of approach gives some indication of the level of adjustment.

The reader is referred to Woltmann[19] for a very thorough and complete discussion of the diagnostic, as well as therapeutic, uses of clay along with numerous illustrative case histories; to Bender[15] and Bender and Woltmann[16] for photographs and descriptions of children's clay products, activities and verbalizations; and to *Break Through the Fog*[18] for a discussion of the sculpture (and painting) of an 18 year old pre-psychotic girl.

In diagnostic use, clay can serve a useful purpose for all children, but especially the very young and/or those who find it difficult to express themselves fluently in verbal or graphic areas. It would also be a particularly appropriate projective medium for use with deaf or blind children.

### *Finger Paint*

The texture and consistency of finger paint make this an easy medium for the quick creation of "pictures" with depth and shading effects. The direct, first-hand use of fingers, hands and arms facilitates freer, and probably more projective, expression than can be obtained with pencils, crayons or paint brushes as intermediate tools.

Although finger paint is generally classified as a graphic medium, the younger and/or more disturbed children frequently regress to a usage resembling plastic manipulation as in the handling of mud or clay. Demands for more and more quantity and colors soon produce a gooey, feces-like mass which stimulates sensuous smearing, squeezing through fingers and "plopping" onto paper or table.

Various criteria have been proposed for analyzing and evaluating the finger painting process and product. Napoli[30] discusses the inherent values of finger painting as a diagnostic medium: it is an easily used material for all ages and mental abilities; the low degree of structure sets up little resistance; the opportunity to choose colors is emotionally stimulating; it lends itself to fantasy productions, free associations and symbolism. He discusses the various motions commonly employed, e.g., smearing, scrubbing, patting, scratching, stubbling, etc., and the emotional implications of each. Other categories of responses include: use of hands, color, rhythm, texture, balance, order, symbolism and verbalization. He suggests securing more than one painting and evaluating the results in terms of the motor act and accompanying verbalizations in addition to the paintings themselves. Either individual or group administration can be used effectively.

Hartley, Frank and Goldenson[29] studied pre-school children's approach to finger painting. At this age, the chief pleasures seem to be the tactile experiences and the joy in "messing" with an acceptable substitute for tabooed bodily products. A progression was noted in finger paint play, with pleasurable sensations leading to further excitement, "frenzied smearing" and finally, release and relaxation.

Arlow and Kadis[28] report the use of finger paints as a projective, diagnostic type of play in child therapy situations. They discuss the facilitation of fantasies via finger paints; the cathartic values of being able to destroy productions and recreate them over and over at will; and the fact that since no skill is necessary there is consequently no need to experience failure. Several case histories are presented in which the child's paintings are discussed in relation to his emotional problems and the course of his therapy.

Alper, Blane and Abrams[27] found differences in the reactions of middle- and lower-class nursery school children to the finger painting situation, which they relate to class differences in toilet training practices. It was found that lower-class children showed a greater tolerance for getting dirty (as measured by less hesitancy in beginning to paint); they were less concerned about washing up during or after the process; and were more inclined to use their whole hands or both hands, and to cover the whole sheet of paper. No class differences were found when these same subjects were given a crayon drawing task. The authors conclude that soiling and smearing generate more anxiety in middle-class children.

Napoli has produced a color film[31] on finger painting which demonstrates techniques, discusses the projective aspects of finger paintings and shows some paintings of various types.

### Play Materials and Manipulation of Objects

#### Family Relations Test

Bene and Anthony,[25,26] of the Institute of Psychiatry in London, have devised a unique test to assess the strength of a child's feelings toward members of his family and his perception of their attitudes toward him. Due to the play nature of the technique and the fact that no verbalization is required, it may often be possible to get an indication of these familial variables from quite young children.

The test materials consist of 20 ambiguously drawn cardboard people of both sexes and various ages, each attached to a box with a slot in the top. The child selects those figures which best represent his family constellation, including a self figure. One additional figure, "Nobody," is always used. Two sets of cards containing printed "messages," suitable for older and younger children, respectively, complete the equipment.

The examiner reads the message to the child, who then drops the card in the slot of the person which it best seems to "fit." If it doesn't fit any member of the family, the item is dropped into "Nobody."

The test items for the younger children (below age six or eight) describe both negative and positive feelings toward others and the attitudes of these others toward various family members. Feelings of dependency are also tapped. Items for the older children are more specific and differentiated and cover such areas as positive attitudes of a mild degree and of a more sensualized nature; negative attitudes ranging from mildly unfriendly to hateful and hostile; attitudes concerning overindulgence and overprotection by the parents.

A few examples of items from the older group will demonstrate the test approach: "This person in the family is very nice"; "I wish this person in the family would care for me more than for anybody else"; "This person in the family sometimes gets too angry"; "Sometimes I wish this person in the family would go away"; "This person in the family likes to tease me"; "Mother worries that this person in the family doesn't eat enough."

The authors point out that in the process of dropping the card in the slot, the child is also releasing the feeling tone associated with that particular message so that there is no visible accumulation of evidence of his negative feelings which might lead to excessive shame or guilt in the test situation.

No recording need be done during the test session as the cards remain in their boxes to be tallied up after the child leaves. A scoring sheet is provided by means of which one can easily determine the relative distribution of both positive and negative outgoing and incoming feelings for each family member.

The test takes 20 to 25 minutes to administer and an additional 15 minutes to score. Validation studies based on psychiatric and case history material are reported in the manual.

## The World Test and the Picture World Test

The World Test, designed by Lowenfeld,[68] consists of numerous miniature objects—houses, stoves, trees, fences, cars, soldiers, people, animals, etc.—which the subject uses in constructing his "world." The test was originally developed for use in diagnostic evaluation of children and for assessing progress during therapy. It has also been used as a projective technique with adults.[66,69]

Bühler et al.[67] summarize standardization studies with children. They list the following kinds of worlds ("symptoms") as signs of emotional disturbance: (1) aggressive—killings, accidents, aggressive content; (2) empty—few pieces and few types of objects, no men or women figures; (3) closed—enclosures of major portion or entire "world"; (4) rigid—exaggerated symmetry, unrealistic orderliness; and (5) disarranged— chaotic, confused.

A study[67] is reported of four groups of 25 children each (normal, withdrawn, retarded and stutterers), between the ages of six and one-half and nine and one-half. It was found that no normals used more than one "symptom" type, while 17 normals did not use any. In contrast, only three children in the remaining groups used no symptoms. The appearance of two

or more symptoms is to be regarded as highly indicative of emotional difficulties.

Symptons not found in the worlds of normal children were: aggressive,
rigid, disarranged, empty. Half of the subjects with psychological problems
produced worlds without using men and women figures. Disorganization was
also a common feature in these groups.

Recently, Bühler and Manson[46] have published the Picture World Test,
a pictorial version to be used with adults or children. Twelve scenes are
presented from which the subject selects those he wishes to incorporate into
his "world." These are pasted onto a large sheet of paper, and the subject
then is encouraged to draw in any persons or objects necessary to complete
the picture. Adults are asked to provide a title and to write a story about
their world, while the child dictates his story to the examiner after the
drawing period.

### The Scenotest

Gerdhild von Staabs,[49] in West Germany, has developed the Scenotest,
which resembles the World Test in that it utilizes family dolls, small furniture, and other objects (e.g., flowers, trees, animals, fish, blocks, dowels,
arches, etc.). From observations of the child's play patterns and general
approach to the materials, evaluations of personality structure can be made.
In discussing this test, Woltmann[50] mentions that four types of play activity
have been noted: objective planning, playfulness, impulsive and overactive,
inhibited. Woltmann also reports several research studies conducted in
Europe which indicate the test's usefulness in diagnosis and therapy.

### The Lowenfeld Mosaic Test

Another gestalt-type method of personality investigation is the Lowenfeld
Mosaic Test.[43,44] The materials consist of 456 small tiles representing five
basic geometric designs (squares, diamonds and three types of triangles) and
six different colors. It is Lowenfeld's contention that the designs produced
with these tiles yield clues to the subject's "reality contact." It does not
tap, as many other projective methods do, the individual's fantasy processes
but helps the examiner to learn what "the individual can actually do."[41]

Two reviews of the literature by Dorken[41,42] indicate that a fair amount
of work with a variety of adult clinical groups has been reported. However,
the paucity of available work with children is readily noted. A study of 100
first grade children was reported by Stewart and Leland.[45] These investigators
classified and obtained patterns in the following categories: prefundamental,
fundamental, hollow-circle, attempt-at-covering-the-tray, representational
and design. They found little relationship between type of design and
intelligence. Children producing prefundamental and rigid, stereotyped
patterns were found to be maladjusted.

Several studies concerning the relationship between the incidence of
different types of design, age and intelligence of children were also reviewed
by Dorken.[42] The results are equivocal and inconclusive. One of the major
difficulties is the lack of a common objective scoring method which would aid
in comparing results from one study to another.

Even when adequate scoring categories do evolve, the theoretical issues remain of concern. The question as to what personality variables are involved should be answered before the method can be meaningfully applied to personality evaluation and assessment. Like the Bender it may be empirically demonstrated to be an adequate tool in differentiating psychopathologic groups, but it is markedly in need of a rationale for relating a variety of design patterns to personality characteristics. This criticism is particularly applicable when the method is employed in the investigation of the young child's personality.

### The Kahn Test of Symbol Arrangement (KTSA)

This test consists of 16 small plastic objects which the author calls "culturally structured object symbols."[38] The objects are: three hearts (differing in color, thickness, size and transparency), three stars, two butterflies, "a green amorphous, phallic symbol which also resembles a parrot," an anchor, a circle, a cross, three dogs (different in size and color), and a sector of a circle which is only used briefly in the testing procedure. The testee is required to place the 15 objects on a strip of felt segmented into 15 consecutively numbered spaces; this procedure is repeated five times. On the first, second and fifth times he may arrange the objects in whatever order he wishes. The third time he is asked to duplicate the second arrangement, and the fourth time he is instructed to arrange the objects along a "like-dislike" continuum.

Naming of objects follows the first arrangement, and an indication of the representational or symbolic meaning of each object is requested following the second arrangement. At the end, the subject is also asked to sort the objects on the back of the record sheet and place them in rectangles marked "Love," "Hate," "Bad," "Good," "Living," "Dead," "Small," "Large." The scoring is much too complicated to be detailed in this brief treatment and may be found in the published manuals.[39,40]

Kahn considers his test "a projective tool which offers objective scoring criteria."[40] The major projective aspects of this method may be found in the symbolization process, especially in what the author calls "unconscious symbolization of objects."[38]

Most of the work with this test has been done with adult normals, psychotics and organics. Some tabular material on normal children (grades 1 to 8) and on emotionally disturbed children has also been reported.[40]

A variety of factors, projective and nonprojective, are involved in this test. Its value for the individual idiographic description in the clinical situation is not yet fully or widely demonstrated.

## References

### Animal Drawings

1. Bender, L. *Child psychiatric techniques.* Springfield, Ill.: C. C Thomas, 1952.
2. ——, & Rapoport, J. Animal drawings of children. *Amer. J. Orthopsychiat.*, 1944, *14*, 521–527.
3. Hammer, E. F. Doodles: an informal projective technique. *In* Hammer, E. F. (Ed.)

*The clinical application of projective drawings.* Springfield, Ill.: C. C Thomas, 1958. Pp. 562–583.

4. Levy, S., & Levy, R. A.  Symbolism in animal drawings. *In* Hammer, E. F. (Ed.) *The clinical application of projective drawings.* Springfield, Ill.: C. C Thomas, 1958. Pp. 311–343.

5. Schwartz, A. A., & Rosenberg, I. H.  Observations on the significance of animal drawings. *Amer. J. Orthopsychiat.*, 1955, *25*, 729–746.

## Bender Visual Motor Gestalt Test

6. Bender, L.  A visual motor gestalt test and its clinical use. *Res. Monogr. Amer. Orthopsychiat. Ass.*, 1938, No. 3.

7. Bell, J. E.  *Projective techniques.* New York: Longmans, Green. 1948.

8. Byrd, E.  The clinical validity of the Bender Gestalt Test with children: a developmental comparison of children in need of psychotherapy and children judged well adjusted. *J. proj. Tech.*, 1956, *20*, 127–136.

9. Clawson, A.  The Bender Visual Motor Gestalt Test as an index of emotional disturbance in children. *J. proj. Tech.*, 1959, *23*, 198–206.

10. Hutt, M. L.  Revised Bender Visual-Motor Gestalt Test. *In* Weider, A. (Ed.)  *Contributions toward medical psychology*, Vol. 2. New York: Ronald Press, 1950. Pp. 660–687.

11. Pascal, G. R., & Suttell, B. J.  *The Bender-Gestalt Test.* New York: Grune & Stratton, 1951.

## Cartoons

12. Haggard, E. A.  A projective technique using comic strip characters. *Charact. & Pers.*, 1942, *10*, 289–295.

13. Kasanin, J., Solomon, J. C., & Axelrod, P.  Extrinsic factors in the treatment of anxiety states in children. *Amer. J. Orthopsychiat.*, 1942, *12*, 439–455.

14. Solomon, J. C.  Therapeutic use of play. *In* Anderson, H. H., & Anderson, G. L. (Eds.) *An introduction to projective techniques.* New York: Prentice-Hall, 1951. Pp. 639–661.

## Clay

15. Bender, L.  *Child psychiatric techniques.* Springfield, Ill.: C. C Thomas, 1952.

16. ——, & Woltmann, A. G.  The use of plastic material as a psychiatric approach to emotional problems in children. *Amer. J. Orthopsychiat.*, 1937, *7*, 283–299.

17. Hartley, R. E., Frank, L. K., & Goldenson, R. M.  *Understanding children's play.* New York: Columbia Univer. Press, 1952.

18. Herskovitz, H. H., Brenner, B. U., & Semple, R. A.  *Break through the fog.* Devon, Pa.: Devereux Found., 1955.

19. Woltmann, A. G.  Mud and clay: their functions as developmental aids and as media of projection. *In* Wolff, W. (Ed.)  *Personality—symposium on topical issues*, No. 2. New York: Grune & Stratton, 1950.

## Drawing-Completion Test

20. Kinget, G. M.  *The Drawing-Completion Test.* New York: Grune & Stratton, 1952.

## Family Drawings

21. Hammer, E. F.  Recent variations of the projective drawing techniques. *In* Hammer, E. F. (Ed.) *The clinical application of projective drawings.* Springfield, Ill.: C. C Thomas, 1958. Pp. 391–438.

22. Hulse, W. C.  The emotionally disturbed child draws his family. *Quart. J. child Behav.*, 1951, *3*, 152–174.

23. ——.  Childhood conflict expressed through family drawings. *J. proj. Tech.*, 1952, *16*, 66–79.

24. Reznikoff, M., & Reznikoff, H. R.  The family drawing test: a comparative study of children's drawings. *J. clin. Psychol.*, 1956, *12*, 167–169.

## Family Relations Test

25. Anthony, J., & Bene, E. A technique for the objective assessment of the child's family relationships. *J. ment. Sci.*, 1957, *103*, 541–555.
26. Bene, E., & Anthony, J. *Manual for the Family Relations Test*. London: Nat'l. Found. for Educ. Res. in England and Wales, 1957.

## Finger Paint

27. Alper, T. G., Blane, H. T., & Abrams, B. K. Reactions of middle and lower class children to finger paints as a function of class differences in child-training practices. *J. abnorm. soc. Psychol.*, 1955, *51*, 439–448.
28. Arlow, J., & Kadis, A. Finger painting in the psychotherapy of children. *Amer. J. Orthopsychiat.*, 1946, *16*, 134–146.
29. Hartley, R. E., Frank, L. K., & Goldenson, R. M. *Understanding children's play*. New York: Columbia Univer. Press, 1952.
30. Napoli, P. J. Finger painting. *In* Anderson, H. H., & Anderson, G. L. (Eds.) *An introduction to projective techniques*. New York: Prentice-Hall, 1951. Pp. 386–415.
31. ——. *Finger painting as a projective technique*. (Film, 16 mm, 21 min., color, sound). University Park, Pa.: Psychological Cinema Register, 1954.

## Horn-Hellersberg Test

32. Ames, L. B., & Hellersberg, E. F. The Horn-Hellersberg Test: responses of three to eleven year old children. *Rorschach Res. Exch. & J. proj. Tech.*, 1949, *13*, 415–432.
33. Frank, L. K., Harrison, R., Hellersberg, E. F., Machover, K., & Steiner, M. Personality development in adolescent girls. *Monogr. Soc. Res. Child Developm.*, 1951, *16*, No. 53.
34. Hellersberg, E. F. The Horn-Hellersberg Test and adjustment to reality. *Amer. J. Orthopsychiat.*, 1945, *15*, 690–710.
35. ——. *The individual's relation to reality in our culture*. Springfield, Ill.: C. C Thomas, 1950.

## It Scale for Children (ITSC)

36. Brown, D. G. Sex-role preference in young children. *Psychol. Monogr.*, 1956, *70*, No. 14 (Whole No. 421).
37. ——. Masculinity-femininity development in children. *J. consult. Psychol.*, 1957, *21*, 197–202.

## Kahn Test of Symbol Arrangement (K.T.S.A.)

38. Kahn, T. C. Personality projection on culturally structured symbols. *J. proj. Tech.*, 1955, *19*, 431–442.
39. ——. Kahn Test of Symbol Arrangement: administration and scoring. *Percept. mot. Skills. Monog. Suppl.*, 1956, *6*, No. 4.
40. ——. The Kahn Test of Symbol Arrangement: clinical manual. *Percept. mot. Skills. Monog. Suppl.*, 1957, *7*, No. 1.

## Lowenfeld Mosaic Test

41. Dorken, H. The Mosaic Test: a review. *J. proj. Tech.*, 1952, *16*, 287–296.
42. ——. The Mosaic Test: a second review. *J. proj. Tech.*, 1956, *20*, 164–171.
43. Lowenfeld, M. The Lowenfeld Mosaic Test. *J. proj. Tech.*, 1952, *16*, 200–202.
44. ——. *The Lowenfeld Mosaic Test*. London: Newman Neame, 1954.
45. Stewart, U., & Leland, L. Lowenfeld Mosaics made by first grade children. *J. proj. Tech.*, 1955, *19*, 62–66.

## Picture World Test

46. Bühler, C., & Manson, M. P. *The Picture World Test*. Los Angeles: Western Psychol. Services, 1956.

## Pigem Test

47. David, H. P.   Brief instructional items: the projective question. *J. proj. Tech.*, 1955, *19*, 292–300.
48. Van Krevelen, D. Arn.   The use of Pigem's test with children. *J. proj. Tech.*, 1956, *20*, 235–242.

## Scenotest

49. von Staabs, Gerdhild.   *Der Sceno Test.* Stuttgart, Germany: S. Hirzel, 1951.
50. Woltmann, A. G.   Play therapy and related techniques. *In* Brower, D., & Abt, L. E. (Eds.)  *Progress in clinical psychology*, Vol. II & III. New York: Grune & Stratton, 1956 & 1958.

## Symbol Elaboration Test (S.E.T.)

51. Krout, J.   Symbol Elaboration Test (S.E.T.): the reliability and validity of a new projective technique. *Psychol. Monogr.*, 1950, *64*, No. 4 (Whole No. 310).

## Szondi Test

52. Borstelmann, L. J., & Klopfer, W. G.   The Szondi Test: a review and critical evaluation. *Psychol. Bull.*, 1953, *50*, 112–132.
53. David, H. P.   A Szondi Test bibliography, 1939–1953. *J. proj. Tech.*, 1954, *18*, 17–32.
54. Deri, S. K.   *Introduction to the Szondi Test: theory and practice.* New York: Grune & Stratton, 1949.
55. ——.   Differential diagnosis of delinquents with the Szondi Test. *J. proj. Tech.*, 1954, *18*, 33–41.
56. Rabin, A. I.   The Szondi Test.  *In* Anderson, H. H., & Anderson, G. L. (Eds.)  *An introduction to projective techniques.* New York: Prentice-Hall, 1951. Pp. 498–513.
57. Schubert, J.   The stimulus value of the Szondi pictures: a theoretical and empirical study. *J. proj. Tech.*, 1954, *18*, 95–106.
58. Scott, E. M.   An investigation of juvenile profiles on the Szondi Test. *J. clin. Psychol.*, 1955, *11*, 46–50.
59. Simpson, W. H., & Hill, V. T.   The effects of verbal reward and punishment upon picture selection on the Szondi Test. *Szondi Newslttr.*, 1953, *4*, 2–15.
60. Spitz, C.   Szondi Test and age—experimental studies of children from 5 to 7 years. *Szondi Newslttr.*, 1950, *2*, 1–4.
61. Szondi, L.   *Experimental diagnostics of drives.* (Transl. by G. Aull) New York: Grune & Stratton, 1952.

## Test of Family Attitudes

62. Jackson, L.   Emotional attitudes towards the family of normal, neurotic and delinquent children. Part I. *Brit. J. Psychol.*, 1950, *41*, 35–51.
63. ——.   Emotional attitudes towards the family of normal, neurotic and delinquent children. Part II. *Brit. J. Psychol.*, 1950, *41*, 173–185.
64. ——.   *A test of family attitudes.* London: Methuen, 1952.
65. ——.   *Aggression and its interpretation.* London: Methuen, 1954.

## World Test

66. Bolgar, H., & Fischer, L.   Personality projection in the World Test. *Amer. J. Orthopsychiat.*, 1947, *17*, 117–128.
67. Bühler, C., Lumry, G. K., & Carrol, H. S.   World Test standardization studies. *J. child Psychiat.*, 1951, *2*, 1–81.
68. Lowenfeld, M.   The World pictures of children. *Brit. J. med. Psychol.*, 1939, *18*, 65–101.
69. Michael, J. C., & Bühler, C.   Experiences with personality testing in the neuropsychiatric department of a general hospital. *Dis. nerv. System*, 1945, *6*, 205–211.

Part VIII:  Projective Processes in the Clinic
and in Research with Children

19

# Projective Techniques in the Clinic Setting

CHARLOTTE H. ALTMAN

BASICALLY, the task of the clinical psychologist in a children's agency does not differ radically from that in an adult setting in applying psychological tests. The purposes of both are to provide a description of the subject's personality, contribute to understanding of his dynamics and to aid in achieving diagnosis, prognosis and recommendations. To accomplish these ends, clinical psychologists customarily utilize a battery of tests instead of relying on a single instrument. Furthermore, they characteristically consider nontest data, facts of the subject's personal history, medical reports, psychiatric evaluation, etc., in arriving at their final, integrated reports. In these respects, the purposes and methods of the psychological diagnostician are the same, whether his subjects are children or adults.

## Evaluation of Children's Test Results

There are, however, some important special considerations which cannot be ignored in evaluating test results of children. While understanding of the developmental process is necessary in work with adults, it forms an inescapable and immediate aspect of work with children which probably transcends any other consideration. Diagnostic evaluations must always be integrated with developmental concepts. In a children's clinic, the psychologist quickly learns that mere lip service to the maxim that "solid knowledge of normal development is fundamental" does not suffice. For him it is crucial to all test interpretation. A review of the characteristics of the "normal" child's personality development serves admirably to demonstrate why this must be a primary consideration in the assessment of any child. Werner,[9] serving as spokesman for the "developmental psychologists," has cogently outlined the most prominent and relevant of these characteristics. They include the relatively syncretic and diffuse structure of the child's personality, the fusion of his ego with its surrounding world, his concreteness, his lack of psychophysical differentiation and his propensity for immediate action. Emotions are immediately and overtly expressed. The child's personality is notable for its lability. Identification with family members, particularly the mother, may be extremely intimate. He "makes little or no distinction between 'inner' and 'outer' aspects, between the behavioral and motivational dynamics of personality" (reference 9, page 443). With increasing individuation, socialization increases.

332

Werner further indicates the critical periods during which sudden transformation takes place in the ego-world relation: (a) the period when the infant is weaned, (b) the resistance period of the young child, and (c) the period of pubescence.

From these aspects of personality development, which must emphatically be borne in mind in assessing children, the factors contributing to the difficulty of the child psychologist's task may be surmised. Primarily, the child's test productions must always be viewed in the light of his relative lack of stability, rapidity of change, lack of clear differentiation and individuation, and the occurrence of sudden changes at certain critical stages. As Gesell[1] observes: "It is difficult to make a sharp distinction between developmental and dynamic psychology, for the simple reason that development is itself a process, an inclusive dynamism, which comprises the total growth complex. . . . maturational mechanisms continue to operate to the age of twenty. . . . Behavior and psyche alike are subject to laws of growth—of developmental morphology. Whether applied to child or to adult, one of the critical tasks . . . is to aid a differential diagnosis of immaturity, abnormality and individuality" (reference 1, page xiii–xiv).

Confronted with the child in the clinic, then, the psychologist recognizes that his test results must be evaluated in terms of norms of development which are not clearly and explicitly defined. His conclusions must be tempered by his knowledge that the personality reflected in his test results has not yet "jelled" but fluctuates and shifts. The child, too, is more reactive than the adult to environmental factors, sometimes transitory, which may therefore receive undue emphasis in test protocols. Further, since the developmental process varies from child to child, the concept of "developmental lags" deserves recognition. In clinic children, the extension of this concept to include that of "developmental vulnerability" may be of even greater significance. As stated by Stone,[8] it is "the idea that there is a crucial need for appropriate stimulation at the appropriate time as well as a crucial sensitivity to the wrong stimulation at specific times. This concept of timing . . . appears to be helpful in understanding various pathologies . . . it seems to help explain the fact that children who appear constitutionally similar and who are exposed to similarly damaging situations do not suffer to the same degree" (reference 8, page 74).

Thus, problems of distinguishing between what is *immature* and what is *aberrant* are correctly regarded as more acute in work with children than in work with adults. The effects of age and maturation per se must be an omnipresent consideration in test evaluation, particularly in comparing results obtained at different times on the same child. Moreover, the meaning of theoretical concepts must be in context. The distinction between *fixation* and *regression*, for example, may have considerably different significance in children from what it has in adults. Sound comprehension of such concepts and their application to children is necessary in understanding and interpreting their test productions. Theoretical considerations of the kinds mentioned are vital to the formulation of the personality picture of the child which is developed from the material he yields.

Having accepted the critical significance of a sound and thorough grasp of normal and abnormal personality development as a foundation for any assessment of problem children, it is pertinent to note some of the implications for the psychologist using the tests in the clinic. As noted, his primary purpose usually is to provide a picture of the child's personality and to help in establishment of the diagnosis as a precursor to making effective plans to help. His selection of tests will be influenced (a) by the specific and unique contribution he expects to make to an understanding of the given child, (b) by the specific purposes of the given examination, (c) by the contributions from examiners of other disciplines associated with him in evaluating the child, (d) by the persons to whom reports are to be submitted and the use to be made of the reports. He must be aware of such practical factors as the brevity of the attention span of children, their relative lack of tolerance for tests, and their greater fatigability. Greater efficiency in test administration is demanded, as well as greater discrimination in test selection. The examiner must cope with unpredictability about the child's responsiveness— the child may produce little (at least of diagnostic value) on one or several projective tests, then unexpectedly pour out rich material on an additional instrument. Even extensive experience with children provides few dependable clues to aid the examiner in predicting this in advance. He will have an advantage if he has a broad armamentarium and is prepared to shift when he is satisfied that the test in use is not eliciting helpful evidence about the child. This is particularly important because he can rarely hope to undertake an exhaustive or very intensive survey, not only because of the child's limitations in capacity to respond, but also because of practical considerations obtaining in most children's settings.

The effects of complicating and obscuring factors must often be considered. Atypical environments or upsetting and unusual experiences will have a more potent effect on children's than on adults' test records, and are far from infrequent in a clinic population. Moreover, the effects on rate and direction of personality development may be modified by such factors as sensory handicaps or cerebral palsy; their consequences for personality can be severe. Modifications in test administration or some form of "adaptive testing" may be required to obtain illuminating results.

In seeking to determine the defense mechanisms, too, the child psychologist may have to tread more warily than the adult psychologist. It frequently appears that the child's mode of reacting is more tentative than the adult's. It is as though he is still experimenting, and his defenses are more varied, less well ingrained; therefore, they can be delineated with much less assurance.

The problems encountered by the child psychologist are further complicated by the difficulties and disparities of practice in diagnosis. There seems to be less agreement and uniformity in classifying children's disorders than those of adults, which are far from a settled state. While there is reason to believe that the current ferment represents a step towards clearer and more meaningful nosology, it does not render the psychologist's task easier at present.

It would be unfair to leave this account of problems confronting the child psychologist without allusion to the factors which may make his task easier than that of the adult psychologist. One of these is that diagnostic evidence may be much more accessible or readily available in children. Often a child responds in a favorable test environment in which an adult's patterns would be too rigidly entrenched to enable him to alter his adjustment to meet the situation as spontaneously and freely as the child. The child is not yet so aware of what to hide; he is not so adept at evasion, concealment and self deception. Even when he has repressed his conflicts, they may not lie so deeply buried. The child may more easily let one see what "makes him tick."

## Some Limitations of Projective Techniques

Although our main concern here is with projective tests, it is important to suggest some instances in which nonprojective tests may yield more valuable results than projectives, as a deterrent to overenthusiasm for the latter. There are at least two large groups of children to whom nonprojective tests may be administered more profitably than projective tests:

### Very Young Children (the Toddlers and Pre-schoolers)

Here, lack of language facility will be a limiting factor in the application of many common projectives. And even after more adequate acquisition of language, the child's developmental level may not permit him to exceed mere enumeration or description when confronted with pictures. The lack of validity in using projective tests with young children has been noted by many workers. Among these are Ames et al. (reference 1, page 285), who state, in evaluating their Rorschach results, that "developmental status may be revealed more clearly than is individual personality structure." They further add: "The child does not simply grow 'better' as he grows older. Behavior does not necessarily become better integrated and better organized. On the contrary, ages of equilibrium to some extent alternate with ages of disequilibrium, ages of expansiveness with ages of inwardizing" (reference 1, page 289).

Beyond this there is an important consideration advanced jointly by the developmental and ego psychologists. Young children express their emotions very directly and very immediately. Repression is rarer and weaker. Conflicts are less apt to be internalized, negative emotions less likely to have become unacceptable. Therefore, young children may be more informative about their problems and conflicts in spontaneous conversation than by the more devious and cumbersome Rorschach or CAT route; it is not necessary to use these devices to learn how the child feels or how he operates in meeting his problems. Moreover, since his personality structure is so fluid, so reactive to temporary factors, interpretations made from personality tests administered on any one day may be misleading; they might change quite significantly if the tests were administered on a different day. These difficulties, according to available evidence, decrease with increasing age, but cannot be ignored in evaluating all young children.

## Extremely Disturbed Children

The second group of children with whom projective tests may be less enlightening than nonprojectives can be the most extremely disturbed children, somewhat surprisingly. These are the children who are so obviously "out-of-contact" and disorganized that it is more helpful to see to what degree they can be "brought back to reality," can organize their thinking, can meet external demands, than to explore their deviations further, which are so extreme as to be patent without the use of tests, in any case. Here the use of intelligence tests and other less ambiguous, more firmly structured, materials can be very informative. It may be a greater contribution to ascertain that such a child has nevertheless learned to read and do arithmetic at his grade level than it is to add to the obvious evidence of his psychopathy. Emphasis is on investigating personality strengths and assets, rather than on underlining weaknesses.

Even in less disturbed children, the capacities and strengths revealed on nonprojective tests, which may differ from those inferred from projectives, must be considered. Both types of tests are needed to complement and supplement each other in the total evaluation. Without either, important information may be lost or obscured, because various psychic levels are not tapped. Rapaport suggests the use of "unstructured tests revealing more the organization and conflict patterns of personality, and structured tests revealing more the strength of socialization and adaptation" (reference 5, page 184).

Thus, the first reason for the use of a battery of tests is to tap different levels or to approach different areas of personality. A second consideration is the difference in the stimulating value any or several of the tests may have for a particular child, and the degree to which any instrument evokes meaningful or helpful information about him. It is comparatively rare to find a clinic in which the same standard battery of tests is administered to every child. Greater flexibility has been found to be warranted for fruitful results.

## Illustrative Case Material*

The following cases are presented to illustrate how material from the various tests is integrated, and how the psychologist's report also may reflect his cognizance of the child's symptoms and data from the social history, in addition to test findings per se. Reports from medical doctors or clinics, schools and other social agencies may be available at the time of the examination.

*Cases cited are from the files of the Institute for Juvenile Research, Chicago, Illinois, and are used with permission of its Superintendent, Raymond E. Robertson, M.D. Examing psychologists for the cases were Irene S. Goldblatt, M.A., and Elise Elkins Lessing, Ph.D., of the Department of Psychology.

In formulating his report, the psychologist aims to make it *child*-oriented rather than *test*-oriented; accordingly, he utilizes pertinent material from all his tests in discussing any particular aspect of the child's personality. For example, in considering intelligence, he examines not only performance on a WISC or Binet, but also the nature and functioning of intelligence as depicted on the projective instruments. Needless to say, he tries to delineate the individual child before him, avoiding generalizations, clichés and jargon, essaying to understand and convey the specifics and the noteworthy about *this* child.

## Case 1

### History

Ted, age 10½, was referred to the clinic at the suggestion of his school. His mind seemed a blank for his schoolwork, and he was inattentive in class. Moreover, for some time he had been making peculiar mouth noises which distracted the class, and was very fidgety with hands and feet. His mother believed that Ted was not aware of the noises he made, nor did he know what made him disobey. "He is not truthful or trustworthy." Achievement in fourth grade was barely passing. His mother found him difficult to manage at home, too, where he also would not pay attention. Things could be going smoothly until an occasion when Ted could not have his own way, when he would have a temper outburst, and go into "a complete rage." No type of punishment was effective, and he felt he did not have to obey, and that nobody wanted him. He had called his parents names and told his mother he didn't want her. His stepfather had spanked him with a strap as well as his hands until Ted had large welts, but without results. The parents were most concerned with the obedience problem and how to discipline Ted. In the previous year, his doctor had prescribed phenobarbital, but this, too, was ineffective. His stepfather added that he was irritated because Ted would not do things by himself, such as building models, and had withdrawn from activity with Ted "to teach him to take responsibility." The boy behaved perfectly with an uncle who gave him attention, such as skating with him. Beyond this, Ted's playmates were three or four year olds, or much older boys.

Ted's parents were English, and he had been born in England. The parents were divorced when Ted was two, after four years of marriage. Mother married stepfather three years later, and the family came to the U. S. Ted had gone to kindergarten here before he and his mother had returned to England because of maternal grandmother's illness and death. He went to first grade there, where he had had difficulty adjusting to school from the outset. After their return he had been in three different parochial schools and a public school, in attempts to improve his adjustment.

Ted's parents had grown up together; "it was sort of planned by our families that we'd marry eventually." The marriage occurred after his father was injured in an accident, mother saying she married him more from pity than love. They enjoyed going out together, and had fun until Ted's birth, when both found parenthood an imposition, particularly resenting that it deprived them of recreation. His father "blew up" over small things after Ted's birth (mother considered Ted very like his father), and things went from bad to worse, with father staying out alone. The mother was obviously upset that Ted's father not only had not contested the divorce, but had not even asked about the boy at the time it was granted. His mother did not want Ted to know that his stepfather was not his real father, although he was five years old at the time of her second marriage. She said Ted referred to his real father as uncle, and insisted Ted had not known him well enough to have any associations.

Her pregnancy and the birth of Ted were normal. He had colic and sleep disturbances to age two (his younger half-brother has the same problems). He walked "on his first birthday" and at 13 months "could sit down and carry on a conversation." He had the usual childhood diseases without complications, and no anomalies of development. He was a good eater between his parents' divorce and the move to the U. S., and then began to have cramps, was "a picky eater" and lost weight (these are still problems). He also began to bite his nails and has continued this habit. The family live in a crowded four-room apartment but in a fairly good neighborhood.

A half-brother was born when Ted was eight years old, and the boys share a room which had been Ted's alone previously.

Ted's mother seemed guarded when she talked to the clinic workers, and she displayed little of her feelings. She described herself as nervous. She said she had "owed responsibility" to Ted, but now owed it to her younger son. She showed no awareness that she might be involved in Ted's problems. In an apparent slip of the tongue, she told the psychiatrist that she had come to the clinic to learn how to "punish" Ted. The stepfather seemed more at ease and more outgoing than she, despite a stutter and grimaces.

## Psychological Examination

Ted was very agreeable, polite, eager in manner. He was critical of his productions and apologetic about his inadequacies, but eager for approval and reassurance. He volunteered information about his problems, centering on his mother, his nervousness and somatic complaints. "Once in a while when mother yells at me I get discouraged and start moaning and groaning. I get fits. I start yelling at my mother and talking back. When mother yells it gets on my nerves." He had some difficulty in consistently maintaining his attention. Once he commented, "I can't hear too good lately." Asked at what times he noticed this, he replied, "When mother talks I can't hear sometimes." He was of average intelligence (Binet IQ 99), but this rating was considered possibly too low.

*Rorschach:* Confronted with Card I, Ted first commented on the tiny spots; after designating the center portion as a crab, he again was distracted from further percepts by noting the shape of the white spots, the presence of a center line, etc. Often he responded to a detail of the cards, and only later noted the same percept on the other side of the card. He identified legs, chair, arms and head on Card IV; only in the inquiry could it be established that he had perceived the whole as a seated giant. The summary follows (Beck scoring):

| | | | | | | |
|---|---|---|---|---|---|---|
| W | 3 | M | 3 | H | 2 | F% | 59 |
| D | 28 | CF | 4 (−, 1) | Hd | 2 (x, 1) | F+ % | 75 |
| Dd | 3 | FC | 4 (−, 1) | A | 6 | A% | 26 |
| | 34 | FY | 1 | Ad | 3 (x, 1) | | |
| | | FV | 1 | Ar | 1 | P | 3 |
| | | FT | 1 | Bt | 4 | | |
| | | F+ | 15 | Cg | 2 | $\dfrac{\text{VIII} - \text{X}}{\text{I} - \text{VII}} = 1.00$ | |
| | | F− | 5 | Hh | 7 | | |
| | | | 34 | Ob | 4 | | |
| | | | | Im | 2 | T/R | 20.2″ |
| | | Exp.: 3/6.0 | | Ge | 1 | T/1R | 5.4″ |
| | | | | | 34 | | |

*Thematic Apperception Test:* Ted's first three stories may suffice to give the "flavor" of his productions.

1. He's trying—he's thinking if he could be able to play, but he doesn't know what to think. Just thinking and thinking if he ought to take a try. He's just sitting there thinking. After a while I think he might try. So after a while he tries and I think he makes it. That's all I can think of. It's pretty tough when you don't know what to do with it.

2. This looks like it's taking place in summer in Europe. They're planting crops for winter. In spring she's thinking how they're going to harvest. Mother (standing by tree) is also thinking. She's trying to think what her daughter's thinking. The daughter's husband is planting all the crops and plowing the land. He just got finished so now is taking the horse and plow to the barn. That's all I can figure out.

3 BM. The boy's crying about something; he's sitting on the floor crying, but I don't know what he's crying about. Looks like a tough one here. He has his head on the bed.

He's crying because his mother went to the hospital and he wants her to come home. He has no father. When he's sleeping one night his mother comes home and then when he gets up in the morning his mother is cooking his breakfast and he wonders what she's doing home. And so he runs up to her and asks, "What are you doing home?" I think that sounds silly. She said she had her operation already and was let out.

Two of the stories tell of a woman and her husband who go to bed, but in the morning the man is missing without explanation. In only one story is the term "father" applied to an adult male, and even this reference is abortive:

7. Looks like a father and son. That's a pretty tough one. The old man was a detective working on a case about a robbery. And so he came to the Wilson's house and he asked John Wilson if he knew anything about the robbery. And the detective asked him a lot of questions, stuff about the robbery. He told him there was two men and he said he never heard of it yet. And finally he confessed he did it. That's about all.

*Figure Drawings:* Four very tiny figures placed far to the left side of the paper and each tilted to the right constituted the family Ted drew. From left to right, they were a baby, aged 2, brother aged 10 (the second largest figure), a mother, aged 33, and a father (largest), aged 40. Rough circles represented the heads, with a scribble for hair (except the father), long necks, circles for trunks, elongated ellipses for arms and legs, dots for eyes and noses, small arcs for mouths.

Asked to draw a boy, he made a similar but much larger figure. Long arms extended upward to the sides, and this time there were fingers added. Legs and feet were very thin and disproportionately small. They extended somewhat out to each side, without a stable base, and the right leg was longer than the left. Following are Ted's associations:

He's happy that his team won in baseball. He won for them.
(Like best?) Likes to play baseball.
(Not like?) Doesn't like to play football.
(Angry?) If his team doesn't win.
(Scared?) If anybody gets hurt in baseball.
(Age?) 11 years old. That's nearly how old I am.

*Bender Gestalt:* No notable anomalies in the drawings. Ted approached this task with the question, "Is it O.K. if I make them small?" He counted the number of dots carefully in the patterns containing dots, was very critical and apologetic about his drawings, very much concerned about how well he was doing.

## Interpretation and Report

In complete form, Ted's productions on the projective tests provided the often hoped-for, but by no means routinely found, opportunity to assess him in several different areas and on several different levels. The Rorschach, which is presumed to explore the deepest, most primitive levels, furnished much information about the personality structure of the boy. The less ambiguous Thematic Apperception Test gave data on the content of his conflicts. Both helped elucidate the nature of his adaptations and defenses. The other tests confirmed hypotheses and served to round out the picture. Integrating them into a whole, the psychologist described him as follows (excerpted from the complete psychological report):

Ted is an insecure, emotionally immature child who is operating under the stress of very primitive, frustrated affectional needs, with resultant hostility and a very pervasive anxiety which restricts his capacity to organize experience. He approaches the world in an unstable, unintegrated manner, hopping anxiously from detail to detail, unable to fully organize and make meaningful the more holistic aspects of experience. To some extent, he handles anxiety by just shutting out aspects of experience from cognitive awareness.

Ted has a cautious, wary approach to the unfamiliar, the unstructured, and an immediate impulse to resist demands made upon him to cope with such situations. However, he has an equivalent need to meet expectations in some fashion, so that his opposition remains covert and is expressed in inadequate productions and feelings of incompetence rather than any direct resistance.

Over-all, Ted's capacity for ego-integrative control is limited. He is labile emotionally, and, when he is not able to ignore them, very much at the mercy of emotionally exciting stimuli. He is unable to experience himself as an integrated whole, perhaps because he is able to defend himself against anxiety only at the expense of blotting out areas of his experience.

Ted's interpretations of situations are generally reality-oriented, but he tends to respond too little in terms of the conventional, matter-of-fact, neutrally toned aspects, and brings to bear more of his own inner wishes and personal associations than would be conducive to the most effective handling of external reality. At times he arrives at interpretations in an alogical manner.

The affective demands Ted wishes to make on his mother, the uncertainty he feels about his position with her, his inability to accept the father as part of the family picture, and his fantasies about the disappearance of husbands, combine to arouse very intense anxiety and guilt. There is a good deal of anxiety over separation from the mother, apparently related both to the present feelings of threat to the hostile-dependent tie, and to Ted's bafflement regarding the tendency of men in mother's life to disappear. He is afraid the family will now get rid of him.

Ted is preoccupied with the past, and perhaps also has some nostalgic feelings about some former life. He alludes often to his English background and appears to be quite identified with his English mother. His passive feminine identification and confusion over sex role represent both a primary clinging to the mother and a defense against the dangers associated with masculinity. Illness, injury and death are fantasied as possible outcomes if Ted should venture to assume a more masculine, assertive and independent role. The father figure is cast in the role of a detective who gets him to confess his guilty secret, that he is a thief.

Ted feels impotent, inferior, in a sense as if he is already emasculated. He is so anxious and guilty that he is unable to cope with the world in any active and effective way.

He shows some strength in his capacity for channeling impulses into fantasy activity, and some tendency toward recovery of his integrative ability as anxiety is diminished. However, the resource suggested by his ability to make empathic identification needs to be qualified in view of the fact that these identifications would seem to be primarily with feminine figures.

Ted seems to want help. Treatment with a male therapist might help him clarify some of the early experiences which seem to have been so confusing, and to deal with his fearful and guilty fantasies so he can move toward a more appropriate identification and acceptance of his sex role.

The examining psychiatrist described Ted as an insecure, scared boy who feels deprived. He protects himself by acting out or fighting, and punishes himself by not eating, although it was speculated that his attitude about food might also contain phobic elements. The mother seemed to be pushing Ted to too-early maturity and responsibility, in addition to her questionable acceptance, and her identification of the boy with his father.

## Comment

In describing this case, the emphasis has been on the final, integrated psychological report, without indication in detail of the source of each of the examiner's statements, since this type of material is available elsewhere. The case illustrates how results of all tests administered are interwoven and commingled, and how conclusions are related to both symptoms or complaints and to the known facts of the child's life. They clearly are neither "blind" analysis, nor attempts to validate the tests; their purpose is to add to the other available information about the child and his problems as much illumination as can be gleaned from the test instruments and the accompanying observations.

To illustrate the importance, if not the indispensability, of the behavioral observations, let us turn to the records of two much younger children.

## Case 2

### History

Seymour, age 4 years, 5 months, was referred primarily because of his attacks on his $1\frac{1}{2}$ year old sister. His mother could never allow the two children together, even in her presence, because he knocked the baby down, hit her on her head or threw things at her. Several times he wrapped a cord around the baby's neck; he also wrapped her head in a blanket and sat on it. He demanded his own way or screamed inordinately, sometimes for two hours at a stretch. His mother had to pour his milk first, or he refused to eat. Things had reached the stage, she said, that if she observed, "It's raining," Seymour would retort, "It's not!" and scream. The parents had tried spanking, ignoring, isolating, bribing, shaking, going to an extreme to give Seymour exactly what they gave to his two sisters—all without effect. The mother tried to show him more love by holding him on her lap, but he merely cried and struggled free or kicked and spat.

Seymour was always a model child outside the home, so that outsiders could not imagine these problems. His father was strict and stronger than the mother; he was somewhat more successful in managing the child, as a consequence, but even he was thoroughly exasperated. In her attempts to avoid partiality, the mother bought new shoes for Seymour when she got them for the girls, even though he did not need them. Seymour's bad tantrums occurred two or three times a day. He had had some before his younger sister's birth, and his mother reported no signs of jealousy at the time of her birth. He tended to follow his $5\frac{1}{2}$-year-old sister around, attempting to imitate her and her friends in all their activities. He wanted to sleep with his parents every night. This had begun six months prior to referral, when he had bad dreams (of snakes, alligators, being chased, being hurt), and because he was allowed in the parental bed then, he had insisted on it since. If he were ever persuaded to sleep alone, he would get up and wander around in the middle of the night. Not long before referral he had asked his mother if he had ever been a baby. He was very interested that everyone had, and in his own baby pictures. His mother thought this meant he wanted to be a baby, and so constantly pointed out to him the advantages of being grown up.

His mother said Seymour had always been a difficult child. At 10 months he could flip out of his crib and go all over the house. He was a big eater and a large baby, bottle fed from the beginning because the older child had lost weight when nursed. Toilet training was a struggle; he screamed and kicked when put on the pot, and had to be held by the mother because he soon broke the straps. It was begun at seven months and completed at $2\frac{1}{2}$ years. There was some smearing of faeces, which the mother was embarrassed to admit. When the younger baby was brought home from the hospital, the mother showed Seymour the diapers and told him he was too old for them; it was then that he was toilet trained. She considered him very different from both of his sisters and from other children. He was an unplanned baby; normal pregnancy and birth. The mother wanted a girl, because she enjoyed dressing them and fixing them up. Her father became ill with cancer when Seymour was three months old, and it was a hectic period, with mother leaving the children with strangers at times while she visited the hospital.

Mother herself had been an only child, and a lonely, shy, retiring one who feared people. She was always an honor student in school. Her father was very conscientious, but lenient with her. Her mother was a strict disciplinarian and very efficient. Towards the end of her interview with the social worker, the mother "confessed" that she and her mother did not get along. The maternal grandmother helped pay for their home, and had an apartment upstairs which was entered through the house. She meddled in the children's discipline and made constant demands on them. She did not have friends of her own and so she tried to run mother's life and competed with her for the children. Mother spoke resentfully of the extra time she had to play with the children because she had little housework to do. And she showed covert gratification in remarking that, although Seymour at one time seemed to prefer his grandmother to his mother, he lately had been kicking, hitting and swearing at her, too. This family had always lived with maternal grandmother, and the mother felt doubtful that she could live apart from her mother.

Father was the older of two boys. His parents quarrelled constantly. His father was selfish, concerned only with his own needs, refusing to work after getting a small inheritance during father's boyhood. As a result, his sons had to assist him; at the time of referral father spent three evenings a week at that home after a $10\frac{1}{2}$ hour working day, which was resented by his wife. Father hated quarrelling and got especially upset by Seymour, "seeing red" because of the dissension he caused. It was interesting that this man, a plant foreman, had obtained a promotion shortly before our contact, because he could "be firm with people."

## Psychological Examination

Seymour was an attractive, rather pale child, who separated from his mother with only mild hesitation. He was consistently alert, attentive, cooperative and interested throughout the examination. His articulation was still infantile, but the content and manner of his conversation were much more mature than expected for his age. He showed a good deal of spontaneity in relating to the examiner, but only through verbalization. In terms of motor behavior, he tended to be overcontrolled. His over-all behavior in the test situation was almost too "good."

*Children's Apperception Test:* The complete stories follow:
1. Three birds, and they didn't have no mommy and they had to cook by themselves but they couldn't cook. (?) There's a big bowl on the table to put food in, but they had no mommy and couldn't cook. One got his finger burned.
2. Both of 'em are pulling and the little bear is pulling and the little bear falled off. At end of rope the papa bear falled off. Mother bear falled off 'cause the rope broke. And all the mother bear's black stuff came off—white stuff. (?) The wind was blowing so hard it all blowed off.
3. I can't say nothing. There was a little mouse hole in the wall, and the little mouse came out and hurt the lion's toe, and then the lion got after him, and the mouse quick ran in the little hole before the lion got him.
4. Kangaroos. A mama and baby and sister kangaroo. The mama is going out to the milk store, buying food for the papa kangaroo. That's all. They came home and found the papa kangaroo home already.
5. The cat had to sleep outside overnight. The crib got broken and the cat didn't know what to sleep in, and had to sleep outside. Her mommy and daddy didn't buy her a new crib. She didn't know what to do. She had to sleep outside in the snow. All the time it snowed. Then the mommy and daddy's bed broke. (?) They had to buy baby kitty's new bed and mommy and daddy's new bed.
6. All the bears are sleeping in a tunnel, and the mama bear came in the middle of the night, and they thought it was some strangers, and they killed her because it was dark in there. And when it was morning and they saw here was the mama bear killed in the night time.
7. This is the jungle. The lion and tiger cage. The lion got a monkey and ate it. Then the monkey got out of the cave when no one was watching the cave: where they put all the animals in, and the people looked at them.
8. One monkey was shaving the little monkey's hair. Then the mama bunny was talking to the papa monkey while the papa—(?) Because his hair was too long. Then the grandpa monkey was talking to the mama, and all of a sudden the zoo people came and put them in a cage at the zoo.
9. There was a baby bunny and was no mommy. She got into bed. Then somebody closed the door and she knew she didn't have no mommy, and she knew it couldn't be her mommy. Then the window even broke. It wasn't her mommy. It was a bear.
10. There was two doggies wrestling, and one went on the potty. The real one. Then one puppy had to go when the other was on the potty. They had a fight. "Where's another potty for me?" Then the doggy was all finished, wiped himself and pulled his trousers up. Then the other dog went on the potty. Then they were wrestling again.

*Figure Drawing:* Circle for head, elongated ellipse for trunk, eyes, nose, mouth indicated, lines for legs, with two-dimensional feet. The entire page covered with lines. It was a picture of "a man locked in jail." Additional pages of more or less indiscriminate scribbles were designated a cowboy, a horse and a map.

*Stanford-Binet:* Very superior intelligence (IQ 149). He was consistently advanced in all areas, with the exception of visual-motor coordination, in which he was about average.

## Psychological Report and Diagnosis

In her report, the psychologist wrote:

Seymour was able to tell stories that were organized, consistently relevant, and revealed a very advanced vocabulary. The themes of both his stories and his drawing suggest a good deal of concern about controlling his "bad" impulses (the man in jail, the animals in cages). Seymour shows some fear of and concern about being deprived of the mother's love and care. He seems to feel that he is "out in the cold" and has no secure place of his own with mother. He sees two possibilities: either to be a baby or to be older and have "a wife, like Roy Rogers does." Seymour expresses his unhappiness over being kept out of the parental bedroom and his babyhood "place" in the story about the cat who has to sleep in the snow because his crib is broken. In conversation prior to this, Seymour had spoken about lying beside mommy that morning, lying in the middle, with daddy on the other side. Asked if he usually slept with his parents, he replied, "When I have a bad dream; otherwise they won't let me in." Seymour's feelings of deprivation and frustration of the wish to have mother's attention provoke anger, which is all the more threatening because of his fear that something might really happen to mother. Some of Seymour's fantasies are suggestive of primal scene material. It would appear that Seymour's problem behavior results from a fusion of thwarted dependency wishes and more "mature" interest in just what does go on in that bedroom, in relation to which he seems to have rather frightening fantasies. Probably Seymour vents his anger on his younger sister because it's safer to try to get back his "baby" place. Consideration of the unusually mature verbal development of this boy suggests the possibility that his parents may tend to overlook some of his four year old limitations. Seymour seems to be a very resourceful child. Therapeutic intervention has an excellent prospect of succeeding.

With the psychiatrist, too, Seymour was compliant and very well behaved. He surveyed the toys in the room, but did not want to touch them. He finally painted, choosing colors carefully and thoughtfully, making balloons; at the end of the interview he did not want to stop painting to leave.

In the diagnostic staff discussion, the dynamics already suggested were generally accepted. There was the added speculation that Seymour might have been a constitutionally active child, which his parents found difficult to accept from the beginning. Their preference for girls, and the mother's statement that girls need more attention and fussing, which couldn't be helped, seemed of greater significance, however. This mother expected Seymour to control himself, to an extent beyond the capacity of a four year old. In attempting to do so, Seymour became too rigid, fearful of expressing any aggression, but when his controls inevitably broke down the tantrums resulted.

## Case 3

In contrast to Seymour, much of what the psychologist learned about Mitchell came from his spontaneous conversation, rather than the Children's Apperception Test given him.

### History

Mitchell, age 4 years 11 months, was referred because he had been masturbating excessively for about a year; this stopped a month or two before referral, but he then began soiling during the day, sometimes as often as three times, and at times he also wet himself. Mitchell's only sibling was a nine year old brother; his mother thought he might have told Mitchell something frightening about masturbation. Mitchell was very dependent on his brother, following him around, fearful of venturing out on his own, refusing to play with other children. He also had nightmares and bad dreams, waking up crying every night. The dreams were of animals and snakes in his bed, or of monsters coming out of the wall. The mother thought she might have given Mitchell too much and spoiled him; she had been too strict with his brother and too lenient with Mitchell, she said. She was very observant of Mitchell's behavior, puzzled by it and anxious to understand it. Mitchell would withhold bowel movements three or four days, to impaction. Just before his clinic examination, Mitchell gave up soiling and wetting, but resumed his masturbation, publicly and at any time of day, although he also frequently retired to his own room, undressed and crawled into bed to masturbate. The problem had begun when he was three and one-half, at the time the family moved into a five-room apartment. Prior to this, Mitchell had slept in the parents' room; he had a twin bed in a room with his brother in the new apartment. His shift from masturbation to soiling occurred when he was almost struck by a truck, an experience which had terrified him.

Mitchell's mother was a clean, fresh-looking young woman who spoke calmly but with nervous gestures. She seemed rather intellectual. In contrast, the father was rugged-looking, and came to the clinic in work clothes which were greasy and dirty, apparently a hard-working, outdoors type of man. The parents disagreed about the implications of Mitchell's symptoms. The mother wanted to understand the cause, and wanted help. The father considered Mitchell "a normal, bratty kid," and thought he would outgrow his symptoms.

Mitchell was a planned child. Delivery was easy and he was a good eater. He was fed from a bottle which was often propped, rather than being held, for eating. He walked at nine months and talked at a year, but his mother felt he still couldn't speak well. Toilet training was begun at two, and not completed until he was three, to mother's obvious irritation. Between two and one-half and three and one-half he had temper tantrums, became very difficult to manage, and seemed to be in revolt against authority. It was immediately following this period that he regressed to soiling. Mother was the chief disciplinarian, using reprimands and threats. Often Mitchell said he didn't like her, and refused to talk to her. He seemed to be a bright child; he could count, knew differences between jet aeroplanes, was able to play games like "Sorry" and "Monopoly." Instead of showing pride in these achievements, both parents felt these things were too advanced for him; he should not be doing them. They had not taught him, and presumed he had picked them up from his brother whom they had taught. Mitchell was still unable to dress himself, however. He was very eager for mother to have another baby, and had asked her to buy one. Told that babies grow inside mothers, he repeatedly asked if she were growing one. He boasted that he would grow bigger than anyone in the family; mother believed he meant his genitals would be biggest.

This seemed to be a middle-class family that lived comfortably. The mother was definitely the dominant parent. In addition to attending to the discipline, she managed the money, decided on moving, decided when new appliances were to be purchased. The father was quiet and submissive, and they never quarrelled. The mother once called herself a "devouring female"; she felt she had been spoiled as a child and was determined not to spoil Mitchell by "giving in to him." The older boy was his father's favorite, and mother thought of Mitchell as hers. The brother treated Mitchell protectively, as an adult would. The mother thought Mitchell might sometimes be jealous of his brother because of his greater proficiency in playing ball and other games. She was quite certain that the older boy was never jealous of Mitchell, however, and seemed surprised to be even asked about this. She said her husband had been fulfilled in the older boy, and not anxious for another child. Both parents had wanted a girl; it took the father a year to recover from his disappointment when they had a second boy.

## Psychological Examination

As noted above, Mitchell's test productions were not particularly informative, in themselves. On the Binet, he was found to be of average intelligence. He counted quickly and casually, and when complimented, replied, "My big brother tell me." Tasks involving motor control were difficult for him; he could not copy a square (Year V) while looking at one, but while trying to copy a circle he produced a quite adequate square. He had great difficulty drawing a cross (Year III-6). His difficulty seemed to involve some lag in the ability to integrate perception, ideation and motor execution.

*Children's Apperception Test:* The complete protocol follows:

1. It's too hard. Ditch-ditch-ditch. Don't know ditch stories. (?) Don't know. Who? The girl, the brother, the frother (father) gets all that. (?) 'Cause the father.
2. Pulling string. Someone's trying to get it. The bears try to get it. A tug of war. (Who?) Two bears and one pratch (Refused to explain).
3. That's a lion. Lion going in the water.
4. He riding a bike.
5. A bed with a window. It's snowing.
6. Bears. They're cheeping. One's sneaking away. (?) Don't know.
7. Tiger taking the bears and he eats 'em up. The lion eats the tiger up.
8. I don't know. The father, the children, mother. Big children.
9. Rabbit. It's snowing.
10. He have to make. Both have to make, the frother and son. The frother spanking boy. (?) Getting real mad.

*Figure drawing:* Mitchell could not produce even the most primitive representation, but his scribbling was accompanied by his verbalizing, "the stomach," "the neck," "the face," "the eyes," "the nose" and "the head."

## Psychological Report and Follow-up

The examining psychologist's report follows:

Mitchell was restless and distractible during the examination, and it was difficult to keep his attention focused on the tasks. His behavior seemed somewhat babyish for his age. His articulation was immature; it was often difficult to understand him. He was impatient when requested to repeat, often replying, "You know" or "You heard," as if he felt the examiner were teasing him. Nonetheless, it was through his conversation that much was learned about him. Particularly when praised, he would assert boastfully, "I know everything." But he often complained about his inadequacies, too. "I don't know how to make a straight line. My big brother calls me a stupid brat." He needed a lot of praise and encouragement, and was inclined to give up quickly and angrily if he encountered difficulties. He was impatient with the CAT and could not be induced to elaborate his stories. However, fantasy material was very readily elicited as he worked on the Binet or his drawings. The major theme of these fantasies was the wish to express his anger by letting loose an overwhelming destructive force, and his consequent great anxiety that some terrible catastrophe would befall him as a result of his angry wishes.

When first asked to draw a person, Mitchell described his production as a "poison rattlesnake." In response to questions about a "person" he drew, he said that the boy would be happiest if he had a bomb, because, "It will blow up 20 million houses; it's gonna blow up the whole world. There will be no more houses, and all the men will be killed." Asked what would make the little boy scared, he replied, "The bombs"; *every-thing* made him scared. He then differentiated between "atomic bombs and hydrogen bombs" which made the boy "real scared," and torpedoes which made him "not so scared." He said the boy would wish most for "an atomic bomb" in order to "blow up the city and our house."

In the CAT pictures, Mitchell paid attention primarily to the male figure and described mostly father-son relationships, largely ignoring the mother-child relationship. One can surmise a wish to ally himself with the father, and some resentment toward the brother. Possibly because of his own confusion, as well as his articulatory inefficiency, it was difficult to tell whether he was referring to father or brother, since he used the word "frother" seemingly interchangeably for them both. He seemed to have an ambivalent relationship with his brother, at times accepting him as a teacher, and at other times viewing him as a competitor whose superiority was resented.

In the opinion of the examining psychiatrist, Mitchell had found some security in masturbation, but the near accident was viewed as punishment, and so he regressed to soiling. He was not getting much gratification in maturing; his mother, too, infantilized him to keep him "hers" (the brother being his father's "property"). She was also unwittingly very seductive with Mitchell (e.g., continuing to hold his penis when he urinated), and this was frightening to the boy, particularly in view of the father's lack of protectiveness.

The mother was accepted for treatment interviews. A month later she reported that Mitchell's symptoms were gone. He had started kindergarten and was adjusting fairly well there, although he did not particularly like it. In all her interviews the mother had concentrated on her own personality problems, scarcely referring to Mitchell. After six interviews, the mother said she knew she needed help for herself, and asked to be referred to an adult psychiatrist. This was arranged for her.

For at least the past decade, there has been clear recognition that the psychological examiner should not limit himself to formal test analysis. In his assessment he builds on, but far exceeds, numerical test scores and raw data. Schafer,[6,7] Rapaport,[4,5] and Hunt[2] were among the early workers to discuss the need for understanding underlying processes, to evidence discontent with mere scores, to note the importance of such factors as the influence of the examiner on test results and to discuss the importance of his insights in structuring and interpreting the findings. The significance of behavioral observations and spontaneously proffered conversation made during the examination will already have been noted, specifically in the interpretations of Mitchell. Perhaps for him this volunteered information can be attributed largely to his age, and consequent greater disposition to spontaneous revelation of his "inner workings." But behavioral observations enhance the picture for all children, and can sometimes be as important or even more important than the test data themselves in the eventual formulation. A case in point is Opal, aged 15 years, 8 months.

## Case 4

As a general rule, when productivity on tests is low, when raw material is sparse, the psychologist must be correspondingly tentative and wary in drawing his conclusions. In extreme cases he may decline to attempt any formulation at all. Opal produced little—only eight responses on the Rorschach, and very brief, descriptive phrases to some of the TAT pictures. Even these scanty results were elicited with great difficulty and with much encouragement by a skilled examiner. The full protocols follow.

*Psychological Examination*
   *Rorschach:*

Rorschach Protocol (Opal)

| | | | | |
|---|---|---|---|---|
| I | 30″ | I don't know what it is. | (Encouraged) | |
| | | A spider (W). | Don't know (Shows wings, | W F − A |
| | | (Encouraged) | head, rest of body). | |
| | | Butterfly (W) | They look the same. | W F + A P |
| | | That's all. | | |
| II | | I don't see nothing on here. (Encouraged. Places card on table, gazes at it. Encouraged). I don't know. (Encouraged.) | | |

|     | 90″ | Two bears, I guess. (D1) (No further response in 140″). | Shape | D F + A P |
|-----|-----|---|---|---|
| III | 16″ | Two people trying to keep warm over fire (D1). (Places card on table). That's all. | Way it looks. Don't know. (?) Looks like smoke (?). It's dark. | D M + H P |
| IV | 28″ | A bear (W). That's all (places card on table). | Don't know. Long claws (D4). (Points out head and feet on request. Can't find arms.) | W F + A P |
| V | 12″ | Looks like a bat (W) That's all. (Places on table, gazes at it) | Looks like it all over (?). Way it's shaped. | W F + A P |
| VI | 30″ | I don't know what this is. (Places card on table. Encouraged) I don't know | | Rejected |
|     | 120″ | I don't know. | | |
| VII | 40″ | I don't know what this is either. (Encouraged) I don't know. | | Rejected |
|     | 120″ | I don't know. | | |
| VIII | 12″ | Looks like two bears trying to climb a mountain (D1) That's all. I don't see nothing else. | They look like climbing a mountain (?). Don't know, don't know. (Points out head when asked.) | D F + A P |
|     | 120″ | | | |
| IX | 35″ | I don't see nothing on here. (Encouraged. Places card on table.) | | Rejected |
|     | 100″ | (Stops looking at it) | | |
| X | 55″ | I see two animals (D8) | I don't know (?) Way it looks (?). I don't know. | |

Rorschach Summary

| W 4 | M 1 | H 1 | P = 6 |
|-----|-----|-----|-------|
| D 4 | F + 6 | A 7 | |
| —  | F − 1 | — | |
| 8 | — | 8 | |
| | 8 | | |

Testing the limits: Unable to form any percept using color—points out VI as "fuzzy."

*Thematic Apperception Test:*

1. Little boy getting ready to play violin. He looks sad. That's all. (Encouraged to tell story with beginning, middle, end.) I don't know.
2. Man is plowing the field. Lady standing and watching, leaning against tree, and girl looks like she's going to school. (?) I don't know nothing else about them.
3BM. I don't know nothing about that picture. A boy, I guess.
4. Don't know about that either. (Happening?) Don't know. (Guess) Don't know.
5. Lady opened door and looked in room. Looks like she's scared. (About?) Don't know. (Encouraged) That's all.
6. Don't know about this.
7GF. Little girl holding a doll and her mother is reading to her. That's all. (Thinking or feeling?) Don't know.

8GF. I don't know about that picture.

9GF. Lady looks like she's running. (Encouraged) This lady standing looking at her, leaning up against a tree. Don't know.

10. (Pause) Two people—looks like they're dancing. That's all.

8BM. Don't know. Two men—looks like getting ready to cut the other man. This little boy watching. (Why?) Don't know.

17GF. Lady's looking into water like she wants to jump in, and these men are bringing cargo from boat. That's all. (Happens?) I guess she jump in. I don't know. (?) Don't know.

13MF. I don't know. I don't like that picture! The man act like he killed the lady.

*Rhode Sentence Completion:* Not very informative. Possibly significant were the following:

5. *The training* school is for girls.

7. *Much of the time* has been wasted.

24. *I fear* being alone.

27. *Many of my dreams* are fearful.

30. *I cannot understand what makes me* have bad dreams and be afraid.

35. *I am very* tired.

*Draw-a-Person:* Carelessly drawn girl, a very immature type of drawing, without many details. Clothing represented by dots for buttons in midline, belt and skirt. Hair scribbled on circumference of head.

## Medical and Historical Note

Six months earlier, Opal had had to have a thyroidectomy. The operation was successful, but three weeks after her return home she began to have "hysterics," would cry, shiver and fall to the floor. She was unable to sleep, and feared dying. Her personality had changed drastically. She asked her mother why others were always talking about her, and was feared by her sisters, who hoped she was not crazy. The doctor who was supervising her medically referred the girl. Postoperatively, it was necessary for Opal to take thyroxin; she showed some signs of myxedema.

## Psychological Report

Opal spoke softly, sat almost motionless in her chair, and was quite unresponsive. Confronted with the tests, she gave up readily and did not respond to encouragement. On the intelligence test, if an answer did not immediately occur to her she lacked the energy to search for it. On some easy items, she amended her usual, "I don't know," to "I done forgot." Usually, though, she seemed unconcerned about her failures and lack of productivity.

The examining psychologist wrote:

In both her behavior and responses, Opal consistently presented the picture of a depressed, severely constricted, anergic child. There were continuous protests of inability. When she responded at all, it was with a very cautious, rigidly accurate adherence to the most obvious, commonplace aspects of the situation. There were no indications of bizarre ideation or intellectual confusion. Opal seemed almost entirely drained of energy. In those few instances where she gave any sign of coming to life or permitting herself some imaginative activity, it was in relation to sad, dysphoric content, e.g., "A lady's looking into the water like she wants to jump in"; "Two people trying to keep warm over a fire." Opal gave no evidence of capacity for normal emotional contact, and seemed quite unable to respond to any pleasurable, emotionally exciting stimuli.

On the more conscious level, she revealed a good deal of concern over her school work, and feelings of inferiority and shame about it. She also had a generalized fearfulness and concern about her "bad dreams," as well as a tendency toward preoccupation with somatic complaints. Most of her energy seems to be channeled into maintaining a rigid psychic vigilance.

The problem of distinguishing the degree to which these reactions were attributable to endocrine dysfunction or readjustment cannot be solved with certainty.

The psychologist concluded, however, that it played a major role, and the examining psychiatrist and staff agreed. The assigned diagnosis was "psychophysiologic endocrine reaction." Opal was followed in 26 treatment interviews. She made considerable progress, with improved school reports and much better relations with her peers. Her rather disturbed relationship to her mother changed little, but since she became increasingly independent it did not affect her so much. Her facial expression was strikingly different; it became lively and vivid. Indications of depression had vanished.

## Summary

While necessarily sketchy and incomplete, these cases give some examples of the problems encountered and of the integration of raw data attempted by the psychologist in the children's clinic. As more knowledge is gained, as greater accuracy and refinements become possible, he may well be held in even higher regard by his colleagues. Even now he is likely to be listened to respectfully, if for no other reason than that he is the sole member of the traditional clinic team with unique diagnostic tools and techniques to apply, however fallible and crude they sometimes appear to be.

## References

1. Ames, L. B., Learned, J., Métraux, R. W., & Walker, R. N.  *Child Rorschach responses: developmental trends from two to ten years.* New York: Hoeber, 1952.

2. Hunt, W. A.  The future of diagnostic testing in clinical psychology. *J. clin. Psychol.*, 1946, *2*, 311–317.

3. Hutt, M. L.  A clinical study of "consecutive" and "adaptive" testing with the Revised Stanford-Binet. *J. consult. Psychol.*, 1946, *11*, 93–103.

4. Rapaport, D., Gill, M., & Schafer, R.  *Diagnostic psychological testing.* Chicago: Year Book, 1946. 2 vols.

5. ——.  The theoretical implications of diagnostic testing procedures. *In* Knight, R. P., & Friedman, C. R. (Eds.)  *Psychoanalytic psychiatry and psychology.* Vol. 1. New York: Int. Univer. Press, 1954. Pp. 173–195.

6. Schafer, R.  *Clinical application of psychological tests.* New York: Int. Univer. Press, 1948.

7. ——.  *Psychoanalytic interpretation in Rorschach testing.* New York: Grune & Stratton, 1954.

8. Stone, L. J.  Recent developments in diagnostic testing of children. *In* Harrower, M. R. (Ed.)  *Recent advances in diagnostic psychological testing.* Springfield, Ill.: C. C Thomas, 1950. Pp. 73–98.

9. Werner, H.  *Comparative psychology of mental development.* (Rev. ed.) New York: Int. Univer. Press, 1957.

**20**

# The Application of Projective Techniques in
# Research with Children

IRVING SIGEL

THE USE of projective tests for personality research with children has been consistently increasing. This growth is no doubt due to the unique properties possessed by projective-type instruments. They tend to elicit rich material, depicting the child's perceptions and interpretations of reality. As the child imposes his own cognitive scheme on stimulus materials, he tends to reveal inner thoughts, feelings and attitudes about various aspects of his world. Such tests enable the examiner to secure material which is unobtainable through other means. This is particularly the case with children. The child, especially the young child, is not amenable to interviewing or direct questioning, since he has difficulty expressing himself solely in verbal terms. Frequently he is unable to understand verbal questions requiring identification of feelings, thoughts and the like. Consequently, it is in an indirect way that the projective test obtains such information. Further, projective tests enable the examiner to get at data which the child might guard against revealing, were he asked directly.

Because projective tests permit the gathering of rich material reflecting the inner life of the child, research workers have found it superior to the more objective methods and the observational approaches.[1] One of the main advantages is that control of stimulus materials and experimental conditions can be maintained to a greater degree than in the case of naturalistic observations. Now the research worker can meet some of the requirements of sound research practice and yet obtain data that are potentially revealing of the covert aspects of the personality.

The relative success of projective tests in clinical settings and the increased usage in research, however, should not keep us from examining the numerous theoretical and methodologic problems that exist, particularly when projective tests are applied to research with children.[1,14,63] This is not to say that such problems do not exist for all users of projective tests. Our concern here, however, is to emphasize those questions relevant to research applications.

The research requirements of an instrument must be stringent. In research a particular measuring device should be as precise a measure of the variables as possible. Projective tests in research require communication of the bases of interpretation, so that replication of the experiment or study is possible.

350

Intuition or clinical hunch is not allowable as a *modus operandi* in research, although it is probably desirable and necessary in clinical situations. The research worker attempting to find modal patterns of behavior is concerned with group differences (although, to be sure, he is interested in individual differences) and so must employ measures which would provide a common or standardized stimulus for his sample. By so doing, he can maintain some of the necessary experimental controls.

These requirements of research thus pose problems which are of considerable import and must be articulated, thereby moving toward some resolution. The fruitfulness of a technique should not be jeopardized by overlooking some of the basic issues involved in assessing its utility and increasing its precision as a research tool.

Awareness of such problems is prevalent in the literature. Numerous writers have pointed out the issues of validity, reliability, complexity and modes of analysis. These discussions have tended to focus on the problems of projectives in general[1,6] or of particular projective tests.[2,3,12] This chapter, however, will attempt to focus on the specific problems involved in employing projective tests with children. As will be shown, unique problems emerge when fantasy-eliciting stimuli are used with children.[7] Some of our discussion will overlap with projective theory in general. The focus will be on theoretical and methodologic problems of projective techniques as sources of data with children. We shall discuss the following questions: (1) What kind of data do projective tests yield? (2) What do the data signify? (3) What factors influence responses on such tests?

## What Types of Data do Projective Tests Yield?

This question may seem obvious. Projective tests yield fantasy material. The responses reflect the child's perception of the stimuli and so are presumed manifestations of the child's inner feelings, states and attitudes.[1]

This is a descriptive statement denoting the general type of material but not what the responses represent, i.e., what is reflected in the fantasy—unconscious material or material reproducing physical and social reality, for example. The answer to this question is important and a necessary prelude to further evaluation of projective test data. To add to the complication, the term "projection" is unclear and not identically defined by all. Some writers confine its use to apperceptive distortion, while others use it to indicate a perceptual-cognitive process employed in organizing and integrating outward and inner reality.[1,6,15] Clarification of this concept, especially for research, is important.

### Concept of Projection

First, it should be made clear that the phenomenon of projection with children cannot be viewed in the same way as in the case of adults. The fact is that children interpret reality in many ways commensurate with their developmental level and, hence, may "distort" reality because of limited experience, knowledge and language facility. The magical thought, the syncretistic reasoning, are both illustrations of "distortions" of physical and social reality by the young child. They cannot be assumed to reflect defensive operations. As Freud has said, "The projection of inner perceptions to the outside is a primitive mechanism which, for instance, also influences our sense-perceptions, so that it normally has the greatest share in shaping our outside world . . . even inner perceptions of ideational and emotional processes are *projected* [italics mine] outwardly, like sense perceptions, and are used to shape the outer world. . . ." (reference 24, page 857) The shift from such an orientation toward a more cognitive view of the world comes about with maturity, and with the formation of language. Thus, this type of mechanism or psychic process is different from that of adults. The bases for distortions, if any, that are observed with children may be derived from factors related to immaturity rather than from conflict and defense.

### Levels of Fantasy Obtained

If the fantasy productions of the child are, in part, indicative of his developmental state, what level of consciousness do these fantasy reports represent? From a psychoanalytic point of view, there should be some correlation between the child's developmental level and the impulse-derived fantasy. That is to say, since the ego develops and provides the child with a progressively increased capacity to view reality in realistic or adult terms, then the young child should in his fantasy produce unrealistic, idiosyncratic responses. Further, there should be less separation of self from material, and the child's fantasy should reflect to a greater degree his own life experience. As he matures, he begins to approach more conventional responses. As we shall see, however, this seems to be a function of the material used.[4,7] Thus, these assumptions may be valid, contingent on the particular test employed.

We need to determine explicitly the level of fantasy particular stimuli can potentially elicit. If a child, for example, in a doll play session gives a story in which the mother doll falls down and is seriously hurt, what does this represent? Conceivably, it could reflect the child's death wishes or hostile feelings against the mother; or it could be a retelling of a situation that had just recently occurred in which the mother did fall down and get hurt. In other words, the child's story may be a reconstruction of his own life experience and his interpretation of reality, or it may be an admixture of reproductive material with unconscious aspects, or it may represent solely the unfulfilled wishes, desires and anxieties which are not conscious. It is because of the difficulty of separating the reconstructive from the unconscious that Anna Freud does not use play techniques as the method for arriving at an understanding of the child's unconscious. "Instead of being invested with symbolic meaning it may sometimes admit of a harmless explanation. . . ." (reference 23, page 29). The symbolic significance of the child's fantasy productions apparently cannot be applied to every act but only to those which are directed by unconscious impulses. As a result, A. Freud[23] prefers such techniques as interpretation of dreams and the use of drawings.

In research, however, we do not have the same goals as the therapist and so cannot rely on the technique used by A. Freud. Nevertheless, her point is well taken when we interpret fantasy material in projective tests and we attempt to determine what its unconscious or latent representations signify.

### Need for Normative Data

To meet these problems, it is necessary to obtain normative data for the various projective techniques. It is necessary to know what constitutes the normal range when a child is compared to other children in his group.[17,25,49,70,73] Further, it is necessary to assess the degree to which the child differs developmentally from other children. In this way we can be more assured as to which responses are significant of apperception or distortion. The degree to which the child deviates from his peers, however, and the place he is on the developmental "curve" can only be determined when we have adequate data by which to make such comparisons. In addition, the norms are necessary to evaluate the degree to which he is expressing his own unique orientation toward reality. Bach,[7] in a comprehensive study of the child's doll play fantasy, points out that 75 per cent are ". . . reproductions of what others have been observed to do, as well as what the child himself has experienced." He concludes that only about one-quarter of the child's fantasy "*cannot* be characterized as rather faithfully reproducing physical or social realities" (reference 7, page 26). Doll play situations, by the way, are notable for the extent to which they have been employed in methodologic studies investigating the kinds of questions posed here.[7,52,59,65,76]

If it is assumed that fantasy production that is stereotyped reflects the modal approach, then nonstereotyped responses would be of particular interest in differentiating individuals. This is, in a sense, Rosenzweig's point[56] when he stresses the need to obtain normative data on projectives. If a large portion of a report is stereotyped and this is known, then what is obtained is a reflection of the broader psychocultural context. Byrd and Witherspoon[14] find, in this connection, that for preschool children on the Children's Apperception Test, oral and aggressive themes are prevalent. The frequency, then, of such thematic material indicates a "normative" trend and limits the potential significance of such material for the individual. Such research indicates that the fantasy level can and does reflect the broader culture.

Numerous studies represent efforts at obtaining what are modal age patterns.[4,14,19,20,30,53,71,73] Similar work should be done with many of the projective techniques which are in wide usage. For such work Rosenzweig[56] offers the suggestion that there is need for two types of norms. One type would be analogous to the Rorschach popular response—stereotyped statements made about the stimulus materials; and the second type of norms would consist of responses (e.g., stories, labeling, drawing, etc.) which characterize the subject. These are subject-oriented as contrasted to the first type, which are test-oriented. Although Rosenzweig refers specifically to the TAT in making his conclusions, the points he makes are relevant to projective techniques in general.

Obtaining such sets of data, then, enables the research worker to identify individuals who reflect the culture and the degree to which others deviate. Parenthetically, it should be pointed out that normative studies involving different age children also offer considerable data on developmental trends. Ideally, these should be longitudinal to yield the maximum data on the developmental pattern.[4,73] But cross sectional samples do have considerable merit in at least suggesting what the course of development seems to be. Thus, normative studies provide us with two sets of data: modal patterns of response and the substantive changes that occur.

In addition to such value, normative studies have general methodologic advantages. Much of the research done with projective tests tends to use small samples of children. Since many of the studies make comparisons between extreme groups, the knowledge of the range of scores from large sample studies is important. It enables the researcher to determine whether his data truly represent extremes relative to the large sample or are merely relevant to his particular sample.

### What do the Data Signify?

Even having normative data, however, still begs the question: To what end fantasy behavior? The assumption seems to be that fantasy is an important area of study because of its underlying relationship to overt behavior. Since fantasy derives from unconscious as well as conscious motivations, its elicitation should yield insights into the covert bases for an individual's actions. Fantasy, therefore, can be presumed to represent an intervening variable—intervening between antecedent variables (e.g., child rearing practices) and overt behaviors (e.g., social interactions). Interest then in studying fantasy becomes twofold: first, to assess the antecedents of the fantasy productions; and, secondly, to predict to the overt behavior of the individual. Thus, given a child in a doll play situation who develops a theme in which destruction and love elements are woven into an elaborate production, we ask: What accounts for the particular thematic organization and content, and what does this information tell us about how that child will behave in particular and specified situations? It might be pointed out that one could also ask: What kind of a person is this child? Phrasing the question in such a general way yields a descriptive diagnostic picture of the child. The validity of the description, however, remains open. Implicit in such descriptions are predictions of the child's behavior. Thus, we need to be specific in order to state under what conditions particular behaviors will emerge, how the child will adapt to particular individuals and situations, etc. Such specificity then presupposes a predictive goal. It is this predictability that is so essential and a primary justification for projective tests.

It should be made clear that prediction can be made not only to future behaviors (i.e., how the individual will behave), but also to past events (i.e., what happened in the past). Although both are important types of prediction, psychologists using projectives are frequently called upon to predict for future events. In order to achieve this, we must continuously assess obtained fantasy production, specify the direction behavior will take, and constantly be sensitive to discriminate between idiosyncratic responses and stereotypic ones. We must also distinguish between reproduction of immediate past events and screened or symbolic material. Some suggestions have already been offered as to how these distinctions can be obtained.

### Relation of Fantasy to Overt Behavior

Research in the past few years has tended increasingly to examine the relationship between fantasy and overt behavior. These are, in part, validation studies of the projective. Doll play, TAT and Rorschach studies have been reported, attempting to find such correlates. Before presenting some of the findings, let us first examine some of the approaches used.

A number of the studies have taken a projective device *in toto*, e.g., Rorschach, and attempted to relate the specific indices with overt manifestations. This assumes, of course, that the concept under study can be adequately measured by the particular projective. This is the taking-over of a technique which has not demonstrated its usefulness for measuring the variable in a particular context. Such practices are apparent in numerous studies.[7,17,29,36,44,45,57,69,74,76]

On the other hand, some notable studies have been done explicitly constructing instruments for the purpose of highlighting the particular variable in question and moved on to test the relationship between overt behavior and fantasy variables.[5,10,12,22,26,31,32,35,46,47,50,63,72]

The results of the first type of endeavor—the employment of a technique *in toto* and predictions to overt behavior—present contradictory findings. Using doll play techniques with preschool children, for example, some writers report that children who demonstrate high and low aggressivity in a preschool situation show high fantasy aggression, more so than children who were only moderately aggressive.[61]

The doll play studies are not as clear-cut as one would like, although Baruch[8] and Sears[61] do find positive relationships between aggressive fantasy and overt aggression. Stolz et al.[67] present data indicating that, for children who were separated from their fathers during the war, the fantasy aggression is high but these children tend to be more often aggressed against than the aggressors. Other studies also point out inconsistencies in predictions of this type.

Smith and Coleman,[66] employing the Rorschach and MAPS, found with the former test curvilinear relationships between hostile content and overt aggression; while for the MAPS, a positive correlation between "the degree to which hostile themes were acted out without modification in the MAPS protocols and overt hostility" was found (reference 66, page 333). The authors also report that using both tests gave better correlations between projective test data and overt behavior, although each of the tests seems to measure different things. Yet, they conclude, "None of the correlations between the hostile projective test content and overt hostility were high enough to make these measures useful as predictive instruments on an individual level" (reference 66, page 333). Valuable, then, as the group results are, we are still faced with solving the problem of how to improve the predictive power of projective test data for the individual.

### The Place of Situationally Relevant Content in Projective Tests

A fruitful approach in resolving some of the problems noted above is the use of stimuli depicting particular situations relevant to the variable under study. One reason for such contradictions may be the ambiguity of the projective test content. It seems reasonable to suggest that unless the content of the projective and the variables measured have some specific relationship, accurate predictions are difficult to make.

There is, fortunately, increased use of projectives depicting particular situations relevant to the problem under study, e.g., mother-child punishment[46,47]; boy-boy aggressivity[32,35]; teacher-child interaction[10]; fear situation[72]; and many others. The techniques are frequently story and sentence completion or of the TAT type. Whatever the projective test employed, the rationale seems to be that the more relevant the projective content to the situation studied, the better. Specificity of content, still allowing for latitude of fantasy expression, should increase our predictive power regarding these particular situations. This, by the way, may well be an effort toward resolving some of the problems posed by the validation studies, when a projective test like the Rorschach or TAT was used in a global way.

When we look at the results of such studies, we have to decide *how* to look at them. Some of the studies, used in the attempt to predict to overt behavior, are successful[13,32,35,48]; others are not.[63,66] Swift,[69] attempting to differentiate between two groups showing different responses to parental rejection, found curvilinear relationships when using story completion tests. Kagan,[32] with a TAT-like test using pictures depicting aggressive situations between peers, found a positive and direct relationship when fantasy suggested an aggressive content, and overt and fantasy behaviors are similar in mode of expression and goal object. Yet Mussen and Naylor[48] also found a direct and positive relationship using the TAT itself. It might be pointed out here that the relationship between aggressive fantasy and overt behavior was found to be high when the fear of punishment was taken into consideration in the Mussen and Naylor study. This effort, including not only the measurement of the variable in question but also those processes that would inhibit expression, is an important procedure. It is a move toward a configurational analysis, at least of those relevant psychic activities.

Other studies do not offer such clear-cut face validity. The degree to which the findings can be accepted varies and, hence, no generalization can be offered that the *more specific* the technique, the *better* the predictive power. The evidence, however, tends to suggest the preference for such specific denotation of projective content specificity and configurational analysis. In a way, the latter aspect is similar to clinical procedures, except that it employs more specified variables and objective measures.

The use of situationally relevant projective content, however, raises a fundamental question, namely, what level of fantasy do such specific projectives elicit? In other words, does this not violate the basic assumption of projective testing: that opportunity be created for the individual to express idiosyncratic fantasy in sufficient quantity to enable one to describe adequately this individual or groups of individuals? The danger, of course, is that the greater the specificity of content, the greater the chance to increase productive, stereotypic material. The increased specificity does not require identity, however, but psychological appropriateness or equivalence. It still can allow for thematic elaboration, idiosyncratic interpretation and employment of defensive modes. To be sure, further research is necessary to assume the degree to which unconscious material in the context is elicited.

It would seem that if a particular variable is specified, the goal toward which the expression of the variable is identified, and the psychological processes impinging on its expression are considered, the predictive power of the instrument could be improved.

### Relation of Fantasy to Antecedent Variables

Turning now to examination of fantasy behavior as the dependent variable, we find that numerous studies have been done assessing the child's life experience, previous interpersonal relationships (e.g., with parents), traumatic experiences (e.g., loss of father), illness, handicaps, etc.[18,29,31,33,42,57,60,62,74,75] Such research, occasionally theoretically based, has on the whole tended to yield inconsistent but low relationships. For example, the study by Sears et al.[62] on dependency and aggression, notable for the explicitness of the theoretical formulations, resulted in relatively few significant findings when predictions were made from maternal behavior to fantasy expression of aggression. On the other hand, when Lesser[35] used a TAT type instrument, positive relationships were found between overt behavior and fantasy under conditions of maternal encouragement of the expression of aggression.

### What are Some of the Factors that Can Influence the Fanasty Production?

The testing situation, whether it be for research or clinical examination, involves an interaction between the child, the testing materials and the examiner. It will behoove us to examine each of these factors individually to highlight some of the particular problems that influence the type, the quality, and the quantity of fantasy productions.

### The Child

First there is need to intensify our knowledge of the child. Although we touched on this throughout the chapter, we merely summarize the points here now. There is need for considerable research on the developmental aspects of fantasy production, with particular reference to the degree to which the child can reflect his own individuality in his handling of projective test materials. There is also considerable need to reexamine some of the assumptions made in the literature about the nature of young children relevant to fantasy productions. It may well be, for example, that the assumptions concerning concretism and lack of thematic approaches are a function of the material.[4,22,30,72]

Other characteristics of the child that must be considered are sex, intellectual ability, verbal facility and fantasy skill.[7,8,9,30,53,59] These types of factors do have some influence on the child's attitude toward the task, his performance and the degree to which he can fulfill the demands. The research worker cannot ignore these variables, which have been demonstrated to have some relationship to fantasy production.[7,59]

One important criterion that has received particular attention to date is the social-class position of the child. Here we are faced with a perplexing problem. Does the difference, if any, in projective test productions of children from different social class groups reflect actual personality differences between the groups; or does it mean that the test is inappropriate for the groups in question? This is a very real problem. Fiedler and Stone[20,21] report that when children of lower socioeconomic status are tested on the Rorschach, their performance differs significantly from the norms presented by Ames[8] and Carlson.[16] In the latter studies, the children predominantly came from middle-class homes, in contrast to the sample used by Fiedler and Stone. Thus, it may be asked, what does this difference represent? The only answer at this time is that the two groups differ. What this difference actually means can only be determined by increased research in such comparisons. It may well be that these are true differences in perceptual-cognitive orientation and, consequently, that the instruments reflect just that. On the other hand, the Mussen and Naylor[48] study does not seem to be different from Kagan's report[32] on the relationship between overt aggression and fantasy. In these cases two different social class groups were used, and the same type of projective task was employed, although they did differ on the specific pictures used. Yet the results indicate at least face validity for the TAT-type measures employed.

Unfortunately, most of the research with young children—pre-schoolers—has tended to be with middle- to upper middle-class groups; thus, there is a considerable class stratification. A study by the Ammons[5] indicates, however, that in a day-care center and public kindergarten they obtained aggressive fantasy material in a modified doll play situation with children from two and one-half to five years of age. Although identification of the social class status of the families of these children is not very precise, the authors state that their occupational level is somewhat above average; but nevertheless, it seems reasonable to conclude that groups in day-care centers and public kindergartens may include more lower social class children than are usually enrolled in university-run nursery schools. The results of this study, according to the authors, agree with similar studies regarding the changes with age of aggressive behavior. These results suggest that the social class variables may not be as critical with pre-school children's display of aggression using doll play materials. Of course, further examination of socioeconomic differences should be done, with the use of more clearly defined status groups.

The evidence seems to point up the need for further investigations in which clarification of the meaning of social class differences, the types of social class differences, and the relevance of particular instruments for different social class groups will result. Essentially, it is necessary to ask whether the differences obtained between the groups is a function of the differential significance and relevance of the instruments employed, or whether the differences are psychologically meaningful and, presumably, a function of one's class position. The answer rests in increased research on projective tests with large, well defined samples of children differing in social class position. Until such work is done, only tenuous generalizations can be made.

### The Test Situation and the Examiner

It is becoming apparent that greater cognizance must be taken of the social situation in which the testing occurs. This holds true for clinical and for research examination.[58] The evidence is piling up that the fantasy production of the child is highly sensitive to the social as well as the physical aspects of the situation. A number of studies have been reported which indicate the sensitivity of the child to the length of the session, the number of sessions required, the presence of significant individuals and the attitude of the experimenter.[37,51,53,65] When the number of sessions increases, contradictory evidence is presented regarding frequency of aggression.[51 65] The use of more sessions is at times not so much intended as an examination of the method as it is a way of testing specific hypotheses regarding extinction of inhibition of aggressive fantasy production.[37,62]

Thus, those studies of aggression which are derived from a learning theory framework have found this a useful tool to explore problems of inhibition, extinction and displacement. Yet on the basis of their findings, other doll play studies were done to test hypotheses which required measures of aggression. Illustrative of this is one[72] which examined measures of aggressive fantasy between accident-prone and nonaccident-prone children between the ages of five and eight; it was reported that doll play was used under permissive conditions in order to facilitate the extinction of aggressive anxiety. Yet, when the hypothesis relevant to aggression anxiety was tested and found to yield limited and inconsistent results, little attention was paid to the role of the doll play as a possible source of error, and attention was focussed on theory construction as the source of error. This common practice presumes validity of the projective test—a questionable assumption.

Thus, serious questions are posed in assuming that the test conditions truly reflect the experimenter's intentions. What is perceived by the experimenter as permissive is not necessarily consistent with the child's perception of the situation and the examiner. Another study[65] poses contradicatory evidence also. From these studies it seems clear that careful methodologic consideration should be given to the experimental conditions in order to ascertain their effect on the fantasy production.

### The Materials

The test materials pose another source of difficulty. Generally we can ask, do all projectives yield the same level of fantasy? Apparently the answer to this is "No." Some of the materials employed, such as the TAT, seem to reflect needs and presses, while other techniques produce more structured cognitive perceptions.[12,28] Some tend to elicit more realistic behavior than others.[7,22,51] It is also clear that, with children, different projectives elicit different types of responses, ranging from primary description to fantasy.[8,14,73] Aside from the age level of the child, the inherent structure of the stimuli has differential pull on the subjects' cognitive orientation.

In general it can be stated that sufficient evidence exists in the literature that status, test conditions and test materials play a potentially significant role in influencing the fantasy production of the child. If this is so, it would seem crucial that more attention be paid to these factors prior to using projective tests for research. The failure to substantiate hypotheses, even though quantities of rich verbal material are available, may be due to the fact that methods did not clearly elicit those data necessary for the experiment. It would be safe to suggest that consideration be made of the methodologic issues before attempting to elaborate *ad hoc* interpretations of the data. The theory may really be correct.

## Conclusion

In this chapter an attempt was made to highlight some of the crucial issues when projective tests are applied to research in personality development with children. The discussion focused on the following questions: What types of data do projective techniques yield? What are some of the methodologic and theoretical problems facing the researcher using such data? What are some of the situational variables influencing the production of fantasy material? The attempt was made to demonstrate these points with relevant studies. It was found, after such analyses, that future research developments may avoid the errors of the past.

The conclusion that can be drawn is that there is much to be done in the field of projective tests to enhance their value. The evidence presented points to the complexity of the entire field. To solve many of the problems posed requires an intensive dedication to re-examination of assumptions, theoretical formulations and experimental designs utilizing projective tests. It seems reasonable to conclude that experiments must be done using adequate controls, larger samples and more rigorous formulations of the variables under examination. In addition, the theoretical developments which must occur—denoting specification and operational definitions of variables and their interaction—would help increase the utility of projective data as well as the value of projective material in studies of personality.

It is time to move away from the old adage that "We are still young," because this may well be self deceiving and rationalizing. Rather, the fact is that increased conceptual and methodologic rigor, as well as a more clear-cut rationale for employment of projective tests, will further the development of a powerful and productive psychological tool.

# References

1. Abt, L. E., & Bellak, L. (Eds.)  *Projective psychology*. New York: Knopf, 1950.
2. Ainsworth, M. D.  Some problems of validation of projective techniques. *Brit. J. med. Psychol.*, 1951, *24*, 151–161.
3. Allen, R.  A longitudinal study of six Rorschach protocols of a three-year-old child. *Child Developm.*, 1951, *22*, 61–70.
4. Ames, L. B., Learned, J., Métraux, R. W., & Walker, R. N.  *Child Rorschach responses: developmental trends from two to ten years*. New York: Hoeber, 1952.
5. Ammons, C. H., & Ammons, R. B.  Aggression in doll play: interviews of two- to six-year-old white males. *J. genet. Psychol.*, 1953, *82*, 205–213.
6. Anderson, H. H., & Anderson, G. L. (Eds.)  *An introduction to projective techniques*. New York: Prentice-Hall, 1951.
7. Bach, G. R.  Young children's play fantasies. *Psychol. Monogr.*, 1945, *59*, No. 2 (Whole No. 272).
8. Baruch, D. W.  Aggression during doll play. *Amer. J. Orthopsychiat.*, 1941, *11*, 252–259.
9. Beier, G., Gorlow, L., & Stacey, C. L.  The fantasy life of the mental defective. *Amer. J. ment. Defic.*, 1951, *55*, 582–589.
10. Biber, B., & Lewis, C.  An experimental study of what young school children expect from their teachers. *Genet. Psychol. Monogr.*, 1949, *40*, 3–97.
11. Block, J., & Martin, B.  Predicting the behavior of children under frustration. *J. abnorm. soc. Psychol.*, 1955, *51*, 281–285.
12. Blum, G. S.  A study of the psychoanalytic theory of psychosexual development. *Genet. Psychol. Monogr.*, 1949, *39*, 3–103.
13. Borenstein, B.  A study of the relationship between Thematic Apperception Test fantasy and overt behavior. Unpublished doctoral dissertation. Univer. of California, 1954.
14. Byrd, E., & Witherspoon, R. L.  Responses of preschool children to the Children's Apperception Test. *Child Develpm.*, 1954, *25*, 35–44.
15. Cattell, R. B.  Principles of design in "projective" or misperceptive tests of personality. *In* Anderson, H. H., & Anderson, G. L. (Eds.)  *An introduction to projective techniques*. New York: Prentice-Hall, 1951. Pp. 55–98.
16. Carlson, R.  A normative study of Rorschach responses of eight-year-old children. *J. proj. Tech.*, 1952, *16*, 56–65.
17. Cox, B., & Sargent, H.  TAT responses of emotionally disturbed and emotionally stable children: clinical judgment versus normative data. *J. proj. Tech.*, 1950, *14*, 61–74.
18. Cox, S. M.  A factorial study of the Rorschach responses of normal and maladjusted boys. *J. genet. Psychol.*, 1951, *79*, 95–115.
19. Elkisch, P.  Children's drawings as a projective technique. *Psychol. Monogr.*, 1945, *58*, No. 1 (Whole No. 266).
20. Fiedler, M. F., & Stone, L. J.  The Rorschachs of selected groups of children in comparison with published norms, I. *J. proj. Tech.*, 1956, *20*, 274–275.
21. ——, & ——.  The Rorschachs of selected groups of children in comparison with published norms, II. *J. proj. Tech.*, 1956, *20*, 276–279.
22. Fishbach, S.  The catharsis hypothesis and some consequences of interaction with aggressive and neutral play objects. *J. Pers.*, 1956, *24*, 449–462.
23. Freud, A.  *The psychoanalytical treatment of children*. London: Imago Publishing Co., Ltd., 1946.
24. Freud, S.  *The basic writings of Sigmund Freud*. New York: Modern Library, 1938.
25. Goodenough, F. L., & Harris, D. B.  Studies in the psychology of children's drawings. II. 1928–1949. *Psychol. Bull.*, 1950, *47*, 369–433.
26. Grace, H. H., & Lohman, J. J.  Children's reactions to stories depicting parent-child conflict situations. *Child Develpm.*, 1952, *23*, 62–74.
27. Gruber, S.  The concept of task orientation in the analysis of play behavior of children entering kindergarten. *Amer. J. Orthopsychiat.*, 1954, *24*, 326–335.
28. Harris, D. B., & Tseng, S. C.  Children's attitudes toward peers and parents as revealed by sentence completions. *Child Develpm.*, 1957, *28*, 401–411.

29. Holden, R. H.   The Children's Apperception Test with cerebral palsied and normal children. *Child Develpm.*, 1956, *27*, 3–8.
30. Honzik, M. P.   Sex differences in the occurrence of materials in the play construction of pre-adolescents. *Child Develpm.*, 1951, *22*, 15–36.
31. Jackson, L.   Emotional attitudes towards the family of normal, neurotic and delinquent children. Part II. *Brit. J. Psychol.* 1950, *41*, 173–185.
32. Kagan, J.   The measurement of overt aggression from fantasy. *J. abnorm. soc. Psychol.*, 1956, *52*, 390–393.
33. Krall, V.   Personality characteristics of accident repeating children. *J. abnorm. soc. Psychol.*, 1953, *48*, 99–107.
34. Lazarus, R.   An experimental analysis of the influence of color on the protocol of the Rorschach test. *J. Pers.*, 1948, *17*, 182–185.
35. Lesser, G.   The relationship between overt and fantasy aggression as a function of maternal response to aggression. *J. abnorm. soc. Psychol.*, 1957, *55*, 218–221.
36. Levin, H., & Sears, R. H.   Identification with parents as a determinant of doll play aggression. *Child Develpm.*, 1956, *27*, 135–153.
37. ——, & Turgeon, V. F.   The influence of the mother's presence on children's doll play aggression. *J. abnorm. soc. Psychol.*, 1957, *55*, 304–308.
38. Liccione, J. V.   The changing family relationships of adolescent girls. *J. abnorm. soc. Psychol.*, 1955, *51*, 421–426.
39. London, I.   The developing personality as a joint function of convergence and divergence, *J. soc. Psychol.*, 1949, *29*, 167–187.
40. McFate, M. Q., & Orr, F. G.   Through adolescence with the Rorschach. *Rorschach Res. Exch. & J. proj. Tech.*, 1949, *13*, 302–319.
41. McLeod, H.   A Rorschach study with preschool children. *J. proj. Tech.*, 1950, *14*, 453–463.
42. Martin, W. E.   Identifying the insecure child. II. The validity of some suggested methods. *J. genet. Psychol.*, 1952, *80*, 25–33.
43. Meyer, R.   Sex role identification in young children. *Genet. Psychol. Monogr.*, 1950, *42*, 81–158.
44. Michal-Smith, H.   The identification of pathological cerebral function through the H-T-P technique. *J. clin. Psychol.*, 1953, *9*, 293–295.
45. Montalto, F. D.   Maternal behavior and child personality: a Rorschach study. *J. proj. Tech.*, 1952, *16*, 151–178.
46. Morgan, P. K., & Gaier, E. L.   The direction of aggression in the mother-child punishment situation. *Child Develpm.*, 1956, *27*, 447–457.
47. ——, & ——.   Types of reactions in punishment situations in the mother-child relationship. *Child Develpm.*, 1957, *28*, 149–160.
48. Mussen, P. H., & Naylor, H. K.   The relationships between overt and fantasy aggression. *J. abnorm. soc. Psychol.*, 1954, *49*, 235–240.
49. Paulsen, A. A.   Personality development in the middle years of childhood: a ten-year longitudinal study of thirty public school children by means of Rorschach tests and social histories. *Amer. J. Orthopsychiat.*, 1954, *24*, 336–350.
50. Payne, D. E., & Mussen, P. H.   Parent-child relations and father identification among adolescent boys. *J. abnorm. soc. Psychol.*, 1956, *52*, 358–362.
51. Phillips, R.   Doll play as a function of the realism of the materials and the length of the experimental session. *Child Develpm.*, 1945, *16*, 123–143.
52. Pintler, M. H., Phillips, R., & Sears, R. R. Sex differences in the projective doll play of preschool children. *J. Psychol.*, 1946, *21*, 73–80.
53. Powell, M.   Age and sex differences in degree of conflict within certain areas of psychological adjustment. *Psychol. Monogr.*, 1955, *69*, No. 2 (Whole No. 387).
54. Raven, J. C.   *Controlled projection for children* (2nd ed.) London: H. K. Lewis, 1951.
55. Reichard, S.   Discussion: projective techniques as a research tool in the study of normal personality development. *J. proj. Tech.*, 1956, *20*, 265–268.
56. Rosenzweig, S.   Apperceptive norms for the Thematic Apperception Test. I. The problem of norms in projective methods. *J. Pers.*, 1949, *17*, 475–482.

57. Schachtel, E. G.   Notes on Rorschach tests of 500 juvenile delinquents and a control group of 500 non-delinquent adolescents. *J. proj. Tech.*, 1951, *15*, 144–172.

58. Schafer, R.   *Psychoanalytic interpretation in Rorschach testing: theory and application.* New York: Grune & Stratton, 1954.

59. Sears, P. S.   Doll play aggression in normal young children: influence of sex, age, sibling status, father's absence. *Psychol. Monogr.*, 1951, *65*, No. 6 (Whole No. 323).

60. Sears, R. R., Pintler, M. H., & Sears, P. S.   Effect of father separation on preschool children's doll play aggression. *Child Develpm.*, 1946, *17*, 219–243.

61. ——.   Relation of fantasy aggression to inter-personal aggression. *Child Develpm.*, 1950, *21*, 5–6.

62. ——, Whiting, J. W. M., Nowlis, V., & Sears, P. S.   Some child-rearing antecedents of aggression and dependency in young children. *Genet. Psychol. Monogr.*, 1953, *47*, 135–234.

63. Seaton, J. K.   A projective experiment using incomplete stories with multiple-choice endings. *Genet. Psychol. Monogr.*, 1949, *40*, 149–228.

64. Siegel, A. E.   Film-mediated fantasy aggression and strength of aggressive drive. *Child Develpm.*, 1956, *27*, 365–378.

65. ——.   Aggressive behavior of young children in the absence of an adult. *Child Develpm.*, 1957, *28*, 371–378.

66. Smith, J. R., & Coleman, J. C.   The relationship between manifestations of hostility on projective tests and overt behavior, *J. proj. Tech.*, 1956, *20*, 327–334.

67. Stolz, L. M., et al.   *Father relations of war-born children.* Stanford, Calif.: Stanford Univer. Press, 1954.

68. Swenson, C. H., Jr.   Empirical evaluation of human figure drawings. *Psychol. Bull.*, 1957, *54*, 431–466.

69. Swift, J. W.   Matching of teacher's descriptions and Rorschach analysis of preschool children. *Child Develpm.*, 1944, *15*, 217–224.

70. ——.   Reliability of Rorschach scoring categories with pre-school children. *Child Develpm.*, 1944, *15*, 207–216.

71. ——.   Rorschach responses of eighty-two preschool children. *Rorschach Res.*, 1945, *9* 74–84.

72. Temple, R., & Amen, E. W.   A study of anxiety reactions in young children by means of a projective technique. *Genet. Psychol. Monogr.*, 1944, *30*, 59–114.

73. Thetford, W. N., Molish, H. B., & Beck, S. J. Developmental aspects of personality structure in normal children. *J. proj. Tech.*, 1951, *15*, 58–78.

74. Wenar, C.   The effects of a motor handicap on personality: III, The effects on certain fantasies and adjustive techniques. *Child Develpm.*, 1956, *27*, 9–15.

75. Winstel, B.   The use of a controlled play situation in determining certain effects of maternal attitudes on children. *Child Develpm.*, 1951, *22*, 299–311.

76. Yarrow, L.   The effect of antecedent frustration on projective play. *Psychol. Monogr.*, 1948, *62*, No. 6 (Whole No. 293).

**21**

# Recent Developments in the Field of Projective Techniques

GERALD F. KING

IN THIS CHAPTER an attempt is made to outline some of the developments, both conceptual and empirical, that have occurred in the field of projective techniques since 1950. Here, conceptual refers to various innovations ranging from concepts of limited scope to more comprehensive theoretical orientations. A few comments, in addition, are devoted to new books, new techniques and the projective community, the latter being a label for the people who use and develop projective tests.

Any review of an extensive field such as this is almost bound to be tinged with a certain amount of arbitrariness and subjectivity. In outlining the developments in projective techniques, the author definitely projects his own orientation into the welter of conceptual and empirical reports. One consequence is that the tone of the chapter is generally critical in nature. There is also the matter of content. The reader may point to the chapter heading as being inaccurate, that "with special reference to the Rorschach and an awareness of the TAT and Blacky" should be added to indicate the restricted coverage. Perhaps, but the reply is that not much really unique or decisive has happened with respect to other projective tests. In a volume on projective techniques with children, this is a chapter that makes only occasional reference to work with children. Again, a similar reply: the minor notice reflects the current contributions to this area.

## Conceptual Trends

Projective techniques present several separate but related theoretical or conceptual issues. The very concept of projection raises a number of questions such as the following one: What are the relationships between Freud's various uses of projection and its various uses in projective techniques? There are the general assumptions utilized in so-called "projective" theory, e.g., responses to projective materials reflect stable, central elements of personality. And finally, each projective technique has additional unique conceptual problems. At the outset it is suggested that, since the introduction of projective techniques, progress in solving these problems has been limited. Further, there are even elements of confusion which hinder their solution.

Perhaps this situation, one of limited progress and confusion, can be illustrated with a brief look at Rorschach history. Using a vague psychoanalytic background, Rorschach[92] introduced in 1921 as an "experiment" a set of ink blots, along with a scoring system and an interpretative outline. It has not been accepted as such, just the opposite. Subsequent clinicians have adopted the Rorschach as a "test," which has tended to freeze the vague theoretical schema, scoring system, and all. It is true that there are presently a number of different scoring systems, but they are all only slight modifications of the original. When exploratory innovations have been made, there has frequently been criticism directed at the offender for departing from the original Rorschach. As it stands, Rorschach would have little difficulty in recognizing his "experiment" at the present time. In a similar vein, Lindzey,[73] in discussing the TAT, wonders: "Why is it that after two decades of thought and investigation we are so near the point at which we began?"

The preceding remarks are not meant to indicate that *no* conceptual developments have occurred since 1950. The purpose was to provide realistic limits for interpreting the discussion that is to follow. It should also be pointed out that these deficiencies are not peculiar to projective techniques, as more basically they reflect the current status of personality theory.

It would not be accurate to say that conceptual problems in projective techniques have been neglected. The recent literature, especially since 1950, shows an ever-growing concern about them. Fragmentary though they may be, there have been a number of attempts to relate projective techniques to a variety of viewpoints (e.g., references 27, 91, 101, 113). In 1953, an APA symposium was focused on projective methods and recent developments in personality theory.[57] And, not exhausting the contributions, Holt[66] has offered a chapter exploring the implications of various personality theories for Rorschach rationale.

The application of psychoanalytic principles to the Rorschach has received serious attention. In Schafer's book[95] can be found the most detailed interpretation of the Rorschach within a psychoanalytic framework. The emphasis is on the recent contributions of psychoanalysis to ego functioning and defense systems. It should be remembered, however, that most of the recent Rorschach volumes, while undoubtedly valuable to the clinician, consist of the traditional patchwork of clinical hypotheses (e.g., references 12, 86).

While the Rorschach has been the object of the major share of the conceptual explorations, a few words might be given to the TAT. Recent volumes[18,52] concerned with matters of interpretation attest to its widespread use among practicing clinicians. The fact that the TAT is not associated with any widely accepted scoring or interpretative system seems to give this instrument a certain amount of flexibility, both conceptually and empirically, in terms of future development. To cite a current example, Davids and Rosenblatt[39] have presented an interesting assessment of the "personality syndrome of alienation" using the TAT.

One might get the impression that projective techniques resemble stranded children searching for conceptual fathers. While this characterization may have general validity, there are exceptions. In the Blacky Pictures,[23] we have a device in which the structure of the stimuli, the scoring and the interpretations all stem directly from the psychoanalytic theory of psychosexual development. The Szondi Test[40] is also the product of a conceptual system, but it is difficult to see how much of this background theory, alien to modern scientific ears, could ever be empirically tested. (Kelly's Role Construct Repertory Test[62] provides an example of a so-called "objective" test that is the direct offspring of a theoretical orientation.) If clinicians develop deeper roots in contemporary personality theory, and there is some evidence for this trend, the expectation might be that future developments in projective techniques would follow more closely the model provided by the Blacky Pictures.

The frame of reference for projective testing has recently been broadened to include "situational" variables. Recognition is given to the possible effects on the subject's responses of the physical environment, instructions, examiner characteristics and other features of the test situation. The importance of this trend is accentuated by the fact that it has led to empirical studies. Sarason[93] and Schafer[95] have provided the most extensive treatments of this problem, with the former emphasizing research strategy and the latter psychoanalytic concepts. The test results obtained with children would seem to be particularly susceptible to the influence of situational variables when one considers all the modifications in test administration that have been used in order to elicit and sustain the attention of children.

There is the matter of conceptual developments of a less global nature, of a lower order (e.g., scoring categories). Actually, conceptual considerations at lower levels are apt to be more closely related to research, as they direct the organization and analysis of data. An earlier reference to the Rorschach indicated that neither the scoring system nor the accompanying interpretations had undergone any pronounced changes since their introduction. Scoring innovations have tended to be restricted to deriving scales from selected clusters of standard formal scores or slight variations thereof, and research findings (e.g., results from factor-analytic studies) have typically been ignored. The interpretations of these standard scores have become fairly well entrenched, again indicating little feedback from research (e.g., negative results with standard interpretations).

What have been some of the Rorschach scoring and interpretative contributions at this level? Although scoring and interpretation are intertwined, a word might be said about one aspect of interpretation first. Some new views on the interpretation of standard scores can be found in books by Phillips and Smith[86] and Piotrowski,[88] and in single studies such as King's,[63] but in general the contributions have been limited. Conceptual innovations stemming from new scoring systems are more evident. Wittenborn and Mettler's perceptual control score[111] represents an outcome of factor-analytic research. Gibby and Stotsky[47] have introduced what they call the "determinant shift" by using the discrepancies between the free association and inquiry scored separately. Klopfer and associates[66] have devised a prognostic scale which uses the interesting concept of "unused ego strength."

A few of the scoring approaches appear to be genuinely fresh. McFarland's experimental scales[79] for investigating perceptual consistency deserve mention in this regard. Fisher and Cleveland[45] focus on Rorschach content in their scoring system for evaluating the individual's "body image." Using both formal characteristics and content, Holt[53] has indicated new directions with his psychoanalytically oriented system for "gauging primary and secondary processes in Rorschach responses." In the author's opinion, the most noteworthy development, one opening new avenues of research, has been reported by Friedman.[46] In Friedman's genetic scoring system, evolved mainly from Werner's theoretical formulations,[109] the stress is on the structural aspects, organization and differentiation, of the perceptual response to ink blots.

Content analysis on the Rorschach, while it is employed in some of the newer scoring systems, has experienced a slow acceptance, presumably because it was not emphasized by Hermann Rorschach. Although suggestions had been offered previously, it was not until 1949 that any systematic treatment of this area appeared, at which time Elizur[43] reported rating scales for anxiety and hostility. In 1952, DeVos[41] attempted to devise a more comprehensive system of content analysis. Since then, increasing attention has been given content analysis. Representing a closely related development is Watkins and Stauffacher's index[105] of pathologic thinking, an attempt to quantify deviant thinking occurring in the Rorschach performance. The author would like to suggest, admittedly not on substantial empirical evidence, that content and related methods of analysis offer more promise than the usual method of determinant analysis.

If the latter statement is true, *part* of the reason may lie in Levin's notion[69] that the Rorschach consists of two tests. According to Levin, Test A is the free association, in which the subject responds primarily with content; while in Test B, the inquiry, the testee in response to questions from the tester gives introspective reports on what were the determinants of the perceptual content. A question immediately arises in regard to the reliability of the data obtained in Test B, i.e., the determinants. This may also account for results indicating a relatively high reliability for the human movement response ($M$), as this "determinant" is not so dependent on the inquiry (Test B), usually being elicited spontaneously in the free association (Test A).

The TAT offers a minor parallel to the Rorschach situation. While Rorschach users until recently have tended to concentrate almost solely on formal characteristics, a similar but opposite trend characterizes the TAT. Content has been emphasized, with formal features being ignored by all but a few users (e.g., reference 112). Most of the "TAT interpretative eggs are still being put in the content basket," but formal features are gradually receiving more and more attention, as attested by recent contributions from Dana,[37] Henry,[52] Holt,[55] and others.

As may readily be seen, most of the discussion in this section has been concerned with the conceptual developments of specific techniques (Rorschach and TAT). What about other conceptual issues? It should be mentioned that the concept of projection in relation to projective techniques has received critical examinations from Bellak,[17] Cattell,[31] and a few others. Then, there are the general assumptions of projective psychology. Macfarlane and Tuddenham[77] and Lindzey,[72] the latter using the TAT as a frame of reference, have conducted the most serious explorations in this area.

More properly, the assumptions of projective psychology are a "conceptual-empirical" problem. First, they must be conceptualized, explicitly stated; then comes empirical substantiation. To paraphrase Macfarlane and Tuddenham,[77] three such assumptions might be stated as follows: (a) projective test protocols sample enough of the subject's personality to permit generalizations, (b) projective responses stem entirely from basic attributes, and (c) projective responses reflect central personality elements equally in different subjects. Although some general notion of "psychic determinism" undoubtedly underlies most orientations toward projective tests, at least implicitly, this assumptive background is rarely specified or delineated. Subjecting projective assumptions to empirical test is even more uncommon; it is as if they were given axiomatic status. Consider the Macfarlane-Tuddenham assumptions. While there is not sufficient evidence for clear evaluations of these assumptions, some comments can be offered. The defense of assumption (a) must take into consideration the fact that certain projective tests such as the Rorschach and TAT, which depend on what the subject will or can produce, not infrequently yield very meager protocols. With regard to assumption (b), if recognition is given to the operation of situational variables, then some qualification is in order. In the case of assumption (c), data obtained by Okarski[84] and others suggest that projective responses do not necessarily reflect basic personality characteristics equally in all subjects. The point to be made is merely that acceptance of this area as a conceptual-empirical problem might well lead to a revision of these assumptions.

An attempt has been made in this section to outline some of the significant conceptual developments in projective techniques, as well as indicate some of the problems. It is the author's opinion that these conceptual problems represent the principal obstacles to further advances. And unfortunately many basic problems have barely been scratched. For example, we have at present only small inklings of the necessary conceptual framework (levels of personality, relevant intervening variables, etc.) for predicting overt behavior from projective responses. This means that many empirical studies are strictly "hit-or-miss" affairs.

### Empirical Trends

Research reports on projective techniques number in the thousands, and the literature is increasing at a steady rate. It has been over 35 years since Rorschach published his monograph; about 20 years since Bender reported the use of certain figures or designs in clinical practice (not originally as projective stimuli, it is true); about 15 years since Murray wrote his manual for the TAT, and so forth. What has happened? What can be said? In the overall picture, one cannot escape being impressed by the vast number of equivocal and negative findings. In the 1958 *Annual Review of Psychology*, Jensen offers the following evaluation:

> In the writer's judgment the standard projective techniques *qua* projective techniques have been a failure methodologically and substantively in personality research. The one exception seems to be the special adaptation of the TAT by McClelland and his associates in their study of motivation. The Rorschach in particular has been worthless as a research instrument. Though claiming for decades to be the method par excellence for studying personality, the Rorschach method has nothing to show for its application in the personality field [reference 59, page 296].*

Perhaps Jensen espouses an extreme view, but it is one that is undoubtedly shared by a large segment of psychologists, particularly nonmembers of the projective community. After discussing the empirical developments since 1950, the author will return to this evaluation and offer some comments.

What about the scientific sophistication of the empirical contributions using projective techniques? Methodologic deficiencies of the following nature, especially in the earlier studies, have been common: inappropriate statistics, failure to collect cross validational data, neglect of reliability (inter-rater), failure to control relevant variables (e.g., number of Rorschach responses). Although studies with these and other deficiencies can still be found, noticeable improvement has occurred. For one thing, investigators have shown a sensitivity to methodologic contributions in this area. Cronbach's articles[33,34] on statistical methods for the Rorschach exerted an almost immediate influence on research. Cronbach and Meehl's discussion[36] delineating types of validation (e.g., construct validity) promises to have a further clarifying effect. The issue of clinical versus statistical prediction, as outlined by Meehl,[80] is beginning to receive attention.[54] Perhaps even the notion of response sets,[35] which has been illustrated in a number of empirical studies of objective tests (particularly in regard to "acquiescence"), will stimulate some interesting methodologic research on projective techniques.

The criterion problem is one that plagues not only empirical studies with projective techniques but all personality research. As emphasized by Levy,[70] prediction is a murky affair when the criteria are not clearly understood. For example, in the attempts to measure anxiety, rigidity, adjustment, and other such variables with projective techniques, the usual implicit assumption is that these variables are unitary in nature. The available evidence indicates just the opposite. Frequently used in research, the standard neuropsychiatric classifications are striking examples of ambiguous criteria. Further illustrations are provided by recent attempts to utilize projective techniques in predicting flying success[56] and missionary success.[96] When research objectives are linked with such vague criteria, it is difficult to see how the typical results can be other than negative. What is involved seems to be the "misuse" of methods, both objective and projective. Tests are not crystal balls.

In terms of substance, the early models for validation studies continue to exert the principal influence on the stream of empirical studies: correlational studies relating projective scores to outside criteria, comparisons of groups, and the like. Occasionally, there has been an experimental study. At best, the results have been equivocal. As indicated in the preceding section, it is the author's opinion that this outcome reflects primarily conceptual and

*Quoted with permission of the publishers of the *Annual Review of Psychology*.

secondarily methodologic deficiencies. Such studies, especially their early counterparts, have been discussed a number of times,[3,26,66] so that there is little need to cover this material again.

A concerted empirical effort to fulfill the long-acknowledged need for normative data has occurred only since 1950. A variety of adult norms have been published since then, especially for the Rorschach[14,30,83] and TAT (e.g., reference 44). In addition, more specialized Rorschach norms have been compiled for children and the aged, particularly by Ames and associates.[1,2] Although most of these reports suffer from major defects (e.g., biased samples), they generally make a solid contribution to a limited number of techniques in a neglected area. There is still the question of the usefulness of norms when they are presented in the usual manner, i.e., means and standard deviations of scores, especially when it is the configuration of scores that supposedly counts.

Another matter sharing an extended history of attention is that of reliability. Most discussions of this topic seem to agree that the standard methods of assessing reliability (e.g., split-half) are not too appropriate for projective techniques. While studies employing the standard methods are still being reported, there seems to be a slight trend to bypass such procedures and to utilize interpretations as the unit of measure for assessing reliability. Recent studies of this nature have been conducted by Palmer,[85] Grant et al.,[49] and Datel and Gengerelli.[38] Actually, the concern, if not overconcern, with reliability seems to have diminished in very recent years. Perhaps, this trend, if it is one, is justified by the consideration that reliability is implied in validity. It does not, however, offer sufficient reason for disregarding the relatively simple, straightforward problem of interscorer reliability.

Research in recent years seems to reflect an increased awareness and interest in the methodologic problems presented by projective techniques. Factor-analytic studies have been reported for the Rorschach,[75,102,110] Bender-Gestalt,[50] Szondi,[48] and undoubtedly others. Strangely, the results have had little or no effect on conceptual trends. There is no development in projective techniques similar to Cattell's program[32] for objective tests. Another approach has been the exploration of the relationships among projective methods on such variables as constriction,[28] movement responses,[84] and psychosexual disturbance.[104] Typically, the interrelationships have been very low or nonexistent. With reliability not necessarily being a factor,[28] the problem seems to lie in the area of conceptualization. Similar problems have also been encountered with objective tests.

Of recent development is the empirical concern with the relationship between projective methods and basic perceptual processes. Following 1948, when Lazarus[68] reported his study of the influence of color on the Rorschach protocol, a trickle of research has been published on the role of the stimulus in Rorschach responses. In this thin number of studies, color has usually been manipulated, but in a few cases other stimulus elements, such as shading and figure-ground, have served as the independent variables. A few studies have dealt with related problems: inter-card comparisons ("card-pull"), card order effects, and similar factors. For individual Rorschach studies, the reader is referred to Baughman's recent review[11] of this area. Other projective techniques have undergone similar empirical scrutiny, with studies being conducted on the "stimulus values" of the TAT,[22] Michigan Picture Test[6] and the Szondi.[103] Weisskopf-Joelson has investigated the effects of ambiguity on projection in the TAT[106] and CAT,[108] as well as variations in bodily similarity between subject and central figure in the TAT.[107] Several studies have been concerned with differential responsiveness of children to animal and human stimuli.[7,21] The lag between empirical and conceptual trends is quite evident in this general area. For example, it seems obvious to suggest that, in terms of developmental sequence, research on response to Rorschach stimulus elements should have preceded the formulation of any elaborate notions about "color shock" or "shading shock."

The conceptual concern with the influence of situational variables (discussed in the previous section) has an empirical counterpart. The effects of various sets (instructions), examiner characteristics and type of examiner-subject interaction on test responses have been investigated with several projective methods. A good picture of this research conducted up to 1954, with special attention to the Rorschach, can be found in Sarason's book.[93] What might be called the influence of "post-test" variables has also come under study, i.e., the interaction between test protocol, personality of the psychologist and diagnostic decisions. A summary of the latter research has been provided by Mintz.[82]

From the extensive research literature, a few studies that seem particularly interesting might be selected for brief mention. Some of these studies also represent conceptual contributions. For example, Jones[60] has presented data for a new version of the TAT, which stems from Freud's concept of negation. The series of studies conducted by Singer, Meltzoff, and others[81,99] on the relationship between Rorschach movement responses ($M$) and motor inhibition come to mind, as well as several studies focused on the relationship between $M$ and certain thinking processes.[20,63,100] Klein and Schlesinger[65] have reported a novel investigation of the relationship between susceptibility to apparent movement (phi) and "form" attitude on the Rorschach. Although not altogether projective in nature, Luborsky and Shevrin's studies[76,97] of the Poetzl phenomenon seem to warrant more than casual attention. In the latter, relationships are obtained between dream imagery and previous perceptual performance (e.g., stimulus elements not reported).

In the author's opinion, the most significant development has been the use of projective techniques as tools for research in motivation, personality and social psychology. New scoring concepts for projective techniques are sometimes evolved in this research, but the conceptual emphasis is on testing nonprojective hypotheses. Here, the principal role of projective techniques is that of fulfilling certain methodologic needs. Of course, the results frequently bear on the construct validity of projective techniques. And a survey of the results that have been obtained seems to show more favorable outcomes than has usually been the case in projective research. This research development is deemed of sufficient importance that a sampling of relevant studies is presented.

Some attention has already been drawn to the special adaptation of the TAT by McClelland et al.[78] in their study of motivation. A rapidly expanding number of studies has found significant correlations between a TAT-scored need for achievement (n Ach) and a variety of variables: academic grades, rate of learning, occupational preferences, recognition thresholds, color preferences, the Zeigarnik effect, and others. At its present stage of development, the research on n Ach has produced a tangle of empirical findings, with serious attempts at conceptualization apparently to come later. With the consideration of additional TAT-derived needs, need for affiliation and need for power, the scope of the research is increasing.[10]

While the TAT is probably more flexible than the average projective technique, its methodologic potential is by no means unique. The Rorschach and Blacky Pictures have been used in a similar manner (as research tools) to investigate psychoanalytic theory. Aronson[8,9] employed both instruments in testing the psychoanalytic theory of paranoia. Rabin[89,90] administered the Rorschach and Blacky to Kibbutz and non-Kibbutz children in Israel in a resourceful investigation of some Freudian notions about the Oedipal situation. Blum,[24,25] by means of the Blacky Pictures, has attempted to relate various psychosexual dimensions of psychoanalytic theory to perceptual vigilance and defense.

The Rorschach has been used as a research tool in a number of other contexts. A cluster of studies has sprung from Friedman's genetic scoring system.[46] This Rorschach method has been used in studies of developmental changes in children's perceptions,[51] cognitive development,[74] social effectiveness,[67] perceptual functioning in paranoid schizophrenia,[98] and others. Becker[15] obtained a product-moment correlation of $-.64$ between genetic level and the process-reaction dimension of schizophrenia! In some intriguing research, Fisher and Cleveland[45] predicted location of psychosomatic symptoms, inner or outer body, from the patient's body image derived from the Rorschach. The Rorschach was one of several methods used by Beck[13] in his interdisciplinary approach to schizophrenic typology.

To round up the research in this area, a few studies employing other projective methods can be cited. In an ambitious, large-scale project, Anderson and Anderson[4] have devised a series of incomplete stories to study differences in cultural reactions to conflict among children of seven countries. Beier and Hanfmann[16] used projective questions to study the personality patterns of former Soviet citizens. Carpenter et al.[29] predicted speed of response to perceptual stimuli on the basis of type of defense classified from sentence completions.

Now, there is the commitment to offer an appraisal of projective techniques from the extensive accumulation of research. While the vast number of equivocal and negative results cannot be ignored, the recent studies using projective methods as research tools in a variety of "nonprojective" areas seem to offer some grounds for optimism. It is the author's belief that any blanket dismissal of projective techniques as failures is not warranted.

Judgment should at least be postponed until there has been enough time to evaluate the aforementioned empirical development. In discounting projective techniques, Jensen offers the work conducted by McClelland and associates with the TAT as an exception. It would seem that if the McClelland TAT research is acceptable, then "logically" the previously cited studies of a similar nature with other projective methods should also be viewed in a positive light.

## New Books and Projective Tests

The years following 1950 have been fertile ones for the publishing of books, many by prominent figures in the projective community. Many of the books can be found in the list of references at the end of this chapter. There is one disconcerting feature about these books that the present author would like to mention. With a few exceptions, the authors have not attempted to integrate the vast reservoir of available research findings into their presentations. It is as if, by ignoring research results, they can reduce the amount of disruption and interference with their interpretations and speculations.

Recent years seem to show a reduction, but not a drastic one, in the number of new projective tests that have been introduced. Apparently, there is more concentration on the conceptual and empirical problems of existing methods. Some of the projective additions are as follows: Kinget's Drawing-Completion Test,[64] the Howard Ink Blot Test,[58] Sargent's Insight Test,[94] the Michigan Picture Test,[5] Phillipson's Object Relations Technique,[87] the Kahn Test of Symbol Arrangement,[61] and Dombrose and Slobin's IES Test,[42] the latter being designed to assess certain psychoanalytic concepts.

New projective techniques, as well as other types of tests, have usually been published on the basis of a limited amount of background data on standardization, reliability and validity. However, this has become standard operating procedure. A test published with adequate background data would be the exception, a real "eye-catcher." It should be remembered that reasonably adequate norms for the Rorschach were not published until 1950.[14] It is the author's opinion that the newer tests, as in the past, will be accepted by practicing clinicians on the basis of their individual appeal rather than on any empirical grounds.

## The Projective Community

In making a minor invasion of the domain of the social psychologist, a few comments will be made about the projective community, the people most closely identified with projective techniques. Fortunate in having strong leaders, the projective community faced an indifferent and more often hostile psychological world in attempting to gain scientific acceptance for its methods of personality evaluation. The strong opposition to the projective movement, frequently based on emotional grounds, elicited in return reactions tinged with defensiveness and dogmatism; and the latter seemed to become accentuated with the flood of negative research results. The extreme adjustment to this situation would have been withdrawal and the transformation of the projective community into a cult. It should be mentioned that some people, presumably critics, have detected such signs. As late as 1958, Levy[70] issued the following warning in reference to the Rorschach: "By prescribing certain research approaches as sterile, rigid, superficial, and irrelevant, Rorschach partisans run the risk of drawing a cloak of immunity from research about the method which may well stifle it. The line between science and mysticism might well be drawn in terms of the number of restrictions put upon methods of inquiry and the tenacity with which a single method alone is held to be permissible."

In recent years, the possible development of a projective cult seems more remote. There appears to be more willingness for the projective community to look at developments with a critical eye and to indulge in self evaluations. An APA symposium recently sponsored by the projective community was devoted to a discussion of "failures with projective techniques."[19] Then too, membership in the projective community has changed; it is more diversified. As one earmark of its success, the projective movement has recruited, in addition to practitioners, individuals with strong scientific interests and backgrounds.

## Summary

The conceptual problems of projective techniques encompass at least the three following issues: (a) the nature of projection, (b) the assumptions of projective theory, and (c) the conceptual problems peculiar to specific techniques. Progress in solving these conceptual problems has been limited, a situation probably attributable more to the current status of personality theory than to that of projective techniques. While in a *post hoc* fashion serious attempts are being made to apply psychoanalytic theory to the Rorschach, most projective techniques are embedded in a hodgepodge of loose clinical hypotheses. An exception is the Blacky Pictures, which were evolved directly from psychoanalytic theory. The general static nature of conceptual developments seems to be illustrated by the fact that even such minor innovations as exploring new scoring categories has only occurred in recent years. Little attention has been given to the basic concept of projection and even less to the assumptions underlying projective theory. As a result, predicting overt behavior from projective responses is usually a haphazard, intuitive affair.

The stream of research employing projective techniques continues, and there is little reason to believe that this empirical productivity will appreciably decline in the near future. Some of the methodologic deficiencies that were common in early research (e.g., inappropriate statistics, control failures) are presently less evident. On the other hand, while the criterion problem is a thorny one for all personality research, studies with projective techniques seem to be especially prone to link research objectives with vague criteria. In the matter of trends, there appears to have been less concern about the issue of reliability and more about the problems of standardization since 1950. Relatively new developments are factor-analytic studies, investigations relating projective methods to basic perceptual processes and other research of a methodologic bent. Although any over-all evaluation of projective techniques cannot sidestep the large number of studies yielding negative and equivocal results, there are some empirical bright spots. Interesting, if not promising, results have been obtained in a number of studies in which a variety of projective methods were adapted and employed as research tools in investigating nonprojective hypotheses.

The years following 1950 have been productive ones for the members of the projective community in terms of new books and new tests. The books add considerable breadth to the projective literature, but most of them fail to take notice of the vast amount of research that has been reported. While some undoubtedly have potential merit, the new tests typically have been published on the basis of very meager background data (e.g., reliability, standardization, etc.). There are also indications that the projective community is beginning to adopt more judicial and objective attitudes towards their methods and practices.

## References

1. Ames, L. B., Learned, J., Métraux, R. W., & Walker, R. N.  *Child Rorschach responses: developmental trends from two to ten years.* New York: Hoeber, 1952.
2. ——, ——, ——, & ——. *Rorschach responses in old age.* New York: Hoeber-Harper, 1954.
3. Anderson, H. H., & Anderson, G. L. (Eds.)  *An introduction to projective techniques.* New York: Prentice-Hall, 1951.
4. ——, & ——. Cultural reactions to conflict: a study of adolescent children in seven countries. *In* Gilbert, G. M. (Ed.)  *Psychological approaches to intergroup and international understanding.* Austin, Tex.: Hogg Foundation, 1956. Pp. 27–32.
5. Andrew, G., Hartwell, S. W., Hutt, M. L., & Walton, R. E. *The Michigan Picture Test.* Chicago: Science Research Assoc., 1953.
6. ——, Walton, R. E., Hartwell, S. W., & Hutt, M. L.  The Michigan Picture Test: the stimulus value of the cards. *J. consult. Psychol.*, 1951, *15*, 51–54.
7. Armstrong, M. A. S.  Children's responses to animal and human figures in thematic pictures. *J. consult. Psychol.*, 1945, *18*, 67–70.
8. Aronson, M. L.  A study of the Freudian theory of paranoia by means of the Rorschach Test. *J. proj. Tech.*, 1952, *16*, 397–411.
9. ——.  A study of the Freudian theory of paranoia by means of the Blacky Pictures. *J. proj. Tech.*, 1953, *17*, 3–19.
10. Atkinson, J. W. (Ed.)  *Motives in fantasy, action, and society.* New York: Van Nostrand, 1958.
11. Baughman, E. E.  The role of the stimulus in Rorschach responses. *Psychol. Bull.*, 1958, *55*, 121–147.
12. Beck, S. J. *Rorschach's Test*, Vol. III. *Advances in interpretation.* New York: Grune & Stratton, 1952
13. ——.  The six schizophrenias. *Res. Monogr. Amer. Orthopsychiat. Ass.*, 1954. No. 6.
14. ——, Rabin, A. I., Thiesen, W. G., Molish, H., & Thetford, W. N.  The normal personality as projected in the Rorschach Test. *J. Psychol.*, 1950, *30*, 241–298.
15. Becker, W. C.  A genetic approach to the interpretation and evaluation of the process-reactive distinction in schizophrenia. *J. abnorm. soc. Psychol.*, 1956, *53*, 229–336.
16. Beier, H., & Hanfmann, E.  Emotional attitudes of former Soviet citizens, as studied by the technique of projective questions. *J. abnorm. soc. Psychol.*, 1956, *53*, 143–153.
17. Bellak, L.  On the problems of the concept of projection. *In* Abt, L. E., & Bellak, L. (Eds.)  *Projective psychology.* New York: Knopf, 1950. Pp. 7–32.

18. ——. *The Thematic Apperception Test and the Children's Apperception Test in clinical use.* New York: Grune & Stratton, 1954.

19. ——, Harrower, M., & Zubin, J.   A symposium on failures with projective techniques. *J. proj. Tech.,* 1954, *18,* 279–315.

20. Bieri, J., & Blacker, E.   The generality of cognitive complexity in the perception of people and inkblots. *J. abnorm. soc. Psychol.,* 1956, *53,* 112–117.

21. Biersdorf, K., & Marcuse, F. L.   Responses of children to human and animal pictures. *J. proj. Tech.,* 1953, *17,* 455–459.

22. Bijou, S. W., & Kenny, D. T.   The ambiguity values of TAT cards. *J. consult. Psychol.,* 1951, *15,* 203–207.

23. Blum, G. S.   *The Blacky Pictures: a technique for the exploration of personality dynamics.* New York: Psychological Corp., 1950.

24. ——.   An experimental reunion of psychoanalytic theory and perceptual vigilance and defense. *J. abnorm. soc. Psychol.,* 1954, *49,* 94–98.

25. ——.   Perceptual defense revisited. *J. abnorm. soc. Psychol.,* 1955, *51,* 24–29.

26. Brower, D., & Abt, L. E. (Eds.)   *Progress in clinical psychology.* Vol. I & II. New York: Grune & Stratton, 1952 & 1956.

27. Brownell, M. H., & Goss, A. E.   Stimulus-response analysis of inferences from projective test behavior. *J. Pers.,* 1957, *25,* 525–538.

28. Carp, F. M. Psychological constriction on several projective tests. *J. consult. Psychol.,* 1950, *17,* 268–275.

29. Carpenter, B., Wiener, M., & Carpenter, J. T.   Predictability of perceptual defense behavior. *J. abnorm. soc. Psychol.,* 1956, *52,* 380–383.

30. Cass, W. A., & McReynolds, P. E.   A contribution to Rorschach norms. *J. consult. Psychol.,* 1951, *15,* 178–184.

31. Cattell, R. B.   Principles of design in "projective" or misperception tests of personality. *In* Anderson, H. H., & Anderson, G. L. (Eds.)   *An introduction to projective techniques.* New York: Prentice-Hall, 1951. Pp. 55–100.

32. ——.   *Personality and motivation structure and measurement.* Yonkers-on-Hudson, N.Y.: World Book Co., 1957.

33. Cronbach, L. J.   "Pattern tabulation": a statistical method for analysis of limited patterns of scores, with particular reference to the Rorschach Test. *Educ. Psychol. Measmt.,* 1949, 9, 149–171.

34. ——.   Statistical methods applied to Rorschach scores: a review. *Psychol. Bull.,* 1949, *46,* 393–429.

35. ——.   Further evidence on response sets and test design. *Educ. Psychol. Measmt.,* 1950, *10,* 3–31.

36. ——, & Meehl, P. E.   Construct validity in psychological tests. *Psychol. Bull.,* 1955, *52,* 281–302.

37. Dana, R. H.   Clinical diagnosis and objective TAT scoring. *J. abnorm. soc. Psychol.,* 1955, *50,* 19–24.

38. Datel, W. E., & Gengerelli, J. A.   Reliability of Rorschach interpretations. *J. proj. Tech.,* 1955, *19,* 372–381.

39. Davids, A., & Rosenblatt, D.   Use of the TAT in assessment of the personality syndrome of alienation. *J. proj. Tech.,* 1958, *22,* 145–152.

40. Deri, S.   *Introduction to the Szondi Test.* New York: Grune & Stratton, 1949.

41. DeVos, G.   A quantitative approach to affective symbolism in Rorschach responses. *J. proj. Tech.,* 1952, *16,* 133–150.

42. Dombrose, L. A., & Slobin, M. S.   The IES Test. *Percept. mot. Skills Monogr. Suppl.,* 1958, *8,* No. 3.

43. Elizur, A.   Content analysis of the Rorschach with regard to anxiety and hostility. *Rorschach Res. Exch. & J. proj. Tech.,* 1949, *13,* 247–284.

44. Eron, L. D.   A normative study of the Thematic Apperception Test. *Psychol. Monogr.,* 1950, *64,* No. 9 (Whole No. 315).

45. Fisher, S., & Cleveland, S. E.   The role of body image in psychosomatic symptom choice. *Psychol. Monogr.,* 1955, *17,* No. 17 (Whole No. 386).

46. Friedman, H.   Perceptual regression in schizophrenia: an hypothesis suggested by the use of the Rorschach Test. *J. proj. Tech.*, 1953, *17*, 151–185.

47. Gibby, R. G., & Stotsky, B. A.   The relation of Rorschach free association to inquiry. *J. consult. Psychol.*, 1953, *17*, 359–363.

48. Gordon, L. V.   A factor analysis of the 48 Szondi pictures. *J. Psychol.*, 1953, *36*, 387–392.

49. Grant, M. Q., Ives, V., & Ranzoni, J. H. Reliability and validity of judges' ratings of adjustment on the Rorschach. *Psychol. Monogr.*, 1952, *66*, No. 2 (Whole No. 334).

50. Guertin, W. H.   A factor analysis of curvilinear distortions on the Bender-Gestalt. *J. clin. Psychol.*, 1954, *10*, 12–17.

51. Hemmendinger, L.   Perceptual organization and development as reflected in the structure of Rorschach Test responses. *J. proj. Tech.*, 1953, *17*, 162–170.

52. Henry, W. E.   *The analysis of fantasy.* New York: John Wiley & Sons, 1956.

53. Holt, R. R.   Gauging primary and secondary processes in Rorschach responses. *J. proj. Tech.*, 1956, *20*, 14–25.

54. ——.   Clinical *and* statistical prediction: a reformulation and some new data. *J. abnorm. soc. Psychol.*, 1958, *56*, 1–12.

55. ——.   Formal aspects of the TAT: a neglected resource. *J. proj. Tech.*, 1958, *22*, 163–172.

56. Holtzman, W. H., & Sell, S. B.   Prediction of flying success by clinical analysis of test protocols. *J. abnorm. soc. Psychol.*, 1954, *49*, 485–490.

57. Holzberg, J. D., Auld, F., Jr., Deutsch, M., Eriksen, C. W., & Schafer, R.   Symposium: Implications for projective methods in recent developments in personality theory. *J. proj. Tech.*, 1954, *18*, 418–447.

58. Howard, J. W.   The Howard Ink Blot Test. *J. clin. Psychol. Monogr. Suppl.*, 1953, No. 10.

59. Jensen, A. R.   Personality. *Ann. Rev. Psychol.*, 1958, *9*, 295–322.

60. Jones, R. M.   The Negation TAT: a projective method for eliciting repressed thought content. *J. proj. Tech.*, 1956, *20*, 297–303.

61. Kahn, T. C.   *Clinical manual: Kahn Test of Symbol Arrangement.* Grand Forks, N.D.: Southern Universities Press, 1957.

62. Kelly, G. A.   *The psychology of personal constructs.* Vol. 1. *A theory of personality.* New York: Norton, 1955.

63. King, G. F.   A theoretical and experimental consideration of the Rorschach human movement response. *Psychol. Monogr.*, 1958, *72*, No. 5 (Whole No. 458).

64. Kinget, G. M.   *The Drawing-Completion Test.* New York: Grune & Stratton, 1952.

65. Klein, G. S., & Schlesinger, H. J.   Perceptual attitudes toward instability: 1. Prediction of apparent movement experiences from Rorschach responses. *J. Pers.*, 1951, *18*, 289–302.

66. Klopfer, B., Ainsworth, M. D., Klopfer, W. G., & Holt, R. R.   *Developments in the Rorschach technique.* Vol. 1. *Technique and theory.* Yonkers-on-Hudson, N. Y.: World Book Co., 1954.

67. Lane, J. E.   Social effectiveness and developmental level. *J. Pers.*, 1955, *23*, 274–284.

68. Lazarus, R. S.   An experimental analysis of the influence of color on the protocol of the Rorschach Test. *J. Pers.*, 1948, *17*, 182–185.

69. Levin, M. M.   The two tests in the Rorschach. *J. proj. Tech.*, 1953, *17*, 471–473.

70. Levy, L. H.   Varieties of Rorschach research. Paper presented at the Midwestern Psychol. Ass. meetings in Detroit, May, 1958.

71. ——, & Dugan, R. D.   A factorial study of personal constructs. *J. consult. Psychol.*, 1956, *20*, 53–57.

72. Lindzey, G.   Thematic Apperception Test: interpretive assumptions and related empirical evidence. *Psychol. Bull.*, 1952, *49*, 1–25.

73. ——.   Thematic Apperception Test: the strategy of research. *J. proj. Tech.*, 1958, *22*, 173–180.

74. Lipton, H., Kaden, S., & Phillips, L.   Rorschach scores and decontextualization: a developmental view. *J. Pers.*, 1958, *26*, 291–302.

75. Lotsof, E. J., Comrey, A., Bogartz, W., & Arnsfield, P.   A factor analysis of the WISC and Rorschach. *J. proj. Tech.*, 1958, *22*, 297–301.

76. Luborsky, L., & Shevrin, H.   Dreams and day-residues: a study of the Poetzl observation. *Bull. Menninger Clin.*, 1956, *20*, 135–148.

77. Macfarlane. J. W., & Tuddenham, R. D.   Problems in the validation of projective techniques. *In* Anderson, H. H., & Anderson, G. L. (Eds.)   *An introduction to projective techniques.* New York: Prentice-Hall, 1951. Pp. 26–54.

78. McClelland, D. C., Atkinson, J. W., Clark, R. A., & Lowell, E. A.   *The achievement motive.* New York: Appleton-Century-Crofts, 1953.

79. McFarland, R. L.   Perceptual consistency in Rorschach-like projective tests. *J. proj. Tech.*, 1954, *18*, 368–378.

80. Meehl, P. E.   *Clinical vs. statistical prediction.* Minneapolis: Univer. Minn. Press, 1954.

81. Meltzoff, J., & Levine, M.   The relationship between motor and cognitive inhibition. *J. consult. Psychol.*, 1954, *18*, 355–358.

82. Mintz, E. E.   Personal problems and diagnostic errors of clinical psychologists. *J. proj. Tech.*, 1957, *21*, 123–128.

83. Neff, W. S., & Lidz, T.   Rorschach patterns of normal subjects of graded intelligence. *J. proj. Tech.*, 1951, *15*, 45–57.

84. Okarski, J. F.   Consistency of projective movement responses. *Psychol. Monogr.*, 1958, *72*, No. 6 (Whole No. 459).

85. Palmer, J. O.   A dual approach to Rorschach validation: a methodological study. *Psychol. Monogr.*, 1951, *65*, No. 8 (Whole No. 325).

86. Phillips, L., & Smith, J. G.   *Rorschach interpretation: advanced technique.* New York: Grune & Stratton, 1953.

87. Phillipson, H.   *Object Relations Technique.* Glencoe, Ill.: Free Press, 1955.

88. Piotrowski, Z. A. *Perceptanalysis.* New York: MacMillan, 1957.

89. Rabin, A. I.   Personality maturity of Kibbutz (Israeli collective settlement) and non-Kibbutz children as reflected in Rorschach findings. *J. proj. Tech.*, 1957, *21*, 148–153.

90. ——.   Some psychosexual differences between Kibbutz and non-Kibbutz Israeli boys. *J. proj. Tech.*, 1958, *22*, 328–332.

91. Rapaport, D.   Projective techniques and the theory of thinking. *J. proj. Tech.*, 1952, *16*, 269–275.

92. Rorschach, H.   *Psychodiagnostics* (Transl. by P. Lemkau & B. Kronenburg). Berne: Hans Huber, 1942.

93. Sarason, S. B.   *The clinical interaction: with special reference to the Rorschach.* New York: Harper, 1954.

94. Sargent, Helen D.   *The Insight Test: a verbal projective test for personality study.* New York: Grune & Stratton, 1953.

95. Schafer, R.   *Psychoanalytic interpretation in Rorschach testing.* New York: Grune & Stratton, 1954.

96. Shah, S. A.   Use of the Inspection Rorschach Technique in analyzing missionary success and failure. *J. proj. Tech.*, 1957, *21*, 69–72.

97. Shevrin, H., & Luborsky, L.   The measurement of preconscious perception in dreams and images: an investigation of the Poetzl phenomenon. *J. abnorm. soc. Psychol.*, 1958, *56*, 285–294.

98. Siegel, E. L.   Genetic parallels of perceptual structuralization in paranoid schizophrenia: an analysis by means of the Rorschach technique. *J. proj. Tech.*, 1953, *17*, 151–161.

99. Singer, J. L., Meltzoff, J., & Goldman, G. C.   Rorschach movement responses following motor inhibition and hyperactivity. *J. consult. Psychol.*, 1952, *16*, 359–364.

100. ——, Wilensky, H., & McCraven, V. G.   Delaying capacity, fantasy, and planning ability: a factorial study of some basic ego functions. *J. consult. Psychol.*, 1956, *20*, 375–383.

101. Spiegelman, M. Jungian theory and the analysis of thematic tests. *J. proj. Tech.*, 1955, *19*, 253–263.

102. Stotsky, B. A.    Factor analysis of Rorschach scores of schizophrenics. *J. clin. Psychol.*, 1957, *13*, 275–278.
103. Szollosi, E., Lamphier, D. E., & Best, H. L.    The stimulus values of the Szondi pictures. *J. consult. Psychol.*, 1951, *15*, 419–424.
104. Tolor, A.    A comparison of several measures of psychosexual disturbance. *J. proj. Tech.*, 1957, *21*, 313–317.
105. Watkins, J. G., & Stauffacher, J. C.    An index of pathological thinking in the Rorschach. *J. proj. Tech.*, 1952, *16*, 276–286.
106. Weisskopf, E. A.    An experimental study of the effect of brightness and ambiguity on projection in the Thematic Apperception Test. *J. Psychol.*, 1950, *29*, 407–416.
107. Weisskopf-Joelson, E. A., & Dunlevy, G. P.    Bodily similarity between subject and central figure in the TAT as an influence on projection. *J. abnorm. soc. Psychol.*, 1952, *47*, 441–445.
108. ———, & Lynn, D. B.    The effect of variations in ambiguity on projection in the Children's Apperception Test. *J. consult. Psychol.*, 1953, *17*, 67–70.
109. Werner, H.    *Comparative psychology and mental development* (rev. ed.). New York: Follett, 1948.
110. Wittenborn, J. R.    A factor analysis of Rorschach scoring categories. *J. consult. Psychol.*, 1950, *14*, 261–267.
111. ———, & Mettler, F. A.    A lack of perceptual control score for the Rorschach Test. *J. clin. Psychol.*, 1951, *7*, 331–334.
112. Wyatt, F.    The scoring and analysis of the Thematic Apperception Test. *J. Psychol.*, 1947, *24*, 319–330.
113. Zelen, S. L.    A systematic orientation to projective methods: principles of interpretation. *J. proj. Tech.*, 1952, *16*, 496–503.

# Appendix

# Authors and Distributors of Test Materials

1. Bender Visual Motor Gestalt Test, 1938, Lauretta Bender
   - *Materials:* Nine test cards
     Booklet of instructions
   - *Publisher:* American Orthopsychiatric Association
   - *Distributor:* Psychological Corporation, 304 E. 45th Street, New York City
   - *Additional manual:* Bender, Lauretta. A visual motor gestalt test and its clinical use. *Res. Monogr. Amer. Orthopsychiat. Ass.*, 1938, No. 3.

2. Blacky Pictures, 1950, Gerald S. Blum
   - *Materials:* Set of 12 pictures
     Inquiry cards
     Record blanks
     Manual
   - *Publisher:* Psychological Corporation
   - *Additional reference:* Blum, G. S. A study of the psychoanalytic theory of psychosexual development. *Genet Psychol. Monogr.*, 1949, *39*, 3–103.

3. Children's Apperception Test (CAT), 1949, Leopold Bellak & Sonya S. Bellak
   - *Materials:* Set of 10 pictures
     Booklet of instructions
     Short Form, Bellak TAT and CAT Blank (1955)
   - *Publisher:* C.P.S. Co., P.O. Box 42, Gracie Station, New York 28, N.Y.
   - *Distributor:* Psychological Corporation
   - *Additional manual:* Bellak, L. *The Thematic Apperception Test and the Children's Apperception Test in clinical use.* New York: Grune & Stratton, 1954.

4. CAT Supplement (CAT-S), 1952, Leopold Bellak & Sonya S. Bellak
   - *Materials:* Set of 10 pictures
     Manual
   - *Publisher:* C.P.S. Co., P.O. Box 42, Gracie Station, New York 28, N. Y.
   - *Distributor:* Psychological Corporation

5. Controlled Projection for Children, 1951, John C. Raven
   - *Manual:* Raven, J. C. *Controlled projection for children.*
     (2nd ed.) London: H. K. Lewis, 1951.
   - *Distributor:* Psychological Corporation

6. Draw-A-Person Test (D-A-P), 1949, Karen Machover
   - *Manual:* Machover, Karen. *Personality projection in the drawing of the human figure: a method of personality investigation.* Springfield, Ill.: C. C Thomas, 1949.

7. Drawing-Completion Test, 1939, Ehrig Wartegg
   - *Materials:* Wartegg's test blanks
     Kinget's scoring sheets

381

Manual: Kinget, G. Marian. *The Drawing-Completion Test: a projective technique for the investigation of personality*, 1952.
Publisher:   Grune & Stratton

8. Family Relations Test, 1957, Eva Bene & James Anthony
    Materials:   20 figures
                 Two sets of test item cards
                 Record sheets for older children
                 Scoring sheets for older children
                 Scoring sheets for young children
                 Manual
    Publisher:   National Foundation for Educational Research in England and Wales, 79 Wimpole Street, London, W.I.

9. Forer Structured Sentence Completion Tests (FSSCT), 1957, Bertram R. Forer
    Materials:   Four test forms: men, boys, women, girls
                 FSSCT check sheets
                 Manual
    Publisher:   Western Psychological Services
                 10655 Santa Monica Blvd., W. Los Angeles 25, Calif.

10. Horn-Hellersberg Test, 1945, Elizabeth F. Hellersberg
    Materials:   Test blanks
                 Manual
    Publisher:   Elizabeth F. Hellersberg
                 641 Whitney Ave., New Haven, Conn.
    Additional manual: Hellersberg, Elizabeth F. *The individual's relation to reality in our culture: an experimental approach by means of the Horn-Hellersberg Test.* Springfield, Ill.: C. C Thomas, 1950.

11. House-Tree-Person Test (H-T-P), 1946, John N. Buck
    Materials:   H-T-P drawing forms
                 Children's Revision, H-T-P Post Drawing Interrogation Folder (Isaac Jolles, 1956)
                 Manual
    Distributor: Western Psychological Services

12. It Scale for Children (ITSC), 1956, Daniel G. Brown
    Materials:   12 sets of pictures
                 Manual
    Distributor: Psychological Test Specialists
                 Box 1441, Missoula, Montana

13. Kahn Test of Symbol Arrangement (KTSA), 1956, Theodore C. Kahn
    Materials:   16 plastic objects, one felt strip
                 Record sheets
                 Work sheet
                 Summary card
                 Two manuals
    Distributor: Psychological Test Specialists

14. Lowenfeld Mosaic Test (L.M.T.), 1930, Margaret Lowenfeld
    Materials:   456 plastic pieces
                 Tray
                 Record forms*
                 Guide booklet*

*Publisher:*   Badger Tests Co., Ltd.
             15-17 Eldon St., London, E.C. 2
  **Distributor:* Western Psychological Services
*Additional manual:* Lowenfeld, Margaret. *The Lowenfeld Mosaic Test.* London:
             Newman Neame, 1954.


15. Make-A-Picture Story Test (MAPS), 1947, Edwin S. Shneidman
    *Materials:*   Figures (67) and backgrounds (22)
                 Theater carrying case
                 Figure Identification Card
                 Figure Location Sheets
                 Manual
    *Publisher:*   Psychological Corporation


16. Michigan Picture Test, 1953, Gwen Andrew, Samuel W. Hartwell, Max L. Hutt, &
    Ralph E. Walton
    *Materials:*   Set of 16 pictures
                 Analysis sheets
                 Manual
                 Rating scales for pupil adjustment
                 Manual for rating scale
    *Publisher:*   Science Research Associates
                 57 W. Grand Ave., Chicago 10, Ill.


17. Picture World Test (PWT), 1956, Charlotte Bühler & Morse P. Manson
    *Materials:*   Pads of World Scenes
                 Symbol sheet
                 Protocol booklets
                 Manual
    *Publisher:*   Western Psychological Services


18. Rock-A-Bye, Baby, 1959, Mary R. Haworth & Adolf G. Woltmann
    *Materials:*   Film (35 min., 16 mm., sound, black & white—available for weekly
                 rental or purchase)
                 Manual (must be ordered prior to film)
    *Distributor:* Psychological Cinema Register
                 The Pennsylvania State University, University Park, Pa.


19. Rorschach, 1921, Hermann Rorschach
    *Materials:*   Ten psychodiagnostic plates
    *Publisher:*   Hans Huber, Bern, Switzerland
    *Distributors:* Grune & Stratton; Psychological Corporation


20. Rosenzweig Picture-Frustration Study (Children's Form), 1948, Saul Rosenzweig
    *Materials:*   Test booklets (Children's Form)
                 Record blanks (Children's Form)
                 Manual
    *Publisher:*   Saul Rosenzweig
                 8029 Washington St., St. Louis 14, Mo.


21. Symbol Elaboration Test (S.E.T.), 1953, Johanna Krout
    *Materials:*   Test booklets
                 Manual
    *Publisher:*   Western Psychological Services

22. Symonds Picture-Story Test, 1948, Percival Symonds
      *Materials:*    Set of 20 pictures
                      Manual
      *Publisher:*    Bureau of Publications, Teachers College, Columbia University
      *Distributor:* Psychological Corporation
      *Additional manual:* Symonds, P. *Adolescent fantasy: an investigation of the picture-
              story method of personality study.* New York: Columbia Univer. Press, 1949.


23. Szondi Test, 1937, Lipot Szondi
      *Materials:*    Set of 48 pictures
                      Profile blanks
                      Manual: Deri, Susan. *Introduction to the Szondi Test: theory and practice,*
                      1949.
      *Publisher:*    Grune & Stratton


24. Test of Family Attitudes, 1952, Lydia Jackson
      *Materials:*    Booklet containing 8 pictures and manual
      *Publisher:*    Methuen & Co., Ltd.
                      36 Essex St., Strand, W.C. 2, London


25. Thematic Apperception Test, 1936, Henry Murray
      *Materials:*    Set of 30 plates
                      Record blanks
                      Manual
      *Distributors:* Psychological Corporation; Grune & Stratton


26. World Test, 1939, Margaret Lowenfeld
      (Toy World Test, 1955, Charlotte Bühler)
      *Materials:*    Test items
                      Record blanks
                      Manual
      *Distributor:* Joyce B. Baisden
                      4570 Mont Eagle Place, Los Angeles 41, Calif.

# Index